Hogan and Weber
CALIFORNIA CIVIL DISCOVERY

Second Edition

VOLUME 1

James E. Hogan
Professor of Law
University of California, Davis

Gregory S. Weber
Professor of Law
McGeorge School of Law

 LexisNexis™

Matthew Bender®

QUESTIONS ABOUT THIS PUBLICATION?

For questions about the **Editorial Content** appearing in these volumes or reprint permission, please call:

Valri Nesbit, J.D., at .... 1-800-424-0651 ext. 3343
E-mail .... cal.custquest@bender.com
Outside the United States and Canada please call .... (415) 908-3200

For assistance with replacement pages, shipments, billing or other customer service matters, please call:

Customer Services Department at .... (800) 833-9844
Outside the United States and Canada, please call .... (518) 487-3000
Fax number .... (518) 487-3584
Customer Service Website .... http://www.lexisnexis.com/custserv/

For information on other Matthew Bender publications, please call
Your account manager or .... (800) 223-1940
Outside the United States and Canada, please call .... (518) 487-3000

LIBRARY OF CONGRESS CATALOGING IN PUBLICATION DATA

Hogan, James E.
    California civil discovery/James E. Hogan, Gregory S. Weber—2nd ed.
      p.   cm.
    Includes index.
    ISBN 0-8205-7515-1 (hardbound)
    1. Discovery (Law)—California. I. Weber, Gregory S., 1956– II. Title.
KFC1020.H63 2005
347.794'072—dc22

2005016317

Originally published in 1972.

Library of Congress Catalog Card Number: 88-071137
ISBN 0-8205-7515-1

MATTHEW◆BENDER

Editorial Offices
744 Broad Street, Newark, NJ 07102 (973) 820-2000
201 Mission St., San Francisco, CA 94105-1831 (415) 908-3200
www.lexis.com

Statement on Fair Use

Matthew Bender recognizes the balance that must be achieved between the operation of the fair use doctrine, whose basis is to avoid the rigid application of the copyright statute, and the protection of the creative rights and economic interests of authors, publishers and other copyright holders.

We are also aware of the countervailing forces that exist between the ever greater technological advances for making both print and electronic copies and the reduction in the value of copyrighted works that must result from a consistent and pervasive reliance on these new copying technologies. It is Matthew Bender's position that if the "progress of science and useful arts" is promoted by granting copyright protection to authors, such progress may well be impeded if copyright protection is diminished in the name of fair use. (See *Nimmer on Copyright* § 13.05[E][1].) This holds true whether the parameters of the fair use doctrine are considered in either the print or the electronic environment as it is the integrity of the copyright that is at issue, not the media under which the protected work may become available. Therefore, the fair use guidelines we propose apply equally to our print and electronic information, and apply, within §§ 107 and 108 of the Copyright Act, regardless of the professional status of the user.

Our draft guidelines would allow for the copying of limited materials, which would include synopses and tables of contents, primary source and government materials that may have a minimal amount of editorial enhancements, individual forms to aid in the drafting of applications and pleadings, and miscellaneous pages from any of our newsletters, treatises and practice guides. This copying would be permitted provided it is performed for internal use and solely for the purpose of facilitating individual research or for creating documents produced in the course of the user's professional practice, and the original from which the copy is made has been purchased or licensed as part of the user's existing in-house collection.

Matthew Bender fully supports educational awareness programs designed to increase the public's recognition of its fair use rights. We also support the operation of collective licensing organizations with regard to our print and electronic information.

Dedication

To my beloved wife, Jan

James E. Hogan

To my wife, Sandy, and my daughters, Alissa and Hallie, with love and thanks
for your patience and support

Gregory S. Weber

v

TABLE OF CONTENTS
VOLUME 1

Chapter 1
INTRODUCTION TO CIVIL DISCOVERY

Chapter 2
ORAL DEPOSITIONS IN CALIFORNIA

Chapter 3
WRITTEN DEPOSITIONS

Chapter 4
OUT-OF-STATE DISCOVERY

Chapter 7
INSPECTIONS OF ITEMS CONTROLLED BY NONPARTIES

Chapter 8
MEDICAL EXAMINATIONS: PHYSICAL AND MENTAL

Table of Contents

Chapter 9
REQUESTS FOR ADMISSION

Chapter 10
EXPERT WITNESS DISCLOSURE

Table of Contents

TABLE OF CONTENTS
VOLUME 2

Chapter 11
DISCOVERY RELEVANCE

Chapter 12
PRIVILEGE

A. In General

B. The Privilege Against Self-Incrimination

C. The Attorney-Client Privilege

Table of Contents

Chapter 13
WORK PRODUCT PROTECTION

Chapter 14
PRE-SUIT AND POST-SUIT DISCOVERY

Chapter 15
SANCTIONS

Table of Contents

CHAPTER 1

INTRODUCTION TO CIVIL DISCOVERY

SYNOPSIS

---

§ 1.1   Purposes of Civil Discovery

The Goal of Civil Litigation: The purpose of a lawsuit is to secure the judicial application of appropriate legal principles to some transaction or event that has occurred in the "real" world. A lawsuit is decided "justly" only if the court applies the *correct* legal principles to the *actual* facts. When the parties to the suit disagree about critical events, a material fact issue exists for trial. Before the correct rules of law can be applied, some judge or jury must determine *now* what actually happened *then*. In this sense, a trial is described as a "truth-seeking" endeavor. The ultimate success of this endeavor depends on the trier of fact's access to witnesses' present memories and to any objects or documents about the underlying events.

The Adversary System: Under our country's justice system, the litigants themselves must assemble and present the pertinent data to the trier of fact. These contending parties are not expected to make a complete and objective presentation of the evidence. Instead, under the adversary system, each side's presentation may be selective and partisan, so long as it is otherwise honest. The trier of fact is expected to arrive at the truth by observing the competing one-sided presentations.

Trial Procedures: Once the case reaches trial, several procedures assist the parties to present their versions of the underlying events. The parties themselves may testify on their own behalf, and they can force each other to take the stand.

They may present the testimony of third persons, and if these individuals are reluctant "to get involved," the court's subpoena power may compel their attendance and testimony. Of course, the parties may cross-examine and impeach each other's witnesses. Finally, where litigants or third parties possess relevant documents and objects, the subpoena power may also compel their production at trial.

"Self Help": A civil procedure system could easily be structured to leave the parties largely to their own devices in collecting their evidence and in preparing to meet their opponent's case. Indeed, without any assistance from judicial processes, counsel still conduct much useful trial preparation.[1]

The pendency of a lawsuit does not prevent a party from carrying on informal discovery activities. In the *Pullin* case,[2] for example, the defendant supermarket in a slip-and-fall case noticed the deposition of the forensic safety engineer whom the plaintiff had designated as his expert concerning the slipperiness of the floor. In advance of the deposition date, defense counsel had refused plaintiff's telephone request for permission to conduct tests on the floor of the store where the fall occurred. Notwithstanding this refusal, plaintiff sent his expert to that store during its business hours. Acting like a customer, the expert proceeded to examine the spot where plaintiff had fallen, used a device to measure the floor's co-efficient of friction, and then left the premises. Characterizing the expert's actions as "secretive," the trial court granted the defense motion to exclude the expert's testimony case.[3]

Reversing this ruling, the appellate court was not troubled by the "secretiveness" of the test:

> All unilateral investigation is by definition conducted outside the presence of the party's adversaries. There is nothing wrong with that. Had [plaintiff's expert] looked at the floor, identified the flooring material, gone and purchased a piece, taken it to a laboratory and tested it, no one from [the defense side] would have been present. As [defendant's] lawyer conceded at oral argument, [plaintiff] could have done just that. Clearly, the issue of "secretiveness" is a red herring.[4]

Nor was the court troubled by plaintiff's failure to have served a discovery inspection demand for access to the premises[5] or by the occurrence of the "self-help" inspection after the cut-off date for formal discovery:

> Our role is to encourage low-cost investigation, not to adopt rules that foster increased reliance on discovery devices that are too often abused.

---

[1] Bause v Anthony Pools, Inc. (1962) 205 Cal App 2d 606, 611, 23 Cal Rptr 265.

[2] Pullin v Superior Court (2000) 81 Cal App 4th 1161, 97 Cal Rptr 2d 447, 447 n 3.

[3] Pullin v Superior Court (2000) 81 Cal App 4th 1161, 1163, 97 Cal Rptr 2d 447.

[4] Pullin v Superior Court (2000) 81 Cal App 4th 1161, 1164 n 3, 97 Cal Rptr 2d 447.

[5] CCP § 2031.010 et seq.

If one lawyer has a genuine concern about the manner in which another lawyer has conducted a test, or if there is something illegal about an investigator's conduct those points may be raised by way of an appropriate in limine motion to exclude evidence on whatever ground may be available. All we are saying in this opinion is that evidence is not made inadmissible by the simple fact that it is obtained by investigation rather than by way of formal discovery.[6]

—Drawbacks: A completely "do-it-yourself" approach to trial preparation has substantial drawbacks. Where litigants do not already possess pertinent information, they must depend on the willingness of others to make their memories and records available. Some of these people will be reluctant to "get involved." Others will be so aligned with the other side that they will be hostile to interviews or to access to their files. Thus, litigants often would have to wait until the trial is underway to learn a great deal about the facts that bear on the issues in the lawsuit.

Three reasons make postponed access to relevant information undesirable. First, it slows the trial. Counsel frequently must ask exploratory questions, many of which will end up leading to an informational dead-end. Second, when attorneys are confronted by previously unknown facts during trial, they lack time either to reflect on the significance of this new information or to find the evidence to counter it. This surprise impairs counsels' ability to represent their clients properly. Third, much relevant information is inadmissible under the rules of evidence applicable at trial. Yet this relevant, though inadmissible, information often leads to evidence that would be admissible. In a system that allowed no discovery, these leads would be unexplored, for the information that would supply them would never come out during the trial.

Value of Discovery: When a jurisdiction includes pretrial discovery in its civil procedure, it has decided that a high level of pretrial access to information helps make the trial not only a truth-*seeking*, but also a truth-*finding* undertaking. This pretrial access helps the respective parties to present at trial their most favorable case. Simultaneously, it reduces the chance that either an unawareness of relevant facts or an opponent's introduction of unanticipated evidence will distort a party's presentation of the underlying events.

Some might contend that a discovery system itself subverts the adversarial nature of civil litigation. In reality, however, these procedures simply try to eliminate an undesirable offshoot of that system: "the sporting theory of litigation—namely, surprise at trial."[7] As Justice Peters stated in the landmark *Greyhound* case, discovery simply tries "to take the 'game' element out of trial preparation while yet retaining the adversary nature of the trial itself."[8]

---

[6] Pullin v Superior Court (2000) 81 Cal App 4th 1161, 1165, 97 Cal Rptr 2d 447.

[7] Chronicle Publishing Co. v Superior Court (1960) 54 Cal 2d 548, 561, 7 Cal Rptr 109, 115, 354 P2d 637, 643.

[8] Greyhound Corp. v Superior Court (1961) 56 Cal 2d 355, 376, 15 Cal Rptr 90, 99, 364 P2d 266.

§ 1.2   By-Products of Civil Discovery

While discovery primarily accomplishes the mutual exchange of relevant information, it also has four useful side-effects: (1) settlement enhancement; (2) issue narrowing; (3) evidence preservation; and (4) pretrial tactical advantages.

Settlement Enhancement: Discovery greatly enhances the prospects for a just settlement. Parties usually settle when their respective evaluations of the actual facts and the applicable legal rules begin to approximate each other. Both in calculating maximum worth of a case and in discounting for the plaintiff's possible defeat, the parties need to analyze as much data as possible. Discovery increases the information available to both sides. It enables the parties to decide the case's value relatively free of the fear that they are not "playing with a full deck" of information.

Narrowing the Issues for Trial: Discovery also helps narrow the issues for trial. As parties learn from each other, they can identify matters about which they agree. Sometimes this information exchange shows that the parties do not dispute *any* material fact. A summary judgment can then resolve the entire case. More often, discovery will segregate agreed matters from disputed ones. The parties can then focus their efforts both during discovery and at trial on the areas of genuine controversy between them.

Evidence Preservation: Discovery also helps preserve evidence. When witnesses have previously testified at a deposition, the resulting transcript can refresh their recollection months or years later as the case approaches trial. The deposition itself may be introduced in evidence if some circumstance makes a person's live trial testimony impractical or impossible. Parties may also use discovery as a way of preserving critical documents or objects from the alteration or destruction that might otherwise have been their fate.

Tactical Advantages: Discovery also provides counsel with legitimate tactical advantages before trial. Early in the litigation, counsel can commit witnesses to a particular version of the events or force their concession that they know nothing about a particular point. Thus pinned down, witnesses are less likely to switch their story at trial. Should they do so, the discovery version can be used to contradict them. Discovery also allows counsel to "size up" witnesses, parties and the opposing attorney. In particular, depositions usually bring counsel face-to-face with the characters that will appear at trial. They can then appraise their demeanor and sense their attitudes. These assessments will strongly influence their decisions about how to handle these persons at trial.

§ 1.3   Evolution of Civil Discovery in California

Pre-1956 Discovery Act: Before the adoption of the Discovery Act of 1956, California civil discovery was significantly more limited in comparison to that in the federal courts. The state's discovery devices were fewer in number and less generous than their federal counterparts.

—Methods of Discovery: With adoption of the Federal Rules of Civil Procedure in 1938 the federal arsenal contained five discovery tools: depositions, interrogatories, inspections, medical examinations and admission requests. As of 1956 the California discovery system contained just three tools: depositions, inspections and medical examinations. It lacked analogs for interrogatories[1] and admission requests.[2] Moreover, of the three discovery tools, only the medical examination had roughly the same dimension as its federal counterpart.[3]

—Scope of Depositions: The availability of depositions in California civil cases depended considerably on the deponent's status in the case. On the one hand, a party had a broad right to depose another party.[4] On the other hand, a party needed to demonstrate special circumstances to depose a nonparty. These included: the deponents' residence outside the forum county, their serious infirmity or their status as the only witness to some material fact. In other words, depositions were only "discovery" devices with respect to party deponents; only such deponents could routinely be asked questions that were not immediately directed at producing admissible evidence for an eventual trial. However, if a party could establish the special circumstances that triggered the right to depose a nonparty, that party was then also free to "discover" the witness's broader knowledge of the lawsuit's subject matter.[5] Thus, discovery from nonparties was more a coincidence than a consequence of the pre-1956 deposition procedures.

—Scope of Inspections: California courts also took a more restrictive approach to document discovery than did the federal courts. On an appropriate showing, the federal courts would allow inspection of documents and things that might be inadmissible at trial, provided they were relevant to the case's general subject matter. In contrast, before allowing such inspections, the California courts required a showing that the desired items contained "competent and admissible evidence which is material to the issues to be tried."[6]

The 1956 Discovery Act: California belatedly entered the modern civil discovery era when it adopted the Civil Discovery Act of 1956. With only few alterations, the Legislature copied this Act from the original discovery rules adopted in 1938 for the federal courts.

The original Discovery Act had three immediate and extensive impacts on California civil litigation. First, it provided two new discovery tools: interrogatories and admission requests. Second, it greatly liberalized the use of the three existing devices: depositions, inspections and medical examinations. Third, it broadened the general scope of discovery. Before the Act, California discovery

---

[1] See Comment, 44 Cal L Rev 909, 933 (1956).

[2] See Note, 42 Cal L Rev 187, 193 (1954).

[3] See Note, 42 Cal L Rev 187, 189–190 (1954).

[4] Ahern v Superior Court (1952) 112 Cal App 2d 27, 31, 245 P2d 568, 571.

[5] Carnation Co. v Superior Court (1950) 96 Cal App 2d 138, 140, 214 P2d 552.

[6] McClatchy Newspapers v Superior Court (1945) 26 Cal 2d 386, 396, 159 P2d 944; see also Comment, 42 Cal L Rev 829, 834–835 (1954).

had focused on providing access to admissible evidence relevant to the actual issues in the lawsuit. The 1956 Act shifted discovery's focus from the lawsuit's specific issues to its general subject matter, and from admissible evidence to information that merely might lead to admissible evidence.

Limitations of the 1956 Act: One major drawback of the original Discovery Act stemmed from California's belated adoption of the then-current federal system. The federal discovery provisions were the products of an earlier generation's thinking. They had been formulated in the years leading up to the 1938 adoption of the Federal Rules of Civil Procedure. Even as California was basing its system on this foundation, the federal courts themselves were beginning to rethink their own discovery provisions. These efforts culminated in 1970 with the adoption of extensive amendments overhauling the federal discovery system.

The Discovery Commission: Over a quarter century after the Legislature adopted the 1956 Act, and over a decade after the federal courts overhauled their discovery rules, a Joint Commission on Discovery of the State Bar and Judicial Council began a top-to-bottom reexamination of California's system civil discovery. The Proposed Civil Discovery Act of 1986 was the product of this Commission's studies, deliberations and proposals. The Commission identified discovery abuses under the 1956 Act. It then developed proposals to eliminate or ameliorate those abuses. In addition, it codified much of the extensive case law that had settled issues arising under the 1956 Act. It thus made the text of the Discovery Act itself a much surer guide to the actual operation of the discovery system. Finally, the Commission reviewed the appropriateness of the 1970 federal discovery amendments for use in this state.

The 1986 Discovery Act: After a two-year study, the Discovery Commission released the Proposed California Civil Discovery Act of 1986. The Legislature adopted much of this proposal. During the legislative process, however, it changed several aspects. The resulting combination of Commission proposal and legislative action produced the Discovery Act of 1986.[7] With some amendments and some judicial amplification, the 1986 Act remains, almost a score of years after it went into effect, the framework for California civil discovery.

The 2005 Reorganization: In 2004, the Legislature partially rearranged the provisions of the 1986 Act to accommodate a shift to a decimalized numbering system. This legislation became effective on July 1, 2005. Although the legislation completely renumbered the Discovery Act's provisions, it expressly states: "Nothing in the act is intended to substantively change the law of civil discovery."[8]

§ 1.4 Methods of Civil Discovery

The Civil Discovery Act provides six "methods"[1] by which litigants can force

---

[7] Although entitled the Civil Discovery Act of 1986, the Act actually took effect on July 1, 1987.

[8] Stats. 2004, ch. 182, § 61.

[1] CCP § 2019.010.

pretrial disclosure of relevant information. These are: (1) depositions, (2) interrogatories, (3) inspections, (4) medical examinations, (5) admission requests and (6) exchanges of expert trial witness information. Parties may use all six of these tools against other parties to the lawsuit. For the most part, however, they may discover information from nonparties only by way of a deposition.[2]

Depositions: A deposition consists of sworn answers to a litigant's questions made before an officer authorized to administer oaths. Usually these answers respond to oral questions asked by counsel for the parties.[3] The questions and answers are reported stenographically and usually transcribed. On rare occasions, counsel compose written questions, for both direct and cross-examination, exchange them among the parties, and forward them to the deposition officer. That officer then propounds them to the deponent.[4]

Counsel may depose any person, including nonparties. Parties to the case, and many persons who are associated with them,[5] must submit to a deposition simply upon proper notice. A subpoena will compel the attendance of those who are not parties to the case. By serving nonparty deponents with a deposition subpoena, a litigant can also direct them to bring to the deposition papers and objects for inspection.[6]

The deposition is both the most expensive and the most effective discovery tool. Unlike the other devices, it allows on-the-spot, face-to-face interrogation and follow-up questioning. In addition, the deposition itself will often be admissible in evidence at trial. A party's deposition is admissible against it under the exception to the hearsay rule for admissions of a party opponent. A nonparty's deposition will be admissible should the deponent, for one of several statutorily defined reasons, be unavailable to testify at trial. In any event, should a witness's trial testimony vary from the deposition testimony, the earlier answers are admissible as prior inconsistent statements. As such, they are usable not only to impeach the trial version, but, in California, also substantively (that is, for the truth of the matter asserted) under a hearsay rule exception.

Interrogatories: Interrogatories are written questions submitted to another party for response under oath.[7] In essence, they provide a means for compelling the party to whom they are propounded to make an affidavit, the topics of which are structured by the party propounding the interrogatories. They have four advantages over depositions as information-gathering devices. First, they are inexpensive to propound. Second, they compel the responding parties to go

---

[2] This includes a "records-only" deposition subpoena to obtain a non-party's documents. For general coverage of document-discovery from nonparties, see Chapter 7.

[3] For general coverage of oral depositions, see Chapter 2.

[4] For general coverage of written depositions, see Chapter 3.

[5] For a discussion of the obligation of party-affiliated deponents to appear for a deposition, see § 2.12.

[6] For general coverage of document-discovery from nonparties, see Chapter 7.

[7] For general coverage of interrogatories to a party, see Chapter 5.

beyond their present memory and to make reasonable inquiries to answer them. Third, they are useful for obtaining noncontroversial details and background information. Often they are a precursor to the taking of the party's oral deposition. Fourth, they allow broader discovery than the deposition. Unlike depositions, interrogatories may seek the other parties' contentions, as well as the facts that support those contentions.

Interrogatories have two principal drawbacks. First, they yield studied responses usually less authored by the answering party and more ghostwritten by its attorney. Second, compared to depositions, follow-up questions are more difficult to pursue.

Inspections: Much relevant information cannot be adequately obtained and evaluated simply by probing the memories of parties and witnesses. It often reposes in documents, tangible objects and places. The inspection demand allows pretrial access to items possessed or controlled by another party to the lawsuit.[8] By using this tool, a litigant may not only look at an adversary's papers, possessions and property, but also copy, photograph, sample and test them.

Medical Examinations: The Discovery Act recognizes that in some cases, especially personal injury actions, proper trial preparation should include a medical examination of an adversary by a doctor not aligned with that party.[9] Such examinations may be physical or mental. The Act allows, upon demand, an initial routine physical examination of a personal injury plaintiff. In all other circumstances, the potential intrusiveness of this form of discovery requires either an agreement among the parties or a court order directing the other party to undergo it. Unlike other discovery devices, compulsory medical examinations are restricted to those conditions that are actually "in controversy" in the lawsuit.

Admission Requests: The preceding four discovery mechanisms help litigants to prepare to try an issue. In contrast, the admission request enables them to prepare *not* to try an issue. In effect, this discovery method pressures another party to stipulate either that a fact is true or that a document is genuine.[10] An unwarranted refusal to make the requested stipulation may shift the expense of proving at trial the fact covered by the request from the party making the request to the party refusing to honor it.

Exchanges of Expert Witness Information: The Discovery Act of 1956 contained no provisions regulating the timing or the extent of discovery about the experts who would be testifying for another party at trial. About twenty years later, the Legislature rectified this omission. It allowed a party to compel an adversary to identify its trial experts, supply information about their background and testimony, obtain their reports and depose them. The 1986 Act retained the core of this scheme and classified it as a sixth discovery method.[11] In essence,

---

[8] For general coverage of inspection demands, see Chapter 6.

[9] For general coverage of compulsory medical examinations, see Chapter 8.

[10] For general coverage of admission requests, see Chapter 9.

[11] For general coverage of exchanges of expert trial witness information, see Chapter 10.

it combines features of three other discovery devices: interrogatories, inspection demands and depositions.

§ 1.5 Scope of Civil Discovery

To be discoverable, information must be: (1) relevant to the subject matter; (2) not privileged; (3) not protected work product; and (4) not unduly burdensome to provide.

Relevance: Parties may only discover "relevant" information. For discovery under California law, "relevance" refers not to the actual "issues" framed by the pleadings, but to the lawsuit's general "subject matter."[1] The information need not be in a form that is admissible at trial. There need only be a reasonable prospect that it might lead to admissible evidence. For example, an out-of-court statement unable to qualify under any of the hearsay rule exceptions is still discoverable if it relates to the subject matter of the case. Once the discovering party discovers the hearsay statement, it can locate and subpoena the speaker or writer so that he or she can make the same statement in a form that fits within the rules of evidence.

Privilege: No matter how relevant information may be to a lawsuit, it is not discoverable if it falls within one of the evidentiary privileges.[2] These include the privilege against self-incrimination, the privilege not to testify against one's spouse, and the privileges accorded to confidential communications such as between husband and wife, attorney and client, and physician or psychotherapist and patient.

Work Product: Even where the information is both relevant and unprivileged, it is still not automatically discoverable. Some of this information has been unearthed or created only through work done by either an adversary or its attorney in anticipation of litigation. On the one hand, if this "work product" were freely discoverable, one side could sit back and "ride free" on the other's efforts. This would reward laziness and penalize diligence. It would dampen and even chill the incentive to investigate the case thoroughly and imaginatively. Moreover, attorneys would become less willing to explore the weaknesses of their case out of fear that anything they turned up would become available to the other side. On the other hand, a blanket "work product" protection would conflict with the civil trial's truth-seeking function. The enterprise or good luck of one litigant might bring into its files information helpful to the other side, but now impossible or quite difficult for that side to obtain on its own.

The attempt to reconcile these competing considerations has resulted in the "work product doctrine."[3] This doctrine charts a continuum of discoverability for different forms of work product. At one end of the continuum full discovery is allowed. For example, the identity and location of any person with, or any

---

[1] For general coverage of "relevance" for discovery, see Chapter 10.

[2] CCP § 2017.010; for general coverage of privilege as a discovery limitation, see Chapter 12.

[3] For general coverage of the work product protection, see Chapter 13.

item containing, relevant information, is fully discoverable.[4] At the other end of the continuum, discovery is prohibited entirely. The impressions, conclusions and legal theories of a litigant's attorney are not directly discoverable.[5] In the middle lie the remainder of an opponent's trial preparation materials. These materials include witness statements, photographs, opinions and reports of experts. Such materials have a qualified or conditional protection: they are only discoverable if the discovering party can show that absent pretrial access to them, unfair prejudice will result.[6] In effect, those seeking discovery of this intermediate form of work product must show the court that, through no fault or laziness on their part, they cannot now duplicate the desired information through a similar expenditure of time, energy and money.

Protective Orders: Once a party has satisfied the trial court that the information sought is relevant, not privileged and not protected work product, one last obstacle remains to its discovery: the trial court's discretion to protect against discovery that it will cause "*unwarranted* annoyance, embarrassment, or oppression, or *undue* burden and expense." A protective order is appropriate where the adverse impact on the one from whom the discovery is sought is out of all proportion to the value of the information to the side seeking it. In such cases, the trial judge can delay, limit, regulate, condition or even deny altogether the desired discovery.

§ 1.6 Applicability of the Discovery Act

The Civil Discovery Act applies in a pending "action."[1] It defines "action" to include both "a civil action" and "a special proceeding of a civil nature."[2] However, like its predecessor, it contains no definition of the latter phrase. This silence has left it to the courts the task of deciding the applicability of the Discovery Act to arbitration, administrative and juvenile proceedings.

Arbitration Proceedings: The question whether the Discovery Act is applicable to an arbitration proceeding depends on the interpretation given to "special proceeding of a civil nature."[3] The *McRae* case[4] held that this language referred to a proceeding in a court of law. In contrast, an arbitration is essentially a dispute-resolution device that *substitutes* for a judicial proceeding. Accordingly, the court held that the Discovery Act does not apply to arbitration proceedings.

McRae merely holds that the Discovery Act does not *by its own terms* apply to arbitrations. Thus, when the Legislature requires arbitration of a particular type

---

[4] CCP § 2017.010.

[5] CCP § 2018.030(a).

[6] CCP § 2018.030(b).

[1] See, e.g., CCP § 2017.010.

[2] CCP § 2016.020(a).

[3] Annotation: Discovery in aid of arbitration proceedings. 98 ALR2d 1247.

[4] McRae v Superior Court (1963) 221 Cal App 2d 166, 170, 34 Cal Rptr 346; see also Brock v Kaiser Foundation Hospitals (1992) 10 Cal App 4th 1790, 1802, 13 Cal Rptr 2d 678.

of controversy, it must give individualized consideration to the extent to which discovery is to be available. For example, with some modifications, it has made the Discovery Act applicable to arbitrations carried out under the Uninsured Motorist Act.[5]

The Legislature has also adopted a discovery system for contractual arbitrations.[6] This provision is mandatory for arbitration agreements regarding personal injury or wrongful death claims.[7] It is available in other contractual arbitrations if the parties so choose.[8] In essence, these statutes afford the arbitrating parties, with one important exception, "the same rights, remedies and procedures," and subject them to "the same duties, liabilities, and obligations" of the Discovery Act "as if the subject matter of the arbitration were pending in a civil action before a superior court of this state."[9] Depositions, however, require the arbitrator's permission.[10] This discovery system is administered not by the court but by the arbitrator. Thus, the arbitrator enforces discovery rights, issues protective orders and imposes sanctions.[11]

The Judicial Arbitration Rules for Civil Cases take the same approach: "The parties to the arbitration shall have the right to take depositions and to obtain discovery, and to that end may exercise all of the same rights, remedies, and procedures, and shall be subject to all of the same duties, liabilities, and obligations as provided in [the Discovery Act] . . . ."[12] The only modifications are the imposition of a deadline for the completion of discovery[13] and a significant liberalization of the right to use depositions instead of live testimony at the hearing itself.[14] Once the arbitrator makes an award, any discovery other than via a demand for an exchange of expert witness information requires leave of court.[15]

A party who is entitled by contract to insist that a particular controversy be submitted to arbitration (with its discovery restrictions) may lose that right if it engages in normal civil discovery before taking steps to compel arbitration.

---

[5] Ins Code § 11580.2(f).

[6] CCP § 1283.05.

[7] CCP § 1283.1(a).

[8] CCP § 1283.1(b).

[9] CCP § 1283.05(a). Of course, the parties to an arbitration agreement may stipulate that all discovery will take place under the Civil Discovery Act. See, e.g., McManus v CIBC World Markets Corp. (2003) 109 Cal App 4th 76, 100, 134 Cal Rptr 2d 446, 464; Schlessinger v Rosenfeld, Meyer & Susman (1995) 40 Cal App 4th 1096, 1101 n 2, 47 Cal Rptr 2d 650, 653 n 2.

[10] CCP § 1283.05(e).

[11] CCP § 1283.05(b)–(c). See, e.g., Long v Hauser (1975) 52 Cal App 3d 490, 492–493, 125 Cal Rptr 125.

[12] Cal Rules of Ct, Rule 1612.

[13] Fifteen days prior to the date set for the arbitration hearing. Cal Rules of Ct, Rule 1612; see Roe v Superior Court (1990) 224 Cal App 3d 642, 646, 273 Cal Rptr 745, 747.

[14] Cal Rules of Ct, Rule 1613(b)(3).

[15] CCP § 1141.24.

In the *Davis* case,[16] an employee sued an airline for failing to control alleged sexual harassment by one of its supervisors. Instead of immediately moving to compel the plaintiff to submit her grievance to arbitration, the airline answered the complaint. Its answer included an affirmative defense that the action was barred because the plaintiff had failed to comply with an alleged agreement to arbitrate such disputes. Over a five-month period, the defendant then carried out a program of "broad-ranging discovery typically undertaken in court litigation and not available in arbitration."[17] It demanded and obtained discovery of documents in 86 categories totaling 1,600 pages, and it later took an extensive videotaped deposition of the plaintiff. Only then did it take steps to implement its claimed right to compel plaintiff to submit her claim to arbitration. The appellate court affirmed the trial judge's conclusion that defendant had waived any right it may have had to compel arbitration:

> The vice involved here, whether characterized as "unreasonable delay," "bad faith misconduct," "gamesmanship" or "unilateral discovery" . . . is that defendants used the discovery processes of the court to gain information about plaintiff's case which defendants could not have gained in arbitration. [They] belatedly sought to change the game to arbitration, where plaintiff would not have equivalent discovery rights. . . . Here, the trial court could reasonably find the discovery conducted was not equivalent for both sides and would work an unfair advantage for defendants if arbitration were ordered. These facts support the trial court's finding of waiver.[18]

Administrative Proceedings: The Discovery Act ordinarily does not apply to administrative proceedings.[19] State Bar disciplinary proceedings are an exception. In *Brotsky v State Bar*,[20] the court held that the State Bar's unique role as an arm of the Supreme Court required use of the same discovery rules applicable to actions brought in a court of law:

> Since [the State Bar] acts herein as an instrument of the courts, its activities should be governed by those statutory principles which have been enacted as rules of procedure for all courts. By whatever name a disciplinary proceeding may be called, whether an action or a special proceeding, it is in essence the initial stage of an action in court. It follows that the discovery act, *in toto*, is applicable thereto.[21]

With several modifications, the attorney discipline system now expressly incorporates the Civil Discovery Act.[22]

---

[16] Davis v Continental Airlines, Inc. (1997) 59 Cal App 4th 205, 69 Cal Rptr 2d 79.

[17] Davis v Continental Airlines, Inc. (1997) 59 Cal App 4th 205, 213, 69 Cal Rptr 2d 79, 84.

[18] Davis v Continental Airlines, Inc. (1997) 59 Cal App 4th 205, 215, 69 Cal Rptr 2d 79, 85–86; see also Guess?, Inc. v Superior Court (2000) 79 Cal App 4th 553, 558, 94 Cal Rptr 2d 201.

[19] See Shively v Stewart (1966) 65 Cal 2d 475, 478–480, 55 Cal Rptr 217, 421 P2d 65.

[20] Brotsky v State Bar (1962) 57 Cal 2d 287, 19 Cal Rptr 153, 368 P2d 697.

[21] Brotsky v State Bar (1962) 57 Cal 2d 287, 301, 19 Cal Rptr 153, 160, 368 P2d 697.

[22] See Rules 150–183 of the Rules of Procedure of the State Bar.

The Discovery Act's inapplicability to administrative proceedings does not mean that these proceedings allow no prehearing discovery. In *Shively v Stewart*,[23] the Supreme Court ruled that the disciplinary proceedings (there, against a doctor) conducted by an administrative agency were sufficiently analogous to a criminal case to require *judicial* development of a system of prehearing discovery.[24] In response, in 1968, the Legislature enacted a system of prehearing discovery.[25] This has superseded the courts' common law powers to craft administrative discovery schemes:

> It is true that *Shively* decided that, in the absence of a discovery statute applicable to administrative proceedings, the court had the authority to authorize the limited use of the subpoena duces tecum and depositions for discovery purposes. . . . [¶] However, the comprehensive exclusive discovery statutes in administrative proceedings (Gov. Code §§ 11507.5–11507.7) were enacted by the Legislature in 1968, thereby supplanting the *Shively* court's holding. Subsequent cases have held that the [administrative] discovery statute is exclusive.[26]

Under this system, a party to an administrative proceeding can "request" in writing to discover the identity of knowledgeable persons and to inspect witness statements, documentary evidence and the content of agency investigative reports. Depositions are only possible if the witness "will be unable or cannot be compelled to attend"[27] the hearing. The constitutionality of this restriction on depositions was challenged on equal protection grounds in a medical disciplinary proceeding. The doctor cited the broader right in attorney disciplinary proceedings to use depositions for discovery. The court found a rational basis to differentiate between the two proceedings.[28]

Juvenile Proceedings: The Legislature has declared that a juvenile court proceeding is not a "criminal proceeding."[29] Moreover, the courts have described these proceedings as "essentially civil [in] nature."[30] Nevertheless, in the *Joe Z.* case,[31] the Supreme Court refused to treat a juvenile proceeding as "a special proceeding of a civil nature."[32] The Court noted that the label "civil" was placed on juvenile proceedings simply for convenience. This should not "obscure the quasi-criminal nature of juvenile proceedings, involving as they often do the

---

[23] Shively v Stewart (1966) 65 Cal 2d 475, 479–480, 55 Cal Rptr 217, 421 P2d 65.

[24] See also Romero v Hern (1969) 276 Cal App 2d 787, 790, 81 Cal Rptr 281; Everett v Gordon (1968) 266 Cal App 2d 667, 670–671, 72 Cal Rptr 379.

[25] See Gov't Code § 11507.6.

[26] Gilbert v Superior Court (1987) 193 Cal App 3d 161, 166, 238 Cal Rptr 220, 222–223.

[27] Gov't Code § 11511.

[28] Kenneally v Medical Bd. (1994) 27 Cal App 4th 489, 499–502, 32 Cal Rptr 2d 504.

[29] Welf & Inst Code § 503.

[30] In re Dennis M. (1969) 70 Cal 2d 444, 462, 75 Cal Rptr 1, 12, 450 P2d 296.

[31] Joe Z. v Superior Court (1970) 3 Cal 3d 797, 91 Cal Rptr 594, 478 P2d 26.

[32] See CCP § 2016.020(a).

possibility of substantial loss of personal freedom."[33] Moreover, the Court found it both unwise and unnecessary to apply the Civil Discovery Act indiscriminately to juvenile proceedings. It felt that broad discovery would prevent expeditious and informal adjudications in juvenile cases. Instead, it applied to juvenile proceedings the essential judicially created discovery rights applicable to adult criminal defendants. Since 1977, a special Rule of Court has comprehensively regulated discovery in juvenile proceedings.[34]

Sexually Violent Predator Act Proceedings: Because a case filed under the Sexually Violent Predator Act contemplates a non-punitive commitment for treatment purposes, it is a "special proceeding of a civil nature" within the meaning of CCP § 2016.020(a), and therefore the Civil Discovery Act applies to it. Accordingly, the *Leake* case[35] held that the respondent in such a matter may compel an exchange of expert witness information under CCP § 2034.210.

§ 1.7 Discovery in "Limited Civil Cases"

Until 1998, superior courts and municipal courts were established for each county in California. Superior courts were courts of general jurisdiction. In contrast, municipal courts' civil jurisdiction was generally limited to actions in which the amount in controversy did not exceed $25,000. In that year, with the advent of county-by-county trial court unification, the municipal courts began to be absorbed into the superior court located in their county. Simultaneously the Legislature introduced the "limited civil case" to describe, in the superior courts, the cases that formerly would have been filed and processed in a municipal court. In general, a case is a "limited civil action" when the amount in controversy does not exceed $25,000.[1] The limitations on civil discovery in municipal court cases were simply exported to the superior courts and made applicable to the "limited civil case."[2]

Severe Restrictions on Most Discovery Methods: The Legislature[3] has severely restricted discovery in suits involving $25,000 or less. In such cases, a litigant can take only one deposition per adverse party.[4] Moreover, a party

---

[33] Joe Z. v Superior Court (1970) 3 Cal 3d 797, 801, 91 Cal Rptr 594, 596, 478 P2d 26.

[34] Cal Rules of Ct, Rule 1420.

[35] Leake v Superior Court (2000) 87 Cal App 4th 675, 682, 104 Cal Rptr 2d 767; see also Baqleh v Superior Court (2002) 100 Cal App 4th 478, 491, 122 Cal Rptr 2d 673 [the civil nature of a hearing under Penal Code § 1368 on the issue of an accused's competency to stand trial on the criminal charges "vests the trial court with authority to utilize appropriate" provisions of the Civil Discovery Act, including those authorizing compulsory psychiatric examinations]; People v Superior Court (2001) 94 Cal App 4th 980, 996, 114 Cal Rptr 2d 980 [trial court erred when it peremptorily quashed inmates' deposition notices].

[1] CCP §§ 85 and 86; see Snukal v Flightways Manufacturing Co. (2000) 23 Cal 4th 754, 763 n 2, 98 Cal Rptr 2d 1, 10 n 2, 3 P3d 286.

[2] CCP § 91(a).

[3] CCP § 94.

[4] CCP § 94(b).

may only propound to each adverse party a *combined* total of 35 interrogatories, inspection demands and admission requests.[5] No interrogatory or admission request may contain "subparts."[6]

Additional Discovery with Leave of Court: A party who wishes to exceed any of these limits must get either a stipulation[7] or court permission.[8] A court may only grant such a request if the moving party shows its inability to proceed effectively without the requested discovery. In reviewing this showing, the court must consider both the applicants' use of the statutorily allotted discovery and their efforts to secure the additional information informally.

List of Witnesses and Exhibits: Once a case receives its first trial date,[9] any party may serve upon other parties a request for the names and addresses of their trial witnesses, a description of any physical evidence and a copy of any documentary evidence they intend to offer.[10]

Small Claims Cases: Discovery is incompatible with the informality of small claims proceedings in the superior courts: "Obviously, formal discovery procedures in the original small claims actions would be completely inconsistent with the goals and procedures of the small claims court and would impose an unacceptable burden on unrepresented litigants."[11] Moreover, discovery is not available in preparation for any superior court trial de novo that results if the defendant appeals from the small claims judgment:

> [T]he Legislature did not intend that formal discovery procedures should be permitted in either the small claims action itself or the de novo proceeding on appeal. . . . Discovery at the appeal level would . . . defeat the object of the entire small claims process.[12]

§ 1.8 Appellate Review of Discovery Rulings

When a party believes that a trial court has erred either in granting or denying discovery, the question arises whether that party may obtain instant appellate review of that ruling, or, as with most other interlocutory rulings, must await final judgment before appealing. There are significant advantages and drawbacks to either alternative.

---

[5] CCP § 94(a).

[6] CCP § 94(a)(1), (3).

[7] CCP § 95(b).

[8] CCP § 95(a).

[9] The request may be made no sooner than 45 days, and no later than 30 days, before the first trial date.

[10] CCP § 95.

[11] Bruno v Superior Court (1990) 219 Cal App 3d 1359, 1363, 269 Cal Rptr 142.

[12] Bruno v Superior Court (1990) 219 Cal App 3d 1359, 1363, 269 Cal Rptr 142, 144; see also Cooper v Pirelli Cable Corp. (1984) 160 Cal App 3d 294, 299, 206 Cal Rptr 581, 584; Burley v Stein (1974) 40 Cal App 3d 752, 757 n 6, 115 Cal Rptr 279.

Delayed Appellate Review: On the one hand, insistence on subjecting discovery rulings to the final judgment requirement has two major advantages. First, it prevents the interruption and delay of the lawsuit in the trial court. Second, it reduces the workload of the appellate court. After all, a substantial number (perhaps an overwhelming majority) of discovery rulings will become moot, either because the case settles or because the party aggrieved by the ruling ultimately prevails on the merits of the lawsuit.

On the other hand, with discovery rulings, appellate review delayed usually means appellate review denied. If one is the victim of an erroneous *grant* of discovery, compliance with the trial court's order "lets the cat out of the bag." There is little point in asking an appellate court months or years later to undo a disclosure that has already occurred. If one is the victim of an erroneous *denial* of discovery, that party may have to prepare for trial without the benefit of all the discovery that the system allows. However, by the time a final judgment allows an appeal from the discovery ruling, the aggrieved party must not only show that the ruling was erroneous, but also that the error was prejudicial, i.e., it affected the outcome in the court below. Besides its adverse impact upon a party aggrieved by a discovery ruling, this approach to appellate review leads to a paucity of appellate opinions on discovery issues. This hinders the jurisdiction in developing a definitive body of case law interpreting its discovery statutes.

Immediate Appellate Review: In contrast, a system that features immediate appellate review of discovery rulings assures that the case will proceed to trial with all litigants receiving the discovery they are entitled to, no more and no less. Moreover, by reviewing these rulings, the jurisdiction will develop a coherent and available body of precedents, thereby supplying its trial courts with a constant flow of direction and guidance. The downside is that instant review spawns piecemeal litigation that can disrupt the calendars of trial and appellate courts alike.

Federal Practice: The federal courts have used the final judgment rule to hold appellate consideration of appellate rulings to a trickle.[1] First, they have tightly restricted the use of extraordinary writs to challenge discovery rulings.[2] For example, the famous "work product" case, *Hickman v Taylor*,[3] received

---

[1] See, e.g., Reise v Board of Regents of University of Wisconsin System (1992, CA7 Wis) 957 F2d 293, 295–296 [order that plaintiff undergo a mental examination is not a final or collateral order, and hence not appealable]; In re National Mort. Equity Corp. Mort. Pool Certificates Litigation (1988, CA9 Cal) 857 F2d 1238, 1239. Cf. Kibrej v Fisher (1983) 148 Cal App 3d 1113, 1115–1116, 196 Cal Rptr 454 [order imposing monetary sanctions for plaintiff's failure to attend and participate in deposition is nonappealable]. See also Thornburg, Interlocutory Review of Discovery Orders: An Idea Whose Time Has Come (1990) 44 Southwestern LJ 1045; Comment, Appellate Review of Discovery Orders in the Federal Courts, 1980 So Ill U LJ 339.

[2] See, e.g., Reise v Board of Regents of University of Wisconsin System (1992, CA7 Wis) 957 F2d 293, 295–296 [denying writ review of order that plaintiff undergo a mental examination]; American Express Warehousing, Ltd. v Transamerica Ins. Co. (1967, CA2 NY) 380 F2d 277, 282–284.

[3] Hickman v Taylor (1947) 329 US 495, 500, 91 L Ed 451, 67 S Ct 385.

immediate appellate review only because an attorney was so convinced that an order directing discovery was erroneous that he was willing to risk a contempt citation to test its validity.

Recently, this attitude has loosened somewhat. A few discovery rulings have qualified as "controlling questions of law" under the restrictive federal procedure for appealing interlocutory orders.[4] Nevertheless, federal appellate courts still conclude only rarely that the novelty of the discovery issue coupled with the burden of an erroneous ruling justifies mandamus review of a discovery ruling.[5]

California Practice: Although the California Legislature enacted a discovery system patterned closely after the federal system, the California Supreme Court has charted its own meandering course over appellate review of discovery orders.

Initially, the Court embraced broad writ review. In the *Greyhound* case, the Court declared in a brief footnote that "an order granting or denying discovery is a proper subject of a prerogative writ."[6] The following year, again in a footnote, the Court revealed some reservations about liberal writ review of discovery rulings. In the *Oceanside Union School Dist.* case, it cautioned that this was to be the exception, and not the rule:

> The prerogative writs have been used frequently to review interim orders in discovery cases. But this does not mean that these discretionary writs will or should issue as of course in all cases where this court may be of the opinion that the interim order of the trial court was erroneous. In most such cases, as is true of most other interim orders, the parties must be relegated to a review of the order on appeal from the final judgment. As inadequate as such review may be in some cases, the prerogative writs should only be used in discovery matters to review questions of first impression that are of general importance to the trial courts and to the profession, and where guidelines can be laid down for future cases.[7]

Nevertheless, during the first dozen years after the adoption of the Discovery Act, neither the Supreme Court nor the Courts of Appeal paid much heed to the *Oceanside* footnote.

---

[4] 28 USC § 1292(b).

[5] See, e.g., Schlagenhauf v Holder (1964) 379 US 104, 110–111, 13 L Ed 2d 152, 85 S Ct 234; In re Puerto Rico Electric Power Authority (1982, CA1 PR) 687 F2d 501, 503–504. See also Haines v Liggett Group, Inc. (1992, CA3 NJ) 975 F2d 81, 88–89; Westinghouse Elec. Corp. v Republic of Philippines (1991, CA3 NJ) 951 F2d 1414, 1422–1423.

[6] Greyhound v Superior Court (1961) 56 Cal 2d 355, 368–369 n 1, 15 Cal Rptr 90, 94 n 1, 364 P2d 266.

[7] Oceanside Union School Dist. v Superior Court (1962) 58 Cal 2d 180, 185–186 n 4, 23 Cal Rptr 375, 378 n 4, 373 P2d 439 [internal citations omitted].

In 1970, in the *Pacific Telephone* case,[8] the Supreme Court ended what was in danger of becoming a system of immediate appellate review of virtually all discovery orders:

> Despite this express declaration [i.e., the *Oceanside* footnote] of the necessary limitations on the availability of the prerogative writs, and our reaffirmance of this standard in subsequent cases, at least some appellate courts have apparently continued to consider prerogative writs as the normal instruments for reviewing discovery orders. . . . [¶] [A]ppellate courts must keep in mind that too lax a view of the "extraordinary" nature of prerogative writs, rendering substantial pretrial delay a usual hazard of the use of discovery, is likely to result in more harm to the judicial process than the denial of immediate relief from less significant errors.[9]

Guidelines for Writ Review: The appellate courts now use four guidelines in deciding whether to provide interlocutory review of a discovery ruling:

(1) Overruling Relevancy Objection: A *grant* of discovery over an objection based only on irrelevancy will almost never be appropriate for writ review:

> The objection to the trial court's grant of discovery on "irrelevancy" grounds . . . generally will not support the issuance of an extraordinary writ. [¶] [T]he burden on the deponent of disclosing matter which is not privileged but only irrelevant to a particular action will generally not be too onerous; we believe he may be required to absorb this burden if the discovery process is to achieve its purposes of improving the efficiency and integrity of the judicial process.[10]

(2) Ruling that an Admission has Occurred: Where the trial court sustains a claim that an admission request has culminated in the admission being made, writ review is often appropriate under generally applicable principles:

> Because requests for admissions are more closely akin to summary-adjudication procedures than to orthodox discovery, being designed not so much to "discover" the facts and to expedite trial preparation as to render it unnecessary to try an otherwise triable issue of fact or law, we do not apply the rule that a reviewing court should rarely interfere with pretrial discovery orders, particularly where such orders operate to grant discovery. Instead, we follow general principles.[11]

---

[8] Pacific Tel. & Tel. Co. v Superior Court (1970) 2 Cal 3d 161, 84 Cal Rptr 718, 465 P2d 854.

[9] Pacific Tel. & Tel. Co. v Superior Court (1970) 2 Cal 3d 161, 169, 84 Cal Rptr 718, 723–724, 465 P2d 854. Cf. Omaha Indemnity Co. v Superior Court (1989) 209 Cal App 3d 1266, 1271–1274, 258 Cal Rptr 66, 68–70 [although this case does not involve discovery issues, it analyzes comprehensively the pro's and con's of writ review of interlocutory rulings].

[10] Pacific Tel. & Tel. Co. v Superior Court (1970) 2 Cal 3d 161, 170–171 n 11, 84 Cal Rptr 718, 724–725 n 11, 465 P2d 854.

[11] Hansen v Superior Court (1983) 149 Cal App 3d 823, 827–828, 197 Cal Rptr 175, 177 [internal citations omitted].

(3) Overruling a Claim of Privilege or Work Product: The type of discovery order most appropriate for writ review is one that overrides a claim of *privilege:*

> The need for the availability of the prerogative writs in discovery cases where an order of the trial court granting discovery allegedly violates a privilege of the party against whom discovery is granted, is obvious. The person seeking to exercise the privilege must either succumb to the court's order and disclose the privileged information, or subject himself to a charge of contempt for his refusal to obey the court's order pending appeal. The first of these alternatives is hardly an adequate remedy and could lead to the disruption of a confidential relationship. The second is clearly inadequate as it would involve the possibility of a jail sentence and additional delay in the principal litigation during review of the contempt order. [12]

Many grants of writ review now involve orders that grant discovery by overruling a claimed evidentiary privilege. [13] Others have involved trial court rulings granting discovery in the face of a claimed constitutional privacy right. [14] Several cases have reviewed orders that grant discovery of information over claims of the "work product" protection. [15]

(4) Other Discovery Rulings: For all other discovery orders, writ review is available only where the issue presented meets these three criteria: it is one of "first impression," of "general importance to the trial courts and to the profession," and capable of providing "general guidelines . . . for future cases."

Decisions Granting Review: The California courts still allow writ review of many discovery orders. When granting such review, however, they customarily preface their opinions with a reminder that only the novelty and general importance of the discovery issue impels them to do so. The following quotations

---

[12] Roberts v Superior Court (1973) 9 Cal 3d 330, 336, 107 Cal Rptr 309, 312, 508 P2d 309. Cf. Phoenix Assurance of Canada v Runck (1982, ND) 317 NW2d 402, 406 [trial court ruling denying party benefit of privilege against self-incrimination is an exception to state's general rule that discovery orders are not appealable].

[13] See, e.g., Davies v Superior Court (1984) 36 Cal 3d 291, 294, 204 Cal Rptr 154, 155, 682 P2d 349; Motown Record Corp. v Superior Court (1984) 155 Cal App 3d 482, 488, 202 Cal Rptr 227, 231; Dickerson v Superior Court (1982) 135 Cal App 3d 93, 97–98, 185 Cal Rptr 97, 99. See also OXY Resources California v Superior Court (2004) 115 Cal App 4th 874, 886–887, 9 Cal Rptr 3d 621; Korea Data Systems Co. v Superior Court (1997) 51 Cal App 4th 1513, 1516, 59 Cal Rptr 2d 925; Palay v Superior Court (1993) 18 Cal App 4th 919, 925, 22 Cal Rptr 2d 839, 842; Hiott v Superior Court (1993) 16 Cal App 4th 712, 716, 20 Cal Rptr 2d 157, 159; Davis v Superior Court (1992) 7 Cal App 4th 1008, 1012, 9 Cal Rptr 2d 331, 333.

[14] See, e.g., Britt v Superior Court (1978) 20 Cal 3d 844, 143 Cal Rptr 695, 574 P2d 766; Valley Bank of Nevada v Superior Court (1975) 15 Cal 3d 652, 125 Cal Rptr 553, 542 P2d 977; Hofmann Corp. v Superior Court (1985) 172 Cal App 3d 357, 218 Cal Rptr 355.

[15] See, e.g., OXY Resources California v Superior Court (2004) 115 Cal App 4th 874, 886–887, 9 Cal Rptr 3d 621; Fellows v Superior Court (1980) 108 Cal App 3d 55, 166 Cal Rptr 274; Glacier General Assur. Co. v Superior Court (1979) 95 Cal App 3d 836, 157 Cal Rptr 435; Long Beach v Superior Court (1976) 64 Cal App 3d 65, 134 Cal Rptr 468.

illustrate the sort of discovery ruling that meets the *Oceanside-Pacific Telephone* criteria for writ review:

> The power of a trial court [in a civil case] to grant a prospective witness [who invokes his privilege against self-incrimination] use immunity and derivative use immunity for the purpose of facilitating discovery by a private party is a question meeting these criteria.[16]

> The novel question confronting us is whether a third party recipient of confidential information from a physician may assert the physician-patient privilege.[17]

> This case . . . presents the question whether the withdrawal of [an] expert witness [by one defendant] on the basis of [an] indemnification agreement [with a co-defendant] reestablishes the privilege against disclosure enjoyed by [that] defendant or leaves the plaintiff free to discover the content of the report. . . . [¶] [W]e granted a hearing in order to resolve the novel issue of work product doctrine which this case presents.[18]

> The question presented is how a plaintiff in a *[Tarasoff]* action . . . can obtain discovery of psychiatric records of defendant's [allegedly "dangerous"] patient without that patient's consent.[19]

> We issued our alternative writ of mandate to examine the single question whether a personal injury litigant may be compelled to submit to a physical examination by a vocational rehabilitation expert who is not a licensed physician.[20]

> This case presents the question whether a taxpayer waives the privilege of confidentiality attaching to his copies of income tax returns when he files a lawsuit placing the contents of those returns directly in issue.[21]

> In this mandamus proceeding we consider whether a trial court in a civil action brought under the Probate Code has the authority to order the exhumation and autopsy of the body of the deceased testator.[22]

> Defendants argue that [the "meet and confer" obligation] does not apply to instances . . . where there has been a total failure to respond to

---

[16] Daly v Superior Court (1977) 19 Cal 3d 132, 140, 137 Cal Rptr 14, 19, 560 P2d 1193.

[17] Rudnick v Superior Court (1974) 11 Cal 3d 924, 928, 114 Cal Rptr 603, 607, 523 P2d 643 [internal citations omitted].

[18] Williamson v Superior Court (1978) 21 Cal 3d 829, 832–833, 148 Cal Rptr 39, 41–42, 582 P2d 126.

[19] Mavroudis v Superior Court (1980) 102 Cal App 3d 594, 598–599, 162 Cal Rptr 724, 728–729.

[20] Browne v Superior Court (1979) 98 Cal App 3d 610, 612–613, 159 Cal Rptr 669, 670–671 [internal citations omitted].

[21] Wilson v Superior Court (1976) 63 Cal App 3d 825, 827, 134 Cal Rptr 130, 131–132.

[22] Holm v Superior Court (1986) 187 Cal App 3d 1241, 1243–1244, 232 Cal Rptr 432, 433–434.

interrogatories within the time prescribed. . . . [¶] . . . This proceeding involves the interpretation of a recently adopted rule of court; the precise issue presented is one of first impression which is likely to arise repeatedly until put to rest.[23]

[The issue presented is whether] under the new discovery act sanctions are mandatory upon the granting of a motion to have requests for admission deemed admitted.[24]

These petitioners raise the novel question of whether a party who has missed the deadline for compelling inspection of documents under [CCP § 2031.010] is barred from requesting that the same document be brought to a deposition [under CCP § 2025.010].[25]

The question confronting us is whether a mother, as a nonlitigant to a medical malpractice action filed on behalf of her infant son, is able to assert a physician-patient privilege to prevent disclosure of her prenatal medical records.[26]

[W]e consider whether a court has the authority to order a deponent to perform a physical reenactment of an event at a deposition.[27]

[The questions of first impression warranting writ review are whether] a party who submits to a medical examination pursuant to [CCP § 2032.220] is entitled a report of that examination on demand even if the examining physician has not prepared one . . . [and] has the right to depose the examining physician in spite of the fact that the party requesting the examination has withdrawn the physician as an expert witness and redesignated him or her as a "consultant."[28]

The issue of whether a corporation that is a defendant in related criminal and civil actions may obtain a stay of discovery in the civil action while the criminal action is pending is, in California, an issue of first impression.[29]

[T]he issues presented are of general importance to the trial courts and to the profession. There is little California case law examining the so-called "common interest" or "joint defense" doctrine as applied to a business transaction.[30]

---

[23] Leach v Superior Court (1980) 111 Cal App 3d 902, 905–906, 169 Cal Rptr 42, 44.

[24] Appleton v Superior Court (1988) 206 Cal App 3d 632, 633–634, 253 Cal Rptr 762, 763.

[25] Carter v Superior Court (1990) 218 Cal App 3d 994, 995–996, 267 Cal Rptr 290.

[26] Palay v Superior Court (1993) 18 Cal App 4th 919, 925, 22 Cal Rptr 2d 839, 842.

[27] Stermer v Superior Court (1993) 20 Cal App 4th 777, 779 n1, 24 Cal Rptr 2d 577, 578 n1.

[28] Kennedy v Superior Court (1999) 64 Cal App 4th 674, 676, 75 Cal Rptr 2d 373.

[29] Avant! Corp. v Superior Court (2000) 79 Cal App 4th 876, 881, 94 Cal Rptr 2d 505, 508.

[30] OXY Resources California v Superior Court (2004) 115 Cal App 4th 874, 887, 9 Cal Rptr 3d 621.

In the present case, California courts have not ruled upon the question of which party should pay when it is necessary to translate electronic data compilations in order to obtain usable information responsive to a discovery request. The question is one that is bound to arise with increasing frequency. Given that the cost of translating such material can be exorbitant, the question of who should bear the cost raises practical concerns as well as complicated policy issues. We believe these issues are sufficiently important to justify review by extraordinary writ.[31]

Decisions Denying Review: Illustrations of discovery questions deemed unworthy of writ review are: whether it was an abuse of discretion to direct a defendant sued for punitive damages to reveal his financial records when trial was still several years away;[32] whether a plaintiff, instead of looking the information up himself in court records, could discover from the defendant the existence of any suits against the latter based on similar tortious acts;[33] and whether a plaintiff undergoing a compulsory medical examination could have not only her attorney present, but also her personal physician.[34]

---

[31] Toshiba America Electronic Components v Superior Court (2004) 124 Cal App 4th 762, 767, 21 Cal Rptr 3d 532. See generally, Arent, Brownstone & Fenwick, E-Discovery: Preserving, Requesting & Producing Electronic Information, 19 Santa Clara Computer & High Tech. L.J. 131 (2002).

[32] City of Alhambra v Superior Court (1980) 110 Cal App 3d 513, 520–521, 168 Cal Rptr 49.

[33] City of Alhambra v Superior Court (1980) 110 Cal App 3d 513, 521, 168 Cal Rptr 49.

[34] Long v Hauser (1975) 52 Cal App 3d 490, 493, 125 Cal Rptr 125.

CHAPTER 2

ORAL DEPOSITIONS IN CALIFORNIA

SYNOPSIS

§ 2.1 In General

Depositions and Affidavits Compared: Depositions and interrogatories are the most commonly used civil discovery methods. A deposition, however, offers several advantages over an interrogatory. Like an affidavit or declaration,[1] a deposition creates a statement under oath detailing the deponent's knowledge about a subject. However, in three ways, a deposition is different. First, an affidavit is the affiant's *voluntary* statement. A court may compel a person to submit to a deposition. Second, an affiant supplies information *narratively*, that is, without an interlocutor's prompts or interruptions. A deponent provides it *testimonially,* that is, in response to counsel's questions. Third, an affiant controls completely the affidavit's topics. A deponent's responses are dictated by the subject matter of the questions asked by counsel for any of the parties to the lawsuit.

Classifications: The depositions authorized by the Civil Discovery Act can be classified from four standpoints: (1) the *mode* of interrogating the deponent (oral examination or written questions); (2) the *location* of the examination (California, or another state or nation); (3) the *sovereign* whose court system is conducting the litigation (California, another state, the United States or another nation); and (4) the *stage* of the litigation (before, during or after the lawsuit).

Dual Role: The 2025 series[2] of statutes serves two purposes in the Discovery Act. First, it comprehensively regulates the manner of conducting the most common form of deposition: an oral deposition taken for discovery within California in a case then pending in the State's court system. Second, it provides the statutory matrix for all other deposition forms: those taken by written

---

[1] Certification or declaration under penalty of perjury. CCP § 2015.5. See Gatton v A.P. Green Services, Inc. (1998) 64 Cal App 4th 688, 695, 75 Cal Rptr 2d 523, 525–527 [comparing deposition testimony to declarations].

[2] CCP §§ 2025.010–2025.620.

questions;[3] those taken in another state[4] or nation;[5] those taken before[6] or after[7] suit; and those taken for use in another jurisdiction.[8]

Regulates Only Deposition Mechanics: The 2025 series[9] deals only with the mechanics of deposition discovery; it does not address the type of information that is discoverable during a deposition. The scope of allowable discovery via deposition is substantially the same as that for other forms of discovery. Accordingly, the reader should refer to the applicable section of the Act and the appropriate chapter of this treatise when an issue arises concerning the relevancy of a particular line of inquiry,[10] the validity of a claim of privilege[11] and the discoverability of an adversary's "work product" materials.[12]

§ 2.2 Commencement of Deposition Discovery

The mere filing of a complaint does not activate a plaintiff's right to start deposition discovery.[1] Instead, it is the date on which a defendant receives process or appears in the action that regulates when litigants may start the deposition-taking process. Section 2025.210 allows a *defendant* to notice a deposition immediately upon being served or entering an appearance in the lawsuit.[2] By contrast, *plaintiffs* may not notice depositions until "20 days after the service of the summons on, or *appearance* by, any defendant."[3] Thus, the California practice differs materially from the current federal practice, which places a hold on all discovery until the parties have met for a discovery conference.[4]

---

[3] CCP §§ 2028.010–2028.080. For a discussion of depositions conducted by written questions, see Chapter 3.

[4] CCP § 2026.010. For a discussion of depositions in a California lawsuit that are conducted in another state, see §§ 4.1–4.2.

[5] CCP § 2027.010. For a discussion of depositions in a California lawsuit that are conducted in another nation, see §§ 4.3–4.4.

[6] CCP §§ 2035.010–2035.060. For a discussion of depositions taken in anticipation of a California lawsuit, see §§ 14.1–14.4.

[7] CCP §§ 2036.010–2036.050. For a discussion of discovery taken while a California action is pending on appeal, see § 14.5.

[8] CCP § 2029.010.

[9] CCP §§ 2025.010–2025.620.

[10] CCP § 2017.010. For coverage of "relevance" in discovery, see Chapter 11.

[11] CCP § 2017.010. For coverage of the discovery of "privileged" materials, see Chapter 12.

[12] CCP § 2018.030. For coverage of the discovery of another party's "work product," see Chapter 13.

[1] California Shellfish Inc. v United Shellfish Co. (1997) 56 Cal App 4th 16, 20, 64 Cal Rptr 2d 797. Cf. Bernson v Browning-Ferris Industries of California, Inc. (1994) 7 Cal 4th 926, 930 n2, 30 Cal Rptr 2d 440 [querying whether the filing of a complaint naming only fictitious defendants gives the right to commence taking depositions].

[2] CCP § 2025.210(a).

[3] CCP § 2025.210(b) (italics added).

[4] FRCivP 26(d).

Immediate Commencement by a Defendant: As soon as a defendant has been served or has appeared, *"that* defendant" may notice a deposition.[5] *Other* defendants may not launch deposition discovery until they have either appeared in the action or received service of process.

Once served, a defendant may begin deposition discovery even before answering the complaint or otherwise formally appearing in the case.[6] However, to preserve an objection to the court's personal jurisdiction, a defendant must confine any deposition examination to jurisdictional matters. The defendant should state this intention in the deposition notices.[7] In *Creed v Schultz*,[8] the court held that the service of a deposition notice can constitute a general appearance in the action.[9]

"Hold" on Plaintiff's Discovery: Plaintiffs must wait until 20 days after some defendant has either been served or entered an appearance before they may notice a deposition.[10] This temporary hobbling of the plaintiffs' right to launch deposition discovery is designed to allow a defendant time to hire an attorney and learn the nature of the suit.[11] Moreover, it provides a brief opportunity for defendants to take the first depositions.[12] This "deposition hold" also prevents a plaintiff from "jumping the gun" by launching discovery before defendants are even aware of the litigation:

> The "hold" on each method of discovery, together with provisions requiring notice when a party initiates discovery by any method, ensures that no discovery is conducted unless some adverse party has notice of the litigation, and an opportunity to protect adversarial interests. . . . [I]t provides the minimum protection that at least one defendant is on notice, and has the opportunity to place some adversarial limits upon the plaintiff's pursuit of discovery. [¶] . . . A calculating litigant might conclude that it could benefit from the opportunity to access information it might not otherwise have if an adversary were on notice of the litigation and able to raise valid objections.[13]

---

[5] CCP § 2025.210(a) (italics added). See Putnam v Clague (1992) 3 Cal App 4th 542, 565, 5 Cal Rptr 2d 25.

[6] Flynn v Superior Court (1979) 89 Cal App 3d 491, 494, 152 Cal Rptr 796.

[7] See Islamic Republic of Iran v Pahlavi (1984) 160 Cal App 3d 620, 628, 206 Cal Rptr 752; 1880 Corp. v Superior Court (1962) 57 Cal 2d 840, 842–843, 22 Cal Rptr 209, 371 P2d 985.

[8] Creed v Schultz (1983) 148 Cal App 3d 733, 739–740, 196 Cal Rptr 252.

[9] Cf. Sanchez v Superior Court (1988) 203 Cal App 3d 1391, 1399, 250 Cal Rptr 787 [submission by unserved defendant to a deposition is not a general appearance in the action].

[10] CCP § 2025.210(b).

[11] Waters v Superior Court (1962) 58 Cal 2d 885, 892, 27 Cal Rptr 153, 377 P2d 265. See also 1970 Advisory Committee Note to FRCivP 30(a).

[12] Waters v Superior Court (1962) 58 Cal 2d 885, 892–893, 27 Cal Rptr 153, 377 P2d 265. For a discussion of priority in taking depositions, see § 2.3.

[13] California Shellfish Inc. v United Shellfish Co. (1997) 56 Cal App 4th 16, 23–24, 64 Cal Rptr 2d 797 [internal citations omitted].

—Multiple Defendants: In the *Waters* case,[14] decided under the 1956 Discovery Act, a plaintiff served deposition notices after serving one of the two defendants named in the complaint. As the statute then read, plaintiffs could not notice depositions until after "*the* defendant"[15] has appeared or received service. The defendant who had been served urged that where there were multiple defendants, a plaintiff must serve all of them before launching deposition discovery. The Supreme Court held, however, that deposition discovery became available when any *one* defendant has been served or has appeared.

Codifying this holding, CCP § 2025.210 now provides that a defendant may notice a deposition after "*that* defendant"[16] has been served or has appeared, and that a plaintiff may do so 20 days after "*any* defendant" has been served or has appeared.[17]

In a lawsuit naming multiple defendants, once the plaintiff has served "any defendant,"[18] the 20-day holding period begins to run as to *all* other defendants. This could cost those other defendants the opportunity to retain counsel and to gain priority in deposition discovery.[19] In *Waters,* the Supreme Court acknowledged this, but concluded that any other rule would be unfair to plaintiffs, who might have difficulty serving all named defendants.[20] The Court did not, however, condone manipulation of the timing of service by plaintiffs to gain priority in discovery over particular defendants. It suggested that defendants who suspect such conduct should seek a protective order.[21]

Leave to Take an Early Deposition: A plaintiff who needs an expedited deposition may apply to the trial court for "leave to serve a deposition notice on an earlier date."[22] A plaintiff may make this motion without notice to the defendant.[23] In that event, however, the federal courts will scrutinize the reasons for not notifying the defendant. As one federal judge put it: "Surely the very requirement . . . that leave be obtained demands the exercise of the court's discretion, which in turn must be based upon a showing of some significant reason for failing to give the opposing party notice and an opportunity to be heard."[24] Where a court has granted permission ex parte to take an early deposition, the

---

[14] Waters v Superior Court (1962) 58 Cal 2d 885, 892–893, 27 Cal Rptr 153, 377 P2d 265.

[15] Former CCP § 2016(a), 1956 Discovery Act, Appendix E (italics added).

[16] CCP § 2025.210(a) (italics added).

[17] CCP § 2025.210(b) (italics added).

[18] CCP § 2025.210(b).

[19] For a discussion of priority in deposition discovery, see § 2.3.

[20] Waters v Superior Court (1962) 58 Cal 2d 885, 892–893, 27 Cal Rptr 153, 377 P2d 265.

[21] Waters v Superior Court (1962) 58 Cal 2d 885, 893, 27 Cal Rptr 153, 377 P2d 265. See, e.g., Caribbean Construction Corp. v Kennedy Van Saun Mfg. & Eng. Corp. (1952, SD NY) 13 FRD 124, 126–127. For a discussion of protective orders in deposition settings, see § 2.14.

[22] CCP § 2025.210(b).

[23] CCP § 2025.210(b).

[24] K. J. Schwartzbaum, Inc. v Evans, Inc. (1968, SD NY) 279 F Supp 422, 423.

defendant, on receipt of the deposition notice, may still challenge the plaintiff's showing by moving to vacate the ex parte order.[25]

—**Good Cause Required:** Whether sought ex parte or after notice, the trial court should not perfunctorily grant a plaintiff leave to take an early deposition.[26] Section 2025.210 requires a plaintiff to show "good cause" for doing so. Federal trial judges have insisted that a plaintiff must provide "some valid, affirmative reason for making an exception to the time limitation."[27] This entails a showing of "urgent circumstances" creating an "emergency situation"[28] that "would be likely to prejudice the plaintiff if he were compelled to await for the required period."[29] They have found such circumstances in the prospective deponent's infirmity or imminent departure to a distant locale.[30] They do not find good cause in a mere desire to better prepare for a hearing on a motion for a preliminary injunction.[31]

§ 2.3 Priority in Deposition Discovery

Tactical Advantage: Parties generally consider it to their advantage to obtain discovery before providing it to their opponents: "Since discovery proceedings can seldom if ever be conducted simultaneously, it is inherent in such proceedings that the party who secures discovery first may derive advantages by securing information from his adversary before he is required to reciprocate by divulging information to him."[1] A party who has undertaken a particular discovery effort, e.g., by noticing a deposition, sometimes argues that this has a "priority" over later-initiated discovery. This claim of priority includes the asserted right to complete that particular discovery before other litigants may carry out any later-initiated discovery.

Priority questions most frequently arise in three situations: (1) when opponents react to a deposition notice by serving one of their own that schedules a deposition for a date earlier than that specified in the notice first served; (2) when a deposition scheduled for an earlier date is not completed by the date set in another

---

[25] See Bank of American Nat. Trust & Sav. Ass'n v Universal Pictures Co. (1952, SD NY) 13 FRD 513.

[26] Babolia v Local 456, Teamsters & Chauffeurs Union (1951, SD NY) 11 FRD 423, 424.

[27] Babolia v Local 456, Teamsters & Chauffeurs Union (1951, SD NY) 11 FRD 423, 424.

[28] K. J. Schwartzbaum, Inc. v Evans, Inc. (1968, SD NY) 279 F Supp 422, 423–424.

[29] Babolia v Local 456, Teamsters & Chauffeurs Union (1951, SD NY) 11 FRD 423, 424.

[30] Babolia v Local 456, Teamsters & Chauffeurs Union (1951, SD NY) 11 FRD 423, 424; Walker v Walker (1941, SD NY) 1 FRD 779; Samuel Goldwyn, Inc. v United Artists Corp. (1940, SD NY) 35 F Supp 633, 638. Under the present federal practice, a party seeking a deposition before the required discovery conference need not obtain leave of court if the deponent is about to leave the United States. In such cases, plaintiff's deposition notice need only certify, with supporting facts, the deponent's imminent departure. FRCivP 30(a)(2)(C).

[31] See, e.g., Pearce v Southeast Banking Corp. (1983, SD Fla) 97 FRD 535, 536–537; Gibson v Bagas Restaurants, Inc. (1980, WD Mo) 87 FRD 60, 61–62.

[1] Rosemont v Superior Court (1964) 60 Cal 2d 709, 714, 36 Cal Rptr 439, 388 P2d 671. See also Note, Developments in the Law—Discovery (1961) 74 Harv L Rev 940, 954.

party's subsequently noticed deposition; and (3) when opponents seek discovery by other methods, such as interrogatories, inspection demands, or admission requests, the response to which is due before the completion of a previously noticed deposition.

Former Federal and California Practice: Neither the original Discovery Act nor its prototype, the original version of the Federal Rules of Civil Procedure, said anything about discovery priority in any of these three situations. The federal trial courts, however, fashioned what became known as "the rule of priority." Under that rule, the first party to notice a deposition obtained the right to *begin* its deposition before any later-noticed deposition could begin.[2] They then extended that rule. No subsequently noticed deposition could start until the *completion* of the one first noticed.[3] In addition, the priority included the right to defer a response to later-served interrogatories, inspection demands and admission requests.[4]

Case law under the former Discovery Act is scant. Passages in two Supreme Court opinions appear to recognize that an earlier deposition notice produced a presumptive a right to complete that deposition before any other party could conduct a later-noticed one.[5]

During the life of the priority rule in the federal courts, it drew sharp criticism: "[T]he whole race of diligence in regard to the service of notice is a throwback to the 'sporting theory' of justice and is unseemly in a system where strategic advantage is to have no place."[6]

Current Federal Practice: In 1970, mindful of these criticisms, the federal rule makers eliminated any general rule of priority. Rule 26 now provides that, absent a protective order, "[the] methods of discovery may be used in any sequence and the fact that a party is conducting discovery, whether by deposition or otherwise, shall not operate to delay another party's discovery."[7] The purpose of this change is "first, to eliminate any fixed priority in the sequence of

---

[2] E.g., Fox v Warner Bros. Pictures, Inc. (1951, D Del) 12 FRD 202, 203.

[3] E.g., Shulman, Inc. v Shertz (1955, ED Pa) 18 FRD 94. A party with priority could forfeit it by failing to complete the deposition diligently. Kurt M. Jachmann Co. v Marine Office of America (1954, SD NY) 16 FRD 381.

[4] E.g., Colonial Airlines, Inc. v Janas (1952, SD NY) 13 FRD 199, 201 [production of documents]; E. I. Du Pont de Nemours & Co. v Phillips Petroleum Co. (1959, D Del) 23 FRD 237 [subsequent written interrogatories].

[5] Waters v Superior Court (1962) 58 Cal 2d 885, 892, 27 Cal Rptr 153, 377 P2d 265 ["Although this priority does not appear to have motivated the 20-day rule, the federal courts have upheld the defendant's right to obtain such priority"]; Rosemont v Superior Court (1964) 60 Cal 2d 709, 714, 36 Cal Rptr 439, 388 P2d 671 ["Parties should be encouraged to expedite discovery and should not needlessly be deprived of the advantages that normally flow from prompt action"].

[6] Yudkin, Some Refinements in Federal Discovery Procedure (1951) 11 Fed BJ 289, 296–297. See also Comment, Tactical Use and Abuse of Depositions Under the Federal Rules (1949) 59 Yale LJ 117, 135.

[7] FRCivP 26(d).

discovery, and second, to make clear and explicit the court's power to establish priority by an order issued in a particular case."[8]

Current California Practice: Section 2019.020 precludes as a general rule any priority claim based solely on a deposition notice's time of service:

> [T]he methods of discovery may be used in any sequence, and the fact that a party is conducting discovery, whether by deposition or another method, shall not operate to delay the discovery of any other party.[9]

This general rule is subject to modification by the Judicial Council or local court rule or policy.[10]

—Protective Order: The needs of a particular case may dictate court supervision of the sequence and timing of discovery, and for good cause the trial court is empowered to establish a different sequence for discovery.[11] A party who needs such supervision should apply to the court for a protective order. The trial court may enter an order that a "deposition be taken at a different time" than that specified in the notice.[12] Even when the California courts were disposed to follow the priority rule, they recognized the trial court's discretion to rearrange the sequence of discovery to prevent one party from obtaining an unfair advantage over another.[13]

De Facto Priority: Although California has copied the essence of the federal "no priority" approach, a first–served defendant who acts promptly may obtain a form of priority from the provisions that place a temporary "hold" on a plaintiff's right to serve interrogatories,[14] inspection demands,[15] and admission requests,[16] or to notice depositions.[17]

To capitalize on this opportunity to take the first deposition, defendants should serve their deposition notices as soon as feasible during the 20 days after being served or appearing in the action.[18] They must also be sure to schedule the

---

[8] 1970 Advisory Committee Note to FRCivP 26(d).

[9] CCP § 2019.020(a).

[10] CCP § 2019.020(a).

[11] CCP § 2019.020(b).

[12] CCP § 2025.420(b)(2). For a discussion of protective orders in a deposition setting, see § 2.14.

[13] Rosemont v Superior Court (1964) 60 Cal 2d 709, 714–715, 36 Cal Rptr 439, 388 P2d 671 [deposition postponed pending production of surreptitious recordings of conversations between the parties in breach of contract action].

[14] CCP § 2030.020(b). For a discussion of when a party may first send interrogatories, see § 5.2.

[15] CCP § 2031.020(b). For a discussion of when a party may first send inspection demands, see § 6.2.

[16] CCP § 2033.020(b). For a discussion of when a party may first send admission requests, see § 9.2.

[17] CCP § 2025.210. For a discussion of when a party may begin the deposition process, see § 2.2.

[18] For a discussion of the 20-day "hold" for plaintiff's deposition notices, see § 2.2.

depositions for the earliest date allowed, usually 10 days after the notice.[19] They should serve the notices personally rather than by mail. Otherwise, plaintiffs may gain priority by immediately making a *personal* service of notices scheduling depositions for an earlier date.

§ 2.4 Contents of Deposition Notice—Basic Components

A party starts the deposition process by serving a written notice.[1] The contents of a notice are minimal for a deposition of a natural person that is to be recorded only stenographically and that will not include a production of documents or other items. Such a deposition notice has only four components: the site of the examination, the time that the deposition will commence, a list of those receiving the notice, and the identity of the deponent.

Deposition Site: The notice must provide the address of the deposition site.[2] Section 2025.220 does not address the precise environment in which a deposition will occur. Most depositions take place in an attorney's office, usually that of the attorney who noticed the deposition. Nothing in the statute, however, prevents the examination from occurring at a court reporter's office, in the local courthouse,[3] in a prison,[4] or in the deponent's home,[5] office or hospital room.[6]

Time of Deposition: The notice must specify the date and hour that the deposition will commence.[7] The date selected must provide the amount of advance notice specified in Section 2025.270 for that type of deposition.[8]

Service List: The notice must also list the parties or attorneys for parties who are receiving notice of the deposition. This list may appear either in the body of the deposition notice itself or in the accompanying proof of service.[9]

Deponent's Identity: The notice must identify the deponent, ordinarily by name.[10] It must also include the address and telephone number, if known, of any deponent who is not a party.[11] The party noticing the deposition will usually have had to learn that person's address to serve the required subpoena.[12]

---

[19] For a discussion of the amount of notice required for a taking a deposition, see § 2.7.

[1] CCP § 2025.220(a).

[2] CCP § 2025.220(a)(1). For a discussion of the extent to which the deponent may be compelled to travel to a deposition site, see §§ 2.13–2.14.

[3] See, e.g., Margolis v Teplin (1958) 163 Cal App 2d 526, 529, 329 P2d 535.

[4] See, e.g., Nizinski v State Bar of California (1975) 14 Cal 3d 587, 590, 121 Cal Rptr 824, 536 P2d 72.

[5] See, e.g., Haley v Friedman (1964, Cal App) 40 Cal Rptr 1, 16.

[6] Cf. Russell v Roberts (1974) 39 Cal App 3d 390, 397, 114 Cal Rptr 305.

[7] CCP § 2025.220(a)(2).

[8] CCP § 2025.270. For a discussion of the time interval between notice and examination, see § 2.7.

[9] CCP § 2025.240(a).

[10] CCP § 2025.220(a)(3).

[11] CCP § 2025.220(a)(3).

[12] For a discussion of the need to subpoena a nonparty deponent, see § 2.9.

Sometimes, however, a party does not know the deponent's name. In such cases, Section 2025.220(a)(3) allows "a general description sufficient to identify the person or the particular class or group to which the person belongs."[13] This provision is only rarely used for nonparty deponents. Interpreting a similar provision,[14] a federal trial court[15] upheld a deposition notice that identified the deponent only as the agent in charge of an insurance carrier's claim file arising out of the injuries suffered by the plaintiff.[16]

More often, a party resorts to such job-function descriptions when the prospective deponent works for a corporate party to the litigation. The party serving the notice may want to depose a certain employee, instead of naming the corporation itself as the deponent and hoping that it will select that individual as its representative.[17] Thus, where that employee is one whom a corporate party must produce for a deposition without a subpoena,[18] the federal courts have upheld the following descriptions: "superintendent or caretaker in charge of [defendant's] premises",[19] the "President" and the "Vice-President" of the defendant corporation,[20] and "the captain or chief officer in charge of" defendant's vessel on a specified date.[21] In contrast, those courts have rejected as too general a notice that tells an organizational party to produce individuals described only by a catchall phrase, such as "persons who have knowledge of the facts relevant to the subject matter of this action,"[22] or "witnesses whose names are unknown to defendants."[23]

—Misnamed Deponents: Occasionally, the notice will misname the intended deponent. If the mistake is not egregious, forgiving courts may still find the notice sufficient to identify the prospective deponent. For example, in a federal case,[24] the plaintiff wanted to depose the founder and president of JOJO Ligne Internationale, Inc., whose name it thought was Mr. JoJo Ligne. Defendant *Joseph*

---

[13] CCP § 2025.220(a)(3).

[14] Fed Rules Civ Proc, Rule 30(b)(1).

[15] Meyer v Zim Israel Navigation Co. (1966, SD Tex) 41 FRD 228. See also Kulich v Murray (1939, SD NY) 28 F Supp 675, 676.

[16] This description was also sufficient for the subpoena used to compel the deponent's attendance.

[17] For a discussion of a deposition notice that names the organization itself as a deponent, see § 2.5.

[18] For a discussion of which employees of a corporate party must attend a deposition without the necessity of a subpoena, see § 2.12.

[19] Burris v American Chicle Co. (1939, ED NY) 1 FRD 9.

[20] Mattingly v Boston Woven Hose & Rubber Co. (1952, SD NY) 12 FRD 266.

[21] Fay v United States (1958, ED NY) 22 FRD 28.

[22] Struthers Scientific & International Corp. v General Foods Corp. (1968, SD Tex) 290 F Supp 122, 127.

[23] Moore v George A. Hormel & Co. (1942, SD NY) 2 FRD 340.

[24] JouJou Designs, Inc. v JoJo Ligne Internationale, Inc. (1992, ND Cal) 821 F Supp 1347, 1350.

(JoJo) Linus received the notice containing this misnomer at his business address and ignored it. The trial court concluded that he had received sufficient notice that the plaintiff wished to depose him.

No Need to Identify the Deposition Officer: Although Section 2025.320 does specify the qualifications of the officer who presides at a deposition,[25] it does not list the identity of that officer among the matters that a deposition notice must "state."[26] Under the similarly worded Rule 30,[27] federal courts have uniformly rejected attacks on deposition notices for failure to identify the officer before whom the examination will occur. A few courts, however, have remarked that it is "better practice" to include this identification.[28] Where the deposition notice does identify the notary-reporter, the substitution of another qualified individual for the person named does not invalidate the deposition.[29]

No Need to State Its Purposes: Some attorneys include in their deposition notices boilerplate language that they are taking the deposition "for discovery or for use as evidence, or for both purposes." Neither the procedure for taking a deposition nor the scope of permissible questioning ordinarily depends on its ultimate purpose. Moreover, no one can decide the admissibility of deposition testimony until someone offers it in evidence at the trial of the case.[30] Accordingly, a deposition notice ordinarily[31] need not specify the purposes for taking the deposition.[32]

No Need to State its Subject Matter: It is usually[33] unnecessary and inappropriate to indicate in the deposition notice the general subject matter that one will be exploring during the oral examination.[34] Nor is it necessary to proclaim in the notice an intent to probe only "nonprivileged matters relevant to the action's subject matter"; courts take this intent for granted.[35]

---

[25] CCP § 2025.320. For a discussion of the qualifications of the officer who presides at the deposition, see § 2.21.

[26] See CCP § 2025.220(a).

[27] FRCivP 30(b)(1).

[28] Yonkers Raceway, Inc. v Standardbred Owners Assn. (1957, SD NY) 21 FRD 3; Zweifler v Sleco Laces, Inc. (1950, SD NY) 11 FRD 202; Norton v Cooper Jarrett, Inc. (1938, ND NY) 1 FRD 92.

[29] Williams v Chadbourne (1856) 6 Cal 559, 561 [noting the inconvenience of the alternative rule], quoted with approval in Reimel v House (1969) 268 Cal App 2d 780, 786, 74 Cal Rptr 345, 348.

[30] Tatman v Collins (1991, CA4 W Va) 938 F2d 509, 510–511. For a discussion of the use of a deposition as evidence at the trial, see § 2.37.

[31] For a discussion of the exception for video recorded depositions of expert trial witnesses, see § 2.41.

[32] CCP § 2025.220.

[33] For a discussion of the exception for organizational deponents, see § 2.5.

[34] Spaeth v Warner Bros. Pictures, Inc. (1941, SD NY) 1 FRD 729, 731.

[35] Goldberg v Raleigh Mfrs., Inc. (1939, D Mass) 28 F Supp 975, 976.

§ 2.5 Special Components

Where a deposition involves an organizational deponent, the recording of the testimony by audio or video, or the production of documents or other items by the deponent, the notice must include more than the four basic deposition notice components.[1]

Organizational Deponents: Section 2025.010 allows a party to depose organizations, such as public or private corporations, partnerships, and government agencies. A deposition notice directed to such an entity must "describe with reasonable particularity the matters on which examination is requested."[2] This enables the entity to produce at the deposition "those of its officers, directors, managing agents, employees, or agents who are most qualified to testify on its behalf as to those matters to the extent of any information known or reasonably available to the deponent."[3] Where the organization is a nonparty, the deposition subpoena must contain a similar description of its topics, and a statement that the organization must produce these employees knowledgeable about these matters.[4]

Audio or Video Recording: The notice requirements also become more complex if the testimony will be recorded not only stenographically, but also on either audio or video.[5] In such cases, the notice must state the party's intention to do so.[6]

The deposition notice also must specify whether the deposing party intends to record the testimony by stenographic method through the instant visual display of the testimony. If so, the party taking the deposition must also give a copy of the notice to the deposition officer. If the deposition officer offers to provide the visual display of the testimony or to provide rough draft transcripts to any party at the deposition, the officer must make the same offer to all parties in attendance.[7]

—Expert Trial Witness: Sometimes a party intends not only to video the testimony of a deponent who is an expert, but also to use the video recorded deposition instead of the expert's live testimony at trial.[8] In this event, the deposition notice must contain a statement of this intention.[9]

Document Production: If the noticing party seeks both the deponent's testimony and a production of documents or other items at the deposition, the

---

[1] For a discussion of the basic components of any deposition notice, see § 2.4.

[2] CCP § 2025.230.

[3] CCP § 2025.230. For a further discussion of depositions of organizations, see §§ 2.9 and 2.14.

[4] CCP § 2020.310(e).

[5] For a discussion of the right to audio or video a deposition, see § 2.33.

[6] CCP § 2025.220(a)(5).

[7] CCP § 2025.220(a)(5).

[8] See CCP § 2025.620(d). For a discussion of the right to offer in evidence an expert's video recorded deposition in lieu of live testimony, see § 2.41.

[9] CCP § 2025.220(a)(6).

notice must specify "with reasonable particularity" the items or categories of items that the deponent is to bring to the deposition session.[10] However, where the *only* purpose of the deposition is to get a copy of a nonparty's business records, a copy of the subpoena served on that party functions as the deposition notice.[11]

§ 2.6 Recipients of the Deposition Notice

Appearance by a Party Governs Right to Notice: Section 2025.210 recognizes the need to allow those parties who have appeared in an action to begin deposition discovery promptly.[1] Section 2025.240 requires service of a deposition notice only on "every other party *who has appeared* in the action."[2] A party who wants to take a deposition no longer needs to serve notice on a party who has not yet appeared in the action,[3] even if that party has been served.

Protections for Non-Appearing Parties: In two ways, the rights of parties who have not yet appeared are protected from suffering prejudice from a deposition of which they did not receive notice. First, these parties are exempted from the prohibition against deposing a person who has already given a deposition in the action.[4] Second, a deposition may not be used at trial against any party who did not receive notice of it.[5] This second provision, however, does not imply that a litigant may deliberately take depositions without notifying parties who have appeared. If the only consequence of failing to notify these parties were the inability to use the depositions against them at trial, a crafty litigant might be willing to chance this to get discovery without an adversary's presence. This practice is unethical:

> If a party were allowed to compel an independent witness to give his deposition, all without notice to the opposing party, a situation not contemplated by the discovery statutes would result. For then a party might resort to all manner of discovery without adequate protection to his opponent, so long as he intended to forego any formal introduction

---

[10] CCP § 2025.220(a)(4).

[11] CCP § 2025.220(b). For a discussion of a "records only" deposition, see § 7.3.

[1] CCP § 2025.210 For a discussion of commencement of deposition discovery, see § 2.2.

[2] CCP § 2025.240(a) (italics added).

[3] Cf. former CCP § 2019(a)(1), 1956 Discovery Act, Appendix E [requiring notice to "every other party" to the action].

[4] CCP § 2025.610(a). For a discussion of the general prohibition against deposing a person who has already given a deposition in the case, see § 2.36.

[5] CCP § 2025.620. E.g., Laesione v Stop-N-Go Foods, Inc. (1990, WD NY) 133 FRD 92, 93–94 [deposition inadmissible against a party who received only oral notice of its taking]; Mature v Stone (1993, Mo App) 856 SW2d 84, 85 [deposition taken before joinder of party in case is generally inadmissible against that party]; Bergsieker v Schnuck Markets, Inc. (1993, Mo App) 849 SW2d 156, 160–163 [prejoinder deposition inadmissible even if new party is not prejudiced]. For a discussion of the use of a deposition at trial, see §§ 2.37–2.42.

of the material at time of trial. This would present an intolerable situation.[6]

However, parties who *have* received notice of a deposition notice do not have standing to block that deposition because others entitled to notice have not received it.[7]

§ 2.7   Time of Taking Deposition

Normal 10-Day Notice: The deposition notice must fix the date on which the examination will begin.[1] In contrast to the federal provision, which requires only a "reasonable" time between the notice and the deposition itself,[2] Section 2025.270 specifies that normally "at least 10 days" must pass between the service of the notice and the start of the deposition.[3] This 10-day period applies even if the deposition notice is one that instructs a party to produce the sort of item that is also obtainable by an inspection demand.[4] The Legislature rejected the Discovery Commission's proposal[5] that a party-deponent directed to produce items receive the same 30-day period allowed for inspection demands.[6]

Exceptions: In four situations, the normal 10-day period does not apply. First, the deposition of one who must produce the "personal records of a consumer" may not occur earlier than 20 days after the issuance of the subpoena for them.[7] Second, mailed service of a deposition notice extends the notice period, usually by five days.[8] Third, in unlawful detainer actions, the deposition date must be 10 days after service of the notice, or five days before trial, whichever is earlier. Finally, upon motion, the trial court may extend or shorten the statutory period.[9]

Objections to the Day or Hour: Parties receiving a deposition notice may object to the time selected for the examination for two reasons: (1) its unusual day or hour, and (2) its violation of the 10-day notice rule. However, in neither situation may they simply ignore the notice. They must take steps to stay the scheduled deposition.

---

[6] Lund v Superior Court (1964) 61 Cal 2d 698, 711, 39 Cal Rptr 891, 394 P2d 707.

[7] Waters v Superior Court (1962) 58 Cal 2d 885, 894, 27 Cal Rptr 153, 377 P2d 265.

[1] CCP § 2025.220(a)(2).

[2] FRCivP 30(b). This usually requires a notice of at least five business days. See 7 Moore's Federal Practice, § 30.20[1].

[3] CCP § 2025.270(a).

[4] See CCP § 2031.260 [allowing 30 days for a party to respond to an inspection demand.] For a further discussion of getting document discovery by a deposition instead of by an inspection demand, see § 6.3.

[5] Proposed Civil Discovery Act of 1986, Section 2025(f), Appendix D.

[6] CCP § 2031.030(c)(2).

[7] CCP § 2025.270.

[8] CCP § 2016.050, referencing CCP § 1013(a).

[9] CCP § 2025.270.

—**Unusual Day or Hour:** Nothing in the statute prevents a party from scheduling a deposition in the evening or on a weekend.[10] In one federal case, however, a party noticed a deposition to begin in midweek and to continue "from day to day" until completed. The court found that such notice did not adequately express an intention to continue through the weekend rather than to resume on Monday.[11] In any event, a party who objects to unusual scheduling should seek a protective order rather than simply ignore the notice.[12]

—**Premature Date:** If a deposition notice schedules the examination for a date before the minimum notice period's expiration, it may be attacked, but it may not be ignored. Section 2025.410 requires the objecting party to serve a written objection at least "three calendar days before the date for which the deposition is scheduled."[13] This objection must specify that the date scheduled is too early.[14] The service of the objection does not itself stay the deposition. At best it will prevent the deposition's use against the objecting party at trial provided the court then rules that the objection was valid.[15] To stay the deposition itself, the objecting party must also move for a protective order.

Motion to Stay Deposition: A party who wishes to stay the taking of a deposition scheduled for a date that is too early should move for a protective order quashing the deposition notice.[16] This motion automatically stays the taking of the deposition pending its determination. The moving party must accompany the motion with a declaration setting forth the informal efforts made to resolve the issues. The party who loses at the hearing on this motion must pay a monetary sanction unless the court finds that there was substantial justification for making or opposing it.[17]

Waiver of Objections: If, without leave of court, a party schedules a deposition on less than ten days' notice, a deponent who nonetheless appears and submits to examination at the scheduled time waives the objection.[18] Similarly, parties receiving notice of the deposition who fail to serve a written objection at least three days before the scheduled examination date also waive any claim of error concerning the premature date.[19]

---

[10] See, e.g., Socha v Webber (1951, D Alaska) 11 FRD 124 [8:00 pm]. Cf. Shenker v United States (1960, ED NY) 25 FRD 96, 98 ["No examination may be held on Sunday"].

[11] Miller v International Paper Co. (1969, CA5 Miss) 408 F2d 283, 293.

[12] CCP § 2025.410. See Socha v Webber (1951, D Alaska) 11 FRD 124.

[13] CCP § 2025.410(a).

[14] CCP § 2025.410(a).

[15] CCP § 2025.410(b).

[16] CCP § 2025.410(c).

[17] CCP § 2020.220(c).

[18] In re Marriage of Lemen (1980) 113 Cal App 3d 769, 779, 170 Cal Rptr 642.

[19] CCP § 2025.410(a).

§ 2.8   Defective Deposition Notice

Examples: A deposition notice might be defective in a host of ways. For instance, it might omit the deposition site, improperly identify the deponent or describe with insufficient particularity the items the deponent must produce.[1] Where the deponent is a corporation or other organization,[2] the notice might fail to describe the areas of proposed inquiry, or to advise a nonparty organization of its duty to designate and produce knowledgeable employees to testify. A deposition notice might also be defective because the party sending it is prematurely commencing discovery by this method,[3] is giving less than the statutorily prescribed notice,[4] or has selected a site that is a greater distance from the deponent than Section 2025.250(a) allows.[5]

Written Objections: Other parties may attack a defective deposition notice, but they ignore it at their peril. Section 2025.410 precludes challenges to "errors or irregularities" in a deposition notice unless a party has served written objections specifying them.[6] The objecting party must serve not only the party who noticed the deposition, but also any party who received that notice.[7] The objecting party must make this service no later than three calendar days before the date set for the deposition. If asserted on the last day for doing so, that party must personally serve the objections on the one who noticed the deposition.

Effect of Serving Objections: The timely service of objections to a notice does not stay the deposition. However, if the objecting party does not then waive the objections by attending the deposition, and if at trial the court finds them meritorious, no one may offer that deposition in evidence against that party.[8]

Motion to Quash Deposition Notice: A party who simply serves objections to a defective deposition notice takes several risks. The party who sent the notice may ignore the objections, go forward with the examination of the witness and obtain at least the discovery value of the deposition. If the objections turn out to lack merit, the party making them may lose the right to depose that witness[9] and to object to use of the deposition at trial.[10]

To avoid these risks, Section 2025.410 allows one who has served a timely objection to a deposition notice to "also move for a protective order staying the

---

[1] For a discussion of the contents of a deposition notice, see §§ 2.4–2.5.

[2] For a discussion of depositions of organizations, see §§ 2.5 and 2.14.

[3] For a discussion of the commencement of deposition discovery, see § 2.2.

[4] For a discussion of the prescribed period between the service of a deposition notice and the examination itself, see § 2.7.

[5] CCP § 2025.250(a). For a discussion of the geographical limits on the place of a deposition, see §§ 2.13–2.14.

[6] CCP § 2025.410(a).

[7] For a discussion of the parties who should receive notice of a deposition, see § 2.6.

[8] CCP § 2025.410(b).

[9] For a discussion of the one-deposition limit, see § 2.36.

[10] For a discussion of the use of depositions at the trial, see §§ 2.37–2.42.

taking of the deposition and quashing the deposition notice."[11] This motion automatically stays the deposition until the court rules on the merits of the objections. The moving party must accompany the motion with a declaration setting forth the informal efforts made to resolve the objections. The party who loses at the hearing on this motion must pay a monetary sanction unless the court finds that there was substantial justification for making or opposing it.[12]

§ 2.9 Compelling Attendance—Nonparty Deponent

A litigant must use court process[1] to compel attendance, testimony and document production by a deponent who is neither a party to the action[2] nor affiliated with a party.[3] Section 2020.020 now provides for three types of "deposition subpoenas," depending on whether the party noticing the deposition seeks only testimony,[4] only production of business records,[5] or both testimony and production.[6] This section of this treatise addresses subpoenas that seek only the testimony of a nonparty deponent. Deposition subpoenas that seek from nonparties only document production[7] or both testimony and document production[8] are covered in Chapter 7.

Issuance of Deposition Subpoenas: No matter where in California the deposition site is, the court of the forum county issues the deposition subpoenas.[9] Instead of a court-issued subpoena, a party's attorney of record may sign and issue a deposition subpoena.[10]

Individual Deponents: A subpoena that commands an individual to attend and testify at a deposition must meet three requirements. First, it must specify the time and the place of the deposition.[11] Second, it must summarize "(1) the

---

[11] CCP § 2025.410(c).

[12] CCP § 2025.410(d).

[1] CCP § 2025.280(b).

[2] For a discussion of ways to compel the attendance of a party deponent, see § 2.10.

[3] See, e.g., People ex rel. Lockyer v Superior Court (2004) 122 Cal App 4th 1060, 1076–1077, 19 Cal Rptr 3d 324 [service of deposition subpoenas is necessary to compel attendance of officials and employees of state agencies, which are not considered to be parties to a civil action brought by the Attorney General on behalf of "the People"]. For a discussion of ways to compel the attendance of a party-affiliated deponent, see § 2.12.

[4] CCP § 2020.020(a).

[5] CCP § 2020.020(b).

[6] CCP § 2020.020(c).

[7] For a discussion of deposition subpoenas that seek only document production, see § 7.3.

[8] For a discussion of deposition subpoenas that seek both testimony and document production, see § 7.2.

[9] CCP § 2020.210(a). Compare Wemyss v Superior Court (1952) 38 Cal 2d 616, 621–622, 241 P2d 525 [under the 1956 Discovery Act, if a nonparty deponent lived in California, but more than 150 miles from the forum county, the court of the county that was the deposition site issued the subpoena].

[10] CCP § 2020.210(b).

[11] CCP § 2020.310(a).

nature of a deposition, (2) the rights and duties of the deponent, and (3) the penalties for disobedience of a deposition subpoena."[12] Finally, it must inform the deponent of any intent to video the testimony.[13]

Organizational Deponents: Section 2025.010 permits parties to a civil action to obtain a deposition not only from individuals but also from "an organization such as a public or private corporation, a partnership, an association, or a governmental agency."[14] An organizational deponent must produce for examination "those of its officers, directors, managing agents, employees, or agents who are most qualified to testify on its behalf"[15] concerning the subjects that the party serving the deposition intends to explore.

Besides the three requirements just described for deposition subpoenas directed to individuals, Section 2020.310 imposes two additional ones for those addressed to a nonparty organization. First, the subpoena must "describe with reasonable particularity" the areas that the party noticing the deposition intends to explore.[16] Second, it must advise the nonparty organization of its duty to produce those of its officers, directors, or employees who are knowledgeable about these subjects.[17]

Open Questions: The Discovery Act unquestionably allows parties to civil suits to depose a nonparty corporation or other organization. However, it does not explicitly deal with three important questions: (1) To what the extent are corporations and other organizations chartered by other states or nations subject to a California court's subpoena during discovery in a case to which they are not a party? (2) How does one serve a deposition subpoena on an organizational deponent? (3) If an organization is subject to a California court's subpoena power, to what extent must it produce knowledgeable officials and employees who are themselves beyond the reach of that power?

—(1) Foreign Organizations: The first issue involves a California court's power to subpoena a nonparty foreign corporation or other organizational entity that has not qualified to do business in California. Case law is scant, but what there is suggests that the organization's contacts with California must at least be sufficient to make it subject to suit here had it been named as a defendant:

> A foreign corporation doing business in a district is subject to all process, including subpoena, in the district . . . . But a corporation not doing business in the district cannot be compelled to respond to such a subpoena. The question of whether a foreign corporation does business within the jurisdiction usually arises in the context of the forum court's

---

12 CCP § 2020.310(b).

13 CCP § 2020.310(c).

14 CCP § 2025.010.

15 CCP § 2025.230.

16 CCP § 2020.310(e), referencing CCP § 2025.230.

17 CCP § 2020.310(e), referencing CCP § 2025.230.

being asked to decide whether it has jurisdiction over the corporation as a party defendant rather than as a non-party witness, and . . . a different (and presumably stricter) standard might apply to *non*-party subpoenas.[18]

—(2) Recipient of Deposition Subpoena: The second question left unanswered is the identity of the person who should receive service of the deposition subpoena for an organization that *is* subject to a California court's subpoena power. Section 1987, incorporated by reference in Section 2020.030, provides that generally one serves a subpoena by delivering it "to the witness personally."[19] Section 1987 does not, however, specify how one is to accomplish this where the witness is not a natural person.

A deposition subpoena is a form of court process. A domestic corporation must file with the Secretary of State a designation of an "agent of such corporation for the purpose of service of *process*."[20] A foreign corporation transacting business in California likewise must designate "an agent upon whom *process* directed to the corporation may be served within this state."[21] Similar provisions apply to domestic unincorporated associations[22] and foreign partnerships doing business in California.[23] The California courts are likely to hold that these designated agents are the proper persons upon whom to serve a deposition subpoena directed to their organization.

Where an organization that is subject to a California court's subpoena power has not designated an agent for service of process, a court may order substitute service of process. If the organization is incorporated or a partnership registered to do business in California, the court may order process served upon the California Secretary of State.[24] If the organization is an unincorporated association, the court may order process served upon any member of the association.[25]

—(3) Individuals Beyond Subpoena Power: The third matter left open by Section 2025 is whether a California court's power to subpoena an organization extends to the production by it of knowledgeable personnel who are *not themselves* subject to that power. Unlike the former statute,[26] Section 2025.230

---

[18] Elder-Beerman Stores Corp. v Federated Dept. Stores, Inc. (1968, SD NY) 45 FRD 515, 516 (original italics). See also Coopman v Superior Court (1965) 237 Cal App 2d 656, 659–661, 47 Cal Rptr 131; Ghandi v Police Dept. of City of Detroit (1977, ED Mich) 74 FRD 115, 121–122; In re Electric & Musical Industries, Ltd. (1957, SD NY) 155 F Supp 892, 894–896.

[19] CCP § 2020.030 referencing CCP § 1987.

[20] Corp Code § 1502(b) (italics added).

[21] Corp Code § 2105(a)(4) (italics added).

[22] Corp Code § 24003.

[23] Corp Code § 15700.

[24] Corp Code § 1702(a) [California corporations], § 2111(a) [foreign corporations] and § 15700 [foreign partnerships].

[25] Corp Code § 24007.

[26] Former CCP § 2019(a)(6), 1956 Discovery Act, Appendix E [requiring the consent of any employee other than an officer, director or managing agent of the organizational deponent].

requires the organization to produce *any* employee who is qualified to testify on the matters described in the deposition subpoena.[27] There is no need to subpoena these individuals. However, the statute does not expressly address the compulsive power of the subpoena served on the organization upon its nonresident personnel.[28]

Fees and Mileage: Any person served with a deposition subpoena that requires actual attendance and testimony is entitled to receive the same witness fees and mileage as if the subpoena required the person to attend and testify before a court.[29] Prospective deponents do not waive their rights if they do not demand this payment when they are served. The statute allows the party taking the deposition to make the payment either at the time of service or at the time the deposition occurs.[30]

Sanctions: Nonparties who ignore a deposition subpoena risk two serious sanctions. First, they expose themselves to punishment for contempt.[31] It is not necessary to obtain a court order compelling their compliance as a precondition for this sanction.[32] Second, they forfeit to the party noticing the deposition $500 and any other damages that party incurred.[33]

§ 2.10   Party Deponent

No Need to Serve Subpoena: The court in which an action is pending already has jurisdiction over plaintiffs and any defendants who have been served. There is no reason to require the rigmarole of serving a subpoena to compel a party to appear for a deposition. Accordingly, where the deponent is a party to the case, Section 2025.280 requires only service of a *notice* of deposition:

> The service of a deposition notice . . . is effective to require any deponent who is a party to the action . . . to attend and to testify, as well as to produce any document or tangible thing for inspection and copying.[1]

Possible Exceptions: In two situations, federal courts have required service of a subpoena upon a party deponent. A deposition subpoena is necessary to compel the attendance of any deponent who is an "involuntary plaintiff"[2] in the

---

[27] CCP § 2025.230.

[28] For a discussion of whether a nonparty organizational deponent must produce knowledgeable employees who are not themselves subject to the court's deposition subpoena power, see § 2.14.

[29] CCP § 2020.230(a).

[30] CCP § 2020.230(a).

[31] E.g., Bankers Trust Co. v Braten (1993, App Div) 598 NYS 2d 498, 498 [nonparty deponents may be held in contempt for failure to appear at deposition in answer to proper subpoena].

[32] CCP § 2020.240. See, e.g., Gregori v Bank of America (1989) 207 Cal App 3d 291, 311, 254 Cal Rptr 853.

[33] CCP § 2020.240, referencing CCP § 1992.

[1] CCP § 2025.280(a).

[2] See CCP § 382. See also FRCivP 19(a).

case.[3] A deposition subpoena is also necessary once a party has been dismissed from the lawsuit.[4] It is likely that a California court would take the same positions.

Fees and Mileage: Unlike a nonparty deponent,[5] a party deponent is not entitled to payment of a witness fee or mileage expenses.[6]

Sanctions: Unlike the 1956 Act,[7] Section 2025.450 does not authorize the immediate imposition of a drastic sanction, such as dismissal or default, upon a party who fails to appear for a noticed deposition. Instead, the one who noticed the deposition must then move for an order compelling the deponent's attendance.[8] Before making this motion, the moving party must have attempted to resolve any issues informally.[9]

If the court grants the motion, it will impose a monetary sanction on the party deponent, unless that party shows that there was substantial justification for not appearing for the deposition.[10] Both the party who noticed the deposition and any other party who attended expecting that the deposition would go forward may seek this sanction.[11]

Only if the party deponent then disobeys the order compelling attendance may the trial court impose a drastic sanction. Even then, however, it has the discretion to impose another monetary sanction and give the party another chance to comply with its order.[12]

§ 2.11 Unnamed Class Members

Deposition Subpoena Not Necessary: The original Discovery Act did not require the service of a subpoena upon a deponent who was "a person for whose

---

[3] See Diebold, Inc. v Record Files, Inc. (1951, ND Ohio) 11 FRD 543.

[4] El Salto, S.A. v PSG Co. (1971, CA9 Or) 444 F2d 477, 484; Sunbeam Corp. v Payless Drug Stores (1953, ND Cal) 113 F Supp 31, 46–47.

[5] For a discussion of the need to subpoena a nonparty deponent and pay that deponent a witness fee and mileage, see § 2.9.

[6] Di Napoli v Superior Court (1967) 252 Cal App 2d 202, 204–205, 60 Cal Rptr 394.

[7] Former CCP § 2034(d), 1956 Discovery Act, Appendix E [requiring finding of "wilful" failure to attend]. See Midwife v Bernal (1988) 203 Cal App 3d 57, 63, 249 Cal Rptr 708 [requiring finding of "wilful" failure to attend deposition under former CCP § 2034(d) before the court could impose a drastic sanction, such as dismissal of the lawsuit].

[8] CCP § 2025.450(a).

[9] CCP § 2025.450(b)(2).

[10] CCP § 2025.450(c)(1).

[11] CCP § 2025.450(c)(2). See also Midwife v Bernal (1988) 203 Cal App 3d 57, 62 n3, 249 Cal Rptr 708 [where a plaintiff's failure to appear for a deposition noticed by one defendant warrants a monetary sanction, that sanction may also run in favor of a co-defendant who did not notice the deposition, but who did appear at the scheduled time and place].

[12] CCP § 2025.450(d).

Annotation: Dismissal of state court action for failure or refusal of plaintiff to appear or answer questions at deposition or oral examination. 32 ALR4th 212.

immediate benefit" the action was being prosecuted.[1] In the *Southern California Edison* case, the Supreme Court held that after certification of a class, its unnamed members fell into this category.[2] Therefore, service of a subpoena on them was not necessary to compel them to appear for a deposition.

Section 2025.280 has dropped all mention of "immediate beneficiaries" of an action from its list of those for whom no subpoena is required to compel their appearance for a deposition.[3] However, this omission does not change the outcome of *Southern California Edison* because it was not necessary for the Court to have rested its holding on the classification of unnamed members as "immediate beneficiaries" of a class action. Section 2025.280 provides that only service of a deposition notice is required to compel the attendance and testimony of "any deponent who is a *party to the action.*"[4] Case law recognizes that after certification of a class, its members become parties to the action and, therefore, must respond to discovery via *interrogatories.*[5] There is no reason to treat these members any differently where the discovery method involved is a deposition. Since it is unnecessary to serve a deposition subpoena on other types of parties to the action, the same should be true of those who are unnamed members of a certified class.

—Discretion to Require Subpoena: Even as *Southern California Edison* was holding that there was no need to serve a deposition subpoena on unnamed class members, it also ruled that the trial court had the discretion to impose this requirement where the particular class is "disorganized and loosely knit."[6] Otherwise, it feared, the ease with which they could arrange to depose class members might tempt defendants to use this form of discovery to undermine the usefulness of class actions:

> [P]laintiffs' attorneys will be forced to expend extraordinary time and effort to round up persons of a disorganized class with whom they probably have had no prior contact; such occurred in the instant case. Prospective deponents who do not heed informal efforts on the part of counsel and do not appear will face potential exclusion. Thus, a defendant can effectively stifle a class action at the discovery stage, either by imposing impossibly expensive burdens on the named plaintiffs

---

[1] Former CCP § 2029(a)(4), 1956 Discovery Act, Appendix E.

[2] Southern California Edison Co. v Superior Court (1972) 7 Cal 3d 832, 839–840, 103 Cal Rptr 709, 500 P2d 621.

[3] CCP § 2025.280(a). See Reporter's Note to Section 2025(h)(1) of the Proposed Civil Discovery Act of 1986, Appendix D.

[4] CCP § 2025.280(a) (italics added). Cf. Collins v Wayland (1944, CA9 Ariz) 139 F2d 677, 678.

[5] Danzig v Superior Court (1978) 87 Cal App 3d 604, 608–609, 151 Cal Rptr 185. For a discussion of interrogatories directed to unnamed class members, see § 5.5.

[6] Southern California Edison Co. v Superior Court (1972) 7 Cal 3d 832, 841 n7, 103 Cal Rptr 709, 500 P2d 621.

or by chipping away at the size of the class through exclusion of the unnamed plaintiffs.[7]

Accordingly, the Court upheld the trial court's discretion, for the "good cause" shown by the attorney for the class, to enter a protective order shifting to the defendant the burden of securing the attendance at depositions of unnamed class members.[8]

Leave of Court Necessary? Quite apart from the need to serve them with a subpoena, an attempt to depose unnamed class members presents a threshold problem, namely, whether they should have to submit to a deposition at all. Federal courts have required defendants to apply for leave to take such depositions and to show, not only their necessity, but the absence of any motive to take advantage of the class members:

> Defendants must have leave of court to take depositions of members of a putative class, other than the named class members—after first showing that discovery is both necessary and for a purpose other than taking undue advantage of class members. The burden is heavy to justify asking questions by interrogatories, even heavier to justify depositions.[9]

§ 2.12 Party-Affiliated Deponent

Deposition of Organizational Party Itself: When an organization, such as a corporation, is a party to a lawsuit, the other parties often need to obtain information from individuals connected with it who are not parties to the action. One way to do this is to depose the organization itself.[1] Since the organization is a party to the case, it need not be served with a deposition subpoena. Service of the deposition notice is "effective" to compel the attendance of "any deponent who is a party to the action."[2] Of course, as an artificial, legal entity, the organization itself will not actually be deposed. Instead, it must produce at the deposition "those of its officers, directors, managing agents, employees, or agents" who are knowledgeable concerning the matters described in the deposition notice.[3] Since these knowledgeable personnel represent the organizational party itself, it is not necessary to serve a subpoena on either them or the organization to compel their attendance.

---

[7] Southern California Edison Co. v Superior Court (1972) 7 Cal 3d 832, 842, 103 Cal Rptr 709, 500 P2d 621.

[8] Southern California Edison Co. v Superior Court (1972) 7 Cal 3d 832, 841 n7, 103 Cal Rptr 709, 500 P2d 621.

[9] Flynn v National Safety Associates (1993, ND Cal) 149 FRD 598, 600. See also Clark v Universal Builders, Inc. (1974, CA7 Ill) 501 F2d 324, 340–341.

[1] See CCP § 2025.210.

[2] CCP § 2025.280(a).

[3] CCP § 2025.230. For a discussion of the contents of a deposition notice directed to an organization, see § 2.5.

Deposition of Officials of an Organizational Party: A party may not be content with deposing only those individuals that an organization might designate in response to a notice to take its deposition. It may prefer to depose a specific individual connected with the organization. In this event, the notice should name that individual, and not the organization itself, as the deponent. It is not necessary to subpoena these nonparty deponents. Section 2025.280 makes the service of a deposition notice on an organizational party "effective" to compel the attendance of any deponent who is an officer, director, or managing agent of a party.[4]

Deposition of "Employee" of an Organizational Party: In a major departure from the pre-1987 California[5] and the present federal law,[6] Section 2025.280 makes the service of a deposition notice "effective" also to compel the attendance of an "employee of a party."[7] This does away with the need to make the slippery distinction between "managing agents" and other employees of an organizational party.[8] It also harmonizes with two other provisions of the Civil Discovery Act: that which requires an organization named as a deponent to designate and produce "employees" who are qualified to testify concerning the matters specified in the deposition notice directed to it;[9] and that which permits at trial the use of a deposition given by a party's employee against the party itself.[10]

Organizational Party's Duty to Produce the Deponents: The corporation or other organization that is a party to the case must compel the attendance of its officers, directors, managing agents and employees. A failure of a party-affiliated deponent to attend is imputed to the organization itself.[11] The organization's ability to compel this attendance is a corollary of its practical control over its officers, directors and subordinates:

> There can be no doubt that a witness . . . who is a director, officer, or managing agent of a party to an action will be under considerable coercion to attend whenever his corporate employer is placed under the severe sanctions authorized by [former CCP § 2034 of the original

---

[4] CCP § 2025.280(a).

[5] Former CCP § 2019(a)(4), 1956 Discovery Act, Appendix E. Cf. Volkswagen of America, Inc. v Superior Court (1971) 18 Cal App 3d 477, 479–480, 96 Cal Rptr 205.

[6] FRCivP 30. E.g., United States v Affram Lines (USA), Ltd. (1994, SD NY) 159 FRD 408, 413.

[7] CCP § 2025.280(a).

[8] See, e.g., Waters v Superior Court (1962) 58 Cal 2d 885, 896, 27 Cal Rptr 153, 377 P2d 265.

Annotation: Who is a "managing agent" of a corporate party (to civil litigation) whose discovery-deposition may be taken under Federal Rules of Civil Procedure or state counterparts. 98 ALR2d 622.

[9] CCP § 2025.230.

[10] CCP § 2025.620(b).

[11] See, e.g., Wanderer v Johnston (1990, CA9 Cal) 910 F2d 652, 657 [where a partnership formed between two corporations was a party, the failure of the representative of one of the corporate partners to respond to a notice naming the partnership as the deponent warranted the imposition of sanctions against the partnership].

Discovery Act]. For example, a witness who refused to obey a reasonable request or command of his employer to attend the taking of a deposition would risk loss of his position or other disciplinary action.[12]

Although a corporate party must produce its current employees for a deposition, it is not required to produce them for pre-deposition interview by another party's counsel, seeking to determine whether a deposition would be worthwhile:

> Nothing in the Civil Discovery Act . . .authorizes a trial court to order a party to make its employees available for interview by its opponent. The fact that the trial court was attempting to fashion a practical solution to accommodate each party's concerns is not controlling.[13]

Subsidiary of an Organizational Party: Arguably, where the named deponent is an officer, director, managing agent or employee of a *subsidiary* of a corporate party, the *parent* corporation must produce that person for a deposition.[14] In the reverse situation, however, some courts have found no obligation for a *subsidiary* that is a party to produce someone in the hierarchy of its *parent* organization.[15] However, the individual deponent's relationship with the particular corporations involved may change this. Thus, one federal court deemed it unnecessary to serve a subpoena on a deponent who was an officer of the European parent of a defendant corporation. The deponent happened to be a former officer of the subsidiary and the son of the president of both corporations.[16]

Former Affiliates: Where the deponent named in the notice is its *former* officer, director, managing agent or employee, an organizational party need not produce that person based on a deposition notice. Ordinarily, the party seeking the deposition must serve a subpoena to compel the deponent's attendance:

> Examination of a party through former officers or managing agents would be unfair both because the party would have no power to secure the attendance of these persons for examination and because it cannot be supposed that these former employees would identify their interests

---

[12] Twin Lock, Inc. v Superior Court County (1959) 52 Cal 2d 754, 759, 344 P2d 788.

[13] Valley Presbyterian Hospital v Superior Court (2000) 79 Cal App 4th 417, 422, 94 Cal Rptr 2d 137.

[14] Cf. Volkswagen of America, Inc. v Superior Court (1971) 18 Cal App 3d 477, 480, 96 Cal Rptr 205; Westinghouse Credit Corp. v Mountain States Mining & Milling Co. (1965, D Colo) 37 FRD 348, 349.

Annotation: Discovery and inspection: compelling party to disclose information in hands of affiliated or subsidiary corporation, or independent contractor, not made party to suit. 19 ALR3d 1134, partially superseded by 145 ALR Red 527 [replacing earlier article's Rule 34 discussion].

[15] Volkswagen of America, Inc. v Superior Court (1971) 18 Cal App 3d 477, 480, 96 Cal Rptr 205; Westinghouse Credit Corp. v Mountain States Mining & Milling Co. (1965, D Colo) 37 FRD 348, 349.

[16] Rehau, Inc. v Colortech, Inc. (1993, WD Mich) 145 FRD 444, 445.

with those of their former employer to such an extent that admissions by them should be held to bind the employer.[17]

However, where the resignation of the deponents is a mere formality[18] or even a ploy to avoid the deposition,[19] the federal courts have required the corporate party to produce them for a deposition.[20]

Corporate Party that is Deponent's Alter Ego: Prior to 1987, it was not necessary to serve a deposition subpoena to compel the attendance of an individual who was "a person for whose immediate benefit an action or proceeding is prosecuted or defended."[21] Persons who were using a corporate party as their alter ego qualified as such an "immediate beneficiary."[22] The Discovery Commission concluded that the slight expansion of the court's power over nonparties that the "immediate beneficiary" concept conferred was not worth the issues it created.[23] The Legislature agreed and dropped this classification from Section 2025.280(a). In most cases this change will have no practical effect. One using a close corporation as an alter ego will usually also be an officer, director, managing agent or employee, whom the corporate party itself must produce in response to a deposition notice.

§ 2.13   Place of Deposition—Individual Deponent

75 and 150 Mile Radius: The notice of deposition of an individual, whether a party to the action or not, may always specify a site that is within 75 miles of that individual's residence.[1] Moreover, the party noticing the deposition always has the option of picking a site that is in the forum county *and* within 150 miles of the deponent's residence.[2]

Measurement: To date, no reported California case has decided whether the respective 75 and 150 mile limits are measured "as the crow flies," or by the

---

[17] Proseus v Anchor Line, Ltd. (1960, SD NY) 26 FRD 165, 167. See also Kolb v A. H. Bull S.S. Co. (1962, ED NY) 31 FRD 252 [former vice-president]; Duncan v United States (1954, SD NY) 16 FRD 568 [former ship captain]; Cohen v Pennsylvania R. Co. (1939, SD NY) 30 F Supp 419, 420 [former vice-president]; Scripto Tokai Corp. v Cayo (1993, Fla App) 628 So2d 828, 828–29 [former corporate director]. For a discussion of the use of a deposition subpoena to compel the attendance of a nonparty deponent, see § 2.9.

[18] Independent Productions Corp. v Loew's, Inc. (1959, SD NY) 24 FRD 19.

[19] Cameo-Parkway Records, Inc. v Premier Albums, Inc. (1967, SD NY) 43 FRD 400.

[20] Cf. Rehau, Inc. v Colortech, Inc. (1993, WD Mich) 145 FRD 444, 445 [compelling deposition without subpoena of former manager of party where deponent worked for the corporation's parent and his father was president of both the parent and the subsidiary].

[21] Former CCP § 2019(a)(4), 1956 Discovery Act, Appendix E.

[22] Waters v Superior Court (1962) 58 Cal 2d 885, 897–898, 27 Cal Rptr 153, 377 P2d 265. See also Volkswagen of America, Inc. v Superior Court (1971) 18 Cal App 3d 477, 96 Cal Rptr 205.

[23] See Reporter's Note to Section 2025(h)(1) of the Proposed Civil Discovery Act of 1986, Appendix D.

[1] CCP § 2025.250(a).

[2] CCP § 2025.250(a).

actual road mileage over the shortest feasible route. The few federal cases that have considered the point calculate the mileage "as the crow flies."[3] This interpretation has the advantage of ease of application: one need only draw a straight line on a map and measure it against the map's mileage scale. The other method, the actual road miles traveled, invites pointless bickering over what is the shortest route to the deposition site.[4] If in a particular case the road miles traveled would be a hardship for the deponent, the court can always grant a motion for a protective order shifting the deposition site.

"Residence": "Residence" in the discovery context means actual residence, not domicile:

> [Residency for purposes of the subpoena power] is residence in fact and not domicile; the subpoena section envisages nothing more than an abode, possibly combined with a professional base of operations, which gives the 'resident' a sojourning connection with the area of a type and duration related to the status of a witness and which makes it not a hardship for him to attend the legal proceedings at which he is commanded to appear.[5]

Increasing the Distance to be Traveled: The court's *trial* subpoena power can compel a "resident" of California to travel anywhere in the state to give live testimony.[6] By contrast, with one important exception,[7] a court is powerless to compel an individual who is neither a party nor affiliated with a party, to travel more than one or the other of distances specified in Section 2025.250 to reach a deposition site.

Parties and Their Affiliates: The trial courts can require a greater travel distance where a deponent is an individual who either is a party to the action or is affiliated with a party (as an officer, director, managing agent or other employee). One who wants to depose these individuals may apply to the court for an order requiring them to attend at a "more distant" deposition site.[8] This motion is subject to a "meet and confer" duty.[9]

---

[3] See, e.g., Cook v Atchison, Topeka & Santa Fe Ry. Co. (1993, D Kan) 816 F Supp 667, 669 [Fed Rules Civ Proc, Rule 45's 100-mile radius is measured by a straight line on the map]; SAM Corp v Xerox Corp. (1977, D Conn) 76 FRD 214, 215 [the 100-mile limits in Fed Rules Civ Proc, Rule 4, 32 and 45 require "a straight line measurement"]. Cf. Langsam-Borenstein Partnership v NOC Enters., Inc. (1990, ED Pa) 137 FRD 217, 218 n3 [interpreting 100 mile provision of Fed Rules Civ Proc, Rule 4 as "a 100-mile radius of the courthouse, measured on a straight line, i.e., by air miles, or 'as the crow flies'"].

[4] But see People v Adams (1987) 196 Cal App 3d 201, 204, 241 Cal Rptr 684 [20-mile radius for drawing juror pool is calculated by actual road miles traveled to the courthouse].

[5] In re Morelli (1970) 11 Cal App 3d 819, 831, 91 Cal Rptr 72.

[6] CCP § 1989.

[7] Members of the California Highway Patrol must appear anywhere in the state for a deposition. Gov't Code §§ 68097.3 and 68097.6.

[8] CCP § 2025.260(a).

[9] CCP § 2025.260(a).

Factors Affecting Court's Decision: Section 2025.260 contains a nonexclusive list of seven factors that the court must consider in exercising its discretion to order travel to deposition sites far from a party-deponent's residence.[10] These include whether the moving party selected the forum; whether the deponent will be available to testify at the trial; the convenience of the deponent; the feasibility of using a written deposition or another method of discovery; the number of applications to remove the travel restrictions on depositions; the expense connected with taking the deposition if the travel restrictions are not lifted; and where the deponent will otherwise be at the time the deposition is scheduled to take place.

—Out-of-State Residence: The mere circumstance that the deponent resides beyond the borders of California does not restrict the trial court's power to order an individual who is a party or employed by a party to travel greater distances than other deponents. The *Glass* case,[11] for example, held that the trial court may require the officers of an Indiana corporate plaintiff to travel to California for depositions. The court rejected the contention that one must depose all nonresident witnesses under the provisions for out-of-state depositions.[12]

—Ordering a Plaintiff to Travel: Of the half-dozen or so factors listed, by far the most important is "[w]hether the moving party selected the forum."[13] Absent a change from the original venue, the party selecting the forum will be, of course, the plaintiff. The placement of this consideration at the front of the list that guides the court's discretion reflects the federal practice: "Generally, a nonresident should make himself available for examination in the forum in which he has brought his action."[14] Federal courts have applied this rule to require plaintiffs to travel at their own expense to the forum for oral depositions not only from distant states,[15] but also from foreign countries.[16] In rationalizing this general rule, the courts frequently refer to the plaintiff's deliberate choice of the forum as the site at which to litigate:

---

[10] CCP § 2025.260(b).

[11] Glass v Superior Court (1988) 204 Cal App 3d 1048, 251 Cal Rptr 690.

[12] See CCP § 2026.010. Cf. Amoco Chemical Co. v Certain Underwriters at Lloyd's of London (1995) 34 Cal App 4th 554, 559, 40 Cal Rptr 2d 80 [nonresident defendant, like any other nonresident witness, cannot be compelled to attend at trial or to produce documents]; Doe v Superior Court (1990) 222 Cal App 3d 1406, 1410 n5, 1414 n3, 272 Cal Rptr 474. For a discussion of depositions taken elsewhere for use in California, see Chapter 4.

[13] CCP § 2025.260(b)(1).

[14] Zweifler v Sleco Laces, Inc. (1950, SD NY) 11 FRD 202, 204. See also Glass v Superior Court (1988) 204 Cal App 3d 1048, 1053, 251 Cal Rptr 690.

[15] E.g., Novel v Garrison (1967, ED La) 42 FRD 234 [from Ohio]; Rifkin v United States Lines Co. (1959, SD NY) 177 F Supp 875, 876 [from California]; Greenberg v Safe Lighting, Inc. (1959, SD NY) 24 FRD 410 [from Kansas]; Pierce v Brovig (1954, SD NY) 16 FRD 569 [from Georgia].

[16] Seuthe v Renwal Products, Inc. (1965, SD NY) 38 FRD 323 [from Germany]; Slade v Transatlantic Financing Corp. (1957, SD NY) 21 FRD 146 [from England].

A Georgia forum would have offered a more convenient, speedier, and possibly less expensive forum. Plaintiff, however, chose to bring the action in this forum. Plaintiff cannot now complain that he should not be examined in this forum.[17]

Where defendants have filed a cross-complaint, especially a permissive one, the court should treat them as plaintiffs in deciding issues as to the right to depose them at the forum.[18]

The rule that nonresident plaintiffs should make themselves available for a deposition at the forum is not inflexible.[19] Varying combinations of the following circumstances have induced federal trial courts to shield a plaintiff from a journey to the forum for a pretrial deposition: (1) the plaintiff's lack of a practical alternative to the forum selected;[20] (2) the forum chosen is more convenient to the defendant;[21] (3) the plaintiff's infirmity makes a journey to the forum painful and hazardous;[22] (4) the plaintiff's finances make travel onerous;[23] (5) the plaintiff's family or business commitments would be disrupted unduly;[24] (6) the

---

[17] Pierce v Brovig (1954, SD NY) 16 FRD 569, 570.

[18] Continental Federal Sav. & Loan Assn. v Delta Corp. of America (1976, WD Okla) 71 FRD 697; Grey v Continental Marketing Associates, Inc. (1970, ND Ga) 315 F Supp 826, 832.

[19] Hyam v American Export Lines, Inc. (1954, CA2 NY) 213 F2d 221 [Indian plaintiff's choice of New York instead of Bombay as forum does not relieve trial judge of duty to weigh burden of travel from India to New York for deposition]. See also Patrnogic v United States Steel Corp. (1967, SD NY) 43 FRD 402 [burden of travel on Yugoslav plaintiff outweighs defendant's desire for oral deposition].

[20] E.g., Abdullah v Sheridan Square Press, Inc. (1994, SD NY) 154 FRD 591, 593 [impoverished plaintiff who sued in New York could not have sued in England, and would lose political asylum claim if he left England]; Patrnogic v United States Steel Corp. (1967, SD NY) 43 FRD 402 [Yugoslav plaintiff injured during sojourn in New York City]; Endte v Hermes Export Corp. (1957, SD NY) 20 FRD 162 [Austrian plaintiff had no choice but to sue defendant at its residence and principal place of business].

[21] O'Hara v United States Lines Co. (1958, SD NY) 164 F Supp 549, 551 [New York forum so convenient to defendant that it resists effort of California plaintiff to transfer case].

[22] Sullivan v Southern Pac. Co. (1947, SD NY) 7 FRD 206 [injury to Minnesota plaintiff had resulted in amputation of portions of each leg]. While the advanced age of the plaintiff is a factor to be considered, it does not alone require a departure from the general rule. See Haviland & Co. v Montgomery Ward & Co. (1962, SD NY) 31 FRD 578 [doctor's certificate insufficient to relieve 80-year old French executive of corporate plaintiff from giving deposition at forum]; Rifkin v United States Lines Co. (1959, SD NY) 177 F Supp 875 [doctor's conclusory certificate insufficient to relieve 70-year old Californian from giving deposition at forum].

[23] E.g., Abdullah v Sheridan Square Press, Inc. (1994, SD NY) 154 FRD 591, 593 [impoverished plaintiff who sued in New York could not have sued in England, and would lose political asylum claim if he left England]; Forde v Urania Transp., Inc. (1958, SD NY) 168 F Supp 240; Endte v Hermes Export Corp. (1957, SD NY) 20 FRD 162; Robinson v Tracy (1954, WD Mo) 16 FRD 113.

[24] E.g., Abdullah v Sheridan Square Press, Inc. (1994, SD NY) 154 FRD 591, 593 [impoverished plaintiff who sued in New York could not have sued in England, and would lose political asylum claim if he left England]; Patrnogic v United States Steel Corp. (1967, SD NY) 43 FRD 402 [foreign law professor's teaching schedule would be disrupted]; Coburn v Warner (1951, SD NY) 12 FRD

plaintiff's lack of personal knowledge about the liability features of the case;[25] (7) the suitability of discovery by interrogatories supplemented by an oral deposition during the week or so before trial.[26] Moreover, the courts have been generally receptive to requiring counsel to travel to the residence of a plaintiff who is willing to pay all the expenses connected with the trip.[27]

The factors favoring travel by a deponent to a distant site, usually in the forum county, may be so strong that a denial of the motion would be an abuse of discretion:

> [Plaintiffs] chose the Orange County forum, and [defendants] offered to schedule the depositions, if possible, at times convenient to all concerned (e.g., when the deponents are in California on [corporate] business). [Defendants] also indicated these might be the only depositions they would take at a distant place [from a deponent's residence]. Depositions are also a preferred method of discovery in this case in light of the complex nature of the lawsuit and the likelihood witness credibility will play a significant role in the litigation. Finally, it will be less expensive to conduct these depositions in California while the deponents are here on business than to require those concerned to travel to Indiana for that purpose.[28]

—**Ordering a Defendant to Travel:** Only a few reported cases have addressed a court's ability to require individual *defendants* to travel to the forum *at their own expense* for a deposition.[29] In one case,[30] a plaintiff sought to force a Michigan defendant in an auto tort case to return to Missouri, the place of the accident, for an oral deposition. Plaintiff argued that the "consent" to jurisdiction implied from defendant's operation of a car in Missouri included a consent to be deposed there. It also argued that the defendant's opportunity to seek

---

188 [Massachusetts plaintiff who is caring for elderly relatives]; Barili v Bianchi (1946, ND Cal) 6 FRD 350 [plaintiff in patent infringement suit would suffer "a real hardship" if compelled to leave his Los Angeles business to attend deposition in San Francisco].

25 Patrnogic v United States Steel Corp. (1967, SD NY) 43 FRD 402 [passenger on bus injured when crane hit its roof]; Robinson v Tracy (1954, WD Mo) 16 FRD 113 [plaintiff in wrongful death action].

26 E.g., Patrnogic v United States Steel Corp. (1967, SD NY) 43 FRD 402; Forde v Urania Transp., Inc. (1958, SD NY) 168 F Supp 240; Pierre v Bernuth, Lembcke Co. (1957, SD NY) 21 FRD 194.

27 Haviland & Co. v Montgomery Ward & Co. (1962, SD NY) 31 FRD 578; Greenberg v Safe Lighting, Inc. (1959, SD NY) 24 FRD 410.

28 Glass v Superior Court (1988) 204 Cal App 3d 1048, 1053, 251 Cal Rptr 690, 693.

29 See Patterson v Williamson (1993, ED Va) 153 BR 32, 33 [noting that "the defendant has no duty or obligation to pay the travel costs associated with his own deposition to be taken by plaintiff"]. Cf. Metrex Research Corp. v United States (1993, D Colo) 151 FRD 122, 124 [noting that, absent special circumstances, where defendant deponent resides far from forum, the deposing party "should be required to take the deposition in the vicinity in which the deponent resides"].

30 Perry v Edwards (1954, WD Mo) 16 FRD 131.

reimbursement for travel expenses from his liability insurance carrier made such travel appropriate. The court rejected both arguments.

In contrast, in a similar case, because a Michigan defendant's driving in Pennsylvania had widowed the plaintiff and left her without funds, the court required him to return at his own expense for a deposition at the forum.[31] In *Housing Authority of Alameda v Gomez,*[32] the court required a defendant who had moved from California to Spain after suit was filed to return for an oral deposition.

§ 2.14 Organizational Deponent

Section 2025.010 permits the deponent named in a deposition notice to be a corporation, partnership or other organizational entity. The notice for such a deposition must specify the subjects that the examination will cover.[1] The organization must then designate and produce for the deposition those of its employees who are most knowledgeable about those subjects.

Those designated by the organization must familiarize themselves with any documents they are instructed to produce and be able to testify about information that is readily available to one in the positions they hold within the organization.[2]

To determine the geographical location for deposing an organization through the employees it selects in response to a deposition notice, two factors must be taken into account: whether the organization, as required by the Corporations Code,[3] has designated a "principal executive or business office" in California; and whether it is a party to the action.

Principal Office Designated: If an organization has designated a "principal executive or business office in California," its status as a party or a nonparty in the lawsuit governs where one may conduct its deposition.

—Parties: If the organizational deponent *is* a party to the action, the one who noticed its deposition has a choice. The deposition site may be a place that is within 75 miles of the "principal executive or business office" designated by the organization. It may also be a place that is within the forum county but not more than 150 miles from that office.[4]

—Nonparty: If the organization is *not* a party to the action, the deposition site must be within 75 miles of its "principal executive or business office in

---

[31] Sowers v General Motors Corp. (1954, ED Pa) 16 FRD 562.

[32] Housing Authority of Alameda v Gomez (1972) 26 Cal App 3d 366, 371, 102 Cal Rptr 657. See also Crummer v Beeler (1960) 185 Cal App 2d 851, 859–860, 8 Cal Rptr 698.

[1] CCP § 2025.230.

[2] See Maldonado v Superior Court (2002) 94 Cal App 4th 1390, 1396, 115 Cal Rptr 2d 137 [company's human resources manager could be expected to answer questions concerning its general employment policies].

[3] This phrase has the same meaning that it has in Corp Code §§ 1502, 2105, 15700 and 24003. See Proposed Civil Discovery Act of 1986, Reporter's Note to Section 2025(2), Appendix D.

[4] CCP § 2025.250(b).

California" unless the organization consents to a more distant place.[5] The party noticing the deposition does not have the option of conducting it at a site within the forum county that is no more than 150 miles from that designated office. In this respect a deposition of a nonparty *organization* differs from that of a nonparty *individual*.[6]

No Principal Office Designated: If the organization, whether a party or not, has *not* designated a "principal executive or business office," the noticing party may choose between two locations: a place within 75 miles of *any* of the organization's California offices, or anywhere within the forum county without regard to the location of its offices.[7]

Compelling the Attendance of Knowledgeable Employees: Section 2025.230 purports to require a nonparty organization to produce *any* employees, whatever their rank, who are qualified to testify on the matters described in the deposition subpoena served on the corporation. In some situations, the organization itself may be subject to the trial court's subpoena power, yet those employees knowledgeable about the subjects specified in the subpoena are not. The present statute differs from its predecessor[8] by not requiring a "consent" to appear from rank-and-file employees. Thus, it slides over the issue of a trial court's power to coerce the attendance of a *nonresident* employee. Interpreting the similar federal provision,[9] the Fifth Circuit has held that a person designated by an organizational deponent "could not be compelled to travel outside the limits" that would apply if that individual were personally served with a subpoena.[10]

§ 2.15   Protective Orders—In General

Section 2025.420 gives the trial court broad power to enter a protective order to prevent deposition discovery from causing "unwarranted annoyance, embarrassment, or oppression, or undue burden and expense."[1]

---

[5] CCP § 2025.250(c).

[6] For a discussion of the option to depose individuals in the forum county but within 150 miles of their residence, see § 2.13.

[7] CCP § 2025.250(c).

[8] Former CCP § 2019(a)(6), 1956 Discovery Act, Appendix E [requiring consent of lower echelon employees to attend for the organization's deposition].

[9] FRCivP 30(b)(6).

[10] Cates v LTV Aerospace Corp. (1973, CA5 Tex) 480 F2d 620, 623. See also Marcoux v Mid-States Livestock (1975, WD Mo) 66 FRD 573, 580; but see Ghandi v Police Dept. of City of Detroit (1977, ED Mich) 74 FRD 115, 119–123 [although not a party to suit, the FBI, served with a deposition subpoena in Detroit, must produce documents located in Washington, D.C.]; Resolution Trust Corporation v Worldwide Insurance Management Corp. (1992, ND Tex) 147 FRD 125, 127–128 [English resident, president of defendant corporation, forced to travel to Texas forum, where forum was location for corporation's headquarters and its counsel]; Less v Taber Instrument Corp. (1971, WD NY) 53 FRD 645 [although board chairman of nonparty corporation, who resides in Los Angeles, is subject to subpoena power based on corporation's activities in New York, trial court has discretion to require deposition to be taken in California].

[1] CCP § 2025.420(b).

Standing: Motions for a protective order are usually made by a party other than the one who noticed the deposition. However, "any" party, including the one taking the deposition, may move for one.[2] The deponent also has standing to make such a motion. Moreover, sometimes the projected discovery will range into sensitive areas that impact some third person.[3] Section 2025.420 now expressly confers standing to move for a protective order on "any other *affected* natural person or organization."[4]

Duty to Meet and Confer: A party or deponent who seeks a protective order must confer informally with the other parties and attempt in good faith to resolve the issues raised by the motion. The moving party must accompany the motion with a declaration detailing these informal efforts.[5]

Timing: A party or a deponent usually seeks a protective order before the oral examination takes place. Section 2025.420, however, also allows one to make the motion "during"[6] or "after"[7] the deposition.[8]

"Good Cause" Required: A trial court may only grant a protective order "for good cause shown."[9] The motion should set forth the specific facts that constitute the "good cause" for granting the protection sought.

Monetary Sanction: One who unsuccessfully makes or opposes a motion for a protective order should expect a monetary sanction unless that party can convince the court that, despite this lack of success, there was "substantial justification" for its position.[10]

Types of Protective Orders: The statute sets forth a nonexclusive list of 16 types of protective orders that might be appropriate.[11] This section of the treatise will briefly discuss most of these protective order categories. The sections that follow cover protective orders restricting depositions of high-ranking officials,[12] limiting attendance at a discovery deposition,[13] keeping the testimony secret,[14] and requiring the taking of the testimony by written questions.[15]

---

[2] CCP § 2025.420(a).

[3] See, e.g., Irwin Memorial Blood Centers v Superior Court (1991) 229 Cal App 3d 151, 157, 279 Cal Rptr 911 [prohibiting anonymous written depositions, behind protective screens, of nonparty HIV positive blood donors].

[4] CCP § 2025.420(a) (italics added).

[5] CCP § 2025.420(a).

[6] For a discussion of motions to terminate or limit a deposition, see § 2.30.

[7] For a discussion of protective orders sealing deposition testimony, see § 2.18.

[8] CCP § 2025.420(a).

[9] CCP § 2025.420(b).

[10] CCP § 2025.420(d).

[11] CCP § 2025.420(b)(1)–(16).

[12] For a discussion of protective orders against deposing high-ranking officials, see § 2.16.

[13] For a discussion of protective orders limiting attendance at a deposition, see § 2.17.

[14] For a discussion of protective orders sealing the testimony or silencing the litigants, see § 2.18.

[15] For a discussion of protective orders substituting a written deposition for an oral one, see § 2.19.

Prohibiting the Deposition: The most extreme form of protective order is one that directs that the deposition "not be taken at all."[16] A clear-cut situation for entering such an order is to prevent the examination of a witness who has already given a deposition in the action.[17] This protective order is also appropriate where the information being sought by the deposition "is unreasonably cumulative or duplicative, or is obtainable from some other source that is more convenient, less burdensome, or less expensive."[18] Moreover, discovery may have gone on to a point where the particular deposition would now be "unduly burdensome or expensive, taking into account the needs of the case, the amount in controversy, and the importance of the issues at stake in the litigation."[19]

Postponing the Deposition: A motion for a protective order is also the way to postpone a deposition.[20] Though the party noticing it has complied with the requirements for commencing deposition discovery[21] and has observed the proper notice periods,[22] the date scheduled may still be undesirable or inconvenient.[23] In addition, if the notice has stated the intention to video an expert's deposition for use instead of live trial testimony,[24] a protective order delaying it will enable other parties to conduct a discovery deposition in preparation for the video recorded session.[25]

Changing the Deposition Site: Even if the specified deposition site is a permissible one, for good cause, the trial court can change it.[26] This power,

---

16 CCP § 2025.420(b)(1). See Home Savings Bank v Gillam (1991, CA9 Alaska) 952 F2d 1152, 1156 [prohibiting a deposition pending a ruling on a motion for a summary judgment, when the proposed testimony was irrelevant to issue of liability]; Friders v Schiltz (1993, SD Iowa) 150 FRD 153, 156 [requiring "extraordinary circumstances" before court will grant the "very unusual" order prohibiting a deposition entirely].

17 CCP § 2025.610. For a discussion of the one-deposition limit, see § 2.36.

18 CCP § 2019.030(a)(1). See In re Marriage of Hixson (2003) 111 Cal App 4th 1116, 1123, 4 Cal Rptr 3d 483 [a party "may obtain an order limiting or even preventing discovery if the proposed discovery exceeds the scope of the statute or is unnecessary under all the circumstances presented."]

19 CCP § 2019.030(a)(2).

20 CCP § 2025.420(b)(2).

21 For a discussion of when parties may start deposition discovery, see § 2.2.

22 For a discussion of the required notice period prior to a deposition, see § 2.7.

23 See Hays v Superior Court (1940) 16 Cal 2d 260, 267–268, 105 P2d 975 [trial court may postpone defendant's deposition pending outcome of appeal dismissing plaintiff's suit]; Bar Association of San Diego v Superior Court (1923) 64 Cal App 590, 592–593, 222 P 185 [trial court has discretion to postpone deposition of critical witness to permit party to recover from illness so that he may be present to assist counsel during cross-examination of deponent]; Neubronner v Milken (1993, CA9 Cal) 6 F3d 666, 671 [finding good cause to postpone deposition until after court ruling on motion to dismiss that might moot the deposition].

24 For a discussion of the use of video recorded depositions of expert witnesses, see § 2.41.

25 CCP § 2025.420(b)(3).

26 Cf. Heda v Superior Court (1990) 225 Cal App 3d 525, 528–529, 275 Cal Rptr 136 [holding that deponent's informal request to change the deposition site for health reasons did not waive any privacy rights he held in his medical records]. For a discussion of the place where a deposition may be taken, see §§ 2.13–2.14.

however, is not unlimited. For example, a party must depose an individual who is not a party either within 75 miles of the deponent's residence, or in the forum county and within 150 miles of that residence.[27]

Changing the Method of Recording the Deposition: A party or the deponent may move for a protective order changing the method of recording the testimony.[28] The trial court may dispense with a stenographic record and allow solely audio or video recording of testimony.[29] Or it may veto an announced plan to make a simultaneous audio or video of the testimony.[30]

Limiting Scope of Deposition: A protective order can also control the permissible topics during the deposition. The trial court may either declare certain subjects out of bounds[31] or allow inquiry only into certain areas.[32] This type of protection is most appropriate where the examination threatens to roam beyond the subject matter of the action,[33] or to explore information covered by some privilege,[34] or invade protected work product.[35] However, for good cause the trial court may even protect one against "attempted discovery which, while it may come within the rules established by the other code sections, offends the sense of justice and reason."[36]

---

[27] CCP § 2025.250(a).

[28] CCP § 2025.420(b)(8).

[29] Cf. Bogan v Northwestern Mut. Life Ins. Co. (1993, SD NY) 152 FRD 9, 11–12 [implying that in unusual cases, such as with preliminary exploratory depositions, where deponent was notified in advance, courts could approve "memory or note-taking" as sole deposition recording method]. For a discussion of the methods for recording deposition testimony, see §§ 2.32–2.33.

[30] See, e.g., Bogan v Northwestern Mut. Life Ins. Co. (1993, SD NY) 145 FRD 642, 642 [upholding magistrate's requirement of stenographic record in contentious multiparty case where clarity was needed]. For a discussion of simultaneous taping of deposition testimony, see §§ 2.32–2.33.

[31] CCP § 2025.420(b)(9). See, e.g., John Z. v Superior Court (1991) 1 Cal App 4th 789, 2 Cal Rptr 2d 556 [order protecting deponent from disclosing the identity of a "whistleblower" in a fraud case]; compare Gonzalez v Superior Court (1995) 33 Cal App 4th 1539, 1546–1547, 39 Cal Rptr 2d 896 [refusing to extend whistleblower protection to whistleblower's accomplice].

[32] CCP § 2025.420(b)(10).

[33] See Smith v Dowson (1994, D Minn) 158 FRD 138, 140–142 [a showing that proposed testimony has no conceivable relevance to the subject matter of the case justifies a protective order stopping the deposition]. For general coverage of the discovery concept of relevance, see Chapter 11.

[34] Cf. Schnabel v Superior Court (1993) 5 Cal 4th 704, 714, 21 Cal Rptr 2d 200, 854 P2d 1117 [in fashioning protective order over "business records only" deposition subpoenas directed to a nonparty, court must balance the discovering party's interest in obtaining information against the nonparty's privacy interest]. For coverage of "business records only" deposition subpoenas directed to nonparties, see § 7.3. For coverage of privilege in the discovery context, see Chapter 12.

[35] For coverage of the work product protection, see Chapter 13.

[36] Greyhound Corp. v Superior Court (1961) 56 Cal 2d 355, 379, 15 Cal Rptr 90, 364 P2d 266.

§ 2.16   Depositions of Attorneys or High-Ranking Officers

Normally, courts are reluctant to preclude altogether the taking of someone's deposition.[1] In three situations, however, they routinely issue orders to that effect. These involve proposed depositions of the attorney for a party to the lawsuit, of a high-level government official, and of an upper-echelon corporate officer or executive. Normally, a court allows such depositions only upon a showing that a party cannot get crucial, nonprivileged information from any other source.[2]

Another Party's Attorney: Courts are very reluctant to let a party depose opposing counsel: "the practice of taking the deposition of opposing counsel should be severely restricted, and permitted only upon showing of extremely good cause."[3] In the *Spectra-Physics* case,[4] the court adopted the following passage from a federal decision:

> Taking the deposition of opposing counsel not only disrupts the adversarial process and lowers the standards of the profession, but it also adds to the already burdensome time and costs of litigation. It is not hard to imagine additional pretrial delays to resolve work-product and attorney-client objections, as well as delays to resolve collateral issues raised by the attorney's testimony. Finally, the practice of deposing opposing counsel detracts from the quality of client representation. Counsel should be free to devote his or her time and efforts to preparing the client's case without fear of being interrogated by his or her opponent. Moreover, the "chilling effect" that such practice will have on the truthful communications from the client to the attorney is obvious.[5]

The court concluded that a party may depose the attorney for another party only on three conditions: "(1) no other means exist to obtain the information than to depose opposing counsel; (2) the information sought is relevant and not privileged; (3) the information is crucial to the preparation of the case."[6] Cases allowing such depositions have generally involved claims of bad faith by an insurance company in which the attorney had acted as the principal negotiator.[7]

---

[1] See, e.g., Friders v Schiltz (1993, SD Iowa) 150 FRD 153, 156 [requiring "extraordinary circumstances" before court will grant the "very unusual" order prohibiting a deposition].

[2] See, e.g., Nagle v Superior Court (1994) 28 Cal App 4th 1465, 1467–68, 34 Cal Rptr 2d 281 [precluding deposition of high governmental official].

[3] Fireman's Fund Ins. Co. v Superior Court (1977) 72 Cal App 3d 786, 790, 140 Cal Rptr 677.

[4] Spectra-Physics, Inc. v Superior Court (1988) 198 Cal App 3d 1487, 1494, 244 Cal Rptr 258.

[5] Shelton v American Motors Corp. (1986, CA8 Ark) 805 F2d 1323, 1327.

[6] Spectra-Physics, Inc. v Superior Court (1988) 198 Cal App 3d 1487, 1496, 244 Cal Rptr 258.

[7] E.g., Fireman's Fund Ins. Co. v Superior Court (1977) 72 Cal App 3d 786, 790, 140 Cal Rptr 677. Cf. Meritplan Ins. Co. v Superior Court (1981) 124 Cal App 3d 237, 241–242, 177 Cal Rptr 236.

In other cases, the courts usually issue a protective order against deposing another party's attorney.[8]

—Exception: Attorneys Acting Pro Se: This prohibition of depositions from the attorney for an opposing party does not, of course, apply to attorneys who are representing themselves in a lawsuit. In such a case they are being deposed in their capacity as a *party,* not as an *attorney.*[9]

High-Level Governmental Officials: In the *Nagle* case, the court refused to allow a party to take the deposition of the director of the California Employment Development Department and the former director of the California Department of Health Services: "It is the general rule in both California and federal courts that the heads of agencies and other top governmental executives are normally not subject to depositions."[10]

The court applied this rule although the deponents were parties to the lawsuit. It noted that it would disrupt the functioning of the agency if every plaintiff filing a complaint against its head could take that official's oral deposition. Moreover, the head of a government agency ordinarily has little or no knowledge of the facts of the case.[11]

Upper-Echelon Corporate Officers and Managers: Courts have fashioned similar protective orders[12] against depositions of the heads of large corporations and other nongovernmental organizations. For example, in the *Liberty Mutual* case,[13] which involved the health care offered to an injured worker, the plaintiff sought immediately to depose the president and CEO of the defendant's compensation carrier. This officer sought a protective order because he had no personal knowledge of, or immediate responsibility for, the processing of insurance claims involved.

The appellate court concluded that the trial court's denial of the protective order was an abuse of discretion. Such a high-ranking officer is usually quite removed from the day-to-day operations of the business:

> The head of a large national corporation will generally not have knowledge of a specific incident or case handled several levels down

---

[8] See Spectra-Physics, Inc. v Superior Court (1988) 198 Cal App 3d 1487, 1494, 244 Cal Rptr 258 [precluding deposition to establish validity of settlement agreement]; Estate of Ruchti (1993) 12 Cal App 4th 1593, 1600–1602, 16 Cal Rptr 2d 151 [precluding deposition to help determine the nature and extent of probate property].

[9] See, e.g., Rifkind v Superior Court (1994) 22 Cal App 4th 1255, 1263, 27 Cal Rptr 822.

[10] Nagle v Superior Court (1994) 28 Cal App 4th 1465, 1467–1468, 34 Cal Rptr 2d 281. See also Church of Scientology of Boston v IRS (1990, D Mass) 138 FRD 9, 12.

[11] See also Union Savings Bank of Patchogue, New York v Saxon (1962, D DC) 209 F Supp 319, 319–320.

[12] For a general discussion of protective orders limiting depositions, see § 2.15.

[13] Liberty Mutual Insur. Co. v Superior Ct. (1992) 10 Cal App 4th 1282, 1289–1290, 13 Cal Rptr 2d 363.

the corporate pyramid. Surely an insurance company's chief will seldom, if at all, be involved in the day-to-day processing of claims.[14]

Moreover, depositions of high corporate officials have a high potential for use as a tool of harassment:

> Vast numbers of personal injury claims could result in the deposition of the president of a national or international company whose product was somehow involved. It would be unreasonable to permit a plaintiff to begin discovery by deposing, for instance, the chief executive officer of a major automobile manufacturer when suing over a design flaw in a brake shoe—especially if we were to accept [plaintiff's] argument that the mere act of copying the chief executive officer with a few pieces of correspondence creates "constructive notice" justifying the deposition.[15]

—**Guidelines:** Using precedents from the federal courts,[16] the court issued guidelines for obtaining a deposition from a high corporate official. In that rare case where the noticing party shows that "the official has unique or superior personal knowledge of discoverable information," the trial court should grant the motion for a protective order.[17]

In the more common case where the noticing party is not presently able to make this showing, "the court should issue the protective order and first require the plaintiff to obtain the necessary discovery through less-intrusive methods."[18] These methods include: "interrogatories directed to the high-level official to explore the state of his or her knowledge or involvement in plaintiff's case; the deposition of lower-level employees with appropriate knowledge and involvement in the subject matter of the litigation; and the organizational deposition of the corporation itself, which will require the corporation to produce for deposition the most qualified officer or employee to testify on its behalf as to the specified matters to be raised at the deposition."[19]

If these less-intrusive means are insufficient, and the noticing party makes "a colorable showing of good cause that the high-level official possesses necessary

---

[14] Liberty Mutual Insur. Co. v Superior Ct. (1992) 10 Cal App 4th 1282, 1287, 13 Cal Rptr 2d 363.

[15] Liberty Mutual Insur. Co. v Superior Ct. (1992) 10 Cal App 4th 1282, 1287, 13 Cal Rptr 2d 363.

[16] E.g., Baine v General Motors Corp. (1991, MD Ala) 141 FRD 332, Travelers Rental Co., Inc. v Ford Motor Co. (1987, D Mass) 116 FRD 140, 145.

[17] Liberty Mutual Insur. Co. v Superior Ct. (1992) 10 Cal App 4th 1282, 1289, 13 Cal Rptr 2d 363.

[18] Liberty Mutual Insur. Co. v Superior Ct. (1992) 10 Cal App 4th 1282, 1289, 13 Cal Rptr 2d 363.

[19] Liberty Mutual Insur. Co. v Superior Ct. (1992) 10 Cal App 4th 1282, 1289, 13 Cal Rptr 2d 363.

information to the case, the trial court may then lift the protective order and allow the deposition to proceed."[20]

§ 2.17 Audience at a Deposition

In most depositions, the only persons present at the oral examination will be the deponent, counsel for the respective parties and the deposition officer. The officer normally doubles as the stenographic reporter of the testimony.[1] In an appropriate case, an interpreter may also have to attend.[2] From time to time, one or more of the parties to the suit may also attend.

Presumptively Open: Occasionally, certain third persons may wish to attend the oral examination: other prospective deponents, employees of a corporate party, consulting experts, relatives of the deponent or of the parties, persons interested in the outcome of the case, members of the public or the media. The Discovery Act does not prohibit the attendance of any of these persons at a deposition. Indeed, as a stage in a lawsuit, a deposition is presumptively open to the public: "As a general proposition, pretrial discovery must take place in the public unless compelling reasons exist for denying the public access to the proceeding."[3]

Consulting with a Deponent: Although as a general rule third persons may attend a deposition, they do not necessarily have a right to speak with the deponent during the questioning. In one federal case, the court precluded the deponent from consulting with his *attorney* during the deposition, unless this consultation involved the possible applicability of a testimonial privilege:

> The underlying purpose of a deposition is to find out what a witness saw, heard, or did—what the witness thinks. A deposition is meant to be a question-and-answer conversation between the deposing lawyer and the witness. . . . The witness comes to the deposition to testify, not to indulge in a parody of Charlie McCarthy, with lawyers coaching or bending the witness's words to mold a legally convenient record.[4]

The court applied this rule even to conferences the client initiates during "the fortuitous occurrence of a coffee break, lunch break, or evening recess."[5] Obviously, if a deponent's attorney has no absolute right to talk to his or her client during a deposition, no other third person has such a right.

---

[20] Liberty Mutual Insur. Co. v Superior Ct. (1992) 10 Cal App 4th 1282, 1289, 13 Cal Rptr 2d 363.

[1] For a discussion of the role of the deposition officer, see § 2.21.

[2] See, e.g., 9th Street Estates, Inc. v Rohatycka (1994, Misc) 610 NYS2d 430, 432 [requiring party to furnish an interpreter for the deponent as a matter of fundamental fairness]. Compare Tagupa v Odo (1994, D Hawaii) 843 F Supp 630, 632–633 [native Hawaiian deponent, fluent in English and a practicing attorney, had no right to testify at deposition in Hawaiian language].

[3] American Telephone & Telegraph Co. v Grady (1979, CA7 Ill) 594 F2d 594, 596.

[4] Hall v Clifton Precision (1993, ED Pa) 150 FRD 525, 528.

[5] Hall v Clifton Precision (1993, ED Pa) 150 FRD 525, 529.

Discretion to Exclude: The trial court may enter a protective order excluding "designated persons" from being present during the oral examination.[6] Normally, the party taking the deposition is the one who seeks the order restricting the attendance of third persons.[7] However, the deponent may also apply for a protective order.[8] Courts do not routinely enter a protective order excluding persons from attending a discovery deposition. As with any other protective order, the moving party must show "good cause."[9]

Sensitive Information Anticipated: "Good cause" for excluding third persons may exist where the deposition is likely to elicit sensitive information. For example, the deponent may testify about trade secrets or confidential business data that competitors might misuse.[10] Alternatively, the deposition may involve other privacy interests of a party.[11] To provide additional protection for such sensitive information, the protective order may direct the sealing of the deposition transcript.[12]

Excluding Potential Deponents: "Good cause" readily appears where the persons whose exclusion is sought are themselves potential deponents. Here, the protective order acts like an order sequestering trial witnesses:[13]

> [S]equestration will deny to the dishonest witness the advantage of observing the experience of other witnesses as they give their testimony on direct examination and are confronted with contradictions or evasions under cross-examination. At the least, it will make available the raw reactions and the individual recollection of each witness unaided by the stimulation of the evidence of any other witness. . . . [¶] In the present case the ten witnesses who have been summoned for examination all have in common their employment by the defendant. They will be testifying regarding a damage claim against their employer. We consider the camaraderie of employees who work together as "good cause" for their separation on their pretrial examination.[14]

---

[6] CCP § 2025.420(b)(12).

[7] Queen City Brewing Co. v Duncan (1966, D Md) 42 FRD 32; Dunlap v Reading Co. (1962, ED Pa) 30 FRD 129; Central Hide & Rendering Co. v B-M-K Corp. (1956, D Del) 19 FRD 296.

[8] Cf. Galella v Onassis (1973, CA2 NY) 487 F2d 986, 997 [granting deponent an order precluding a third person's attendance].

[9] CCP § 2025.420(b). See Skidmore v Northwest Engineering Co. (1981, SD Fla) 90 FRD 75 [no good cause for excluding plaintiff's expert from attendance at deposition of defendant's employee].

[10] See Uinta Oil Refining Co. v Continental Oil Co. (1964, D Utah) 36 FRD 176, 184; Marshwood Co. v Jamie Mills, Inc. (1950, ND Ohio) 10 FRD 386.

[11] E.g., Gottlieb v County of Orange (1993, SD NY) 151 FRD 258, 260 [in a case involving allegations of sexual abuse of a minor, the court restricted attendance to the deponent, his counsel, the court reporter, and the attorneys for the other parties].

[12] For a discussion of a protective order sealing a deposition, see § 2.18.

[13] See Evid Code § 777.

[14] Dunlap v Reading Co. (1962, ED Pa) 30 FRD 129, 131.

Excluding the Press: When a lawsuit arises out of a newsworthy event, members of the press often want to attend the depositions. An order barring the public and the press from the deposition process has constitutional implications. Arguably, since the public and the press would have a right to attend the eventual trial of the case, they could have a concomitant right to attend the pretrial depositions. However, because discoverable evidence includes a much broader range than that which is merely admissible at trial, the courts have rejected this analogy between the depositions and the trial:

> [D]epositions before a qualified officer in an equity or law case are not a judicial trial, nor a part of a trial, but a proceeding preliminary to a trial, and neither the public nor representatives of the press have a right to be present at such taking. Until a deposition has been presented to the court (not the Clerk), and ordered opened, it does not become evidence in the case, nor has either party until then an opportunity to be heard upon the question of the competency, materiality, or relevancy of the statements made by the witness, and the public can have no right to know what the testimony is until the court knows what it is.[15]

Parties to the Case: A court has no power to exclude from attendance at a deposition those who are "parties to the action."[16] In the *Willoughby* case,[17] the plaintiff sought to exclude from her own deposition two defendants whose alleged conduct was the focus of her employment harassment claim. These defendants had been her supervisors on the job, and the trial court found that their presence would rattle her. Nevertheless, the appellate court directed the trial court to vacate its protective order excluding them from her deposition:

> To prevent a client's presence during the cross-examination of the opposing party at deposition would significantly and unreasonably impair trial counsel's ability to effectively represent his client. In many cases it is critical for counsel to be able to confer with his client at his side concerning responses being received during the course of a deposition.[18]

Officers of a Party: Section 2025.420 prohibits the exclusion of the "officers" of a party from attending a deposition.[19] In the *Lowy Development Corp.* case,[20]

---

[15] Times Newspapers, Ltd. v McDonnell Douglas Corp. (1974, CD Cal) 387 F Supp 189, 197 [press has no right to attend depositions in lawsuits arising out of Paris jet aircraft crash in which 350 persons were killed]. Cf. In re "Agent Orange" Product Liability Litigation (1983, ED NY) 96 FRD 582, 583–584 [nonparty news network has no independent right of access to documents produced during discovery by one of the parties, but not made part of the public record of the lawsuit].

[16] CCP § 2025.420(b)(12). Cf. Fed Rules Civ Proc, Rule 26(c), which allows the exclusion of a party from a deposition.

[17] Willoughby v Superior Court (1985) 172 Cal App 3d 890, 218 Cal Rptr 486.

[18] Willoughby v Superior Court (1985) 172 Cal App 3d 890, 892, 218 Cal Rptr 486.

[19] CCP § 2025.420(b)(12).

[20] Lowy Development Corp. v Superior Court (1987) 190 Cal App 3d 317, 235 Cal Rptr 401.

a small, closely held corporation maintained that this meant it had the right to have all of its officers present during each other's deposition. The court declined to read the plural "officers" literally. It noted "the chaos that would result if a large corporation adopted [the same] position," and expressed its concern that even with a small corporation, as in the case before it, "the presence at each deposition of closely allied prospective deponents could foster collusive testimony . . . ."[21] It allowed the corporation to designate *one* officer to attend *all* depositions, and another officer to attend the deposition of that designee.

Occasionally, the deponent may seek to exclude the particular corporate officer designated to sit in on depositions. For example, in a federal class action against Shell Oil Refinery brought by its employees,[22] the defendant corporation had selected the supervisor of a certain deponent to attend depositions in the case. The court, however, excluded him from this deposition because of the possibility that the deponent would feel intimidated and the likelihood that the supervisor would be a witness at trial.

§ 2.18　Sealing a Deposition

Sealing the Transcript Distinguished: Very often a deposition will yield sensitive personal or business information. In such circumstances, Section 2025.410 authorizes the trial court to enter a protective order that "the deposition be sealed and thereafter opened only on order of the court."[1] This type of order is quite different from the routine sealing of the *transcript.* Section 2025.550 directs the deposition officer to "securely seal" the deposition transcript "in an envelope" and "transmit it to the attorney for the party who noticed the deposition."[2] This is done simply to ensure that the transcript will arrive intact, free from tampering. In contrast, a protective order sealing a deposition directs counsel and the parties not to publish or disclose the *information* contained in the testimony.[3]

Good Cause: As with any other protective order, there must be "good cause" for sealing a deposition. This generally requires a showing that disclosure of the testimony would produce more than the embarrassment or invasion of privacy normally incident to any public judicial proceeding.[4] For example, good cause may exist to seal the deposition of the donor of contaminated blood.[5] In contrast,

---

[21] Lowy Development Corp. v Superior Court (1987) 190 Cal App 3d 317, 321, 235 Cal Rptr 401.

[22] In Re Shell Oil Refinery (1991, ED La) 136 FRD 615.

[1] CCP § 2025.420(b)(15). Cf. In re Providian Credit Card Cases (2002) 96 Cal App 4th 292, 296, 116 Cal Rptr 2d 833 [party responding to inspection demand initially allowed to designate documents as "Confidential Material" and to file them under seal].

[2] CCP § 2025.550(a). For a discussion of the custody of the deposition transcript, see § 2.35.

[3] See, e.g., Moskowitz v Superior Court (1982) 137 Cal App 3d 313, 187 Cal Rptr 4; International Products Corp. v Koons (1963, CA2 NY) 325 F2d 403, 404 n1.

[4] Hawley v Hall (1990, D Nev) 131 FRD 578, 584–585 [finding no "serious embarrassment" sufficient to justify protective order].

[5] E.g., Marcella v Brandywine Hospital (1995, CA3 Pa) 47 F3d 618, 626–627 [suggesting that, on remand, the trial court might find it appropriate to seal the deposition].

the political embarrassment incident to disclosure of the testimony of elected officials sued for civil rights violations does not justify sealing their depositions.[6]

First Amendment Concerns: During their trial preparation parties often find out sensitive information by their own investigation and without resort to the discovery process. A protective order purporting to prohibit disclosure of this information trenches on First Amendment rights: "[N]either the parties nor their counsel implicitly waive their First Amendment rights to disclose or disseminate information or matters obtained independent of the court's processes."[7]

However, where discovery develops information of doubtful admissibility at trial, an order prohibiting pretrial revelation of this information to third persons does not invade their First Amendment rights:

> [D]iscovery rules are liberal, giving parties broad powers to gather information. As a result, a deponent may be obliged to reveal information that will not be admissible at trial. Unlike evidence at trial, it has not passed the strict threshold tests of relevance and admissibility, yet it has been compelled by dint of legal process. The information revealed may be irrelevant, prejudicial, or pose an undue invasion of an individual's privacy. [¶] Such undigested matter, forced from the mouth of an unwilling deponent, is hardly material encompassed within a broad public "right to know." Its disclosure would not advance the informed civic and political discussion that the First Amendment is intended to protect. . . . [A]lthough there is a First Amendment interest in information produced at trial that warrants full protection, a judicially-powered process compelling information that has not yet passed through the adversary-judicial filter for testing admissibility does not create communications that deserve full protection.[8]

—The *Seattle Times* Case: In *Seattle Times Co. v Rhinehart*,[9] a religious leader's defamation suit against newspapers and reporters warranted defendants' discovery of the identity of the religion's members and financial supporters. However, the trial court directed the defendants to neither divulge this information to the public nor use it other than for trial preparation. The defendants

6 E.g., Hawley v Hall (1990, D Nevada) 131 FRD 578, 584–585.

7 Rodgers v United States Steel Corp. (1976, CA3) 536 F2d 1001, 1006–1007. See also International Products Corp. v Koons (1963, CA2 NY) 325 F2d 403, 408.

Annotation: Restriction on dissemination of information obtained through pretrial discovery proceedings as violating Federal Constitution's First Amendment—federal cases. 81 ALR Fed 471. See generally, Miller, Confidentiality, Protective Orders, and Public Access to the Courts (1991) 105 Harvard LR 427; see also Note: Products Liability Litigation and Third-Party Harm: The Ethics of Nondisclosure (1991) 5 Georgetown Jour. of Legal Ethics 435; Note: Trade Secrets in Discovery: From First Amendment Disclosure to Fifth Amendment Protection (1991) 104 Harvard LR 1330.

8 In re San Juan Star Co. (1981, CA1 PR) 662 F2d 108, 115. See also In re "Agent Orange" Product Liability Litigation (1983, ED NY) 96 FRD 582, 584–585 [nonparty news network has no standing to challenge protective order restricting rights of litigants to disseminate products of discovery procedures].

9 Seattle Times Co. v Rhinehart (1984) 467 US 20, 81 L Ed 2d 17, 104 S Ct 2199.

attacked this restriction as an unconstitutional prior restraint on their right of freedom of expression.

The United States Supreme Court upheld the order. It found only a minimal impairment of the defendants' free expression rights. After all, they got the information covered by the protective order only with the help of the court that imposed the restriction. In addition, the liberality of the scope of discovery creates "an opportunity . . . for litigants to obtain—incidentally or purposefully—information that not only is irrelevant but if publicly released could be damaging to reputation and privacy."[10] There is a strong governmental interest in preventing the discovery process from causing unnecessary embarrassment and intrusion on privacy.

Disclosure to Clients: The trial court can even enter a protective order prohibiting counsel from revealing to their own clients information obtained via discovery.[11] Such orders are common for information concerning a defendant's financial worth made relevant only by the plaintiff's claim for punitive damages.[12]

§ 2.19 Substituting Written Questions

Requiring Use of Interrogatories: An oral deposition is not the only formal method by which a party can get information from another person. Where the one with the information is a party to the case, the other parties can obtain it through "interrogatories to a party."[1] Upon a showing of "good cause," the trial court has the power to compel a party to proceed via written interrogatories instead of an oral deposition.[2]

Requiring Written Deposition: Where the knowledgeable person is not a party to the case, one seeking the information must proceed by deposition. However, a party can take a deposition either by an oral examination or by a written one.[3] Upon a showing of "good cause," the trial court may compel a party to proceed by a written, instead of an oral, examination.[4]

Deference to the Party's Choice of Method: Although trial courts do not give a party an "absolute right" to select the method for obtaining discovery,[5] they usually defer to the choice made by the party seeking discovery: "[T]he court should ordinarily allow the examining party to choose his own mode of

---

[10] Seattle Times Co. v Rhinehart (1984) 467 US 20, 35, 81 L Ed 2d 17, 104 S Ct 2199.

[11] CCP § 2025.420(b)(13). See, e.g., GT, Inc. v Superior Court (1984) 151 Cal App 3d 748, 755–756, 198 Cal Rptr 892.

[12] Richards v Superior Court (1978) 86 Cal App 3d 265, 272, 150 Cal Rptr 77. For a further discussion of discovery of a party's financial worth, see § 11.7.

[1] See CCP §§ 2030.010–2030.410. For coverage of interrogatories to a party, see Chapter 5.

[2] CCP § 2025.420(b)(7).

[3] See CCP § 2028.010. For coverage of written depositions, see Chapter 3.

[4] CCP § 2025.420(b)(6).

[5] Colonial Capital Co. v General Motors Corp. (1961, D Conn) 29 FRD 514, 518.

examination."[6] This deference for a litigant's choice of examination method is especially strong when a party is asking the court to substitute "a tool of discovery very inferior,"[7] namely, written questions, for "the more complete technique of oral deposition."[8] The courts have explained:

> Under ordinary circumstances the advantages of oral examination over the rigidity of written interrogatories are readily acknowledged. Cross-examination of a witness who may be evasive, recalcitrant or nonresponsive to questions is an essential in ferreting out facts, particularly of an adverse party or witness.[9]

> Answers given by a witness to particular questions often suggest additional questions or another line of inquiry. In the deposition process, these additional questions can immediately be posed or the other line of inquiry pursued on the spot. Such is not the case with interrogatories unless the questioner who prepares the interrogatories possesses a prescience or an ability to anticipate answers which is seldom possessed by mere mortals.[10]

> Depositions are also a preferred method of discovery in this case in light of the complex nature of the lawsuit and the likelihood witness credibility will play a significant role in the litigation.[11]

Exception—Extensive Travel: A protective order substituting written for oral questioning is most often sought when either counsel or the deponent must spend much time and money to travel to the site proposed for the oral deposition. Sometimes a court will direct the parties to try to get the information they are seeking by asking their questions in writing.[12] If this proves unsuccessful, the court can reconsider allowing an oral deposition.[13] Other times, the court may give the side insisting upon the oral deposition the option either of paying the travel expenses of the deponent or opposing counsel, or of conducting the discovery by written questions.[14]

---

[6] Interlego A. G. v Leslie-Henry Co. (1963, MD Pa) 32 FRD 9, 11.

[7] Perry v Edwards (1954, WD Mo) 16 FRD 131, 133.

[8] Williams F. Jobbins, Inc. v American Export Lines, Inc. (1954, SD NY) 16 FRD 178, 179.

[9] V. O. Machinoimport v Clark Equipment Co. (1951, SD NY) 11 FRD 55, 58.

[10] Meritplan Insurance Co. v Superior Court (1981) 124 Cal App 3d 237, 241–242, 177 Cal Rptr 236.

[11] Glass v Superior Court (1988) 204 Cal App 3d 1048, 1053, 251 Cal Rptr 690.

[12] For coverage of written depositions, see Chapter 3.

[13] E.g., Mitchell v American Tobacco Co. (1963, MD Pa) 33 FRD 262; Colonial Capital Co. v General Motors Corp. (1961, D Conn) 29 FRD 514, 518; Kurt M. Jachmann Co. v Hartley, Cooper & Co. (1954, SD NY) 16 FRD 565.

[14] See, e.g., In re China Merchants Steam Navigation Co. (1966, SD NY) 259 F Supp 75, 78; Fisser v International Bank (1957, SD NY) 20 FRD 419; Jones v Pennsylvania Greyhound Lines, Inc. (1950, ED Pa) 10 FRD 153.

Written Cross-Examination at an Oral Deposition: A party can participate in an oral deposition without expending the time, money and energy to travel to its site. A party who is not present at the oral examination may conduct a cross-examination of sorts by submitting written questions for the deposition officer to propound to the deponent.[15]

Protecting Deponent's Anonymity: A federal case has approved a trial court's use of the written deposition procedure to preserve a nonparty deponent's anonymity.[16] The deponent was a blood donor whose blood may have transmitted HIV to the decedent in a wrongful death case. However, the California statutes protecting the confidentiality of blood donor's identity prevent its courts from following this case.[17] Though the written deposition procedure may not meet the particular concerns triggered by blood transfusion cases, it may be appropriate in other cases raising privacy or confidentiality concerns.

Deposition of an Opposing Attorney: Another federal case has upheld the substitution of written for oral examination when the plaintiffs sought to depose the defendants' attorneys in complex RICO litigation.[18] The trial court *sua sponte* had entered this protective order because it was "convinced that these depositions, absent firm control by the court, would almost certainly have been attended by continuing disputes and might have required supervision by a judicial officer."[19]

§ 2.20 Failure to Attend Deposition

A deposition may abort because the party scheduling it or the deponent simply fails to appear at the time and place specified in the notice. Litigants adjust their schedules and incur legal fees and travel expenses in reliance on deposition notices. Parties receiving a deposition notice may justifiably assume, until told otherwise, that it will take place at the scheduled time and place. They may further assume that the noticing party will have taken any steps necessary to compel the deponent's attendance. The court may impose sanctions against the noticing party or a recalcitrant witness responsible for derailing the deposition.[1]

Cancellation of a Deposition: A party who has served a deposition notice may not cancel it without informing the other parties. Nor may that party simply decide not to appear at the time and place in the notice. In either event, the trial court can impose a monetary sanction "in favor of any party attending in person or by attorney."[2] However, a deponent who appears in response to a subpoena

---

[15] See CCP § 2025.330(e). For a discussion of the use of written cross-examination questions in lieu of personal attendance at the oral examination, see § 2.23.

[16] Watson v Lowcountry Red Cross (1992, CA4 SC) 974 F2d 482, 487–488.

[17] See Irwin Memorial Blood Centers v Superior Court (1991) 229 Cal App 3d 151, 279 Cal Rptr 911.

[18] Cox v Administrator, U.S. Steel & Carnegie (1994, CA11 Ala) 17 F3d 1386. For a discussion of the ability of one party to depose another party's attorneys, see § 2.16.

[19] Cox v Administrator, U.S. Steel & Carnegie (1994, CA11 Ala) 17 F3d 1386, 1423.

[1] CCP §§ 2025.430–2025.450.

[2] CCP § 2025.430.

for a deposition that fails to go forward can receive only the statutory witness fee and mileage. This is true even if that deponent happens also to be the attorney for a party.[3]

A party who improperly aborts a noticed deposition may avoid the monetary sanction by persuading the court that there was "substantial justification" for this happening.[4] Giving notice of the cancellation of a deposition does not automatically avoid the sanction. The party must give this notice in time to prevent others from incurring expenses. In a federal case,[5] a team of attorneys journeyed from Pennsylvania to Los Angeles to participate in a deposition noticed by the other side. On the day set for the deposition, their opponents informed them that they had decided to cancel it. The court ordered reimbursement of the substantial travel expenses incurred.

Failure of a Nonparty Deponent to Attend: A deposition may abort because the witness either does not attend or refuses to be sworn.[6] To compel their attendance and testimony at a deposition, nonparties must be served with a deposition subpoena.[7]

—Deponent under Subpoena: Nonparties who ignore a deposition subpoena risk two serious sanctions. First, they expose themselves to contempt.[8] No court order compelling their compliance is required as precondition for this sanction.[9] Second, they forfeit to the party noticing the deposition $500 and any other damages that party incurred.[10]

—Deponent Not under Subpoena: A party noticing a deposition sometimes does not bother serving a subpoena on a cooperative witness. That party then must accept the consequences if that deponent does not appear or refuses to be sworn. In the *Rosen* case,[11] for example, defense counsel traveled from California to New York only to learn that the deponent, who was not under subpoena, was insisting on a postponement of several days. When plaintiff foolishly refused his demand for the cost of staying over to the new date, the defense attorney

---

[3] Poe v Diamond (1987) 191 Cal App 3d 1394, 1399–1400, 237 Cal Rptr 80.

[4] CCP § 2025.430.

[5] Baldwin-Lima-Hamilton Corp. v Tatnall Measuring Systems Co. (1958, ED Pa) 22 FRD 12. See also Detsch & Co. v American Products Co. (1944, CA9 Cal) 141 F2d 662.

[6] See, e.g., Aziz v Wright (1994, CA8 Mo) 34 F3d 587, 589 [finding that refusal of inmate deponent to answer questions until his handcuffs were removed was not a failure to appear, but a failure to proceed justifying dismissal for failure to prosecute].

[7] For a discussion of the use of a deposition subpoena to compel attendance of a nonparty at a discovery deposition, see § 2.9.

[8] E.g., Bankers Trust Co. v Braten (1993, App Div) 598 NYS 2d 498, 498 [nonparty deponents may be held in contempt for failure to appear at deposition in answer to proper subpoena].

[9] CCP § 2020.240. See, e.g., Gregori v Bank of America (1989) 207 Cal App 3d 291, 311, 254 Cal Rptr 853.

[10] CCP § 2025.440, referencing CCP § 2020.240.

[11] Rosen v Superior Court (1966) 244 Cal App 2d 586, 53 Cal Rptr 347. See also Crippen v Superior Court (1984) 159 Cal App 3d 254, 261, 205 Cal Rptr 477.

returned to California. The court held that it was an abuse of discretion to deny that attorney's motion for reimbursement for the entire cost of the trip.

—Sanctions: Section 2025.440 provides that "[if] a deponent does not appear for a deposition because the party giving notice of the deposition failed to serve a required deposition subpoena," the trial court can impose a monetary sanction on that party and on the attorney for that party.[12] This sanction runs in favor of other parties or their attorneys who attended at the time and place specified in the deposition notice "in the expectation that the deponent's testimony would be taken." The court must impose this sanction unless the party who noticed the deposition can convince it that there was "substantial justification" for the failure to subpoena the deponent.

Failure of a Party Deponent to Attend: It is not necessary to subpoena a party to the lawsuit to compel their appearance at a deposition. Parties must appear in response to the deposition notice itself.[13] Individuals who are parties and who fail to appear become vulnerable to a near-certain imposition of a monetary sanction.[14] This is also true where a corporation or other organization is a party, and an officer, director, managing agent or employee of that organization fails to appear in response to a notice naming that person as the deponent.[15] In addition, where the notice names the organizational party as the deponent, and that organization does not produce those employees most knowledgeable about the areas specified in the deposition notice, that organization exposes itself to the risk of a monetary sanction.[16]

—Sanctions: In a departure from the pre-1987 statute,[17] Section 2025.450 does not authorize the immediate imposition of a drastic sanction, such as dismissal or default, upon a party who, personally or through an employee, fails, even wilfully, to appear for a noticed deposition. Instead, the one who noticed the deposition must move for an order compelling the deponent's attendance.[18] Before making this motion, the party who noticed the deposition must attempt to contact the deponent to inquire about the nonappearance.[19] Implicit in this requirement to inquire is an obligation to listen to the reasons offered for the

---

[12] See CCP § 2025.440(a).

[13] For a discussion of compelling the attendance of a party for a deposition, see § 2.10.

[14] CCP § 2025.450.

[15] For a discussion of compelling the attendance of those affiliated with a party for a deposition, see § 2.12.

[16] Wanderer v Johnston (1990, CA9 Cal) 910 F2d 652, 657 [organizational party bore responsibility for its representative's failure to appear]. For a discussion of depositions of an organizational deponent, see §§ 2.5. 2.9, 2.12 and 2.14.

[17] Former CCP § 2034(d) [requiring finding of "wilful" failure to attend]. See Midwife v Bernal (1988) 203 Cal App 3d 57, 63, 249 Cal Rptr 708 [requiring finding of "wilful" failure to attend deposition under former CCP § 2034(d) before the court could impose a drastic sanction, such as dismissal of the lawsuit].

[18] CCP § 2025.450(a).

[19] CCP § 2025.450(b)(2).

nonappearance and to try in good faith to resolve the issue. A party who files a motion to compel without first complying with the specifics of this "meet and confer" obligation may expose itself to a monetary sanction.[20]

If the court grants the motion, it will impose a monetary sanction on the party deponent, unless that party shows that there was substantial justification for not appearing for the deposition.[21] Not only the party who noticed the deposition but also any other party who attended with the expectation that the deposition would go forward may seek this monetary sanction.[22]

Only if the party deponent then disobeys the order compelling attendance may the trial court impose a drastic sanction. Even then, however, it has the discretion to impose another monetary sanction and give the party another chance to comply with its order.[23]

§ 2.21 Deposition Officer

Section 2025.320 requires that an oral discovery deposition be supervised by an officer "who is authorized to administer an oath."

Notary Public: In most situations the officer for a deposition taken in California[1] will be a notary public. One statutory function of a notary public is to "take depositions . . . and administer oaths and affirmations . . . to be used before any court, judge, officer, or board."[2] Usually, the deposition officer will also double as the deposition reporter.[3]

Disqualifications: Any individual who is "financially interested in the action," is "a relative or employee of any attorney of any of the parties," or is "a relative or employee of any . . . of the parties" may not preside at a deposition.[4] The

---

[20] Leko v Cornerstone Bldg. Inspection Service (2000) 86 Cal App 4th 1109, 1124, 103 Cal Rptr 2d 858.

[21] CCP § 2025.450(c)(1).

[22] CCP § 2025.450(c)(2). See also Midwife v Bernal (1988) 203 Cal App 3d 57, 62 n3, 249 Cal Rptr 708 [where a plaintiff's failure to appear for a deposition noticed by one defendant warrants a monetary sanction, that sanction may also run in favor of a co-defendant who did not notice the deposition, but who did appear at the scheduled time and place].

Annotation: Dismissal of state court action for failure or refusal of plaintiff to appear or answer questions at deposition or oral examination. 32 ALR4th 212.

[23] CCP § 2025.450(d).

[1] Special provision is made for the officer to supervise a deposition taken in another state [CCP § 2026.010(d)] or in another nation [CCP § 2027.010(d)]. For a discussion of out-of-state depositions, see §§ 4.1–4.2.

[2] Gov't Code § 8205(a)(3).

[3] E.g., United States ex rel. Burch v Piqua Engineering, Inc. (1993, SD Ohio) 152 FRD 565, 566–567 [deposition officer was independent court reporter, licensed as a notary public under state law].

[4] CCP § 2025.320(a).

Annotation: Disqualification of attorney, otherwise qualified, to take oath or acknowledgment from client. 21 ALR3d 483, 497–500.

parties, however, may stipulate in writing to allow an otherwise disqualified person to preside at a deposition.[5]

Objections: Parties must make any objections to a deposition officer's qualifications "before the deposition begins or as soon after that as the ground for that objection becomes known or could be discovered by reasonable diligence."[6] Failure to timely object waives all challenges. This waiver will occur even where the deposition officer is disqualified, and the parties have not stipulated to waive the disqualification.[7] Moreover, absent prejudice, even a timely objection does not invalidate a deposition that is only "technically flawed." For example, in *Banks v McMorris*,[8] the officer involved, although empowered to administer an oath, was not authorized to preside at a deposition. Nevertheless, the court refused to invalidate the deposition where no prejudice resulted from the officer's lack of that qualification.

Changing the Deposition Officer: Where the deposition notice specifies a certain individual as the deposition officer,[9] and someone otherwise qualified appears in that person's stead, this substitution furnishes no ground for objection:

> [P]ublic convenience would seem to demand that in the [event of the] sickness or absence of the officer designated, any other empowered by law might be substituted. . . . [I]t would certainly be a matter of small importance who should take the deposition, particularly in view of the inconvenience and delay which would result from a different rule.[10]

Duties of the Deposition Officer: Deposition officers may perform as many as eight duties. First, they administer the oath to the deponent.[11] Second, they propound written cross-examination questions for parties who have submitted them in advance instead of attending the examination in person.[12] Third, they suspend the taking of testimony on demand of a party or the deponent so that the objector may move for a protective order against an abusive examination.[13] Fourth, if a deponent declines to answer a question or produce an item, and the attorney seeking the information orally notifies the deponent of an intention to

---

[5] See CCP § 2016.030.

[6] CCP § 2025.320(e).

[7] See Reimel v House (1969) 268 Cal App 2d 780, 787, 74 Cal Rptr 345.

[8] Banks v McMorris (1975) 47 Cal App 3d 723, 729–730, 121 Cal Rptr 185 [oath administered by referee instead of notary or judge as required by former CCP § 2018(a)].

[9] For a discussion of whether such a designation in the deposition notice is necessary, see § 2.4.

[10] Williams v Chadbourne (1856) 6 Cal 559, 561, quoted with approval in Reimel v House (1969) 268 Cal App 2d 780, 786, 74 Cal Rptr 345.

[11] CCP § 2025.330(a). Cf. United States v Kramer (1990, SD Fla) 741 F Supp 893, 894–895 [failure to administer oath to translators at a deposition in a foreign country was not fatal to deposition's admissibility at trial, where the translators could be sworn and examined at the trial itself].

[12] CCP § 2025.330(e). For a discussion of cross-examination in absentia, see § 2.23.

[13] CCP § 2025.470. For a discussion of motions to terminate or limit a deposition, see § 2.30.

move to compel discovery, the deposition officer directs the deponent to attend that court session.[14] It is not, however, the officer's role to certify a question to the court for a ruling on its propriety.[15] Fifth, deposition officers notify the deponent and the parties when the deposition transcript becomes available for the deponent's review and signature.[16] Sixth, they record the deponent's response to this notification.[17] Seventh, they certify that the transcript of the deposition is correct.[18] And finally, they seal the transcript and transmit it to the attorney who noticed the deposition.[19]

§ 2.22 Recording the Testimony

Required Stenographic Record: Section 2025.330 requires a stenographic record of the deposition "[u]nless the parties agree or the court orders otherwise."[1] The dictionary defines "stenography" as "shorthand writing." The Business and Professions Code defines the practice of this shorthand reporting as "the making by means of written symbols or abbreviations in shorthand or machine shorthand writing of a verbatim record of any oral . . . deposition."[2]

Supplemental Recording: Besides the required stenographic record, a party who is taking a deposition may simultaneously audio or video the testimony. However, that party must announce this intent in the deposition notice.[3] If the deponent is not a party to the case, the deposition subpoena must contain the same information.[4]

Other parties may also simultaneously audio or video the deposition testimony. To do so, they must give written notice of that intent, no later than three calendar

---

[14] CCP § 2025.480(c). For a discussion of motions to compel answers and production, see § 2.29.

[15] Gall v Saint Elizabeth Medical Center (1990, SD Ohio) 130 FRD 85, 86–87 [rejecting Ohio practice permitting notaries to certify questions to the court before they exercise their statutory powers to punish deponents who refuse to testify].

[16] CCP §§ 2025.520–2025.530. For a discussion of the submission of the deposition to the deponent for reading and signing, see §§ 2.31–2.32.

[17] CCP §§ 2025.520(e) and 2025.530(c). See United States ex rel. Burch v Piqua Engineering, Inc. (1993, SD Ohio) 152 FRD 565, 566–567 [deposition transcript changes had to be made by deposition officer, not the deponent].

[18] CCP § 2025.540(a). For a discussion of the certification of the deposition record, see § 2.34.

[19] CCP § 2025.550(a). For a discussion of the custody of the deposition record, see § 2.34.

[1] CCP § 2025.330(b). See Bogan v Northwestern Mut. Life Ins. Co. (1993, SD NY) 152 FRD 9, 11–12 [implying that in unusual cases, such as with preliminary exploratory depositions, where deponent was notified in advance, courts could approve "memory or note-taking" as sole deposition recording method].

[2] Bus and Prof Code § 8017. Cf. Saunders v Superior Court (1994) 27 Cal App 4th 832, 841–842, 33 Cal Rptr 2d 438 [considering propriety, under unfair competition laws, of certified court reporters' "direct contracts" with insurers for deposition recording].

[3] CCP § 2025.330(c).

Annotation: Use of videotape to take deposition for presentation at civil trial in state court. 66 ALR3d 637. Survey: The Video Deposition as a Deposition Tool (1991) 13 Campbell LR 375.

[4] CCP § 2020.310(c).

days before the deposition, to the attorney who noticed the deposition, to all other parties who received the deposition notice and to any nonparty deponent.[5]

Procedures at a Recorded Deposition: Section 2025.340 contains an elaborate set of procedures for taping deposition testimony. The operator of the electronic equipment must be "competent to set up, operate, and monitor" it.[6] As long as someone else is serving as the deposition officer,[7] the operator usually may be an employee of the attorney taking the deposition.[8] One federal trial judge, however, balked at letting a party to the lawsuit operate the recording equipment.[9] Where a party is videotaping the deposition of an expert for use at trial instead of the expert's live testimony,[10] the equipment operator must have the same qualifications as a deposition officer.[11] During the questioning the operator may not use recording techniques that distort the appearance or the demeanor of the participants in the deposition.[12]

The room in which the deposition occurs must be "suitably large, adequately lighted, and reasonably quiet."[13] The deposition must begin with a statement on the record identifying the operator, the lawsuit, the deponent, the party noticing the deposition, and its date, time and place.[14] After that, the attorneys for each party must identify themselves on the camera or the audio.[15] The administration of the oath[16] and any stipulations[17] made by the parties must also be Recorded.

—Camera Focus: One matter that Section 2025.340 does not address is where the camera may focus during a video deposition.[18] Several courts require the camera to remain focused at all times on the deponent, instead of turning to an attorney asking a question or objecting.[19]

---

[5] CCP § 2025.330(c). See Green v GTE California (1994) 29 Cal App 4th 407, 410, 34 Cal Rptr 2d 517.

[6] CCP § 2025.340(b).

[7] For a discussion of the deposition officer's qualifications, see § 2.20.

[8] CCP § 2025.340(b).

[9] Sheppard v Beerman (1993, ED NY) 822 F Supp 931, 941–942 [distinguishing cases where nonparty attorney permitted to operate the recording machines].

[10] For a discussion of the use of video recorded depositions of expert witnesses at trial, see § 2.39.

[11] For a discussion of a deposition officer's qualifications, see § 2.20.

[12] CCP § 2025.340(g).

[13] CCP § 2025.340(a).

[14] CCP § 2025.340(h).

[15] CCP § 2025.340(i).

[16] CCP § 2025.340(j).

[17] CCP § 2025.340(h)–(l).

[18] See Green v GTE California (1994) 29 Cal App 4th 407, 410, 34 Cal Rptr 2d 517 ["it is questionable whether the statute applies to videotaping opposing counsel instead of the witness"].

[19] See, e.g., Rice's Toyota World v S.E. Toyota Distributors, Inc. (1987, MD NC) 114 FRD 647, 652; State ex rel. Williams v Mauer (1986, Mo) 772 SW2d 296, 304.

Recorded Reenactments: In the *Stermer* case,[20] a products liability action arising from injury caused by an infant seat, defense counsel during a video recorded deposition asked the child's mother to demonstrate on camera, with the aid of a similar seat and a plastic doll, how she had secured her child in the seat. The mother refused. The defendants then got a court order compelling this reenactment.

The appellate court overturned this order, in part because then-applicable Section 2025(o) authorized a trial court to compel deponents only to give an "answer" to a "question":

> [A] reenactment at a deposition requires something more than a mere answer—it requires that the deponent perform a host of nonverbal actions that go well beyond answering questions. In other words, the reenactment necessarily includes a series of acts by the deponent which are not of a verbal nature.[21]

Four years after *Stermer*, the Supreme Court considered the same issue in the *Emerson Electric* case.[22] It disapproved *Stermer* for three reasons: (1) one of the dictionary definitions of "answer" is "to act in response to a request"; (2) reenactments are permitted during a trial, and the Discovery Act provides that the examination of a deponent is to "proceed as permitted at trial";[23] and (3) this interpretation furthers the goal of discovery to educate the parties concerning each other's claims and defenses.

§ 2.23 Cross-Examination in Absentia

Section 2025.330 allows what amounts to an *in absentia* cross-examination at an oral deposition: "In lieu of participating in the oral examination, parties may transmit written questions . . . for delivery to the deposition officer, who shall . . . propound them to the deponent after the oral examination has been completed."[1] This provision was rarely used, probably because it was little known. It has probably become obsolete now that Section 2025.310 permits parties, in lieu of personal appearance at the deposition site, to participate in an oral deposition of any person "by telephone or other remote electronic means."[2]

§ 2.24 Objections to Questions—In General

Trial Procedure Compared: Frequently, during an oral deposition, counsel will ask the deponent a question that an attorney for another party considers objectionable. If someone were to ask the same question to a trial witness, the

---

[20] Stermer v Superior Court (1993) 20 Cal App 4th 777, 24 Cal Rptr 2d 577.

[21] Stermer v Superior Court (1993) 20 Cal App 4th 777, 781, 24 Cal Rptr 2d 577.

[22] Emerson Electric Co. v Superior Court (1997) 16 Cal 4th 1101, 68 Cal Rptr 2d 883, 946 P2d 841.

[23] CCP § 2025.330(d).

[1] CCP § 2025.330(e).

[2] CCP § 2025.310(a).

attorney could simply object to it. Moreover, the attorney would be aware that a failure to timely and specifically object will usually waive the objection.[1] The trial court would rule on the objection. If it is sustained, the witness does not answer the question.

Several features peculiar to depositions preclude a simple transplantation of this trial procedure. The scope of pretrial discovery is significantly broader than the scope of trial admissibility.[2] A question that would be objectionable at trial may be quite proper during discovery.[3] Moreover, an attorney aware of these differing standards must still consider whether it is necessary to "note an objection for the record" to preserve the right to object later to the same question at the trial.

Questioning Outside Scope of Discovery: Where a question calls for information beyond the legitimate scope of discovery, counsel must give attention to three matters: (1) Does a failure to object to discovery make the information admissible at the trial? (2) Does an objection during a deposition preserve the ground stated when the case comes to trial, or must counsel also instruct the witness not to answer the question? (3) Questions of waiver aside, how can one stop a deponent from supplying information that is outside the scope of discovery, since the deposition officer cannot make a ruling on the objection?[4]

Because the specific ground for the objection affects the answer to these three questions, the following four sections discuss separately objections based on: the irrelevance of the inquiry,[5] the inadmissibility of the information at trial,[6] a claim of privilege or the work product protection[7] and the form of the question.[8]

§ 2.25 "Irrelevant"

Three-Step Inquiry: During a deposition, an attorney may believe that a question put to the deponent by another attorney would elicit only "irrelevant" information. A simple, three-step inquiry should inform counsel's reaction to the question. (1) Is the information truly "irrelevant?" (2) If it *is* irrelevant, must the attorney object at the deposition to preserve the objection at the trial? (3) Is the line of questioning so outside the bounds of relevancy that a motion to limit the examination is in order?

(1) Is the Matter "Irrelevant?" Counsel should reflect carefully on whether the information sought really *is* irrelevant. "Relevance" is a broad concept. Information is relevant to a fact if it has "*any* tendency in reason to prove or

---

[1] See Evid Code § 353. See also McCormick, Evidence § 55 (5th Ed 1999).

[2] For general coverage of the scope of discovery, see Chapters 11–13.

[3] For a discussion of the use of depositions as evidence at trial, see §§ 2.37–2.42.

[4] For a discussion of motions to terminate or limit a deposition, see § 2.30.

[5] See § 2.25.

[6] See § 2.26.

[7] See § 2.27.

[8] See § 2.28.

disprove" that fact.[1] Stated another way, it is relevant if it has "*any* tendency to make the existence" of that fact "more probable or less probable than it would be without the evidence."[2]

A more informed analysis of a relevance objection will often reveal that its real basis is not that the information has no value for proving a certain fact. Rather, it is that the fact it tends to prove is not material because, even if proved, it is of no "consequence to the determination of the action."[3]

A fact that is not material in this sense may still be part of the broader subject matter of the action. At trial, the *admissibility* of a matter depends *not only* on whether it tends to prove a certain fact *but also* on whether that fact has any legal significance to the issues being tried. By contrast, during a deposition, its *discoverability* depends on whether it tends to prove a fact that has anything to do with the broad "subject matter involved in the pending action."[4]

(2) Should One Object? If counsel concludes that an objection to the relevance of a question relates only to the *admissibility* at trial of the information it seeks, there is no need to object at the deposition. The failure to make an objection on this ground does not waive the right to do so at trial: "Objections . . . to the relevancy, materiality, or admissibility at trial of the testimony or of the materials produced are unnecessary and are not waived by failure to make them . . . before or during the taking of the deposition."[5]

Although it is not necessary to make this objection during the deposition, counsel should consider making it "for the record" as a reminder to object to that portion of the testimony should someone later offer the deposition in evidence. This may also underscore the importance of the objection when counsel renews it at trial, and it may even subliminally affect the trial judge's ruling.

Where the relevance objection goes not just to the ultimate admissibility of a line of inquiry, but also to its discoverability, counsel should object during the deposition. As discussed below, this objection will not prevent the deponent from answering. However, it may lead the questioner to abandon the line of inquiry. It may also lay the groundwork for a protective order.

(3) Should One Move to Terminate the Deposition? Standing alone, an objection to the relevance of a line of questioning to the subject matter of the case does not prevent the deponent from answering. The presiding officer will "note" the objection in the record, but will not rule on it.[6] The federal courts have consistently held that the deponent should answer the question once the objection has been noted:

---

[1] See Evid Code § 210 (italics added).

[2] See Fed Rules Evid, Rule 401 (italics added).

[3] See Evid Code § 210.

[4] CCP § 2017.010. For a discussion of "relevance" for discovery, see § 11.1.

[5] CCP § 2025.460(c).

[6] See CCP § 2025.460(b).

The harm caused by being required to take additional depositions of a witness who fails to answer a question based on an improperly asserted objection far exceeds the mere inconvenience of a witness having to answer a question which may not be admissible at the trial of the action. . . . In regard to routine objections based on relevancy, such objections should be noted on the record and witnesses should thereafter answer the question.[7]

A federal appellate court has strongly condemned the practice of instructing a deponent not to answer an allegedly irrelevant line of inquiry. It branded the practice "indefensible," "highly improper," and "utterly at variance" with the provision that evidence objected to "shall be taken subject to the objections."[8]

Under this approach, the objecting party should let the deponent answer the objectionable questions unless they reach the point where "the examination is being conducted in bad faith or in a manner that unreasonably annoys, embarrasses, or oppresses" that party.[9] In that event, the objecting party should demand suspension of the examination pending a motion to terminate or limit the deposition.[10]

The *Stewart* case has read the Discovery Act's objection procedure in much the same way as the approach followed in the federal court:

Deposing counsel's insistence on inquiring into irrelevant areas could justify suspension [of the deposition], but only if it reaches the point where it could legitimately be said that counsel's intent was to harass, annoy, embarrass, or oppress. Taken as a whole, these provisions clearly contemplate that deponents not be prevented by counsel from answering a question unless it pertains to privileged matters or deposing counsel's conduct has reached a state where suspension is warranted. The fact that suspension is available only where an interrogation into improper matters reveals an underlying purpose to harass, annoy, etc., indicates that witnesses are expected to endure an occasional irrelevant question without disrupting the deposition process.[11]

---

[7] W. R. Grace & Co. v Pullman, Inc. (1977, WD Okla) 74 FRD 80, 84.

[8] Ralston Purina Co. v McFarland (1977, CA4 NC) 550 F2d 967, 973. See also International Union of Electrical, etc. Workers v Westinghouse Electric Corp. (1981, D DC) 91 FRD 277. Cf. Kerper & Stuart, Rambo Bites the Dust: Current Trends in Deposition Ethics, 22 J. Legal Prof. 103 (1998).

[9] CCP § 2025.470.

[10] See Smith v Dowson (1994, D Minn) 158 FRD 138, 140–142 [granting mid-deposition protective order to preclude irrelevant line of inquiry]; W. R. Grace & Co. v Pullman, Inc. (1977, WD Okla) 74 FRD 80, 84; Shapiro v Freeman (1965, SD NY) 38 FRD 308, 311–312. Cf. Board of Supervisors v Superior Court (1995) 32 Cal App 4th 1616, 1626–1627, 38 Cal Rptr 2d 876 [party cannot circumvent prohibition against inquiry into local legislators' thought processes by deposing county sheriff who communicated with them]; County of Los Angeles v Superior Court (1975) 13 Cal 3d 721, 727–729, 119 Cal Rptr 631, 532 P2d 495 [taxpayer may not inquire into legislators' thought processes]. For a discussion of motions to terminate or limit a deposition, see § 2.30.

[11] Stewart v Colonial Western Agency, Inc. (2000) 87 Cal App 4th 1006, 1015, 105 Cal Rptr 2d 115.

§ 2.26 "Inadmissible"

A question asked during a deposition may be proper in form and may seek information that is both relevant to the subject matter of the case[1] and not within any evidentiary privilege or the work product protection.[2] Yet the question is one that the rules of evidence would make objectionable if asked at trial. The prejudicial impact of the evidence may outweigh its probative value.[3] Or the question may call for an impermissible opinion.[4] Or it may elicit a hearsay statement that is not within any of the hearsay exceptions.[5] Or it may seek information that falls under an exclusionary rule implementing social policies extrinsic to the law of evidence, such as the one restricting evidence of repairs or other safety measures taken after an accident.[6]

Confronted with this sort of question, counsel must consider: (1) whether to object, and (2) whether to go further and ask the deposition officer to suspend the deposition while counsel seeks a court to prohibiting the line of questioning.

(1) Should Counsel Object? The correctness of and the necessity for an objection turn on the distinction between the *admissibility* and the *discoverability* of the information sought by the question.

On the one hand, where a matter is relevant to the subject matter of the case, yet objectionable under the rules of evidence, an objection during the deposition is not necessary and may not even be correct. Many items of information that would be inadmissible at trial are nonetheless subject to discovery. Section 2017.010 allows discovery of a matter that "*either* is itself admissible in evidence *or* appears reasonably calculated to lead to the discovery of admissible evidence."[7] Accordingly, objections to the "admissibility at trial of the testimony or of the materials produced are unnecessary and are not waived by failure to make them before or during the deposition."[8]

Some attorneys are more comfortable when they make these evidentiary objections "for the record" during the deposition. If nothing else, they serve as printed reminders to object to those parts of the testimony if someone later offers the deposition in evidence.

---

[1] For a discussion of objections to deposition questions as irrelevant, see § 2.25.

[2] For a discussion of objections to deposition questions on the ground of privilege or the work product protection, see § 2.27.

[3] See Evid Code § 352.

[4] See Evid Code §§ 800–801.

[5] See Evid Code § 1200. See, e.g., Jordan v Medley (1983, CA DC) 711 F2d 211, 217–219 [evidence that criminal charges had been filed against defendant-deponent for the conduct involved in the pending civil assault case]; Schalkofski v Lawrence (1972) 37 Mich App 686, 195 NW2d 292 [hearsay].

[6] See Evid Code § 1151.

[7] CCP § 2017.010 (italics added). For a discussion of when items that may lead to admissible evidence, see §§ 11.1–11.3.

[8] CCP § 2025.460(c). See, e.g., Johnson v Nationwide Mut. Ins. Co. (1960, CA4 Va) 276 F2d 574, 578–579 [objection to hearsay not waived].

On the other hand, counsel may challenge whether a line of inquiry has any reasonable prospect of turning up admissible evidence. In that event, they should object at the deposition and advise the witness to refuse to answer. If the deponent obeys this instruction, this will force the examining party to abandon the line of inquiry or move for an order compelling an answer.[9]

(2) Should Counsel Move to Terminate? An objection that a line of inquiry is not reasonably calculated to produce admissible evidence does not stop the deponent from responding. Even an instruction to the deponent not to answer the question is ineffective if the deponent chooses to disobey it. An objecting party who wants to cut off the inquiry must then demand the suspension of the examination pending a motion to terminate or limit the deposition.[10]

§ 2.27 "Privileged" or "Work Product"

When a deposition question calls for privileged information, it is, of course, objectionable on that ground.[1] A deposition question is also objectionable when it asks for information covered by the work product protection.[2]

Waiver: In contrast to other deposition questions calling for inadmissible information,[3] Section 2025.460 now makes explicit previous case law[4] that required a prompt objection to questions intruding upon a privilege or protected work product. Failure to make a timely objection waives the evidentiary privilege or work product protection:

> The protection of information from discovery on the ground that it is privileged or that it is protected work product . . . is waived unless a specific objection to its disclosure is timely made during the deposition.[5]

Instruction Not to Answer: By itself, the assertion of an objection is not enough to preserve a privilege or the work product protection: "A strict application of the provisions . . . that evidence objected to shall be taken subject to objections being noted cannot be followed as to a privilege asserted during a deposition because such disclosure would undermine the protection afforded

---

[9] For a discussion of motions to compel answers, see § 2.29.

[10] CCP § 2025.460(b). For a discussion of motions to terminate or limit a deposition, see § 2.30.

[1] See CCP § 2017.010. See also Fed Rules Civ Proc, Rule 26(b)(1). For coverage of these evidentiary privileges, see Chapter 12.

[2] For coverage of the "work-product" protection, see Chapter 13.

[3] For discussion of objections to deposition questions on the ground of irrelevance, see § 2.25. For discussion of objections to deposition questions on the ground of inadmissibility, see § 2.26.

[4] Schaff v Superior Court (1983) 146 Cal App 3d 921, 923, 194 Cal Rptr 546. See also Rosenfeld v Ungar (1960, SD Ia) 25 FRD 340.

[5] CCP § 2025.460(a). See Morganroth & Morganroth v DeLorean (1997, CA6 Mich) 123 F3d 374, 383 [privilege for confidential marital communications is waived at trial by husband's failure to object during deposition of ex-wife].

by the privilege and would constitute a waiver of such privilege."[6] Counsel must take the additional step of instructing the deponent not to answer the question.

—Unrepresented Deponents: On some occasions a deponent who is not a party may be asked for information that is protected by a privilege held either by the deponent or some third person. In *Sabado v Moraga,*[7] for example, the plaintiff subpoenaed the defendant's wife for a deposition. At the outset of the session, his attorney, who did not represent the wife, advised her of her privilege not to testify against her husband.[8] Even though the advice was correct, the trial judge sanctioned the husband's attorney for telling her about the privilege. The appellate court held that this was error:

> An attorney who, while acting presumably in the best interest of his own client, offers gratuitous information to an unrepresented witness of possible legal rights should not have to fear punishment if the witness chooses to exercise those rights. The best interests of our judicial system are not served by keeping our uninformed citizens in the dark. . . . [S]anctions may be appropriate if an attorney offers meritless legal advice to a witness which results in a delay in the proceedings . . . .[9]

—Deponent Obeys the Instruction: Often the deponent receiving the instruction not to answer is a client, or an employee of a client, of the attorney making the objection. Such a deponent expectably will decline to respond. Even a deponent who is not connected with the party making the objection may decide to heed the instruction.[10] Unless willing to abandon the line of inquiry, the party asking the question will have to test the claim of privilege or work product by moving to compel an answer.[11]

—Deponent Disobeys the Instruction: The statute does not tell counsel what to do if the deponent, in the face of the objection and an instruction not to answer, indicates an intention to divulge the information anyway. In such cases, the objecting party, to avoid a waiver, probably has to demand that the deposition officer suspend the examination to permit the filing of a motion for an order to limit the deposition.[12]

Appellate Review: If the trial court overrules a claim of privilege or work product, a deponent may not persist in refusing to answer just because the ruling

---

[6] W. R. Grace & Co. v Pullman, Inc. (1977, WD Okla) 74 FRD 80, 85. See also Preyer v United States Lines, Inc. (1973, ED Pa) 64 FRD 430, 431.

[7] Sabado v Moraga (1987) 189 Cal App 3d 1, 234 Cal Rptr 249.

[8] For a discussion of the spousal privilege, see § 12.13.

[9] Sabado v Moraga (1987) 189 Cal App 3d 1, 9, 234 Cal Rptr 249.

[10] See, e.g., Sabado v Moraga (1987) 189 Cal App 3d 1, 234 Cal Rptr 249.

[11] For a discussion of motions to compel an answer to a deposition question, see § 2.29.

[12] Cf. Perrignon v Bergen Brunswig Corp. (1978, ND Cal) 77 FRD 455, 460–461. For a discussion of suspending a deposition pending a motion to limit inquiry, see § 2.30. For a discussion of the duties of the deposition officer, see § 2.21.

is erroneous. An objecting party who wishes to challenge the order should seek immediate appellate review via petition for writ of mandate.[13]

The failure to seek writ review does not waive any error committed in overruling the claim of privilege or work product. However, disobedience of a court order, even an erroneous one, may expose counsel or the deponent to sanctions. "[T]he failure to comply with a court order which is within the jurisdiction of the court, where appellate review is available but not sought in a timely manner, justifies the imposition of sanctions whether or not the order is subsequently determined on appeal to have been erroneous."[14]

§ 2.28 "The Form of the Question"

The rules that govern the phrasing of questions at trial also apply during a deposition: "Examination and cross-examination of the deponent shall proceed as permitted at trial under the provisions of the Evidence Code."[1]

Examples: This provision imports into discovery practice the right to object to questions that are "ambiguous or unintelligible," "argumentative," "compound" or "too general." Other objections may challenge the form of a question that unnecessarily "calls for a narrative answer," "lacks the proper foundation," has been "asked and answered," "misquotes a witness," "leads" a friendly or neutral witness, "assumes a fact not in evidence" or "calls for speculation."[2] It is, of course, inappropriate for attorneys to use objections to the form of questions as a way either of suggesting answers or of "testifying" themselves.[3]

Waiver: In contrast to objections based on irrelevancy[4] or inadmissibility,[5] a party must challenge the form of questions when they are asked: "Errors or irregularities of any kind occurring at the oral examination that *might be cured if promptly presented* are waived unless a specific objection to them is timely made during the deposition."[6] Among the curable errors that the statute lists as waived by a failure to assert them are those "to the form of any question."[7] The most common curable objections forfeited under this rule are to questions that

---

[13] For a discussion of "writ review" of rulings overruling a claim of privilege or work product, see § 1.8.

[14] In re Marriage of Niklas (1989) 211 Cal App 3d 28, 36 n4, 258 Cal Rptr 921.

[1] CCP § 2025.330(d).

[2] Chavez v Zapata Ocean Resources, Inc. (1984) 155 Cal App 3d 115,125, 201 Cal Rptr 887. For an excellent analysis of objections to the form of questions, see Blitch, California Trial Objections §§ 7.1–16.7 (10th Ed. Cal CEB 2004).

[3] Chavez v Zapata Ocean Resources, Inc. (1984) 155 Cal App 3d 115, 125, 201 Cal Rptr 887; see also Johnson v Wayne Manor Apartments (1993, ED Pa) 152 FRD 56, 59.

[4] For a discussion of objections to deposition questions on the ground of irrelevance, see § 2.25.

[5] For a discussion of objections to deposition questions on the ground of inadmissibility, see § 2.26.

[6] CCP § 2025.460(b) (italics added).

[7] CCP § 2025.460(b). See, e.g., Batelli v Kagan & Gaines Co. (1956, CA9 Cal) 236 F2d 167, 169–170.

are leading[8] or unclear.[9] A party who has failed to object to the form of a question during the deposition cannot make that objection should another party later offer the answer in evidence at trial.

—Objections to the Answer: Although a deposition question itself may be proper, the form of the *answer* to it may not be, as where it is not "responsive" to that question. Counsel must make an objection "to the form of any . . . answer"[10] at the time the deponent gives it. Otherwise, the objecting party will waive the right to object to the use of that answer at trial.[11]

Instruction Not to Answer: It is rarely appropriate to accompany an objection to the form of a question with an instruction to the deponent not to answer it. The most likely justification for such an instruction is that the question is ambiguous or misleading. This sort of question can be a trap for unwary deponents. Moreover, if the ambiguity or deceptiveness is unintentional, the examining party can rephrase the question to eliminate it.

Generally, however, once a party makes an objection to the form of a question, the deponent should answer it over that objection.[12] One state court has held that a party may ask *any* deponent leading questions for discovery purposes, if that party is willing to risk the answers being ruled inadmissible at the trial on that ground:

> [T]he oral examination of *any* deponent shall proceed to completion, subject to recorded objections subsequently to be resolved by the court, and all reasonably relevant questions, leading or otherwise, must be answered unless privileged whether or not such answers themselves, or other evidence toward which they may lead, would be admissible at trial. Again, the distinction between acquiring evidence and *using* it must be emphasized. . . . Discovering evidence is one thing, admitting it at trial is quite another.[13]

§ 2.29 Motion to Compel Answer or Production

Two Options: When a deponent fails to answer any question, or to produce any item specified in a deposition notice or subpoena, the party seeking the answer or the production has two options: to adjourn the deposition and move to compel the discovery, or to complete the deposition on other matters, and then

---

[8] See Evid Code §§ 764 [defining "leading question"] and 767 [describing permitted and prohibited leading questions]. See, e.g., Oberlin v Marlin American Corp. (1979, CA7 Ind) 596 F2d 1322, 1328; Houser v Snap-on Tools Corp. (1962, D Md) 202 F Supp 181, 187–188.

[9] E.g., Aetna Cas. & Surety Co. v Aceves (1991) 233 Cal App 3d 544, 558, 284 Cal Rptr 477 [objection to vagueness of question waived unless made at the deposition].

[10] CCP § 2025.460(b).

[11] Kirschner v Broadhead (1981, CA7 Ind) 671 F2d 1034, 1037–1038.

[12] See, e.g., Gall v Saint Elizabeth Medical Center (1990, SD Ohio) 130 FRD 85, 87 [an objection to the form of a question, such as unduly "repetitive," is insufficient reason to instruct the deponent not to answer it].

[13] Jones v Seaboard C. L. R. Co. (1974, Fla App) 297 So 2d 861, 864 (original italics).

make the motion.[1] In either event, the court in which the action is pending will hear the motion, no matter in which county the deposition took place.[2]

—Immediate Motion to Compel: When a deponent frustrates a party's discovery efforts by refusing to answer a question or produce an item, that party may immediately "adjourn" the deposition[3] to apply for a court order compelling the discovery sought.[4] When taking this route, it is wise to announce on the record that counsel does not consider the deposition to be "completed on other matters." This may prevent a squabble later over the scope of the resumed examination.

—Deferred Motion to Compel: Instead of adjourning the deposition the party seeking discovery has the alternative of "complet[ing] the examination on other matters."[5] By doing so, there is no waiver of the right to make a later motion to compel.[6] Unless all further examination hinges on an answer to a certain question or the production of a certain item, an attorney normally completes the deposition on other matters.

Notice of the Motion: A party who intends to make a motion to compel must give notice to *both* the deponent and the parties.[7] Counsel may notify them either orally at the deposition itself or in writing later.

—Oral Notice: Where a party elects to give the notice "orally at the examination,"[8] the deposition officer must direct the deponent to attend, at a time then specified, a session of the court in which the action is pending.[9] Before fixing this date, counsel should find out from the reporter when a transcript of the deposition will be ready. A party making a motion to compel must lodge with the court those parts of the stenographic transcript that pertain to the motion within five days of the hearing date.[10]

—Written Notice: A party who elects not to give notice of the motion to compel during the deposition may do so through a "subsequent service in writing."[11] A motion to compel must be made no later than 60 days "after the completion of the record of the deposition."[12] Within five days of the hearing

---

[1] CCP § 2025.460(d).

[2] CCP § 2025.480(a) provides simply that a party may move "the court" for an order compelling discovery. CCP § 2016.020(b) provides: "'Court' means the trial court in which the action is pending, unless otherwise specified."

[3] CCP § 2025.460(d).

[4] CCP § 2025.480(a).

[5] CCP § 2025.460(d).

[6] CCP § 2025.460(d).

[7] CCP § 2025.480(c).

[8] CCP § 2025.480(c). The Legislature did not adopt the Discovery Commission's recommendation to eliminate the oral-notice procedure. Proposed Civil Discovery Act of 1986, Reporter's Note to Section 2025(o), Appendix D.

[9] For a discussion of the duties of the deposition officer, see § 2.21.

[10] CCP § 2025.480(d).

[11] CCP § 2025.480(c).

[12] CCP § 2025.480(b).

date, the moving party must lodge with the court those parts of the stenographic transcript that pertain to the discovery being sought. [13]

Duty to Meet and Confer: Before making a motion to compel, a party must confer informally with the other parties and attempt in good faith to resolve the dispute. [14] The moving party must accompany the motion with a declaration detailing these informal efforts. A party who gives oral notice of the motion to compel during the deposition should be sure that the transcript will reflect a reasonable attempt to work out the dispute with the deponent and the other parties.

—Bickering During Deposition Does Not Suffice: Compliance with the "meet and confer" duty requires "a serious effort at negotiation and informal resolution." [15] When an objection is made during a deposition, it is *possible* to carry out then and there the required attempt to resolve the dispute informally:

> Depositions differ from other manner of discovery mechanisms in that counsel for both parties are present. The immediacy of counsel allows for the instantaneous discussion of an objection and attempts at informal resolution. [16]

Often, however, the argument between counsel following an objection and instruction not to answer does not qualify as the required effort at informal resolution: "Argument is not the same as informal resolution." [17] Where the deposition record shows only verbal sparring and heated exchanges, a later attempt to resolve the dispute must be made before seeking court intervention:

> It is the collective experience of lawyers and judges that too often the ego and emotions of counsel and client are involved at depositions. . . . [C]ounsel can become blinded by the combative nature of the proceeding and be rendered incapable of informally resolving a disagreement. It is for this reason that a brief cooling-off period is sometimes necessary. [18]

Nonparty Deponents: A nonparty deponent is entitled to notice of the motion to compel. [19] However, if that deponent appeared for the deposition in response to a subpoena, no additional subpoena is necessary to compel his or her presence at the hearing of the motion. A deposition subpoena also compels "the deponent's attendance at a court session to consider any issue arising out of the deponent's refusal to be sworn, or to answer any question, or to produce specified items,

---

[13] CCP § 2025.480(d). Cf. Ascherman v Superior Court (1967) 254 Cal App 2d 506, 514, 62 Cal Rptr 547.

[14] CCP § 2025.480(b).

[15] Townsend v Superior Court (1998) 61 Cal App 4th 1431, 1438, 72 Cal Rptr 2d 333.

[16] Townsend v Superior Court (1998) 61 Cal App 4th 1431, 1436, 72 Cal Rptr 2d 333.

[17] Townsend v Superior Court (1998) 61 Cal App 4th 1431, 1437, 72 Cal Rptr 2d 333.

[18] Townsend v Superior Court (1998) 61 Cal App 4th 1431, 1436, 72 Cal Rptr 2d 333.

[19] CCP § 2025.480(c).

or to permit inspection or specified testing and sampling of the items produced."[20]

Sanctions: "[A]ny party, person, or attorney" who unsuccessfully makes or opposes a motion to compel should expect a monetary sanction unless the court finds that, despite this lack of success, there was "substantial justification" for the position taken.[21]

If the court orders the deponent to answer certain questions or to produce certain items, it may treat any disobedience of this order as a contempt.[22] However, where the deponent is a party to the action, or an officer, director, managing agent or employee of a party, the availability of evidence, issue and terminating sanctions[23] arguably makes the contempt sanction inappropriate:

> The trial court here had available many alternative solutions other than adding to the already overcrowded jail population. . . . Imposition of a jail sentence to enforce civil discovery against a party to the lawsuit strikes us as unnecessary and overbearing. Use of this most extreme sanction should be reserved for situations where the court's dignity is truly compromised and no other suitable penalty can be found.[24]

Instead of these drastic sanctions, the trial court has the discretion to deal with the disobedience by a monetary sanction.[25]

§ 2.30   Motion to Terminate or Limit a Deposition

Controlling Abuse: Both the breadth of permissible inquiry and the liberality of the examination procedures under the Discovery Act create enormous potential for abuse by any attorney so inclined. Objections coupled with instructions to the deponent not to answer will control most abusive questioning. Sometimes, however, they are not enough to rein in an attorney bent on eliciting privileged or sensitive information. Moreover, by themselves, they will not put an end to an examination that is being needlessly and unproductively prolonged. On the contrary, the repeated objections may exacerbate the problem. Section 2025.470 contains a device for putting a stop to abusive questioning: an order terminating or limiting a deposition.[1]

Protective Order: Deponents or parties who feel that deposition questioning is being "conducted in bad faith or in a manner that unreasonably annoys, embarrasses, or oppresses" them may "demand" that the deposition officer suspend the examination so that they can move for a protective order.[2] A party

---

[20] CCP § 2020.220(c)(3).

[21] CCP § 2025.480(f).

[22] CCP § 2025.480(g).

[23] For a discussion of these drastic sanctions, see § 15.5.

[24] In re de la Parra (1986) 184 Cal App 3d 139, 144–145, 228 Cal Rptr 864.

[25] CCP § 2025.480(g).

[1] CCP § 2025.470.

[2] CCP § 2025.470.

seeking such an order must accompany the motion with a declaration reciting efforts to resolve the dispute informally. A court may not grant the motion ex parte; it must hear any opposition from the party desiring to continue the deposition.[3] After this hearing, the trial court may limit the topics covered by the oral examination or may even terminate the deposition altogether.

Privilege: Motions to terminate or limit a deposition often are the result of a dispute over the existence or scope of a privilege: "[The] insistent questioning of the deponent as to a privileged matter may justify a motion to terminate or limit the scope of the examination."[4] Parties have used such motions to get rulings on objections asserting the privilege against self-incrimination,[5] the "speech and debate" privilege of members of Congress,[6] the physician-patient privilege[7] and the newsperson's privilege and shield.[8] Parties have also used the motion to test the scope of the work-product protection.[9]

Extensive Questioning: The trial court's power to terminate a deposition because of oppressive length "should be exercised sparingly lest it cripple the broad discovery intended."[10] Transcript length alone does not justify a termination order.[11] Nevertheless, a trial court should step in when counsel has adequately explored all nooks and crannies and the examination is beginning to "trespass upon eternity":

> The transcript contains about 1,000 pages. [Counsel's] examination progressed from interest to boredom, and thence to a certain amount of shock. . . . Granting that [Fed Rules Civ Proc, Rule] 26 has a tendency somewhat to encourage fishing expeditions, still the fishing

---

[3] St. Paul Fire & Marine Ins. Co. v Superior Court (1984) 156 Cal App 3d 82, 85–86, 202 Cal Rptr 571.

[4] Broadbent v Moore-McCormack Lines, Inc. (1946, ED Pa) 5 FRD 220, 222.

Annotation: Construction and effect of Rules 30(b), (d), 31(d), of the Federal Rules of Civil Procedure, and similar state statutes and rules, relating to preventing, limiting, or terminating the taking of depositions. 70 ALR2d 685, 788–797.

[5] Blackburn v Superior Court (1993) 21 Cal App 4th 414, 420–421, 425–426, 27 Cal Rptr 2d 204; National Discount Corp. v Holzbaugh (1952, ED Mich) 13 FRD 236.

[6] Smith v Crown Publishers, Inc. (1953, SD NY) 14 FRD 514.

[7] Cf. Ross v Cities Service Gas Co. (1957, WD Mo) 21 FRD 34.

[8] Garland v Torre (1958, CA2 NY) 259 F2d 545, 550.

[9] French v Zalstem-Zalessky (1940, SD NY) 1 FRD 508; Schweinert v Insurance Co. of North America (1940, SD NY) 1 FRD 247. For a discussion of objections based on the work-product protection, see § 2.27. For coverage of the work-product protection, see Chapter 13.

[10] Schwartz v Broadcast Music, Inc. (1954, SD NY) 16 FRD 31, 33. See also Idle Wild Farm, Inc. v W. R. Grace & Co. (1958, SD NY) 22 FRD 334; Miller v Sun Chemical Corp. (1952, D NJ) 12 FRD 181; Michel v Meier (1948, WD Pa) 8 FRD 464, 472.

[11] See, e.g., Nickerson v Volt Delta Resources, Inc. (1993, App Div) 606 NYS2d 156, 157–158 [mere three-day length of deposition, which generated 500 transcript pages, did not justify protective order precluding additional testimony].

is subject to some license and limit, and should not be continued day after day when the catch is composed of minnows.[12]

Protective orders terminating depositions are most often directed against the party who noticed the deposition. In one case, however, a federal trial judge issued such an order to halt the prolonged cross-examination of an elderly deponent in delicate health.[13]

Counterparts: A motion by the deponent or the objecting party to limit a deposition is the counterpart of a motion by the examining party to compel an answer.[14] Indeed, one motion often draws the other as a cross-motion.[15]

The motion to limit the deposition also serves as a belated way to obtain a protective order that the movant could have sought before the deposition began.[16]

§ 2.31 Transcribing the Testimony

Once the reporter has taken down the deponent's testimony in shorthand, issues may arise about whether the notes must be transcribed and who must pay for doing so.

Transcription Usually Required: Section 2025.510 continues the requirement that the reporter prepare a printed transcription of any testimony recorded stenographically.[1] However, the parties may stipulate that the reporter need not transcribe the stenographic notes.[2] Alternatively, they may agree to postpone transcription. This agreement need not be in writing, but it is good practice for the party noticing the deposition to confirm an oral agreement by a letter to all parties. This may prevent disputes about the existence or the terms of the stipulation.

Party Taking Deposition Usually Pays Transcription Cost: The reporter's charge for the original transcript is significantly more than that made for a copy of it.[3] Since any party may insist upon a transcription of deposition testimony, it is important to know who must pay the cost of the original. Section 2025.510

---

12 Heiner v North American Coal Corp. (1942, WD Pa) 3 FRD 64, 65. See also Pittsburgh Plate Glass Co. v Allied Chemical Alkali Workers (1951, ND Ohio) 11 FRD 518.

13 De Wagenknecht v Stinnes (1957) 243 F2d 413, 417.

14 For a discussion of the motion to compel an answer at a deposition, see § 2.29.

15 See, e.g., Idle Wild Farm, Inc. v W. R. Grace & Co. (1958, SD NY) 22 FRD 334; Schwartz v Broadcast Music, Inc. (1954, SD NY) 16 FRD 31.

16 See CCP § 2025.420(b)(9). For a discussion of pre-deposition motions for protective orders, see § 2.15.

1 CCP § 2025.510(a). For a discussion of when deposition testimony must be recorded stenographically, see § 2.22.

2 CCP § 2025.510(a).

3 See, e.g., Burke v Central-Illinois Secur. Corp. (1949, D Del) 9 FRD 426 [cost of the originals of a series of depositions estimated at $1,400, whereas copies cost only $250].

specifies that normally it is the party who noticed the deposition who bears the cost of transcribing it.[4]

—Exception: Section 2025.510 authorizes the trial court to shift all or part of the transcription costs. It may order that "the cost be borne or shared by another party" if the party noticing the deposition establishes "good cause" for doing so.[5] Examples of such good cause might include a showing that another party engaged in a prolonged and harassing cross-examination designed to build up the deposition cost;[6] or the deposing party is unable to afford the transcription costs.[7]

Section 2025.510 gives all parties to a lawsuit a right to obtain a copy of a deposition transcript.[8] However, there is no statute fixing the fee that a court reporter may exact for providing that copy: "Deposition reporters are free to charge all the market will bear."[9] Nor may a party escape a court reporter's exorbitant charge by issuing a "business records only" deposition subpoena calling for private copying of the transcript. The transcript is not considered a "business record" of the court reporter, but rather a product of that business.[10]

Right of Others to Obtain a Copy of Transcript: "[A]ny person" is entitled to request a copy of a transcript from the deposition officer.[11] However, before a deposition officer complies with that request, he must give notice of the request to the deponent and to the parties,[12] after which any of them has 30 days in which to obtain a protective order.[13]

Retention of Original Notes: Section 2025.510 requires deposition reporters to retain their stenographic notes. If no transcript is prepared, they must keep them for eight years after the deposition. If a transcript is made, they must preserve them for one year after preparing it. Reporters may keep their notes on paper, or on electronic media that "allows for satisfactory production of a transcript at any time during the [two specified] periods."[14]

---

[4] CCP § 2025.510(b). For a discussion of the recovery of deposition transcription expenses as "costs," see § 2.42.

[5] CCP § 2025.510(b).

[6] Kolosci v Lindquist (1969, ND Ind) 47 FRD 319, 321.

[7] See Dall v Pearson (1963, D DC) 34 FRD 511; Odum v Willard Stores, Inc. (1941, D DC) 1 FRD 680.

[8] CCP § 2025.510(b).

[9] Urban Pacific Equities Corp. v Superior Court (1997) 59 Cal App 4th 688, 692, 69 Cal Rptr 2d 635.

[10] Urban Pacific Equities Corp. v Superior Court (1997) 59 Cal App 4th 688, 692, 69 Cal Rptr 2d 635.

[11] CCP § 2025.570(a).

[12] CCP § 2025.570(b).

[13] CCP § 2025.510(c).

[14] CCP § 2025.510(e).

§ 2.32 Submission to the Deponent—Stenographic Transcript

Deposition testimony usually is taken down "stenographically."[1] This is true even when the deposition is simultaneously video recorded or audio recorded.[2] After the shorthand reporter has transcribed the testimony,[3] he or she submits the transcript to the deponent for reading, correction and signature.[4] To accomplish this, the deposition officer sends a written notice to the deponent that the transcript is ready for reading and signing. All parties who attended the oral examination receive the same notice.

Importance of the Deponent's Signature: The deponent's signature consummates the deposition process. Without it, or its legal equivalent,[5] the deposition remains incomplete. California defines a "deposition" as: "a *written* declaration, under oath, made upon notice to the adverse party, for the purpose of enabling him to attend and cross-examine."[6] Therefore, the oral testimony before the notary-reporter is only the embryo of the deposition. Unless the deponent, with the consent of all parties, waives reading and signing at the end of the oral examination,[7] there is no "deposition" until the reporter transcribes the shorthand notes *and* the witness has had an opportunity to read and sign it:

> Since it is an intermediary who makes the writing which becomes the testimony, it is specially necessary to be certain that this writing shall represent precisely the statements for which the witness stands responsible. . . . Because the writing is to stand as the witness' own words and there is always an inherent possibility of error in the transcription, a final opportunity for correction of the writing as completed should be given by the reading [of the transcript] to or by the witness. The witness' signature may be regarded either as necessary to constitute the writing his by adoption, or as symbolically equivalent to a knowing assent to its tenor . . . .[8]

—False Testimony by Deponent: One who knowingly gives false deposition testimony may commit perjury, a felony.[9] However, unlike a witness at a trial or hearing, a person who has knowingly given untruthful answers during the

---

[1] CCP § 2025.330(b). For a discussion of the recording of deposition testimony, see § 2.22.

[2] CCP § 2025.330(c).

[3] For a discussion of the requirement that the stenographic notes of deposition testimony be transcribed, see § 2.31.

[4] CCP § 2025.520(a).

[5] See CCP § 2025.520(f).

[6] CCP § 2004 (italics added).

[7] CCP § 2025.520(a).

[8] Voorheis v Hawthorne-Michaels Co. (1957) 151 Cal App 2d 688, 692–693, 312 P2d 51. See also Coy v Superior Court (1962) 58 Cal 2d 210, 218–219, 23 Cal Rptr 393, 373 P2d 457; Reimel v House (1969) 268 Cal App 2d 780, 786, 74 Cal Rptr 345; People v Hjelm (1964) 224 Cal App 2d 649, 37 Cal Rptr 36.

[9] Depositions are expressly covered by the definition of perjury in Penal Code § 118.

taking of his deposition is not *ipso facto* guilty of perjury. Under the Penal Code a deposition is not considered to be "complete,"for purposes of a perjury prosecution, until "it is delivered by the accused to any other person, with the intent that it be uttered or published as true."[10] In the *Collins* case,[11] an employer deposed a workers' compensation claimant concerning the extent to which his work-related injury had resulted in physical limitations. A later investigation revealed that the worker was engaging in physical activities that were inconsistent with the limitations he had described during his deposition testimony. The employer reported this discrepancy the district attorney, who charged the claimant with giving perjurious answers at his deposition.

It developed, however, that although the reporter had sent the transcript of the oral deposition testimony to the claimant's attorney, the deponent had never seen it, let alone signed it. Nor had the deposition been used in any proceeding. The court held that even if the deponent had given knowingly false answers during his oral examination, the crime of perjury had not yet been committed:

> The prosecution asserts that the crime of perjury occurs the moment a deponent willfully gives false testimony. This assertion underscores a basic misunderstanding of the nature of a deposition. "The term 'deposition' is now confined in meaning to testimony delivered in writing; testimony which in legal contemplation does not exist apart from a writing made or adopted by the witness." (*Voorheis v Hawthorne-Michaels Co.* (1957) 151 Cal App 2d 688, 692, 312 P2d 51.) As with an affidavit or certificate [under penalty of perjury] it is the finality of the writing and its delivery, and not merely speaking the false words, which constitutes an essential element of the crime of perjury. This is to be distinguished from the giving of false testimony before the judge, jury, or tribunal responsible for deciding the matter at issue. Such testimony constitutes perjury when the words are spoken . . . .[12]

As the court acknowledged, the Civil Discovery Act does provide that if a deponent does not sign the deposition within 30 days after notification of its availability, "the deposition shall be given the same force and effect as though signed."[13] However, this later provision did not supplant Penal Code § 124:

> The pertinent question is not whether [the claimant's] deposition could be put to use in a civil matter, but whether this document had been completed and delivered as required by [Penal Code] Section 124. [¶] Simply stated, a deposition may be final and legally conclusive, but

---

[10] Penal Code § 124.

[11] Collins v Superior Court (2001) 89 Cal App 4th 1244, 108 Cal Rptr 2d 123.

[12] Collins v Superior Court (2001) 89 Cal App 4th 1244, 1247, 108 Cal Rptr 2d 123. See also People v Post (2001) 94 Cal App 4th 467, 476–484, 114 Cal Rptr 2d 356 [reluctantly agreeing with *Collins* that there is no perjury until deponent signs and delivers the deposition transcript, but holding that the deponent is nonetheless guilty of attempted perjury].

[13] CCP § 2025.520(f).

remain undelivered. So long as this deposition remains in the office of counsel of the deponent, and so long as no one attempts to make use of the document, the crime of perjury is not committed.[14]

Deponents' Options: Deponents have 30 days[15] after the reporter sends notice of the transcript's readiness to react in any of four ways: (1) approve and sign the original as transcribed; (2) correct the original and sign it as changed;[16] (3) expressly refuse to approve the transcript; or (4) simply fail to respond to the notice.[17]

Deponents may visit the reporter's office to read, correct and sign the original transcript. Alternatively, they may send the deposition officer a signed letter stating their position concerning the accuracy of the transcript: approval *in toto*, approval as corrected[18] or refusal to sign.[19]

—Conferring with Counsel before Signing: The response-by-letter procedure implies that the deponent will already have had access to the transcript. This is because the reporter customarily sends a copy of the unsigned transcript to counsel when notifying the deponent that the original is ready. Counsel may then arrange for the deponent to read that copy. This provides an opportunity for the attorney who took the deposition to confer with the witness about the accuracy not only of the transcript but also of the answers recorded. A federal case[20] has upheld the propriety of such post-deposition conferences against the argument that it is comparable to conferring with a trial witness whose testimony is still in progress:

> [A]s a general rule this court approves the practice of permitting all counsel to have a copy of the deposition and of permitting any of them to have a private conference with the deponent before he states any changes which he may desire to make. In many instances counsel would be able to discover obvious or latent errors in the reporting which the deponent might not have the ability to discover.[21]

Refusal to Sign: A deponent may also, in person[22] or by letter, refuse to sign the deposition. This refusal, however, is tantamount to a signature of the transcript: "When a deponent . . . expressly disapproves the accuracy of the

---

[14] Collins v Superior Court (2001) 89 Cal App 4th 1244, 1249, 108 Cal Rptr 2d 123.

[15] The trial court may shorten this time for good cause. CCP § 2025.520.

[16] For a discussion of the deponent's right to change the deposition testimony, see § 2.34.

[17] Cf. Northwest Airlines, Inc. v American Airlines, Inc. (1994, D Minn) 870 F Supp 1504, 1508 [deposition transcript errata sheet was not untimely where party challenging it did not show when the transcript was made available to the deponent].

[18] For a discussion of the deponent's right to change the deposition testimony, see § 2.34.

[19] CCP § 2025.520(c).

[20] Erstad v Curtis Bay Towing Co. (1961, D Md) 28 FRD 583, 584.

[21] Erstad v Curtis Bay Towing Co. (1961, D Md) 28 FRD 583, 584.

[22] CCP § 2025.520(b).

transcript by refusing to sign it, the deposition shall be given the same effect as though signed."[23] In addition, by itself, the refusal does not prevent the deposition's use at trial. Rather, to preclude such use, the deponent or a party must present its reasons to the court in a timely motion to suppress the deposition: "[O]n seasonable motion to suppress the deposition, . . . the court may determine that the reasons given for the refusal to sign require rejection of the deposition in whole or in part."[24] The failure to move promptly will waive any challenge to the deposition's use.[25]

Before making a motion to suppress a deposition, the parties must attempt to resolve the dispute informally.[26] The trial court will usually impose a monetary sanction on the party who loses at the hearing of the motion, unless that party establishes substantial justification for filing or opposing the motion.[27]

Where an unsigned deposition is used during the trial, the trial court does not inform the jury that the deponent refused to sign the transcript: "The reading of the reporter's certificate [containing a recital of the deponent's refusal to sign] to the jury could have served no purpose other than to invite the jury to speculate with respect to a subject beyond the jury's concern."[28]

Deponent Unavailable to Sign: The death or disappearance of the deponent after the oral examination but before signing the deposition poses a difficult question if a party later wants to offer that unsigned deposition in evidence. In *Chavez v Zapata Ocean Resources, Inc.,*[29] a nonparty deponent disappeared before he could read and sign the deposition transcript. The appellate court upheld the use of the deposition as evidence at the trial. It stressed the absence of any objections to the testimony when it was given, and the reporter's certification that the transcript was "a true record" of the deponent's oral testimony:

> The deposition testimony, absent objections to questions or answers, is not denigrated by [the deponent's] failure to review, correct, sign or refuse to sign. Surely, his signature is not necessary to the truthfulness of his assertions. Here, the pen is not mightier than the word.[30]

---

[23] CCP § 2025.520(f).

[24] CCP § 2025.520(g). Cf. People v Hjelm (1964) 224 Cal App 2d 649, 657, 37 Cal Rptr 36 [under pre-1987 law, distinguishing the use in civil cases of an unsigned deposition and concluding that false statements in an unsigned deposition by a deponent who had not waived the right to change the transcript could not form the basis for a perjury prosecution].

[25] See, e.g., In re Ashley (1990, CA9 Cal) 903 F2d 599, 603 [failure to timely move to suppress deponent's unsigned deposition waived any defect in the submission process]. Cf. Longo v McLaren (1992, ND Ohio) 136 BR 705, 719 [deponent waived any challenge to his unsigned deposition's use by first submitting and relying upon that unsigned deposition himself].

[26] CCP § 2025.520(g).

[27] CCP § 2025.520(h).

[28] Ikerd v Lapworth (1970, CA7 Ind) 435 F2d 197, 207.

[29] Chavez v Zapata Ocean Resources, Inc. (1984) 155 Cal App 3d 115, 201 Cal Rptr 887.

[30] Chavez v Zapata Ocean Resources, Inc. (1984) 155 Cal App 3d 115, 122, 201 Cal Rptr 887.

A federal decision sensibly accommodates the competing concerns. It suggests that the deponent's unavailability for signature affects not the deposition's admissibility, but only its weight.[31]

Failure to Respond: A deponent's failure to communicate with the officer either in person or in writing during the 30 days after notice of the transcript's readiness is tantamount to approving and signing the testimony as transcribed: "When a deponent fails to contact the officer within the allotted period, . . . the deposition shall be given the same force and effect as though signed."[32]

Stipulations: The statutory procedure for submission of the deposition transcript to the deponent need not be followed if "the deponent and the attending parties agree on the record [during the deposition] to waive the reading and signing of the transcript of the testimony."[33] Although parties and deponents commonly make such a stipulation, the court will not imply one simply because nothing was said to the contrary during the oral examination.[34]

§ 2.33 Audio or Video

Where the oral examination was either audio recorded or video recorded to *supplement* the stenographic recording, the procedures for submitting a stenographic transcript to the deponent still apply.[1] However, the parties may stipulate that the *only* recording of the oral examination will be via audio or video.[2] In such a case, at the conclusion of oral examination, the deponent and the parties may agree on the record to waive the hearing or viewing of the recording. Absent such an agreement, the deponent must have the opportunity to hear or view the recording before approving it.[3]

Review of Recording: The deposition officer must send the deponent written notice of the recording's availability for hearing or viewing.[4] The deponent then has 30 days "to change the substance"[5] of any answers to any questions[6] and to sign a statement identifying the deposition as his or her own. To do so, the deponent may either appear in person before the deposition officer or send a written and signed letter containing the changes. If the deponent makes any changes, the deposition officer must write them down in a document that will

---

[31] Bernstein v Brenner (1970, D DC) 51 FRD 9, 12–14 [trial court may decline to suppress the unsigned deposition of one who died months later, since the transcript revealed the deponent's impartiality, and the direct and cross-examination had been careful and thorough].

[32] CCP § 2025.520(f). Cf. Gray v Reeves (1977) 76 Cal App 3d 567, 572, 142 Cal Rptr 716.

[33] See Topanga Corp. v Gentile (1967) 249 Cal App 2d 681, 690, 58 Cal Rptr 713.

[34] See Bernstein v Brenner (1970, D DC) 51 FRD 9, 11.

[1] For a discussion of the submission of the stenographic transcript to the deponent, see § 2.32.

[2] CCP § 2025.330(b).

[3] CCP § 2025.530(a).

[4] CCP § 2025.530(a).

[5] CCP § 2025.530(b).

[6] For a discussion of the deponent's right to change the answers given during the oral examination, see § 2.34.

thereafter accompany the deposition recording.[7] A refusal to sign the identifying writing or a failure to contact the deposition officer within 30 days gives the deposition the same effect as if the deponent had signed the deposition.[8] However, any party may move to suppress the deposition.[9] The procedures connected with such a motion are essentially the same as those for a stenographically recorded deposition.[10]

§ 2.34 Correcting the Transcript

The submission of the transcript[1] allows deponents to exercise their important right to change the answers they gave during the oral examination.[2] When deponents exercise this right, the deposition officer must show the changes on the original.[3] However, Section 2025.520 does not adopt the federal practice, which requires the deponent to give "a statement of the reasons"[4] for making the changes.

Substantive Changes: The right of correction allows changes in the "substance"[5] of the answer to any question. An early federal case, *De Seversky v Republic Aviation Corp.*,[6] describes the breadth of this right. It applies when: (1) the deponent has misunderstood a question; (2) the reporter has misunderstood or mistranscribed an answer; (3) the deponent wants to supplement an answer; and (4) the deponent now recollects the facts differently. The federal courts accord this scope to the right of correction despite their rule that requires the deponent to give reasons for making changes in the testimony.[7] *A fortiori*, the California courts should give it the same scope since Section 2025.520 does not require any such explanations.[8]

Broad as the right to correct deposition testimony is, it is not absolute. It almost certainly does not extend to the retroactive assertion of a privilege.[9] Nor should

---

[7] CCP § 2025.530(c).

[8] CCP § 2025.530(d).

[9] CCP § 2025.530(g).

[10] For a discussion of the procedures for suppressing a deposition, see § 2.32.

[1] For a discussion of the procedure for submitting the deposition transcript to the deponent, see § 2.32.

[2] CCP § 2025.520(b).

[3] CCP § 2025.520(e).

[4] See Fed Rules Civ Proc, Rule 30(e). See Architectural League of New York v Bartos (1975, SD NY) 404 F Supp 304, 311 n7; Colin v Thompson (1954, WD Mo) 16 FRD 194.

[5] CCP § 2025.520(b).

[6] De Seversky v Republic Aviation Corp. (1941, ED NY) 2 FRD 113. See also Lugtig v Thomas (1981, ND Ill) 89 FRD 639.

[7] See Fed Rules Civ Proc, Rule 30(e).

[8] See Weber, Lipshie & Co. v Christian (1997) 52 Cal App 4th 645, 656, 60 Cal Rptr 2d 677; Todd v Dow (1993) 19 Cal App 4th 253, 257 n1, 23 Cal Rptr 2d 490.

[9] See SEC v Parkersburg Wireless Ltd. (1994, D DC) 156 FRD 529, 535–536 [rule allowing deponent to change deposition testimony does not allow belated assertion of privilege against self-incrimination].

parties make such extensive changes that they convert an oral deposition into a series of written interrogatories. As one federal judge remarked: "A deposition is not a take-home examination."[10]

Effect of Changing Deposition Testimony: When deponents make substantive changes to their deposition answers, three collateral questions may arise: (1) May a party reopen the examination? (2) What is the status of the original answer? (3) What use may be made of that original answer at trial?

—Reopening the Deposition: A party may wish to reopen the deposition to cross-examine the witness in light of the new answers. Courts decide, case-by-case, whether the changes have affected usefulness of the original oral examination.[11]

—Status of Original Answer: Once a deponent changes an answer, the witness's oath attaches to the new response. However, the original answer should remain on the face of the transcript. The reporter should draw a line through it instead of erasing it or blacking it out.[12]

—Use of the Original Answer: The most important question that arises when deponents change their answers is the effect of the original answer if at trial deponents testify or if their deposition is placed in evidence.[13] In a federal case,[14] for example, plaintiff testified during his deposition that he could not recall any previous injury to his leg. Before signing the deposition, he changed this answer. This change evidently helped the *defense's* position, and his trial testimony was consistent with the answer as changed. Nevertheless, the appellate court ruled that the defense could ask him about his original deposition answer, presumably to let the jury know that the plaintiff had switched answers:

> Any out-of-court statement by a party is an admission; the original answer should have been admitted. Of course, the plaintiff would then be free to introduce the amended answer and explain the reasons for the change.[15]

There is no reason to treat a changed answer by a *nonparty* deponent any differently:

---

[10] Greenway v International Paper Co. (1992, WD La) 144 FRD 322, 323–325.

[11] See, e.g., Hawthorne Partners v AT&T Technologies, Inc. (1993, ND Ill) 831 F Supp 1398, 1406–1407 [deposition not reopened even though deponent made 41 changes since changes did not make transcript useless or incomplete]; Allen & Co. v Occidental Petroleum Corp. (1970, SD NY) 49 FRD 337 [no need to reopen deposition where changes simply eliminated an inconsistency in two of the original answers; the very nature of that change means that counsel will have had an opportunity to examine as to both versions]; Turchan v Bailey Meter Co. (1957, D Del) 21 FRD 232 [deposition reopened when a "no" answer was changed to a "yes"].

[12] See Allen & Co. v Occidental Petroleum Corp. (1970, SD NY) 49 FRD 337, 340.

[13] For a discussion of when a deposition may be offered in evidence, see §§ 2.37–2.42.

[14] Usiak v New York Tank Barge Co. (1962, CA2 NY) 299 F2d 808.

[15] Usiak v New York Tank Barge Co. (1962, CA2 NY) 299 F2d 808, 810. See also Noah v Black & White Cab Co. (1931) 138 Cal App 236, 239, 32 P2d 437.

The witness who changes his or her testimony on a material matter between the giving of the deposition and appearance at the trial may be impeached by the former answers, and the cross-examiner and the jury are likely to be keenly interested in the reasons for the changing testimony. There is no apparent reason why the witness who has a change of mind between the giving of the deposition and its transcription should be treated differently. [16]

—**The *Gray* Case:** In *Gray v Reeves*,[17] a medical malpractice case, plaintiff claimed that his delayed discovery of his injuries had tolled the statute of limitations. During his deposition, however, he gave answers that placed the date of discovery well before the expiration of limitations. Plaintiff then delayed signing the transcript containing these answers for almost two years. Defendant eventually moved for summary judgment based on the oral deposition answers. On the day of the hearing of that motion, plaintiff "corrected" the answers the defense was relying on in a way that would salvage his cause of action under the date-of-discovery exception to the limitations defense. He then signed the deposition. However, the trial court relied on the original answers and entered summary judgment.

In upholding the summary judgment, the *Gray* court saw an analogy to cases involving initial responses to admission requests. Several courts have held that a party's later affidavit repudiating damaging admissions does not necessarily prevent a grant of summary judgment based on the original responses.[18] *Gray* ruled that the corrected deposition answers similarly did not preclude the trial court from using the initial oral responses to grant summary judgment against the deponent:

> There is no reason to draw a distinction between an attempt to counter an admission by affidavit and an attempt to counter an admission by changing the content of an answer given by a party directly in the deposition, especially where there is no assertion the original answer was incorrectly transcribed or the question was misleading or ambiguous. In both the changed affidavit and changed deposition cases the credibility of the parties is held up for examination by the contradicting statements, the first of which constitutes a reliable admission against interest. The trial court may accept the first and reject the later of these contrary positions. This choice is particularly called for where, as here, the deponent waits 19 months to make the changes and is then inspired

---

[16] 8A Wright & Miller, Federal Practice & Procedure § 2118 (1994). Cf. Bennett v Superior Court (1950) 99 Cal App 2d 585, 593, 222 P2d 276.

[17] Gray v Reeves (1977) 76 Cal App 3d 567, 142 Cal Rptr 716.

[18] D'Amico v Board of Medical Examiners (1974) 11 Cal 3d 1, 21–22, 112 Cal Rptr 786, 520 P2d 10; Leasman v Beech Aircraft Corp. (1975) 48 Cal App 3d 376, 381–384, 121 Cal Rptr 768.

to make the changes by pressures attending an apparently grantable motion for summary judgment.[19]

§ 2.35 Certification and Custody of Deposition

Certification: Once the deposition officer has "submitted" the record of the oral examination to the deponent,[1] the officer must "certify" that record. This certification attests that the deponent was under oath during the oral examination, and that the transcript, video or audio correctly reflects the deponent's testimony.[2]

—Stenographic Recording: If, as usually happens, a reporter has taken down the testimony stenographically[3] and then transcribed it,[4] the officer makes the certification on the transcript. This is true even if the testimony was *also* simultaneously recorded by audio or video, for in such cases "the stenographic transcript is the official record of that testimony."[5]

—Audio or Video Recording: If, through court order or stipulation,[6] the *only* record of the deposition is an audio or a video, the officer makes the certification in the same writing that reflects the deponent's actions approving, changing and signing the deposition.[7]

Custody: Whether the official deposition record takes the form of a stenographic transcript, an audio or a video, the deposition officer does not file it with the court.[8]

—Written Transcript: If the official record is a stenographic transcript, the deposition officer must "securely seal" it in an envelope or package. That envelope must bear the case title, show that it contains a deposition and identify the deponent. The officer then transmits the record to the attorney for the party

---

[19] Gray v Reeves (1977) 76 Cal App 3d 567, 574, 142 Cal Rptr 716. See also Rios v Welch (1994, D Kan) 856 F Supp 1499, 1502 [impermissible for deponent to rewrite practically the entire transcript, particularly after opposing party relied on it in summary judgment motion]; Slowiak v Land O'Lakes, Inc. (1993, CA7 Wis) 987 F2d 1293, 1296–1297 [self-serving affidavits that change critical deposition testimony without explanation cannot create a triable issue of material fact in opposition to a summary judgment motion that relied on the original testimony]; Workman v Chinchinian (1992, ED Wash) 807 F Supp 634, 644–645 [change in critical deposition answers after discovery is closed would prejudice party who had relied on the oral statements]. Cf. Burgon v Kaiser Foundation Hospitals (1979) 93 Cal App 3d 813, 822–823, 155 Cal Rptr 763.

[1] For a discussion of the submission of the record to the deponent, see §§ 2.32–2.33.

[2] CCP § 2025.540(a).

[3] For a discussion of the requirement to record deposition testimony stenographically, see § 2.22.

[4] For a discussion of the requirement that a transcript of the oral examination be made, see § 2.31.

[5] CCP § 2025.510.

[6] For a discussion of dispensing with a stenographic recording of deposition testimony by court order or stipulation, see § 2.22.

[7] For a discussion of the writing created by the deposition officer as an adjunct to a recorded deposition, see § 2.33.

[8] CCP §§ 2025.550(a), 2025.560(a).

who noticed the deposition. This attorney must store it under conditions that will prevent its loss, destruction or tampering.[9]

The attorney must retain the deposition transcript until six months after the final disposition of the action. Then, absent a court order directing longer preservation, the attorney may destroy the transcript.[10]

—Audio or Video Records: An audio or a video of a deposition, whether made besides or instead of a stenographic record, is retained by the taping equipment operator.[11] The custodian must store the recording under conditions that will prevent its loss, destruction or tampering, and will preserve as far as practicable its quality and the integrity of the words and images it contains.[12]

If requested, the operator must let the deponent and any party to the action, even one who did not attend the oral examination, hear or view the recording. The operator may demand advance payment of a reasonable fee for providing listening or viewing facilities. Upon receipt of a reasonable duplication fee, the operator must furnish a copy of the recording to the deponent and to any party who requests it.[13]

The operator must retain the audio or video until six months after the final disposition of the action. Then, absent a court order directing longer preservation, the operator may destroy or erase the recording.[14]

§ 2.36 One-Deposition Limit

No Limit on Number of Deponents: The Discovery Act does not impose a presumptive limit on the total number of depositions that a party or a side may take. However, deposition discovery, like any other discovery method, is subject to the trial court's power to limit case-by-case its "frequency or extent."[1] Thus, a trial court may restrict the number of depositions if they are becoming cumulative or duplicative or are not the most efficient means of getting the information sought.[2] It may also decide that this method of discovery entails burden and cost disproportionate to what is at stake in the particular case.[3]

By contrast, the Federal Rules, since 1993, do presumptively limit to ten the oral or written depositions that each *side* may take. If the plaintiffs, the defendants or third-party defendants, respectively, want to take additional depositions, they must obtain leave of court.[4]

---

[9] CCP § 2025.550(a).

[10] CCP § 2025.550(a).

[11] See CCP § 2025.560(a).

[12] CCP § 2025.560(a).

[13] CCP § 2025.560(b).

[14] CCP § 2025.560(c).

[1] CCP § 2019.030(a).

[2] CCP § 2019.030(a)(1).

[3] CCP § 2019.030(a)(2).

[4] Fed Rules Civ Proc, Rule 30(a)(2)(A).

One Deposition Per Witness: Section 2025.610 provides that a "natural person" need ordinarily only submit to one deposition during a lawsuit.[5] Even those parties who did not notice the original deposition may not compel the deponent to undergo another examination. Moreover, this one-deposition limit applies whether the deponent is a party or a nonparty.

This restriction reflects much the same concerns about cost and potential abuse that led the Legislature to impose presumptive numerical limits on two other discovery methods: interrogatories[6] and admission requests.[7] Since 1993 the Federal Rules have contained a similar limit on the number of times a person must submit to a deposition.[8]

—Protective Orders: The one-deposition-per-witness limit reduces both the time and money expended in deposition discovery, and the disruption and inconvenience it causes deponents. However, just because one party is prepared to depose a witness does not mean that every other party is or can be ready to do so as quickly. A trial judge should factor in this one-deposition limit when considering motions for a protective order postponing a deposition.[9]

Six Exceptions: There are six exceptions to the one-deposition limit:

(1) The limit applies only when the deponent is a "natural person."[10] There is no presumptive limit on the number of times parties may depose organizations.[11]

(2) The one-deposition limit does not apply to a party who did not receive notice of the original deposition.[12] One who had not yet appeared in the action when the deposition of someone was taken, or who has later become a party, may still depose that witness.

(3) The one-deposition limit does not prevent a second deposition of a natural person who has already undergone examination as a designee of an organizational deponent.[13]

(4) The parties may stipulate to additional depositions of a witness. However, if the deponent is a nonparty, he or she must also agree to the additional examination.[14]

---

[5] CCP § 2025.610(a).

[6] For a discussion of the presumptive limit on the number of interrogatories, see § 5.6.

[7] For a discussion of the presumptive limit on the number of admission requests, see § 9.4.

[8] Fed Rules Civ Proc, Rule 30(a)(2)(B).

[9] For a discussion of protective orders postponing depositions, see § 2.15.

[10] CCP § 2025.610(a).

[11] For a discussion of depositions of organizations, see §§ 2.5, 2.9, and 2.12

[12] CCP § 2025.610(a). For a discussion of who is entitled to notice of a deposition, see § 2.6.

[13] CCP § 2025.610(c)(1). For a discussion of the duty of an organizational deponent to designate knowledgeable personnel, see § 2.5.

[14] CCP § 2025.610(b).

(5) The trial court may grant leave to conduct an additional examination of a witness. [15] Good cause for another deposition should be easier to show if the deponent is a party or if the moving party did not notice the original deposition.

(6) If a deponent was examined pursuant to a court order for the limited purpose of discovering the identity, location, and value of property in which that deponent has an interest, [16] that person may be deposed again, [17] but only on other issues in the case. [18]

§ 2.37   Use at Trial—In General

In contrast to its broad and liberal license to *take* depositions, Section 2025 tightly restricts a litigant's rights to *use* them as trial evidence. This section addresses issues that are common to any attempt to offer deposition testimony into evidence. [1] The sections that follow discuss the use of depositions: (1) against a party deponent; [2] (2) to impeach a trial witness; [3] (3) as a substitute for an unavailable witness; [4] (4) in place of the live testimony of an expert witness; [5] and (5) when taken in another action. [6]

Pretrial Use as Evidence: Section 2025.620 regulates the use of deposition testimony only when it is offered as evidence *at the trial* of a case. Since deponents are under oath, nothing stops a trial court from treating depositions the same as affidavits or declarations under penalty of perjury when considering, for instance, a summary judgment motion. [7] On the contrary, the statute regulating summary judgment motions allows them to be "supported or opposed by affidavits, declarations, admissions, answers to interrogatories, *depositions* and matters of which judicial notice may be taken." [8] The same should be true of motions for a preliminary injunction. [9]

---

[15] CCP § 2025.610(b).

[16] See CCP § 485.230.

[17] CCP § 2025.610(c).

[18] CCP § 2025.610(d).

[1] Annotation: Propriety and effect of jury in civil case taking depositions to jury room during deliberations. 57 ALR2d 1011. Annotation: Admissibility of Depositions Under Federal Evidence Rule 804(b)(1). 84 ALR Fed. 668.

[2] For a discussion of the use of depositions at trial against a party deponent, see § 2.38.

[3] For a discussion of the use of depositions at trial to impeach a witness, see § 2.39.

[4] For a discussion of the use of the deposition of a person who is unavailable to testify at trial, see § 2.40.

[5] For a discussion of the use at trial of video recorded depositions of experts, see § 2.41.

[6] For a discussion of the use of deposition testimony taken in another action, see § 2.42.

[7] See, e.g., Tormo v Yormark (1975, D NJ) 398 F Supp 1159, 1168 [federal discovery rules do not govern "the use of deposition testimony at a hearing or a proceeding at which evidence in affidavit form is admissible"].

[8] CCP § 437c(b) (italics added).

[9] See United States v Fox (1962, ED La) 211 F Supp 25, 30.

Use at Trial Differentiated: Where a party offers deposition testimony *at trial*, two considerations require restrictions: (1) a deposition is a form of hearsay evidence; and (2) the scope of discovery is much broader than the scope of admissibility at trial.

—Hearsay: Evidence law considers a deposition to be inferior to live testimony: "The deposition has always been, and still is, treated as a substitute, a second-best, not to be used when the original is at hand."[10] After all, deposition testimony, though given under oath and subject to cross-examination, is nonetheless hearsay evidence: "When offered to prove the truth of what it asserts, [a deposition] is hearsay, and may be received in evidence only if it is admissible under an exception to the hearsay rule."[11] Reading a transcript of deposition testimony into evidence at trial deprives the trier of fact of the opportunity to use demeanor in assessing the deponent's credibility:

> Demeanor is of the utmost importance in the determination of the credibility of a witness. The innumerable telltale indications which fall from a witness during the course of his examination are often much more of an indication to judge or jury of his credibility and the reliability of his evidence than is the literal meaning of his words.[12]

Despite this shortcoming, however, the oath and the opportunity for cross-examination do make deposition testimony much more reliable than most other forms of hearsay evidence.

—Scope of Inquiry: The other reason for restricting use of a discovery deposition at the trial is the difference between the questions and the answers allowed during a deposition and those allowed during a trial. The test for measuring relevance is dissimilar at these two stages of the lawsuit. Relevance "to the *subject matter*"[13] is the discovery criterion,[14] while relevance to the *issues* is the trial standard.[15] Moreover, during a deposition, the examiner may elicit relevant information although it is in a form, e.g., hearsay, that would require its exclusion at trial.

Consequently, to the extent that Section 2025.620 lets a party use deposition testimony at trial, it first filters it through the evidence rules.[16] When one party offers a deposition at trial, any other party may, with two exceptions, object to

---

[10] Napier v Bossard (1939, CA2 NY) 102 F2d 467, 469. See also Arnstein v Porter (1946, CA2 NY) 154 F2d 464, 470.

[11] Jobse v Connolly (1969, Misc) 302 NYS2d 35, 37.

[12] Government of Virgin Islands v Aquino (1967, CA3) 378 F2d 540, 548.

[13] CCP § 2017.010 (italics added).

[14] For a discussion of "relevance" for discovery, see Chapter 11.

[15] Evid Code §§ 210, 350.

[16] CCP § 2025.620(a).

Annotation: Former testimony used at subsequent trial as subject to ordinary objections and exceptions. 40 ALR 4th 514.

a question or answer as if "the deponent were then present and testifying as a witness."[17] The two exceptions are an objection claiming a privilege and one challenging the form of the question, each of which a party waives by not making it during the deposition.[18]

When another party objects at trial, the court must exclude those portions of a deposition that contain inadmissible hearsay,[19] inadmissible opinions and conclusions[20] or improper impeachment.[21] Moreover, though a deposition otherwise meets all the requirements for use at trial, the court may still exclude it entirely if the information it contains is merely cumulative of testimony already received.[22]

Prerequisite: One may offer a deposition in evidence only against a party who had an opportunity to question the deponent. This includes not only a party "who was present or represented at the taking of the deposition," but also one "who had due notice of the deposition and did not serve a valid objection" to its taking.[23] Thus, ordinarily,[24] a party may not use a deposition against: (1) a party brought into the case later (unless it is someone who has been substituted for a party);[25] (2) a party who had not yet been served or made an appearance in the case,[26] (3) a party who received no notice of the deposition;[27] or (4) a party who validly objected to the taking of the deposition.[28]

Purpose of Taking Deposition Does Not Control Use at Trial: A deposition does not "belong" to the party who noticed it.[29] Thus, if the deposition is

---

[17] CCP § 2025.620(a).

[18] See CCP § 2025.460(a). For a discussion of when the failure to object during the deposition will result in a waiver, see §§ 2.24–2.28.

[19] See Johnson v Nationwide Mut. Ins. Co. (1960, CA4 Va) 276 F2d 574, 578–579.

[20] Estate of Murphy (1976) 15 Cal 3d 907, 919, 126 Cal Rptr 820, 544 P2d 956.

[21] See Stroud v Dorr-Oliver, Inc. (1975, Ariz) 542 P2d 1102, 1113–1114; Westinghouse Electric Crop. v Wray Equipment Corp. (1961, CA1 Mass) 286 F2d 491, 493.

[22] Estate of Murphy (1976) 15 Cal 3d 907, 919, 126 Cal Rptr 820, 544 P2d 956. See also Fenstermacher v Philadelphia Nat. Bank (1974, CA3 Pa) 493 F2d 333, 338; Pepsi-Cola Metropolitan Bottling Co. v Pleasure Island, Inc. (1965, CA1 Mass) 345 F2d 617, 624.

[23] CCP § 2025.620.

[24] For a discussion of the use of the "former testimony" exception to circumvent this restriction in limited circumstances, see § 2.42.

[25] CCP § 2025.620(f).

[26] See Glass v. Superior Court (1988) 204 Cal App 3d 1048, 251 Cal Rptr 690.

[27] See N.N.V. v American Assn. of Blood Banks (1999) 75 Cal App 4th 1358, 1395–1396, 89 Cal Rptr 2d 885 [where copy of notice of a pre-suit deposition to perpetuate testimony is sent to a potential adversary at an address where she was not employed, the notice was inadequate, and the deposition, which she did not attend, may not be used against her at trial]; Lauson v Stop-N-Go Foods, Inc. (1990, WD NY) 133 FRD 92, 93–94 [deposition inadmissible against a party who received only oral notice of its taking]. For a discussion of persons entitled to deposition notice, see § 2.6.

[28] For a discussion of objections based on a defective deposition notice, see § 2.8.

[29] Mondello v General Electric Co. (1994, Maine) 650 A2d 941, 943 [rejecting trial court's conclusion that "each party owns the questions that they asked"].

otherwise admissible under Section 2025.620, *any* party may offer it. In one federal case,[30] an injured taxi passenger sued the cab company, but not its driver. The plaintiff noticed a deposition of the cabdriver "solely for purposes of discovery." Defense counsel attended but asked no questions. The driver died before the case came to trial. When the defense offered the deposition of the driver as evidence,[31] the plaintiff tried unsuccessfully to persuade the trial judge that the limitation in the deposition notice barred such use: "[Fed Rules Civ Proc, Rule 26(d)] does not evince a distinction as to admissibility at trial between a deposition taken solely for purposes of discovery and one taken for use at trial, and I am not empowered to read a restriction into the Rule which does not exist."[32] Another federal court reached the same conclusion: "[A district court] cannot exclude deposition testimony on the basis that the defendant intended that the deposition be taken for discovery purposes and did not expect that it would be used at trial."[33]

Offer of Deposition as Evidence is Essential: Even where circumstances exist that would qualify a deposition for use at trial, a party must still formally offer it into evidence: "Unless someone offered [the deposition] in evidence on the trial it was not evidence in the case, nor was it proper to be transmitted as such with the record on appeal."[34] For example, no party may attack the granting of a directed verdict by pointing to a part of a deposition that was not offered in evidence.[35] Even in a nonjury trial, a party may neither attack[36] nor support[37] findings by references to deposition testimony never offered in evidence. *Howe v Pioneer Mfg. Co.*[38] carried this rule a step further: a grant of summary judgment must stand or fall on the basis of "those portions of the depositions which were abstracted and placed before the court in the affidavit and in the declaration filed in connection with the motion."

Rule of Completeness: Depositions are often quite lengthy. A party offering one in evidence should select just the portions that are directly relevant to what

---

[30] Rosenthal v Peoples Cab Co. (1960, WD Pa) 26 FRD 116.

[31] For a discussion of the use of the deposition testimony of a person unavailable to testify at trial, see § 2.40.

[32] Rosenthal v Peoples Cab Co. (1960, WD Pa) 26 FRD 116, 117. See also Savoie v Lafourche Boat Rentals, Inc. (1980, CA5 La) 627 F2d 722, 724 [one may use the deposition of his own expert, unavailable to testify at trial, even though the deposition was taken solely for discovery purposes by an adversary]; McVay v Cincinnati Union Terminal Co. (1969, CA6 Ohio) 416 F2d 853, 856 ["Any party may use a deposition, not merely the party taking it"].

Annotation: Introduction of deposition by party other than the one at whose instance it was taken. 134 ALR 212.

[33] Tatman v Collins (1991, CA4 WVa) 938 F2d 509, 511.

[34] United States v City of Brookhaven (1943, CA5 Miss) 134 F2d 442, 447.

[35] See Worsham v Duke (1955, CA6 Ky) 220 F2d 506, 509.

[36] See United States v City of Brookhaven (1943, CA5 Miss) 134 F2d 442, 446–447.

[37] See Salsman v Witt (1972, CA10 Okla) 466 F2d 76, 79; Processteel, Inc. v Mosley Machinery Co. (1970, CA6 Ky) 421 F2d 1074, 1076.

[38] Howe v Pioneer Mfg. Co. (1968) 262 Cal App 2d 330, 336, 68 Cal Rptr 617.

that party wants to prove. Section 2025.620 provides that one may offer in evidence "all or *any part* of a deposition."[39] However, this right to pick the favorable parts of the deposition does not include the distortion of the deponent's meaning. The antidote for this abuse is the "rule of completeness": "[I]f the party introduces only part of the deposition, any party may introduce any other parts that are relevant to the parts introduced."[40] This rule prevents a deponent's testimony from being taken out of context:

> The rule provides a method for averting, so far as possible, any misimpressions from selective use of deposition testimony. The opposing party is entitled under the rule to have the context of any statement, or any qualifications made as a part of the deponent's testimony also put into evidence.[41]

The court has no duty to admit sua sponte the parts necessary to provide context. The opposing party must move to supplement the testimony already admitted.[42]

—**"Relevance"**: The portions of the deposition admitted as context must be "relevant to the parts introduced" initially.[43] This prevents another party from introducing hundreds of pages of otherwise inadmissible evidence, none of which clarifies the part already in evidence.[44] This "relevance" restriction on context evidence echoes a similar requirement in the Evidence Code.[45]

Although *Witt v Jackson*[46] did not involve use of a deposition, it exemplifies the proper functioning of the rule of completeness. In a statement, the plaintiff had described two separate facts related to the same accident. When his trial testimony as to the first fact varied from that statement, the defense impeached him by reading from the statement only the part containing the different version. The plaintiff's lawyer then wanted read into evidence the remainder of the statement, which described the second fact in a way favorable to the plaintiff. The Supreme Court upheld the trial court's ruling that this part of the statement was not admissible. It acknowledged that where one party has offered part of

---

[39] CCP § 2025.620(e) (italics added). See Pursche v Atlas Scraper & Engineering Co. (1961, CA9 Cal) 300 F2d 467, 488.

[40] CCP § 2025.620(e).

[41] Westinghouse Electric Crop. v Wray Equipment Corp. (1961, CA1 Mass) 286 F2d 491, 494. See, e.g., De Jesus v Ridder (1969, CA7 Ill) 411 F2d 560.

[42] Paul Arpin Van Lines, Inc. v Universal Transportation Services, Inc. (1993, CA1 RI) 988 F2d 288, 294.

[43] CCP § 2025.620(e).

[44] See Sprague v Equifax, Inc. (1985) 166 Cal App 3d 1012, 1035–1036, 213 Cal Rptr 69 [where part of a conversation is introduced, the balance of it is admissible, if this is necessary to forestall the inference that the part offered contains the whole conversation].

[45] Evid Code § 356 ["Where part of an act, declaration, conversation, or writing is given in evidence by one party, the whole on the same subject may be inquired into by an adverse party . . ."].

[46] Witt v Jackson (1961) 57 Cal 2d 57, 66–67, 17 Cal Rptr 369, 366 P2d 641.

a statement, the opposing party may introduce the balance of it. However, it excluded from this rule those portions of the statement that are irrelevant to matters covered in the part introduced.

—**Timing:** Section 2025.620 does not address the timing of an opposing party's right to introduce these other portions of the deposition.[47] First impressions are difficult to erase. It is not fair to let the deponent's answers remain out of their context for any appreciable length of time. A federal court has discerned the danger that, especially in lengthy trials, the trier of fact may not connect the later portions with the segment heard earlier:

> [T]he spirit of the rule dictates that the opposing party should be able to require the introduction of the relevant parts of the deposition testimony at least at the conclusion of the reading of the deposition. In the instant case the supplementary relevant testimony authorized by the rule was separated by more than 1,000 pages of transcript from the deposition testimony introduced by the plaintiff. . . . [S]uch wide separation of the relevant parts of a deposition unduly impedes the orderly consideration of the deposition testimony, even in a non-jury case.[48]

A California case, *Conderback, Inc. v Standard Oil Co.*,[49] goes a step further. It empowers the trial court to require *the party offering part of an answer* to read the rest of it "in order to obviate immediately any false or distorted impression the jury might receive from a fragmentary introduction."

Recorded Depositions: Section 2025.340 contains a four-step procedure for a party who intends to offer an audio or video recording of a deposition at trial.[50] (1) If no stenographic record of that deposition[51] has been made, the party who intends to use the recording at trial must prepare a written transcript of the testimony. (2) In any event, that party must give written notice to the trial court and to all parties of the intention to offer in evidence a video or audio recorded deposition. (3) This notice must specify the parts of the deposition that will be offered. (4) The party must give this notice a "sufficient time" in advance to allow appropriate steps to insure that the jury sees or hears what it should of the deposition testimony, but nothing more. Therefore, the other parties need enough time to object to the parts designated and to make their own designations of testimony. In addition, the notice should be early enough for the trial court to rule on any objections and for the preparation, if necessary, of an edited version of the deposition.[52]

---

[47] See CCP § 2025.620(e).

[48] Westinghouse Electric Crop. v Wray Equipment Corp. (1961, CA1 Mass) 286 F2d 491, 494.

[49] Conderback, Inc. v Standard Oil Co. (1966) 239 Cal App 2d 664, 686, 48 Cal Rptr 901.

[50] CCP § 2025.340(m).

[51] For a discussion of when a deposition may be taken without making a simultaneous stenographic record of the testimony, see § 2.22.

[52] The parties must, however, preserve unaltered the original recording of the deposition. CCP § 2025.340(m).

§ 2.38 Against a Party Deponent

An adverse party may "use for any purpose, a deposition of a party to the action."[1] This simply applies to deposition testimony "the long recognized rule of evidence that statements of a party which are inconsistent with his claim in litigation are substantively admissible against him."[2]

Traditional Hearsay Exception for Admissions: The hearsay rule is the major obstacle to the admissibility at trial of someone's prior out-of-court statement. The hearsay barrier collapses, however, where two circumstances coincide: the person who made the earlier statement is a party to the lawsuit *and* the statement is offered *against* that party. As an admission of a party-opponent, such statements are universally exempted from the hearsay rule. The federal evidence rules accomplish this by defining hearsay itself to exclude a party-opponent's admissions.[3] California reaches the same result more conventionally. It leaves admissions within the hearsay *definition*,[4] but then removes them from the hearsay *rule*[5] by recognizing an exception for out-of-court statements made by a party-opponent: "Evidence of a statement is not made inadmissible by the hearsay rule when offered against the declarant in an action to which he is a party . . . ."[6]

—Rationale for the Admissions Exception: This freeing of party admissions from the general rule against hearsay evidence recognizes that the rule responds to the danger that attends proof of a fact against one person by the extrajudicial say-so *of other people.* The hearsay rule is not concerned about protecting litigants from their own tongue or pen: "The rationale underlying this exception [i.e., for admissions of a party] is that the party cannot object to the lack of the right to cross-examine the declarant since the party himself made the statement."[7]

—Application to Depositions: The admissions exception overcomes the hearsay objection to even the most offhand remarks that an opposing party has made. A *fortiori*, it covers statements that parties make during a pretrial deposition. Fully aware of the litigation and in their attorney's presence, parties give sworn answers, which are instantly and precisely recorded by a certified shorthand reporter, and sometimes also on an audio or video recording.[8] Section 2025.620 simply applies specifically to depositions the same treatment that the Evidence Code already provides generally for all statements of a party-opponent.

---

[1] CCP § 2025.620(b).

[2] Community Counseling Service, Inc. v Reilly (1963, CA4 Va) 317 F2d 239, 243 [discussing Fed Rules Civ Proc, Rule 32(a)(2), the federal analog of CCP § 2025.620(b)].

[3] See Fed Rules Evid, Rule 801(d)(2).

[4] See Evid Code § 1200(a).

[5] See Evid Code § 1200(b) (italics added).

[6] Evid Code § 1220.

[7] Evid Code § 1220, Law Revision Comm'n Comment.

[8] For a discussion of the permitted methods of recording a deposition, see § 2.22.

Permissible Purposes: The Civil Discovery Act gives a sweeping license to a party to use another party's deposition at trial. As one court described it:

> [T]he deposition of a party may be used by an adverse party for any purpose. There is no limitation. Consequently, it may be used to establish any material fact, a prima facie case, or even to prove the whole case.[9]

Codifying well-settled case law,[10] Section 2025.620 allows such a use even where the party deponent is available to testify at trial: "It is not ground for objection to the use of a deposition of a party . . . by an adverse party that the deponent is available to testify, has testified, or will testify at the trial or other hearing."[11] Parties may even open their case-in-chief by reading into the record excerpts from an adversary's pretrial deposition.[12]

—Evidentiary versus Conclusive: Although the deposition answers of parties to a lawsuit are admissible in evidence against them, they are only evidentiary admissions, not the judicial admissions that result from admission requests. Thus, absent some abuse of the discovery process, these answers are not conclusive at trial: "[A] court abuses its discretion when it precludes a party from trying a case on a theory consistent with existing evidence, even though the pretrial testimony of the party relating to how the accident occurred is contrary to the theory."[13]

—Cumulative Use of Opponent's Deposition: Although the hearsay rule does not bar a party's use of an adversary's deposition as evidence at trial, in a particular case, the general rule against cumulative evidence may do so. Once adverse parties have testified at trial, a later offer of excerpts from their depositions is "subject to the court's right to exclude such parts thereof as might be unnecessarily repetitious in relation to the witness's testimony on the stand."[14] Conversely, a party who first introduces an opponent's deposition testimony

---

[9] Murry v Manley (1959) 170 Cal App 2d 364, 367, 338 P2d 976. See also Alvarez v Felker Mfg. Co. (1964) 230 Cal App 2d 987, 1002, 41 Cal Rptr 514 [even where parties repudiate the version of the facts in their pretrial depositions, the jury is free to disbelieve their trial testimony and to credit the deposition version].

[10] Mayhood v La Rosa (1962) 58 Cal 2d 498, 500–501, 24 Cal Rptr 837, 374 P2d 805; Hurtel v Albert Cohn, Inc. (1936) 5 Cal 2d 145, 149, 52 P2d 922; Robinson v North American Life & Casualty Co. (1963) 215 Cal App 2d 111, 115, 30 Cal Rptr 57. See also Fey v Walston & Co. (1974, CA7 Ill) 493 F2d 1036, 1046; Pursche v Atlas Scraper & Engineering Co. (1961, CA9 Cal) 300 F2d 467, 488.

[11] CCP § 2025.620(b). For a discussion of the use of an adverse party's answers to interrogatories as evidence at trial, see § 5.22.

[12] See, e.g., Young v Liddington (1957, Wash) 309 P2d 761, 762.

[13] Kelly v New West Federal Savings (1996) 49 Cal App 4th 659, 672–673, 56 Cal Rptr 2d 803 [plaintiff who mistakenly identified the smaller of two elevators as the one in which she fell is not precluded from presenting evidence at trial that it was the larger one].

[14] Merchants Motor Freight, Inc. v Downing (1955, CA8 Iowa) 227 F2d 247, 250. See also Fey v Walston & Co. (1974, CA7 Ill) 493 F2d 1036, 1046.

should expect judicial resistance to a later effort to plow the same ground with unduly repetitive live testimony from that opponent.

—Harmless Error: Unquestionably, a trial court errs if it limits the use of an adverse party's deposition testimony simply because that party is available for live testimony. This error, however, is likely to be harmless. Confronted with such an erroneous ruling, counsel usually puts the adverse party on the witness stand and elicits the same information through a direct examination supplemented by impeachment from the deposition. This procedure may not have the same impact on the trier-of-fact that the reading of the deposition itself would. The party-opponent may communicate more effectively as a "live" witness than he or she did during the deposition. Still, an appellate court is not likely to find that this possible difference in the two performances was prejudicial: "The district judge's refusal to permit the introduction of the depositions into evidence was not prejudicial, however, since the depositions do not appear to add any information to that given in oral testimony by the deponents and otherwise developed at the hearing."[15]

Party Representatives: Insofar as Section 2025.620[16] allows use of their depositions against parties at trial, it simply applies the general hearsay exception for a party-opponent's admissions. The statute has an added dimension, however, when it allows the use against an adverse party of the deposition of any persons who were officers, directors, managing agents, employees or agents of that party when their deposition was taken. Moreover, where the party-deponent is a corporation or other type of organization,[17] the testimony of those whom it designated to testify on its behalf at the deposition is also admissible against that organization. This right to use the depositions of a party-opponent's employees is broader than that allowed in the federal courts. There, the rule applies not to all "employees," but only to those who were officers, directors, managing agents or designated representatives.[18]

Multi-Party Litigation: Courts should go slowly when considering the use of a party-opponent's deposition in multi-party litigation. Suppose a pedestrian has sued two drivers for injuries. One motorist has given a statement about the accident to a police officer. In it that motorist addressed a circumstance, such as the color of a traffic light or the condition of the pavement, that reflected adversely on both drivers. This statement is, of course, admissible at trial against the party who made it. However, unless it happens also to qualify under another hearsay exception, the statement of one driver will not be admissible against the *other* driver:

---

[15] Fenstermacher v Philadelphia Nat. Bank (1974, CA3 Pa) 493 F2d 333, 338. See also Spector v El Ranco, Inc. (1959, CA9 Nev) 263 F2d 143, 145. For a rare holding that the trial testimony of the adverse party did not make the error in excluding his deposition harmless, see Barker v New (1954, Mun Ct App DC) 107 A2d 779.

[16] CCP § 2025.620(b).

[17] For a discussion of depositions of corporations or other organizations, see § 2.5.

[18] Fed Rules Civ Proc, Rule 32(a)(2).

If there are several parties on one side of the litigation, whether plaintiffs or defendants, the admission of one of these co-parties is admissible only against himself. It is not admissible merely by virtue of the co-party relationship against the other parties with whom he is aligned.[19]

Where the hypothetical motorist's statement, implicating not only the speaker but also a co-party, occurs in a deposition, the result should be no different. The statement should be inadmissible even if that co-party attended the deposition. The permission to introduce deposition testimony at trial extends only "so far as admissible under the rules of evidence applied as though the deponent were then present and testifying as a witness . . . ."[20] Since other types of statements by a party are *not* admissible against a co-party, a statement in a deposition should receive no different treatment.[21]

—**Exceptions:** In three situations, the deposition testimony of one party may be used against a co-party:

(1) The party deponent might give trial testimony that clashes with the deposition. This would make the deposition testimony admissible to impeach,[22] since it has now become a form of prior inconsistent statement.[23] Moreover, the Evidence Code makes *any* prior inconsistent statement that is used to impeach a trial witness admissible substantively against *all* parties to the case.[24]

(2) The party-opponent may at the time of the deposition have had such a relationship to some co-party that the deposition testimony of one becomes a vicarious admission of the other.[25] For example, the party-opponent may have been the co-party's managing agent or employee.

(3) By the time of the trial, a party deponent may have become unavailable as a witness for a reason specified in Section 2025.620.[26] If so, the deposition testimony is admissible independently of the unavailable deponent's status as a party to the case.[27]

---

[19] McCormick, Evidence § 262 (4th Ed 1992).

[20] CCP § 2025.620.

[21] Ghezzi v Holly (1970, Mich App) 177 NW2d 247, 252; Davis v Sedalia Yellow Cab Co. (1955, Mo App) 280 SW2d 869; Napier v Bossard (1939, CA2 NY) 102 F2d 467, 468. Cf. Keen v Prisinzano (1972) 23 Cal App 3d 275, 283 n4, 100 Cal Rptr 82 [in a malpractice action against two doctors, plaintiff used one physician's deposition to establish a fact against the other, but the court noted that the co-party had not objected to this use].

Annotation: Admissibility in evidence of deposition as against one not a party at time of its taking. 4 ALR3d 1075.

[22] CCP § 2025.620(a). For a discussion of the use of their deposition testimony to impeach trial witnesses, see § 2.39.

[23] See Evid Code § 780(g).

[24] See Evid Code § 1235. For a discussion of the use of deposition testimony to impeach the trial testimony of the deponent, see § 2.39.

[25] CCP § 2025.620(b).

[26] CCP § 2025.620(c).

[27] For a discussion of the use at trial of the deposition of one who has become unavailable as a witness, see § 2.40.

§ 2.39 Impeachment of the Deponent

Any time witnesses testify at trial, they place their credibility in issue. A powerful way to attack credibility is to show that the witnesses have made earlier statements that are inconsistent with their present trial testimony. People hesitate to believe those who have given two different versions of the same event.

The Evidence Code explicitly recognizes the right to impeach a witness by a prior inconsistent statement.[1] The provision which allows impeachment by a witness's inconsistent *deposition testimony* is simply a specific application of this rule: "Any party may use a deposition for the purpose of contradicting or impeaching the testimony of the deponent as a witness . . . ."[2] Accordingly, much of the general case law on the use for impeachment of a witness's earlier inconsistent statement will apply *a fortiori* to answers given during a deposition.

A review of the general principles governing impeachment by prior inconsistent statements is beyond this treatise's scope. Instead, this section focuses on four problems that are peculiar to prior inconsistent statements contained in discovery depositions.

(1) Absence of Adverse Party from Deposition: Section 2025.620 purports to allow the use of depositions only "against any party who was present or represented at the taking of the deposition or who had due notice of the deposition."[3] However, it makes no sense to apply this general restriction to those depositions offered solely to impeach the deponent.

A prior inconsistent statement made in a *non*-deposition setting may be used to impeach the declarant though none of the parties to the case was present when the declarant uttered the statement. The earlier statement's impeachment value stems from the difference between it and the witness's trial testimony. This value is not affected by who was present when the witness made the earlier statement. Indeed, no one need be present at all, as where the inconsistent statement is in writing.

Therefore, when a party objects to the impeachment of a witness by an answer given in a deposition of which that party had no notice, the court should ignore the restrictive language of Section 2025.620 and rely instead on the Evidence Code, which contains no such limitation on prior inconsistent statements.[4] An identical restriction in Fed Rules Civ Proc, Rule 32 did not stop Professor Moore from stating that "a deposition may be used by any party for the purpose of contradicting or impeaching the testimony of the deponent as a witness, *irrespective of whether parties other than the one taking the deposition were present or represented at the taking of the deposition or had due notice thereof.*"[5]

---

[1] See Evid Code § 780(h). See also Evid Code §§ 769, 770.

[2] CCP § 2025.620(a).

[3] CCP § 2025.620.

[4] See Evid Code § 780(g).

[5] 4A Moore's Federal Practice § 32.02[2] (1991) (italics added). The current edition omits the italicized language. 7 Moore's Federal Practice § 32.02[2][c] (2005). See also Osborne v Bessonette (1973, Ore) 508 P2d 185, 188–189.

(2) **Revised Deposition Transcripts:** Once the reporter has prepared the transcript of the oral examination, the deponent may change the substance of answers before signing it.[6] Usually the witness's later trial testimony will be consistent with the changed transcript but inconsistent with the answer given during the oral examination. This creates an issue concerning the use of the original oral answer to impeach the deponent at trial. Had the witness made the original statement in a *non*-deposition setting, it would be usable to impeach trial testimony that differed from it. The rule should be the same when the statement was made during a deposition session and later changed in the transcript:

> The witness who changes his or her testimony on a material matter between the giving of the deposition and appearance at the trial may be impeached by the former answers, and the cross-examiner and the jury are likely to be keenly interested in the reasons for the changing testimony. There is no apparent reason why the witness who has a change of mind between the giving of the deposition and its transcription should be treated differently.[7]

Deponents are only "bound" by the deposition as signed. This means only that any perjury prosecution would have to be based on the answer as changed. However, this should not affect the use of the original oral answer for impeachment. In *Gasquet v Pechin*,[8] a witness had stated during her oral examination: "I ought to pay whatever I can toward this debt." She later struck "debt" before signing the transcript. The trial court's exclusion of the original version from evidence was error:

> [T]he [trial] court refused to allow it, assigning as the reason for the ruling that the witness was bound only by the terms of the deposition as finally corrected before signing. This ruling was erroneous and the reason given fallacious. If her original statement was as claimed, and was inconsistent with the testimony given on the trial on a material point, it could be proven for the purposes of impeachment, regardless of the occasion upon which the original statement was made . . . .[9]

(3) **Unsigned Transcripts:** A deponent sometimes refuses or neglects to sign the deposition transcript. In such cases, absent a successful motion to suppress, the deposition has the same effect as if signed.[10] Therefore, the lack of a signature

---

[6] For a discussion of the deponent's right to make substantive changes to the deposition transcript, see § 2.34.

[7] 8A Wright & Miller, Federal Practice and Procedure § 2118 (1994). Cf. Bennett v Superior Court (1950) 99 Cal App 2d 585, 593, 222 P2d 276.

[8] Gasquet v Pechin (1904) 143 Cal 515, 77 P 481.

[9] Gasquet v Pechin (1904) 143 Cal 515, 521, 77 P 481. See also Lewis v Western Truck Line (1941) 44 Cal App 2d 455, 460–461, 112 P2d 747.

[10] CCP § 2025.520(f). For a discussion of the effect of a deponent's refusal or neglect to sign the deposition transcript, see § 2.32.

on the transcript does not prevent its use to impeach any trial testimony by the deponent that varies from the answers given during the oral examination.[11]

(4) Substantive Use: Suppose a witness testifies at trial that a traffic light was red. Suppose further that before trial the witness had said that the light was green. Use of the prior statement to *impeach* the witness aims to persuade the fact-finder to disregard the witness as a reliable source of information about the light's color. Use of the prior statement *substantively* would aim to persuade the fact-finder that the light was indeed green.

Traditionally, the hearsay rule prevented substantive use of a prior inconsistent statement.[12] The Evidence Code overturns this rule by excepting from the hearsay rule all prior inconsistent statements: "Evidence of a statement made by a witness is not made inadmissible by the hearsay rule if the statement is inconsistent with his testimony at the hearing . . . ."[13] Section 2025.620 incorporates this exception when it allows use of a deposition not only to impeach or contradict a witness, but also "for any other purpose permitted by the Evidence Code."[14] Thus, whenever a portion of a deposition is received in evidence to impeach the deponent's credibility, the trier of fact may also use that deposition testimony substantively, that is, as the correct account of the facts involved.

§ 2.40   Unavailable Deponent

Deposition testimony becomes admissible when the deponent is unavailable to testify at trial.[1] In language similar to its Evidence Code counterpart,[2] the Civil Discovery Act specifies six types of unavailability.[3] Unless the party offering the deposition can fit the deponent into one of these categories,[4] or qualify it under another exception,[5] deposition testimony remains inadmissible hearsay.

---

[11] Bennett v Superior Court (1950) 99 Cal App 2d 585, 593, 222 P2d 276. For a general discussion of the effect of an unsigned deposition transcript, see § 2.32.

[12] See McCormick on Evidence § 34 (5th Ed 1999).

[13] Evid Code § 1235.

[14] CCP § 2025.620(a).

[1] CCP § 2025.620(c).

[2] Evid Code § 240.

[3] CCP § 2025.620(c)(2).

[4] Moore v Mississippi Valley State University (1989, CA5 Miss) 871 F2d 545, 551–552 [deposition may not be offered without explaining absence of deponent from trial]; Nanda v Ford Motor Co. (1974, CA7 Ill) 509 F2d 213, 224; Andrews v Hotel Sherman, Inc. (1943, CA7 Ill) 138 F2d 524, 528–529.

Annotation: Admissibility of Depositions under Federal Evidence Rule 804(b)(1). 84 ALR Fed 668.

[5] E.g., CCP §§ 2025.620(a) [prior inconsistent statements], 2025.620(b) [use against a party deponent]. For a discussion of the use of a deposition to impeach a witness at trial, see § 2.39. For a discussion of the use of a deposition against the party-deponent, see § 2.38.

Eligible Types of Unavailability: A deponent is unavailable to testify at the trial if he or she is dead,[6] seriously ill,[7] located beyond the court's subpoena power,[8] missing,[9] validly asserting a privilege,[10] or disqualified as a witness.[11] This unavailability, however, must not result from "the procurement or wrongdoing of the proponent of the deposition for the purpose of preventing testimony in open court."[12] Whether a deponent fits under any of these categories of unavailability is "a preliminary fact to be established to the satisfaction of the trial court by the proponent of the evidence."[13]

Deponent's Serious Illness: A party who claims that a deponent is now too ill to appear as a trial witness usually needs the support of a doctor or a psychotherapist. In *Sanchez v Bagues & Sons Mortuaries*,[14] counsel tried to make the showing only by some statements about his health made by the very elderly deponent. The appellate court upheld the trial court's insistence on medical testimony:

> There was no testimony of a doctor or nurse that the witness could not appear in court. On cross-examination, plaintiff's counsel admitted that he had not spoken with any doctors of the witness, and admitted that he knew of no medical evidence that precluded the witness from being brought to court to testify. . . . The court's requirement that medical evidence be produced to establish nonavailability cannot be said to be unreasonable.[15]

---

[6] CCP § 2025.620(c)(2). See, e.g., O'Mary v Mitsubishi Electronics America, Inc. (1997) 59 Cal App 4th 563, 567, 69 Cal Rptr 2d 389, 392.

[7] "[U]nable to attend or testify because of existing physical or mental illness or infirmity." CCP § 2025.620(c)(2)(C). See Note, Dead Men Tell No Tales: Admissibility of Civil Depositions upon Failure of Cross-examination (1979) 65 Va L Rev 153.

[8] "[A]bsent from the trial or other hearing and the court is unable to compel the deponent's attendance by its process." CCP § 2025.620(c)(2)(D).

Annotation: Admissibility of deposition, under Rule 32(a)(3)(B) of Federal Rules of Civil Procedure, where court finds that witness is more than 100 miles from place of trial or hearing. 71 ALR Fed 382.

[9] "[A]bsent from the trial or other hearing and the proponent of the deposition has exercised reasonable diligence but has been unable to procure the deponent's attendance by the court's process." CCP § 2025.620(c)(2)(E). See, e.g., Chavez v Zapata Ocean Resources, Inc. (1984) 155 Cal App 3d 115, 118, 201 Cal Rptr 887.

[10] "[E]xempted or precluded on the ground of privilege from testifying concerning the matter to which the deponent's testimony is relevant." CCP § 2025.620(c)(2)(A).

[11] "[D]isqualified from testifying." CCP § 2025.620(c)(2)(B).

[12] CCP § 2025.620(c)(2).

[13] Sanchez v Bagues & Sons Mortuaries (1969) 271 Cal App 2d 188, 194, 76 Cal Rptr 372, 375. See Evid Code § 405.

[14] Sanchez v Bagues & Sons Mortuaries (1969) 271 Cal App 2d 188, 76 Cal Rptr 372.

[15] Sanchez v Bagues & Sons Mortuaries (1969) 271 Cal App 2d 188, 194, 76 Cal Rptr 372, 375.

Distant Deponent: In two overlapping situations the geographical location of deponents qualifies them as "unavailable" for trial testimony: (1) they are outside the court's civil subpoena power;[16] or (2) they reside "more than 150 miles from the place of the trial or other hearing."[17]

—150-Mile Limit: To compute the 150-mile distance, the "place of the trial" is probably measured from the courthouse rather than from the border of the county where the trial is being held. This is the interpretation given to the identical phrase in Fed Rules Civ Proc, Rule 32:

> [F]or purposes of applying the rule the place of trial is the courthouse where the trial takes place. It is apparent that the rule is intended to protect the convenience of the witness and the parties, and that the limit of convenience is measured by the [specified] distance. To measure a distance from the borders of the district . . . rather than from the courthouse, would provide a variable standard of convenience, depending on the size of the district, the location of the trial, and the location of the witness.[18]

—Showing Deponent's Location: A party may use hearsay and reasonable inference to show that a person resides either beyond the court's subpoena power or more than 150 miles from the place of trial.[19] The court may take judicial notice of the distance between the witness's home and the trial site.[20] The deposition itself may show that the deponent then resided either outside California or more than 150 miles from the courthouse. This should be a sufficient circumstantial showing to allow use of the deposition at trial, absent anything to suggest that the witness has later moved. This is especially true where the interval between the deposition and the trial is only a matter of months.[21] Having made the required showing of the deponent's location, the party offering the deposition in evidence need not use "due diligence" to induce the deponent to testify in person.[22]

---

[16] CCP § 2025.620(c)(2)(D).

[17] CCP § 2025.620(c)(1).

[18] Tatman v Collins (1991, CA4 W Va) 938 F2d 509, 511 [interpreting Fed Rules Civ Proc, Rule 32(a)(3)(B)].

[19] See, e.g., Topanga Corp. v Gentile (1967) 249 Cal App 2d 681, 690, 58 Cal Rptr 713.

[20] See Hartman v United States (1976, CA8 Mo) 538 F2d 1336, 1346; Ikerd v Lapworth (1970, CA7 Ind) 435 F2d 197, 205.

[21] Hartman v United States (1976, CA8 Mo) 538 F2d 1336, 1346; Ikerd v Lapworth (1970, CA7 Ind) 435 F2d 197, 205.

Annotation: Construction of statute or rule admitting in evidence deposition of witness absent or distant from place of trial. 94 ALR2d 1172.

[22] Compare CCP §§ 2025.620(c)(1) and 2025.620(c)(2)(D) [no mention of "reasonable diligence"] with CCP § 2025.620(c)(2)(E) [requiring "reasonable diligence" to locate any deponent not shown to be beyond the court's subpoena power or the 150 mile limit]. Cf. Hansen v Abrasive Engineering & Manufacturing, Inc. (1993, Ore) 856 P2d 625, 631–633 [no showing of exceptional efforts required to meet general hearsay exception for unavailable witness where deponent was beyond the reach of the court's subpoena power].

Missing Deponent: A party who claims an inability to find deponents must show "reasonable diligence" to locate and subpoena them.[23] Whether the party's efforts add up to due diligence is a factual question. Appellate courts will reverse the trial court's evaluation only for an abuse of discretion.[24]

—Showing Diligent Search: "Reasonable diligence" cannot be reduced to a formula; it is decided case-by-case:

> The term is incapable of a mechanical definition. It has been said that the word "diligence" connotes persevering application, untiring efforts in good earnest, efforts of a substantial character. The totality of efforts of the proponent to achieve presence of the witness must be considered by the court. Prior decisions have taken into consideration not only the character of the proponent's affirmative efforts but such matters as whether he reasonably believed prior to trial that the witness would appear willingly and therefore did not subpoena him when he was available, whether the search was timely begun, and whether the witness would have been produced if reasonable diligence had been exercised.[25]

At a minimum, the efforts to find the deponent must be current as of the trial date. It does not suffice merely to show that the telephone book does not list the deponent.[26] It is good practice to direct a subpoena to the deponent's last-known address, even where counsel is sure the deponent no longer lives there. However, this is probably neither a required nor, by itself, an adequate effort.[27]

—Use of Precedents from Criminal Cases: Civil litigants should proceed cautiously before relying on decisions in criminal cases evaluating *prosecution* efforts to search for missing persons. Because the accused has a constitutional right to confront the prosecution's witnesses, the measure of due diligence will be tougher for a criminal case than for its civil counterpart.[28] Efforts by the People to locate a witness that the courts have deemed to show "reasonable diligence" will suffice *a fortiori* for a civil case. However, a search for a prosecution witness that a court considered to fall short of due diligence may be adequate in a *civil* case.

---

[23] CCP § 2025.620(c)(2)(E).

[24] Gorgon v D & G Escrow Corp. (1975) 48 Cal App 3d 616, 624, 122 Cal Rptr 150, 155.

[25] People v Linder (1971) 5 Cal 3d 342, 346–347, 96 Cal Rptr 26, 28–29, 486 P2d 1226, 1228–1229 (internal citations omitted).

Annotation: Sufficiency of efforts to procure missing witness's attendance to justify admission of his former testimony—state cases. 3 ALR4th 87.

[26] Gorgon v D & G Escrow Corp. (1975) 48 Cal App 3d 616, 624–625, 122 Cal Rptr 150, 155–156.

[27] Cf. Matter of Respondent C (1991) 1 Cal State Bar Ct Rptr 439 [examiner's failure to show due diligence to obtain investigator's trial attendance, despite subpoena of investigator, precluded use of investigator's deposition at State Bar Court hearing]; People v Linder (1971) 5 Cal 3d 342, 347 n1, 96 Cal Rptr 26, 29 n1, 486 P2d 1226, 1229 n1.

[28] Cf. People v Linder (1971) 5 Cal 3d 342, 348 n3, 96 Cal Rptr 26, 30 n3, 486 P2d 1226, 1230 n3. See also Ohio v Roberts (1980) 448 US 56, 65 L Ed 2d 597, 100 S Ct 2531.

Catch-All Provision: Even where the witness does not fit within any of the six listed categories of unavailability,[29] the trial court may still let a party use a deposition if, "with due regard to the importance of presenting the testimony of witnesses orally in open court," it finds that "[e]xceptional circumstances" make it "in the interests of justice" to do so.[30] Only one California case has addressed such "exceptional circumstances." In *Jordan v Warnke*,[31] the deponent was an attorney who was in trial in another county. The deposition was offered against the party who had taken it. The court ruled that the deposition was properly received in place of the attorney's live testimony.[32]

Unavailable *Party* Deponents: Litigants most frequently cite a deponent's unavailability when they are trying to admit into evidence the deposition of a nonparty. However, there is explicit authorization to use at trial of the deposition of "any party to the action" who fits within a category of unavailability.[33] Of course, the use of a deposition *against* the party who gave it does not require any showing of unavailability.[34] But where a party deponent fits under one of the statutory categories, this opens other avenues of admissibility for the deposition.

—Multi-Party Litigation: In litigation involving more than one plaintiff or defendant, the deposition of a party deponent who is now unavailable for live testimony may be offered in evidence by any party against any other party.

—Parties' Use of Their Own Depositions: Normally, when parties offer their own depositions into evidence, they are excluded as inadmissible hearsay. However, when party deponents fall under one of the unavailability categories, their own attorney may introduce their deposition in evidence. This is certainly justified where the party deponent dies between the deposition and the trial,[35] or is now too ill to testify in person.[36]

—Distant Party-Deponents: It is harder to justify a rule that lets an attorney offer a client's deposition simply because he or she resides outside California, or lives more than 150 miles from the courthouse. Nevertheless, on its face, Section 2025.620 would allow the receipt of the deposition testimony into

---

[29] CCP § 2025.620(c)(2).

[30] CCP § 2025.620(c)(3).

[31] Jordan v Warnke (1962) 205 Cal App 2d 621, 630–631, 23 Cal Rptr 300.

[32] But see Allgeier v United States (1990, CA6 Ky) 909 F2d 869, 876 [abuse of discretion to permit automatic use of deposition of a doctor who is located within range of court's subpoena power]. See also Tatman v Collins (1991, CA4 W Va) 938 F2d 509, 510–511.

Annotation: Admissibility of former testimony of nonparty witness, present in jurisdiction, who refuses to testify at subsequent trial without making claim of privilege. 92 ALR3d 1138.

[33] CCP § 2025.620(c).

[34] For a discussion of the use of a deposition against the party-deponent, see § 2.38.

[35] See, e.g., Derewecki v Pennsylvania R. Co. (1965, CA3 Pa) 353 F2d 436 [in personal injury case administrator or executor of plaintiff may put in evidence the decedent's deposition].

[36] Cf. Ray v Henderson (1963) 212 Cal App 2d 192, 194–195, 27 Cal Rptr 847 [rightly decided, but wrongly reasoned]. See, e.g., Parrott v Wilson (1983, CA11 Ga) 707 F2d 1262, 1268–1269.

evidence.[37] A federal decision, *Richmond v Brooks,*[38] well illustrates the problem.[39] The California plaintiff, having sued in New York City, was unwilling to travel there to testify at the trial, although she could well afford the trip. To save her from making a cross-country journey, her own attorney deposed her via written questions.[40] At trial that attorney offered in evidence this deposition of the absent plaintiff. The trial court overruled a defense objection that it "was entitled to require the presence of the plaintiff as a part of her case and the opportunity to cross-examine her before the jury."[41]

Affirming this ruling, the appellate court could "find no occasion to add something to the rule which is not there and which effectually distorts its purpose and utility."[42] It concluded that the disadvantage to the plaintiff of presenting her case in this fashion more than offset any suffered by the defendant from his inability to conduct a live cross-examination: "The tactical burden assumed by the plaintiff in proceeding to trial in her absence . . . is likely to limit frequent resort to this course . . . ."[43]

Other federal cases[44] and several states have reached the same result.[45] By contrast, three states take the opposite view.[46] They are concerned that allowing parties to offer their own deposition simply because of their distance from the forum deprives the trier of fact of the opportunity to observe their demeanor during direct and cross-examination:

> When the plaintiff failed to appear at the trial of his case he thereby voluntarily caused or brought about his absence from the trial, and he thereby prevented his examination as a witness by his own counsel and

---

[37] See CCP § 2025.620(c)(1).

[38] Richmond v Brooks (1955, CA2 NY) 227 F2d 490. See also Note (1956) 69 Harv L Rev 1503; Note (1956) 4 UCLA L Rev 150.

[39] Fed Rules Civ Proc, Rule 32(a)(3) also allows the use in evidence of the deposition of an unavailable witness "whether or not a party."

[40] For coverage of depositions taken via written questions, see Chapter 3.

[41] Richmond v Brooks (1955, CA2 NY) 227 F2d 490, 491.

[42] Richmond v Brooks (1955, CA2 NY) 227 F2d 490, 492.

[43] Richmond v Brooks (1955, CA2 NY) 227 F2d 490, 492.

[44] Stewart v Meyers (1965, CA7 Ill) 353 F2d 691, 696; Houser v Snap-on Tools Corp. (1962, D Md) 202 F Supp 181, 189; Weiss v Weiner (1950, D Md) 10 FRD 387. But see Vevelstad v Flynn (1956, CA9 Alaska) 230 F2d 695, 702.

[45] In re Adoption of IJW (1977, Alaska) 565 P2d 842; Hiltibrand v Brown (1951, Colo) 234 P2d 618; Ross v Lewin (1964, NJ Super) 200 A2d 335; Aircraft Radio Industries, Inc. v M. V. Palmer, Inc. (1954, Wash) 277 P2d 737, 743. But see Avis Rent-A-Car, Inc. v Cooper (1994, NJ App Div) 641 A2d 570, 572 [corporate plaintiff's nonresident deponent employee was not "unavailable" where corporation could have procured witness's transportation to trial].

[46] Bartell v Bartell (1976, Md) 357 A2d 343, 348–349; Jobse v Connolly (1969, NY Misc) 302 NYS2d 35; King v International Harvester Co. (1971, Va) 181 SE2d 656.

Annotation: Party's right to use, as evidence in civil trial, his own testimony given upon interrogatories or depositions taken by opponent. 13 ALR3d 1312.

by counsel for defendants. He deprived the jury and the trial judge of the benefit of such information as they would have obtained by his presence on the witness stand.[47]

In effect, these courts find that healthy parties who fail to attend the trial are "procuring" their own unavailability.[48]

There is little to recommend a rule that allows a litigant to camp just outside the court's reach and thereby escape a live examination. A sounder approach would be a flexible rule giving the trial court discretion to allow parties to put their own depositions in evidence where there are "exceptional circumstances" making it "in the interests of justice" to do so.[49] These circumstances might be found where: (1) the matters known to the absent party are peripheral or uncontested; or (2) that party is a long distance from the forum; or (3) the amount involved in the case is small as compared to the cost of travel and the press of other commitments; or (4) the party is simply too poor to incur the cost of the trip.

General Requirements: Besides the specific statutory criteria,[50] an unavailable witness's deposition must meet two general requirements contained in the introductory or umbrella clause of Section 2025.620. First, the parts of the deposition offered must be "admissible under the rules of evidence." Second, unless it otherwise qualifies under the former testimony exception to the hearsay rule,[51] the deposition may be offered only against "any party who was present or represented at the taking of the deposition or who had due notice of the deposition and did not serve a valid objection" to the taking of the deposition.[52]

—Prior Examination Opportunity: A litigant is allowed to use the deposition of an unavailable deponent because of the special reliability that attends hearsay statements offered against someone who had an *opportunity* to cross-examine the deponent when they were made.[53] However, the party against whom the deposition is offered need not have *actually* examined the witness or attended the deposition. All that is required is that that party had a chance to do so.[54]

Where a party dies before the completion of his or her deposition, it may be used against the party who was taking it; the incompleteness affects only its

---

[47] King v International Harvester Co. (1971, Va) 181 SE2d 656, 661.

[48] See CCP § 2025.620(c)(2) [precluding use of deposition testimony where party offering deposition procured the witness's unavailability]. See also Avis Rent-A-Car, Inc. v Cooper (1994, NJ Super Ct, App Div) 641 A2d 570, 572 [corporate plaintiff's nonresident deponent employee was not "unavailable" where corporation could have procured witness's transportation to trial].

[49] CCP § 2025.620(c)(3).

[50] See CCP § 2025.620(c).

[51] For a general discussion of "former testimony," see § 2.42.

[52] For a general discussion of the parties against whom a deposition may be offered, see § 2.37.

[53] Taylor v Rederi A/S Volo (1966, ED Pa) 249 F Supp 326, 328.

[54] See Wong Ho v Dulles (1958, CA9 Cal) 261 F2d 456, 460.

weight.[55] However, where a party terminates a key witness's deposition during the other side's direct examination, and then refuses to produce that witness to resume the questioning, that party forfeits the right to use the partial testimony.[56]

§ 2.41   Video Recorded Deposition of Expert

A party may offer in evidence at trial certain video recorded depositions given by doctors and other expert witnesses: "Any party may use a video [recording of a] deposition of a treating or consulting physician or of any expert witness even though the deponent is available to testify if the deposition notice . . . reserved the right to use the deposition at trial . . . ."[1] If the recording meets the statutory requirements, a party may use it at trial even if the expert witness is otherwise available to testify in person.[2] In essence, then, this provision creates a new exception to the hearsay rule.

Advantages: This right to substitute at trial a video recording of a deposition for the live testimony of an expert witness has two important effects: (1) it ameliorates the disruptive effect of courtroom appearances on the practice of doctors and other professionals, and (2) it reduces significantly the costs connected with the presentation of expert testimony.

Courtroom appearances pull doctors and other professionals away from their daily practices. Often the live testimony they give is uncontroversial and cumulative of that of other professionals. Moreover, courtroom appearances may play havoc with the schedule of a busy doctor or other professional. This in turn delays, inconveniences and sometimes even endangers others who need the services of that professional. Exacerbating the disruption that attends any live testimony by a professional is the difficulty in many counties of pinpointing when the trial will start and when a party can anticipate putting the expert on the witness stand.

In addition, the substitution of a video recorded deposition for the live testimony of an expert may cut litigation costs substantially. Doctors and other experts frequently charge large fees for the time lost from their practices to give trial testimony. These fees are often much higher than the comparable charges for deposition testimony, especially for those taken in their office.

Special Procedures: Ordinarily, a deposition need not state that a party is taking it for use as trial evidence.[3] However, to use at trial video recorded

---

[55] Derewecki v Pennsylvania R. Co. (1965, CA3 Pa) 353 F2d 436, 442–443. See also Daigle v Maine Medical Center, Inc. (1994, CA1 NH) 14 F3d 684, 692 [where witness more than 100 miles from trial site, okay to admit incomplete deposition].

[56] Sprague v Equifax, Inc. (1985) 166 Cal App 3d 1012, 1041–1043, 213 Cal Rptr 69, 87–89.

[1] CCP § 2025.620(d).

[2] Cf. Clarksville-Montgomery County School System v United States Gypsum Co. (1991, CA6 Tenn) 925 F2d 993, 997–999 [expert's deposition admissible without a showing of unavailability where deposition notice reserved right to introduce it at trial and opposing party failed to object to such trial use by deadline specified in pretrial order].

[3] For a discussion of the basic components of a deposition notice, see § 2.4.

depositions of experts without regard to their availability for live testimony, a party must expressly state this intention in the deposition notice. Of course, that party must later comply with the procedures that regulate the use of any video recorded depositions at trial.[4] In addition, the party must be sure that the operator of the video camera during the expert's testimony is a person authorized to administer an oath and is neither financially interested in the case nor an employee or relative of any attorney for any of the parties.[5]

Preparatory Deposition: Other litigants may need to take a discovery deposition better to prepare for the video recorded one that may substitute for the personal appearance of an expert at trial. Upon receiving notice of such a deposition, they may apply for a protective order postponing that deposition.[6] This postponement allows time for other parties to conduct a *discovery* deposition of that expert. This will enable them to get ready for what may turn out to be the only cross-examination of that expert that the trier of fact will see.

Live Trial Testimony Not Precluded: A party who videos an expert's deposition for possible trial use retains the option of calling that expert to provide live testimony at trial. The deposition notice for such a deposition forewarns other parties that a party is *contemplating* such use of the video, but it does not guarantee the video will be used in lieu of the live testimony of the expert.[7]

§ 2.42 Deposition From Another Lawsuit

Prior Suit Involving Same Claim and Parties: Occasionally, the cause of action involved in a pending case will have been the subject of previous litigation between the present parties or their predecessors in interest. This earlier action may have been in a federal court, in the court of another state, or even in a California court where it was dismissed without prejudice. Before it was aborted, this earlier proceeding may have reached a point where depositions were taken. Such depositions can become evidence in subsequent litigation between the same parties.[1]

A party may use such depositions as evidence in the later case "as if originally taken" in that later case.[2] Their admission into evidence at trial is subject to the same restrictions and uses that apply to depositions taken in the pending case.[3]

---

[4] See CCP § 2025.340(m). For a discussion of the prerequisites to the offer of *any* video recorded deposition, see § 2.37.

[5] CCP § 2025.220(a)(6).

[6] CCP § 2025.420(b)(3).

[7] CCP § 2025.220(a)(6).

[1] CCP § 2025.620(g). It suffices if the present action is between "representatives or successors in interest" of parties to the previous lawsuit.

[2] CCP § 2025.620(g). See Gatton v A.P. Green Services, Inc. (1998) 64 Cal App 4th 688, 692–695, 75 Cal Rptr 2d 523, 525–527 [rejecting contention that a 10-year-old deposition from an earlier lawsuit involving different parties was akin to a declaration filed in the instant case].

[3] For a discussion of these restrictions and uses, see §§ 2.37–2.41.

Former Testimony Exception: The Evidence Code's "former testimony" exception to the hearsay rule includes "[a] deposition taken in compliance with law in another action."[4] This exception requires that the deponent now be "unavailable as a witness."[5] However, in two respects the former testimony exception is a broader avenue for admissibility of depositions from other cases. First, it does not require that the deponent have testified in a case "involving the same subject matter"[6] as the present case. The information contained in the deposition need only be relevant to the issues in the present case. Second, it is not essential that the party against whom one is now offering the deposition have also been a party to the earlier action. It suffices that some party to that other action had an opportunity to cross-examine the deponent with an interest and motive "similar" to that of the party against whom another party now wants to use the deposition.[7]

—Use against Parties Added Later: The former testimony exception is also broad enough to allow the use against a present party of a deposition taken in the *instant* action, but before joinder of that party. Suppose A sues B, and then deposes X. Later C becomes a party to the case. The deposition would not be admissible against C under Section 2025.620 because, as a nonparty, C had no opportunity to attend the deposition and question X.

However, if X's deposition, taken when only A and B were parties, is now offered against C, it should qualify as one taken "in another action."[8] Therefore, if X is now unavailable as a witness,[9] the deposition may be admissible against C under the former testimony exception.[10] All that one offering it need show is that at the deposition either A or B had an interest and motive in probing X's testimony similar to the interest and motive that C would now have at the trial.[11]

§ 2.43 Recovery of Deposition Expenses as Costs

Expenses Connected with Depositions: Depositions are the most expensive discovery method. If the deponents are not parties to the action, the deposing party must pay both to subpoena them and for their statutory witness fee.[1] That party must also pay the reporter to attend and record the deposition.[2] The reporter

---

[4] Evid Code § 1290(c).

[5] Evid Code §§ 240, 1291 and 1292.

[6] See CCP § 2025.620(g).

[7] Evid Code § 1292(a)(3). See Gatton v A.P. Green Services, Inc. (1998) 64 Cal App 4th 688, 692–695, 75 Cal Rptr 2d 523 [rejecting contention that a 10-year-old deposition from an earlier lawsuit involving different parties was akin to a declaration filed in the instant case].

[8] See Evid Code § 1290(c).

[9] For a discussion of what constitutes unavailability of a deponent, see § 2.40.

[10] See Evid Code § 1292.

[11] Ikerd v Lapworth (1970, CA7 Ind) 435 F2d 197, 205–206.

[1] For a discussion of the need to subpoena a nonparty deponent, see § 2.9

[2] See Gov't Code § 8211.5. For a discussion of the recording of depositions, see § 2.22.

will charge a substantial fee for any transcription of the oral examination.[3] The attorney taking the deposition and most other counsel will usually purchase a copy of the transcript for trial preparation.[4] When deponents reside far from the forum, counsel will incur travel expenses to attend the deposition.[5] At the case's conclusion, the victor will surely try to recoup these expenses as part of its judgment for "costs."

Cost Recovery Statute: The Discovery Act itself does not address recovery of any discovery expenses. However, another statute lists as an "allowable" cost "[t]aking, videotaping, and transcribing necessary depositions including the original and one copy of those taken by the claimant and one copy of depositions taken by the party against whom costs are allowed."[6] Deposition transcription costs include the expenses incurred in copying exhibits marked for identification during the deponent's examination.[7]

—Video Recorded Depositions: Unless the parties agree to dispense with it, a stenographic record is made during a video recorded deposition.[8] Both the costs of videotaping and of transcribing the deposition appear to be recoverable since the statute is worded conjunctively.[9] Similarly, where a recorded deposition is later transcribed to qualify its use at trial,[10] the transcription costs should also be recoverable.[11]

"Necessary" Depositions Only: The prevailing party may only recover expenses incurred in taking "necessary" depositions.[12] The losing party bears the burden of establishing that any particular deposition cost was incurred unnecessarily.[13] Three examples of a "necessary" deposition are: (1) one received

---

[3] See Gov't Code § 8211.5. For a discussion of the deposing party's obligation to have the deposition testimony transcribed, see § 2.31.

[4] See Gov't Code § 8211.5.

[5] See also County of Kern v Ginn (1983) 146 Cal App 3d 1107, 1114, 194 Cal Rptr 512, 512–516.

[6] CCP § 1033.5. That section has been the subject of efforts to recover expert witness fees and discovery special master fees. See, e.g., Baker-Hoey v Lockheed Martin Corp. (2003) 111 Cal App 4th 592, 604–605, 3 Cal Rptr 3d 593, 602–603 [special master fees not recoverable as deposition fees or expert witness fee]. Cf. Winston Square Homeowner's Ass'n v Centex West, Inc. (1989) 213 Cal App 3d 282, 293, 261 Cal Rptr 605 [trial court has discretion to apportion discovery special master fees as costs].

[7] People ex rel. Mosk v Barenfeld (1962) 203 Cal App 2d 166, 184, 21 Cal Rptr 501 [decided under former CCP § 1032.7].

[8] CCP § 2025.330. For a discussion of videotaped depositions and their transcription, see §§ 2.22 and 2.33.

[9] CCP § 1033.5.

[10] CCP § 2025.330.

[11] Compare Commercial Credit Equipment Corp. v Stamps (1990, CA7 Ill) 920 F2d 1361, 1367–1369 [reading former Fed Rules Civ Proc, Rule 30(b)(4) to require parties to bear their own transcription costs for video recorded depositions].

[12] CCP § 1033.5.

[13] See Glass v Gulf Oil Corp. (1970) 12 Cal App 3d 412, 439–440, 89 Cal Rptr 514, 533; Horner v Marine Engineers' Beneficial Assn. (1959) 175 Cal App 2d 837, 844, 1 Cal Rptr 113, 117 [decided under former CCP § 1032.7].

in evidence at trial; (2) one used to support a successful summary judgment motion; and (3) one that would have been used at trial had not the prevailing party's motion for a nonsuit been granted.

This list does not exhaust the category of "necessary" depositions. For instance, *Brake v Beech Aircraft Corp.* [14] held that the prevailing party may recover the costs of deposing an opponent's trial experts although that party did not later dispute those experts' testimony during the trial:

> [P]laintiffs are legally mistaken to assert that costs of deposing experts are "unnecessary" where their testimony is ultimately not disputed at trial. The need for a deposition must be viewed from the pretrial vantage point of a litigant who does not yet know whether or not to oppose the expert's opinions. [15]

Travel Expenses: The current statute expressly includes as an allowable cost "travel expenses to attend depositions." [16] An early case upheld the trial court's discretion to allow as a "cost" the expenses incurred by the prevailing party's attorney in journeying from California to New York to attend a deposition scheduled by the other side. [17] More recently, *Thon v Thompson* [18] upheld the trial court's discretion to award as costs the airfare of out-of-county counsel who journeyed to the forum county for depositions. The appellate court, however, found improper the recovery of the cost of chartering a plane since travel by commercial airline was feasible, though more time-consuming and inconvenient.

Subpoena Costs: Where a party must subpoena deponents to compel their attendance, [19] the cost of "[s]ervice of process by a public officer" is a recoverable cost. [20]

---

[14] Brake v Beech Aircraft Corp. (1986) 184 Cal App 3d 930, 229 Cal Rptr 336.

[15] Brake v Beech Aircraft Corp. (1986) 184 Cal App 3d 930, 940, 229 Cal Rptr 336, 341.

[16] CCP § 1033.5.

[17] Hoge v Lava Cap Gold Mining Corp. (1942) 55 Cal App 2d 176, 186–188, 130 P2d 470, 475–477. For a discussion of the imposition of travel costs on a party who does not serve a deposition subpoena on a witness who fails to appear, see § 2.19.

[18] Thon v Thompson (1994) 29 Cal App 4th 1546, 35 Cal Rptr 2d 346.

[19] For a discussion of when a subpoena is necessary to compel a deponent's attendance, see §§ 2.8–2.10.

[20] CCP § 1033.5.

CHAPTER 3

WRITTEN DEPOSITIONS

SYNOPSIS

§ 3.1　General Nature and Function

Overlooked Alternative: Almost all depositions involve the witness's *oral* examination, which is covered in the Civil Discovery Act by the Section 2025 series of statutes.[1] In everyday legal parlance "deposition" has come to connote a *face-to-face* questioning of the deponent by the attorneys in the lawsuit. An often overlooked alternative, however, exists. Section 2028.010 authorizes a "deposition by written questions." This method has limited but genuine utility. In particular, it does not require that the examining attorneys and the deponent be present at the same time and place.

Focus of this Chapter: This chapter focuses on topics peculiar to the written deposition. Chapter 2 discusses topics common to *any* deposition, oral or written. The scope of allowable discovery by a written deposition is the same as for other forms of discovery. Accordingly, one should refer to the appropriate chapters of this treatise when an issue arises concerning the relevancy of a particular line of inquiry,[2] the validity of a claim of privilege,[3] or the discoverability of an adversary's "work product" materials.[4]

---

[1] CCP §§ 2025.010–2025.620. For an overview of oral depositions, see Chapter 2.

[2] For coverage of "relevance" for discovery, see Chapter 11.

[3] For coverage of privilege in discovery, see Chapter 12.

[4] For coverage of the discoverability of another party's "work product," see Chapter 13.

Overview: A party who wishes to take a written deposition must serve written notice on all other parties in the lawsuit. The questions for direct examination accompany this notice. Other parties have a specified time to prepare and serve written questions for cross-examination. They must serve these cross-questions on the party noticing the deposition and all other parties. Shorter periods govern the exchange of any redirect and recross questions. After the parties complete this interchange of written questions, the party who noticed the deposition forwards the questions to a person qualified to act as a deposition officer. At the deposition, that officer reads to the deponent the questions and records the answers verbatim.[5]

Contrast with Interrogatories: Since both sides to the litigation can draft questions for the witness, this process produces a "deposition" in every sense of the term: "A deposition on [written questions] is but another method of obtaining the same information that might be procured by an oral examination . . . ."[6] This *bilateral* questioning sets the "deposition on written questions" sharply apart from the quite different discovery tool, "written interrogatories to a party." These involve an entirely *one-sided* questioning process.[7] In addition, unlike written depositions, a party may only propound interrogatories to *another party*.[8]

—Nomenclature: The 1956 Discovery Act denominated discovery via written depositions as a "*deposition* upon written *interrogatories*."[9] This unfortunate word choice invited confusion between the written deposition and the "written interrogatory." Although they describe two quite different discovery methods, each does involve the propounding of written questions. In line with the current federal approach,[10] Section 2028.010 eliminates this potential confusion by simply renaming the written deposition as a "deposition by written *questions*."

Cross-References: The Section 2028 series of statutes[11] does not itself contain many of the provisions that govern written depositions. Instead, an attorney planning to take this type of deposition must extensively consult the Section 2025 series,[12] primarily regulating oral depositions. That series provides the statutory matrix for any deposition, written or oral. Section 2028.010 incorporates these procedures except as "modified."

The written deposition is often the most practical, convenient, and inexpensive method for deposing persons residing outside California. Sections 2026.010 and

---

[5] See Schmertz, Written Depositions under Federal and State Rules (1970) 16 Villanova L Rev 7, 9.

[6] Cronan v Dewavrin (1949, SD NY) 9 FRD 337, 339.

[7] For coverage of discovery by interrogatories to a party, see Chapter 5.

[8] CCP § 2030.010(a) authorizes the propounding of interrogatories only "to any other *party*." (Italics added.)

[9] Former CCP § 2020, 1956 Discovery Act, Appendix E (italics added).

[10] See Fed Rules Civ Proc, Rule 31.

[11] CCP §§ 2028.010–2028.080.

[12] CCP §§ 2025.010–2025.620.

2027.010 govern depositions conducted, respectively, in another state[13] or in another nation.[14] Section 2028.010 also incorporates these provisions except "as modified."

§ 3.2 Advantages and Disadvantages

Undoubtedly the deposition on written questions is "one of the least used of the discovery tools."[1] One author has estimated that attorneys take only one deposition out of fifty in this way.[2] The scarcity of California appellate cases involving written depositions also suggests that attorneys here seldom use it.[3] This meager use is undoubtably attributable to the advantages offered by an oral deposition. In limited cases, however, the written deposition's advantages significantly outweigh its disadvantages.

Advantages of Oral Depositions: Courts and attorneys have "readily acknowledged"[4] the advantages an oral examination of a witness offers over examination by written questions. For the most part, these advantages stem from the opportunity for an interrogator and a witness who are face-to-face to observe and react to one another.

—Clarifying Questions and Answers: During an oral examination, a deponent who finds a question unclear can say so; the interrogator can then clarify its meaning. Moreover, the wording of an answer may need clarification by follow-up questions. This give-and-take is impossible with written depositions. If a question asked during a written deposition is unclear, the best that can happen is that the witness will say so and not answer it. The worst result occurs if, without indicating any doubt as to the question's meaning, the witness interprets the words in his or her own way. In these latter instances, the witness may end up answering a different question than was asked.

—Follow-up Inquiry: A witness's deposition answer often suggests the need for the questioner to follow up with additional questions. A deposition taken by written questions leaves these new areas unexplored. As one federal judge put it: "From my long experience at the Bar, I can readily agree that the device of taking a deposition upon written [questions] under Rule 31, except for the proof of formal matters, is a tool of discovery very inferior to oral examination."[5]

—Sizing Up the Deponent: An oral deposition gives counsel a chance to assess the deponent's performance as a potential trial witness. In particular, it

---

[13] For a discussion of depositions taken in another state, see §§ 4.1–4.2.

[14] For a discussion of depositions taken in another nation, see §§ 4.3–4.4.

[1] Schmertz, Written Depositions under Federal and State Rules (1970) 16 Villanova L Rev 7, 8–9.

[2] Glaser, Pretrial Discovery and the Adversary System 53 (1966).

[3] Chronicle Publishing Co. v Superior Court (1960) 54 Cal 2d 548, 7 Cal Rptr 109, 354 P2d 637 involved a written deposition. However, the point decided there—a privilege issue—was unaffected by the deposition mode.

[4] E.g., V.O. Machinoimport v Clark Equipment Co. (1951, SD NY) 11 FRD 55, 58.

[5] Perry v Edwards (1954, WD Mo) 16 FRD 131, 133.

allows counsel to gauge firsthand the deponent's demeanor and the likelihood that the trier-of-fact will later find the witness credible.[6] In contrast, the faceless and often rehearsed[7] answers to written deposition questions provide an attorney little opportunity to make such pretrial evaluations.

Disadvantages of Oral Depositions: Counsel's physical presence is the major advantage to conducting an oral deposition. However, sometimes this can also be its greatest drawback.[8] Occasionally, the witness's testimony, while important, is cut-and-dried. Busy trial attorneys are wasting time, energy and money if they attend a deposition only to propound a few routine, simple questions, the answers to which they already know. This disadvantage increases markedly where counsel must travel far to attend such a perfunctory deposition.

Advantages of Written Depositions: Where a great geographical distance separates the forum and a deponent who has predictable and undisputed information, attorneys are most likely to consider the written deposition.[9] Not surprisingly, almost all cases interpreting the federal provision governing written depositions[10] have involved witnesses in foreign countries.[11] The written deposition is particularly useful in three situations: (1) for obtaining undisputed information from a cooperative but distant deponents; (2) for deposing someone who is likely to claim some privilege in response to most questions; and (3) for protecting a deponent's identity.

—Distant but Cooperative Deponents: The written deposition is most useful when three factors coincide: (1) the witness is friendly or cooperative; (2) the witness resides a considerable distance from the forum; and (3) the information sought is either formal or of the name-date-time-place variety. Here, a written deposition simply and efficiently gets the same information from the witness for a fraction of an oral deposition's cost.

—Anticipated Claim of Privilege: The written deposition is also useful where a distant deponent is likely to invoke a privilege in response to most of the questions that will be asked. Counsel need not to travel to the witness's locale only to encounter an anticipated privilege claim. Such a claim would force the

---

[6] Mill-Run Tours, Inc. v Khashoggi (1989, SD NY) 124 FRD 547, 549.

[7] Mill-Run Tours, Inc. v Khashoggi (1989, SD NY) 124 FRD 547, 549.

For a discussion of the propriety of a deponent's previewing the written deposition questions, see § 3.7.

[8] See, e.g. Wood v Pompey (1995, ND Cal) 1996 US App Lexis 24404, *1 [involving attempts to take written depositions by a federal inmate who had filed from prison a civil rights action *pro se*].

[9] For a discussion of the procedures for conducting a deposition in another state, see §§ 4.1–4.2.

For a discussion of the procedures for conducting a deposition in another country, see §§ 4.3–4.4

[10] Fed Rules Civ Proc, Rule 31.

[11] E.g., DBMS Consultants Ltd. v Computer Associates International, Inc. (1990, D Mass) 131 FRD 367, 370 [Australia]; Hamdi & Ibrahim Mango Co. v Fire Assn. of Philadelphia (1957, SD NY) 20 FRD 181 [Lebanon]; Gill v Stolow (1954, SD NY) 16 FRD 9 [Germany, Israel].

almost immediate adjournment of the deposition for a court ruling on its validity. [12]

The decision to proceed by a written, as opposed to an oral, deposition, however, is for counsel to make. Deponents have no right to stop an oral deposition and insist upon written questions so that they may, for example, better decide, question by question, whether to assert a privilege. [13]

—**Anonymous Deponents:** To protect the deponent's identity, several federal courts have ordered counsel to depose a witness by written questions instead of an oral examination. For example, several cases involving the source of HIV-tainted blood have resorted to a written deposition as a way of preserving the anonymity of a nonparty blood donor. [14] In the *Irwin Memorial Blood Centers* case, [15] however, the court ruled that, even if a screen were to be placed between the deponent and the deposition officer, the Health and Safety Code provisions barring revelation of a blood donor's identity would preclude even a written deposition of an allegedly HIV-tainted blood donor.

§ 3.3 Direct Examination Preparation

The uncomplicated nature of the information sought or the distance between the forum and the witness often leads a party to decide upon a deposition by written questions. [1] Many procedures for arranging it are the same as for an oral deposition. One must prepare and serve a deposition notice, [2] take steps to assure the deponent's attendance, [3] and arrange for the services of a qualified presiding officer, reporter and, if necessary, interpreter. [4]

---

[12] Goodwill, Inc. v Forest Hill State Bank (1985, D Md) 104 FRD 580; American Standard Inc. v Bandeaux Corp. (WD Mo, 1978) 80 FRD 706.

[13] Irwin Memorial Blood Centers v Superior Court (1991) 229 Cal App 3d 151, 279 Cal Rptr 911; National Life Ins. Co. v Hartford Accident & Indemnity Co. (1980, CA3 Pa) 615 F2d 595, 599–600; Mill-Run Tours, Inc. v Khashoggi (1989, SD NY) 124 FRD 547, 549.

[14] Watson v Lowcountry Red Cross (1992, CA4 SC) 974 F2d 482; 483 n3. Boutte v Blood Systems, Inc. (1989, WD La) 127 FRD 122, 126. Cf. Borzillieri v American Nat. Red Cross (1991, WD NY) 139 FRD 284, 287.

[15] Irwin Memorial Blood Centers v Superior Court (1991) 229 Cal App 3d 151, 279 Cal Rptr 911.

[1] For a discussion of the advantages of a written deposition in such situations, see § 3.2.

[2] For a discussion of the contents and service of the notice of deposition, see §§ 2.4–2.6.

[3] For a discussion of the need to subpoena a deponent for a deposition taken within California, see §§ 2.9–2.12.

For a discussion of the means of compelling the deponent's attendance at a deposition taken in another state, see §§ 4.1–4.2.

For a discussion of the means of compelling the deponent's attendance at a deposition taken in another country, see §§ 4.3–4.4.

[4] For a discussion of the presiding officer's qualifications for a deposition taken within California, see § 2.1.

For a discussion of the presiding officer's qualifications for a deposition taken in another state, see §§ 4.1–4.2.

For a discussion of the presiding officer's qualifications for a deposition taken in another nation, see §§ 4.3–4.4.

Special Deposition Notice Requirements: Section 2028.020 makes two modifications to the usual contents of a deposition notice. First, the notice must state the deposition officer's name or descriptive title.[5] Second, it may leave the deposition's date, time and place for that officer's later determination.[6] This second modification recognizes that the exchange of the written questions and the possibility of objections to some of them make it difficult to settle these logistical matters at the time a party notices the deposition.

Preparation Time: Both the extent and timing of question preparation differ considerably depending on whether a party is taking an oral or a written deposition. For oral depositions, the attorney usually postpones detailed question preparation until near the deposition date. Even then, most lawyers only outline the general areas they plan to pursue. They then rely on their experience, their spontaneous inspiration, and the witness's answers to develop the particular questions they ask.

In contrast, for written depositions, a copy of the direct examination questions must accompany the deposition notice.[7] Thus, question preparation must occur much earlier than the deposition date itself. Moreover, the attorneys cannot rely on a general outline; they must decide on and phrase the questions for the entire deposition.

Preparation Method: The drafting of the individual questions will generally prove to be much easier than one might suppose. Counsel will usually have contacted the witness by letter or telephone. This will have provided the outlines and many details of the deponent's information. Armed with this background information, attorneys should simply imagine that the deponents are present in their office for an oral deposition. With this vision in mind, they should write out the very questions that they would put to the deponent orally.

—Simple Questions: In phrasing the questions, attorneys should use everyday language. Each question should elicit one narrow fact. They "must be carefully constructed to elicit specific facts, not conclusory generalities."[8] It is helpful to imagine the precise response anticipated from the witness. This will help to detect ambiguities in the phrasing of the question and to suggest follow-up questions.

—Leading Questions: As with oral depositions, leading questions are objectionable.[9] Since opposing counsel gets the text of each question in advance, one must use special care to avoid wording that could draw this objection. An objection might force the deposition's postponement and rescheduling.

—Foundational Requirements: Parties often resort to written depositions less for discovery of new information and more for their eventual use at trial instead

---

[5] CCP § 2028.020(a).

[6] CCP § 2028.020(b).

[7] CCP § 2028.030(a).

[8] Molignaro v Dutton (1967, CA5 Ga) 373 F2d 729, 731.

[9] For a discussion of an objection that a written deposition question is leading, see § 3.5.

of the live testimony of that witness.[10] The questions therefore should include the foundational requirements imposed by evidence law. At the minimum, they should let the deponents show that they are answering from their personal knowledge. Where counsel anticipates more intricate evidentiary objections, such as hearsay, counsel should ask questions that will allow the deponents to supply any foundational facts that support the testimony's ultimate admissibility under some exception to the hearsay rule.[11]

Service: Once drafted, the direct examination questions should be typed under the case caption. Counsel should then forward a copy of them, as an enclosure to the deposition notice, to all parties who have appeared in the law suit.[12]

§ 3.4 Protective Orders

Section 2028.070 incorporates by reference the protective order provisions of Section 2025.420, which governs oral depositions. Broadly speaking, the court may enter any order necessary to prevent a written deposition from causing "unwarranted annoyance, embarrassment, or oppression, or undue burden and expense."[1] Specifically, it may enter any order on Section 2025's lengthy illustrative list that would also be suited to a written deposition.[2] In addition, Section 2028.070 contains its own nonexclusive list of protective orders particularly appropriate for written depositions.[3]

Meet and Confer Duty: A party or deponent who seeks a protective order must confer informally with the other parties and attempt in good faith to resolve the issues raised by the motion. The moving party must accompany the motion with a declaration detailing these informal efforts.[4]

Oral Examination Substituted: When a party proposes to depose someone by written questions, the trial court can direct that the testimony "be taken by oral, instead of written, examination."[5] To date, no reported California case has considered such an order. Federal cases provide some guidance.

—Cross-Questioning Difficulties: Those who have sought such an order in federal cases most frequently base their request on the difficulty of drafting cross-questions before the witness has testified. This awkwardness, however, is

---

[10] For a discussion of the use at trial of an unavailable witness's deposition testimony, see § 2.40.

[11] See generally, Imwinkelried, Wydick and Hogan, California Evidentiary Foundations 3d (2000, Lexis Publishing).

[12] CCP § 2028.030(a).

[1] CCP § 2025.420(b).

[2] CCP § 2025.420(b)(1)–(16).

For a discussion of protective orders against oral depositions, see §§ 2.15–2.19.

[3] CCP §§ 2028.070(a)–(d).

[4] CCP § 2025.420(a).

[5] CCP § 2028.070(a).

For a discussion of a protective order to direct that a deposition be taken via *written* questions, in lieu of an *oral* examination, see § 2.19.

endemic to most written depositions. If courts routinely accept this argument, they will virtually eliminate the written deposition as a discovery device. Thus, the federal courts have usually required the parties to at least attempt written cross-questions.

In one case,[6] for example, a sailor sued for injuries sustained in France in a dockside accident that occurred as he was returning from shore leave. Defendant claimed that these injuries resulted from plaintiff's intoxication. It sought to support this defense by deposing three French citizens via written questions. Plaintiff opposed the written deposition. He sought an order requiring the defendant to pay the expenses for his attorney to travel to France to conduct an oral cross-examination. In support of this order he argued "that the difficulties normally encountered in framing cross-[questions] are multiplied here because the French concept of intoxication is different from the American concept; the questions will have to be interpreted from English to French; a long time has elapsed since the occurrence of the accident; and further that the witnesses sought to be examined were interviewed [a few months earlier] by defendant's counsel."[7] This argument did not persuade the trial court: "The issue of plaintiff's alleged intoxication on the night of the accident is not so complex that the need for an oral cross-examination is evident at this time. Plaintiff should first attempt to conduct his examination by cross-[questions]."[8]

—**Complex Information:** The type of information sought during some depositions makes the written question mode inappropriate. For example, where the deponent is an expert witness, the technical nature of the questions would place an opponent at "a distinct disadvantage" in the preparation of cross-examination. The court will usually require a party to conduct such a deposition by oral examination.[9] Sometimes the number of the proposed direct examination questions shows the unsuitability of this mode.[10] In addition, where the range of inquiry is wide and relatively complex, the anticipated testimony critically important, and the deponent aligned with the side seeking the deposition, courts are more willing to order the deposition conducted by oral examination.

A federal case[11] provides an example. A seaman sought to recover for a shipboard injury. The defendant noticed the written deposition of the vessel's chief mate at the time of the accident, who now lived in San Francisco. The direct examination questions that accompanied the deposition notice showed the court that the interrogation would cover areas of vital importance in the litigation. These included the key negligence allegation: a failure, despite prior complaints,

---

[6] Wheeler v West India S. S. Co. (1951, SD NY) 11 FRD 396.

[7] Wheeler v West India S. S. Co. (1951, SD NY) 11 FRD 396, 397.

[8] Wheeler v West India S. S. Co. (1951, SD NY) 11 FRD 396, 398.

[9] Obis McAllister & Co. v The S.S. Marchovelette (1961, SD NY) 200 F Supp 695.

[10] Fall Corp. v Yount-Lee Oil Co. (1938, ED Tex) 24 F Supp 765 [106 questions seeking to prove heirship]; Lago Oil & Transport Co. v United States (1951, SD NY) 97 F Supp 438 [146 questions, some with subdivisions, seeking to elicit the details of a maritime salvage effort].

[11] Vareltzis v Luckenbach S. S. Co. (1956, SD NY) 20 FRD 383.

to sand the ship's decks under icy conditions. The trial court directed that the defendant conduct an oral deposition:

> The details of conversations, oral reports, inspections, the use of protective materials and similar matters, can be better brought out by oral examination than by written [questions]. It would be almost impossible for plaintiff to frame cross-[questions] which would provide adequate cross-examination on such details. Plaintiff is entitled to his right of cross-examination, and such right can be exercised adequately only if he is permitted oral cross-examination after oral direct examination . . . .[12]

—Expenses Paid: Parties seeking to substitute an oral examination for a written one will improve their chances of obtaining that protective order if they are willing to absorb some of the other parties' expenses of attending an oral deposition. For example, they might offer to pay the other side's expenses for travel to the witness's location.[13] Alternatively, they might offer to share the cost of bringing the witness to the forum.[14]

Attending the Deposition Session: An opposing party who wants to conduct an oral cross-examination of the deponent may seek a protective order that stops short of prohibiting a written deposition. That party may simply seek permission to attend the written deposition and cross-examine the deponent orally.[15] Such requests have received a mixed reaction from federal trial judges.[16]

Challenging the Deposition Officer: Section 2028.020 requires the notice for a written deposition to name or describe the deposition officer.[17] A party who objects to the designated officer can move for an order that "the deposition be taken before an officer other than the one named or described in the deposition notice."[18]

---

[12] Vareltzis v Luckenbach S. S. Co. (1956, SD NY) 20 FRD 383, 384. See also Lago Oil & Transport Co. v United States (1951, SD NY) 97 F Supp 438 [written questions inappropriate for deposition in the West Indies of the captain of plaintiff's vessel, who would be describing the maneuvers during a salvage operation on the high seas]; V.O. Machinoimport v Clark Equipment Co. (1951, SD NY) 11 FRD 55 [issues in breach of contract case involving almost $2,500,000 claim created a "greater need than in the ordinary one for a face-to-face questioning"]; Oscar Gruss & Son v Lumbermens Mutual Casualty Co. (1966, SD NY) 41 FRD 279 [written questions inappropriate for deposition of witnesses in Switzerland who would be describing their own intricate financial maneuvers, which cross-examining party claimed were fraudulent].

[13] See Houghton Mifflin Co. v Stackpole Sons, Inc. (1940, SD NY) 1 FRD 506.

[14] Lago Oil & Transport Co. v United States (1951, SD NY) 97 F Supp 438, 439–40.

[15] CCP § 2028.070(b)

[16] Baron v Leo Feist, Inc. (1946, SD NY) 7 FRD 71 [oral cross-examination denied]; United States v National City Bank of New York (1940, SD NY) 1 FRD 367 [oral cross-examination denied]; Winograd Bros., Inc. v Chase Bank (1939, SD NY) 31 F Supp 91 [oral cross-examination permitted].

[17] CCP § 2028.020(a).

[18] CCP § 2028.070(d).

Rulings on Objections: Unlike other discovery methods,[19] written depositions allow a party to use a motion for a protective order to get an advance ruling on the validity of objections it is making. Indeed, the objecting party must seek a protective order to preserve an objection to the form of a question.[20] And the propounding party must seek one to override an objection based on privilege or the work product protection. Unless this is done, Section 2028.050 prohibits the deposition officer from propounding the question to the deponent.[21]

§ 3.5 Objections to Particular Questions

The bases for objecting to questions during a written deposition are essentially the same as those for an oral deposition. Section 2028.010 generally incorporates by reference the provisions of Section 2025.460 regulating objections during an oral deposition.[1] However, depending on the ground for the particular objection, the procedure for obtaining a judicial ruling on it differs substantially from the procedure for oral depositions.

Objections to Admissibility: Although parties frequently take written depositions for eventual use at trial, they may still ask individual questions solely for discovery purposes.[2] Accordingly, if a particular question "appears reasonably calculated to lead to the discovery of admissible evidence,"[3] it is not objectionable on relevancy grounds although the testimony it elicits would later be inadmissible at trial. Moreover, objections based on competency, relevancy, materiality and admissibility are preserved for trial even if not made before the written deposition.[4]

—Pre-Deposition Rulings: Because discoverability is broader than admissibility, the courts have consistently refused to rule on objections such as competency, relevancy and materiality before the written deposition occurs:

> [They] are saved for the parties and may be made at the trial. [¶] They cannot prevent a party from propounding [questions]. The consideration of these objections is therefore premature at this time.[5] [7]

---

[19] See, e.g., § 5.14 [*Interrogatories*]; § 6.11 [*Inspections*]; § 9.8 [*Admission Requests*].

[20] CCP §§ 2028.070(c) and 2028.040(a).

[21] CCP §§ 2028.070(c) and 2028.050(b). For a discussion of the procedure for objecting to questions submitted for a written deposition, see § 3.5.

[1] CCP § 2025.460.

[2] Tsangarakis v Panama S.S. Co. (1966, ED Pa) 41 FRD 219.

[3] CCP § 2017.010.

[4] CCP § 2025.460(c). For a discussion of such objections during an oral examination, see §§ 2.24–2.26.

[5] Eyiutuoyo Awani v Public Nat. Bank of New York (1952, SD NY) 12 FRD 263, 265. See also Houghton Mifflin Co. v Stackpole Sons, Inc. (1940, SD NY) 1 FRD 506, 507; Tsangarakis v Panama S.S. Co. (1966, ED Pa) 41 FRD 219; Cronan v Dewavrin (1949, SD NY) 9 FRD 337.

[7] Wm. A. Hausman Co. v United States (1966, Cust Ct) 260 F Supp 860, 863–865.

For a discussion of the use of deposition testimony at trial, see §§ 2.37–2.42.

Thus, as in an oral deposition, unless the deponents themselves balk, they must answer any question that asks for arguably irrelevant or immaterial information.[6] If the deposition is ultimately offered at trial, objection may then be made, and the trial judge will rule then on the admissibility of that question and answer.

Objections to the Form of the Question: Section 2028.040 specially provides for objections based on the form of a question, e.g., it is leading, compound or argumentative. A party receiving questions that are not in proper form must serve a specific objection to them on all parties within 15 days.[8] This period is increased, usually by five days, if the objectionable question was served by mail.[9] This gives the questioner an opportunity to cure any error by rephrasing the question. A party who fails to make a timely objection to the form of a written question waives that objection.[10]

In addition, the *objecting* party must "promptly" seek a court ruling on the objection's validity.[11] Unless the court has sustained the objection, the deposition officer will propound the question despite the objection.[12]

—Federal Practice: By providing a pre-deposition hearing on objections to form, the California practice differs from federal practice. The federal courts do not rule on the validity of objections when they are served, unless the defects reach the point of oppression of the witness. The objections simply alert the party propounding the question to the claimed defect. That party may either reframe the question or risk a later adverse ruling at trial.[13]

Privilege and Work Product Objections: Section 2028.050 creates a special procedure for objections based on privilege or the work product protection. If a party has an objection to a particular question on either ground, that party must serve a specific objection to it on all parties entitled to notice of the deposition.[14] This objection must be within 15 days after service of the written questions.[15]

Unlike the procedure for objections based on form,[16] the *propounding* party must seek a court ruling on the claim of privilege or work product protection.[17]

---

[6] For a discussion of relevancy objections during an oral examination, see § 2.25.

[8] CCP § 2028.040(a).

[9] CCP § 2016.050, referencing CCP § 1013(a).

[10] CCP § 2028.040(a).

[11] CCP § 2028.040(b).

[12] CCP § 2028.040(b).

[13] E.g., Baranowski v National Union Fire Insurance Co. of Pittsburgh (1992, ND Tex) 141 FRD 55, 56; United States v The LV No. 134 (1953, SD NY) 14 FRD 261; Eyiutuoyo Awani v Public Nat. Bank of New York (1952, SD NY) 12 FRD 263.

[14] CCP § 2028.050(a).

[15] CCP § 2028.050(a).

[16] See CCP § 2028.040(b).

[17] CCP § 2028.050(b).

Unless that party both seeks and obtains an order overruling the objection, the deposition officer will propound the question involved to the deponent.[18]

—Standing: Where the deponent or some third person holds the privilege, the deponent must assert it.[19] Accordingly, courts will not entertain an objection on this ground made before the deposition by a litigant who is not the holder of the privilege.[20] As with any such claim,[21] deponents who first object, but then divulge the privileged information, will have waived the privilege.[22]

Meet and Confer Duty: A party or a deponent who seeks a ruling on any objection must first confer informally with the other parties and attempt in good faith to resolve the issues raised by the objection. The moving party must accompany the motion with a declaration detailing these informal efforts.[23]

Sanctions: Those who unsuccessfully make or oppose motions to sustain[24] or to overrule[25] objections to a written deposition question expose themselves to a monetary sanction unless the court finds that they acted with substantial justification or that other circumstances would make the imposition of the sanction unjust.[26]

§ 3.6   Cross, Redirect and Recross Questions

Each proposed direct-examination question must accompany the notice of written deposition. Service of these questions allows other parties to seek a protective order[1] or to object to the questions' form.[2] In addition, it enables them to better prepare their own cross-examination questions.

Preparation: Although awkward, opposing counsel can frame a cross-examination to probe answers that a deponent has yet to give. Counsel should study the direct-examination questions and try to anticipate the likely answers. With these possible answers in mind, counsel can draft suitable cross-questions.[3]

---

[18] CCP § 2028.050(a). For a discussion of privilege or work product objections during an oral deposition, see § 2.27.

[19] See, e.g., Chronicle Publishing Co. v Superior Court (1960) 54 Cal 2d 548, 565, 7 Cal Rptr 109, 354 P2d 637.

[20] Cronan v Dewavrin (1949, SD NY) 9 FRD 337.

[21] CCP § 2028.050(b).

[22] For a discussion of situations where the privilege is held by a nonparty deponent, see § 2.27.

[23] CCP §§ 2028.040(b) and 2028.050(b).

[24] CCP § 2028.040(c).

[25] CCP § 2028.050(c).

[26] See, e.g., Chronicle Publishing Co. v Superior Court (1960) 54 Cal 2d 548, 565, 7 Cal Rptr 109, 354 P2d 637.

[1] For a discussion of protective orders for a written deposition, see § 3.4.

[2] For a discussion of objections to written deposition questions, see § 3.5.

[3] See, e.g., Hamdi & Ibrahim Mango Co. v Fire Assn. of Philadelphia (1957, SD NY) 20 FRD 181, 182 [where a deposition taken in Lebanon concerning "rather complicated transactions occurring in the Near East more than seven years" earlier consisted of 35 subdivided questions on direct and 119 cross-questions].

—Deferred Preparation: Occasionally, attorneys have asked the court to allow them to defer the preparation of their cross-questions until after they have received the answers to the direct examination. Courts, however, have responded lukewarmly to these efforts to cause a piecemeal deposition.[4]

Service: Once prepared, the party serves the cross-questions on the party noticing the deposition and all other parties to the case.[5] This allows these other parties to prepare and serve redirect questions.[6] In turn, such redirect questions may lead to recross-questions.[7] This exchange of questions must run its full course before the deposition can begin. In one federal case,[8] the party arranging the deposition received the cross-questions, drafted and served redirect questions. Then, without waiting for recross-questions, that party forwarded the three sets of questions to the deposition officer. After the deposition was offered at trial, the court tried to cure the absence of answers to the recross-questions by simply excluding the redirect examination from evidence. The appellate court, however, ruled that this departure resulted in a deposition that was "incomplete and improper" and "contrary both to the letter and spirit of [Fed Rules Civ Proc] 31."

Time: Section 2028.030 allows 30 days for service of cross-questions,[9] 15 days for redirect questions,[10] and 15 days for recross-questions.[11] Service of a set of questions by mail expands these times, usually by five days.[12] For good reason, the trial may extend or shorten the time periods for the interchange of the questions.[13]

§ 3.7 Deponent's Preview of Deposition Questions

The attorney who initiates a written deposition acts as a depository for all sets of questions before their transmission to the deposition officer.[1] With the exact text of the questioning sequence in hand, counsel will naturally contemplate forwarding a copy of all the questions to the deponents. This would allow them to study the questions, seek any necessary clarification of their meaning and reflect carefully on the answers they will give.[2]

---

[4] See Baron v Leo Feist, Inc. (1946, SD NY) 7 FRD 71 [request denied, but with leave to file supplemental questions if answers received are not adequate]; Spotts v O'Neil (1939, SD NY) 30 F Supp 669 [request denied, except that witness required to answer one preliminary question before cross-questions are prepared].

[5] CCP § 2028.030(b).

[6] CCP § 2028.030(c).

[7] CCP § 2028.030(d).

[8] Lipscomb v Groves (1951, CA3 Pa) 187 F2d 40, 44–45.

[9] CCP § 2028.030(b).

[10] CCP § 2028.030(c).

[11] CCP § 2028.030(d).

[12] CCP 2016.050(e), referencing CCP § 1013(a).

[13] CCP § 2028.030(e).

[1] See CCP § 2028.080.

[2] See, e.g., Gill v Stolow (1954, SD NY) 16 FRD 9.

Preview Debated: At one time Professor Moore, a leading scholar of Federal Civil Procedure, condemned any such preview as an "improper practice."[3] Other commentators have echoed this view.[4] However, the only reported case to deal with this issue disagreed with these judgments, at least where the forwarding parties send only their own questions to the witness:

> It is usual and legitimate practice for ethical and diligent counsel to confer with a witness whom he is about to call prior to his giving testimony, whether the testimony is to be given on deposition or at trial. . . . In such a preliminary conference counsel will usually, in more or less general terms, ask the witness the same questions as he expects to put to him on the stand. . . . This sort of preparation is essential to the proper presentation of a case and to avoid surprise.[5]

To this federal trial judge, the previewing of the questions by the deponent affected the weight but not the admissibility of the answers. Other parties, after all, remain free to use their cross-questions to learn the nature and extent of any such advance preparation of the deponent.

Perhaps influenced by this judicial approval of the practice, Professor Moore softened his criticism. He still disapproves of such previews by the witness: "If [Fed Rules Civ Proc, Rule 31 is] to be an adequate substitute for oral depositions, the maximum spontaneity of the answers should be preserved and the questions should not be provided to the deponent in advance of the examination."[6] However, he acknowledges that, at least as far as the direct examination of a cooperative witness is concerned, the spontaneous deposition answer is a will-o'-the-wisp. In such cases, deponent's counsel can prepare the witness "with an eye to the questions he knows will be asked, even if he does not provide him with the questions in haec verba."[7]

Limited Preview Permitted: Trial lawyers have enough genuine ethical problems to concern themselves without worrying about one like this. Hence, Section 2028.060 expressly permits the party taking the deposition to forward a copy of its direct examination to the deponent.[8] However, it prohibits all parties from letting that deponent preview either the form or the substance of any cross, re-direct, or recross-questions.[9]

---

[3] See 4A Moore's Federal Practice, ¶ 31.02 n3 (2d ed.).

[4] 8A Wright and Miller, Federal Practice and Procedure, § 2133 (1994); Schmertz, Written Depositions under Federal and State Rules (1970) 16 Villanova L Rev 7, 9.

[5] Hamdi & Ibrahim Mango Co. v Fire Assn. of Philadelphia (1957, SD NY) 20 FRD 181, 182–83. See also Homan v Wayer (1908) 9 Cal App 123, 130, 98 P 80, 83.

[6] 4A Moore's Federal Practice ¶ 31.02 (2d. ed.).

[7] 4A Moore's Federal Practice ¶ 31.02 (2d. ed.).

[8] CCP § 2028.060(a).

[9] CCP § 2028.060(b).

§ 3.8   Conducting the Deposition

The deposition officer generally performs the same functions at oral and written depositions.[1] However, there are a few differences.

Time Frame: The notice for a written deposition need not specify the date, time and place it is to occur. Accordingly, on receipt of all questions, the deposition officer must set the deposition time. The statute simply requires the officer to propound the questions to the deponent "promptly" after receiving the questions.[2]

Role of the Deposition Officer: Since the attorneys for the respective parties are not present for written depositions, situations may arise where the officer may be inclined to do more than the purely ministerial tasks of swearing the witness, reading the questions and recording the answers that are the norm at an oral deposition.

—Examples: In one case, the Japanese judge conducting the deposition expanded counsels' ten questions into 43![3] Later, a party tried to introduce the deposition at trial. Most of the judge's supplemental questions called for hearsay. Accordingly, the federal court excluded them on that ground, without ruling on the propriety of the deposition officer's conduct.

In another case,[4] a consular officer, conducting a deposition in Germany, recorded three bits of information that would otherwise not have appeared in the record: (1) the deponent's preliminary comment that his memory had not been good since he had been injured in an automobile accident; (2) the deponent's constant need to refresh his recollection by reference to his notes; and (3) the deponent's consumption of hazel nuts during the deposition to calm his nervousness. The trial judge reacted severely to the deposition officer's conduct:

> [T]hese comments were comments of the Vice Consul offered gratuitously and were not in answer to any of the [questions]. Since the deposition was taken on written [questions], it was not possible for the parties to interrogate the witness concerning the matters which were commented upon in this statement by the Vice Consul. [¶] The Rules do not permit the officer before whom the deposition is taken to add his own gratuitous comments on the demeanor of the witness or on answers or statements made by the witness other than those included in the written [questions].[5]

—Flexibility Desirable: This total disapproval of the deposition officer's conduct seems unwarranted. Suppose the witness appears for a deposition intoxicated. If the officer functions in the robot-like manner that the court

---

[1] For a discussion of the deposition officer's duties, see § 2.21.

[2] CCP § 2028.080.

[3] Wm A. Hausman Co. v United States (1966, Cust Ct) 260 F Supp 860, 863.

[4] Gill v Stolow (1954, SD NY) 16 FRD 9.

[5] Gill v Stolow (1954, SD NY) 16 FRD 9, 10.

envisions, the record would not reveal this. Moreover, this would seriously mislead those parties who used the answers later assuming that a sober person had given them. Of course, officers for a written deposition should not act like attorneys during an oral deposition. Yet, where their perceptions are relevant to credibility or to describe the circumstances under which the deposition is occurring, court and counsel should have the benefit of them. The court can always screen out comments that reflect an officer's subjective reactions, inferences and conclusions. It can retain those notations that record events about which impartial observers would not likely differ.

CHAPTER 4

Out-of-State Discovery

SYNOPSIS

§ 4.1   Discovery in Another State: From a Party

Increasingly, attorneys in cases pending in California must conduct discovery activities with out-of-state ramifications. [1] Where those from whom the discovery is sought are parties to the case, their residence in another state presents few complications.

Jurisdiction: Parties to a lawsuit pending in California have no basis for jurisdictional objections when asked to provide discovery. Nonresident plaintiffs have already submitted themselves to California's judicial procedures by invoking the aid of its court system to vindicate their claims. Once nonresident defendants are validly served with process or appear in the case, they, too, become subject to the jurisdiction of the California courts.

Out-of-State Depositions: Section 2026.010 authorizes conducting in other states the oral depositions of parties to California lawsuits: "Any party may obtain discovery by taking an oral deposition, as described in Section 2025.010, in another state of the United States, or in a territory or an insular possession subject to its jurisdiction." [2] Section 2025.010, in turn, authorizes the depositions "of any person, *including any party to the action*." [3]

---

[1] For a discussion of the taking of depositions within California but outside the boundaries of the county where the case is pending, see §§ 2.12–2.13.

[2] CCP § 2026.010(a).

[3] CCP § 2026.010 (emphasis added).

Nonresident parties, however, need not always be deposed in their home state. Upon a proper showing, a California court may require a party to come *to* California to submit to an oral examination.[4]

> [C]ounsel may follow the procedures prescribed by [former] section 2025 and obtain an order to depose an out-of-state resident in California. Alternatively, counsel may travel to the witness' home state or territory and depose the witness within 75 miles of his or her residence pursuant to [former] section 2026. In short, [former] section 2026 is merely permissive; it does not require nonresidents [to] be deposed outside California.[5]

—No Subpoena Required: Even where the deposition of a nonresident party is taken in that party's home state, service of a deposition notice suffices to compel that party to attend; counsel need not subpoena the deponent: "If a deponent is a party to the action . . ., the service of the deposition notice is effective to compel that deponent to attend and to testify, as well as to produce any document or tangible thing for inspection and copying."[6] The same is true for a party-affiliated deponent, such as "an officer, director, managing agent, or employee of a party."[7]

—No Commission or Letters Rogatory Required: A "discovery commission"[8] or "letters rogatory"[9] are devices that another state may require to enlist the aid of its court system in compelling a deponent's attendance. However, Section 2026.010, by obliging nonresident parties in California litigation to appear in response to a deposition notice, in effect eliminates any need *under California law* to obtain a discovery commission or letters rogatory.[10]

---

[4] CCP § 2025.260(a).

For a discussion of the trial court's discretion to order a nonresident party to submit to a deposition within California, see §§ 2.13–2.14.

[5] Glass v Superior Court (1988) 204 Cal App 3d 1048, 1052–1053, 251 Cal Rptr 690, 692 (internal citations omitted).

[6] CCP § 2026.010(b).

For a discussion of the procedure for arranging a nonparty's out-of-state deposition, see § 4.2.

[7] CCP § 2026.010(b).

For a discussion of how to compel a party-affiliated deponent's attendance at an oral deposition in California, see § 2.12.

[8] A discovery "commission" is the forum court's authorization of a designated individual to take a named witness's deposition. See Volkswagenwerk A.G. v Superior Court (1973) 33 Cal App 3d 503, 506, 109 Cal Rptr 219, 221.

[9] "Letters rogatory" are a formal communication from the forum court to a court in another state or nation requesting that the testimony of a witness residing in that state or nation be taken under the direction of the court addressed, and then transmitted to the requesting court. See Volkswagenwerk A.G. v Superior Court (1973) 33 Cal App 3d 503, 506–507, 109 Cal Rptr 219, 221.

[10] For a discussion of the need for a commission or letters rogatory to depose a nonparty out-of-state, see § 4.2.

—**Site of Deposition:** Section 2026.010 restricts the distance that a party or party-affiliated deponent must travel to reach an out-of-state deposition site. The deposition must be taken at a place that is both within the state where the deponent resides, and no more than 75 miles from the deponent's home or business office.[11]

Other Discovery Methods: Interrogatories, admission requests and exchanges of expert witness information pose no special problems when directed to out-of-state parties. The party seeking discovery deals with the local attorneys for the responding parties. These attorneys must cope with the logistics created by the location of their clients outside California.

—**Inspection Demands:** Sometimes the item demanded for inspection is located far from the forum. Controversies may arise over whether the responding party must transport it to the forum, or whether the party seeking the inspection must journey to its location. In deciding which of these two places—the forum or the item's situs—is the "reasonable"one for a discovery inspection, the courts are more ready to give the choice to defendants, whether they are a demanding or a responding party. As one federal court remarked: "Plaintiff, who has elected to bring suit in this district, may not compel defendants to produce documents, or copies, outside the district except at his sole cost and expense."[12] Other courts have ruled similarly. For example, in two federal cases litigated in the eastern United States,[13] the plaintiffs sought voluminous records located on the west coast. Each trial judge refused to order the defendants to bring the records to the forum. Although neither mentioned the matter, it seems beyond a coincidence that the party seeking the production was a plaintiff.[14] Similarly when a defendant insists on inspecting an item at the forum, the out-of-state plaintiff must bring it there.[15]

—**Medical Examinations:** A party seeking a discovery medical examination in a California case rarely wants to conduct it at a location that is far from the county where the case is pending. Usually controversies over the site of a medical examination involve the existence of good cause to require the examinee to travel from another state to California to submit to the examination.[16]

---

[11] CCP § 2026.010(b).

For a discussion of the distance a party or a "party-affiliated" deponent must travel for a deposition in California, see §§ 2.13–2.14.

[12] Trieschmann v 347-349 E. 53rd St. Owners, Inc. (1992, SD NY) 1992 US Dist. Lexis 19966, 2.

[13] Lundberg v Welles (1950, SD NY) 93 F Supp 359, 363; Niagara Duplicator Co. v Shackleford (1947, CAD) 160 F2d 25.

[14] See also Mid-America Facilities, Inc. v Argonaut Ins. Co. (1978, ED Wis) 78 FRD 497, 499.

[15] Monks v Hurley (1939, D Mass) 28 F Supp 600. For further discussion of the site for carrying out discovery inspections, see § 6.10.

[16] For further discussion of the site for court-ordered medical examinations, see § 8.11.

§ 4.2 From a Nonparty

The only discovery devices available against a nonparty are oral[1] and written[2] depositions. However, one may also use these devices to obtain an inspection, during the deposition, of documents or other tangible things under the deponent's control.[3] Section 2026.010 authorizes taking oral depositions of nonparties in other states: "Any party may obtain discovery by taking an oral deposition, as described in Section 2025.010, in another state of the United States, or in a territory or an insular possession subject to its jurisdiction."[4] Section 2025.010, in turn, authorizes taking depositions "of any person."[5] Moreover, Section 2028.010, by its incorporation of Section 2026.010, authorizes written depositions in another state.[6]

California Procedures Apply: In essence, Sections 2025.010, 2026.010 and 2028.010 collectively say that, *as far as California is concerned*, a party who wishes to depose a nonparty *outside* California is to follow the same procedures used for a nonparty's deposition *within* California: "In designating the procedure to be followed for such out-of-state depositions as that set forth in [the original Discovery Act], the Legislature has thus provided that the procedure for taking depositions out of this state, but within the United States, is identical to taking them within this state."[7] However, since a California litigant is taking the deposition within another sovereign state, that state's laws may require some supplementation of these procedures.

Subpoenas: California courts cannot compel a nonparty located beyond the state's borders to appear for a deposition in California or any other state, including the state of his residence. Instead, they must rely on the courts at the deposition site to issue a subpoena. Moreover, a party must seek the aid of that state's court system if the deponent refuses to provide discovery.[8]

—Cooperative Deponents: A deponent's promise to appear voluntarily for the deposition may tempt the party taking the deposition not to go to the trouble of serving a subpoena.[9] However, if the deponent fails to appear, that party could end up paying the attorney fees and expenses of parties who journeyed to the out-of-state deposition site. Section 2026.010[10] incorporates by reference this

---

[1] For general coverage of oral depositions, see Chapter 2.

[2] For general coverage of written depositions, see Chapter 3.

[3] For general coverage of document discovery from nonparties, see Chapter 7.

[4] CCP § 2026.010(a). See, e.g., Rodriquez v McDonnell Douglas Corp. (1978) 87 Cal App 3d 626, 646, 151 Cal Rptr 399, 409.

[5] CCP § 2025.010.

[6] CCP § 2028.010. For a discussion of written depositions, see Chapter 3.

[7] Snyder v Superior Court (1970) 9 Cal App 3d 579, 584, 89 Cal Rptr 534, 537.

[8] Cf. Warford v Medeiros (1984) 160 Cal App 3d 1035, 1038–1041, 207 Cal Rptr 94.

[9] For a discussion of out-of-state depositions of party or party-affiliated deponents, see § 4.1.

[10] CCP § 2026.010.

provision of Section 2025.440: "If a deponent does not appear for a deposition because the party giving notice of the deposition failed to serve a required deposition subpoena, the court shall impose a monetary sanction . . . against that party, or the attorney for that party, or both, in favor of any other party who, in person or by attorney, attended at the time and place specified in the deposition notice in the expectation that the deponent's testimony would be taken . . . ."[11]

In the *Rosen* case,[12] for instance, the plaintiff in a California lawsuit noticed a nonparty's deposition in New York City, but did not bother subpoenaing the deponent. Defense counsel traveled to New York for the deposition, only to learn upon his arrival that the deponent had insisted on a postponement of several days. The California trial court ordered the plaintiff to pay the expenses incurred by the opposition's attorney in connection with the aborted deposition.[13]

—Uniform Foreign Deposition Act: To facilitate the deposing of their residents in cases pending elsewhere, many states, including California, have adopted the Uniform Foreign Deposition Act. The California version of this Act provides:

> Whenever any mandate, writ, letters rogatory, letter of request, or commission is issued out of any court of record in any other state, territory, or district of the United States, or in a foreign nation, or whenever, on notice or agreement, it is required to take the oral or written deposition of a natural person in California, the deponent may be compelled to appear and testify, and to produce documents and things, in the same manner, and by the same process as may be employed for the purpose of taking testimony in actions pending in California.[14]

Although this statute has no application to cases pending in California, its equivalent is likely to be in effect in the jurisdiction where a nonparty deponent resides.[15] Attorneys should consult the Law Digests volume of the Martindale-Hubbell Law Directory under the heading "Depositions" to find out whether the state where the deponent resides has adopted the Uniform Act or any cognate statute.

Commission: Section 2026.010 requires one who wishes to depose a nonparty in another state to "use any process and procedures required and available under [that state's] laws" to compel the deponent's attendance.[16] If the state or territory has adopted the Uniform Foreign Deposition Act or its equivalent, its courts

---

[11] CCP § 2025.440(a).

[12] Rosen v Superior Court (1966) 244 Cal App 2d 586, 53 Cal Rptr 347.

[13] For a discussion of procedures when a deponent fails to attend a deposition, see § 2.20.

[14] CCP § 2029.010.

See, e.g., Warford v Medeiros (1984) 160 Cal App 3d 1035, 1038–1041, 207 Cal Rptr 94.

[15] See generally Mullin, Interstate Deposition Statutes: Survey and Analysis (1981) 11 U Baltimore L Rev 1 [comprehensive coverage].

[16] CCP § 2026.010(c).

should issue a subpoena for the deponent's attendance simply upon a showing that a party in a California case has noticed the deposition. Some states, however, may condition the issuance of a subpoena upon proof that the court where the case is pending has issued a commission for the deposition. [17] Although California never *requires* a commission for an out-of-state deposition, Section 2026.010 authorizes the issuance of one when "necessary or convenient." [18] This would cover those states that still insist on a commission before they will compel one of their residents to submit to a deposition in a case pending elsewhere.

California Discovery Provisions Apply: Although a deposition in a California case is being taken in another state, the parties themselves remain subject to California discovery law. In the *International Insurance* case, [19] a litigant in a California lawsuit scheduled the deposition of a nonparty in Connecticut. Before the deposition, that party had shown some of its documents to the deponent to refresh his recollection. During the deposition, the other party demanded to see these documents. Connecticut law requires application to the court to inspect documents shown to a witness. California law, in contrast, confers an immediate right to inspect the documents used to refresh the deponent's memory. [20] The California court ruled that California law applied:

> [E]xcept as expressly provided otherwise in the Discovery Act, California law governs discovery in California cases, including depositions. See [former] § 2025. Thus, although [former] section 2026 compelled [plaintiff] to follow Connecticut law in noticing [the deponent's] deposition, California law governs [its] request to [defendant] for the documents used by [the deponent] to refresh his recollection. [21]

§ 4.3 Discovery in Another Nation: From a Party

The great expansion of international trade and travel over the last 60 years has produced an increasing number of lawsuits in California between American citizens and foreign nationals. Sometimes, the foreign nationals are plaintiffs. In most cases, however, they are defendants that have become subject to the jurisdiction of the California court system because of their contacts with this state.

Potential Issues: In a California lawsuit that involves a foreign national as a party questions often arise about the applicability of this state's discovery procedures to that party. [1] For example, must the foreign national or its employees

---

[17] A discovery "commission" is the forum court's authorization of a designated individual to take a named witness's deposition. See Volkswagenwerk A.G. v Superior Court (1973) 33 Cal App 3d 503, 506, 109 Cal Rptr 219, 221.

[18] CCP § 2026.010(d).

[19] International Ins. Co. v Montrose Chemical Corp. (1991) 231 Cal App 3d 1367, 282 Cal Rptr 783.

[20] Evid Code § 771.

[21] International Ins. Co. v Montrose Chemical Corp. (1991) 231 Cal App 3d 1367, 1371, 282 Cal Rptr 783, 785.

[1] See generally, Smalley, How to Conduct International Discovery (1999) 71 Am Jur Trials 1-110.

submit, like any other litigant,[2] to a deposition in California? Does a deposition notice suffice to compel a foreign party or its employees to submit to depositions in their home country?[3] Must a foreign party answer interrogatories[4] or admission requests[5] when the necessary information is in another nation? Must a foreign national comply with an inspection demand by producing in California documents or things that are in the foreign land?[6] Must a foreign national submit to an inspection of its factories or buildings in another country?[7]

Pre-1987 California Case Law: The original Discovery Act had no specific provisions governing procedures for obtaining discovery from foreign national parties. Thus, the Act left it to the courts to adjust those procedures as required.

—Volkswagenwerk I: The first case to consider the applicability of California discovery procedures to foreign national parties was *Volkswagenwerk I*.[8] There, the plaintiff in a product liability case sought to depose in Germany seven officials and employees of the German defendant. The plaintiff also sought to inspect its manufacturing plant. Defendant Volkswagen convinced the California appellate court that Germany would regard the deposition, even from a party to the case, as an encroachment on its judicial sovereignty:

> [C]ommon law nations regard the deposition of a willing witness as a private, relatively informal matter in which their courts have no interest. A different view is taken by civil law nations such as Germany. There, a deposition in aid of a foreign proceeding is a public matter, requiring the participation and consent of their own courts; the activity of a commissioner appointed abroad represents an intrusion upon the "judicial sovereignty" of such a nation; thus a letter rogatory is the usual and accepted method of taking depositions in a civil law nation.[9]

The court declared it to be California's policy to avoid "international discovery methods that cause friction with the procedures of host nations."[10] It even stated: "International discovery activities under California law may be conducted only

---

[2] For a discussion of the permissible California locations for the deposition of a party or a party-affiliated deponent, see §§ 2.13–2.14.

[3] For a discussion of the obligation of a defendant to produce for a deposition its officers and employees, see § 2.12.

[4] For general coverage of interrogatories, see Chapter 5.

[5] For general coverage of admission requests, see Chapter 9.

[6] For general coverage of inspection demands, see Chapter 6.

[7] For a discussion of demands to inspect property or the activities conducted on it, see § 6.9.

[8] Volkswagenwerk A.G. v Superior Court (1973) 33 Cal App 3d 503, 109 Cal Rptr 219.

[9] Volkswagenwerk A.G. v Superior Court (1973) 33 Cal App 3d 503, 507, 109 Cal Rptr 219, 221.

See also Comment, Obtaining Testimony Outside the United States: Problem for the California Practitioner (1978) 29 Hastings LJ 1237, 1243–1244.

[10] Volkswagenwerk A.G. v Superior Court (1973) 33 Cal App 3d 503, 508, 109 Cal Rptr 219, 222.

within channels and procedures established by the host nation."[11] In its view, since German law required letters rogatory,[12] it was irrelevant that California did not: "Whatever the generous provisions of the California discovery statutes, courts ordering discovery abroad must conform to the channels and procedures established by the host nation."[13]

The court warned, however, that while California litigants may have to give up the simplicity of its discovery procedures to conduct discovery in another nation, a foreign party may not use this additional red tape to frustrate permissible discovery altogether: "Should a foreign-based litigant . . . hide behind diplomatic walls, the California courts may deal with that situation when it appears."[14]

—*Volkswagenwerk II:* Seven years later, in another case involving the same German auto manufacturer,[15] a California court reexamined the impact that another nation's restrictive laws should have upon discovery otherwise permissible under California law. Unlike the previous case, this court did not agree that a foreign party could object to any particular mode of discovery simply by showing that its procedures were frowned upon under the law of its sovereign:

> That VWAG should have been chartered by, and should maintain its manufacturing facility in, a jurisdiction which would regard these California discovery orders as violations of its sovereignty seems happenstance so far as the California action is concerned: A strong argument can be made that as a legitimate party to a California action VWAG may be required to elect between the demands of the California court and the sensitivities of the . . . German government, and to risk the sanctions authorized by California law should it elect not to give the required discovery.[16]

Nevertheless, in deference to international comity, the court ruled that a California trial court must initially structure its discovery orders to accommodate the foreign state's notion of its sovereignty in any way that is consistent with their efficacy. An order that does not make this accommodation is improper, though it would otherwise be proper under California law.[17] For example, where

---

[11] Volkswagenwerk A.G. v Superior Court (1973) 33 Cal App 3d 503, 507, 109 Cal Rptr 219, 221.

[12] A letter rogatory is a judicial request addressed to a foreign court that a witness be examined within its territorial limits.

[13] Volkswagenwerk A.G. v Superior Court (1973) 33 Cal App 3d 503, 508, 109 Cal Rptr 219, 222.

[14] Volkswagenwerk A.G. v Superior Court (1973) 33 Cal App 3d 503, 508, 109 Cal Rptr 219, 222.

[15] Volkswagenwerk A.G. v Superior Court (1981) 123 Cal App 3d 840, 176 Cal Rptr 874.

[16] Volkswagenwerk A.G. v Superior Court (1981) 123 Cal App 3d 840, 857, 176 Cal Rptr 874, 884.

[17] Volkswagenwerk A.G. v Superior Court (1981) 123 Cal App 3d 840, 859, 176 Cal Rptr 874, 885.

the foreign sovereign has signed the Hague Convention, the California trial courts should follow its procedures in the first instance.[18]

The *Pierburg* case[19] extended the principle of "first use" of the Hague Convention to a case involving interrogatories. There, a plaintiff propounded interrogatories to a German corporate defendant, a form of discovery that normally operates extrajudicially.[20] The appellate court, however, ordered the trial court to follow the Convention by submitting a "letter of request" to West German judicial authorities.

Discovery Act of 1986: Initially, the California Discovery Commission recommended codification of the state's case law requiring "first use" of the Hague Convention, in accord with *Volkswagenwerk II* and *Pierburg*.[21] This recommendation comported with the Commission's practice of identifying and codifying discovery issues that California case law had settled. The Commission later withdrew its proposal, however, to await the outcome of the then-pending *Aerospatiale* case.

Aerospatiale: In 1987, the United States Supreme Court addressed the Hague Convention's interaction with the more liberal federal discovery procedures otherwise available against a party. The *Aerospatiale* case[22] was a product liability action that arose from the crash of a private plane. Following the federal rules, the plaintiff propounded interrogatories, inspection requests and admission requests to the defendant French manufacturer. This defendant objected that "the Hague Convention dictated the exclusive procedures that must be followed for pretrial discovery."[23]

—Bright-Line Solutions Rejected: The Court rejected three approaches to the applicability of the Hague Convention, each of which had offered simplicity: (1) the Convention preempts the discovery provisions of the Federal Rules; (2) the Convention has no role to play where discovery is sought from a foreign national that is a party to the lawsuit; and (3) the courts must "first use" the Convention procedures before resorting to their own discovery procedures.

—Individualized Analysis: Instead of any of these categorical approaches, the Court directed federal trial judges to examine, case by case, three factors:

---

[18] Comment, The Hague Convention on the Taking of Evidence Abroad in Civil or Commercial Matters: The Exclusive and Mandatory Procedures for Discovery Abroad (1984) 132 U Pa L Rev 1461.

[19] Pierburg GmbH & Co. KG v Superior Court (1982) 137 Cal App 3d 238, 247, 186 Cal Rptr 876, 882.

[20] For a discussion of the extrajudicial operation of interrogatories, see § 5.2.

[21] Proposed Civil Discovery Act of 1986, Section 2022, Appendix D.

[22] Societe Nationale Industrielle Aerospatiale v United States Dist. Court for Southern Dist. (1987) 482 US 522, 96 L Ed 2d 461, 107 S Ct 2542.

See Note, Discovery in France and the Hague Convention: The Search for a French Connection (1989) 64 NYU LR 1073.

[23] Societe Nationale Industrielle Aerospatiale v United States Dist. Court for Southern Dist. (1987) 482 US 522, 526, 96 L Ed 2d 461, 461, 107 S Ct 2542, 2553.

(1) the particular facts of the lawsuit; (2) the respective interests of the United States and the other sovereign; and (3) the likelihood that Convention procedures will provide effective discovery.[24]

The Court gave some direction for carrying out this three-sided analysis. On the one hand, it saw no need to even consider the Convention procedures for interrogatories or admission requests.[25] On the other hand, the analysis is appropriate where a party seeks discovery by more intrusive methods, such as inspection demands or depositions: "The foreign litigant should be afforded a full and fair opportunity to demonstrate appropriate reasons for employing Convention procedures in the first instance, for some aspects of the discovery process."[26]

However, the foreign party now must move for a protective order directing that the party seeking discovery comply with the Convention's procedures. The foreign party must show why these should prevail over the Federal Rules.[27] For example, the foreign party might show that "the additional cost of transportation of documents or witnesses to or from foreign locations may increase the danger that discovery may be sought for the improper purpose of motivating a settlement, rather than finding relevant and probative evidence."[28] Most federal courts applying the three-step analysis of *Aerospatiale* have concluded that resort to the Hague Convention was not appropriate.[29]

In the *American Home Insurance* case,[30] the court concluded that *Aerospatiale* had superseded the "First resort to the Hague Convention" rule of

[24] Societe Nationale Industrielle Aerospatiale v United States Dist. Court for Southern Dist. (1987) 482 US 522, 544, 96 L Ed 2d 461, 484, 107 S Ct 2542, 2555–2556.

[25] Societe Nationale Industrielle Aerospatiale v United States Dist. Court for Southern Dist. (1987) 482 US 522, 545–546, 96 L Ed 2d 461, 485–486, 107 S Ct 2542, 2556.

[26] Societe Nationale Industrielle Aerospatiale v United States Dist. Court for Southern Dist. (1987) 482 US 522, 546–547, 96 L Ed 2d 461, 485–486, 107 S Ct 2542, 2557.

See Comment, Five Years After *Aerospatiale*: Rethinking Discovery Abroad in Civil and Commercial Litigation under the Hague Convention and the Federal Rules of Civil Procedure (1992) 13 U Pa J Intl Bus L 425.

[27] Societe Nationale Industrielle Aerospatiale v United States Dist. Court for Southern Dist. (1987) 482 US 522, 546–547, 96 L Ed 2d 461, 485–486, 107 S Ct 2542, 2557.

[28] Societe Nationale Industrielle Aerospatiale v United States Dist. Court for Southern Dist. (1987) 482 US 522, 546–547, 96 L Ed 2d 461, 485–486, 107 S Ct 2542, 2557.

[29] In re Perrier Bottled Water Litigation (1991, D Conn) 138 FRD 348, 353–354 [requiring Convention procedures although noting that most trial courts have ruled differently].

See, e.g., Doster v Schenk (1991, MD NC) 141 FRD 50, 52–55 [after extensive analysis, finding Convention procedures inappropriate]; Rich v KIS California, Inc. (1988, MD NC) 121 FRD 254, 258–260 [Convention procedures are inappropriate where party sought answers to 10 interrogatories relevant to jurisdictional issues]; Benton Graphics v Uddeholm Corp. (1987, D NJ) 118 FRD 386, 390–392 [finding Convention procedures inappropriate]. But see Hudson v Herman Pfauter GmbH & Co. (1987, ND NY) 117 FRD 33, 35–40 [in a questionable analysis, finding Convention procedures appropriate].

[30] American Home Assurance Co. v Societe Commerciale Toutelectric (2002) 104 Cal App 406, 421–427, 128 Cal Rptr 2d 430, 442–447.

Volkswagenwerk II and *Pierburg*. That court also held that the party invoking the Hague Convention must persuade the trial court that considerations of comity make the Convention's more cumbersome procedures applicable.[31] In addition, it ruled that a party, by not timely invoking the Convention, waives those procedures, even though they might otherwise have been appropriate.[32]

§ 4.4 From a Nonparty

Depositions in Foreign Lands Authorized: Given the globalization of trade and commerce, an attorney preparing a California case for trial may well want to depose a nonparty who is physically located in another nation.[1] The Discovery Act authorizes parties to civil cases to try to obtain such depositions and contains provisions that aim to facilitate their taking. Section 2027.010 provides: "Any party may obtain discovery by taking an oral deposition, as described in Section 2025.010, in a foreign nation."[2] By its incorporation of Section 2027.010, Section 2028.010 permits written depositions in foreign nations.[3]

To facilitate the taking of nonparty depositions in foreign nations, Section 2027.010 authorizes the trial court to "issue a commission, letters rogatory, or a letter of request, if it determines that one is necessary or convenient."[4] A "discovery commission"[5] or "letters rogatory"[6] are devices that another nation may require to enlist the aid of its court system in compelling a deponent's attendance. A "letter of request" is the method contained in the Hague Convention.[7] In addition, Section 2027.010 requires the party proposing to take the deposition to "use any process and procedures required and available under the laws of the foreign nation where the deposition is to be taken" to secure the deponent's attendance.[8]

---

[31] American Home Assurance Co. v Societe Commerciale Toutelectric (2002) 104 Cal App 406, 427, 128 Cal Rptr 2d 430, 447.

[32] American Home Assurance Co. v Societe Commerciale Toutelectric (2002) 104 Cal App 406, 427–430, 128 Cal Rptr 2d 430, 447–449.

[1] See generally, Smalley, How to Conduct International Discovery (1999) 71 Am Jur Trials 1-110.

[2] CCP § 2027.010(a).

[3] CCP § 2027.010. For coverage of written depositions, see Chapter 3.

[4] CCP § 2027.010(e).

[5] A discovery "commission" is the forum court's authorization of a designated individual to take a named witness's deposition. See Volkswagenwerk A.G. v Superior Court (1973) 33 Cal App 3d 503, 506, 109 Cal Rptr 219, 221.

[6] "Letters rogatory" are a formal communication from the forum court to a court in another state or nation requesting that the testimony of a witness residing in that state or nation be taken under the direction of the court addressed, and then transmitted to the requesting court. See Volkswagenwerk A.G. v Superior Court (1973) 33 Cal App 3d 503, 506–507, 109 Cal Rptr 219, 221.

[7] The Hague Convention on the Taking of Evidence Abroad in Civil or Commercial Matters.

[8] CCP § 2027.010(c).

Attitude of the Host Nation: The attitude of the country where the deposition will occur toward the taking of depositions within its borders is crucial. This nation may restrict or even prohibit the taking of testimony on its soil. An attorney contemplating a deposition in a foreign land in connection with a California case should consider at least 10 factors that might impact the undertaking:

(1) Does the host nation permit depositions at all? In this type of lawsuit? For discovery?

(2) Is the host nation a common law or a civil law country?

(3) Does counsel seek discovery from an American citizen or from a foreign national?

(4) Will the witness appear for the deposition voluntarily, or must counsel use some form of compulsory process to secure the deponent's attendance?

(5) Does the witness speak English?

(6) Does the host nation permit a deposition to be taken on the basis of a mere notice, or must counsel have a court issue a commission, letters rogatory or a letter of request?

(7) Will the host nation require retention of local counsel?

(8) Does the host nation's procedure for interrogating a deponent depart so much from California's procedure that the deposition testimony will be inadmissible at trial?

(9) Does counsel seek to inspect documents in addition to obtaining the witness's testimony?

(10) Has the host nation signed[9] the Hague Convention?[10] Since a California court has no jurisdiction at all over a nonparty foreign national, resort to the Convention's procedures are probably necessary whenever the deposition is to occur in a country that is a signatory of the Convention.[11]

---

[9] As of 2005, the ratifying countries are Anguilla, Argentina (excludes recognition of the extension of the Convention by the United Kingdom to the Malvinas, South Georgia and South Sandwich Islands), Aruba, Australia, Barbados, Bulgaria, Cayman Islands, China, Cyprus, Czech Republic, Denmark, Djibouti, Estonia, Falkland Islands, Finland, France, French Guiana, French Polynesia, Germany, Gibraltar, Guadeloupe, Guernsey, Hong Kong SAR, Isle of Man, Israel, Italy, Jersey, Latvia, Luxembourg, Macao SAR, Martinique, Mexico, Monaco, Netherlands, Norway, Poland, Portugal, Saint Pierre and Miquelon, Singapore, Slovak Republic, Sovereign Base Areas of Akrotiri and Dhekelia, Spain, Sweden, Switzerland, United Kingdom, United States, and Venezuela. However, the signatories are often in flux as countries change.

[10] The Hague Convention on the Taking of Evidence Abroad in Civil or Commercial Matters. See Comment, Obtaining Testimony Outside the United States: Problem for the California Practitioner (1978) 29 Hastings LJ 1237, 1251–1255; Note, Discovery in France and the Hague Convention: The Search for a French Connection (1989) 64 NYU LR 1073.

[11] Cf. Jenco v Martech Intern., Inc. (1988, ED La) 1988 US Dist LExis 4727, 1 [upholding magistrate's order that depositions of *nonparty* foreign nationals should proceed under Hague Convention, while depositions of foreign national *parties* could proceed under federal rules].

State Department Help: With the above factors in mind, a California attorney who wants to take a nonparty's deposition in a foreign land should contact the United States Department of State, Bureau of Consular Affairs. The Bureau's Office of Overseas Citizens Services is staffed by personnel who are experts about the deposition procedures of the nations in their assigned areas. At present, the Office of Overseas Citizens Services has five divisions: the Africa Division, the East Asia and Pacific Division, the Europe and Canada Division, the Latin America Division, and the Near East and South Asia Division. These staff officers can inform counsel of the host nations' procedures. The two major factors that will affect the procedures for a deposition in a foreign land are whether the deponents are willing or reluctant witnesses, and whether they are United States citizens or citizens of some other nation.

CHAPTER 5

INTERROGATORIES TO A PARTY

SYNOPSIS

§ 5.1   General Nature and Function

Akin to a Coerced Affidavit: Section 2030.010 authorizes a litigant to obtain discovery by submitting a series of written questions, called "interrogatories,"[1] to another party to the action: "Any party may obtain discovery . . . . by propounding to any other party to the action written interrogatories to be answered

---

[1] For a discussion of the infrequently used and substantially different "written deposition," see Chapter 3.

under oath."[2] In effect, this enables the propounding party to select the topics for an affidavit, and then compel the responding party to supply the specifics of those topics under oath.[3]

Advantages: There are five substantial advantages to using interrogatories for discovery. First, for certain types of data, interrogatories are superior to depositions for obtaining the desired information. During a deposition parties are not likely to remember all relevant names, dates and details spanning relatively long periods. In contrast, interrogatories give responding parties time to search their memory and records for the desired information. Consequently, a party is far less likely to give "I don't remember" answers to interrogatories than to deposition questions.

Second, interrogatories search the collective knowledge of the responding parties, their attorneys[4] and their insurance carriers;[5] deposition questions probe only for facts of which a responding party has personal knowledge. Furthermore, interrogatories oblige the recipients to reasonably investigate other sources that may contain the information needed for an adequate response.[6] This obligation can be quite important if the responding party is a corporation or other institutional entity.[7] Again, an "I don't know" answer is less likely to be a legitimate response to an interrogatory than to a deposition question.

Third, interrogatories are especially valuable to break the trail for other methods of discovery. Litigants can use them to learn which facts are not controversial and which facts need exploration in a deposition.[8] They are also useful for learning the identity and location of knowledgeable persons, who then become candidates for a deposition. Interrogatories commonly precede inspection demands,[9] since they enable the propounding party to learn the existence, location and custodian of books, records, tangible things and places.[10] Often, the answers obtained via interrogatories will enable a party to compose admission requests.[11]

---

[2] CCP § 2030.010(a).

[3] Estate of Horman (1968) 265 Cal App 2d 796, 805, 71 Cal Rptr 780, 786.

[4] Smith v Superior Court (1961) 189 Cal App 2d 6, 12, 11 Cal Rptr 165, 169.

[5] Unger v Los Angeles Transit Lines (1960) 180 Cal App 2d 172, 175, 4 Cal Rptr 370, 372–373.

[6] For a discussion of the responding party's duty to consult outside sources in order to answer an interrogatory, see § 5.16.

[7] For a discussion of the procedure for taking the deposition of a corporation or other institutional entity, see §§ 2.5, 2.9, 2.12 and 2.14.

[8] For coverage of oral depositions, see Chapter 2.

[9] See, e.g., Smith v Superior Court (1961) 189 Cal App 2d 6, 12, 11 Cal Rptr 165, 169.
For coverage of inspection demands, see Chapter 6.

[10] Strictly speaking, a party may not use interrogatories to secure the production of documents themselves. There is, however, no harm in inviting opponents to attach a copy of those documents to their response. See, e.g., Hernandez v Superior Court (2003) 112 Cal App 4th 285, 293, 4 Cal Rptr 3d 883, 890. Cf. Gene Compton's Corp. v Superior Court (1962) 205 Cal App 2d 365, 367, 23 Cal Rptr 250, 252.

[11] For coverage of admission requests, see Chapter 9.

These in turn may obviate proof at trial or shift to an adversary the expenses of such proof.

Fourth, in an interrogatory, a party may ask whether an opponent is making certain legal contentions, and the factual bases for them,[12] a type of question that is objectionable during a deposition.[13] Thus, contention interrogatories shift from the pleadings stage to the discovery stage the particularization of an opponent's claims and defenses. In this way they reduce the need for special demurrers on the ground of uncertainty.

Finally, interrogatories are economical. The only out-of-pocket expenditure incurred in propounding them is usually the cost of a postage stamp.[14]

Disadvantages: Although interrogatories have many advantages, they have three principal shortcomings. First, unlike depositions, interrogatories are available only against a party to the action.[15] Second, the answers obtained differ greatly from the spontaneous replies secured during a deposition. Indeed, the responding party's attorney usually ghostwrites the answers for the client's adoption.[16] A set of answers slanted towards the responding side's position inevitably results. Finally, it is cumbersome and time-consuming to explore by subsequent interrogatories the avenues of inquiry suggested by the initial answers.

Focus of Chapter: This chapter focuses on topics peculiar to the *mechanics* of interrogatories. Other chapters discuss matters and issues common to the entire discovery process. Thus, the reader should refer to the appropriate chapters of this treatise when, during the use of this discovery device, an issue arises concerning the *relevancy* of a particular line of inquiry,[17] the validity of a claim of *privilege*[18] or the discoverability of an adversary's *"work product"* materials.[19]

§ 5.2 Initiation and Cutoff

Extrajudicial Operation: Discovery via interrogatories operates extrajudicially. Thus, a party normally[1] need not seek court authorization to use this tool.[2]

—Initiation by Plaintiffs: Plaintiffs must wait until 10 days after a particular defendant either has been served or has appeared before propounding

---

[12] For a discussion of the propriety of contention interrogatories, see §§ 5.8–5.13.

[13] Rifkind v Superior Court (1994) 22 Cal App 4th 1255, 27 Cal Rptr 822.

[14] See Ellison v Runyan (1993, SD Ind) 147 FRD 186, 189 n4.

[15] For a discussion of those to whom interrogatories may be directed, see §§ 5.4–5.5.

[16] Cf. Greyhound Corp. v Superior Court (1961) 56 Cal 2d 355, 392 n16, 15 Cal Rptr 90, 109–110 n16, 364 P2d 266, 285–286 n16.

[17] See Chapter 11.

[18] See Chapter 12.

[19] See Chapter 13.

[1] For a discussion of the need for court permission to propound interrogatories to unnamed members in a class action, see § 5.5.

[2] See Coy v Superior Court (1962) 58 Cal 2d 210, 220, 23 Cal Rptr 393, 398, 373 P2d 457, 462.

interrogatories to that party. Section 2030.020 implicitly prohibits the propounding of interrogatories to defendants who have neither received service nor appeared:

> A plaintiff may propound interrogatories to a party . . . . at any time that is 10 days after the service of the summons on, ... or appearance by, *that* party, whichever occurs first. [3]

However, where a suit names several defendants, a plaintiff need not wait until the court acquires jurisdiction over all of them before propounding interrogatories to those already served or appearing in the case. [4] Moreover, a plaintiff remains a "party," entitled to propound interrogatories, even after the court has sustained a demurrer to the complaint if it has granted leave to amend. [5]

—**Initiation by Defendants:** Unlike plaintiffs, defendants need not wait before propounding interrogatories. They may serve them "at any time." [6] Therefore, a defendant who acts promptly during the 10 days immediately after service of process can get a head start in the use of this discovery device. [7] However, a defendant who intends to challenge the court's personal jurisdiction should limit any interrogatories to matters that bear on jurisdiction. [8] The service of interrogatories dealing with matters that go to the merits of the case may constitute a general appearance. [9] Moreover, an unserved defendant who answers interrogatories addressed to it thereby makes a general appearance in the lawsuit:

> The act of filing and serving [answers to interrogatories] is evidently predicated on the assumption that the court has jurisdiction over the answering party—otherwise, there would be no need for the answers. [T]he only hypothesis upon which answers to interrogatories are

---

[3] CCP § 2030.020(b) (italics added).

A plaintiff, however, may apply for leave of court to serve interrogatories earlier. CCP § 2030.020(c).

Annotation: Time for filing and serving discovery interrogatories. 74 ALR2d 534.

[4] Cf. Waters v Superior Court (1962) 58 Cal 2d 885, 891–892, 27 Cal Rptr 153, 156, 377 P2d 265, 268.

For a discussion of the right to initiate deposition discovery without waiting until all defendants have been served, see § 2.2.

[5] See Budget Finance Plan v Superior Court (1973) 34 Cal App 3d 794, 797–798, 110 Cal Rptr 302.

[6] CCP § 2030.020(a). See Putnam v Clague (1992) 3 Cal App 4th 542, 565, 5 Cal Rptr 2d 25, 39–40.

[7] For a discussion of "priority" in conducting discovery, see § 2.3.

[8] See 1880 Corp.v Superior Court (1962) 57 Cal 2d 840, 842–843, 22 Cal Rptr 209, 210–211, 371 P2d 985, 986–987; Islamic Republic of Iran v Pahlavi (1984) 160 Cal App 3d 620, 628, 206 Cal Rptr 752, 756–757.

[9] Cf. Creed v Schultz (1983) 148 Cal App 3d 733, 739–740, 196 Cal Rptr 252, 256 [serving notice of deposition constitutes a general appearance].

prepared, filed and served is that the answering party is subject to the court's jurisdiction.[10]

Discovery Cutoff: Discovery as a matter of right must be "completed" 30 days "before the date initially set for trial of the action."[11]

In limiting discovery in some circumstances by reference to the date initially set for trial, the Legislature is doubtless aware of the possibilities for abuse and for interference with the orderly preparation for trial, if a party is freely permitted to recommence discovery after every delay in trial, however trivial.[12]

Arguably, discovery by interrogatories is "completed" not when a party *serves* the questions but when the answers *are due*. A federal court interpreted a court-ordered discovery cutoff date in this way:

Common sense dictates that any request for discovery must be made in sufficient time to allow the opposing party to respond before the termination of discovery. . . . . When the court sets a date for the termination of discovery, the parties should heed the logical import of such a deadline: the parties should complete discovery on or before that date and will not receive the benefit of court supervision of discovery which is to occur after that date.[13]

Since the responding party has 30 days to answer interrogatories,[14] the propounding party should serve them by the 60th day before the initial trial date.[15] A party using the mails to serve them should post them by the 65th day before that trial date.[16]

Discovery Reopened: In the *Fairmont Ins. Co.* case,[17] the Supreme Court considered the meaning of the phrase "date initially set for the trial of the action" in situations where there has been a mistrial, an order granting a new trial, or

---

[10] Chitwood v County of Los Angeles (1971) 14 Cal App 3d 522, 528, 92 Cal Rptr 441, 445.

Under the 1993 amendments to the Federal Rules of Civil Procedure, discovery via interrogatories continues to operate extrajudicially. Fed Rules Civ Proc, Rule 33(a). However, without obtaining leave of court, no party may propound interrogatories (or engage in any other form of discovery) until the parties have met and conferred to develop a proposed discovery plan. Fed Rules Civ Proc, Rule 26(d) and (f).

[11] CCP § 2024.020(a).

[12] Roe v Superior Court (1990) 224 Cal App 3d 642, 646, 273 Cal Rptr 745, 747.

[13] Northern Indiana Public Service Co. v Colorado Westmoreland, Inc. (1986, ND Ind) 112 FRD 423, 424.

[14] CCP § 2030.260(a).

[15] Cf. Beller v Credit Alliance Corp. (1985, ND Ga) 106 FRD 557, 560 [where local rule requires discovery to be "completed" within a four-month period, interrogatories must be served by the end of the third month, "thereby allowing the opposing party its full thirty days to respond"].

[16] CCP § 2016.050, referencing CCP § 1013(a).

[17] Fairmont Ins. Co. v Superior Court (2000) 22 Cal 4th 245, 92 Cal Rptr 2d 70, 991 P2d 156.

a remand for a new trial after reversal of a judgment on appeal. It held that in such cases discovery is reopened and the cutoff date is calculated based on the date initially set for the *new* trial.

§ 5.3 Mechanics of Preparation, Service and Filing

Format: Interrogatories must begin by identifying the party who is propounding them and the party who is to respond to them.[1] Each set must be numbered consecutively.[2] A set of interrogatories may not include a preface or special instructions for answering,[3] unless it is one contained in the Judicial Council's Official Forms.[4] A propounding party may specially define a term that is to be repeated several times in a set of interrogatories. However, each time that term thereafter appears in any individual interrogatory, it must be printed in capital letters to remind the other party of that special definition.[5] Each interrogatory in a set must bear its own identifying number or letter.[6]

—Interspersed Requests for Admissions Prohibited: Under the original Discovery Act attorneys often interspersed admission requests with interrogatories.[7] The responding party was to answer any individual interrogatory only if unwilling to make the corresponding admission.[8] Section 2033.060 now prohibits the mixing of other discovery methods with admission requests: "No party shall combine in a single document requests for admission with any other method of discovery."[9] Therefore, a party propounding an interrogatory no longer may precede it with a related admission request and an instruction not to answer it if that admission is made.

Text: Each interrogatory must be so composed that it is "full and complete"[10] by itself. For example, a single interrogatory that asks "which of the answers given during an eight-day deposition the responding party considers to be untrue" is not "full and complete in and of itself" because resort to the deposition would be necessary to know what the interrogatory meant.[11] If the interrogatory is "specially prepared,"[12] as opposed to a Judicial Council Official Form

---

[1] CCP § 2030.060(b).

[2] CCP § 2030.060(a).

[3] CCP § 2030.060(d).

[4] CCP §§ 2030.060(d) and 2033.710.

[5] CCP § 2030.060(e).

[6] CCP § 2030.060(c).

[7] See, e.g., Enfantino v Superior Court (1984) 162 Cal App 3d 1110, 1112, 208 Cal Rptr 829, 830.

[8] Cf. Imwinkelried and Blumoff, Pretrial Discovery—Strategy and Tactics § 11.02 (2004) [discussing the former practice].

[9] CCP § 2033.060(h). For further discussion of the prohibition of combining admission requests with interrogatories in the same document, see § 9.3.

[10] CCP § 2030.060(d).

[11] Catanese v Superior Court (1996) 46 Cal App 4th 1159, 1164, 54 Cal Rptr 2d 280, 283.

[12] See CCP § 2030.030(a)(1).

Interrogatory, it may not contain subparts. Nor may it contain compound, conjunctive or disjunctive wording.[13] These restrictions prevent evasion of the statutory limit on the number of interrogatories that one party may propound to another.[14]

Judicial Council Form Interrogatories: As indicated above, the Legislature directed the Judicial Council to prepare "official" form interrogatories suitable for use in personal injury, wrongful death, breach of contract and any other civil actions it deems appropriate.[15] The Judicial Council has carried out this mandate by producing thoughtful, comprehensive and well-worded interrogatories for various types of cases. The use of these form interrogatories is optional, thus leaving counsel free to use different or additional interrogatories appropriate to a particular case.

Service: The party sending interrogatories must, of course, serve a copy of them on the responding party.[16] That propounding party must also serve an informational copy of them on all other parties who have appeared in the action.[17] If these other parties are many and the interrogatories deal with matters of no immediate concern to them, the propounding party may apply to the court for relief from this requirement.[18]

Custody: The party propounding a set of interrogatories does not file the original with the court. Instead, that party must preserve it, with original proof of service attached, until six months after the case is over.[19]

§ 5.4 Proper Recipients of Interrogatories

Permitted Only Against a Party: Although depositions and interrogatories differ in several ways,[1] the most significant one is that counsel may use depositions to obtain information from third persons as well as from parties. In contrast, counsel may only use written interrogatories against a party to the case: "Any party may obtain discovery . . . . by propounding *to any other party to the action* written interrogatories . . . ."[2]

---

[13] CCP § 2030.060(f).

[14] For a discussion of the presumptive numerical limit on the number of interrogatories, see § 5.6.

[15] CCP § 2033.710.

[16] CCP § 2030.080(a).

[17] CCP § 2030.080(b).

[18] CCP § 2030.080(b). Compare CCP § 2033.070 [containing no provision for relieving a party from the requirement of serving informational copies of admission requests]. See § 9.3.

[19] CCP § 2030.280(b). For a discussion of custody of the original of the response to interrogatories, see § 5.15.

[1] For a discussion contrasting these two discovery devices, see § 5.1.

[2] CCP § 2030.010(a) (italics added). See Ellison v Runyan (1993, SD Ind) 147 FRD 186 [although corporation was a party to suit on date interrogatories were propounded, it is not required to answer them once it has been dismissed from the case]. For a discussion of whether interrogatories may be propounded to unnamed members in a class action, see § 5.5.

Although the attorney for the responding party usually drafts the answers to interrogatories, it is technically improper to address them to that attorney,[3] or to phrase any particular interrogatory so that it asks a party for information "known to you *or your attorneys.*"[4]

Institutional Parties: Since a corporation, partnership, association, or governmental agency may be a "party" to a lawsuit, interrogatories may, of course, be propounded to such institutional parties.[5] Interrogatories have been served on such governmental entities as the Regents of the University of California,[6] the State Bar,[7] the Division of Industrial Safety,[8] a public utility district,[9] a flood control district,[10] and a city or county.[11] Although interrogatories to an institutional defendant must be answered by some agent for that entity,[12] the propounding party may not direct which agent shall provide the response:

> Interrogatories, like requests for admission, are addressed to the adverse party, not to his witnesses. Their proper use is not in substitution of the right to obtain information by deposition. It shocks one's sense of fairness to affirm a proposition that an opponent should have the right to select the representative of a corporate, partnership, or association adversary to give answers which will not only bind such adversary but, also, under some circumstances, subject it to serious sanctions. And it is to accuse the legislature of rank discrimination to contend that it intended so to penalize partnerships, associations and corporations, including public entities, in favor of individual parties.[13]

Parties Need Not be Adverse: Section 2030.010 authorizes the propounding of interrogatories to "any other" party in the lawsuit.[14] This wording carries over

---

[3] See Steelman v United States Fidelity & Guaranty Co. (1964, WD Mo) 35 FRD 120. See also Hickman v Taylor (1947) 329 US 495, 504, 91 L Ed 451, 458, 67 S Ct 385, 390.

[4] Smith v Superior Court (1961) 189 Cal App 2d 6, 11–12, 11 Cal Rptr 165, 169. For a discussion of the duty of parties to go beyond their own personal knowledge in answering interrogatories put to them, see § 5.16.

[5] See CCP § 2030.250(b). Cf. Dahlquist v State (1966) 243 Cal App 2d 208, 212–213, 52 Cal Rptr 324, 327 (italics added).

[6] See, e.g., Gorman Rupp Industries, Inc. v Superior Court (1971) 20 Cal App 3d 28, 97 Cal Rptr 377.

[7] See, e.g., Brotsky v State Bar of California (1962) 57 Cal 2d 287, 302–303, 19 Cal Rptr 153, 368 P2d 697.

[8] See, e.g., State ex rel. Division of Industrial Safety v Superior Court (1974) 43 Cal App 3d 778, 117 Cal Rptr 726.

[9] See, e.g., Mowry v Superior Court (1962) 202 Cal App 2d 229, 234, 20 Cal Rptr 698.

[10] See, e.g., Chitwood v County of Los Angeles (1971) 14 Cal App 3d 522, 92 Cal Rptr 441.

[11] See, e.g., San Francisco v Superior Court (1958) 161 Cal App 2d 653, 327 P2d 195.

[12] CCP § 2030.250(b).

[13] Mowry v Superior Court (1962) 202 Cal App 2d 229, 235, 20 Cal Rptr 698, 701 [interrogatories may not be addressed to an appraiser for condemning authority].

[14] CCP § 2030.010.

from a 1971 amendment to its predecessor[15] in the original Discovery Act. The history of this amendment shows that its meaning is as sweeping as the phrase indicates. Before the 1971 amendment, interrogatories could be directed only to a party who was "adverse" to the one propounding them. In multi-party litigation, arguably, only a pleading that created a formal issue between them would make parties "adverse." Indeed, some federal courts, interpreting the same language in the original version of Rule 33,[16] had ruled that, absent a cross-claim, co-defendants could not propound interrogatories to each other.[17] Other federal courts had relied on the word "adverse" to bar discovery by interrogatories between the original plaintiff and a third-party defendant in impleader situations.[18]

However, the first California case[19] to consider the issue liberally interpreted "adverse party." The court ruled that where one co-defendant was blaming another co-defendant for the plaintiff's injuries, the two were sufficiently "adverse," even though neither was seeking a judgment against the other. In reaching this result, the court relied strongly on a federal decision that had allowed a third-party defendant to serve interrogatories on the original plaintiff.[20] The court also suggested that California emulate the "progressive step"[21] taken in the federal system in 1970 when Rule 33 was amended to replace "any adverse party" with the phrase "any other party."[22] The Legislature immediately implemented this suggestion.[23]

Class Actions: The most troublesome issue concerning those to whom interrogatories may be directed is whether they may be propounded to unnamed members in a class action. The next section discusses this issue.

§ 5.5 Class Actions

Class actions present unique issues with respect to the duty to answer interrogatories. The Civil Discovery Act still contains no specially tailored provisions concerning discovery in class actions. Accordingly, the case law that developed under the original Discovery Act should remain controlling under the current one.[1]

---

[15] Former CCP § 2030(a), 1956 Discovery Act, Appendix E.

[16] Fed Rules Civ Proc, Rule 33(a).

[17] See, e.g., Biddle v Hutchinson (1959, MD Pa) 24 FRD 256.

[18] See, e.g., Mozeika v Kaufman Constr. Co. (1960, ED Pa) 25 FRD 233.

[19] Gorman Rupp Industries, Inc. v Superior Court (1971) 20 Cal App 3d 28, 97 Cal Rptr 377.

[20] Carey v Schuldt (1967, ED La) 42 FRD 390.

[21] Gorman Rupp Industries, Inc. v Superior Court (1971) 20 Cal App 3d 28, 30 n2, 97 Cal Rptr 377, 379 n2.

[22] Fed Rules Civ Proc, Rule 33(a).

[23] Cf. Levy-Zentner Co. v Southern Pacific Transportation Co. (1977) 74 Cal App 3d 762, 790, 142 Cal Rptr 1, 19–20.

[1] Cf. Marina Point, Ltd. v Wolfson (1982) 30 Cal 3d 721, 734, 180 Cal Rptr 496, 504, 640 P2d 115, 123; Laddon v Superior Court (1959) 167 Cal App 2d 391, 394–395, 334 P2d 638, 639–640.

Class Representatives: Unquestionably, the class representatives themselves must somehow respond to interrogatories. The problem is pinpointing the extent of their duty to supply information about the *unnamed or absent* class members. This question received careful consideration in the *Alpine Mutual Water Co.* case.[2] This was a class action claiming that the defendants had slandered the title of over a thousand homeowners by recording an invalid assessment and lien against their property. The defendants addressed interrogatories to the class representative that sought detailed information about each of the thousand-plus houses: the identity of the legal owners and of any other person in possession, its purchase price, its mortgage balance and its present market value. Another interrogatory also asked the class representatives to state the factual basis for their allegation that the value of each house and lot had diminished by $1,000.

The court decided to "chart a middle course" between the one extreme of requiring the class representatives "to answer detailed interrogatories concerning the class members and their respective interests,"[3] and the other, of not requiring them to answer any questions at all. Following this "middle course," it ruled that the class representatives must supply information concerning the unnamed class members only if that information is: (1) presently in their possession or readily obtainable; or (2) directly bears on their standing to sue, on the existence of an ascertainable class, or on the presence of the community of interest required for a class action.

Applying this approach, the court directed the class representative to reveal the basis for his allegation that the recording of the invalid assessment and lien had caused $1,000 in damages to each homeowner. This allegation bore directly on the class issues. However, the court held that the class representative need not supply detailed background data concerning any house and lot other than his own. The additional information would become pertinent only in the event the plaintiff was successful on the class issues.

Unnamed or Absent Class Members: Because of the limited scope of the class representative's obligation to supply information about unnamed or absent class members, a litigant may consider directing the interrogatories to those members.[4] This strategy would work only if an unnamed class member is considered a "party" under Section 2030.010.[5] In the *Danzig* case,[6] five of 60 limited partners filed a class action against their general partner, alleging that he had induced them to invest in a certain venture by fraudulent misrepresentations. Defendant addressed written interrogatories to all class members, including the unnamed ones, none of whom had opted out of the class or retained separate

---

[2] Alpine Mutual Water Co. v Superior Court (1968) 259 Cal App 2d 45, 66 Cal Rptr 250.

[3] Alpine Mutual Water Co. v Superior Court (1968) 259 Cal App 2d 45, 54, 66 Cal Rptr 250, 256.

[4] Annotation: Absent or unnamed class members in class action in state court as subject to discovery. 28 ALR4th 986.

[5] CCP § 2030.010.

[6] Danzig v Superior Court (1978) 87 Cal App 3d 604, 151 Cal Rptr 185.

counsel. These interrogatories called for each class member to detail the information relied on by that individual in joining the partnership.

The limited partners named as class representatives each answered the interrogatories as far as they sought information about their own decisions to join the partnership. However, they objected to answering on behalf of unnamed members on the ground that these were not "parties" for this purpose. Relying heavily on federal cases that had faced the same issue under Rule 33, the court ruled that a party may serve interrogatories on unnamed class members.

Simultaneously, the court pointed out that unnamed class members do not "stand on the same footing as named parties"[7] as far as the obligation to respond to interrogatories is concerned. It recognized that interrogatories, if allowed to operate on unnamed class members just as with any other "party" to the case, could undermine the benefits of class actions:

> The purpose of the device is not only to relieve the courts of the burdens of repetitive litigation and multiple named plaintiffs; it is also to relieve the absent members of the burden of participating in the action. Where, for example, each class member's individual claim is small, the absent class members might not consider it worth their while to answer detailed interrogatories, a task that may require the assistance of counsel. In such a case, defendants could effectively use interrogatory discovery to decrease the size of a plaintiff class. In any class action, unnecessary interrogatories might be used effectively to delay the action, or to harass the absent members of the plaintiff class.[8]

These concerns mandate close trial court supervision of interrogatories in class actions. Accordingly, although this device normally operates extrajudicially, two California cases have indicated that a court order is necessary before one may propound interrogatories to unnamed or absent class members.[9]

§ 5.6 Presumptive Numerical Limit

Abuses Under the Original Discovery Act: The original Discovery Act did not limit the number of interrogatories that one party could serve on another. Indeed, it expressly provided no limit either on the number of interrogatories in a set, or on the number of sets that one party could propound to another: "The number of interrogatories or of sets of interrogatories to be served is not limited . . . . except as justice requires to protect the party from annoyance, expense, embarrassment or oppression."[1] Thus, if the recipient of interrogatories

---

[7] Danzig v Superior Court (1978) 87 Cal App 3d 604, 612, 151 Cal Rptr 185, 190.

[8] Danzig v Superior Court (1978) 87 Cal App 3d 604, 612, 151 Cal Rptr 185, 190–191 (internal citation omitted).

[9] Spoon v Superior Court (1982) 130 Cal App 3d 735, 740, 182 Cal Rptr 44, 47; Danzig v Superior Court (1978) 87 Cal App 3d 604, 614, 151 Cal Rptr 185, 191.

[1] Former CCP § 2030(c), 1956 Discovery Act, Appendix E.

considered that their quantity was excessive, the only recourse was a motion for a protective order. This almost unrestricted license produced two related discovery abuses: voluminous and boilerplate interrogatories.

—**Voluminous Interrogatories:** The discovery abuse resulting from an excessive number of questions is illustrated by the reaction of one federal judge in 1975 to "a behemoth set of interrogatories."[2] These came before him when the Federal Rules of Civil Procedure also contained no fixed limits on the number of interrogatories:[3]

> The set of interrogatories is two inches high, 381 pages long, and contains a total of 2,736 questions and subparts . . . . . If an attorney takes ten minutes to answer each . . . . and charges $50.00 an hour, his fee will be $22,800. At three answers to a page the answers will fill 916 pages and measure six inches high. To mail copies to the sixty-seven parties on the service list, it will be necessary to reproduce a total of 60,192 pages. At $.03 a page, copying will cost $1,800. A conservative estimate of the total cost of answering is $24,000.

> The above statistics pertain to answering one set of interrogatories . . . . If now every defendant proceeds to indiscriminately interrogate cross-claiming defendants the barrage of useless paperwork will be insurmountable. There are in excess of 300 cross-claims in this litigation. If 300 interrogatories of 381 pages are sent to each of the sixty-seven parties on the service list, the Xerox machines will have to grind out 7,535,800 pieces of paper which will occupy 3,768 linear feet of storage space. Answering will of course involve a proportionately greater volume of paperwork.[4]

—**Boilerplate Interrogatories:** The abuse caused by voluminous interrogatories frequently is linked with another potential abuse: boilerplate or canned interrogatories. Attorneys often find that they are propounding the same questions in case after case. This tempts them to print interrogatories in advance with only the caption of the case left blank.

The use of preprinted or form interrogatories does not by itself abuse discovery. Many questions preprinted or found in form books pertain to most cases of the type covered and are ones that the courts have repeatedly approved.[5] Indeed, the Legislature has directed the Judicial Council to develop official form

---

2 In Re U. S. Financial Secur. Litigation (1975, SD Cal) 74 FRD 497.

3 See former Fed Rules Civ Proc, Rule 26(a).

4 In Re U. S. Financial Secur. Litigation (1975, SD Cal) 74 FRD 497, 497–498. See also Day v Rosenthal (1985) 170 Cal App 3d 1125, 1172, 217 Cal Rptr 89, 119 [court estimated that answering just the first of nine sets of interrogatories would have required more than 1600 hours of preparation time].

5 See Pankola v Texaco, Inc. (1960, ED Pa) 25 FRD 184. See Culhane, Model Interrogatories (1987) [comprehensive, precisely drafted form interrogatories for use in personal injury actions arising out of vehicular negligence, premises liability and product liability].

interrogatories for use in the more common types of litigation, such as personal injury, breach of contract and unlawful detainer, and for any other type of civil litigation it deems appropriate.[6]

However, preprinted or form interrogatories become oppressive when routinely used without any tailoring to an individual lawsuit. In *Wooldridge v Mounts,*[7] the appellate court showed considerable sympathy for the trial judge who struck an entire set of interrogatories for this reason:

> It is understandable that trial courts, when faced with reviewing a multitude of printed form interrogatories, many of which have no relevance to the subject matter of the action, on occasion lose patience with such practices. They constitute an abuse of the discovery procedure. They are an imposition upon the witness being interrogated and upon opposing counsel. In addition, it is an unwarranted trespass upon the time of the courts and other litigants.[8]

One federal judge has condemned the indiscriminate use of "canned or form interrogatories" as "an unprofessional and insulting practice":[9]

> I have seen defendants served with hundreds of irrelevant canned questions that have been cut and pasted together by a paralegal or other staff assistant . . . , , I do not mean that form questions are *per se* inappropriate. However, if used at all, the form or canned questions must be used selectively, must be germane to the case, must be prepared by a lawyer or under his direction, must be a reasonable number given the nature of the case, and must be consecutively numbered.[10]

Evolution of the 35-Question Limit: To curb the twin abuses of voluminous and boilerplate interrogatories, the Discovery Commission in 1986 proposed a presumptive limit of 35 on the number of interrogatories that one party could propound to another.[11] The Commission realized that this number would be grossly inadequate for many lawsuits. Its thought was that in most of those instances the need to exceed this limit would be mutual. Therefore, the parties would agree to waive or raise the statutory limit. If an opponent balked at lifting

---

6 CCP § 2033.710.

7 Wooldridge v Mounts (1962) 199 Cal App 2d 620, 18 Cal Rptr 806.

8 Wooldridge v Mounts (1962) 199 Cal App 2d 620, 626–627, 18 Cal Rptr 806, 810.

9 SCM Societa Commerciale S.P.A. v Industrial & Commercial Research Corp. (1976, ND Tex) 72 FRD 110, 113 n5.

10 72 FRD at 113 n5. See, e.g., Cabrera v Evans (1975, Fla App) 322 So2d 559 [an individual plaintiff, involved in a traffic accident, was served with 37 pages of interrogatories that included questions relating to plaintiff's corporate structure].

11 Proposed Civil Discovery Act of 1986, Section 2030(c)(1), Appendix D. The 1993 amendments to Fed Rules Civ Proc, Rule 33(a) impose a limit of 25 interrogatories, "including all discrete subparts," absent a stipulation or leave of court.

the limit, however, this would force a party wanting to exceed it to file a motion for relief from the limitation.[12]

The Legislature was not as optimistic as the Discovery Commission that the courts could depend on litigants to agree, where appropriate, to accommodate each other's needs for more than 35 interrogatories. It also feared that motions for relief from the presumptive limit would clog the law and motion calendars. Moreover, it was not persuaded that a limit as low as 35 was a realistic one. Nevertheless, the Legislature was not willing to abandon any effort to impose some curbs in this area. The compromise that eventually emerged has four features.

(1) Thirty-five "Specially Prepared" Questions: In any lawsuit, each party may propound to any other party 35 "specially prepared" interrogatories. If the initial set of interrogatories does not exhaust this 35-question limit, a later set may use the balance. One who receives, unsupported by a declaration of necessity,[13] a set of specially prepared interrogatories that, either alone or in combination with previous sets, exceeds the presumptive limit "need only respond to the first 35 specially prepared interrogatories."[14] The response should then state simply that the recipient objects to the balance because they exceed the statutory limit.[15]

One court confronted a novel attempt to avoid the presumptive limit. The *Catanese* case held that counsel may not undermine the prescribed limit by submitting a single interrogatory that asks which of the 2,500 answers given during a deposition does the responding party contend are untrue.[16]

(2) Official Form Interrogatories: The Judicial Council's official form interrogatories cover many categories of lawsuits. These include personal injury, wrongful death, breach of contract, and unlawful detainer actions.[17] A party may propound to another *any* number of these questions, provided they are relevant to the particular case.[18] Furthermore, the use of a Judicial Council interrogatory does not count against the presumptive limit of 35 specially prepared ones. However, approval of an interrogatory by the Judicial Council does not make it invulnerable to any other objection.[19]

---

[12] Proposed Civil Discovery Act of 1986, Section 2030(c)(2), Appendix D.

[13] See CCP § 2030(c)(3). The use of a declaration of necessity when propounding more than 35 specially prepared interrogatories is discussed later in this section.

[14] CCP § 2030.030(c).

[15] CCP § 2030.030(c).

[16] Catanese v Superior Court (1996) 46 Cal App 4th 1159, 1164–1166, 54 Cal Rptr 2d 280, 283–284.

[17] See CCP § 2033.710.

[18] CCP § 2030.030(a)(2).

[19] Nacht & Lewis Architects, Inc. v Superior Court (1996) 47 Cal App 4th 214, 216–217, 54 Cal Rptr 2d 575, 576 [Form Interrogatory 12.2, asking the identity of witnesses an opponent has *interviewed*, intrudes upon the work product protection].

(3) Overcoming Presumptive Limit: A party who wishes to propound more than 35 "specially prepared" interrogatories must overcome this presumptive limit. Section 2030.040 lists the three factors that might warrant service of additional questions. Counsel probably most frequently rely upon "the complexity or the quantity of the existing and potential issues in the particular case."[20] This ground, of course, has more force if no official form interrogatories exist for the particular kind of lawsuit involved. A second justification for exceeding the presumptive limit is "the financial burden" that obtaining the information by oral deposition would impose.[21] Finally, counsel may cite the advantage of interrogatories where the information sought necessitates the making of inquiries or a search of records.[22]

—Supporting Declaration: A party who wants to exceed the presumptive numerical limit need not apply to the court for leave to do so. Instead, it simply serves specially prepared interrogatories that exceed this limit. However, the party must attach a "Declaration for Additional Discovery" stating the circumstances that warrant the additional questions.[23]

As originally adopted, this declaration required little in the way of justification. Counsel could simply recite that the information sought was necessary for the proper preparation of the case and that this number of questions was reasonably required to obtain it. However, during the extensive amendment process between initial passage of the 1986 Discovery Act and its effective date, the Legislature put some teeth into the declaration. Counsel for the propounding party must state which of the three statutory "factors" warrant the additional number of interrogatories, and then must specify "the reasons why" each factor is applicable to the present lawsuit.[24]

(4) Motion for Protective Order: If the required declaration accompanies the additional number of specially prepared interrogatories, a responding party who considers this quantity excessive must move for a protective order.[25] The moving party must accompany this motion with a declaration showing the steps taken to resolve the dispute informally.[26] In most other discovery disputes, the moving party establishes the need for a protective order. However, where a motion for a protective order challenges the need for more than 35 specially prepared interrogatories, "the propounding party shall have the burden of justifying" them.[27]

---

[20] CCP § 2030.040(a)(1).

[21] CCP § 2030.040(a)(2).

[22] CCP § 2030.040(a)(3).

[23] See CCP § 2030.050.

[24] Paragraph 8 of Supporting Declaration, CCP § 2030.050.

[25] CCP § 2030.090(b)(2).

[26] CCP § 2030.090(b)(2).

[27] CCP § 2030.040(b).

Increasing Limit by Stipulation: The Civil Discovery Act gives the parties the right "by written stipulation" to "modify the procedures" for any discovery method.[28] Accordingly, any two parties could agree to raise or to waive altogether the statutory limit on the number of specially prepared interrogatories that each of them may propound to the other.

§ 5.7 "Continuing" and "Supplemental" Interrogatories

"Continuing" Interrogatories Prohibited: Answers to interrogatories must, of course, reflect the responding party's knowledge on the date it serves those answers. But what if later information, developments, insights or tactical decisions would now require a different answer to the identical question if it were propounded at a later stage in the discovery process? May the propounding party, by specifying that certain or all of the interrogatories are "continuing," impose a duty to update, supplement or correct an answer that the responding party subsequently learns has become incomplete, misleading or outright wrong?[1]

The original Discovery Act's silence on this question left it to the courts to assess the propriety of "continuing" interrogatories. In 1961 when this matter first came before a California appellate court, former CCP § 2030 was still restricting a litigant to a single set of interrogatories.[2] Because the court in the *Smith* case[3] viewed the "continuing interrogatory" as a circumvention of this restriction, it held that a party needed leave of court to use this device. The vitality of the *Smith* decision became doubtful two years later, when an amendment eliminated the single-set limitation.[4] This change led one court to remark that the status of the continuing interrogatory in California discovery practice was "apparently an open question."[5]

The Discovery Commission deemed it unfair to require the responding party to constantly review and supplement prior answers. Accordingly, the Commission proposed,[6] and the Legislature adopted, an explicit prohibition against use of "continuing" interrogatories:

> An interrogatory may not be made a continuing one so as to impose on the party responding to it a duty to supplement an answer to it that was initially correct and complete with later acquired information.[7]

---

[28] CCP § 2016.030.

[1] Annotation: Propriety of discovery interrogatories calling for continuing answers. 88 ALR2d 657.

[2] The original version of former CCP § 2030(a) stated: "No party may serve more than one set of interrogatories to be answered by the same adverse party, except with leave of court obtained on motion after notice."

[3] Smith v Superior Court (1961) 189 Cal App 2d 6, 10–11, 11 Cal Rptr 165, 168–169.

[4] Former CCP § 2030(c), 1956 Discovery Act, Appendix E.

[5] Rangel v Graybar Electric Co. (1977) 70 Cal App 3d 943, 950 n6, 139 Cal Rptr 191, 195 n6. See also Deyo v Kilbourne (1978) 84 Cal App 3d 771, 782 n6, 149 Cal Rptr 499, 508 n6.

[6] Proposed Civil Discovery Act of 1986, Section 2030(c)(6), Appendix D.

[7] CCP § 2030.060(g).

Supplemental Interrogatories Permitted: Although the Discovery Commission condemned "continuing" interrogatories, it acknowledged that the propounding party needs to update the answers previously received. The imposition of a presumptive numerical limit on interrogatories accentuated this need for current information.[8] To compensate for the prohibition of the "continuing" interrogatory, the Commission recommended, and the Legislature adopted, the use of a "supplemental" interrogatory:

> [A] party may propound a supplemental interrogatory to elicit any later acquired information bearing on all answers previously made by any party in response to interrogatories . . . .[9]

> The Federal Rules of Civil Procedure in effect make all interrogatories "continuing" ones. A responding party who learns that an earlier answer to an interrogatory "is in some material respect incomplete or incorrect" must on its own initiative "seasonably" amend that response.[10]

The only difference between the "continuing" and the "supplemental" interrogatory is that the latter shifts the burden of seeking updated answers to the party who propounded them.[11]

A party may serve a supplemental interrogatory "twice prior to the initial setting of a trial date."[12] Once the initial trial date has been set, a party may propound one more supplemental interrogatory.[13] The court may allow additional supplemental interrogatories "for good cause shown."[14] Supplemental interrogatories do not count against the presumptive limit of 35 specially-prepared interrogatories.[15]

A party who wishes to propound a supplemental interrogatory after the setting of the initial trial date must act promptly. Section 2024.020 requires the completion of all discovery as a matter of right 30 days "before the date initially set for trial of the action."[16] Discovery by interrogatories would appear to be "completed" not on the date a party serves the supplemental interrogatory, but on the date the answer to it is due.[17] Since the responding party has 30 days

---

[8] For a discussion of the presumptive numerical limit on interrogatories, see § 5.6.

[9] CCP § 2030.070(a).

[10] Fed Rules Civ Proc, Rule 26(e)(2).

[11] See Biles v Exxon Mobil Corp. (2004) 124 Cal App 4th 1315, 1328–1329, 22 Cal Rptr 3d 282, 291–292 [in contrast to the federal practices, a responding party in a California case has no affirmative duty to supplement a response to an interrogatory that was honest at the time of the response when new information later comes into that party's possession].

[12] CCP § 2030.070(b).

[13] CCP § 2030.070(b).

[14] CCP § 2030.070(c).

[15] See CCP § 2030.070(a).

For a discussion of the presumptive numerical limit on interrogatories, see § 5.6.

[16] CCP § 2024.020(a).

[17] For a discussion of the discovery cut-off for interrogatories, see § 5.2.

to answer the supplemental interrogatory,[18] the propounding party should serve it by the 60th day before that trial date. A party using the mails to serve it should post it by 65th day before that trial date.[19]

Discovery Reopened: In the *Fairmont Ins. Co.* case,[20] the Supreme Court considered the meaning of "date initially set for the trial of the action" where there has been a mistrial, an order granting a new trial, or a remand for a new trial after reversal of a judgment on appeal. It held that in such cases discovery is reopened and the cutoff date is calculated based on the date initially set for the *new* trial.

§ 5.8 "Contention" Interrogatories

Four Types: The most-litigated issue concerning the scope of interrogatory discovery is the extent to which interrogatories can elicit answers that would not simply divulge facts, but would require an opinion or conclusion. Such questions are commonly called "contention" interrogatories.[1] This umbrella term covers at least four different types of interrogatory.[2]

—(1) Outright Opinion: An interrogatory may openly ask the responding party to express an opinion about the events involved in the litigation. For example, counsel might command: "State what, in your opinion, was the nature and cause of the alleged unsafe or defective condition in the fishing boat's machinery or motor."[3]

—(2) Factual Basis: An interrogatory may ask for the factual basis of some claim or defense that the adversary has made, usually in the pleadings. For example, counsel might command: "State in detail all facts forming the basis of the allegation in the complaint that defendant operated its train negligently"[4] or "State what facts form the basis for the affirmative defense of assumption of risk."[5]

—(3) Issue Identification: An interrogatory may inquire into legal contentions that the pleadings, because of their generality, do not reveal. For example, counsel might ask: "Does defendant liability carrier contend that there was any legal consideration given to the insured when a later endorsement to the policy reduced its coverage?"[6]

---

[18] CCP § 2030.260(a).

[19] CCP § 2016.050, referencing CCP §§ 1013(a).

[20] Fairmont Ins. Co. v Superior Court (2000) 22 Cal 4th 245, 92 Cal Rptr 2d 70, 991 P2d 156.

[1] Less frequently, courts use the term "substantive" interrogatory. See In re Convergent Technologies Securities Litigation (1985, ND Cal) 108 FRD 328, 332, 335.

[2] See In re Convergent Technologies Securities Litigation (1985, ND Cal) 108 FRD 328, 332.

[3] See Landry v O'Hara Vessels, Inc. (1939, D Mass) 29 F Supp 423, 425.

[4] See Southern Pacific Co. v Superior Court (1969) 3 Cal App 3d 195, 197, 83 Cal Rptr 231.

[5] See Singer v Superior Court (1960) 54 Cal 2d 318, 325–326, 5 Cal Rptr 697, 353 P2d 305.

[6] See Universal Underwriters Ins. Co. v Superior Court (1967) 250 Cal App 2d 722, 728–729, 58 Cal Rptr 870.

—(4) **Legal Reasoning:** An interrogatory may seek the legal reasoning by which the responding party supports a particular contention. For example, counsel might command: "State the reasons for your contention that the complaint fails to state facts sufficient to constitute a cause of action."[7]

Explicit Authorization: The original Discovery Act gave no explicit guidance on contention interrogatories. An early decision, *Rust v Roberts*,[8] held that the landowner in a condemnation case could not ask the State whether it was contending that the best use of the acreage involved was not as a residential subdivision, and if so, what was the basis for this contention. However, the Supreme Court quickly disapproved this case.[9] Simultaneously, in another decision it signaled that an interrogatory was not objectionable merely because it called for an opinion:

> [E]ven if . . . . the question does call for an opinion and conclusion, that fact, *of itself*, is not a proper objection to an interrogatory. Such objection may be proper when the answer is intended to have probative value, but it may not be utilized on discovery as a means of preventing a party from obtaining information that will lead him to probative facts.[10]

Section 2030.010, following the lead of the Federal Rules,[11] expressly authorizes "contention" interrogatories:

> An interrogatory may relate to whether another party is making a certain contention, or to the facts, witnesses, and writings on which a contention is based. An interrogatory is not objectionable because an answer to it involves an opinion or contention that relates to fact or the application of law to fact, or would be based on information obtained or legal theories developed in anticipation of litigation or in preparation for trial.[12]

This does not represent a change in the pre-1987 discovery practice. As the sections immediately following will explain, it simply codifies the California case law liberally embracing three of the four types of "contention" interrogatories described above, and rejecting the fourth.[13]

---

[7] See Flora Crane Service, Inc. v Superior Court (1965) 234 Cal App 2d 767, 780, 45 Cal Rptr 79, 86.

[8] Rust v Roberts (1959) 171 Cal App 2d 772, 341 P2d 46.

[9] Greyhound Corp. v Superior Court (1961) 56 Cal 2d 355, 381, 15 Cal Rptr 90, 102, 364 P2d 266, 278.

[10] West Pico Furniture Co. v Superior Court (1961) 56 Cal 2d 407, 417, 15 Cal Rptr 119, 123, 364 P2d 295, 299 (original italics).

[11] Fed Rules Civ Proc, Rule 33(b).

[12] CCP § 2030.010(b).

[13] For a discussion of interrogatories that ask for the expression of an opinion about facts within the responding party's personal knowledge, see § 5.9. For a discussion of interrogatories that probe

§ 5.9   Fact-Based Opinions

Some interrogatories unquestionably call for the expression of an opinion concerning events known to the responding party. An obvious example is one that asks for an estimate of the speed at which vehicles were traveling.[1]

Prior Case Law Codified: The original Discovery Act gave little guidance concerning the propriety of an interrogatory that calls for an "opinion" or a "conclusion" by the responding party. It simply said that interrogatories "may relate to any matter which can be inquired into" during a deposition.[2] Only one reported California case considered an objection that an interrogatory violated the "opinion rule." In the *West Pico Furniture* case,[3] defendant was asked which of its employees had engaged in certain commercial paper transactions, when they did so, and what duties they performed. Defendant objected that "it calls for the opinions and conclusions of the answering party, both as to the duties of the employees and as to the periods of time during which each participated."[4] Although the Court held that the interrogatory did not really call for an opinion, it remarked that even if it did, this would not be a reason for resisting a response.[5]

Section 2030.010,[6] taking its cue from the *West Pico Furniture* case and the 1970 amendments to Federal Rule 33,[7] permits interrogatories that call for an opinion about relevant facts: "An interrogatory is not objectionable because an answer to it involves an opinion . . . . that relates to fact . . . ."[8]

Conforms to the Law of Evidence: A brief examination of the present-day status of the so-called "opinion rule" in the law of evidence shows the wisdom of allowing interrogatories to call for fact-based opinions or conclusions. Modern courts have come to realize that even during a trial the foundation for the opinion rule is an illusion. An attempt to apply it "on the assumption that 'fact' and

---

for the factual bases of an adversary's allegations and contentions, see § 5.10. For a discussion of interrogatories that seek to ascertain an adversary's contentions, see § 5.11. For a discussion of interrogatories that ask for an explanation of an adversary's legal theories or reasoning, see § 5.12.

[1] See, e.g., Moorman v Simon (1947, WD Mo) 8 FRD 328. See also Advanced Cardiovascular Systems v C.R. Bard, Inc. (1992, ND Cal) 144 FRD 372, 378–379 [inventors asked to state their understanding of the terms used in their claims of patent]; Goodman v International Business Machine Corp. (1973, ND Ill) 59 FRD 278 [defendant asked to explain, if it knows, how certain material happened to fall from its property into the street below].

[2] Former CCP § 2030(c), 1956 Discovery Act, Appendix E.

[3] West Pico Furniture Co. v Superior Court (1961) 56 Cal 2d 407, 15 Cal Rptr 119, 364 P2d 295.

[4] West Pico Furniture Co. v Superior Court (1961) 56 Cal 2d 407, 416, 15 Cal Rptr 119, 123, 364 P2d 295, 299.

[5] West Pico Furniture Co. v Superior Court (1961) 56 Cal 2d 407, 416, 15 Cal Rptr 119, 123, 364 P2d 295, 299.

[6] CCP § 2030.010(b).

[7] Fed Rules Civ Proc, Rule 33(b).

[8] CCP § 2030.010(b).

'opinion' stand in contrast and hence are readily distinguishable" will produce "one of the clumsiest tools for regulating the examination of witnesses."[9] Over the years the courts have whittled a wooden rule excluding answers expressed in opinion form down to a mere policy preferring testimony that is as specific as the circumstances of the described event will allow. In the words of Professor McCormick: "[T]he prevailing practice in respect to the admission of lay opinions should be described not as a rigid rule excluding opinions, but as a rule of preference. The more concrete description is preferred to the more abstract."[10]

The Evidence Code reflects this approach. It does not contain a general rule prohibiting opinion-type testimony from lay witnesses. Instead, Section 800 "limits" the admissibility of lay opinions to those that are at once "rationally based on the perception of the witness," and "helpful to a clear understanding of his testimony."[11]

Since opinion testimony is often quite proper at trial, any such opinion should, of course, be discoverable.[12] Moreover, even where the admissibility of a particular opinion is debatable, knowledge of that opinion might lead to the discovery of admissible evidence:

> [E]ven if it be conceded that the question does call for an opinion and conclusion, that fact, *of itself*, is not a proper objection to an interrogatory. Such objection may be proper when the answer is intended to have probative value, but it may not be utilized on discovery as a means of preventing a party from obtaining information that will lead him to probative facts.[13]

This simply applies the principle that allows discovery of a "matter" that "either is itself admissible in evidence or appears reasonably calculated to lead to the discovery of admissible evidence."[14]

§ 5.10 Factual Basis of Contentions

Improper Question During Deposition: A party who sees that an adversary is making a certain contention (for example, that the defendant operated its train negligently,[1] or that the plaintiff's own negligence contributed to his injury)[2]

---

[9] McCormick on Evidence § 11 (5th Ed 1999).

[10] McCormick on Evidence § 11 (5th Ed 1999).

[11] Evid Code § 800. See also FRE 701.

[12] See, e.g., Advanced Cardiovascular Systems v C.R. Bard, Inc. (1992, ND Cal) 144 FRD 372, 378–379 [inventors properly asked to state their understanding of the key phrases in their patent claims].

[13] West Pico Furniture Co. v Superior Court (1961) 56 Cal 2d 407, 417, 15 Cal Rptr 119, 123, 364 P2d 295, 299 (original italics).

[14] CCP § 2017.010.

[1] See, e.g., Southern Pacific Co. v Superior Court (1969) 3 Cal App 3d 195, 197, 83 Cal Rptr 231.

[2] See, e.g., Singer v Superior Court (1960) 54 Cal 2d 318, 325–326, 5 Cal Rptr 697, 353 P2d 305.

will understandably be curious about the facts that the other party intends to use to support that contention. Taking the oral deposition of the adverse party is neither a satisfactory nor a proper way to satisfy this curiosity. Answering a question about the factual basis of a legal contention requires a law-to-fact application beyond the competence of a layperson. One federal trial judge explained:

> Plaintiff seeks from a seller of peanut butter sandwiches, crackers, cakes and cookies facts upon which the latter asserts, for example, that an affidavit under Paragraphs 8 and 15 of the Trade-Mark Act of 1946 is invalid. It seems to us that this, at the least, is unrealistic. It would be like asking a railroad brakeman the facts on which he alleged that a defendant railroad violated the Safety Appliance Acts . . . . To be sure, the client presumably knows the facts (although not always), but he can hardly be expected to know their legal consequences. This is what lawyers are for. . . . . [T]he cause of justice and the fruitful advancement of discovery will be better served by refusing plaintiff's motion to compel answers on depositions to inquiries on the factual basis of conclusionary allegations.[3]

The *Rifkind* case[4] adopted and extended this position for California discovery practice. The court held that even where the party-deponent is a lawyer, that deponent may not be asked questions that would require application of law to fact: "A lawyer who is sued or is suing someone else, and who places his or her cause in the hands of an attorney, is not less entitled to have that attorney attend to legal and quasi-legal aspects of the case than is a layperson."[5]

Suitable for Interrogatory: An interrogatory is the ideal discovery device for probing the factual bases of an opponent's contentions. It allows both time for reflection and the assistance of counsel in formulating a reply. Admittedly, interrogatory discovery takes on an added dimension when used for this purpose. It goes beyond an oral deposition's discovery of what a party has done, seen or heard. Instead, it forces one's opponent (or, more realistically, the opponent's attorney) to engage in sophisticated legal reasoning. To respond to such an interrogatory, the opponent must sort through the available information and match it to the various contentions.

The *Singer* Case: The original Discovery Act did not explicitly authorize interrogatories concerning the factual basis for another party's allegations or contentions. To the contrary, it tied the scope of interrogatories to the scope of

[3] Lance, Inc. v Ginsburg (1962, ED Pa) 32 FRD 51, 53. See also Davis v Lower Bucks Hospital (1972, ED Pa) 56 FRD 21 [improper to ask defendant-deponent in medical malpractice case to explain legal theories]. Cf. Pember v Superior Court (1967) 66 Cal 2d 601, 604, 58 Cal Rptr 567, 569, 427 P2d 167, 169.

[4] Rifkind v Superior Court (1994) 22 Cal App 4th 1255, 1260–1261, 27 Cal Rptr 2d 822, 825.

[5] 22 Cal App 4th at 1263, 27 Cal Rptr 2d at 827.

depositions.[6] Thus, arguably, because such questioning was improper during a deposition,[7] it was similarly improper for interrogatories.

The propriety of using interrogatories to ascertain the factual support for an adversary's contentions came before the Supreme Court soon after the original Discovery Act went into effect. In the *Singer* case,[8] a complaint for personal injuries in a shipboard accident met with an answer setting up the affirmative defenses of contributory negligence and assumption of risk. The plaintiff then propounded interrogatories that asked "what fact or facts form the basis" for these defenses. The defendant maintained that the interrogatories improperly sought discovery of conclusions and opinions rather than facts.

The Court, however, regarded these interrogatories as a way to compensate for a system of pleading that tolerated, especially in negligence cases, conclusory allegations in complaints and answers:

> Such general allegations do not apprise the plaintiff of matters which may lead him "to the discovery of admissible evidence." It follows that, in California, discovery proceedings provide a most important method of obtaining knowledge of such facts as may exist and on which the protagonist relies.[9]

Section 2030.010 codifies *Singer:* "An interrogatory may relate . . . . to the facts, witnesses, and writings on which a contention is based."[10]

Contentions in Pleadings: In *Singer* the plaintiff was using interrogatories to obtain the specifics of affirmative defenses. This device is, of course, also available to defendants wanting to know the basis for the allegations in a complaint. For example, *Petersen v Vallejo*[11] held that the State of California had "the unquestionable right"[12] to receive an answer to the following interrogatory: "State in detail the factual basis for your allegation that the State of California 'negligently and carelessly controlled, maintained, repaired and constructed'" a certain road and overpass.[13] And the *Southern Pacific* case[14] upheld the railroad's interrogatories calling on the plaintiff to state all facts forming the basis of allegations that the railroad was negligent in the operation of its train, the maintenance of its right of way, the design, maintenance and construction of its crossing warning signs, and its compliance with a specified PUC order.

---

[6] Former CCP §§ 2030(c) and 2016(b), 1956 Discovery Act, Appendix E.

[7] See Lance, Inc. v Ginsburg (1962, ED Pa) 32 FRD 51.

[8] Singer v Superior Court (1960) 54 Cal 2d 318, 5 Cal Rptr 697, 353 P2d 305.

[9] Singer v Superior Court (1960) 54 Cal 2d 318, 324, 5 Cal Rptr 697, 700, 353 P2d 305, 308 (internal citation omitted).

[10] CCP § 2030.010(b).

[11] Petersen v Vallejo (1968) 259 Cal App 2d 757, 66 Cal Rptr 776.

[12] Petersen v Vallejo (1968) 259 Cal App 2d 757, 781, 66 Cal Rptr 776, 791.

[13] Petersen v Vallejo (1968) 259 Cal App 2d 757, 778–779, 66 Cal Rptr 776, 790.

[14] Southern Pacific Co. v Superior Court (1969) 3 Cal App 3d 195, 197, 83 Cal Rptr 231.

—Negative Defenses: A party may also use interrogatories to explore the factual basis for negative defenses, i.e., defenses that contradict elements of an opponent's prima facie case. In the *Burke* case,[15] an action against a bonding company for a wrongful attachment, the defendant responded to an unverified complaint with a one-paragraph answer denying its allegations. Seeking to pinpoint just which of the allegations in the complaint the defendant was really contesting, the plaintiff served an interrogatory probing for the factual basis for this general denial. The Supreme Court approved this use of interrogatories: "[N]o reason appears why such an interrogatory should not be permitted . . . . where, as here, the answer consists solely of a disfavored overbroad general denial which gives the plaintiff no guidance whatsoever regarding what specific matters legitimately are at issue and warrant discovery."[16]

Contentions Outside the Pleadings: A party may also use interrogatories to discover the factual underpinnings of contentions that appear during the discovery process itself.[17] In one case, for example, the plaintiffs learned from the answer to an earlier interrogatory that the defendants were contending that those pumping ground water in a certain region were not all tapping a common source of supply. The court upheld the plaintiffs' follow-up interrogatory seeking "the hydrological and geological asserted facts" that were the foundation for this claim.[18]

Overcoming a "Work Product" Objection: Interrogatories seeking supporting facts have also come under attack as an invasion of the "work product" of one's opponent. Answering such an interrogatory undisputably requires a party to use facts and legal theories developed during trial preparation. In the *Southern Pacific* case[19] a California court first considered whether this type of interrogatory impermissibly intrudes upon an opponent's work product. There, the plaintiff objected that an interrogatory about the factual basis for her negligence claim necessarily inquired into facts gathered in anticipation of litigation. The court acknowledged that the trial preparation *materials* that contained such facts, such as reports of experts and investigators, diagrams and the like, might well be protected "work-product." It ruled, however, that the facts themselves, *even though derived from work product materials*, were discoverable:

> The facts sought, those presently relied upon by plaintiffs to prove their
> case, are discoverable no matter how they came into the attorney's

---

[15] Burke v Superior Court (1969) 71 Cal 2d 276, 78 Cal Rptr 481, 455 P2d 409.

[16] Burke v Superior Court (1969) 71 Cal 2d 276, 285, 78 Cal Rptr 481, 490, 455 P2d 409, 418. See also Durst v Superior Court (1963) 218 Cal App 2d 460, 32 Cal Rptr 627 [objection overruled to interrogatory asking defendant to "state separately and with particularity all facts known to (it) which will prove or tend to prove, in whole or in part, that the plaintiff did not suffer or sustain" three specified injuries].

[17] For a discussion of the use of interrogatories to learn the contentions of one's adversary that are not reflected in the pleadings, see § 5.11.

[18] Tehachapi-Cummings County Water District v Superior Court (1968) 267 Cal App 2d 42, 44, 72 Cal Rptr 589, 590.

[19] Southern Pacific Co. v Superior Court (1969) 3 Cal App 3d 195, 83 Cal Rptr 231.

possession. Plaintiffs will ultimately disclose these facts at the trial. Surprise is the only objective of withholding these facts pending the trial. That objective is contrary to the spirit and letter of the discovery statutes. [20]

Section 2030.010 codifies *Southern Pacific:* "An interrogatory is not objectionable because an answer to it . . . . would be based on information obtained or legal theories developed in anticipation of litigation or in preparation for trial." [21]

—Derivative Material: However, where an interrogatory seeks the material from which the facts supporting a contention have been derived, it is objectionable. In the *Sheets* case, [22] one partner in a building construction venture sued the other for an accounting. The defendant was not content with discovery of which book entries and expenditures the plaintiff was questioning. Instead he sought to learn what plaintiff's expert had reported in these respects:

> Instead of asking [plaintiff] directly to state the facts now known to him upon which he presently relies to prove the allegations of his amended complaint, [the] interrogatories . . . . call on him to state whether . . . . the certified public accountant discovered and reported any discrepancies or false entries in the books. Again, [the] interrogatories . . . . do not call for a statement of the facts on which [plaintiff] intends to rely; instead, they call on him to state whether the accountant "reported any facts or information" which tend to support the allegations of the amended complaint, that [defendant] has diverted partnership funds and property to his own use. [23]

The court sustained objections to these interrogatories because "they call on [plaintiff] to disclose the analysis and evaluation of [the accountant's] report which his lawyer has made on behalf of [plaintiff] in the course of his preparation for the trial of the case." [24] If the defendant wished to see the accountant's report itself, the court said, he should file a motion for its production, and thereby give the plaintiff an opportunity to argue that it was protected work product.

Evasive Responses: Interrogatories seeking the factual support for contentions are not to be evaded by responses containing generalities. In *Petersen v Vallejo,* [25]

---

[20] Southern Pacific Co. v Superior Court (1969) 3 Cal App 3d 195, 199, 83 Cal Rptr 231, 233 (internal citation omitted). See also Mead Corp. v Riverwood Natural Resources Corp. (1992, D Minn) 145 FRD 512, 516–518.

[21] CCP § 2030.010(b).

[22] Sheets v Superior Court (1967) 257 Cal App 2d 1, 64 Cal Rptr 753.

[23] Sheets v Superior Court (1967) 257 Cal App 2d 1, 9, 64 Cal Rptr 753, 758.

[24] Sheets v Superior Court (1967) 257 Cal App 2d 1, 9, 64 Cal Rptr 753, 758.

[25] Petersen v Vallejo (1968) 259 Cal App 2d 757, 777–784, 66 Cal Rptr 776, 788–794. See also Juarez v Boy Scouts of America, Inc. (2000) 81 Cal App 4th 377, 385–392, 97 Cal Rptr 2d 12, 17–22 [plaintiff persisted in making evasive responses to defendants' interrogatories seeking evidence that he would rely on to support his claim that defendants knew or should have known that scoutmaster was a pedophile; this warranted a sanction conclusively establishing that defendants had no prior access to any information that would have caused them to suspect the scoutmaster's propensities].

a defendant served an interrogatory asking for a statement of the factual basis for the complaint's allegation "that the State of California 'negligently and carelessly controlled, maintained, repaired and constructed'" a certain road and overpass. Plaintiff answered that the State "allowed certain road markings and directional guides to remain on said roadway" that were "hazardous" to drivers "under the conditions which prevailed on the evening" of the accident. Directed by the trial court to describe the location of the "certain road markings and directional guides," the plaintiff added only that the State, "either during the time of construction or repairs of this roadway, allowed two divider strippings to remain on said roadway," and that these "would and did create confusion as to which direction the roadway led." These answers were also deemed inadequate and evasive.

§ 5.11 Contentions Not Reflected in the Pleadings

Reduced Role of Pleadings in Framing Issues: In a procedural system that rigorously required the pleadings to frame the trial issues, each side's assertions would require the other side's responsive pleading that admitted, denied, or avoided the assertion. To simplify and accelerate the pleadings, however, the Code of Civil Procedure has taken three steps that collectively de-emphasize the pleadings' role in framing the trial issues. First, where a party does not verify a complaint or a cross-complaint, code pleading tolerates a general denial,[1] "which gives the plaintiff no guidance whatsoever regarding what specific matters legitimately are at issue and warrant discovery."[2] Second, when an answer sets up "new matter" constituting some affirmative defense, these allegations are automatically deemed denied.[3] Third, California lacks a pleading that replies to affirmative defenses in a defendant's answer. Thus, even if the plaintiff will rely on additional facts to avoid an affirmative defense (e.g., "fraud in the inducement" to overcome a defense of "release"), no pleading notifies defendant of these additional facts.[4]

Interrogatories as an Adjunct to the Pleadings: Commentators have long urged that interrogatories should fill these gaps left after the pleadings have been closed:

> Liberal use of interrogatories for the purpose of clarifying and narrowing the issues made by the pleadings should be permitted and encouraged by the courts. Only in this manner can the proper interrelations between the pleading and the discovery rules be maintained.[5]

---

[1] See CCP § 431.30.

[2] Burke v Superior Court (1969) 71 Cal 2d 276, 285, 78 Cal Rptr 481, 490, 455 P2d 409, 418.

[3] See CCP § 431.20(b).

[4] California has no counterpart to Fed Rules Civ Proc, Rule 7(a), which permits the trial court to "order a reply to an answer . . . ."

[5] 4A Moore's Federal Practice ¶ 33.17 (2d ed.), quoted with approval in Universal Underwriters Ins. Co. v Superior Court (1967) 250 Cal App 2d 722, 729, 58 Cal Rptr 870, 874. See now 7 Moore's Federal Practice § 33.03. See also Burke v Superior Court (1969) 71 Cal 2d 276, 281, 78 Cal Rptr 481, 487, 455 P2d 409, 415.

In the *Burke* case,[6] the Supreme Court considered whether interrogatories should play this role in California discovery. There, plaintiffs sued to recover the legal expenses incurred in defending an earlier lawsuit in which the principal of the defendant bonding company had wrongfully attached certain property. An interrogatory asked whether the bonding company was contending that plaintiffs should have mitigated the damage from the attachment by a pretrial motion to dissolve it. The Court rejected defendant's challenge to this interrogatory:

> [A] defendant in California may be required to disclose . . . . whether or not he makes a particular contention, either as to the facts or as to possible issues in the case. . . . . [¶] The interrogatories in question ask . . . . "Do you contend that . . . .?" They seek simple yes or no answers which [plaintiffs] are entitled to have. . . . . [O]nly if the question of inability to challenge the attachment prior to trial is in good faith contested should [plaintiffs] be required to prove it at trial.[7]

Section 2030.010 expressly allows interrogatories that seek to learn whether another party is making a particular contention: "An interrogatory may relate to whether another party is making a certain contention . . . . ."[8]

§ 5.12 Legal Theories or Reasoning

Need for Distinctions: Where an interrogatory seeks an adversary's contentions, court and counsel must carefully distinguish several matters. As developed in the two preceding sections, a party may use interrogatories both to learn the contentions of the other side,[1] and to learn the factual support for them.[2] But a party may not use an interrogatory to ask about the legal reasoning that leads an adversary either to make a certain contention or to believe that certain facts support it.

Intrusion on Work Product: An interrogatory that seeks to elicit an opponent's legal theories runs afoul of the work product doctrine. This doctrine absolutely protects an attorney's thoughts and reasoning during case preparation: "A writing that reflects an attorney's impressions, conclusions, opinions, or legal research or theories is not discoverable under any circumstances."[3] This language

---

[6] Burke v Superior Court (1969) 71 Cal 2d 276, 78 Cal Rptr 481, 455 P2d 409.

[7] Burke v Superior Court (1969) 71 Cal 2d 276, 281–283, 78 Cal Rptr 481, 488–489, 455 P2d 409, 416–417 (internal citations omitted). See also Tehachapi-Cummings County Water District v Superior Court (1968) 267 Cal App 2d 42, 43, 72 Cal Rptr 589, 590; Universal Underwriters Ins. Co. v Superior Court (1967) 250 Cal App 2d 722, 725–726, 58 Cal Rptr 870, 872.

[8] CCP § 2030.010(b). For a discussion of interrogatories that probe for the factual basis of another party's contentions, see § 5.10.

[1] For a discussion of the use of interrogatories to learn the contentions of one's opponent, see § 5.11.

[2] For a discussion of the use of interrogatories to learn the facts relied on to support the contentions of one's opponent, see § 5.10.

[3] CCP § 2018.030(a). For a discussion of the restrictions on discovery of the opinions, theories and legal research of an opponent's attorney, see § 13.16.

seems to deal only with an already-existing "writing." Nevertheless, the courts, interpreting identical language in the 1956 Discovery Act,[4] have found in the penumbra of the statute a prohibition against the direct divulgence of "an opponent's legal reasoning or theories."[5]

Pre-1986 Case Law: Several decisions under the 1956 Discovery Act[6] condemned interrogatories that essentially required answers setting forth the legal theories behind an opponent's contentions. For example, in the *State of California* case,[7] unsuccessful applicants for a permit to develop certain land within the Coastal Zone challenged the ruling against them. They propounded interrogatories asking the State to set forth: (1) "each and every reason" in support of its position that the dividing line for application of the Coastal Zone Conservation Act was "1000 yards from the mean high tide line of the Pacific Ocean," (2) "every State purpose to be furthered by" such classification and (3) "every compelling interest of the State" that would justify and support the Act. The Supreme Court directed the trial court to set aside its order compelling answers to these interrogatories: "The objections to these interrogatories should have been sustained because they seek to determine opinions of the Commission regarding the constitutionality of the Act, and such opinions have no relevance whatever to the purely legal problem of determining the validity of the Act on its face."[8]

In the *Sav-On Drugs* case,[9] a class action against several retailers for charging excessive sales taxes to their customers, the plaintiffs were not content to ask for the specific adjustments or deductions that a retailer had made on its sales tax returns. Another interrogatory sought to identify the law or regulation that, in the defendant's view, permitted those adjustments or deductions. The Supreme Court ruled that this interrogatory was objectionable:

> Both the California Revenue and Taxation Code and the California Administrative Code are as readily available to [plaintiffs] as to [defendant] and no purpose of discovery is served by compelling the latter to perform legal research for the former. Further, the request in essence seeks the legal reasoning and theories behind [defendant's] contention that any sales tax deductions it took are proper. A party's contention may be the subject of discovery, but not the legal reasoning or theory behind the contention.[10]

---

[4] Former CCP § 2016(b), 1956 Discovery Act, Appendix E.

[5] See Burke v Superior Court (1969) 71 Cal 2d 276, 284, 78 Cal Rptr 481, 490, 455 P2d 409, 418. See also CCP § 2018.040.

[6] Former CCP § 2030, 1956 Discovery Act, Appendix E.

[7] State of California v Superior Court (1974) 12 Cal 3d 237, 115 Cal Rptr 497, 524 P2d 1281.

[8] State of California v Superior Court (1974) 12 Cal 3d 237, 256, 115 Cal Rptr 497, 509, 524 P2d 1281, 1293.

[9] Sav-On Drugs, Inc. v Superior Court (1975) 15 Cal 3d 1, 123 Cal Rptr 283, 538 P2d 739.

[10] Sav-On Drugs, Inc. v Superior Court (1975) 15 Cal 3d 1, 5, 123 Cal Rptr 283, 286, 538 P2d 739, 742 (internal citation omitted). See also Flora Crane Service, Inc. v Superior Court (1965) 234 Cal App 2d 767, 780–782, 45 Cal Rptr 79, 85–87 [interrogatory improper that asks defendant

The *Burke* case [11] is also instructive. There, one of the plaintiffs' interrogatories asked for the "facts, grounds, and evidence" on which the defendant bonding company was basing one of its contentions. That portion of the interrogatory that asked for the "grounds and evidence" that would support the contention troubled the Court:

> It is possible that the interrogatories could be construed as requesting, inter alia, the bonding company's legal reasoning or theories. Therefore the trial court would be warranted in ruling that *insofar as they do* they need not be answered. . . . . For example, the bonding company may be required to divulge whether it contends that there is a defect in the undertaking or affidavit supporting the attachment, although it need not divulge the legal theory or reasoning process underlying a contention that there is such a defect. [12]

Not Permitted by the Current Statute: Section 2030.010 [13] now broadly authorizes the use of "contention" interrogatories. However, a careful reading discloses that it does not override the previous case law condemning interrogatories that ask for an opponent's legal reasoning: "An interrogatory is not objectionable because an answer to it . . . . would be *based on* . . . . legal theories developed in anticipation of litigation or in preparation for trial." [14] Almost any answer to a contention interrogatory will be "based on" the responding party's legal theories. This wording precludes an objection for that reason alone. It simply codifies the *Southern Pacific* holding [15] that a contention interrogatory is not objectionable simply because an answer to it might draw on legal conclusions and theories developed in preparation for trial. [16]

Moreover, the statute contains no wording authorizing interrogatories that ask opponents to set out the legal reasoning behind their contentions. This is in harmony with the present version of Federal Rule 33, which also does not permit interrogatories that "extend to matters of 'pure law,' i.e., legal issues unrelated to the facts of the case." [17]

---

to state why defendant claimed that the facts in the complaint did not constitute a cause of action]; Farnham v Superior Court (1961) 188 Cal App 2d 451, 454–455, 10 Cal Rptr 615, 616–617 [interrogatory improper that asks adverse party whether it fully performed its contract].

[11] Burke v Superior Court (1969) 71 Cal 2d 276, 78 Cal Rptr 481, 455 P2d 409 (originial italics).

[12] Burke v Superior Court (1969) 71 Cal 2d 276, 285, 78 Cal Rptr 481, 490, 455 P2d 409, 418.

[13] CCP § 2030.010(b).

[14] CCP § 2030.010(b) (Italics added).

[15] Southern Pacific Co. v Superior Court (1969) 3 Cal App 3d 195, 83 Cal Rptr 231. For a discussion of the *Southern Pacific* case, see § 5.10.

[16] For a further discussion of the relationship between "contention" interrogatories and the work product protection, see § 5.10.

[17] Advisory Committee Note to 1970 Amendments to Fed Rules Civ Proc, Rule 33(b). See Alta Health Strategies, Inc. v Kennedy (1992, D Utah) 790 F Supp 1085, 1098–1100 [interrogatory improper that asks party to explain how certain statements by others can be deemed an admission

§ 5.13 Timing

Federal Approach: While interrogatories may probe the factual basis for an opponent's contentions, their use early in the litigation poses other issues. In the *Convergent Technologies* case, a federal magistrate in California vividly described the dangers posed by the early use of contention interrogatories:

> [T]here is substantial reason to believe that the *early* knee jerk filing of sets of contention interrogatories that systematically track all the allegations in an opposing party's pleadings is a serious form of discovery abuse. Such comprehensive sets of contention interrogatories can be almost mindlessly generated, can be used to impose great burdens on opponents, and can generate a great deal of counterproductive friction between parties and counsel.[1]

In addition, he concluded that early contention interrogatories cause far more trouble than they are worth:

> Counsel drafting responses to these kinds of interrogatories early in the pretrial period may fear being boxed into a position that later embarrasses them, or that might be used to try to limit the subject areas of their subsequent discovery. Lawyers generally attempt to maximize and preserve their options while providing as little tactical help to their opponents as possible; so motivated they are likely to search for ways to give opponents as little information as they can get away with when they respond to contention interrogatories early in the trial period. The "substance" of their responses to such questions might reduce to phrases like "research and investigation continuing."[2]

He also stressed that although Federal Rule 33 provides that contention interrogatories "are not necessarily objectionable,"[3] it also empowers the trial court in its discretion "to order that such an interrogatory need not be answered until after designated discovery has been completed or until a pre-trial conference or until a later time."

Unwilling to proscribe altogether early contention interrogatories, this magistrate would instead have allowed a limited set of hand-crafted questions. However, if these met with objection, he would have placed the burden of justifying the timing of them on the propounding party. This burden would

binding on plaintiff]; Kendrick v Sullivan (1989, D DC) 125 FRD 1, 3 [interrogatory improper that asks party to express legal position on hypothetical factual scenarios]; O'Brien v International Brotherhood of Electrical Workers (1977, ND Ga) 443 F Supp 1182, 1187–1188 [interrogatory improper that asked a party to "state and explain the reason why" a particular federal statute did not invalidate certain provisions in a labor union's constitution].

[1] In re Convergent Technologies Securities Lit. (1985, ND Cal) 108 FRD 328, 337 (original italics).

[2] In re Convergent Technologies Securities Lit. (1985, ND Cal) 108 FRD 328, 338.

[3] Fed Rules Civ Proc, Rule 33(c).

include a showing of good reason to believe that early answers to these contention interrogatories will clarify or narrow the issues, promote settlement or expose frivolous positions. Several federal judges and magistrates have now followed this approach.[4]

California Approach: When the question of the validity of contention interrogatories first came before the Supreme Court in the *Singer* case,[5] one of the main objections to making them a part of California discovery practice was the claim that they would prematurely lock opponents into a particular theory and thereby deny them the benefit of subsequently developed information and insights. The Court categorically rejected this argument:

> The answers to these interrogatories would not have that legal effect. Answers to these interrogatories now, if compelled, will not prevent the defendant at the trial from relying on subsequently discovered facts, including facts produced at the trial by plaintiff or his witnesses, or by any of the other parties to this lawsuit, or their witnesses. In fact, such answers would not even prevent production of facts now known to defendant but not included in the answers, upon a proper showing that the oversight was in good faith.[6]

Section 2030.010 codifies the previous California case law relating to contention interrogatories.[7] Unlike Federal Rule 33, this provision does not in so many words give the trial court discretion to defer answers.

§ 5.14 Protective Orders

Grounds for Protective Orders: Under Section 2030.090, to prevent "unwarranted annoyance, embarrassment, or oppression, or undue burden or expense," the trial court can relieve a party from the need to respond to interrogatories.[1] This provision differs from its predecessor in the 1956 Discovery Act[2] in four minor respects. First, it adds to the original trio of annoyance, embarrassment and oppression a fourth ground for seeking the court's protection, namely, the "undue burden and expense" that a response will entail. Second, it uses the adjective "unwarranted" to underscore that mere "annoyance" and "embarrassment" are not grounds for avoiding an answer. Third, it includes a nonexclusive list of the protections that a responding party may request. Finally, it clarifies

---

[4] See B. Braun Medical Inc. v Abbott Laboratories (1994, ED Pa) 155 FRD 525; Fischer and Porter Co. v Tolson (1992, ED Pa) 143 FRD 93; Nestle Foods Corp. v Aetna Casualty & Surety Co. (1990, D NJ) 135 FRD 101; but see In re One Bancorp Securities Litigation (D Maine) 134 FRD 4, 7.

[5] Singer v Superior Court (1960) 54 Cal 2d 318, 5 Cal Rptr 697, 353 P2d 305.

[6] Singer v Superior Court (1960) 54 Cal 2d 318, 325, 5 Cal Rptr 697, 701, 353 P2d 305, 309. For a discussion of the use of a supplemental interrogatory to obtain this later-acquired information, see § 5.7.

[7] CCP § 2030.010(b).

[1] CCP § 2030.090(b).

[2] Former CCP 2030(c), 1956 Discovery Act, Appendix E.

that not only the responding party, but also other parties to the lawsuit and even "affected" nonparties, may seek a protective order.[3]

—Challenging the Need to Exceed Presumptive Limit: Section 2030.030 allows a party to propound more than the presumptive limit of 35 "specially prepared" interrogatories if an accompanying declaration sets forth the necessity for exceeding that limit.[4] The recipient of such a set of interrogatories may challenge that declaration by a motion for a protective order.[5]

—Eleventh-Hour Interrogatories: Even though timely under the discovery cut-off provision,[6] an eleventh-hour set of interrogatories may be oppressive and unduly burdensome. In that case, the trial court can order that the interrogatories "need not be answered."[7] For example, in *Day v Rosenthal,*[8] a complex case that had been pending for several years, a defendant waited until the trial date was only a few months away to serve nine sets of voluminous interrogatories. The appellate court upheld the protective order that relieved the plaintiffs of the need to respond:

> [T]he interrogatories came very late in the proceedings, were volumi-
> nous, would require so much time to answer that the trial would
> inevitably have to be postponed, and were without focus. In addition,
> the interrogatories were, in very large measure, inquiries concerning
> allegations which had been in the pleadings for as long as five years.
> The trial court should rightly have been concerned that perhaps the
> reason for the rush to discovery was less to obtain information than to
> overburden the [plaintiffs].[9]

—Possibility of Mootness: The recipient of a set of interrogatories may wish to postpone answering some or all of them until the court has ruled on a pending motion that could moot the need for the information sought. A motion for a protective order can accomplish this postponement. Class actions provide an example. The trial court may rule that a party need not respond to interrogatories probing the merits of the underlying cause of action until it has decided whether the case may proceed as a class action.[10] It may also postpone answers to merits-related interrogatories pending its disposition of a jurisdictional challenge[11] or a motion to stay or dismiss for forum non conveniens.[12]

---

[3] CCP § 2030.090(a).

[4] For a discussion of the presumptive numerical limit on interrogatories, see § 5.6.

[5] CCP § 2030.090(b)(2).

[6] CCP § 2024.020(a).

[7] CCP § 2030.090(b)(1).

[8] Day v Rosenthal (1985) 170 Cal App 3d 1125, 1169–1173, 217 Cal Rptr 89, 117–120.

[9] Day v Rosenthal (1985) 170 Cal App 3d 1125, 1172, 217 Cal Rptr 89, 119.

[10] See Coriell v Superior Court (1974) 39 Cal App 3d 487, 493, 114 Cal Rptr 310, 315.

[11] Cf. Investment Properties Intl., Ltd. v IOS, Ltd. (1972 CA2 NY) 459 F2d 705 [quashing deposition notices].

[12] Cf. Fitzgerald v Texaco, Inc. (1975 CA2 NY) 521 F2d 448, 451 n3 [denying document production].

—**Confidential Information:** Interrogatories may pertain to information that, while otherwise discoverable, is nevertheless quite sensitive or confidential. Trade secrets are the classic examples. The trial court can seal or restrict access to answers involving such material.[13]

—**Extensions of Time:** The responding party may need more than 30-days for serving a response.[14] If the propounding party will not agree to an extension, a motion for a protective order can get this additional time.[15]

Burden of Persuasion: Normally, the party seeking some protection against answering interrogatories must persuade the court that the task would cause unwarranted annoyance, embarrassment, oppression, or undue burden and expense.[16] Where, however, a party seeks to propound more than the presumptive limit of 35 "specially prepared" interrogatories, Section 2030.040 squarely requires the propounding party to convince the court that the greater number is necessary:

> If the responding party seeks a protective order on the ground that the number of specially prepared interrogatories is unwarranted, the propounding party shall have the burden of justifying the number of these interrogatories.[17]

"Objections" and "Protection" Distinguished: Strictly speaking, "objections" to interrogatories and protective order motions are not interchangeable. A motion for a protective order is improper when the only ground for resisting discovery is that an interrogatory seeks irrelevant or privileged material. In such cases, the responding party should serve a "response" that includes an "objection" to any questions that are outside the scope of permissible discovery.[18] Moreover, where a party propounds more than 35 "specially prepared" interrogatories *without* the required justifying declaration, the responding party should state in the "response" an "objection" to all interrogatories over the statutory limit.[19]

Protective orders are better reserved for interrogatories that are, at least arguably, within the scope of allowable discovery, yet nonetheless warrant trial court intervention because they are, for example, burdensome. However, as long as the motion for a protective order clearly informs the other party of the basis

---

[13] CCP §§ 2030.090(b)(6) and (7). Cf. Ryan v Superior Court (1960) 186 Cal App 2d 813, 820, 9 Cal Rptr 147, 152.

[14] CCP § 2030.260(a).

[15] CCP § 2030.090(b)(3).

[16] Coriell v Superior Court (1974) 39 Cal App 3d 487, 492–493, 114 Cal Rptr 310, 314–315; People v Superior Court (Witzerman) (1967) 248 Cal App 2d 276, 280, 56 Cal Rptr 393, 397.

[17] CCP § 2030.040(b).

[18] See CCP § 2030.210. For a discussion of a response that objects to an interrogatory, see § 5.18.

[19] CCP § 2030.030(c). For a discussion of interrogatories exceeding the 35-question limit, see § 5.6.

for objecting to an interrogatory, it would elevate form over substance to deny the motion simply because the "response" is the correct vehicle for raising it.[20]

The reverse situation raises different concerns. Courts have sometimes been reluctant to consider "objections," in a "response," that a discovery request would be annoying, embarrassing, oppressive or burdensome. There are two reasons for this strict attitude. First, before moving for a protective order, a party must consider the prospect of a monetary sanction if the court finds no substantial justification for the motion. The deterrent effect of this threat might be lost if a party could raise by objection an issue such as the annoyance, embarrassment, oppression, burden or expense of responding to interrogatories.[21] Second, a protective order motion is subject to a "meet and confer" requirement;[22] an objection is not.[23]

Nevertheless, in the *Coy* case,[24] defendants "objected" to certain interrogatories on the ground that they had already supplied the same information during their depositions. Adverting to the protective order provision, the Supreme Court remarked that "defendants made no motion to protect their rights as required by the code section."[25] Despite this procedural misstep, the Court considered the merits of the "objection."[26]

Duty to Meet and Confer: Before moving for a protective order, the party receiving interrogatories must try to work out informally the points of dispute with the one propounding party them. A declaration setting forth these efforts must accompany the motion.[27]

Sanction: One who unsuccessfully makes or opposes a motion for a protective order should expect a monetary sanction unless that party can convince the court that, despite this lack of success, there was "substantial justification" for making or opposing the motion.[28]

---

[20] See, e.g., Brown v Superior Court (1963) 218 Cal App 2d 430, 32 Cal Rptr 527 [ruling on the merits of objections to interrogatories, although they were raised via motion to quash]; but see Ryan v Superior Court (1960) 186 Cal App 2d 813, 820, 9 Cal Rptr 147, 152 [if responding party claims that an interrogatory calls for confidential information in the nature of a trade secret, it should move for a protective order instead of lodging an objection to the interrogatory].

[21] Coy v Superior Court (1962) 58 Cal 2d 210, 218, 23 Cal Rptr 393, 396, 373 P2d 457, 460 [objection that an *interrogatory* covered same matters as did previous deposition should have been raised by a motion for a protective order]; Zellerino v Brown (1991) 235 Cal App 3d 1097, 1101–1102, 1 Cal Rptr 2d 222, 224 [remedy of party receiving a premature *demand to exchange expert witness information* is a motion for a protective order, not an objection to the demand].

[22] CCP § 2030.090(a).

[23] See Zellerino v Brown (1991) 235 Cal App 3d 1097, 1101–1102, 1 Cal Rptr 2d 222, 224.

[24] Coy v Superior Court (1962) 58 Cal 2d 210, 23 Cal Rptr 393, 373 P2d 457.

[25] Coy v Superior Court (1962) 58 Cal 2d 210, 218, 23 Cal Rptr 393, 396, 373 P2d 457, 460.

[26] See also Durst v Superior Court (1963) 218 Cal App 2d 460, 466–468, 32 Cal Rptr 627, 631–632 [claim that interrogatories were oppressive and burdensome raised by objection instead of by motion for protective order].

[27] CCP § 2030.090(a).

[28] CCP § 2030.090(d).

§ 5.15 Response: Format, Signature and Service

Format: Absent circumstances warranting a protective order,[1] a party served with a set of interrogatories must prepare a "response."[2] Immediately below the title of the case, there should appear the name of the responding party, the name of the propounding party, and the same identifying number that appears on the set of interrogatories itself. After that, the answering party must respond "separately" to each interrogatory in the set. That answer must arrange the individual responses in the same sequence and identify them by the same number or letter as the corresponding interrogatory. It helps to retype the text of each interrogatory before answering it, but this is not required.

Three Types of Response: The answering party must make some "response" to each individual interrogatory. The term "response" in Section 2030.210[3] has a triple meaning: an "answer,"[4] a tender of access to records from which the answer can be derived,[5] or an "objection."[6]

—Nitpicking Prohibited: The current statutes reflect two serious legislative efforts to eliminate hypertechnical, nitpicking interpretations of interrogatories. First, if only part of an interrogatory is objectionable, a party must still answer the rest of the question.[7] Second, a party who is unable to answer a particular interrogatory completely must answer it to the extent possible.[8]

Signing the Response: The nature of the responses to individual interrogatories affects who must sign the response document.[9] If the "response" consists entirely of objections, then only the attorney need sign the document. If it consists entirely of "answers" or records-access tenders, then only the answering party must sign it; the attorney need not. If the response includes not only answers and records-access tenders, but also objections, then both the party and the attorney must sign the document. In addition, the party must swear to the factual information in the answers and tenders. However, the lack of the party's signature and oath on a timely response that includes such a mixture does not waive the objections it contains:

> The provision that a response consisting solely of objections need not
> be verified confirms that an objection in an unverified "hybrid" response
> is nonetheless effective. The verification requirement for a response

---

[1] For a discussion of protective orders against interrogatories, see § 5.14.

[2] CCP § 2030.210(a).

[3] CCP § 2030.210(a).

[4] See § 5.16.

[5] See § 5.16.

[6] See § 5.17.

[7] CCP § 2030.240(a).

[8] CCP § 2030.220(b). For a discussion of the duty to supplement an incomplete response, see § 5.7.

[9] CCP § 2030.250.

which contains matter other than objections operates to support the *other* statements in the response. The objections themselves do not require a verification in order to be preserved. [¶] . . . . . The statutes reflect the recognition that objections are legal conclusions interposed by counsel, not factual assertions by a party, making their verification unnecessary.[10]

This interpretation was followed in *Food 4 Less Supermarkets,* which rejected an argument that the lack of verification rendered the objections untimely:

[T]here is no need to verify that portion of the response containing the objections. Thus, if the response is served within the statutory time period, that portion of the response must be considered timely notwithstanding the lack of verification. The omission of the verification in the portion of the response containing fact specific responses merely renders *that* portion of the response untimely and therefore only creates a right to move for orders and sanctions . . . . *as to those responses* but does not result in a waiver of the objections made.[11]

—**Institutional Parties:** Where the responding party is an entity (for example, a corporation, partnership, or governmental agency), one of its officers or agents must sign for that party.[12] This agent may be an attorney for the entity, but in that event a limited waiver of the lawyer-client privilege and the work product protection occurs. The answering party may not later use either to block efforts to learn from that attorney "the identity of the sources" used by the attorney to obtain the information contained in any of the answers.[13]

Wards: Section 2030.250 requires interrogatories to be signed by "the party" to whom they are directed.[14] In the *Regency Health Service* case,[15] the plaintiff, injured while a patient in a nursing home, was incompetent, and the court had appointed a guardian ad litem for her. The guardian ad litem persuaded the trial court that plaintiff's incompetence prevented her from verifying the response, and that the guardian had neither the duty nor the authority to verify the response on her behalf. The appellate court, recognizing that such a ruling would effectively insulate incompetent parties from providing discovery, held that "a

[10] Blue Ridge Ins. Co. v Superior Court (1988) 202 Cal App 3d 339, 344–345, 248 Cal Rptr 346, 349–350 [dealing with a response to an *inspection demand*].

[11] Food 4 Less Supermarkets v Superior Court (1995) 40 Cal App 4th 651, 657–658, 46 Cal Rptr 2d 925, 928–929 [unverified response to an *inspection demand* (original italics)].

[12] By signing interrogatories on behalf of an entity, an officer or agent also named as a party, but as yet unserved, does not make an appearance in the action. See Semole v Sansoucie (1972) 28 Cal App 3d 714, 723–724, 104 Cal Rptr 897, 903 [interpreting CCP § 2030 of the 1956 Discovery Act].

[13] CCP § 2030.250(b).

[14] CCP § 2030.250(a).

[15] Regency Health Services, Inc. v Superior Court (1998) 64 Cal App 4th 1496, 76 Cal Rptr 2d 95.

ward has no general right to evade discovery and that a guardian ad litem has the authority, subject to the court's ultimate supervision, to verify proper responses to interrogatories on behalf of the ward."[16]

Oath: Where the response requires the signature of a party, it must be under oath or it is "legally invalid."[17] A "response" to interrogatories is unlike an answer to a complaint, which the attorney for a party may "verify" when the client resides outside the county of the attorney's office.[18] Where an attorney has had a client sign several undated, blank verification forms, that attorney may not prepare answers to interrogatories and then, without consulting the client about their accuracy, simply attach a presigned verification to these answers and serve them on opposing counsel: "The *use* of a presigned verification in discovery proceedings, without first consulting with the client to assure that any assertions of fact are true, is a clear and serious violation of the statutes and the rules."[19]

Time for Response: The response is normally due 30 days after service of the interrogatories.[20] Service of the response by mail increases this period, however, usually by five days.[21] The propounding and the responding parties may agree to extend this period without court approval.[22] The agreement may be informal, but the parties must confirm it in a writing that specifies the date agreed on for a response.[23] Unless the agreement specifies to the contrary, it preserves not only the right to "answer" an interrogatory, but also to object and to tender records-access.[24]

Service and Custody of Response: The answering party must serve the original of the response on the party who served the interrogatories and simultaneously must send an informational copy to all other parties.[25] The propounding party must retain the originals both of the interrogatories and of the response to them until six months after the case is over.[26]

---

[16] Regency Health Services, Inc. v Superior Court (1998) 64 Cal App 4th 1496, 1504–1505, 76 Cal Rptr 2d 95, 100.

[17] See Laguna Auto Body v Farmers Ins. Exchange (1991) 231 Cal App 3d 481, 489, 282 Cal Rptr 530, 536.

[18] CCP § 446. Cf. Steele v Totah (1986) 180 Cal App 3d 545, 550, 225 Cal Rptr 635, 637 [CCP § 446 does not apply to a response to admission requests].

[19] See Drociak v State Bar (1991) 52 Cal 3d 1085, 1090, 278 Cal Rptr 86, 89, 804 P2d 711, 714 [not realizing that his inability to contact his client was because she had died, plaintiff's attorney prepared answers to interrogatories and attached presigned declaration].

[20] CCP § 2030.260(a). On motion the court may shorten or extend this time period.

[21] CCP § 2016.050, referencing CCP § 1013(a).

[22] CCP § 2030.270(a).

[23] CCP § 2030.270(b).

[24] CCP § 2030.270(c).

[25] CCP § 2030.260(b).

[26] CCP § 2030.280(b).

§ 5.16 Answers

Basic Requirement: A party must "respond"[1] to each interrogatory in one of three ways: an "answer," a "tender of access to records,"[2] or an "objection"[3] An "answer" is a "response" that supplies the information sought by the particular interrogatory. Section 2030.220 requires that an answer be a "complete and straightforward" reply to the interrogatory.[4] Compliance with this provision requires more than a gesture.[5] A reply that is nonresponsive, incomplete or evasive,[6] of course, fails this requirement.

> Parties, like witnesses, are required to state the truth, the whole truth, and nothing but the truth in answering interrogatories. Where the question is specific and explicit, an answer that supplies only a portion of the information sought is wholly insufficient.[7]

For example, an answer that simply tells the propounding parties where they may find the desired information is not "complete": "[I]t is not proper to answer by stating, 'See my deposition,' 'See my pleading,' or 'See the financial statement.'"[8]

Evasive Answer: An "evasive" reply misuses discovery[9] and warrants a sanction upon the responding party. Case law illustrates evasive interrogatory answers. For example, one may not duck an answer to an interrogatory seeking the identity of certain persons by stating simply that the records containing such information have been destroyed: "[Defendant's] sworn answers to these interrogatories refer *only* to the unavailability of information because certain documents were not available, but make no mention of defendant's *personal* knowledge of

---

[1] CCP § 2030.210(a). For a discussion of the general format of the "response" to interrogatories, see § 5.15.

[2] For a discussion of a response that tenders access to records, see § 5.17.

[3] For a discussion of objections to interrogatories, see § 5.18.

[4] CCP § 2030.220(a). See Olmstead v Arthur J. Gallagher & Co. (2002) 104 Cal App 4th 858, 868, 128 Cal Rptr 2d 573, 580 [an answer to an interrogatory that is "blatantly false" certainly does not meet this requirement].

[5] See, e.g., Herdlein Technologies v Century Contractors (1993, WD NC) 147 FRD 103; Jefferson v Davis (1990, ND Ill) 131 FRD 522, 529–532.

[6] See, e.g., Stein v Hassen (1973) 34 Cal App 3d 294, 300 n6, 109 Cal Rptr 321, 325 n6; Fuss v Superior Court (1969) 273 Cal App 2d 807, 816–817, 78 Cal Rptr 583, 589.

[7] Deyo v Kilbourne (1978) 84 Cal App 3d 771, 783, 149 Cal Rptr 499, 509 [internal citation omitted].

[8] Deyo v Kilbourne (1978) 84 Cal App 3d 771, 783–784, 149 Cal Rptr 499, 510. See also Mahoney v Kempton (1992, D Mass) 142 FRD 32, 33 ["interrogatory answers must be complete in and of themselves; other documents or pleadings may not be incorporated into an answer by reference"]; Jefferson v Davis (1990, ND Ill) 131 FRD 522, 527 [answer directing propounding party to look at certain investigative reports to obtain the information sought is "incomplete"]. Annotation: Propriety of answer to interrogatory merely referring to other documents or sources of information. 96 ALR2d 598. For a discussion of the sufficiency of an answer tendering the responding party's records, see § 5.17.

[9] CCP § 2023.010(f).

the information sought."[10] And when a party is asked how it performed a certain contract, an answer that it "did everything required" contributes nothing.[11]

An answer that is based on a deliberate and hypertechnical misreading of an interrogatory is evasive. For instance, where a party inquired about the dollar volume of "sales of bolted steel tanks made outside of the United States," the defendant responded as if the word "made" modified "tanks" instead of "sales." It simply stated that it made no tanks outside of the United States. The trial court deemed this a "deliberate misconstruction" of the interrogatory.[12]

Nor may the responding party reshape the question by prefatory language, and then answer only in terms of its own version of the interrogatory. For example, in *Dollar v Long Mfg., Inc.*,[13] an interrogatory in a product liability case sought information as to *all* accidents involving its product known to the manufacturer. An answer that expressly limited itself to accidents occurring *before* the one involved in the lawsuit was deemed evasive:

> Discovery by interrogatory requires candor in responding. . . . . The candor required is a candid statement of the information sought or of the fact that objection is made to furnishing the information. A partial answer by a party reserving an undisclosed objection to answering fully is not candid. It is evasive.[14]

More frequently, "deftly worded conclusionary answers"[15] signal an evasive response. In *Petersen v Vallejo*,[16] for example, the State asked the plaintiff to supply "in detail the factual basis" for her allegations that it had negligently controlled a certain highway.[17] The plaintiff answered only that the road "was allowed to become and was a hazard to people using it for its intended purpose, to-wit: as a thoroughfare for automobiles."[18] Ordered to amplify this answer, plaintiff responded that the State "allowed certain road markings and directional guides to remain on said roadway" that were "hazardous to people operating their automobiles under the conditions that prevailed" at the time of the accident.[19]

---

[10] Alliance to End Repression v Rochford (1976, ND Ill) 75 FRD 438, 440 (original italics). See also Welgoss v End (1967) 252 Cal App 2d 982, 984 n2, 61 Cal Rptr 52, 54 n2.

[11] Kieran v Johnson-March Corp. (1945, ED NY) 7 FRD 128, 131.

[12] Hunter v International Systems & Controls Corp. (1970, WD Mo) 51 FRD 251, 257, cited with approval in Deyo v Kilbourne (1978) 84 Cal App 3d 771, 783, 149 Cal Rptr 499, 509. See also Mead Corp. v Riverwood Natural Resources Corp. (1992, D Minn) 145 FRD 512, 516 ["interrogatories should be reasonably interpreted in light of both the letter and spirit of the Discovery rules. . . . . [T]his court looks askance at total resistance to discovery predicated upon semantic games"].

[13] Dollar v Long Mfg. (1977, CA5 Ga) 561 F2d 613.

[14] Dollar v Long Mfg. (1977, CA5 Ga) 561 F2d 613, 616–617.

[15] Deyo v Kilbourne (1978) 84 Cal App 3d 771, 783, 149 Cal Rptr 499, 509.

[16] Petersen v Vallejo (1968) 259 Cal App 2d 757, 66 Cal Rptr 776.

[17] Petersen v Vallejo (1968) 259 Cal App 2d 757, 778–779, 66 Cal Rptr 776, 790.

[18] Petersen v Vallejo (1968) 259 Cal App 2d 757, 779, 66 Cal Rptr 776, 790.

[19] Petersen v Vallejo (1968) 259 Cal App 2d 757, 779, 66 Cal Rptr 776, 790.

Directed to describe the markings and directional guides and to specify their location, plaintiff answered only that the State "allowed two divider strippings to remain" on the roadway, and that these "would and did create confusion as to which direction the roadway led."[20] This, too, the court deemed insufficient.[21]

Duty to Inquire of Third Persons: The most frequently raised issue about the adequacy of an "answer" to an interrogatory involves the responding party's efforts to limit its response to information it personally knows. The original Discovery Act was rather vague concerning a party's obligation to go beyond its personal knowledge in order to answer an interrogatory. It stated simply that one must "furnish such information as is *available* to the party."[22] In several cases, the California courts recognized that a mere profession of lack of personal knowledge did not automatically constitute an adequate answer to an interrogatory.[23]

The current provision explicitly recognizes that parties may not limit interrogatory answers to information then within their personal knowledge:

> If the responding party does not have personal knowledge sufficient to respond fully to an interrogatory, that party shall so state, but shall make a reasonable and good faith effort to obtain the information by inquiry to other natural persons or organizations, except where the information is equally available to the propounding party.[24]

The current statute clarifies five matters. First, a party does not always discharge its duty to answer an interrogatory simply by supplying all information within its personal knowledge at the time of the answer.

> Information regarding the number of patrons, accidents, employees on a given day . . . . is information that is usually documented by a large business operation in its business records. For [defendant] to intimate that it does not know or cannot give approximate answers to such questions makes it appear as if defendant is attempting to be evasive in its answers, or that it has not done a reasonable review of its business records for such answers.[25]

---

[20] Petersen v Vallejo (1968) 259 Cal App 2d 757, 778–779, 66 Cal Rptr 776, 790.

[21] Petersen v Vallejo (1968) 259 Cal App 2d 757, 784, 66 Cal Rptr 776, 793–794. See also Stein v Hassen (1973) 34 Cal App 3d 294, 109 Cal Rptr 321; Fuss v Superior Court (1969) 273 Cal App 2d 807, 78 Cal Rptr 583; Caryl Richards, Inc. v Superior Court (1961) 188 Cal App 2d 300, 10 Cal Rptr 377.

[22] Former CCP § 2030(a), 1956 Discovery Act, Appendix E (italics added).

[23] Jones v Superior Court (1981) 119 Cal App 3d 534, 174 Cal Rptr 148; Sigerseth v Superior Court (1972) 23 Cal App 3d 427, 100 Cal Rptr 185; Pantzalas v Superior Court (1969) 272 Cal App 2d 499, 77 Cal Rptr 354; Unger v Los Angeles Transit Lines (1960) 180 Cal App 2d 172, 4 Cal Rptr 370.

[24] CCP § 2030.220(c).

[25] Hickman v Wal-Mart Stores, Inc. (1993, MD Fla) 152 FRD 216, 222–223.

Second, a "complete" interrogatory answer may require some inquiry of other persons. Third, the duty to inquire is limited: the responding party need make only "a reasonable and good faith effort". Fourth, the responding party need make no inquiry where the information sought is equally available to the propounding party. Finally, the responding party must identify any part of an answer that is not based on personal knowledge.

Reasonable Inquiry: Although the statute answers these five questions, it leaves one major bone of contention: what constitutes a "reasonable" inquiry. The cases decided under the former statute provide considerable guidance. In the five cases summarized below, the critical factor seems to be the existence of a connection or relationship between the responding party and the knowledgeable third person that makes it likely that the latter will honor a request for the information.

In the *Sigerseth* case,[26] for example, the defendant received an interrogatory concerning the extent of his trial expert's experience, training and education. He answered that all he knew was that the expert was a licensed professional engineer, and he refused to expend either the time or the money to secure from the expert himself further details. The court held that he must make this effort: "[T]here is no rule which holds that proper discovery is limited to interrogatories which may be answered without effort or loss of time."[27]

In the *Pantzalas* case,[28] a group insurer insisted that the master policy expressly excluded from its coverage an accidental death in a plane crash. The plaintiff propounded an interrogatory asking whether a copy of that policy had been provided to the insured employee. The insurance company's answer merely referred the plaintiffs to the decedent's employer, which, under the agreement with the defendant, had promised to deliver individual certificates to its employees. The court held that the insurance company had to make the inquiries necessary to determine whether the employer had fulfilled this delegated duty: "While it may impose a burden on the insurer to do the necessary research to obtain the requested information as to whether an individual certificate was issued to [the insured], it is a burden which is inherent in the way [defendant] has elected to do business."[29]

In the *Unger* case,[30] the court held that the responding party had to procure from his insurance carrier the information necessary to answer an interrogatory.

The *Jones* case[31] involved a plaintiff who claimed injury to herself from her mother's ingestion of a drug while the daughter was *in utero*. The appellate court

[26] Sigerseth v Superior Court (1972) 23 Cal App 3d 427, 100 Cal Rptr 185.

[27] Sigerseth v Superior Court (1972) 23 Cal App 3d 427, 433, 100 Cal Rptr 185, 188.

[28] Pantzalas v Superior Court (1969) 272 Cal App 2d 499, 77 Cal Rptr 354.

[29] Pantzalas v Superior Court (1969) 272 Cal App 2d 499, 504, 77 Cal Rptr 354, 358. See also Zervos v S.S. Sam Houston (1978, SD NY) 79 FRD 593 [party must request internal memoranda from its Swiss bank].

[30] Unger v Los Angeles Transit Lines (1960) 180 Cal App 2d 172, 175, 4 Cal Rptr 370, 372–373.

[31] Jones v Superior Court (1981) 119 Cal App 3d 534, 174 Cal Rptr 148.

upheld the trial court's order that plaintiff at least make a good faith effort to get from her mother the information about the latter's medical history needed to answer interrogatories:

> We, of course, do not suggest that a mother's information is necessarily or even typically within the power of her daughter to obtain for the asking. The relationship of mothers and daughters is undoubtedly as varied as human beings upon the earth, and certainly beyond the power of courts to predict, much less to control . . . . But from the record before the court, it appears that plaintiff's mother has been cooperating closely in her daughter's lawsuit; the making of inquiry posed no discernible burden upon the plaintiff . . . . Of course, her mother was and is free to say no for privacy reasons or any reasons.[32]

A California court would probably agree with the federal trial judge who held that personal injury plaintiffs, asked to itemize their medical expenses, may not respond that as yet they have received no bill for these services:

> The plaintiff's answer . . . to the effect that he has not received bills for charges made to him for treatments is insufficient and this interrogatory should be answered to the extent reasonably possible as a result of inquiries by him to his physicians.[33]

Indeed, Section 2030.220 provides that if a complete answer cannot be provided to a particular interrogatory, it should be answered "to the extent possible."[34]

By contrast, it would be unfair to permit one party, by simply propounding an interrogatory, to require another party to engage in extraordinary investigations to answer it. The *Holguin* case[35] involved a medical malpractice claim arising out of a mother's death during childbirth. The plaintiff propounded interrogatories to the attending physician and the anesthetist seeking facts relating to the autopsy performed by the coroner's office. The doctors answered that they did not know this information since they had not attended the procedure. The court held that they were under no obligation to inquire of those who had performed the autopsy:

> We do not believe that plaintiffs had a right to different answers. They seem to take the position that the propounding of the interrogatories created a duty in defendants to start an investigation with the various persons in the coroner's office who participated in the autopsy and then to answer in accordance with the information thus gathered, even if the facts learned were antagonistic to their trial posture. We know of no

---

[32] Jones v Superior Court (1981) 119 Cal App 3d 534, 552–553, 174 Cal Rptr 148, 159 (internal citation omitted).

[33] Lowe v Greyhound Corp. (1938, DC Mass) 25 F Supp 643, 646. See also Hodge v Osteopathic General Hospital (1969, RI) 249 A2d 81.

[34] CCP § 2030.220(b).

[35] Holguin v Superior Court (1972) 22 Cal App 3d 812, 99 Cal Rptr 653.

principle of discovery law which thus compels a party not only to prepare his opponent's case, but also to stipulate away his own.[36]

Where, even after inquiry to any reasonably available sources, a party still cannot answer a particular interrogatory, it is, of course, permissible to so state in the response. However, the answer must also "set forth the efforts made to secure the information."[37]

§ 5.17 Tender of Access to Records

Information Requiring a Records Search: Much information relevant to a lawsuit reposes in the parties' files and records. Litigants who want to examine these records for themselves should serve an inspection demand.[1] In many situations, however, a party does not want access to the records themselves, but simply wants the information that they contain. As long as this information is simple and the records containing it are readily accessible, a party should be able to discover it by an interrogatory rather than by a demand to inspect those records.

Sometimes, however, a litigant would be able to supply the information called for by an interrogatory only by sorting through its records and compiling or summarizing their contents. For example, in the *West Pico Furniture* case,[2] plaintiff furniture company sought the names and addresses of all employees of defendant finance company who had participated in certain transactions with plaintiff. An answer to this interrogatory would have required the finance company to compile records located in over 75 branch offices.[3]

A federal case[4] provides another example: almost 100 factory workers, suing to recover portal-to-portal pay for a six-year period, sought by an interrogatory to learn from their employer the hours each had worked every day during this time. An answer to this interrogatory would require, first, a sorting out of their clock times from those of other employees on 60,000 clock tapes, each containing 150,000 entries, and then an analysis of each of the quarter of a million entries that would pertain to the plaintiffs.[5]

---

[36] Holguin v Superior Court (1972) 22 Cal App 3d 812, 821, 99 Cal Rptr 653, 658. See also Alpine Mutual Water Co. v Superior Court (1968) 259 Cal App 2d 45, 53–54, 66 Cal Rptr 250, 255.

[37] Deyo v Kilbourne (1978) 84 Cal App 3d 771, 782, 149 Cal Rptr 499, 509. See also International Fertilizer & Chemical Corp. v Brasileiro (1957, SD NY) 21 FRD 193, 194.

[1] For a discussion of inspection demands as a method of discovery, see Chapter 6.

[2] West Pico Furniture Co. v Superior Court (1961) 56 Cal 2d 407, 15 Cal Rptr 119, 364 P2d 295.

[3] Instead of tendering access to its records as permitted by former CCP § 2030(c), defendant unsuccessfully objected to the interrogatory on the ground that answering it would be "burdensome." West Pico Furniture Co. v Superior Court (1961) 56 Cal 2d 407, 420, 15 Cal Rptr 119, 125, 364 P2d 295, 301.

[4] Adelman v Nordberg Mfg. Co. (1947, ED Wis) 6 FRD 383.

[5] Because Fed Rules Civ Proc, Rule 33 then contained no provision for tendering access to records, the trial court ordered defendant to search its records and supply the information sought.

Option of Making Records Available: If no other way existed to handle such an interrogatory, the responding party would almost inevitably either move for a protective order[6] or object[7] because of the undue burden and expense connected with answering it. Section 2030.230, however, allows[8] the responding party to avoid the expenditure of the time, energy and money that an "answer"[9] to such an interrogatory would entail. In effect, it lets the responding party tells the propounding party to "do it yourself." Instead of supplying the information from its records, the responding party simply offers access to those records so that the propounding party may ferret out and compile the information itself.[10] The option naturally makes it considerably less likely that an objection or a motion for a protective order directed at the burdensomeness of the interrogatory would be successful.[11]

Answer Must Entail a Compilation: This option is not available every time a responding party would have to consult its records to supply the information called for in an interrogatory. A responding party may invoke this option only where "the answer to an interrogatory would necessitate the preparation or the making of a compilation, abstract, audit, or summary of or from" those records.[12] The *Kaiser Foundation Hospitals* case[13] exemplifies the proper use of this option. A medical facility, sued for alleged malpractice during the birth of a child, was asked to "state in exact detail all of the facts and circumstances leading up to the delivery" of the child, as well as "the course and progress" of both the labor and the delivery. The hospital responded that its patient records contained this information and offered to make these records accessible. The court sustained its response:

> Normally, each significant event in a medical procedure is recorded, and the recording is done as nearly contemporaneously as possible with the event itself. Ordinarily, the written record is far more accurate and contains far more detail than the personal recollection of a participant in the event.[14]

---

[6] For a discussion of protective orders against answering interrogatories, see § 5.14.

[7] For a discussion of objections to interrogatories, see § 5.18.

[8] A similar option was provided by the 1956 Discovery Act. Former CCP § 2030(d), 1956 Discovery Act, Appendix E.

[9] For a discussion of the answer to an interrogatory, see § 5.16.

[10] CCP § 2030.230. Annotation: Propriety of answer to interrogatory merely referring to other documents or sources of information. 96 ALR2d 598.

[11] See West Pico Furniture Co. v Superior Court (1961) 56 Cal 2d 407, 420, 15 Cal Rptr 119, 125, 364 P2d 295, 301; Flora Crane Service, Inc. v Superior Court (1965) 234 Cal App 2d 767, 779–780, 45 Cal Rptr 79, 85.

[12] CCP § 2030.230.

[13] Kaiser Foundation Hospitals v Superior Court (1969) 275 Cal App 2d 801, 802, 80 Cal Rptr 263, 264.

[14] Kaiser Foundation Hospitals v Superior Court (1969) 275 Cal App 2d 801, 804, 80 Cal Rptr 263, 265.

Equality of Burden of Records Search: A party may not invoke the tender-of-records option simply because an interrogatory would require a compilation from or a summary of its records.[15] Like its federal counterpart,[16] this option only exists "if the burden or expense" of doing so "would be substantially the same for the party propounding the interrogatory as for the responding party."[17]

Requirements: Section 2030.230 sets out the requirements for the tender-of-records option. It is available only when the information sought by an interrogatory reposes in the records "of the party to whom the interrogatory is directed."[18] Accordingly, the responding party may not direct the propounding party to its own records.[19]

The written response to the interrogatory must refer to Section 2030.230, and "specify" the records from which the information sought "may be derived or ascertained." This specification must contain "sufficient detail" to enable the propounding party to locate and identify the pertinent records with the same facility as the responding party can. This requirement prevents a responding party from making a propounding party search through a haystack of records looking for a needle of information. In the words of one court: "A broad statement that the information is available from a mass of documents is insufficient."[20]

Improper Use of Option: A responding party may not use the option to send the propounding party on a wild goose chase. For example, in a federal antitrust case,[21] an interrogatory probed for the details of any market-allocation agreements that the defendant might have reached with its distributors. The defendant answered that "if and to the extent that defendant entered into any" such agreements, the information would be contained in its plant files. It then offered to make these files available to the propounding party. The court ruled that the tender-of-records option does not allow a party to offer access to records without representing that they contain the information sought:

> [The option] does not shift to the interrogating party the obligation to find out *whether* sought after information is ascertainable from the files tendered, but only permits a shift of the burden to dig it out once the respondents have specified the records from "where the answer" can

[15] Annotation: Propriety of answer to interrogatory merely referring to other documents or sources of information. 96 ALR2d 598.

[16] Fed Rules Civ Proc, Rule 33(c).

[17] CCP § 2030.230. See, e.g., T.N. Taube Corp. v Marine Midland Mortgage Corp. (1991, WD NC) 136 FRD 449 [responding party's familiarity with its own records makes it less burdensome for it to research them for the information sought].

[18] CCP § 2030.230.

[19] See E.E.O.C. v General Dynamics Corp. (1993, CA5 Tex) 999 F2d 113, 118.

[20] Deyo v Kilbourne (1978) 84 Cal App 3d 771, 784, 149 Cal Rptr 499, 510. See also Holben v Coopervision, Inc. (1988, ED Pa) 120 FRD 32, 34 [improper to dump "several volumes of unspecified information" on opposing counsel].

[21] In Re Master Key (1971, D Conn) 53 FRD 87.

be derived or ascertained. If the answers lie in the records of the defendants, they should say so; and, if, on the other side, they do not, they should say that.[22]

The *Fuss* case[23] illustrates another improper use of the tender-of-records option. There, a law firm sued to collect from a motion picture director and producer a legal fee for $150,000 based on 18 categories of services allegedly rendered over a three-year period. The clients propounded interrogatories aimed at ascertaining the particular attorneys who performed the services, the date of their performance, the amount of time spent on and the precise nature of the services, and the amount of the total claim allocable to each of the 18 categories.

The law firm replied that the requested information would require a compilation of data reposing in its "services performed" sheets, time records, appointment books and telephone records, as well as the recollections of those who did the work. It tendered what it termed "pertinent and proper portions" of these records for examination by the defendant. The court deemed this effort to use the tender-of-records option deficient in two respects. First, as the law firm's response conceded, the information sought required access not only to the tendered records but also to the recollections of people. This fact alone made the interrogatory ineligible for this type of response. Second, the tender-of-records was found to be impermissibly restrictive: "An opportunity to examine records and files which the opposing party to the litigation deems pertinent and proper is no opportunity at all for the purpose of civil discovery."[24]

§ 5.18   Objections

The Third Type of "Response": A party who receives an objectionable interrogatory need not "answer" it.[1] It may not, however, ignore it. On the contrary, Section 2030.210[2] requires some "response" to every interrogatory, no matter how objectionable it may be. Although "response" and "answer" are synonyms in everyday usage, they are not equivalents in the interrogatory provisions of the Civil Discovery Act. These contemplate three types of "response" to interrogatories: an "answer,"[3] a tender of access to records,[4] or an "objection."[5] A party who has not sought a protective order[6] must use the "response" to assert objections to interrogatories.

---

[22] In Re Master Key (1971, D Conn) 53 FRD 87, 90 (original italics).

[23] Fuss v Superior Court (1969) 273 Cal App 2d 807, 78 Cal Rptr 583.

[24] Fuss v Superior Court (1969) 273 Cal App 2d 807, 815, 78 Cal Rptr 583, 588.

[1] CCP § 2030(f)(1) describes the meaning of "answer."

[2] CCP § 2030.210(a).

[3] CCP §§ 2030(a)(1) and 2030.220. For a discussion of an answer, see § 5.16.

[4] CCP §§ 2030.210(a)(2) and 2030.230. For a discussion of a tender of access to records, see § 5.17.

[5] CCP §§ 2030.210(a)(3) and 2030.240.

[6] For a discussion of protective orders against interrogatories, see § 5.14.

Method of Objecting: The "response" should be a single document, containing answers or tenders of records to those interrogatories that are proper, and objections to any that are not. Although it would be helpful, the response need not repeat the text of the interrogatory.[7] However, the response must identify each individual interrogatory in the set by its assigned number or letter and deal with it "separately."[8] Sometimes a particular interrogatory is only partially objectionable. The response to it should "answer" any part that is not vulnerable to the objection and object to the rest.[9] Though several interrogatories may be objectionable on the same ground, with one exception, they may not be objected to as a group.[10] The one exception applies to those specially prepared interrogatories in a set that exceed the presumptive limit of 35 and are unaccompanied by the required declaration.[11] Here, the responding party need only state "an objection to the balance . . . on the ground that the limit has been exceeded."[12] The responding party's attorney must sign any response that contains an objection.[13]

Specification of Ground for Objection: A party may not respond to an interrogatory with the single word "Objection." On the contrary, Section 2030.240 requires that the "specific ground for the objection shall be set forth clearly in the response."[14] This phrasing is almost identical to that used in the Evidence Code to preserve a trial objection for appeal.[15] Moreover, where a party objects because of a privilege, it may not simply state: "Objection: Privileged." The statute requires an identification of the "particular privilege invoked."[16] Since the work product doctrine is not truly a "privilege,"[17] an objection based on that ground must be "expressly asserted."[18] An objection that claims only the attorney-client *privilege* does not assert the work product *protection.*[19] One

---

[7] CCP § 2030.210.

[8] CCP § 2030.210.

[9] Now that CCP § 2030.060(d) requires each interrogatory to be "full and complete in and of itself," and CCP § 2030.060(f) prohibits an interrogatory that is "compound, conjunctive, or disjunctive," it should be rare that only a part of an interrogatory is objectionable.

[10] CCP § 2030.210(c).

[11] For a discussion of the presumptive limit of 35 specially prepared interrogatories, see § 5.6.

[12] CCP § 2030.030(c).

[13] CCP § 2030.250(c).

[14] CCP § 2030.240(b).

[15] Evid Code § 353.

[16] CCP § 2030.240(b). See Hernandez v Superior Court (2003) 112 Cal App 4th 285, 293, 4 Cal Rptr 3d 883, 890 ["In short, a responding party may object to an interrogatory that seeks privileged *information* by clearly stating the objection and the particular privilege invoked. But the *existence* of a document containing privileged information is not privileged."]

[17] For a general discussion of the work product doctrine, see § 13.1.

[18] CCP § 2030.240(b). Nacht & Lewis Architects, Inc. v Superior Court (1996) 47 Cal App 4th 214, 216–217, 54 Cal Rptr 2d 575, 576.

[19] Nacht & Lewis Architects, Inc. v Superior Court (1996) 47 Cal App 4th 214, 216–217, 54 Cal Rptr 2d 575, 576; Sheets v Superior Court (1967) 257 Cal App 2d 1, 8, 64 Cal Rptr 753, 757.

may not make piecemeal objections to an interrogatory. The response must state all grounds for objection. Those not stated are waived.[20]

Validity of Ground for Objecting: An interrogatory is, of course, objectionable if the information it seeks is irrelevant.[21] However, in assessing the validity of a relevancy objection, the responding party should keep in mind the broad scope of discovery. The test for discovery is not whether the information sought is relevant to a material *issue* in the case. Rather, it is whether that information is relevant to the general *subject matter* of the suit.[22]

In the same vein, counsel should not object to an interrogatory simply because the information sought, although relevant, would be inadmissible at trial under some rule of evidence, such as the hearsay rule.[23] By answering an interrogatory a party is not conceding that the answer itself, or the information it contains, is admissible at trial.[24]

A party may object to the *form* of the question, i.e., it is argumentative,[25] contains subparts, is compound, or is phrased disjunctively or conjunctively.[26]

Waiver of Objection by Untimely Response: A party wishing to object to an interrogatory must serve a "timely" response, that is, one made within 30 days after service of the interrogatories.[27] Section 2030.290 codifies the case law[28] to the effect that failure to serve a timely response waives all objections, including those based on privilege or on the work product protection.[29] This waiver occurs even when the privilege involved has a constitutional dimension, for example, the privilege against self-incrimination.[30]

—Verification Not Required: Where a response consists entirely of objections, Section 2030.050 makes unnecessary the responding party's signature and

---

[20] Cf. Scottsdale Ins. Co. v Superior Court (1997) 59 Cal App 4th 263, 273, 69 Cal Rptr 2d 112, 118 [timely response to inspection demand asserting objection based only on burdensomeness waived any later objection based on attorney-client privilege].

[21] See, e.g., Columbia Broadcasting System, Inc. v Superior Court (1968) 263 Cal App 2d 12, 20–21, 69 Cal Rptr 348, 353–354.

[22] See, e.g., Perkins v Superior Court (1981) 118 Cal App 3d 761, 173 Cal Rptr 596; Columbia Broadcasting System, Inc. v Superior Court (1968) 263 Cal App 2d 12, 22–23, 69 Cal Rptr 348, 354–355; Coffelt v Superior Court (1967) 254 Cal App 2d 884, 886–887, 62 Cal Rptr 636, 638. For coverage of "relevance" during discovery, see Chapter 11.

[23] Smith v Superior Court (1961) 189 Cal App 2d 6, 12, 11 Cal Rptr 165, 169.

[24] For a discussion of the use of answers to interrogatories as evidence at trial, see § 5.20.

[25] Sheets v Superior Court (1967) 257 Cal App 2d 1, 13, 64 Cal Rptr 753, 761.

[26] See CCP § 2030.060(f).

[27] CCP § 2030.260(a). For a further discussion of the time for responding to interrogatories, see § 5.15.

[28] E.g., Coy v Superior Court (1962) 58 Cal 2d 210, 216–217, 23 Cal Rptr 393, 395–396, 373 P2d 457, 459–460; Leach v Superior Court (1980) 111 Cal App 3d 902, 905–906, 169 Cal Rptr 42, 43–44; Fuss v Superior Court (1969) 273 Cal App 2d 807, 817, 78 Cal Rptr 583, 589.

[29] CCP § 2030.290(a). See Laguna Auto Body v Farmers Ins. Exchange (1991) 231 Cal App 3d 481, 488, 282 Cal Rptr 530, 535.

[30] Brown v Superior Court (1986) 180 Cal App 3d 701, 708–712, 226 Cal Rptr 10, 13–16.

oath.[31] This provision clearly implies that, although improper, an unverified response that answers some interrogatories and objects to some others does not waive those objections. Indeed, the *Food 4 Less Supermarkets* case gave the same interpretation to the identical inspection demand provision.[32] The court rejected the argument that a timely but unverified response waived the objections that it contained:

> [T]here is no need to verify that portion of the response containing the objections. Thus, if the response is served within the statutory time period, that portion of the response must be considered timely notwith-standing the lack of verification. The omission of the verification in the portion of the response containing fact specific responses merely renders *that* portion of the response untimely and therefore only creates a right to move for orders and sanctions . . . . *as to those responses* but does not result in a waiver of the objections made.[33]

—Effect of Extensions of Time to Respond: Under the 1956 Discovery Act some question existed about the impact of an agreement to extend the time for response on the right to object. Section 2030.270 now clarifies that no waiver occurs unless the extension agreement specifies that it does.[34] Otherwise, that statute "preserves" the right to "respond" in any "manner" permitted by Section 2030.210. An objection under Section 2030.240 is a permitted manner of "responding."

Preserving Waiver of Objections: To take advantage of the waiver of objections that results from an untimely response to interrogatories, the propounding party itself must file a timely motion to compel further response.[35] Failure to do so waives the waiver of objections.[36]

Relief from Waiver of Objections: The case law under the 1956 Discovery Act recognized the trial court's discretion to relieve a responding party from the waiver of objections that would otherwise result from its belated assertion.[37] Section 2030.290 now specifies that a party may obtain relief from this waiver by showing that its failure to respond on time was traceable to "mistake,

---

[31] CCP § 2030.250(a).

[32] CCP § 2031.250(c).

[33] Food 4 Less Supermarkets v Superior Court (1995) 40 Cal App 4th 651, 657–658, 46 Cal Rptr 2d 925, 928–929 [unverified response to an *inspection demand* (original italics)]. See also Blue Ridge Ins. Co. v Superior Court (1988) 202 Cal App 3d 339, 344–345, 248 Cal Rptr 346, 349–350 [involving a response to an *inspection demand* that objected to certain items].

[34] CCP § 2030.270(c).

[35] For a discussion of the time limit for a motion to compel further response to interrogatories, see § 5.20.

[36] Vidal Sassoon, Inc. v Superior Court (1983) 147 Cal App 3d 681, 195 Cal Rptr 295.

[37] Borse v Superior Court (1970) 7 Cal App 3d 286, 86 Cal Rptr 559; Zonver v Superior Court (1969) 270 Cal App 2d 613, 622–623, 76 Cal Rptr 10, 15–16. See also West Pico Furniture Co. v Superior Court (1961) 56 Cal 2d 407, 414, 15 Cal Rptr 119, 121–122, 364 P2d 295, 297–298.

inadvertence, or excusable neglect," and that it has now filed a belated response that substantially complies with the applicable provisions. [38]

§ 5.19 Failure to Serve Timely Response

Immediate Consequences of Failure to Respond: A party served with a set of interrogatories must "respond"[1] to each question within 30 days. Section 2030.290 describes the two immediate consequences of either ignoring altogether particular interrogatories in a set[2] or an entire set of interrogatories or of disregarding the time limit for serving a timely, sworn response to them.[3] First, the delinquent party waives any right to object to that interrogatory.[4] Indeed, the statute explicitly extends the waiver to objections based on privilege or on the work product protection.[5] Second, the failure to respond forfeits any tender-of-records option that might have been available.[6]

—Codification of Prior Case Law: Section 2030.290 does not materially change the case law that had developed under the 1956 Discovery Act. The courts had held the failure to make a timely, sworn response to a discovery request waived the right to object to it.[7] They had also held that this was the sort of default from which one could be relieved under either CCP § 473 or the trial court's inherent power to set aside a default judgment that had resulted from "extrinsic fraud or mistake."[8] Nevertheless, the articulation of this waiver on the face of the current statute should spur parties who receive a set of interrogatories to serve a timely response.

—Relief from Consequences: Neither the waiver of objections nor the forfeiture of the tender-of-records option is carved in stone. The delinquent party may move for relief from either. To be successful, it must convince the court that the failure to serve a timely, sworn response resulted from "mistake,

---

[38] CCP § 2030.290(a).

[1] For a discussion of the responses to interrogatories, see §§ 5.15–5.18.

[2] A "response" that simply ignores an individual question in a set of interrogatories is tantamount to a failure to respond to that question. Coy v Superior Court (1962) 58 Cal 2d 210, 216–217, 23 Cal Rptr 393, 395–396, 373 P2d 457, 459–460.

[3] CCP § 2030.290(a), referencing CCP § 2030.230. For a discussion of the remedy for a timely response that fails to provide a *proper* answer to one or more interrogatories, see § 5.20.

[4] Cf. City of Fresno v Superior Court (1988) 205 Cal App 3d 1459, 1466–1467, 253 Cal Rptr 296, 299–300 [involving untimely response to *inspection demand*]. See also Davis v Fendler (1981, CA9 Ariz) 650 F2d 1154, 1160; Scott v Arex, Inc. (1989, D Conn) 124 FRD 39, 41; Turick by Turick v Yamaha Motor Corp., USA (1988, SD NY) 121 FRD 32, 36.

[5] CCP § 2030.290(a).

[6] For a discussion of a response in the form of a tender of access to records, see § 5.17.

[7] Coy v Superior Court (1962) 58 Cal 2d 210, 216–217, 23 Cal Rptr 393, 395–396, 373 P2d 457, 459–460.

[8] Palmer v Moore (1968) 266 Cal App 2d 134, 140–141, 71 Cal Rptr 801, 805 [defense counsel failed to appear at hearing on motion for default because clerical staff had not noted hearing date on his calendar].

inadvertence, or excusable neglect."[9] As a prerequisite to any such relief, the moving party must prepare and serve a belated response. That response must otherwise substantially comply with the requirements for a proper response.[10]

In the *City of Fresno* case,[11] an attorney who had failed to respond timely to an *inspection demand* sought relief from the consequent waiver of objections. The motion relied on two grounds: his failure to study carefully the time limits in the then-recently adopted Discovery Act of 1986, and his distraction by the imminent trial of another case. The appellate court upheld the trial court's refusal to grant relief for either of these reasons. Presumably the same holding would have resulted had the case involved an untimely response to *interrogatories*.

—Drastic Sanction Eliminated: As severe as the consequences spelled out in Section 2030.290 are,[12] they are milder than the sanction available under the 1956 Discovery Act. Under that act, a court could have immediately imposed a drastic sanction for a failure to serve a timely response to a set of interrogatories.[13] The trial court could have struck a delinquent party's complaint[14] or answer.[15] If this sanction seemed too severe, the court could have imposed an "issue" or an "evidence" sanction on that party. Imposition of one of these drastic sanctions, however, required the court to find a "willful" delinquency."[16] In practice, a trial court seldom imposed a drastic sanction in the first instance; it would merely assess a monetary sanction and order the delinquent party to respond. In the few cases where the trial court did immediately impose a drastic sanction, the appellate court would usually find the sanction an abuse of discretion.[17] Accordingly, the more lenient approach now taken in Section 2030.290, which does not allow immediate resort to a drastic sanction,[18] represents no major departure from the realities of the older discovery practice.

---

[9] CCP § 2030.290(a)(2). Cf. City of Fresno v Superior Court (1988) 205 Cal App 3d 1459, 1466–1467, 253 Cal Rptr 296, 299–300 [involving untimely response to *inspection demand*].

[10] CCP § 2030.290(a)(1), referencing CCP §§ 2030.210–2030.240. For a discussion of the contents of a proper response, see §§ 5.15–5.18.

[11] City of Fresno v Superior Court (1988) 205 Cal App 3d 1459, 1466–1467, 253 Cal Rptr 296, 299–300.

[12] CCP § 2030.290.

[13] Former CCP § 2034(d), 1956 Discovery Act, Appendix E.

[14] See, e.g., Frates v Treder (1967) 249 Cal App 2d 199, 57 Cal Rptr 383; Thompson v Vallembois (1963) 216 Cal App 2d 21, 30 Cal Rptr 796. Annotation: Dismissal of state court action for failure or refusal of plaintiff to answer written interrogatories. 56 ALR3d 1109.

[15] Annotation: Judgment in favor of plaintiff in state court action for defendant's failure to obey request or order to answer interrogatories or other discovery questions. 30 ALR4th 9.

[16] Frates v Treder (1967) 249 Cal App 2d 199, 57 Cal Rptr 383; Thompson v Vallembois (1963) 216 Cal App 2d 21, 30 Cal Rptr 796.

[17] See, e.g., Thomas v Luong (1986) 187 Cal App 3d 76, 231 Cal Rptr 631; Garza v Delano Union Elementary School Dist. (1980) 110 Cal App 3d 303, 314–315, 167 Cal Rptr 629, 635; Cornwall v Santa Monica Dairy Co. (1977) 66 Cal App 3d 250, 135 Cal Rptr 761.

[18] See CCP § 2030.290.

Motion to Compel Response: Section 2030.290 specifies the remedy available to the propounding party who fails to receive any response.[19] That party should move to compel a response.[20] In keeping with the earlier case law[21] governing total failures to respond to discovery requests, the propounding party need not "meet and confer" with the recipient of the interrogatories before making this motion.

—Monetary Sanction: If this motion is granted, the trial court's order should contain two provisions. First, it should order answers to the interrogatories. Second, it should impose a monetary sanction on the party in default unless it finds "substantial justification" for the noncompliance.[22]

Disobedience of Order to Respond: Once the trial court transmutes the obligation to serve a response from a statutory duty into a judicial order, further noncompliance exposes the disobedient party to the more drastic "issue," "evidence," or "terminating" sanctions.[23] However, the trial court still may deal more leniently with the disobedience of its order. It may simply impose another monetary sanction and give the party a second chance to comply with its order to compel answers to the interrogatories.[24]

§ 5.20   Compelling Further Response

Unsatisfactory Response to Interrogatories: Upon receiving a timely response to interrogatories, the propounding party may not be satisfied with its contents.[1] That party may consider the response's objections to be meritless,[2] its answers evasive or incomplete,"[3] or its tender of access to records inappropriate.[4]

Motion to Compel Further Response: When a response to interrogatories is improper in some respect, the propounding party must seek a court ruling on the adequacy of the response. Section 2030.300 spells out the procedure both

---

[19] CCP § 2030.290.

[20] CCP § 2030.290(b).

[21] Cf. Leach v Superior Court (1980) 111 Cal App 3d 902, 905–906, 169 Cal Rptr 42, 43–44.

[22] CCP § 2030.290(c). For a discussion of the current Civil Discovery Act's approach to "substantial justification," see § 15.4.

[23] CCP § 2030.290(c) and CCP §§ 2023.030(b)–2023.030(d). See, e.g., Morgan v Southern Cal. Rapid Transit Dist. (1987) 192 Cal App 3d 976, 981–984, 237 Cal Rptr 756, 760–762.

[24] CCP § 2030.290(c).

[1] For a discussion of a response in the form of an objection, see § 5.18

[2] See, e.g., Coffelt v Superior Court (1967) 254 Cal App 2d 884, 886–887, 62 Cal Rptr 636, 638. For a discussion of answers in a response to interrogatories that are evasive or incomplete, see § 5.16.

[3] CCP § 2030.300(a)(1). See, e.g., Stein v Hassen (1973) 34 Cal App 3d 294, 297, 109 Cal Rptr 321, 323; Bunnell v Superior Court (1967) 254 Cal App 2d 720, 721, 62 Cal Rptr 458, 460. For a discussion of the requirements for a proper answer to an interrogatory, see § 5.16.

[4] Cf. Bunnell v Superior Court (1967) 254 Cal App 2d 720, 723–734, 62 Cal Rptr 458, 461–462. For a discussion of a response to an interrogatory that tenders access to records, see § 5.17.

for overcoming objections,[5] for obtaining "complete and straightforward" answers,[6] and for challenging an exercise of the tender-of-records options.[7] The propounding party should apply to the trial court for an order compelling a *further* response.[8] Before resorting to this motion, however, that party must meet and confer with the responding party to try to work out informally the dispute.

—**Critical Time Limit:** A motion to compel a further response to interrogatories is subject to an important time limit. The propounding party must serve notice of the motion no later than 45 days after the unsatisfactory response has been served.[9] This period is extended, usually by five days, if the response was served by mail.[10] The time consumed in trying to resolve the dispute informally is *not* deducted from the 45-day time limit for noticing the motion.[11] Unless this motion is timely made, the propounding party waives any right to compel a further response to the interrogatories.[12] This waiver occurs even though the responding party's written opposition to the motion to compel further response does not raise an issue as to its timing.[13] One who has allowed the 45-day period to expire may not avoid the waiver by including the same interrogatory in a later set:

> [I]t would be an absurdity to say that a party who fails to meet the time limits of section 2030 may avoid the consequences of his delay and lack of diligence by propounding the same question again. Such a construction of the statute would obviously encourage delay and provide no incentive to attempt to resolve any dispute with the opposing party. The Legislature has explicitly stated that unless a party moves to compel further response within forty-five days of the unsatisfactory response, he waives *any* right to compel a further response. We hold that it means what it says . . . .[14]

However, propounding parties may extricate themselves from this predicament by deposing the responding party and asking the same questions.[15]

---

[5] CCP § 2030.300(a)(3).

[6] CCP § 2030.300(a)(1).

[7] CCP § 2030.300(a)(2).

[8] CCP § 2030.300(a).

[9] CCP § 2030.300(c).

[10] See CCP § 2016.050, referencing CCP § 1013(a). See also Karz v Karl (1982) 137 Cal App 3d 637, 646, 187 Cal Rptr 183, 188; California Accounts, Inc. v Superior Court (1975) 50 Cal App 3d 483, 123 Cal Rptr 304.

[11] Vidal Sassoon, Inc. v Superior Court (1983) 147 Cal App 3d 681, 195 Cal Rptr 295.

[12] CCP § 2030.300(c). See Trail v Cornwell (1984) 161 Cal App 3d 477, 488, 207 Cal Rptr 679, 685; Vidal Sassoon, Inc. v Superior Court (1983) 147 Cal App 3d 681, 195 Cal Rptr 295; Karz v Karl (1982) 137 Cal App 3d 637, 646, 187 Cal Rptr 183, 188.

[13] Cf. Sexton v Superior Court (1997) 58 Cal App 4th 1403, 68 Cal Rptr 2d 708 [involving *inspection demand*].

[14] Professional Career Colleges, Magna Institute, Inc. v Superior Court (1989) 207 Cal App 3d 490, 493–494, 255 Cal Rptr 5, 7–8 (original italics).

[15] Cf. Carter v Superior Court (1990) 218 Cal App 3d 994, 997, 267 Cal Rptr 290, 291–292 [one who has allowed 45-day period for objecting to response to *inspection demand to lapse* may seek the same information via deposition].

Burden on Responding Party: At the hearing on the motion to compel a further response, the responding party must justify the objection.[16] A party who unsuccessfully makes or opposes a motion to compel a further response must pay a monetary sanction unless it can persuade the trial court that there was substantial justification for its position.[17]

Disobedience of Order for Further Response: A successful motion to compel a further response transmutes the duty to respond from a statutory one to a judicial command. Disobedience of a court order exposes the responding party to an appropriate[18] drastic sanction.[19] However, the trial court may not anticipate such disobedience by a proviso that failure to comply will result automatically in a drastic sanction.[20]

The 45-day time limit for a party to move to compel[21] does not apply to the later effort of the propounding party to enforce a court order compelling further response or to obtain sanctions for its disobedience.[22]

Of course, the trial court may not impose any sanction if the reason for the failure to comply with the order to answer is that the responding party was trying, even unsuccessfully, to obtain appellate review of that order. Instead, the trial court should fix a new date for compliance with its order.[23]

The trial court may choose to deal leniently with disobedience of its order to respond further to interrogatories. Instead of resorting immediately to a drastic sanction, it may impose another monetary sanction and give the disobedient party another chance to comply with its order.[24]

§ 5.21 Correcting Answer to Interrogatory

Gap in Former Statute: Occasionally, after providing a good faith answer to a particular interrogatory, the responding party learns that the answer given was not or is no longer correct. This raises two related issues: (1) *may* a party amend its original answer to set forth the more accurate information? and (2)

---

[16] Columbia Broadcasting System, Inc. v Superior Court (1968) 263 Cal App 2d 12, 18, 69 Cal Rptr 348, 352.

[17] CCP § 2030.300(e).

Cf. Stein v Hassen (1973) 34 Cal App 3d 294, 297, 109 Cal Rptr 321, 323.

[18] See Caryl Richards, Inc. v Superior Court (1961) 188 Cal App 2d 300, 10 Cal Rptr 377.

[19] CCP § 2030.300(e). See, e.g., Calvert Fire Ins. Co. v Cropper (1983) 141 Cal App 3d 901, 904, 190 Cal Rptr 593, 594 [dismissal]; Karz v Karl (1982) 137 Cal App 3d 637, 648–651, 187 Cal Rptr 183, 190–192 [issue preclusion]; Stein v Hassen (1973) 34 Cal App 3d 294, 302, 109 Cal Rptr 321, 327 [default].

[20] Duggan v Moss (1979) 98 Cal App 3d 735, 743, 159 Cal Rptr 425, 430.

[21] See CCP § 2030.300(e).

[22] Morgan v Southern Cal. Rapid Transit Dist. (1987) 192 Cal App 3d 976, 981, 237 Cal Rptr 756, 759.

[23] See Fairfield v Superior Court (1966) 246 Cal App 2d 113, 121–122, 54 Cal Rptr 721, 726–727.

[24] CCP § 2030.300(e). Cf. Welgoss v End (1967) 252 Cal App 2d 982, 61 Cal Rptr 52.

must that party do so before offering evidence that varies from the original answer?

Guzman v General Motors Corp.[1] vividy illustrates the problem. At one of its plants, defendant used three paste machines, one of which it had built itself. A worker, injured while operating one of these machines, tried to escape the limited worker's compensation recovery on the ground that he was using the one manufactured by his employer. The defendant-employer first responded to interrogatories by admitting that the plaintiff had sustained his injury on the machine it had made. Later it learned that the plaintiff had been using a machine that it had purchased. Thus, it was immune from liability in plaintiff's personal injury action. The defendant sought leave to amend its interrogatory answer to reflect this new information.

The appellate court noted the silence of the original version of Section 2030 concerning "the necessity of, and method by which, a party who has incorrectly responded to interrogatories may change, amend, or supplement those answers."[2] It filled this statutory gap by holding that "a party wishing to amend its answers to interrogatories need only serve the corrected answers on the proponent."[3] Moreover, it ruled that, absent evidence that the original answer was wilfully false or that there was no "substantial justification" for the mistake, the propounding party was not entitled to any sanction to compensate it for the inconvenience and expense caused by the correction. The court acknowledged that this approach produced inequities for the propounding party and it recommended that the Legislature give "attention to this situation."[4]

Evidentiary Admission: Section 2030.310 now deals with the amendment of interrogatory answers. It codifies the *Guzman* holding by allowing the responding party to initiate the amendment:

> Without leave of court, a party may serve an amended answer to any interrogatory that contains information subsequently discovered, inadvertently omitted, or mistakenly stated in the initial interrogatory.[5]

Moreover, when a responding party serves an amended answer, the statute allows the propounding party to use the original answer as an *evidentiary* admission at trial.[6] In that event the responding party may counter with its amended answer.

Judicial Admission: In some situations, allowing a party to amend an interrogatory answer may substantially prejudice the propounding party. In the

---

[1] Guzman v General Motors Corp. (1984) 154 Cal App 3d 438, 201 Cal Rptr 246.

[2] Guzman v General Motors Corp. (1984) 154 Cal App 3d 438, 442, 201 Cal Rptr 246, 248.

[3] Guzman v General Motors Corp. (1984) 154 Cal App 3d 438, 444, 201 Cal Rptr 246, 250.

[4] Guzman v General Motors Corp. (1984) 154 Cal App 3d 438, 446 n16, 201 Cal Rptr 246, 252 n16.

[5] CCP § 2030.310(a).

[6] Cf. Freitas v Emhart Corp. (1989, D Mass) 715 F Supp 1149, 1151.

Gordon case,[7] for example, defendant answered interrogatories by stating that at the time of the accident its employee and co-defendant was driving her auto on an errand for it. The trial court later dismissed the claim against that employee because of a delay in serving process. Defendant then amended its interrogatory answers to say that the employee was not on an errand for it. It attributed this switch in position to the bad faith of another employee, who had signed the original answers. Under these circumstances, the appellate court ruled that a trial court could impose "the sanction of treating the [initial] answers as binding admissions,"[8] which was tantamount to an "issue" sanction.[9]

Section 2030.310 now expressly permits the recipient of an amended interrogatory answer to move for a court order binding the responding party to the original answer.[10] To succeed on this motion, the propounding party must convince the trial court that: (1) the switch in position has created prejudice;[11] (2) the responding party has not shown any substantial justification for the original incorrect answer;[12] and (3) neither further discovery nor use of the original answer as an evidentiary admission will overcome the resulting prejudice.[13]

Variance between Interrogatory Answer and Trial Evidence: A change in position by the responding party poses a more serious prospect of prejudice where that party, without having amended the original answer to an interrogatory, presents evidence at trial that is inconsistent with it.[14] When this situation arises, the court's response will depend upon the reason for the discrepancy.

—Answer Correct When Originally Made: Where the variance between the interrogatory answer and the trial evidence results from information acquired after the serving of the answer, the following passage from *Singer v Superior Court* becomes pertinent:

> Certainly, it should not be the law that interrogatories can be used as a trap so as to limit the person answering to the facts then known and to prevent him from producing subsequently discovered facts. . . . The answers to these interrogatories would not have that legal effect. Answers to these interrogatories now, if compelled, will not prevent the defendant at the trial from relying on subsequently discovered facts
> . . . .[15]

---

[7] Gordon v Superior Court (1984) 161 Cal App 3d 157, 207 Cal Rptr 327.

[8] Gordon v Superior Court (1984) 161 Cal App 3d 157, 167, 207 Cal Rptr 327, 333.

[9] See CCP § 2030.030(b).

[10] CCP § 2030.310(b). An attempt to "meet and confer" is a prerequisite for this motion. See CCP § 2016.040.

[11] CCP § 2030.310(c)(1).

[12] CCP § 2030.310(c)(2).

[13] CCP § 2030.310(c)(3).

[14] Annotation: Answers to interrogatories as limiting answering party's proof at state trial. 86 ALR3d 1089.

[15] Singer v Superior Court (1960) 54 Cal 2d 318, 325, 5 Cal Rptr 697, 701, 353 P2d 305, 309.

When the difference between an interrogatory answer and the later proof at trial is traceable to after-acquired information, the propounding party usually could have learned this new information by propounding supplemental interrogatories.[16]

—**Honest and Harmless Mistake:** Even when the answer to an interrogatory was wrong at the very time it was given, the responding party may still be able to present at trial evidence inconsistent with that answer. As the Court observed in *Singer:* "[S]uch answers [to interrogatories] would not even prevent production of facts now known to defendant but not included in the answers, upon a proper showing that the oversight was in good faith."[17] In *Milton v Montgomery Ward & Co., Inc.,*[18] for instance, plaintiff, who had fallen in an auto repair facility, was asked to state whether "any party or witness known to you" was claiming to have heard any of defendant's employees discuss how the fall had occurred. Plaintiff answered: "None known at this time," because he had construed these words to inquire only as to statements overheard by other people. At trial plaintiff proposed to testify that *he* had heard the defendant's service manager admit that before the fall he had seen grease or oil on the floor. The court concluded that plaintiff should have realized that the interrogatory embraced statements heard by him, and not just those heard by third persons. However, it also noted that he had mentioned during his deposition that he had overheard the service manager's statement. This indicated both that the incorrect answer to the interrogatory was inadvertent, and that plaintiff's trial testimony neither surprised nor prejudiced the defendant:

> In the instant case [plaintiff] testified that he thought interrogatory No. 23 referred to witnesses other than himself. His inadvertent failure to respond with technical perfection is very different from a wilful failure to respond to an unambiguous interrogatory.[19]

In *Phillips v Cooper Laboratories, Inc.,*[20] plaintiff in a products liability action sued a successor corporation for a defective product manufactured by its predecessor. To an interrogatory asking whether it had assumed the debts and liabilities of the acquired company, defendant answered simply: "Yes." At trial, however, its president qualified this response by adding that it had assumed only liabilities that it actually knew of at the time of the acquisition. The trial court's ruling that plaintiff was not prejudiced by this substantial variance was upheld on appeal:

---

[16] For a discussion of supplemental interrogatories, see § 5.7.

[17] Singer v Superior Court (1960) 54 Cal 2d 318, 325, 5 Cal Rptr 697, 701, 353 P2d 305, 309.

[18] Milton v Montgomery Ward & Co., Inc. (1973) 33 Cal App 3d 133, 108 Cal Rptr 726.

[19] Milton v Montgomery Ward & Co., Inc. (1973) 33 Cal App 3d 133, 140, 108 Cal Rptr 726, 730.

[20] Phillips v Cooper Laboratories, Inc. (1989) 215 Cal App 3d 1648, 264 Cal Rptr 311.

The contradiction between an answer to an interrogatory and a witness' testimony at trial does not in itself affect the latter's admissibility. Absent significant prejudice to the opponent, a party may present evidence at variance to prior answers to interrogatories. [21]

—Honest but Harmful Mistake: Even though a responding party did not wilfully answer an interrogatory incorrectly, a misleading answer may still surprise and prejudice the propounding party. In *Campain v Safeway Stores, Inc.,* [22] a personal injury plaintiff had answered "No" to an interrogatory asking whether she was "making any claim for loss of wages, earnings or earning capacity" because of the accident. At trial she then testified that, although unemployed for many years before the accident, she was injured just as she was about to start a new job. The trial court, evidently concluding that the erroneous answer was inadvertent, overruled defendant's objection to this testimony. This did not, however, eliminate the surprise to the defendant. The appellate court ordered a retrial of the damages issue to take place after defendant had an opportunity to conduct further discovery concerning her claim of lost earnings.

—Deliberate Error: Where the variance between the position taken in an answer to an interrogatory and that taken at trial results from an effort to deceive, more severe consequences follow. In *Thoren v Johnston & Washer,* [23] where the trial court found that a plaintiff had wilfully concealed the identity of a key witness, it refused to let that witness testify at the trial, although without this testimony a nonsuit resulted. On appeal, the court reasoned that a wilfully false answer to an interrogatory was tantamount to not answering it all.

—Treating Variance as an Amendment: Section 2030.310 does not explicitly cover variances between a responding party's interrogatory answer and its position at trial. The variance can reasonably be treated as the functional equivalent of an amended answer to the interrogatory. [24] This would entitle the responding party either to use the original answer as an evidentiary admission, [25] or to make the showing required for treating it as a binding admission. [26]

§ 5.22   Use of Answers as Evidence at Trial

Unlike Deposition Answers: One of the deficiencies in the 1956 Discovery Act was its lack of a specially crafted provision regulating the use of interrogatory answers as evidence. Copying the approach of the original version of the Federal Rules, [1] it simply incorporated by reference the provision regulating the use of

---

[21] Phillips v Cooper Laboratories, Inc. (1989) 215 Cal App 3d 1648, 1661, 264 Cal Rptr 311, 318–319 (internal citations omitted).

[22] Campain v Safeway Stores, Inc. (1972) 29 Cal App 3d 362, 104 Cal Rptr 752.

[23] Thoren v Johnston & Washer (1972) 29 Cal App 3d 270, 105 Cal Rptr 276.

[24] See CCP § 2030.310.

[25] CCP § 2030.310(a).

[26] CCP §§ 2030.310(b) and 2030.310(c).

[1] Former Fed Rules Civ Proc, Rule 33(b).

depositions as evidence: "[T]he answers [to interrogatories] may be used to the same extent as provided . . . . for the use of the deposition of a party."[2]

By 1970 the federal courts had realized that the differences between depositions and interrogatories were significant enough to require separate treatment of the admissibility of the latter at trial: "The provisions governing use of depositions, to which Rule 33 presently refers, are not entirely apposite to answers to interrogatories, since deposition practice contemplates that all parties will ordinarily participate through cross-examination."[3] Accordingly, Fed Rules Civ Proc, Rule 33(b) was amended to provide simply that "the answers may be used to the extent permitted by the rules of evidence."

The Civil Discovery Act now contains a specially crafted provision, Section 2030.410, governing the use of interrogatory answers as evidence. As developed below, it codifies the case law that developed to cope with the original statute's shortcomings.

Use against Responding Party: When an answer to an interrogatory is offered *against* the party making it, few problems arise. The answer, which is given under oath, is a superior species of admission of a party-opponent. Thus, it would be admissible even if the Discovery Act were silent on the matter.[4] In *Mayhood v La Rosa*,[5] the Supreme Court held that other parties could offer interrogatory answers directly into evidence against the responding party. They need not have called the responding party as a witness and the court need not restrict the use of the answers to impeachment of inconsistent testimony. Section 2030.410 embodies this holding: it allows the use of answers to interrogatories "against the responding party," although "the responding party is available to testify, has testified, or will testify at the trial or other hearing."

—Institutional Party: Where the responding party is a corporation or other institutional party, the individual signing the answers is making an "authorized admission."[6] Hence, lack of personal knowledge by the individual who signed the answers is not a valid objection. As one federal trial judge expressed it:

> [T]he agents of the defendant made statements to the defendant's attorney which were then used as the basis of answers to interrogatories. If these answers were held inadmissible on the basis of hearsay, it is conceivable that no corporation could ever be bound by its answers, since all corporate answers must of necessity be based on statements of employees. Such a ruling would defeat the purpose of interrogatories as addressed to corporations and cannot be tolerated. Therefore, we conclude that answers to interrogatories posited to a corporation are

---

[2] Former CCP § 2030(c), 1956 Discovery Act, Appendix E.

[3] 1970 Advisory Committee Note to amended Fed Rules Civ Proc, Rule 33.

[4] See Evid Code § 1220. For a discussion of the use against a party of its answers given during a *deposition*, see §§ 2.37–2.42.

[5] Mayhood v La Rosa (1962) 58 Cal 2d 498, 500–501, 24 Cal Rptr 837, 374 P2d 805.

[6] Evid Code § 1222.

admissible where they are based on the statements of corporate agents given within the scope of their authority.[7]

—**Use by a Non-Propounding Party:** Answers to interrogatories are admissions of a party-opponent under Evid Code § 1220.[8] Therefore, any one, even someone other than the party who propounded the interrogatories, may offer them in evidence.[9] Section 2030.410 removes any doubt on this score. It specifies that interrogatory answers may be used not only by the propounding party, but by "any other party than the responding party."[10]

—**Limitations on Use:** A party contemplating use of another party's interrogatory answers as evidence should keep three things in mind. First, answers to interrogatories are not automatically part of the trial record; they must be offered in evidence.[11] Second, since the scope of pretrial discovery is much broader than the range of admissibility under the rules of evidence, an interrogatory that is unobjectionable during discovery will frequently yield an answer that is inadmissible at trial. Section 2030.410 takes this into account: it permits the use of answers to interrogatories only "as far as admissible under the rules of evidence."[12] Third, in contrast to the product of an admission request,[13] a party is not "bound" by its answers to interrogatories. They are evidentiary admissions, not judicial ones:

> An answer to an interrogatory is comparable to answers, which may be mistaken, given in deposition testimony or during the course of the trial itself. Answers to interrogatories must often be supplied before investigation is completed and can rest only upon knowledge which is available at the time. When there is conflict between answers supplied in response to interrogatories and answers obtained through other questioning, either in deposition or trial, the finder of fact must weigh all of the answers and resolve the conflict.[14]

---

[7] Mangual v Prudential Lines, Inc. (1971, ED Pa) 53 FRD 301, 302. See also Castaline v Los Angeles (1975) 47 Cal App 3d 580, 588 n7, 1 21 Cal Rptr 786, 791 n7.

[8] Although Section 2030.410 does not mention the use in evidence of answers to interrogatories given by a party in another lawsuit, such answers are also a form of admission of a party-opponent under Evid Code § 1220. Cf. Heilig v Studebaker Corp. (1965, CA10 Okla) 347 F2d 686, 689–690.

[9] Cf. Gadaleta v Nederlandsch-Amerekaansche Stoomvart (1961, CA2 NY) 291 F2d 212, 213. See also Rosenthal v Peoples Cab Co. (1960, ED Pa) 26 FRD 116.

[10] CCP § 2030.410.

[11] Cf. Heilig v Studebaker Corp. (1965, CA10 Okla) 347 F2d 686, 689–690.

[12] CCP § 2030.410.

[13] For a discussion of the effect of an admission obtained as a result of a discovery request made, see § 9.20.

[14] Victory Carriers, Inc. v Stockton Stevedoring Co. (1968, CA9 Cal) 388 F2d 955, 959. Cf. Kelly v New West Federal Savings (1996) 49 Cal App 4th 659, 672–673, 56 Cal Rptr 2d 803, 810 [plaintiff who at deposition mistakenly identified the smaller of two elevators as the one in which she fell is not precluded from presenting evidence at trial that it was the larger one]. See also Freed v Erie Lackawanna R. Co. (1971, CA6 Ohio) 445 F2d 619.

Not Admissible against Other Parties: When answers to interrogatories are offered *against the party giving them,* the hearsay objection is dissolved by the exception for admissions of a party opponent. However, when the answers are offered *against another party,* the hearsay objection retains its force. Here, the difference between deposition testimony and answers to interrogatories becomes most significant. Although answers to interrogatories resemble deposition testimony in that both are under oath, the latter is given in a setting where it is subject to cross-examination. This opportunity for cross-examination does not cure its hearsay nature, but it does give the resultant testimony special reliability that sets it apart from ordinary hearsay. If the deponent is unavailable as a live witness at the trial, the deposition may qualify as an exception to the hearsay rule.[15]

Answers to interrogatories are altogether different. The lack of opportunity to cross-examine the responding party leaves them within the hearsay rule. Thus, *Rimmele v Northridge Hospital Foundation,*[16] a medical malpractice case, held that an interrogatory answer by a hospital defendant was not admissible against a doctor co-defendant. And *Castaline v Los Angeles*[17] held that it was error to allow a plaintiff to use the interrogatory answers of the state and the county as evidence that the co-defendant city owned the street sweeping machine that had caused a freeway collision.[18]

—Responding Party Now Unavailable: The rule that one party's answers to interrogatories may not be offered against other parties in the case is followed even when the responding party later proves to be unavailable as a witness at the trial of the case. In *Associates Discount Corp. v Tobb Co.,*[19] a defendant who had answered interrogatories submitted by a co-defendant died before the case came to trial. When that co-defendant offered these answers against the plaintiff, the trial court refused to receive them. On appeal the co-defendant argued that answers to interrogatories should be admissible to the same extent as the deposition of a party. Since any deposition may be used when the deponent is unavailable as a trial witness, appellant continued, the answers of a deceased party should receive the same treatment. Stressing that the one against whom the answers were being offered had no opportunity to participate in the exchange of questions and answers, the court refused to give such a reading to the Discovery Act:

> It would be unreasonable and absurd to permit questions and answers
> respectively propounded and received in an interrogatory proceeding

---

[15] For a discussion of the use in evidence of a deposition of one who is now unavailable as a witness, see § 2.40.

[16] Rimmele v Northridge Hospital Foundation (1975) 46 Cal App 3d 123, 129, 120 Cal Rptr 39.

[17] Castaline v Los Angeles (1975) 47 Cal App 3d 580, 588–590, 121 Cal Rptr 786.

[18] See also Shoei Kako Co. v Superior Court (1973) 33 Cal App 3d 808, 813, 109 Cal Rptr 402, 405–406; Petersen v City of Vallejo (1968) 259 Cal App 2d 757, 66 Cal Rptr 776.

[19] Associates Discount Corp. v Tobb Co. (1966) 241 Cal App 2d 541, 50 Cal Rptr 738.

between two parties to be used against a third party when the latter is not given the right to propound cross-interrogatories or to exercise the privilege conferred upon the [propounding] party . . . . to require the adverse party to whom the interrogatories are directed to make a further response.[20]

—Not Admissible against Propounding Party: In each of the three cases just described, the party against whom the interrogatories were offered was neither the propounding nor the responding party. A later case, *Levy-Zentner Co. v Southern Pacific Transportation Co.*,[21] attempted to distinguish a so-called "bystander party" who offers the answers of another litigant against the party who propounded the interrogatories. There, one co-defendant served interrogatories on the other and received an answer that was not to its liking. At trial the plaintiffs sought to use this answer against the propounding party:

> Unlike [the cases] where the issue was whether party A could introduce the responses furnished by party B in answer to interrogatories propounded by party A for use in evidence against a "bystander" party C, the instant case concerns C's introduction of the fruits of discovery conducted between A and B, to be used in evidence against A. This configuration is important . . . .[22]

The opportunity for the propounding party to use follow-up interrogatories to probe the answers initially received, and the lack of any need for "a concern over a collusive and conclusive use of discovery methods against an unaware third party" warranted, in the court's view, a different result.

This decision was misguided. Carried to its logical conclusion, it would let even responding parties use their own answers in evidence against the propounding party, for here, too, the latter could submit further interrogatories and there would be no danger of a collusive use against a nonparticipating litigant. Moreover, the court failed to consider the chilling effect that its holding would have on the use of interrogatories, at least in multi-party litigation. One contemplating discovery via interrogatories would have to weigh the risk that some other litigant would seize upon a self-serving answer and offer it in evidence against the one propounding the interrogatory. Section 2030.410 effectively annuls the holding in *Levy-Zentner*; it allows use of answers to interrogatories "*only* against the responding party."[23]

—Responding Party May Not Use: The offer into evidence of answers to interrogatories by the very party who gave them is a classic illustration of

---

[20] Associates Discount Corp. v Tobb Co. (1966) 241 Cal App 2d 541, 551–552, 50 Cal Rptr 738, 745.

[21] Levy-Zentner Co. v Southern Pacific Transportation Co. (1977) 74 Cal App 3d 762, 142 Cal Rptr 1.

[22] Levy-Zentner Co. v Southern Pacific Transportation Co. (1977) 74 Cal App 3d 762, 789, 142 Cal Rptr 1, 19.

[23] CCP § 2030.410 (italics added).

"self-serving" hearsay.[24] In *Giesler v Berman*,[25] the trial court's failure to perceive the inadmissibility of such answers led to a reversal.[26]

—Responding Party Now Unavailable: The unavailability of the responding party for trial testimony does not change this result. In *Estate of Horman*,[27] the State of California propounded interrogatories to certain claimants to an estate who were domiciled in the Soviet Union. In due course they answered. When the claimants could not attend the trial, their attorney offered in evidence their answers to these interrogatories. On appeal from the action of the trial judge in excluding this evidence, the court noted the hearsay nature of these answers:

> The answers to the interrogatories are no more than affidavits of interested persons. By their very nature, such statements contain self-serving facts. In the absence of statutory permission, an affidavit is not competent evidence, although made under oath, because it is hearsay.[28]

The court observed that the federal courts, interpreting "discovery statutes almost identical to those existing in California," had refused to allow a responding party to secure the admission in evidence of his own answers to interrogatories. For two reasons, it adopted the same rule for California. First, it noted the lack of an opportunity for cross-examination. Second, it realized that such "practice, if countenanced, would greatly inhibit the use of discovery procedures, thereby thwarting the purpose of the Legislature."[29]

—Exceptions: There are two exceptions to the rule that answers to interrogatories may be offered in evidence only against parties giving them. First, if parties testify at trial in a way that is inconsistent with their answers to interrogatories, those answers will be admissible not only to impeach that trial testimony, but also as substantive evidence under California's exception to the hearsay rule for prior inconsistent statements.[30] Second, where a party has corrected an earlier answer to an interrogatory, and an adversary insists on introducing the original answer as an admission, that party may counter this by introducing the corrected answer, no matter how self-serving it may be.[31]

---

[24] Annotation: Party's right to use, as evidence in civil trial, his own testimony given upon interrogatories or depositions taken by opponent. 13 ALR3d 1312.

[25] Giesler v Berman (1970) 6 Cal App 3d 919, 929–930, 86 Cal Rptr 205.

[26] See also Haskell Plumbing & Heating Co. v Weeks (1956, CA9 Alaska) 237 F2d 263, 266–267; Lobel v American Airlines, Inc. (1951, CA2 NY) 192 F2d 217, 221.

[27] Estate of Horman (1968) 265 Cal App 2d 796, 71 Cal Rptr 780.

[28] Estate of Horman (1968) 265 Cal App 2d 796, 805, 71 Cal Rptr 780, 786.

[29] Estate of Horman (1968) 265 Cal App 2d 796, 805, 71 Cal Rptr 780, 786.

[30] See Evid Code § 1235. Cf. Le Grand v Yellow Cab Co. (1970) 8 Cal App 3d 125, 87 Cal Rptr 292. For a discussion of the impact of this exception to the hearsay rule on deposition testimony, see § 2.39.

[31] CCP § 2030.310(a). See also Grace & Co. v Los Angeles (1960, CA9 Cal) 278 F2d 771, 776. For a discussion of amendments to answers to interrogatories, see § 5.21.

CHAPTER 6

INSPECTION DEMANDS

SYNOPSIS

§ 6.1   In General

An Essential Form of Discovery: At trial, an opponent's evidence usually includes not only the testimony of witnesses but also the introduction of exhibits. A civil discovery system would be feeble indeed if it did not provide litigants with pretrial access to documents and tangible things that will become exhibits at trial. Moreover, even items that are themselves inadmissible may contain clues to admissible evidence. A mature discovery system must include methods for parties to compel pretrial inspection of relevant items so that they may then pursue any leads they supply.

Party or Nonparty? A party who wants to discover a document, place or thing must first determine whether that item is possessed or controlled by a party or a nonparty. The filing of a lawsuit subjects a plaintiff to the trial court's jurisdiction; service of process or a voluntary appearance does the same for a defendant. Jurisdiction over the parties permits a simple and direct procedure for obtaining discovery inspections from them. In contrast, the need to subject nonparties to the trial court's power complicates obtaining this type of discovery from them.[1]

This chapter focuses on the pretrial inspection of documents, things, and places possessed or controlled by a *party* to the case. The next chapter deals with the procedures that apply when the item a party wants to inspect is possessed or controlled by a *nonparty*.

Limitations: Inspection demands do not provide access to every document or thing that another party possesses or controls. The item sought for inspection must have some *relevance* to the subject matter of the lawsuit.[2] Moreover, it must not be insulated from disclosure by any of the evidentiary *privileges*.[3] And even where the party seeking an inspection can clear the hurdles of relevance and privilege, the *work product protection* may restrict or preclude discovery of the item sought.[4]

§ 6.2 Alternate Procedures

Two Methods: The Civil Discovery Act provides two different tools for obtaining pretrial inspections from a party to a lawsuit. The more direct method is the service of a demand that the other party produce and permit inspection of some item. The more circuitous alternative entails a notice to take the other party's deposition, which notice includes an instruction to produce the desired item at the deposition.

Demand for Inspection: The inspection demand provisions[1] contain a comprehensive scheme for discovery of items that another party to the lawsuit possesses or controls. This discovery tool is the conventional method for obtaining a pretrial inspection of documents,[2] tangible things[3] and land or other property.[4] Although use of this device originally required leave of court,[5] since 1974 it has been self-executing: a party simply serves a "demand"[6] that another

---

[1] Cf. Carlton v Superior Court (1968) 261 Cal App 2d 282, 287, 67 Cal Rptr 568, 571.

[2] See, e.g., Quotron Systems, Inc. v Automatic Data Processing, Inc. (1992, SD NY) 141 FRD 37, 41 [relevance for document production measured broadly by reference to the subject matter of the suit, not just the specific issues in the pleadings].

For a discussion of standard of relevance for discovery purposes, see Chapter 11.

[3] For a discussion of the concept of privilege in the discovery context, see Chapter 12.

[4] For a discussion of the work product protection, see Chapter 13.

[1] CCP §§ 2031.010–2031.510.

[2] CCP § 2031.010(b).

[3] CCP § 2031.010(c).

[4] CCP § 2031.010(d).

[5] Former CCP § 2031 originally required a party seeking an inspection to make a *motion* to produce.

[6] The 1974 amendment to former CCP § 2031 described this as a "request" to produce. The Civil Discovery Act of 1986 renamed this a "demand."

party produce an item for inspection.[7] Only in unusual circumstances does a party seeking this type of discovery resort to a motion instead of a demand.[8]

Deposition-Notice Procedure: The Civil Discovery Act perpetuates a long-standing practice[9] that bypasses the inspection demand scheme. A litigant serves a notice to take the deposition of the party who possesses or controls certain documents or things. The notice includes an instruction that the deponent bring specified items to the deposition.[10] No subpoena is needed to compel production of an item by a party to the case.[11] The deposition notice itself obligates the party-deponent not only to produce the described items, but also to allow an inspection and copying of them:

> The service of a deposition notice . . . is effective to require any deponent who is a party to the action . . . to attend and to testify, as well as to produce any document or tangible thing for inspection and copying.[12]

Advantages of the Demand Procedure: There are three advantages to using inspection demands to obtain a discovery from a party. First, a party wanting to sample or test property may have no choice: only the demand procedure explicitly authorizes "sampling" and "testing" of a produced item.[13] Second, this procedure allows one to obtain items before deposing a party. A leisurely study of these items should result in better questions during the deposition. Finally, use of an inspection demand avoids using up the one-deposition limit.[14] For these

---

[7] See People ex rel. Dept. of Transportation v Superior Court (1976) 60 Cal App 3d 352, 358, 131 Cal Rptr 476, 480 [this method of discovery was made self-executing "to free the trial court from the unreasonable burden of hearing on motion every case in which production of documentary material is sought"].

[8] County of Los Angeles v Superior Court (1990) 219 Cal App 3d 1605, 1610–1611, 269 Cal Rptr 187, 190 [in a civil action arising out of a collision with a police car, a litigant seeking access to the personnel records of the officer-driver must file a motion]; City of Fresno v Superior Court (1988) 205 Cal App 3d 1459, 1473–1477, 253 Cal Rptr 296, 303–306 [in a civil action based on alleged excessive force in making an arrest, plaintiff seeking discovery of records of citizen complaints of officer's misconduct must file a motion]; Volkswagenwerk A.G. v Superior Court (1981) 123 Cal App 3d 840, 851, 176 Cal Rptr 874, 880 [where the history of discovery efforts in a case demonstrates that an opponent is likely to refuse any inspection demand, the trial court has the discretion to let the party seeking an inspection speed up the process by resorting immediately to a motion].

[9] See, e.g., Filipoff v Superior Court (1961) 56 Cal 2d 443, 15 Cal Rptr 139, 364 P2d 315 [the same alternative was available under the 1956 Discovery Act].

[10] CCP §§ 2025.220(a)(4) and 2025.280(a).

[11] Cf. CCP § 2025.280(b), which requires the service of a subpoena to compel a nonparty deponent to produce an item for inspection at a deposition.

[12] CCP § 2025.280(a).

[13] For a discussion of the extent to which an item produced for inspection under Chapter 14 may be subjected to testing, see §§ 6.8–6.9.

[14] CCP § 2025.610(a).

For a discussion of the one-deposition limitation, see § 2.36.

reasons, litigants generally prefer inspection demands to depositions for obtaining discovery inspections from a party.

Advantages of Deposition-Notice Procedure: Under the 1956 Discovery Act inspections required advance approval from the trial court. In contrast, depositions of a party required only service of a notice, and there was then no limit on their number. These differences often made it advantageous to bypass the inspection method and use deposition-notices to obtain document discovery. A 1974 amendment to the original Section 2031 ended its requirement of a motion by permitting a party to serve a production "request." (The present statutes rename this a "demand" for production.) Once the inspection device became self-executing, a major advantage of the deposition-notice procedure evaporated.

At present, the main reason for resorting to the deposition procedure is to accelerate the inspection itself. Under the demand procedure, the party seeking an inspection usually must wait 30 days after service of the demand.[15] In contrast, one need only give ten days notice to take a deposition, including one that requires a party[16] to produce documents or things.[17]

—Second Bite at the Apple: The deposition route may also rescue a party who has lost the right to compel an inspection of a certain item under the demand procedures. When an inspection demand meets with a formal objection, the party seeking the inspection must move to compel an inspection within 45 days.[18] Failure to do so forfeits the right to use that demand or any later one to inspect the specified items.[19] However, the inspection demand and the deposition, even one including a production of specified items, are technically discrete discovery methods: "the inspection of documents procedure is quite different from a deposition at which a party is required to bring documents."[20] This difference creates a loophole for parties whose delay in filing a motion to compel has cost them the right to enforce an inspection demand. They may extricate themselves from this plight by simply noticing a deposition of the party and instructing the deponent to produce the same items. Nothing in either the deposition procedure or the inspection demand procedure "suggests that seeking documents under one

---

[15] CCP § 2031.030(c)(2).

[16] For a discussion of the longer time required where production is sought from a nonparty deponent, see § 7.3.

[17] CCP § 2025.270(a).

In adopting this provision, the Legislature rejected a Discovery Commission proposal to require 30 days notice before a deposition that included an inspection demand. See Proposed Civil Discovery Act of 1986, Section 2025(f), Appendix D.

Cf. FRCivP 30(b)(5) [procedures for document production under FRCivP 34 govern deposition notices to produce to a party].

[18] CCP § 2031.310.

[19] For a discussion of the consequences of a failure to make a timely motion for further response to an inspection demand, see § 6.14.

[20] Carter v Superior Court (1990) 218 Cal App 3d 994, 997, 267 Cal Rptr 290, 291–292.

statutory procedure bars a litigant from seeking the same documents under the other."[21]

The remedy for any abuse of this loophole lies in a motion for a protective order against "unreasonably cumulative or duplicative" use of discovery methods[22] under Section 2019.030, or against "unwarranted annoyance."[23]

§ 6.3 Mechanics of Inspection Demand

Self-Executing Procedure: The inspection demand, the conventional method[1] for obtaining a pretrial access to documents,[2] tangible things[3] and land or other property[4] from another party to a lawsuit, is a self-executing discovery tool: a party simply serves a "demand"[5] that another party produce an item for inspection.[6] Only in unusual circumstances need or should a party seeking this type of discovery resort to a motion instead of a demand.[7]

Timing: Generally, if discovery remains open,[8] a party may serve an inspection demand "without leave of court" and "at any time."[9] The one exception applies to a plaintiff. During the first 10 days after the court has obtained jurisdiction over a defendant, a plaintiff must obtain court permission

---

[21] Carter v Superior Court (1990) 218 Cal App 3d 994, 997, 267 Cal Rptr 290, 291–292.

[22] CCP § 2019.030(a)(1).

[23] CCP § 2025.420(b).

See Carter v Superior Court (1990) 218 Cal App 3d 994, 998, 267 Cal Rptr 290, 292.

[1] For a discussion of the alternate deposition-notice route, see § 6.2.

[2] CCP § 2031.010(b).

[3] CCP § 2031.010(c).

[4] CCP § 2031.010(d).

[5] The 1974 amendment to the original CCP § 2031 described this as a "request" to produce. The Civil Discovery Act of 1986 renamed this a "demand."

[6] See People ex rel. Dept. of Transportation v Superior Court (1976) 60 Cal App 3d 352, 358, 131 Cal Rptr 476, 480 [the Legislature made this method of discovery self-executing "to free the trial court from the unreasonable burden of hearing on motion every case in which production of documentary material is sought"].

[7] County of Los Angeles v Superior Court (1990) 219 Cal App 3d 1605, 1610–1611, 269 Cal Rptr 187, 190 [in a civil action arising out of a collision with a police car, a litigant seeking access to the personnel records of the officer-driver must file a motion]; City of Fresno v Superior Court (1988) 205 Cal App 3d 1459, 1473–1477, 253 Cal Rptr 296, 303–306 [in a civil action based on alleged excessive force in making an arrest, a plaintiff seeking discovery of records of citizen complaints of officer's misconduct must file a motion]; Volkswagenwerk A.G. v Superior Court (1981) 123 Cal App 3d 840, 851, 176 Cal Rptr 874, 880 [where the history of discovery efforts in a case demonstrates that an opponent is likely to refuse any inspection demand, the trial court has the discretion to let the party seeking an inspection to speed up the process by resorting immediately to a motion].

[8] See CCP § 2024.010.

[9] CCP § 2031.020(a).

See Putnam v Clague (1992) 3 Cal App 4th 542, 565, 5 Cal Rptr 2d 25, 39–40.

before serving an inspection demand upon that defendant.[10] The plaintiff may get such permission by an unnoticed motion.[11]

Format and Content: Section 2031.030 regulates an inspection demand's format and content. The document must start with the case title.[12] Below this should first appear the demanding party's name, then the producing party's name.[13] Next should come the set number.[14] During discovery, a party may serve several sets of inspection demands. Consequently, the statute requires the assignment to each demand of a number that is consecutive with the demand that preceded it.[15]

The body of the demand must separately identify and number (or letter) each item and each category of item.[16]

Time, Place, and Manner of Inspection: The demand must specify the date on which the inspection is to take place. Ordinarily, this date may be no sooner than 30 days after the service of the demand.[17] Mail service extends this period, usually by five days.[18] The demand must also state where the inspection will take place.[19] Finally, if the party making the demand seeks to do anything more than visually inspect the item, the demand must specify the nature of this "related activity."[20] For example, the demand must specify that the party wishes to photograph, sample, test, measure or survey specified real or personal property. Moreover, if this "related activity" will permanently change or destroy the item, the inspection demand must state that this is an anticipated consequence of the testing.[21]

---

[10] CCP § 2031.020(b).

Unlawful detainer plaintiffs need only wait five days. CCP § 2031.020(b).

Cf. California Shellfish Inc. v United Shellfish Co. (1997) 56 Cal App 4th 16, 22, 64 Cal Rptr 2d 797, 799.

[11] CCP § 2031.020(c).

[12] CCP § 2031.030(b).

[13] CCP § 2031.030(b).

[14] CCP § 2031.030(b).

[15] CCP § 2031.030(a).

[16] CCP § 2031.030(c).

For a discussion of the requirement to "designate" these items with particularity, see § 6.5.

[17] CCP § 2031.030(c)(2).

Plaintiffs in unlawful detainer actions may demand that the inspection occur as soon as five days after service of the notice. CCP § 2031.030(c)(2).

In all cases, the court may shorten time for "good cause." CCP § 2031.030(c)(2).

[18] CCP § 2016.050, referencing CCP § 1013(a).

[19] CCP § 2031.030(c)(3).

For a discussion of a "reasonable place" for the inspection, see § 6.10.

[20] CCP § 2031.030(c)(4).

For a discussion of what may be done in addition to an inspection of the item produced, see §§ 6.8–6.9.

[21] CCP § 2031.030(c)(4).

For a discussion of the extent to which an inspection may include "destructive testing," see § 6.8.

Service and Custody of Original: A copy of the demand must be served not only on the producing party, but also on every other party who has appeared in the action. [22] Neither the original of the demand nor the original of the response to it is to be filed with the court. [23] The demanding party must retain both the original of the demand and the proof of service, as well as the original of the response, until six months after final disposition of the action. At that time, all may be destroyed. [24]

§ 6.4 Designation of Items

Categories Permitted: Continuing longstanding California practice, [1] and following comparable federal practice under current Federal Rule of Civil Procedure 34, [2] Section 2031.030 [3] does not require the demanding party to pinpoint the very document or thing to be produced. Rather, a demand need only identify categories of items sought. As explained by the Supreme Court in the *Union Trust Co.* case: [4]

> [A]ll that should be required of a party litigant in his endeavor to obtain an inspection of records . . . is that in his attempt to do so, he describe them with such certainty only as will or should reasonably apprise his legal opponent, or the custodian of such records, of that which may be desired. . . . Whether the description of records is sufficient . . . presents a question merely of whether . . . [the responding party] ought to recognize and be able to distinguish or identify the particular thing that is required. [5]

---

[22] CCP § 2031.040.

[23] CCP § 2031.290(a).

[24] CCP § 2031.290(b).

On motion and for good cause, the trial court may order that the originals be preserved for a longer period. CCP § 2031.290(b).

[1] See Section § 2031 of the Discovery Act of 1956, as amended in 1975, Appendix E.

See also West Pico Furniture Co. v Superior Court (1961) 56 Cal 2d 407, 419–420, 15 Cal Rptr 119, 125, 364 P2d 295, 301 [similar result under original text of 1956 Discovery Act]; Union Trust Co. v Superior Court (1938) 11 Cal 2d 449, 458, 81 P2d 150, 155 [similar practice established long before 1956 Act].

[2] As amended in 1974, FRCivP 34(b) allows items to be designated "either by individual item or category." These amendments resolved a split among federal courts over the degree of particularity required. Compare United States v National Steel Corp. (1960, SD Tex) 26 FRD 607, 610 [finding inadequate the request for "[a]ll correspondence passing between National and Metallic during [a specified 5-year period] which refers to the existence of competition between Metallic dealers and Stran-Steel dealers in the sale of metal buildings"] with United States v Certain Parcels of Land (1953, CD Cal) 15 FRD 224, 227 [finding adequate in an eminent domain action the request for "all appraisals, appraisal reports and other documents containing written communications, facts, figures and photographs relating to the [property's] value"].

[3] CCP § 2031.030(c)(1).

[4] Union Trust Co. v Superior Court (1938) 11 Cal 2d 449, 81 P2d 150.

[5] Union Trust Co. v Superior Court (1938) 11 Cal 2d 449, 458, 81 P2d 150, 155.

In the Court's view, as long as the responding party can understand what the demanding party is seeking, the designation need not be comprehensible "to persons other than those who may be directly concerned in the compliance with [it]."[6] Nor is it fatal that the documents are "not described in accordance with the [other party's] appellation of them."[7]

Blanket Demands: The liberal approach to the "designation" requirement does not mean that the courts will enforce "blanket" or "omnibus" inspection demands:

> [I]dentification may be inadequate . . . when the books and documents sought to be produced are designated by or included within a so-called omnibus description. The unlimited characteristics of such a description may impair or destroy exactitude so that the custodian of the records is not reasonably apprised of what he must produce.[8]

For example, in a federal hazardous waste cleanup case, plaintiffs made a request that would have forced another party to produce all writings relating to any cleanups, removal actions, remedial investigations, or feasibility studies involving it regardless of whether the attendant circumstances bore any similarity to the instant case. The court concluded: "The request . . . represents not merely a 'fishing expedition,' but, as one court described it, an effort to 'drain the pond and collect the fish from the bottom.' "[9]

Instead of making blanket demands, a party must reasonably particularize the categories of materials sought for inspection. This rules out dragnet demands such as one for "all of plaintiff's books and records showing the transaction with the defendant,"[10] or for all documents that "may be material to the issues,"[11]

---

[6] Union Trust Co. v Superior Court (1938) 11 Cal 2d 449, 458, 81 P2d 150, 155.

[7] Union Trust Co. v Superior Court (1938) 11 Cal 2d 449, 458, 81 P2d 150, 155.

[8] Flora Crane Service, Inc. v Superior Court (1965) 234 Cal App 2d 767, 786–787, 45 Cal Rptr 79, 89–90 (internal citations omitted).

See also Calcor Space Facility, Inc. v Superior Court (1997) 53 Cal App 4th 216, 222, 61 Cal Rptr 2d 567, 571 [12-page demand, including three pages of "instructions" and a three-page "definition," was in reality a blanket demand for all records on a broad subject]; Pacific Auto Ins. Co. v Superior Court (1969) 273 Cal App 2d 61, 68–70, 77 Cal Rptr 836, 841–842; Twin Lock, Inc. v Superior Court (1959) 171 Cal App 2d 236, 240–241, 340 P2d 748, 751.

[9] Amcast Industrial Corp. v Detrex Corp. (1991, ND Ind) 138 FRD 115, 121, quoting In re IBM Peripheral EDP Devices Anti-Trust Litigation (1977, ND Cal) 77 FRD 39, 41–42.

[10] Frank v Tinicum Metal Co. (1950, ED Pa) 11 FRD 83, 85.

See also Standard Chlorine of Delaware, Inc. v Sinibaldi (1992, D Del) 821 F Supp 232, 258 [finding overly broad a request for all documents dealing both with the business relationship between one party and its parent corporation and with the parent's sales to plaintiff]. Cf. Navajo Express v Superior Court (1986) 186 Cal App 3d 981, 986, 231 Cal Rptr 165, 168 [in proceeding seeking release of juvenile court records, request for "any and all records" concerning the juvenile upheld where requesting party informed court of the specific issues relevant to the request and court could conduct an in camera inspection prior to the records' release].

[11] Mercantile Metal & Ore Corp. v American General Supply Corp. (1952, SD NY) 12 FRD 345, 346.

or that an opposing party intends to use at trial.[12] Also inadequate are overly broad categories: "Though the documents in question . . . are limited to 'financial records' that designation would seem to embrace every paper from sales stubs on a spike through the annual report."[13] However, this judicial hostility to blanket requests does not mean the mere use of "all" or "each and every" in a demand is automatically objectionable.[14]

Lists of Responsive Items: A 1980 amendment to the original Section 2031 allowed a party to include in an inspection request what was, in effect, an interrogatory. Under that practice, the responding party could be forced to "identify" any item that fell within any category described in the request. Section 2031.030 scraps this feature. One who wishes to obtain a list of responsive items in a described category should proceed by written interrogatory, and not by an inspection demand.[15]

§ 6.5 "Possession, Custody or Control" by a Party

Parties need only produce a demanded item or grant access to land if they have the power to do so. Under Section 2031.010, they must have "possession, custody, or control"[1] of the demanded document, thing, or place. The party seeking discovery must establish the responding party's power.[2] This section discusses some general issues of possession and control. The next section takes up some specific frequently encountered issues of "control."

"Possession" and "Custody": Determination of a party's "possession" or "custody" of an item presents mainly a factual inquiry. On the one hand, physical possession is generally enough to require a party to produce it. Thus, a party who possesses an item may not refuse to produce it just because some nonparty

---

[12] In re Kolinsky (1992, SD NY) 140 BR 79, 87.

[13] Richland Wholesale Liquors, Inc. v Joseph E. Seagram & Sons, Inc. (1966, D SC) 40 FRD 480, 481.

See also Buntzman v Springfield Redevelopment Authority (1993, D Mass) 146 FRD 30, 33 [request for unspecified "financial statements" too vague].

[14] See, e.g., Data-Link Systems, Inc. v Data Line Service Co. (1992, ND Ind) 148 FRD 225, 228 [although "sweeping in scope," extensive document production requests "were not overly broad in light of the issues in the case"].

Cf. Taylor v Florida Atlantic University (1990, SD Fla) 132 FRD 304, 305 [deposition subpoena that asked for "all notes, charts, records, correspondence, memoranda, etc." that deponent had regarding two named parties held sufficiently particular]; RKB Enterprises, Inc. v Ernst & Young (1993, NY Sup, App Div) 600 NYS2d 793, 794 [use of "all" in request for "all written agreements" between the parties is permissible "in a narrowly defined category"]; Slutzky v Aron Estates Corp. (1993, NY Sup) 597 NYS2d 997, 1003 [request for " 'any', 'all', 'each' and 'every' document of a certain kind" is not per se overly broad].

[15] The responding party can be required to identify items within a demanded category only where that party objects formally to the production of that category. See CCP § 2031.060(b)(3). For a discussion of this requirement, see § 6.12.

[1] CCP § 2031.010(a).

[2] See, e.g., Burton Mechanical Contractors, Inc. v Foreman (1992, ND Ind) 148 FRD 230, 236.

owns it.[3] In such a case, however, the inspecting party probably should notify the nonparty owner.[4]

On the other hand, an inspection demand may not oblige a party who once possessed or controlled an item, but no longer does, to retrieve it. For example, in a federal case,[5] an insured sued her carrier to recover the value of a badly damaged auto. Then, after appropriately signaling her intentions, she sold the car as junk to someone in another jurisdiction. She could not, of course, comply with a later court order that she allow the insurance company to test the car to find out whether it was repairable. The retaliatory dismissal of her complaint by an irate trial judge was reversed:

> [I]t is necessary that the object sought to be examined must at the time the order is entered be in the possession, custody, or control of plaintiff. There was no showing of that fact. Actually the court had already been advised . . . that the automobile had been sold as junk. . . . [T]his sale was not surreptitious . . . . Accordingly, there was no basis in Rule 34 for the entry of the order.[6]

—Improper Destruction: Destruction of an item that forestalls a discovery inspection may lead to sanctions. A deliberate destruction to frustrate discovery justifies a drastic sanction.[7] Even a negligent destruction of an item *before* service of the inspection demand may warrant a sanction. For example, in the *Puritan Insurance Co.* case,[8] a party's expert had lost the piece of machinery whose alleged defect was the central issue in the case. The case upheld the trial court's imposition of an "evidence" sanction: the exclusion of that expert's opinion to the extent that he was basing it on his examination of the missing piece. Moreover, although the Civil Discovery Act does not explicitly require an

---

[3] Kirkland v Superior Court (2002) 95 Cal App 4th 92, 115 Cal Rptr 2d 279 [defendant who possessed relevant documents and transcripts from SEC investigation required to produce them in subsequent civil fraud suit].

See also Mead Corp. v Riverwood Natural Resources Corp. (1992, D Minn) 145 FRD 512, 522 [holding that "a contention that the requested documents have been obtained from another source will not relieve a party from the obligation to properly respond to a proper Request"]; Mullen v Mullen (1953, D Alaska) 14 FRD 142.

[4] Alma-Schuhfabrik Ag. v Rosenthal (1960, ED NY) 25 FRD 100, 101.

Cf. Valley Bank of Nevada v Superior Court (1975) 15 Cal 3d 652, 658, 125 Cal Rptr 553, 556, 542 P2d 977, 980.

[5] Fisher v United States Fidelity & Guaranty Co. (1957, CA7 Ill) 246 F2d 344.

[6] Fisher v United States Fidelity & Guaranty Co. (1957, CA7 Ill) 246 F2d 344, 349–350.

[7] See, e.g., Valenstein v Bayonne Bolt Corp. (1946, ED NY) 6 FRD 363.

For a discussion of sanctions for noncompliance with a demand for inspection, see § 6.15.

[8] Puritan Insurance Co. v Superior Court (1985) 171 Cal App 3d 877, 217 Cal Rptr 602.

Compare Beil v Lakewood Engineering & Manufacturing Co. (1994, CA6 Ky) 15 F3d 546, 552 [sanctions under FRCivP 37 not available for destruction of evidence before suit was filed].

adversary to preserve an item in its possession or under its control, a party may obtain a preliminary injunction ordering an opponent to do so.[9]

"Control": A party who does not possess an item covered by an inspection demand may nonetheless "control" it. The obligation to produce items extends to those that a party controls. The courts have expended significant energy wrestling with the meaning of "control" for inspection discovery.[10]

—Two Approaches: Two lines of cases have emerged. The stricter courts require the party seeking discovery to show something *more* than that the opposing party could have obtained the desired materials "if it tried hard enough."[11] To them, "control" implies the responding party's *right* to demand that the nonparty in possession of the item surrender it.[12] Another line of cases takes a more practical approach: a party demanding an inspection shows "control" simply by showing the *likelihood* that the nonparty in actual possession would honor a request for the item.[13]

Of course, a party's unsuccessful effort to persuade the nonparty in possession of records to make them available shows that party's lack of "control" over them. In one case, a client asked his former attorney to make the client's records available for inspection by an opponent. The attorney, however, asserted a possessory lien over these papers as security for his fee. The court held that it would be an abuse of discretion to sanction the party for failing to produce these documents for pretrial inspection.[14]

§ 6.6 Frequently Encountered "Control" Issues

Courts have repeatedly addressed the meaning of "control" over items possessed by nonparties in cases involving corporations, attorneys, insurers, governmental agencies, doctors, and hospitals.

Corporations: Questions involving "control" of a demanded item held by a nonparty have surfaced in three principal areas involving corporations: (1) access

---

[9] Dodge, Warren & Peters Insurance Services, Inc. v Riley (2003) 105 Cal App 4th 1414, 130 Cal Rptr 2d 385 [preliminary injunction ordered recipient of an inspection demand not to destroy electronic data that is the subject of the demands].

See generally Arent, Brownstone and Fenwick, E-Discovery: Preserving, Requesting and Producing Electronic Information, 19 Santa Clara Computer and High Tech. L.J. 131 (2002).

[10] For a discussion of frequently encountered situations raising the issue of "control," see § 6.6.

[11] Chaveriat v Williams Pipe Line Co. (1993, CA7 Ill) 11 F3d 1420, 1427 [party's need to ask nonparty to give it or sell it requested materials demonstrated party's *lack* of possession, custody, or control].

[12] Green v Fulton (1994, D Me) 157 FRD 136, 142 [defendant police chief sued in official capacity had authority to obtain requested police records].

[13] Herbst v Able (1972, SD NY) 63 FRD 135 [willingness of nonparty governmental agency to honor a party's request for a transcript of its secret hearing sufficiently demonstrated his "control"].

[14] Williams v Consolidated Investors, Inc. (1970, Kan) 472 P2d 248.

See also Searock v Stripling (1984, CA11 Fla) 736 F2d 650, 654.

by a corporate party to the records of its affiliates; (2) access by one of its officers, managers, or shareholders who is a party to the records of a nonparty corporation; and (3) access by a corporate party to items possessed by its employees and agents.

—Affiliated Corporations: The courts have consistently ruled that a corporate party has sufficient "control" of the books and records of its subsidiaries and affiliates to require it to obtain and produce those records for a discovery inspection:

> It is true that [Federal] Rule 34 applies only to parties, but here the corporate defendant owns 100% of the stock of Polyglass, both corporations occupied the same premises, and the office manager of the corporate defendant is "in charge and control" of the books and records of Polyglass. In view of these facts, for the purpose of applying Rule 34, we think Polyglass and the corporate defendant are "substantially one."[1]

Although the question is a tougher one, courts have frequently found that a *subsidiary* has control of a parent corporation's records.[2]

—Officers, Shareholders, and Mangers: Courts have sometimes ordered a party to produce records possessed by a nonparty close corporation of which that party is an officer, director, or substantial shareholder.[3] Indeed, one state court, applying the broader, practical notion of "control," upheld the dismissal of a suit because the plaintiff failed to produce the records of a nonparty corporation that he managed.[4] The defendants had shown that he had failed to use his "influence" over the corporation's officers to induce them to turn the records over to him.[5]

---

[1] Standard Ins. Co. v Pittsburgh Electrical Insulation, Inc. (1961, WD Pa) 29 FRD 185, 188.

See also West v Johnson & Johnson Products, Inc. (1985) 174 Cal App 3d 831, 874, 220 Cal Rptr 437, 463–464; Societe Internationale Pour Participations Industrielles et Commerciales, S. A. v Rogers (1958) 357 US 197, 204, 2 L Ed 2d 1255, 1262, 78 S Ct 1087, 1091; Cooper Industries, Inc. v British Aerospace, Inc. (1984 SD NY) 102 FRD 918. Cf. In re Perrier Bottled Water Litigation (1991, D Conn) 138 FRD 348, 350–351 [corporate party need not obtain records where affiliate is a co-party].

Annotation: Discovery and inspection: Compelling party to disclose information in hands of affiliated or subsidiary corporation, or independent contractor, not made party to suit. 19 ALR3d 1134, partially superseded by 145 ALR Fed 527.

Annotation: Who has possession, custody, or control of corporate books or records for purposes of order to produce. 47 ALR3d 676.

[2] See, e.g., Gerling Intern. Insur. Co. v C.I.R. (1988, CA3) 839 F2d 131, 140–141; Japan Halon Co., Ltd. v Great Lakes Chemical Corp. (1993, ND Ind) 155 FRD 626, 628–629; Camden Iron & Metal, Inc. v Marubeni America Corp. (1991, D NJ) 138 FRD 438, 441–442.

[3] General Environmental Science Corp. v Horsfall (1991, ND Ohio) 136 FRD 130, 133–134 [compelling managing director and owners of majority of shares of nonparty corporation to produce documents possessed by that corporation].

[4] For a general description of the broad and narrow approaches to "control," see § 6.5.

[5] Hart v Wolff (1971, Alaska) 489 P2d 114.

—**Employees and Agents:** "Control" may become more difficult to establish when a corporate party is asked to produce something that belongs to and is possessed by one of its agents or employees. In one case, a federal court concluded that a corporation lacked sufficient control over its nonparty employees to make them submit to fingerprint tests in response to an inspection demand.[6] In another case, however, a federal court ordered a corporate party to allow a plaintiff access to the pier where he was injured even though it was now leased to a nonparty. Here, however, the plaintiff succeeded in showing that the lessee was actually operating the pier as the corporate defendant's agent.[7]

Attorneys: Issues of control frequently arise when the opposing party's attorney possesses an item sought for a discovery inspection. Courts uniformly find that the client "controls" these items. This result applies both to items delivered to an attorney by the client,[8] and to those received by counsel from some third person.[9] In the latter instance, however, the attorney must have obtained the records in the course of employment by the party, not by another client.[10]

Insurers: For an inspection demand, a party also "controls" relevant items possessed by its insurance carrier. For example, in the *Clark* case,[11] the defendants resisted production of a document that neither they nor their attorney possessed. The defendants' insurer had generated the document during its investigation of plaintiff's claim, and it remained in its general counsel's possession. The court concluded:

> [T]he liability insurance carrier is defending the personal injury action under the terms of the defendants' policy of insurance. In such a situation the attorneys for the insurance company must be treated as the defendants' attorney and any material which is in their possession, custody or control solely because of this relationship is also in the possession, custody, or control of the defendants, and therefore is reachable [by an

---

[6] Nalco Chemical Co. v Hydro Technologies, Inc. (1993, ED Wis) 148 FRD 608, 619 [granting protective order against demanded production of fingerprint exemplars from 9 nonparty employees].

[7] Martin v N.V. Nederlandsche Amerikaansche Stoomvaart Maatchappij (1948, SD NY) 8 FRD 363.

Annotation: Discovery and inspection of article or premises the condition of which is alleged to have caused personal injury or death. 13 ALR2d 657.

Annotation: Discovery and inspection of articles and premises in civil actions other than for personal injury or death. 4 ALR3d 762.

[8] Bifferato v States Marine Corp. (1951, SD NY) 11 FRD 44, 46.

See also Gray v Faulkner (1992, ND Ind) 148 FRD 220, 223 [any documents possessed by state's attorney general are within control of its prison officials].

[9] Hanson v Gartland S.S. Co. (1964, ND Ohio) 34 FRD 493, 495–496.

Such items, however, may be insulated from discovery on some other basis, such as the work product protection. For coverage of the work product protection, see Chapter 13.

[10] Poppino v Jones Store Co. (1940, WD Mo) 1 FRD 215, 219.

[11] Clark v Superior Court (1960) 177 Cal App 2d 577, 2 Cal Rptr 375.

inspection demand]. To hold otherwise would allow parties to defeat the purpose of the statute.[12]

Governmental Documents: Courts have considered "control" issues concerning documents in the custody of a nonparty governmental agency in two recurring situations.

—Tax Records: In a federal case,[13] a plaintiff resisted production of her income tax returns since she had not retained copies of them. Government regulations, however, permit the taxpayer, and only the taxpayer, to receive a copy of a return upon request. The trial court ruled that the plaintiff had enough "control" over the returns to require their production:

> The potential right to the custody and control of the copies may be converted into an actual custody and control solely upon the exercise of the option of the taxpayer. If the copies were not required to be obtained and produced and such copies could not be obtained by anyone other than the taxpayer, then a taxpayer who retained no copies would be in an immeasurably better position than the careful person who retained such copies.[14]

Thus, the taxpayer's right to receive on demand a copy of the return from the Internal Revenue Service would have satisfied even those courts that follow the narrow approach to the concept of "control."[15]

—Interagency Control: A second problem involves the control exercisable by a party governmental agency over records possessed by a nonparty agency of the same government. In one federal case,[16] the Federal Deposit Insurance Corporation (FDIC) cited its difficulties in obtaining records from other federal agencies. Although the court acknowledged "the Kafkaesque [maze] that is endemic to governmental bureaucracy and that retards even inter-governmental

---

[12] Clark v Superior Court (1960) 177 Cal App 2d 577, 579, 2 Cal Rptr 375, 377.

Federal cases have reached the same conclusion under FRCivP 34. See, e.g., Bingle v Liggett Drug Co. (1951, D Mass) 11 FRD 593; Simper v Trimble (1949, D Mo) 9 FRD 598; Martin v N.V. Nederlandsche Amerikaansche Stoomvart Maatchappij (1948, SD NY) 8 FRD 363.

Such items, however, may be insulated from discovery on some other basis, such as the work product protection. For a discussion of the extent to which materials generated by the liability insurance carrier of a party qualify for this protection, see § 13.8.

[13] Reeves v Pennsylvania R. Co. (1948, D Del) 80 F Supp 107.

[14] Reeves v Pennsylvania R. Co. (1948, D Del) 80 F Supp 107, 109.

See also United States v Weinblatt (1951, SD NY) 11 FRD 398.

In California, however, a taxpayer has in many situations a privilege to refuse discovery of his state and federal tax returns. For a discussion of the "taxpayer's privilege," see §§ 12.35–12.36.

Annotation: Discovery and inspection of income tax returns in actions between private individuals. 70 ALR2d 240.

[15] For a description of the narrow and broad interpretations of control, see § 6.5.

[16] Comeau v Rupp (1992, D Kan) 810 F Supp 1127.

requests for information,"[17] this did not preclude the FDIC's "control" of these records:

> Although the FDIC is part of a complex regulatory banking scheme that involves other agencies, the FDIC, as an arm of the government, is in a superior position to gain access to the documents of these other agencies. Because of this superior position, the court will not accept a naked averment by the FDIC that a particular document is not within its "possession." . . . . "[C]ontrol" comprehends not only possession but also the right, authority, or ability to obtain the documents. Thus, . . . the FDIC [must] make reasonable, diligent inquiries, and, if applicable, demands of other agencies in order to obtain documents within the possession of such other agencies.[18]

In another federal case, involving investments in the DeLorean motor car company, however, the court took a narrower view of "control." The case involved fraud claims by an agency of the British government against an American accounting firm.[19] The defendant requested the plaintiff agency to produce the records of an investigation conducted by the British police. Citing the legal independence of the English police force from other officers of the Crown, the federal court concluded that the plaintiff agency did not control these records.[20]

Just because the People of California are parties to a case, they are not in possession, custody, or control of the documents of all state agencies. They thus need not produce all documents from those agencies that an opposing party demands:

> Indeed, the very nature of state agencies supports a finding that the People should not be deemed to have possession, custody or control over their documents. Each agency or department of the state is established as a separate entity, under various state laws or constitutional provisions.[21]

> It would be unduly burdensome if any time the People are a party to litigation they are required to search for documents from any and all state agencies that the propounding party demands.[22]

---

[17] Comeau v Rupp (1992, D Kan) 810 F Supp 1127, 1166.

[18] Comeau v Rupp (1992, D Kan) 810 F Supp 1127, 1166 (internal citations omitted).

[19] Department of Economic Development v Arthur Anderson & Co. (USA) (1991, SD NY) 139 FRD 295.

[20] Department of Economic Development v Arthur Anderson & Co. (USA) (1991, SD NY) 139 FRD 295, 301.

[21] People ex rel. Lockyer v Superior Court (2004) 122 Cal App 4th 1060, 1078, 19 Cal Rptr 3d 324, 337–338.

[22] People ex rel. Lockyer v Superior Court (2004) 122 Cal App 4th 1060, 1079, 19 Cal Rptr 3d 324, 338.

Medical Records: Several cases have addressed whether party-patients "control" the medical records of their doctors and hospitals. These cases turn on whether the court follows the narrow or the liberal approach to "control."[23] Courts that believe that "control" connotes a legal *right* to obtain the item from another will not require parties to produce the records of doctors or hospitals. For example, the same federal judge who ruled that a plaintiff's tax returns were under her control refused to require her to ask her treating physician for X-ray photographs:

> The defendant suggests that a request of the plaintiff [to her doctor] for the custody of the photographs would probably be complied with. No right is shown to exist in the plaintiff to enforce a demand for such X-ray photographs from the person having the possession, custody or control and the lack of a right to enforce the demand negatives the legal right of custody or control.[24]

This same reasoning supports rulings that parties need not request a copy of the office records of their treating physician.[25]

Other courts have taken the more practical view of "control" over medical records held by a nonparty. Thus, a few federal and state courts have ordered a personal injury plaintiff to sign an authorization for the release of medical records.[26]

In California Section 1158 of the Evidence Code and Section 1795.12 of the Health and Safety Code now give patients the right to demand an inspection of their medical records. Therefore these records should be considered under their "control" if an adversary demands to inspect them during discovery.[27]

---

[23] For a description of the narrow and broad interpretations of control, see § 6.5.

[24] Reeves v Pennsylvania R. Co. (1948, D Del) 80 F Supp 107, 109.

[25] Greene v Sears, Roebuck & Co. (1966, ND Ohio) 40 FRD 14.

See also Neal v Boulder (1992, D Colo) 142 FRD 325, 327 [defendants cannot compel medical malpractice plaintiff to sign blank releases authorizing access to medical files held by nonparty]; Nitzel v Jackson (1994, Okla) 879 P2d 1222, 1223 [court lacked authority to require plaintiff to sign blank medical authorization requests].

Cf. Santa Fe International Corp. v Potashnick (1979, ED La) 83 FRD 299 [one litigating with a general contractor could not compel that party to exercise its right to inspect the work of its nonparty subcontractor in order to provide an opportunity to enter the nonparty's premises].

[26] Schwartz v Travelers Ins. Co. (1954, CD NY) 17 FRD 330; Rojas v Ryder Truck Rental, Inc. (1994, Fla) 641 So2d 855.

Cf. Securities & Exchange Comm'n v College Bound, Inc. (1994, D DC) 155 FRD 1, 2 [trial court can order party to sign blank consent directives seeking release of documents held by nonparty foreign banks]; Fields v McNamara (1975, Colo) 540 P2d 327 [party can be compelled to provide releases to an opposing party's counsel].

[27] Cf. Person v Farmers Ins. Group of Companies (1997) 52 Cal App 4th 813, 61 Cal Rptr 2d 30 [health care practitioners may not refuse their patients' requests to inspect their medical records unless and until their bill is paid or they are given a lien for the amount of it].

§ 6.7 Inspection of Documents

Documents are the most common target of inspection demands.[1] Section 2031.010 expressly authorizes inspection of "documents,"[2] which the Civil Discovery Act defines[3] by reference to the Evidence Code's definition of "writing":

> 'Writing' means handwriting, typewriting, printing, photostating, photographing, and every other means of recording upon any tangible thing any form of communication or representation, including letters, words, pictures, sounds, or symbols, or combinations thereof.[4]

The Law Revision Commission Comment to this statute says only that "writing" is "defined very broadly to include all forms of tangible expression, including pictures and sound recordings."

Application: The Evidence Code definition of "writing" leaves no room to argue that traditional paper documents, however produced or bound, do not fall within its scope. Thus, papers, books, accounts, letters and photographs unquestionably are covered.[5] In addition, California courts have extended the definition to motion picture film,[6] phonograph records,[7] audio recordings,[8] video recordings,[9] and artist sketches of a criminal suspect.[10]

—Computerized Records: The *Aguimatang* case[11] held that computerized records are "writings" under the business record exception to the hearsay rule.[12] The court noted that the definition of "writing" in the Evidence Code "is not

---

[1] CCP § 2031.010(a).

For a discussion of production and inspection of tangible things, see § 6.8.

For a discussion of entry of property for inspection, see § 6.9.

[2] CCP § 2031.010(a).

[3] CCP § 2016.020(c).

Cf. Former CCP § 2031(a), 1956 Discovery Act, AppendixE [authorizing inspection of "documents, papers, books, accounts, letters, (and) photographs"] and FRCivP 34(a), specifying that "documents" includes "writings, drawings, graphs, charts, photographs, phono-records, and other data compilations from which information can be obtained."

[4] Evid Code § 250.

[5] Cf. Steele v Superior Court (1961) 56 Cal 2d 402, 15 Cal Rptr 116, 364 P2d 292 [an unsigned transcript of a deposition taken in another action treated as a "document" for purposes of 1956 version of CCP § 2031]; Price v Superior Court (1958) 161 Cal App 2d 650, 327 P2d 203 [transcript of a tape-recorded witness statement deemed a "document" under 1956 version of CCP § 2031].

[6] People v Enskat (1971) 20 Cal App 3d Supp 1, 3, 98 Cal Rptr 646.

[7] People v Manson (1976) 61 Cal App 3d 102, 215, 132 Cal Rptr 265.

[8] People v Patton (1976) 63 Cal App 3d 211, 133 Cal Rptr 533.

[9] Jones v City of Los Angeles (1993) 20 Cal App 4th 436, 24 Cal Rptr 2d 528.

[10] People v Garcia (1988) 201 Cal App 3d 325, 328–329, 247 Cal Rptr 94.

[11] Aguimatang v California State Lottery (1991) 234 Cal App 3d 769, 286 Cal Rptr 57.

[12] Evid Code § 1271.

limited to the commonly understood forms of writing,"[13] but is broad enough to include a magnetic tape.

Where a party seeks to inspect computerized records, Section 2031.280 requires the responding party to use its own "detection devices" where necessary to "translate any data compilations included in the demand into reasonably usable form."[14] This language comes from Federal Rule of Civil Procedure 34, where it was inserted in 1970 to adapt inspection demands to the computer age.[15] However, unlike the federal rule, Section 2031.280(b) places on the demanding party the "reasonable expenses" of recovering the electronic data from the responding party's devices for storing them.[16]

Foreign Language Documents: With the increase in international trade, parties seeking to inspect documents often find that they are written in a foreign language. This raises the question whether one responding to an inspection demand must furnish an English translation. The 1970 amendment to Federal Rule of Civil Procedure 34 has confused this issue by its use of the verb "translate" in describing the responding party's obligation to convert its computerized information into a form usable by the demanding party. This wording led a federal trial court in a product liability case to require a Japanese manufacturer, as part of the price for doing business in the United States, to pay for the translation of its product's specifications into English.[17]

In another case, however, a federal appellate court confined the duty to "translate" records in Rule 34 to computerized information:

> Congress thus had in mind computerized data or the like which could be presented *only* by use of a machine ("detection device") which respondent alone controlled. In such situations, the data would be valueless unless respondent cooperated in rendering it intelligible. Nothing in the Advisory Committee's comments suggests that the amended Rule 34 was intended to apply outside the specialized situation described . . . . The rule speaks specifically only of "data compilations" translated through "detection devices." There is no hint of a more general principle requiring respondents to translate documents not written in the discovering party's native tongue—nor, indeed, would there be any need to so extend the rule given the general availability of translators.[18]

Since Section 2031.280 derives its use of "translate"[19] from Federal Rule 34,

---

[13] Aguimatang v California State Lottery (1991) 234 Cal App 3d 769, 798, 286 Cal Rptr 57, 73.

[14] CCP § 2031.280(b).

[15] 1970 Advisory Committee Note to amended FRCivP 34.

[16] Aguimatang v California State Lottery (1991) 234 Cal App 3d 769, 286 Cal Rptr 57.

[17] Stapleton v Kawasaki Heavy Industries, Ltd. (1975, ND Ga) 69 FRD 489.

[18] In re Puerto Rico Electric Power Authority (1982, CA1 PR) 687 F2d 501, 508 (original italics).

[19] CCP § 2031.280(b).

See Toshiba America Electronic Components v Superior Court (2004) 124 Cal App 4th 762, 770, 21 Cal Rptr 3d 532, 539.

California courts should carefully consider this appellate level decision restricting that word to computerized data.

Duplication: Section 2031.010 gives a party not only the right to "inspect," that is, look at or read, the document involved, but also the right to "copy" it.[20] This "copy," of course, may be a photocopy; it need not be a manual one.[21]

§ 6.8 Inspection of Things

Undoubtedly the vast majority of inspection demands seek a document of some sort.[1] However, this device can also compel another party to produce "tangible things"[2] for inspection.

Examples: A sampling of the wide variety of items that federal and state courts have included within its scope best illustrates the phrase's breadth: the passenger bus involved in an accident,[3] a bus like the one involved in an accident,[4] a steamship,[5] automobile wreckage,[6] a conveyor belt's drive shaft,[7] livestock,[8] livestock carcasses,[9] tape recordings of conversations,[10] a surveillance motion picture of a personal injury plaintiff,[11] a personal computer with the information stored on its hard drive,[12] the clothing worn by a defendant at the time of the alleged tort,[13] even the production of the parties themselves.[14]

---

[20] CCP § 2031.010(b).

Cf. Financial Holding Corp. v Garnac Grain Co. (1991, WD Mo) 1991 US Dist Lexis 11028, **8–9 [unless party expressly requests production of document originals, production of copies is sufficient].

[21] Diapulse Corp. of America v Curtis Publishing Co. (1967, CA2 NY) 374 F2d 442, 445.

[1] For a discussion of document inspection, see § 6.7.

For a discussion of entry on property for inspection, see § 6.9.

[2] CCP § 2031.010(a).

The original version of the statute referred redundantly to "objects or tangible things." Former CCP § 2031(a), 1956 Discovery Act, Appendix E.

FRCivP 34(a) now also refers simply to "tangible things."

[3] Sacco v Greyhound Corp. (1959, WD Pa) 24 FRD 257, 259–260.

[4] Lauritzen v Atlantic Greyhound Corp. (1948, D Tenn) 8 FRD 237, 238.

[5] Canty v Great Lakes Transit Corp. (1941, WD NY) 2 FRD 156.

[6] Cf. Fisher v United States Fidelity & Guaranty Co. (1957, CA7 Ill) 246 F2d 344.

[7] Puritan Insurance Co. v Superior Court (1985) 171 Cal App 3d 877, 217 Cal Rptr 602.

[8] Martin v Reynolds Metals Corp. (1961, CA9 Or) 297 F2d 49, 57.

[9] Martin v Reynolds Metals Corp. (1961, CA9 Or) 297 F2d 49, 57.

[10] Rosemont v Superior Court (1964) 60 Cal 2d 709, 36 Cal Rptr 439, 388 P2d 671; Poeschl v Superior Court (1964) 229 Cal App 2d 383, 40 Cal Rptr 697.

[11] Suezaki v Superior Court (1962) 58 Cal 2d 166, 172, 23 Cal Rptr 368, 373 P2d 432. Cf. Atchison, T. & S.F. R. Co. v Superior Court (1962) 208 Cal App 2d 73, 25 Cal Rptr 54.

Annotation: Photographs of civil litigant realized by opponent's surveillance as subject to pretrial discovery. 19 ALR4th 1236.

[12] TBG Ins. Services Corp. v Superior Court (2002) 96 Cal App 4th 443, 117 Cal Rptr 2d 155.

[13] Shepherd v Superior Court (1976) 17 Cal 3d 107, 118, 130 Cal Rptr 257, 262, 550 P2d 161, 166.

—Defective Products: Product liability parties frequently seek inspections of the allegedly defective product. For example, parties have sought to inspect: an automobile's carburetor,[15] a handbrake assembly,[16] a bicycle,[17] a furnace's component,[18] a shotgun and its shells,[19] the remnants of a burned blouse,[20] an allegedly chipped hammer,[21] an intramedullary pin that broke after insertion in the patient,[22] and a ruptured propane gas cylinder.[23]

—Corpses: Everything has its limits, however. In the *Holm* case,[24] will contestants argued that an autopsy of the testator's body might reveal that he had had Alzheimer's disease when he signed the will. The trial court ordered the body exhumed. The appellate court, however, refused to allow inspection discovery to extend this far: "Given the extremely sensitive nature of the interests which are infringed when the remains of the dead are disturbed, we are reluctant in the absence of legislative guidance to extend the meaning of the phrase 'objects or tangible things' to include interred human bodies."[25]

Related Activities: The most recurrent controversy connected with inspections of tangible things concerns the extent of the "related activities,"[26] beyond a mere visual inspection, that a party may undertake with the demanded item. The 1956 Discovery Act expressly authorized only the "photographing" of an item.[27]

---

[14] Shepherd v Superior Court (1976) 17 Cal 3d 107, 118, 130 Cal Rptr 257, 262, 550 P2d 161, 166; Alford v Northeast Ins. Co., Inc. (1984, ND Fla) 102 FRD 99.

Annotation: Discovery and inspection of article or premises the condition of which is alleged to have caused personal injury or death. 13 ALR2d 657.

Annotation: Discovery and inspection of article and premises in civil actions other than for personal injury or death. 4 ALR3d 762.

[15] State ex rel. State Farm Mutual Auto. Ins. Co. v Rickhoff (1974, Mo App) 509 SW2d 485.

[16] Quinn v Chrysler Corp. (1964, WD Pa) 35 FRD 34.

[17] Wilson v Naifeh (1975, Okla) 539 P2d 390.

[18] Arney v Bryant Sheet Metal, Inc. (1982, ED Tenn) 96 FRD 544.

[19] State ex rel. Remington Arms Co., Inc. v Powers (1976, Okla) 552 P2d 1150; Toorchen v Olin Industries, Inc. (1946, ED NY) 6 FRD 20.

[20] Cf. Sladen v Girltown, Inc. (1970, CA7 Ill) 425 F2d 24, 25.

[21] Sarver v Barrett Ace Hardware, Inc. (1976, Ill) 349 NE2d 28.

[22] Edwardes v Southampton Hospital Assoc. (1967, Misc) 278 NYS2d 283.

[23] Foster-Lipkins Corp. v Suburban Propane Gas Corp. (1973, Misc) 339 NYS2d 581.

Annotation: Discovery and inspection of article or premises the condition of which is alleged to have caused personal injury or death. 13 ALR2d 657.

[24] Holm v Superior Court (1986) 187 Cal App 3d 1241, 232 Cal Rptr 432.

[25] Holm v Superior Court (1986) 187 Cal App 3d 1241, 1248, 232 Cal Rptr 432, 437.

Cf. Walsh v Caidin (1991) 232 Cal App 3d 159, 283 Cal Rptr 326 [defendants in medical malpractice have no cause of action against plaintiff-widow because her decision to cremate their deceased patient's remains has precluded an autopsy].

[26] See CCP §§ 2031.210 and 2031.220.

[27] Former CCP § 2031(a), 1956 Discovery Act, Appendix D.

However, Section 2031.010 allows the inspecting party to "photograph, test, or sample" it.[28]

Photographs: Under the authorization to "photograph" the item produced, courts have let pictures be taken of the interior of a ship,[29] and of the brake mechanism, mirrors, windshield, lights, and interior of a bus.[30]

The most expansive interpretation of the right to "photograph" a produced item is the Supreme Court's ruling in the *Shepherd* case.[31] There, wrongful death plaintiffs wished to confirm the identity of the police officers who had shot their son. The Court upheld an order that compelled the defendant officers to have their picture taken after donning the clothing they were wearing on the day of the shooting:

> California discovery statutes are to be construed liberally . . . . So construing the terms "objects or tangible things," we conclude that the photographing of the face and body of a person is well within the contemplation of the statute.[32]

Compelled Reenactments: The California courts have balked at allowing an inspection demand to compel a party during discovery to reenact the underlying events in a lawsuit. In the *Bailey* case,[33] the product liability defendants wanted to require a plaintiff to demonstrate in front of a video camera just how he had been using a radial saw at the time it severed some of his fingers. A divided Court of Appeal refused. The majority pointed out that a party engaging actively in a reenactment, unlike one passively submitting to photography, would be making a nonverbal statement:

> The distinction between *Shepherd* and the instant case is clear. There, the order sought did not require a reenactment of any activities. Compliance with the order took a purely nontestimonial form. The officers were simply sought as physical objects or sources of evidence, as in, for example, a blood sample, a photographic identification, or an

---

[28] CCP § 2031.010(c).

Compare FRCivP 34(a)(1) [authorizing a party to "copy, test, or sample"].

[29] Rosenthal v Compagnie Generale Transatlantique (1953, SD NY) 14 FRD 336.

See also Vermilyea v Chesapeake & Ohio R. Co. (1951, WD Mich) 11 FRD 255; Canty v Great Lakes Transit Corp. (1941, WD NY) 2 FRD 156.

[30] Sacco v Greyhound Corp. (1959, WD Pa) 24 FRD 257, 259–260.

[31] Shepherd v Superior Court (1976) 17 Cal 3d 107, 130 Cal Rptr 257, 550 P2d 161.

[32] Shepherd v Superior Court (1976) 17 Cal 3d 107, 118, 130 Cal Rptr 257, 262, 550 P2d 161, 166.

See also Alford v Northeast Ins. Co., Inc. (1984, ND Fla) 102 FRD 99 [a fire insurance carrier, defending on the ground that the plaintiff-insured set the fire deliberately, was entitled to compel him to submit to fingerprinting so that his prints could be compared with those lifted from incendiary devices found on the burned premises].

[33] Bailey v Superior Court (1978) 79 Cal App 3d 444, 144 Cal Rptr 875.

in-person identification. In the instant case, the order requires a testimonial compliance.[34]

Depositions[35] and interrogatories are, in the court's view, the exclusive discovery mechanisms for obtaining testimony. The present version of the inspection demand neither codifies nor rejects *Bailey*.[36]

Testing: Quite often the party seeking production of a "tangible thing" wishes to experiment on, test, sample, or take specimens of it. Section 2031.010[37] permits a party to "test" and "sample" the item produced.[38]

—**Examples:** Many courts have considered requests to test produced items. For example, an insurance company, sued under its auto theft policy, wished to replace missing engine parts to see whether a wrecked and stripped car was operable.[39] An automobile manufacturer, sued for a claimed defect in a handbrake system, wanted to install that system in a similar car to test its functioning.[40] The manufacturer of a shotgun that exploded wanted an opportunity to test-fire the weapon and the remaining shells.[41] An aluminum manufacturer, accused of polluting a nearby livestock farm, wanted to sample the water, soil, air, feed, and forage from the farm. In addition, it sought to obtain urine samples from the living cattle and to perform autopsies on the dead ones.[42] Finally, a fire insurance carrier, claiming that the plaintiff-insured had set the blaze himself, sought to take his fingerprints.[43]

---

[34] Bailey v Superior Court (1978) 79 Cal App 3d 444, 447, 144 Cal Rptr 875.

Cf. Stermer v Superior Court (1993) 20 Cal App 4th 777, 780, 24 Cal Rptr 2d 577, 578–579.

[35] But see Stermer v Superior Court (1993) 20 Cal App 4th 777, 24 Cal Rptr 2d 577 [a deponent, even one who is a party, may refuse reenact an event]. The Supreme Court has disapproved *Stermer*. Emerson Electric Co. v Superior Court (1997) 16 Cal 4th 1101, 1106–1107, 68 Cal Rptr 2d 883, 946 P2d 841 [a deponent may be compelled to reenact an event].

For a discussion of compelled reenactments by a *deponent*, see § 2.22.

[36] See CCP § 2031.010(c).

[37] CCP § 2031.010(c).

[38] See Martin v Reynolds Metals Corp. (1961, CA9 Or) 297 F2d 49, 53 n1 [although original version of FRCivP 34 authorized only "inspection and copying," an "inspection" could include testing and sampling if necessary for a complete inspection of the item produced].

See also O'Hare v Peacock Dairies, Inc. (1938) 26 Cal App 2d 345, 353, 79 P2d 433, 438 [the word "inspection" in a contract relating to the sale of milk included not just "optical observations" but also "tests and examinations" as well.]

[39] Fisher v United States Fidelity & Guaranty Co. (1957, CA7 Ill) 246 F2d 344, 347.

[40] Quinn v Chrysler Corp. (1964, WD Pa) 35 FRD 34.

[41] State ex rel. Remington Arms Co., Inc. v Powers (1976, Okla) 552 P2d 1150, 1152.

See also Wilson v Naifeh (1975, Okla) 539 P2d 390 [bicycle]; State ex rel. State Farm Mutual Auto. Ins. Co. v Rickhoff (1974, Mo App) 509 SW2d 485 [carburetor].

[42] Martin v Reynolds Metals Corp. (1961, CA9 Or) 297 F2d 49, 53 n1.

[43] Alford v Northeast Ins. Co., Inc. (1984, ND Fla) 102 FRD 99.

—**Destructive Testing:** The most difficult issues concerning inspection involve so-called "destructive testing."[44] This signifies a testing procedure that either alters the item's appearance, or destroys it altogether. For example, in an Illinois product liability case,[45] where the plaintiff was claiming that a chip of metal from the hammer he was using had injured his eye, the manufacturer showed the need for its expert to cut a piece of metal from the hammer for testing. An order that permitted this slight alteration of the hammer, after photographing it in its original condition, was upheld:

> [T]he hammer will still be available for viewing by the jury after completion of the testing. While a small, pie-shaped wedge will have been removed from the hammer's striking face, the jury will still be able to observe the general condition of most of the striking face, and they will have macrophotos of the hammer's face in its original condition.[46]

A New York trial court permitted a much more extensive "destructive test." The action sought damages from a fire allegedly caused by a leaking propane gas cylinder. The judge authorized a test that entailed removing the body and stem of the main valve from the cylinder, cutting the valve in half down its center, and then taking microsections from the two halves:

> The administration of justice profits by the progress of science. Resort should be had to scientific tests whenever the results disclosed by the tests can aid or elucidate the just determination of legal controversies. The defense of the action seems fundamentally to be dependent upon the results of such tests as are sought. This Court is of the opinion that plaintiff's interests will not be prejudiced if the tests take place before the exhibit is shown to the jury at a trial.[47]

No reported case in California has considered whether a court may compel a party to permit destructive testing. Section 2031.030 requires a demanding party

---

[44] Annotation: Propriety of discovery order permitting "destructive testing" of chattel in civil case. 11 ALR4th 1245.

As to the right of the one in control of the item to conduct tests that alter or destroy it, see Puritan Insurance Co. v Superior Court (1985) 171 Cal App 3d 877, 217 Cal Rptr 602 and Cameron v District Court (1977, Colo) 565 P2d 925. Cf. Petruk v South Ferry Realty Co. (1956, Misc) 157 NYS2d 249.

[45] Sarver v Barrett Ace Hardware, Inc. (1976, Ill) 349 NE2d 28.

[46] Sarver v Barrett Ace Hardware, Inc. (1976, Ill) 349 NE2d 28, 30–31.

See also Note, Partially Destructive Testing is Within the Scope of the Illinois Discovery Rules (1977) 26 DePaul L Rev 408.

[47] Foster-Lipkins Corp. v Suburban Propane Gas Corp. (1973) 339 NYS2d 581, 582–583 (internal citations omitted).

See also Spell v Kendall-Futuro Co. (1994, ED Tex) 155 FRD 587, 587 [destructive testing of allegedly defective cane permitted]; Edwardes v Southampton Hospital Assn. (1967) 278 NYS2d 283 ["destructive testing" of intramedullary surgical pin permitted].

to specify whether that party intends to perform any activity that will permanently "alter or destroy"[48] the desired item. This implies that "destructive testing" is permissible in an appropriate case. However, the responding party is entitled to advance notice of the contemplated testing. This notice gives the responding party an opportunity either to object to the test or to seek a protective order setting forth the ground rules for its performance.

—Responding Party Need Not Conduct Test: Occasionally, a party tries to use an inspection demand to compel an opponent to test items under the opponent's control.[49] For example, in a federal case,[50] the manufacturer of a blouse that allegedly burst into flames tried to compel the plaintiff to conduct flammability tests on the remnants of the garment. The court refused to require plaintiff to test the item. Similarly, in air crash litigation, the plaintiffs demanded that the defendant manufacturer test an airliner identical to the one that crashed.[51] Since the plaintiffs could lease and then test such a plane themselves, the court refused to require the defendant to perform the tests for them.

Although destructive testing may be appropriate in a particular case, a court may not order a party who does not seek such testing to share in its cost, even though the testing may well yield information beneficial to that party.[52]

§ 6.9 Inspection of Land

An inspection demand may reach beyond documents[1] and tangible things.[2] It may also allow a party to enter an opponent's "land or other property."[3]

Examples: Few California decisions involve entries on land or other property.[4]

---

48 CCP § 2031.030(c)(4).

49 As to the right of the one in control of an item to conduct tests that alter or destroy it, see Puritan Insurance Co. v Superior Court (1985) 171 Cal App 3d 877, 217 Cal Rptr 602; Cameron v District Court (1977, Colo) 565 P2d 925. Cf. Petruk v South Ferry Realty Co. (1956) 157 NYS2d 249.

50 Sladen v Girltown, Inc. (1970, CA7 Ill) 425 F2d 24.

51 In re Air Crash Disaster at Sioux City, Iowa (1991, ND Ill) 1991 US Dist Lexis 10372, *6–7 [defendant not required to provide DC 10 aircraft and flight crew to simulate the conditions of aircraft that crashed].

52 San Diego Unified Port District v Douglas E. Barnhart, Inc. (2002) 95 Cal App 4th 1400, 116 Cal Rptr 2d 65.

1 For a discussion of document inspections, see § 6.7.

2 For a discussion of inspections of tangible things, see § 6.8.

3 CCP § 2031.010(d).

Annotation: Discovery and inspection of article or premises the condition of which is alleged to have caused personal injury or death. 13 ALR2d 657.

Annotation: Discovery and inspection of article and premises in civil actions other than for personal injury or death. 4 ALR2d 762.

4 The principal case is Volkswagenwerk A.G. v Superior Court (1981) 123 Cal App 3d 840, 176 Cal Rptr 874. Cf. Manzetti v Superior Court (1993) 21 Cal App 4th 373, 380–381, 25 Cal Rptr 2d 857, 862 [finding frivolous a second writ petition challenging an order permitting inspection and videotaping of defendant's nickel plating operations].

However, a survey of federal and state decisions applying similar provisions[5] reveals the wide range of access that an inspection demand provides. Through this discovery device, parties have gained entrance to: large tracts of unimproved land,[6] a livestock ranch,[7] an improved lot,[8] an oil and gas well,[9] a pier,[10] a ship,[11] an offshore drilling rig,[12] a prison facility,[13] a mental institution,[14] and a manufacturing plant.[15]

Related Activities: Besides a visual examination of an opponent's property, Section 2031.010 authorizes a trial court to allow the inspecting party to carry out "related activities,"[16] e.g., to "measure," "survey," "photograph,"[17] "test,"[18] or "sample" the property.[19] The court may go further and let the inspecting party perform the same sort of activities upon a "designated object"[20] located on the property.

—Examples: In a leading federal case, a company accused of discharging fluorides from an aluminum plant onto a livestock ranch and into its water supply obtained the right to enter the ranch repeatedly. During these entries, the company sampled the soil, water, air, forage, and cattle feed; examined cattle visually and

---

[5] See, e.g., FRCivP 34(a).

[6] Arkansas State Highway Com. v Stanley (1962, Ark) 353 SW2d 173, 176.

[7] State ex rel. State Highway Com. v District Court (1966, Mont) 412 P2d 832; Martin v Reynolds Metals Corp. (1961, CA9 Or) 297 F2d 49, 56–57.

[8] Borland v Dunn (1974, RI) 321 A2d 96.

[9] Williams v Continental Oil Co. (1954, CA10 Okla) 215 F2d 4.

[10] Martin v N. V. Nederlandsche Amerikaansche Stoomvaart Maatchappij (1948, SD NY) 8 FRD 363.

[11] Ferro Union Corp. v SS Ionic Coast (1967, SD Tex) 43 FRD 11; Rosenthal v Compagnie Generale Transatlantique (1953, SD NY) 14 FRD 336; Vermilyea v Chesapeake & O. R. Co. (1951, WD Mich) 11 FRD 255, 258.

[12] See Guidry v Continental Oil Co. (1981, CA5 La) 640 F2d 523, 533.

[13] Morales v. Turman (1972, ED Tex) 59 FRD 157.

[14] New York State Ass'n for Retarded Children v Carey (1983, CA2 NY) 706 F2d 956, 960–961.

[15] See Volkswagenwerk A.G. v Superior Court (1981) 123 Cal App 3d 840, 176 Cal Rptr 874. Cf. Manzetti v Superior Court (1993) 21 Cal App 4th 373, 380–381, 25 Cal Rptr 2d 857, 862 [finding frivolous a second writ petition challenging an order permitting inspection and videotaping of defendant's nickel plating operations].

See also Eirhart v Libbey-Owens-Ford Co. (1981, ND Ill) 93 FRD 370; Dow Chemical Co. v Monsanto Co. (1966, SD Ohio) 256 F Supp 315; Cox v E. I. Du Pont de Nemours & Co. (1965, D SC) 38 FRD 396.

[16] CCP § 2031.210(a)(1).

[17] Cf. Manzetti v Superior Court (1993) 21 Cal App 4th 373, 380–381, 25 Cal Rptr 2d 857, 862 [finding frivolous a second writ petition challenging an order permitting inspection and videotaping of defendant's nickel plating operations].

[18] Former CCP § 2031 did not expressly authorize "testing." See former CCP § 2031(a), 1956 Discovery Act, Appendix E.

[19] CCP § 2031.010(d).

[20] CCP § 2031.010(d).

physically, including taking urine samples; conducted post-mortem examinations on any dead animals; and removed portions of the carcasses for analysis.[21]

Other cases have authorized: (1) a homeowner, claiming that a neighbor's cesspool was polluting his artesian well, to place a vegetable dye in that cesspool to test whether it would later appear in his water supply;[22] (2) a building contractor, sued for installing defective material in a roof, to remove and test one of its panels;[23] (3) a landowner, claiming that a nearby oil well was drawing its production from under his land, to survey the well's directional path;[24] and (4) a condemning authority, taking a small part of a ranch for a highway project, to drill two wells near a house to find out whether it would leave the main house without a water supply.[25]

—Observing Operations: Beyond an inspection of the property entered or the physical things located on it, Section 2031.010 authorizes a litigant to observe an "operation"[26] underway there. In product liability actions, plaintiffs often find it useful to watch the manufacturer's assembly line in action.[27] Similarly, viewing working conditions may be useful to plaintiffs in employment discrimination cases.[28] In two civil rights cases challenging the conditions in a youth correctional facility[29] and in a school for the mentally retarded,[30] the court allowed a party to send in experts to observe the institutions' daily routine.

—Informal Interviews: Often, a party observing an "operation" on an opponent's property will wish to speak informally with people while they are carrying on those activities. The interviewees may be employees, customers, or inmates.[31] The party conducting the "operation" may object to such interviews

---

21 Martin v Reynolds Metals Corp (1961, CA9 Or) 297 F2d 49, 56–57.

22 Borland v Dunn (1974, RI) 321 A2d 96.

See also United States v Bunker Hill Co. (1976, DC Idaho) 417 F Supp 332.

23 Kingsport v SCM Corp. (1972, ED Tenn) 352 F Supp 287, 288.

24 Williams v Continental Oil Co. (1954, CA10 Okla) 215 F2d 4; cf. Union Oil Co. v Reconstruction Oil Co. (1935) 4 Cal 2d 541, 51 P2d 81.

25 State ex rel. State Highway Com. v District Court (1966, Mont) 412 P2d 832.

See also Arkansas State Highway Com. v Stanley (1962, Ark) 353 SW2d 173, 176 [even where severance damages are waived, a condemning authority was permitted to enter the balance of the tract to make test drillings in an effort show that its abundant gravel deposits substantially reduced the value of those on the part taken].

26 CCP § 2031.010(d).

27 See, e.g., Volkswagenwerk A.G. v Superior Court (1981) 123 Cal App 3d 840, 176 Cal Rptr 874. Cf. Volkswagenwerk A.G. v Superior Court (1973) 33 Cal App 3d 503, 109 Cal Rptr 219.

28 See, e.g., Eirhart v Libbey-Owens-Ford Co. (1981, ND Ill) 93 FRD 370 [in a case based on the use of minimum height and weight requirements to discriminate against women, an employer was required to permit the plaintiffs' attorneys and experts to observe its production line in operation].

29 Morales v Turman (1972, ED Tex) 59 FRD 157.

30 New York State Ass'n for Retarded Children v Carey (1983, CA2 NY) 706 F2d 956, 960–961.

31 See, e.g., New York State Ass'n for Retarded Children v Carey (1983, CA2 NY) 706 F2d

for two reasons: (1) their potential for disruption of the operation outweighs their potential for discovery;[32] and (2) a court-ordered informal interview is "tantamount to a roving deposition, taken without notice, throughout the [facility], of persons who were not sworn and whose testimony was not recorded, and without any right by [that party] to make any objection to the questions asked."[33]

The few federal cases that have considered such informal interviews during a discovery inspection have disagreed.[34] The *Volkswagenwerk* case[35] is the only reported California opinion on the question. There the trial court had allowed counsel for the plaintiff in a products case not only to enter the defendant's plant but also to interview its employees. It even directed the defendant to tell its employees to submit to the interviews. The appellate court, however, ruled that the discovery inspections could not extend to compelled informal interviews.[36]

§ 6.10   Situs of Production

Using longstanding statutory language,[1] Section 2031.030 simply requires that the demanding party "[s]pecify a reasonable place for making the inspection, copying, and performing any related activity."[2]

Normal Practice: The dearth of case law on the topic suggests that the selection of an appropriate place for the production and copying of documents usually presents no problem. Doubtless, the vast majority of document productions occur at the office of the attorney for either the demanding or the responding party. Occasionally, they may occur at a local printing and copying company. The records, however, may be voluminous or needed for daily business. In such cases, the responding party's office is the better place for the inspection.[3] Where

---

956, 960 [staff, employees, and inmates of mental institution]; Belcher v Bassett Furniture Industries, Inc. (1978, CA4 Va) 588 F2d 904, 906 [supervisors and employees of a factory assembly line]; Morales v Turman (1972, ED Tex) 59 FRD 157, 159 [staff and inmates of a youth correctional facility].

[32] See Belcher v Bassett Furniture Industries, Inc. (1978, CA4 Va) 588 F2d 904, 907.

[33] Belcher v Bassett Furniture Industries, Inc. (1978, CA4 Va) 588 F2d 904, 907.

[34] Compare New York State Ass'n for Retarded Children v Carey (1983, CA2 NY) 706 F2d 956, 960–961 [order permitting interviewing of inmates, staff members, and employees of state mental institution upheld] and Morales v Turman (1972, ED Tex) 59 FRD 157, 159 [interviews with inmates and staff of youth correctional facility permitted] with Belcher v Bassett Furniture Industries, Inc. (1978, CA4 Va) 588 F2d 904, 907 [order permitting interviews with supervisors and employees of factory assembly line set aside as "improvident"].

[35] Volkswagenwerk A.G. v Superior Court (1981) 123 Cal App 3d 840, 176 Cal Rptr 874.

[36] 123 Cal App 3d at 849, 176 Cal Rptr at 879; see also Valley Presbyterian Hospital v Superior Court (2000) 79 Cal App 4th 417, 422, 94 Cal Rptr 2d 137, 140.

[1] Former CCP § 2031, 1956 Discovery Act, Appendix E, contained substantially similar language. The Discovery Commission proposed giving the responding party the right to choose either its attorney's office or the demanded item's situs as the place for discovery. See Proposed California Civil Discovery Act of 1986, §§ 2031(c) and (f)(1), Appendix D.

[2] CCP § 2031.030(c)(3).

[3] See, e.g., Caruso v Coleman Co. (1994, ED Pa) 157 FRD 344, 349–350 [defendant allowed

the responding party needs the records for its daily operations, an inspection of the original may never occur. A photocopy of the records will usually satisfy counsel for the demanding party.[4]

Out-of-Forum Items: Sometimes the item demanded for inspection is located far from the forum. Controversies may arise over whether the responding party must transport the item to the forum, or whether the demanding party must journey to its location.

—Within the United States: In deciding which of these two places—the forum or the situs of the item—is the "reasonable" one for a discovery inspection, the courts are more ready to give the choice to defendants, whether they are a demanding or a responding party. For example, in two federal cases litigated in the eastern United States,[5] the plaintiffs sought voluminous records located in California. Each trial judge refused to order the defendants to bring the records to the forum. Although neither mentioned the matter, it seems more than coincidental that the party seeking the production was a plaintiff.[6] Similarly, when a defendant insists on inspecting an item at the forum, the out-of-state plaintiff must bring it there.[7]

—Items Abroad: Where records are located in a foreign country, however, American courts are inclined to order their production at the forum.[8] This occurs even where the records are those of a foreign defendant.[9]

Surrender of Item for Testing: The place of production will often become a substantial issue where the party seeking discovery wants to test an item.[10]

---

to make documents available to plaintiff at place convenient to defendant]; Bercow v Kidder, Peabody & Co. (1965, SD NY) 39 FRD 357; Harris v Sunset Oil Co. (1941, WD Wash) 2 FRD 93. Cf. Krypton Broadcasting of Jacksonville, Inc. v MGM-Pathe Communications Co. (1993, Fla App) 629 So2d 852, 855–856 [if demanding party wishes records to be brought to its offices, absent unusual circumstances, it must pay cost of transporting the records].

[4] See Financial Holding Corp. v Garnac Grain Co. (1991, WD Mo) 1991 US Dist Lexis 11028, *8–90. [unless party expressly requests production of document originals, production of copies is sufficient].

[5] Lundberg v Welles (1950, SD NY) 93 F Supp 359, 363; Niagara Duplicator Co. v Shackleford (1947, CADC) 160 F2d 25.

[6] See also Mid-America Facilities, Inc. v Argonaut Ins. Co. (1978, ED Wis) 78 FRD 497, 499.

[7] Monks v Hurley (1939, D Mass) 28 F Supp 600.

[8] See, e.g., La Chemise Lacoste v General Mills, Inc. (1971, D Del) 53 FRD 596, 604, affd (CA3 Del) 487 F2d 312 [plaintiff ordered to bring records from France, especially since no showing as to their bulk or cost of shipping them was made by the responding party]; Bernstein v N.V. Nederlandsche-Amerikaansche Stoomvart Maatschappij (1953, SD NY) 15 FRD 32, 35 [third-party plaintiff required to bring records from Holland for inspection by third-party defendant].

[9] See Compagnie des Bauxites de Guinea v Insurance Co. of North America (1981, CA3 Pa) 651 F2d 877, 883–884; Arthur Andersen & Co. v Finesilver (1976, CA10 Colo) 546 F2d 338; Securities & Exchange Comm. v Minas de Artemisa, S.A. (1945, CA9 Ariz) 150 F2d 215.

For a discussion of the extent to which either the Hague Convention or international comity affects the court's discretion to order a foreign party to bring its records to the forum, see § 4.3.

[10] For a discussion of the extent to which an item produced for inspection may be tested, see § 6.8.

To conduct such testing, the demanding party, or its expert, may need to obtain physical possession of the item. The 1956 Discovery Act spoke only of "copying or photographing"[11] a document or object produced for inspection. Other courts, interpreting similar language in their discovery provisions, have disagreed over their authority to order the responding party to surrender the item produced. On the one hand, some courts have concluded:

> "Produce" is defined [by the dictionary] as "to bring forward; lead forth; offer to view or notice; exhibit; show" . . . . It is not a synonym for "turn over" or "give." The rule contemplates that the possession, custody and control shall remain in the party producing, and the moving party shall have the opportunity to inspect, copy or photograph. The rule does not contemplate that the moving party shall receive the possession, custody or control of the thing produced.[12]

On the other hand, one state trial court directed a product liability plaintiff to deliver the allegedly defective product to the defendant's expert for testing.[13]

—Within California: Section 2031.010 explicitly permits the demanding party to test or sample the item.[14] To facilitate such testing or sampling, the trial court may order the responding party to transfer possession of the item for testing within California. Where it orders such a transfer, the court should impose conditions to safeguard the item and to restrict the length of time it is surrendered. If the demanding party loses or destroys the item, the court could mitigate any prejudice to the responding party by an "evidence" or an "issue" sanction.[15]

—Outside California: Where the demanding party seeks to test the item outside California, the court should be extremely cautious before ordering the responding party to surrender it. The few courts in other states that have considered the matter have found it an abuse of discretion to require a party to surrender an item for shipment outside the trial court's subpoena power, whether to another state[16] or to another nation.[17]

---

[11] Former CCP § 2031(a), 1956 Discovery Act, Appendix E.

[12] State ex rel. Emge v Corcoran (1971, Mo App) 468 SW2d 724, 725–726 [a party may not be compelled to deliver its books and records to another party].

[13] Nasoff v Hills Supermarket, Inc. (1963, Misc) 243 NYS2d 64.

For a discussion of the extent to which tests may conducted on an item produced for inspection, see § 6.8.

[14] CCP § 2031.010(c).

[15] Cf. Puritan Insurance Co. v Superior Court (1985) 171 Cal App 3d 877, 217 Cal Rptr 602.

For a discussion of "evidence" and "issue" sanctions, see § 15.5.

[16] See, e.g., State ex rel. State Farm Mut. Auto. Ins. Co. v Rickhoff (1974, Mo App) 509 SW2d 485 [shipment of carburetor from Missouri to defendant's plant in Michigan refused].

[17] Wilson v Naifeh (1975, Okla) 539 P2d 390 [shipment of bicycle from Oklahoma to defendant's plant in Mexico refused]; Equitable Life Assur. Soc. v MacMahon (1949, Mich) 37 NW2d 769 [shipment of allegedly forged change-of-beneficiary form to a questioned document expert in Canada refused].

§ 6.11 Protective Orders

Role of Protective Orders: The recipient of an inspection demand may challenge it on the ground that it is not in the required form,[1] or that the items sought are irrelevant,[2] privileged,[3] or protected work product.[4] The appropriate way to raise these issues is by an "objection" in the written "response" to the demand.[5] A protective order is best reserved for resisting inspection demands that are in proper form and, at least arguably, within the scope of allowable discovery, yet nonetheless warrant intervention by the trial court. However, as long as the motion for a protective order clearly informs the other party of the basis for objecting to an inspection demand, it would elevate form over substance to deny the motion simply because the "response" is the correct vehicle for raising it.[6]

Section 2031.060 authorizes the trial court to override or adjust a facially proper inspection demand where its operation in a particular case would cause "unwarranted annoyance, embarrassment, or oppression, or undue burden and expense."[7] It provides a non-exhaustive list of six permissible grounds for a protective order.

Modifications to Demand: By issuing a protective order, the trial court may regulate the way the demanding party conducts the inspection. It may change the date[8] or the place for the inspection.[9] It may forbid or regulate the conduct

---

[1] For a discussion of the format for an inspection demand, see § 6.3.

[2] For coverage of relevance for discovery, see Chapter 11.

[3] For coverage of privilege as limitation of discovery, see Chapter 12.

[4] For coverage of the work product protection, see Chapter 13.

[5] CCP § 2031.210(a)(3).

See also Stadish v Superior Court (1999) 71 Cal App 4th 1130, 1142–1144, 84 Cal Rptr 2d 350, 357–358 [protective order to govern dissemination of trade secrets was proper despite party's waiver of trade secret privilege].

For a discussion of the "response" to an inspection demand, see § 6.12.

[6] See, e.g., Brown v Superior Court (1963) 218 Cal App 2d 430, 32 Cal Rptr 527 [ruling on the merits of objections to interrogatories, although they were raised via motion to quash]; but see Ryan v Superior Court (1960) 186 Cal App 2d 813, 820, 9 Cal Rptr 147, 152 [if responding party claims that an interrogatory calls for confidential information in the nature of a trade secret, it should move for a protective order instead of lodging an objection to the interrogatory].

[7] CCP § 2031.060(b).

Cf. In re Shell Oil Refinery (1992, ED La) 143 FRD 105, 108 [the power under FRCivP 26 to issue a protective order precluding the release of confidential information is limited to materials obtained during discovery].

[8] CCP § 2031.060(b)(2).

For a discussion of the normal date of a discovery inspection, see § 6.3.

See, e.g., Todd v Merrell Dow Pharmaceuticals, Inc. (1991, CA7 Ind) 942 F2d 1173, 1178 [finding no abuse of discretion in trial court's decision to delay document production for 75 days while parties proceeded on threshold issues]. Cf. In re Shell Oil Refinery (1992, ED La) 144 FRD 75, 77 [court may issue protective order delaying disclosure of nonparty witness statements].

[9] CCP § 2031.060(b)(3).

For a discussion of the place of inspection, see § 6.10.

of a demanded "related activity,"[10] such as testing, upon the items.

Trade Secrets: Where the demands seek trade secrets[11] or confidential information,[12] the trial court may screen[13] them in camera and then limit the dissemination of any materials that it orders produced.[14]

In the *Stadish* case,[15] the appellate court upheld the use of a protective order in a trade secret dispute. The court found the order appropriate even though the moving party had waived the trade secret privilege by its prior responses to an inspection demand. The court first concluded that the waiver of the privilege required the production of the documents to the requesting party. But it then found that the waiver did not preclude the responding party from seeking an order restricting the public dissemination of the produced materials.[16]

The court also specified the procedure that trial courts should use when considering protective orders in trade secrets disputes. They must follow the procedures established by Evidence Code § 1061 for criminal cases. Under that procedure, the moving party must submit nonconclusory affidavits that demonstrate the existence of a trade secret. Where the trade secret touches upon public health matters, the court must balance public and private interests before issuing its order.[17]

If a trial court initially allows a party, claiming that documents contain trade secrets, to file them under seal, it may later entertain an opponent's or an intervener's motion to unseal them if it turns out that they are not eligible for trade secret protection.[18]

---

[10] See CCP § 2031.210(a)(1).

[11] In re Worlds of Wonder Securities Litigation (1992, ND Cal) 147 FRD 214, 216 [the burden is on the party seeking a protective order to demonstrate the existence of a trade secret the disclosure of which would cause harm; the burden then shifts to the inspecting party to establish the relevance and the necessity for its disclosure].

[12] Fireman's Fund Ins. Co. v Superior Court (1991) 233 Cal App 3d 1138, 1141, 286 Cal Rptr 50, 51 [trial court erred by ordering production of allegedly confidential reinsurance agreements without reviewing documents in camera].

[13] CCP § 2031.060(b)(4).

[14] CCP §§ 2031.060(b)(5) and (6).

Raymond Handling Concepts Corp. v Superior Court (1995) 39 Cal App 4th 584, 45 Cal Rptr 2d 885 [the trial court may enter a protective order that permits a party obtaining discovery of confidential information, such as trade secrets, to disclose that information to litigants in similar litigation who stipulate that they will not disclose it to competitors]; Westinghouse Electric Corp. v Newman & Holtzinger (1995) 39 Cal App 4th 1194, 1208 n6, 46 Cal Rptr 2d 151, 160 n6 [absent a protective order to the contrary, "nothing in California law would prohibit a party's sharing documents obtained through discovery with a nonparty"].

[15] Stadish v Superior Court (1999) 71 Cal App 4th 1130, 84 Cal Rptr 2d 350.

[16] Stadish v Superior Court (1999) 71 Cal App 4th 1130, 1142–1144, 84 Cal Rptr 2d 350, 357–358.

[17] Stadish v Superior Court (1999) 71 Cal App 4th 1130, 1144–1145, 84 Cal Rptr 2d 350, 358–359.

[18] In re Providian Credit Card Cases (2002) 96 Cal App 4th 292, 116 Cal Rptr 2d 833.

Denial of Inspection: Section 2031.060 allows the trial court to order that "all or some of the items in the inspection demand need not be produced at all."[19] This provision would be redundant[20] if it applied only to demands for irrelevant, privileged, or protected work product items. It signifies that even if an inspection demand is unobjectionable on those three grounds, the court may still deny it.[21] To obtain such relief, the responding party must show how, in the particular case,[22] the demand would cause "unwarranted annoyance, embarrassment, or oppression, or undue burden and expense."[23]

Burden of Persuasion: Normally, the party seeking some protection against inspection must persuade the court that the task would cause unwarranted annoyance, embarrassment, or oppression, or undue burden and expense.[24]

Time for Motion: Section 2031.060 requires only that the responding party move "promptly"[25] for a protective order. Certainly, a motion made within the time to serve a "response" to the demand would be timely.[26] Federal cases have found a motion made before the date set for production to be timely,[27] and a motion filed two months after that date to be untimely.[28]

---

[19] CCP § 2031.060(b)(1).

[20] See CCP § 2031.240.

[21] See, e.g., Harding Lawson Assoc. v Superior Court (1992) 10 Cal App 4th 7, 9–10, 12 Cal Rptr 2d 538, 539–540 [plaintiff showed neither compelling need to order production of defendant's files on nonparty employees, nor the unavailability of the information through depositions or other nonconfidential sources].

[22] Nestle Foods Corp. v Aetna Cas. & Surety Co. (1990, D NJ) 129 FRD 483, 485–486 [vague, conclusory, and general allegations of harm insufficient to justify protective order under FRCivP 26].

Cf. Diamond State Ins. Co. v Rebel Oil Co. (1994, D Nev) 157 FRD 691, 700 [party seeking in camera review to resist subpoena demanding document production must submit affidavits or other evidence that are sufficient to justify the request for protection].

[23] Compare Monaghan v SZS 33 Assoc., LP (1993, SD NY) 148 FRD 500, 512 [where responding party claimed it had 500,000 relevant documents kept in shifting locations, court refused to grant protective order that would have forced the inspecting party to locate, identify, and organize these "wandering haystacks of matter unorganized"] with Nugget Hydroelectric, L.P. v Pacific Gas & Electric Co. (1992, CA9 Cal) 981 F2d 429, 438–439 [request for "millions of pages of documents concerning every aspect of (defendant's) relationships with private power suppliers" properly found "unnecessarily burdensome and overly broad"].

[24] Cf. Coriell v Superior Court (1974) 39 Cal App 3d 487, 492–493, 114 Cal Rptr 310, 314–315 [party seeking protective order postponing need to answer *interrogatories* has burden of showing good cause]; People v Superior Court (Witzerman) (1967) 248 Cal App 2d 276, 280, 56 Cal Rptr 393, 397 [party seeking protective order sealing its answers to *interrogatories* has burden of showing good cause].

[25] CCP § 2031.060(a).

[26] CCP § 2031.260 allows a party 30 days to prepare a "response" to an inspection demand in most situations.

[27] Brittain v Stroh Brewery Co. (1991, MD NC) 136 FRD 408, 413 [untimely motion may be excused for good cause].

[28] Nestle Foods Corp. v Aetna Cas. & Surety Co. (1990, D NJ) 129 FRD 483, 486–487.

See also United States v Panhandle Eastern Corp. (1988, D Del) 118 FRD 346, 350–351 [finding untimely a motion made three weeks after date set for production].

Duty to Meet and Confer: Before resorting to a motion for a protective order, a party receiving an inspection demand must try to work out informally the points of dispute with the party making the demand. A declaration setting forth these efforts must accompany the motion.[29]

Monetary Sanction: One who unsuccessfully makes or opposes a motion for a protective order runs the risk of incurring a monetary sanction. The party can avoid the sanction by convincing the trial court that, despite this lack of success, there was "substantial justification or that other circumstances make the imposition of the sanction unjust."[30]

Abuse of Elders and Dependent Adults: In 2003, the legislature added two new sections to the Discovery Act that address settlement agreements and protective orders in cases of alleged abuse of elders or dependent adults. Section 2017.310 addresses confidential settlement agreements in such cases.[31] Section 2017.320 deals with stipulated protective orders.[32] Neither of these provisions is applicable to malpractice actions against health care providers.

Section 2017.310 establishes a policy disfavoring confidential settlement agreements in these abuse cases.[33] It specifically forbids the enforcement of any such agreements except for provisions that involve privileged matters,[34] do not involve evidence of abuse,[35] or would probably cause prejudice if the agreement were made public.[36] Where information is made public, the court may not seal or redact the defendant's name.[37] The statute does allow, however, the terms of any monetary settlement to remain confidential.[38]

Section 2017.320 sets out the situations where stipulated protective orders against disclosure of information obtained through discovery may be enforced. It sets out a procedure whereby information that does not involve abuse is first redacted from the discovery materials and then the remaining information is filed with the court.[39] Unless the party from whom the information showing abuse was received successfully obtains a protective order, the information filed with the court becomes public.[40] In effect, a protective order can be issued in the same circumstances in which a confidential settlement agreement is enforceable under Section 2017.310. The party seeking judicial protection bears the burden

---

[29] CCP § 2031.060(a).

[30] CCP § 2031.060(d).

[31] CCP § 2017.310, formerly CCP § 2031.1.

[32] CCP § 2017.320, formerly CCP § 2031.2.

[33] CCP § 2017.310(a).

[34] CCP § 2017.310(b)(1).

[35] CCP § 2017.310(b)(2).

[36] CCP § 2017.310(b)(3).

[37] CCP § 2017.310(c).

[38] CCP § 2017.310(e).

[39] CCP § 2017.320(a).

[40] CCP § 2017.320(c).

of proof.[41] Again, as with Section 2017.310, for those protective orders meeting one of these criteria, under Section 2017.320, the court may not seal or redact the defendant's name.[42]

§ 6.12   Response to Inspection Demand

Response Document: The party who receives an inspection demand must respond to it in writing. Section 2031.210 outlines the formal requirements for the response document.[1] Under the title of the case, the document must identify the responding party, the set number of the inspection demand, and the demanding party.[2] It must refer to each item or category by the same number or letter used in the inspection demand, though it need not repeat the text in which that item or category is demanded.[3] It must respond separately to each item or category demanded.[4] It must state as to each item or category that the party (1) *will* produce it,[5] (2) *cannot* produce it,[6] or (3) *objects* to producing it.[7]

(1) Compliance with Demand: If the party is willing to produce the item, the response should state this intention.[8] If the demand seeks a category of items, the response must state specifically whether the party will produce all items falling within that category.[9] Unlike the 1956 Act,[10] Section 2031.220 does not contain a requirement that the response list each item that fits the demanded category. If the demand seeks anything more than a visual inspection of the item, the response must state the extent to which the party will allow any demanded testing, sampling, or other "related activity."[11]

---

[41] CCP § 2017.320(e).

[42] CCP § 2017.320(f).

[1] CCP § 2031.210.

[2] CCP § 2031.210(b).

[3] CCP § 2031.210(c).

[4] CCP § 2031.210(a).

[5] CCP § 2031.210(a)(1).

[6] CCP § 2031.210(a)(2).

[7] CCP § 2031.210(a)(3).

Alternatively, in appropriate cases, the responding party, instead of making an objection in the response, can move for a protective order. See Gray v Faulkner (1992, ND Ind) 148 FRD 220, 222 [it is inappropriate for the responding party to condition production on the demanding party's agreement to keep documents confidential; the proper response is either an objection or a motion for a protective order].

For a discussion of the appropriate use of the motion for a protective order, see § 6.11.

[8] CCP § 2031.220.

Cf. Rayman v American Charter Fed S & L Ass'n (1993, D Neb) 148 FRD 647, 651 [under FRCivP 34, where responding party claims that it has *already* produced the documents now being requested, it must so answer under oath].

[9] CCP § 2031.220.

[10] Former CCP § 2031(b), 1956 Discovery Act, Appendix E.

[11] CCP § 2031.220.

For a discussion of testing and sampling personal and real property, see §§ 6.8–6.9.

—**Mode of Compliance:** At the time set for production, compliance may occur in two ways.[12] The responding party may produce documents as they are usually arranged. Alternatively, that party may organize and label the items in a way that corresponds to the categories demanded. If the demanded information is on a computer, the responding party must print it out at the demanding party's expense.[13]

(2) Inability to Produce: A party who does not have "possession, custody, or control"[14] of an item need not produce it in response to an inspection demand. In such cases, however, Section 2031.230 requires more than a bare statement to that effect.[15] If the party does not now have the item, the response must state whether it was ever in its possession, custody, or control. Additionally, the party must identify anyone known or believed to possess or control the item. If no such item ever existed, or if the item did exist, but has been destroyed, lost, misplaced, or stolen, the responding party must so state.[16] A responding party acts in bad faith if it conceals an item's loss or destruction by objecting to production on grounds of irrelevance or privilege.[17]

(3) Objection: The "response" to an inspection demand is the proper place to lodge an objection to production of an item.[18] Section 2031.240 specifies the form of an objection. It must "identify with particularity" the objectionable item.[19] If the demand seeks a category of items, the response must identify each relevant document, thing, or property under the responding party's control to which the objection applies.[20] This should eliminate battles over the discoverability of nonexistent items. If the objection applies only to part of a demanded item or category, then the response must either state that the party will produce the remainder, or set forth the reasons for any inability to do so.[21]

---

[12] CCP §§ 2031.220 and 2031.280(a)

Compare Board of Educ. v Admiral Heating and Ventilating Co. (1984, ND Ill) 104 FRD 23, 36 [to prevent the responding party from burying responsive materials in midst of irrelevant materials, under comparable language in FRCivP 34(b), *demanding* party has the option to indicate whether documents will be produced as kept in the course of business, or segregated to correspond to specific demands].

Cf. T.V. Taupe Corp. v Marine Midland Mortgage Corp. (1991, WD NC) 136 FRD 449, 456 [where court doubted that responding party ordinarily kept records in cardboard box as produced, responding party was ordered to separate them to correspond to specific demands].

[13] CCP § 2031.280(b).

For a discussion of the obligation to "translate" computerized information, see § 6.7.

[14] For a discussion of "possession, custody, or control" of an item, see § 6.6.

[15] CCP § 2031.230.

[16] See Laguna Auto Body v Farmers Insur. Exch. (1991) 231 Cal App 3d 481, 485 n3 [verified statement that records were destroyed by fire would comply].

[17] Bihun v AT&T Information Systems, Inc. (1993) 13 Cal App 4th 976, 991–992 n5, 16 Cal Rptr 2d 787, 794–795 n5.

[18] CCP § 2031.210(a)(3).

[19] CCP § 2031.240(b)(1).

[20] CCP § 2031.240(b)(1).

[21] CCP § 2031.240(a).

Once the response has identified the objectionable item or category, it must "set forth clearly the extent of, and the specific ground for, the objection."[22] A party claiming a privilege must state the particular one relied on.[23] Similarly, the response must expressly set forth any work product protection claim. Counsel should remember that the attorney-client privilege differs from the work product protection.[24] A claim of one does not assert the other.

A response to an inspection demand that contains objections based on the attorney-client privilege or the work product protection should include a so-called "privilege log." This identifies the items claimed to be covered by the privilege or protection. Although the court may impose sanctions for failure to serve a timely privilege log, it may not treat this delinquency as a waiver, if the response itself was timely.[25] The term "privilege log" does not appear in the provisions governing inspection demands or anywhere else in the Discovery Act. "The expression is jargon, commonly used by courts and attorneys to express the requirements of [Section 2031.240(b)(2)]."[26]

A party who timely responds with certain objections waives any additional grounds for objection. In the *Scottsdale Ins. Co.* case, for example, an insurer responded to a demand for inspection of its claims file with only the objections that the demand was overbroad, oppressive, and burdensome. After these objections were overruled, it objected that the materials were privileged under the attorney-client privilege. The failure to include this ground for objection in its original response waived the privilege:

> [Petitioner's] argument makes no sense. It would allow piecemeal and seriatim doling out of objections to legitimate discovery requests whenever a timely response, no matter how insubstantial, is served. It is clear from the [Discovery] Act that the Legislature intended that any and all objections are to be made at the earliest timely response.[27]

Signature and Oath: Section 2031.250 requires the responding party's signature under oath for a response document that contains anything other than objections.[28] If the party is a public or private corporation, an officer or agent

---

[22] CCP § 2031.240(b).

Cf. Rayman v American Charter Fed S & L Ass'n (1993, D Neb) 148 FRD 647, 651 [response that documents have *already* been produced is not an objection].

[23] Compare Miller v Pancucci (1992, CD Cal) 141 FRD 292, 302 [boilerplate privilege objections insufficient] with Rodger v Electronic Data Systems Corp. (1994, ED NC) 155 FRD 537, 542–543 [log of privileged documents meets requirements of FRCivP 26(b)(5) to provide demanding party with enough information to assess propriety of claimed privilege].

[24] Cf. Sheets v Superior Court (1967) 257 Cal App 2d 1, 7–8, 64 Cal Rptr 753, 757.

[25] Korea Data Systems v Superior Court (1997) 51 Cal App 4th 1513, 59 Cal Rptr 2d 925.

[26] Hernandez v Superior Court (2003) 112 Cal App 4th 285, 292, 4 Cal Rptr 3d 883, 889.

[27] Scottsdale Ins. Co. v Superior Court (1997) 59 Cal App 4th 263, 273, 69 Cal Rptr 2d 112, 118.

[28] CCP § 2031.250(a).

may sign and swear to its response.[29] This officer or agent may be an attorney. However, in this event, that attorney may not assert the attorney-client privilege or the work product protection if the demanding party later tries to discover the identity of those supplying the information in the response.[30]

Counsel should resist the temptation to have the client sign undated, blank verification forms. An attorney may act unethically by attaching such a form to a response that makes factual representations:

> The *use* of a presigned verification in discovery proceedings, without first consulting with the client to assure that any assertions of fact are true, is a clear and serious violation of the statutes and rules.[31]

—Objections: Any response containing an objection must be signed by the responding party's attorney. Only the attorney need sign a response consisting entirely of objections.[32]

If the response includes statements of compliance or inability to comply as well as objections, then both the party and the attorney must sign. In addition, the party's signature must be under oath. However, the lack of the party's signature and oath on a timely response that includes such a mixture does not waive[33] the objections it contains, provided the response has been signed by the party's attorney:

> The provision that a response consisting solely of objections need not be verified confirms that an objection in an unverified "hybrid" response is nonetheless effective. The verification requirement for a response which contains matter other than objections operates to support the *other* statements in the response. The objections themselves do not require a verification in order to be preserved. [¶] . . . . The statutes reflect the recognition that objections are legal conclusions interposed by counsel, not factual assertions by a party, making their verification unnecessary.[34]

This interpretation was followed in *Food 4 Less Supermarkets,* which rejected an argument that the lack of verification rendered the objections untimely:

Cf. Rayman v American Charter Fed S & L Ass'n (1993, D Neb) 148 FRD 647, 651 [under FRCivP 34, where responding party claims that it has *already* produced the demanded documents, it must so answer under oath].

[29] CCP § 2031.250(b).

[30] CCP § 2031.250(b).

[31] Cf. Drociak v State Bar (1991) 52 Cal 3d 1085, 1090, 278 Cal Rptr 86, 89, 804 P2d 711, 714 [not realizing that his client's death was the reason for his inability to contact her, plaintiff's attorney prepared answers to *interrogatories* and attached presigned verification].

[32] CCP § 2031.250(c).

[33] For a discussion of the waiver of an objection by a failure to assert it in a response, see § 6.13.

[34] Blue Ridge Ins. Co. v Superior Court (1988) 202 Cal App 3d 339, 344–345, 248 Cal Rptr 346, 349–350 (original italics).

[T]here is no need to verify that portion of the response containing the objections. Thus, if the response is served within the statutory time period, that portion of the response must be considered timely notwithstanding the lack of verification. The omission of the verification in the portion of the response containing fact specific responses merely renders *that* portion of the response untimely and therefore only creates a right to move for orders and sanctions . . . *as to those responses* but does not result in a waiver of the objections made.[35]

Timing: The response is ordinarily due 30 days after service of the demand.[36] Service of the demand by mail increases this period, however, usually by five days.[37] The demanding and responding parties may agree to extend this period.[38] The agreement may be informal, but the parties must confirm it in a writing that specifies the date agreed on for a response.[39] Unless the agreement provides to the contrary, the responding party retains the right to object to any item in the demand.[40]

Service: The responding party must serve not only the demanding party but also all other parties who have appeared in the case.[41] The original response is sent to the demanding party. This party must then retain it, along with the original of the inspection demand itself, until six months after the case is over.[42] Neither document gets filed with the court.[43]

§ 6.13   Failure to Respond to Inspection Demand

Section 2031.300 comprehensively covers both the consequences of and the remedy for a party's failure to respond (either on time or at all) to an inspection demand.[1]

Waiver of Objections: Following earlier case law,[2] the failure to serve any response within the 30-day period[3] waives any objection a party might otherwise

---

[35] Food 4 Less Supermarkets v Superior Court (1995) 40 Cal App 4th 651, 657–658, 46 Cal Rptr 2d 925, 928–929 (original italics).

[36] CCP § 2031.260. In unlawful detainer actions, the response must be served within five days.

For a discussion of consequences of failing to serve a timely response to an inspection demand, see § 6.13.

[37] CCP § 2016.050, referencing CCP § 1013(a).

[38] CCP § 2031.270(a).

[39] CCP § 2031.270(b).

[40] CCP § 2031.270(c).

[41] CCP § 2031.260.

[42] CCP § 2031.290(b).

[43] CCP § 2031.290(a).

[1] For a discussion of the remedy for a timely but inadequate response, see § 6.14.

[2] Cf. Coy v Superior Court (1962) 58 Cal 2d 210, 216–217, 23 Cal Rptr 393, 395–396, 373 P2d 457, 459–460 [under former CCP § 2030 of the original Discovery Act, objections were waived if not served on time].

[3] See CCP §§ 2031.260 and 2031.300. In unlawful detainer cases, the response must be served within five days.

have to the demand.[4] This waiver expressly includes objections based on privilege and the work product protection.[5] However, a timely response that lacks a party's required signature and oath[6] does not waive[7] any objections stated in it, provided the party's attorney has signed it:

> The provision that a response consisting solely of objections need not be verified confirms that an objection in an unverified "hybrid" response is nonetheless effective. The verification requirement for a response which contains matter other than objections operates to support the *other* statements in the response. The objections themselves do not require a verification in order to be preserved. [¶] . . . The statutes reflect the recognition that objections are legal conclusions interposed by counsel, not factual assertions by a party, making their verification unnecessary.[8]

This interpretation was followed in *Food 4 Less Supermarkets,* which also rejected an argument that a timely but unverified response waived the objections that it contained:

> [T]here is no need to verify that portion of the response containing the objections. Thus, if the response is served within the statutory time period, that portion of the response must be considered timely notwithstanding the lack of verification. The omission of the verification in the portion of the response containing fact specific responses merely renders *that* portion of the response untimely and therefore only creates a right to move for orders and sanctions . . . *as to those responses* but does not result in a waiver of the objections made.[9]

Relief from Waiver: Parties who delay in responding to an inspection demand may avoid the automatic waiver of their objections by: (1) filing a late response that otherwise substantially complies with the Civil Discovery Act;[10] (2) moving

---

See also City of Fresno v Superior Court (1988) 205 Cal App 3d 1459, 1466, 253 Cal Rptr 296, 299.

For a discussion of the time limit for serving a response to an inspection demand, see § 6.12.

[4] CCP § 2031.300(a).

City of Fresno v Superior Court (1988) 205 Cal App 3d 1459, 1466, 253 Cal Rptr 296, 299.

[5] See CCP § 2031.300(a).

See also City of Fresno v Superior Court (1988) 205 Cal App 3d 1459, 1466, 253 Cal Rptr 296, 299.

[6] For a discussion of the requirement that a party sign a response under oath, see § 6.12.

[7] For a discussion of the waiver of an objection by a failure to assert it in a response, see § 6.13.

[8] Blue Ridge Ins. Co. v Superior Court (1988) 202 Cal App 3d 339, 344–345, 248 Cal Rptr 346, 349–350.

[9] Food 4 Less Supermarkets v Superior Court (1995) 40 Cal App 4th 651, 657–658, 46 Cal Rptr 2d 925, 928–929 (original italics).

[10] CCP § 2031.300(a)(1), referencing CCP §§ 2031.210, 2031.220, 2031.230, 2031.240 and 2031.280.

for relief from the waiver; and (3) persuading the trial court that their failure to respond timely resulted from "mistake, inadvertence, or excusable neglect."[11]

Relief from this waiver is hardly automatic. In the *City of Fresno* case,[12] an attorney who had failed to timely respond to an inspection demand sought relief from the consequent waiver of objections. The motion relied on two grounds: his failure to study carefully the time limits in then recently adopted Discovery Act of 1986, and his distraction by the imminent trial of another case. The appellate court upheld the trial court's refusal to grant relief for either of these reasons:

> As the [trial] judge observed in denying [the defendant's] motion for relief: "[I]f we are going to simply find that being busy, or not fully understanding the provisions of a code section, or whatever it is, constitutes excusable neglect, why, you know, we just don't have any rules."[13]

Motion to Compel: Section 2031.300 specifies the remedy available to the demanding party who fails to receive any response.[14] That party moves to compel a response.[15] A demanding party has always the right to receive a response, even where the items sought are not discoverable. Therefore, following prior case law governing total failures to respond to discover requests,[16] Section 2031.300 does not require the demanding party to first "meet and confer" with the delinquent party before making this motion.

If the court grants the motion, the order should contain two provisions. First, it should order a response to the demands. Second, it should impose a monetary sanction on the party in default unless it finds some "substantial justification" for the noncompliance.[17] However, even if the delinquent party has had a history[18] of noncompliance with discovery, the court may not yet impose a drastic sanction:[19]

---

[11] CCP § 2031.300(a)(2).

This provision supplants the discretion the court would otherwise have under CCP § 473. Zellerino v Brown (1991) 235 Cal App 3d 1097, 1107, 1 Cal Rptr 2d 222, 228 ["the Legislature's use of section 473 language in parts of the discovery act evidences its intent to supplant the application of section 473 pro tanto."]

[12] City of Fresno v Superior Court (1988) 205 Cal App 3d 1459, 1465–1467, 253 Cal Rptr 296, 298–300.

[13] 205 Cal App 3d at 1467, 253 Cal Rptr at 300.

[14] CCP § 2031.300(b).

[15] CCP § 2031.300(b).

For a discussion of the motion to compel *further* response, see § 6.14.

[16] Cf. Leach v Superior Court (1980) 111 Cal App 3d 902, 906, 169 Cal Rptr 42, 44.

[17] CCP § 2031.300(c).

[18] Ruvalcaba v Government Employees Insur. Co. (1990) 222 Cal App 3d 1579, 1583, 272 Cal Rptr 541, 544.

[19] For a discussion of the "drastic" sanctions, see § 15.5.

Here, [plaintiff] did not timely respond to a demand for inspection documents . . . . Thus, the court could have ordered [plaintiff] to respond to the discovery request and could have imposed a monetary sanction. . . . Without the prior order directing [plaintiff] to comply, however, it was inappropriate for the court to dismiss the matter.[20]

Once the trial court transmutes the obligation to serve a response from a statutory duty into a judicial order, further disobedience exposes the recalcitrant party to the more drastic "issue," "evidence," or even "terminating" sanctions.[21] However, the trial court may deal more leniently with the disobedience of its order. It may simply impose a monetary sanction and give the party a second chance to comply with its order to compel a response.[22]

§ 6.14 Compelling Further Response

Upon receiving a timely response to an inspection demand, the demanding party may not be satisfied with its contents.[1] The statements of compliance may fall short of the inspection demanded.[2] Its statements of inability to comply may not support the responding party's claim of lack of control over the demanded items.[3] Most often, however, the demanding party considers the response's objections to be meritless.[4] The demanding party must then move for an order compelling *further* response to the demand.[5]

---

[20] Ruvalcaba v Government Employees Insur. Co. (1990) 222 Cal App 3d 1579, 1583, 272 Cal Rptr 541, 543–544.

[21] CCP § 2031.300(c).

For a discussion of the "drastic" sanctions, see § 15.5.

Cf. Constitution Bank v Levine (1993, ED Pa) 151 FRD 278, 279 [on a motion for sanctions for disobedience of a discovery order, the propriety of that discovery is not an issue].

[22] CCP § 2031.300(c).

[1] For a discussion of the procedures when *no* timely response is made to an inspection demand, see § 6.13.

[2] CCP § 2031.310(a)(1).

See, e.g., London v Dri-Honing Corp. (2004) 117 Cal App 4th 999, 1002, 12 Cal Rptr 3d 240, 242.

For a discussion of the requirements for a statement of compliance in a response to an inspection demand, see § 6.12.

[3] CCP § 2031.310(a)(2).

For a discussion of the requirement of an explanation of a party's inability to produce an item, see § 6.12.

For a discussion of what constitutes "control" over a demanded item, see §§ 6.5–6.6.

[4] CCP § 2031.310(a)(3).

Cf. Mann v University of Cincinnati (1993, SD Ohio) 824 F Supp 1190, 1201 [before ruling on a motion to compel, the court may conduct in camera review of documents to assess claims of privilege].

For a discussion of the requirements for objections in a response to a demand, see § 6.12.

[5] CCP § 2031.310(a).

See, e.g., London v Dri-Honing Corp. (2004) 117 Cal App 4th 999, 12 Cal Rptr 3d 240.

Time Limit: In contrast to motions to compel an initial response to,[6] or a compliance with, an inspection demand,[7] the demanding party must move to compel a *further* response within 45 days.[8] This period runs not from the date that the demand has specified for production of the items,[9] but from the date of service of the unsatisfactory response:

> [Defendant's] motion was made less than 45 days after the date for *production*, but more than 45 days after the *response* date. A careful reading of the statute compels the conclusion that the motion was untimely.[10]

Once this period has expired, "the demanding party waives any right to compel a further response to the inspection demand."[11] This waiver occurs even though the responding party's written opposition to the motion to compel further response does not raise an issue as to its timing.[12]

—Extending Time for Motion: Three situations may extend the 45-day limit. First, the parties may agree in writing to a specified later date.[13] Second, the responding party, usually because of the parties' "meet and confer" efforts, may serve a supplemental response. If this supplemental response is unsatisfactory, the demanding party will have 45 days after its service to move to compel further response.[14] Third, service of either an initial or a supplemental response by mail extends the period by five additional days.[15]

Circumventing Waiver: After expiration of the 45-day period, the demanding party may not avoid the waiver of its right to compel production simply by demanding the same materials in another inspection demand.[16] However,

---

[6] For a discussion of the motion to compel a response to an inspection demand, see § 6.13.

[7] For a discussion of the motion to compel compliance with an inspection demand, see § 6.15.

[8] CCP § 2031.310(c).

[9] For a discussion of the requirement that the demand specify a date for the inspection to occur, see § 6.3.

[10] Standon Co. v Superior Court (1990) 225 Cal App 3d 898, 902, 275 Cal Rptr 833, 835.

[11] CCP § 2031.310(c).

Sperber v Robinson (1994) 26 Cal App 4th 736, 745–746, 31 Cal Rptr 2d 659, 664; Standon Co. v Superior Court (1990) 225 Cal App 3d 898, 275 Cal Rptr 833, 903.

[12] Sexton v Superior Court (1997) 58 Cal App 4th 1403, 68 Cal Rptr 2d 708. Note that in this case the petitioner orally raised the objection as to timeliness at the hearing on the motion. In a footnote (58 Cal App 4th at 1410, fn. 4), the court stated: "Arguably, if petitioner had not raised the objection as he did and allowed the hearing to go forward to see how the ruling came out, he might be estopped, but we are not confronted by that circumstance and do not decide the issue."

[13] CCP § 2031.310(c).

[14] CCP § 2031.310(c).

[15] CCP § 2016.050, referencing CCP § 1013(a).

See, e.g., Sperber v Robinson (1994) 26 Cal App 4th 736, 745, 31 Cal Rptr 2d 659, 664.

[16] Cf. Professional Career Colleges, Magna Institute, Inc. v Superior Court (1989) 207 Cal App 3d 490, 493–494, 255 Cal Rptr 5, 7–8 [one who has allowed the 45 day period for compelling a further response to *interrogatories* to expire may not "reset the clock" by including the same interrogatory in a later set].

demanding parties may depose the custodian of the items sought in the inspection demand and include in the deposition notice an instruction to bring those items to that deposition:

> [Defendant] argues that [plaintiffs] have employed only one discovery "method" which is available under two separate statutes. But the inspection of documents procedure is quite different from a deposition at which a party is required to bring documents. Nothing in either [former] section 2025 or [former] section 2031 suggests that seeking documents under one statutory procedure bars a litigant from seeking the same documents under the other.[17]

The remedy for any abuse of this loophole lies in a motion for a protective order against "unreasonably cumulative or duplicative" use of discovery methods, under Section 2019.030,[18] or against "unwarranted annoyance" under Section 2025.420.[19]

"Good Cause": A motion to compel a further response to an inspection demand differs in an important respect from one to compel further response to interrogatories[20] or to admission requests:[21] the motion must "set forth specific facts showing good cause justifying the discovery sought."[22]

The 1956 Discovery Act conditioned the right to an inspection "upon a showing of good cause."[23] This "good cause" requirement allowed trial courts to restrict discovery of materials prepared in anticipation of litigation by *parties* or by their *liability carriers* before the hiring of an attorney. An obvious example of such materials is a third-party witness statement obtained by a potential defendant's insurance carrier. Since the client or the carrier generated the statement, it is not an *attorney's* statutorily protected work product. Nevertheless, the courts recognized that many policies behind the attorney work product doctrine applied to the work product of clients and liability carriers. They thus interpreted "good cause" as requiring a special showing before an opponent could discover such materials.[24]

---

[17] Carter v Superior Court (1990) 218 Cal App 3d 994, 997, 267 Cal Rptr 290, 291–292.

For a discussion of the use of depositions to obtain an inspection, see § 6.2.

[18] CCP § 2019.030(a)(1).

[19] CCP § 2025.420(b).

Carter v Superior Court (1990) 218 Cal App 3d 994, 998, 267 Cal Rptr 290, 292.

[20] CCP § 2030.290.

[21] CCP § 2033.290.

[22] CCP § 2031.310(b)(1).

Cf. Harding Lawson Assoc. v Superior Court (1992) 10 Cal App 4th 7, 9–10, 12 Cal Rptr 2d 538, 539–540 [plaintiff neither demonstrated compelling need to order production of defendant's files on nonparty employees, nor showed the unavailability of the information through depositions or other nonconfidential sources].

[23] Former CCP § 2034(a), 1956 Discovery Act, Appendix E.

[24] For a discussion of the special protection given to witness statements obtained by a party or its insurance carrier in anticipation of litigation, see § 13.8.

The 1970 amendments to the Federal Rules expressly extended protection to the materials generated by a client or a liability carrier in anticipation of litigation.[25] The Discovery Commission proposed to replace the "good cause" phrase with a similar direct statement restricting discovery of such materials.[26] However, the Legislature ultimately[27] decided to stay with the existing approach. Accordingly, the work product statute, Section 2018.030, continues to speak only of an *attorney's* activities. However, it also states that it "is not intended to expand or reduce the extent to which work product is discoverable under existing law in any action."[28] Thus, it preserves the case law restricting discovery of trial preparation materials generated by clients and their carriers. The Legislature underscored this by inserting the "good cause" language from the 1956 Discovery Act[29] into Section 2031.310.[30]

Meet and Confer: Unlike the motion to compel a response to an inspection demand,[31] or a compliance with that demand,[32] a motion to compel a further response is subject to a "meet and confer" condition. Before filing this motion, a party who considers the response inadequate must try to work out informally the points in dispute with the responding party. A declaration setting forth these efforts must accompany the motion.[33]

Sanctions: A party who unsuccessfully makes[34] or opposes[35] a motion to compel further response risks a monetary sanction.[36] The party making a motion to compel should couple it with a motion for a monetary sanction in the event it is successful. However, the sanction motion may also be made after the court has granted the motion to compel. It is not subject to the 45-day limit that applies to the motion to compel.[37]

The unsuccessful party can avoid the sanction by showing "substantial justification for making or opposing the motion.[38] However, the trial court may

---

[25] FRCivP 26(b)(3).

[26] See Proposed Civil Discovery Act of 1986, CCP § 2018(a), Appendix D.

[27] Initially, the Legislature enacted the Commission's recommendation. See Stats. 1986, ch. 1334, § 2.

[28] CCP § 2018.040.

[29] Former CCP § 2034(a), 1956 Discovery Act, Appendix E.

[30] CCP § 2031.310(b)(1).

[31] For a discussion of the motion to compel a response to an inspection demand, see § 6.13.

[32] For a discussion of the motion to compel compliance with an inspection demand, see § 6.15.

[33] CCP § 2031.310(b)(2).

[34] See, e.g., Mattco Forge, Inc. v Arthur Young & Co. (1990) 223 Cal App 3d 1429, 1436, 273 Cal Rptr 262, 265.

[35] See, e.g., Standon Co. v Superior Court (1990) 225 Cal App 3d 898, 904, 275 Cal Rptr 833, 837.

[36] CCP § 2031.310(d).

[37] London v Dri-Honing Corp. (2004) 117 Cal App 4th 999, 1002–1009, 12 Cal Rptr 3d 240, 242–248.

[38] Compare Standon Co. v Superior Court (1990) 225 Cal App 3d 898, 904, 275 Cal Rptr 833,

not at that point impose a drastic sanction upon a party whose response it finds deficient.[39]

Once the trial court transmutes the obligation to serve a response from a statutory duty into a judicial order, further disobedience exposes the recalcitrant party to the more drastic "issue," "evidence," or even "terminating" sanctions.[40] However, the trial court may deal more leniently with the disobedience of its order. It may simply impose a monetary sanction and give the party a second chance to comply with its order to compel a response.[41]

§ 6.15 Failure to Comply with Inspection Demand

Although a responding party may have promised full compliance with an inspection demand,[1] problems may occur on the inspection date. The responding party may not show up, may not turn over some or all of the demanded materials, or may refuse to allow demanded "related activities." In such circumstances, the demanding party should move to compel compliance.[2]

No Time Limit: In contrast to a motion to compel a further response,[3] no statutory time limit exists for the motion to compel a party to comply with its response:

[A] failure in the actual compliance with the demand is governed by [Section 2031.320]. Under that subdivision, a party may seek to compel "compliance" with the demand if "a party filing a response . . . thereafter fails to permit

---

837 [court not required to impose monetary sanction where motion to compel was meritorious, but untimely, since there had been no appellate interpretation of new statutory time limit] with Mattco Forge, Inc. v Arthur Young & Co. (1990) 223 Cal App 3d 1429, 1436, 273 Cal Rptr 262, 265 [possibility that a pending demurrer may moot plaintiff's inspection demand did not justify defendants' refusal to meet and confer concerning the adequacy of their response to that demand].

For a discussion of "substantial justification," see § 15.4.

[39] Ruvalcaba v Government Employees Insur. Co. (1990) 222 Cal App 3d 1579, 1583, 272 Cal Rptr 541, 543–544 [prior order to compel is necessary before a court may impose a terminating sanction for failure to respond to an inspection demand].

[40] CCP § 2031.300(c).

For a discussion of the "drastic" sanctions, see § 15.5.

Cf. Constitution Bank v Levine (1993, ED Pa) 151 FRD 278, 279 [on a motion for sanctions for disobedience of a discovery order, the propriety of that discovery is not an issue].

[41] CCP § 2031.310(e).

See, e.g., Estate of Ivey v DiLeonardo (1994) 22 Cal App 4th 873, 878–879, 28 Cal Rptr 2d 16, 18 [since demanded documents were critical to the decision of the issue before the court, an "issue" sanction was appropriate for disobedience of order compelling their production].

For a discussion of these drastic sanctions, see § 15.5.

[1] For a discussion of a response that contains a statement of compliance with an inspection demand, see § 6.12.

[2] CCP § 2031.320(a).

[3] For discussion of the time limit for a motion to compel further response to an inspection demand, see § 6.14.

the inspection in accordance with that party's statement of compliance." No time limit is placed on the motion.[4]

No Duty to Meet and Confer: Once the responding party promises compliance with an inspection, the demanding party has a right to insist upon that compliance. Therefore, following prior case law,[5] Section 2031.320 does not require the demanding party to first "meet and confer" with the delinquent party before filing the motion.[6]

Sanctions: One who unsuccessfully makes or opposes a motion to compel compliance risks a monetary sanction.[7] That party can avoid the sanction by showing "substantial justification for making or opposing the motion."[8] However, no matter how flagrant the noncompliance may be, the trial court may not at that stage impose a drastic sanction upon the recalcitrant party.[9]

Once the trial court transmutes the obligation to comply from a statutory duty into a judicial order, further disobedience exposes the recalcitrant party to the more drastic "issue," "evidence," or even "terminating" sanctions.[10] However, the trial court may deal more leniently with the disobedience of its order. It may simply impose a monetary sanction and give the party a second chance to comply with its order to compel a response.[11]

---

[4] Standon v Superior Court (1990) 225 Cal App 3d 898, 903, 275 Cal Rptr 835, 836.

[5] Cf. Leach v Superior Court (1980) 111 Cal App 3d 902, 906, 169 Cal Rptr 42, 44.

[6] Compare CCP § 2031.310(b)(2) [meet and confer requirement for motions to compel *response*] with CCP § 2031.320 [no meet and confer requirement stated for motions to compel *compliance* with response].

[7] CCP § 2031.320(b).

[8] For a discussion of "substantial justification," see § 15.4.

[9] Ruvalcaba v Government Employees Insur. Co. (1990) 222 Cal App 3d 1579, 1583, 272 Cal Rptr 541, 543–544 [prior order to compel needed before court can order terminating sanctions for failure to respond to inspection demand].

[10] CCP § 2031.320(c).

E.g., Estate of Ivey v DiLeonardo (1994) 22 Cal App 4th 873, 878–879, 28 Cal Rptr 2d 16, 18 [since the demanded documents were critical to the decision of the issue before the court, an "issue" sanction was appropriate for disobedience of an order compelling their production].

For a discussion of these "drastic" sanctions, see § 15.5.

[11] CCP § 2031.310(e).

CHAPTER 7

INSPECTIONS OF ITEMS CONTROLLED BY NONPARTIES

SYNOPSIS

---

§ 7.1   In General

Frequently, parties to a lawsuit cannot complete their trial preparations unless they can obtain materials that a nonparty controls. The inspection-demand procedure of the Civil Discovery Act, however, applies only to parties.[1] Instead, separate provisions govern document discovery from nonparties.[2]

Deposition Subpoenas: Section 2020.010 creates the "deposition subpoena" to compel nonparties to provide discovery.[3] A deposition subpoena has three functions. First, it can compel a nonparty to appear and provide deposition testimony.[4] Second, it can compel a nonparty to produce at a deposition specified records, documents, and things for inspection and copying.[5] Third, where a party is seeking only "business records" themselves, and not their custodian's attendance, the deposition subpoena becomes the functional equivalent of an inspection demand to a nonparty.[6]

---

[1] Cf. Botsford v Pascoe (1979) 94 Cal App 3d 62, 69, 156 Cal Rptr 177, 181.

For general coverage of inspection demands, see Chapter 6.

[2] CCP §§ 2020.010–2020.510.

[3] CCP § 2020.010(b).

[4] CCP §§ 2020.310(a)(1) and (2) and 2020.310(b).

For a discussion of compelling the attendance of nonparties for a discovery deposition, see §§ 2.9 and 2.12.

[5] CCP § 2020.510.

For discussion of this form of nonparty document discovery, see § 7.2.

[6] CCP § 2020.410.

For a discussion of this way to discover a nonparty's records, see § 7.3.

Incorporation of Other Statutes: The Civil Discovery Act's provisions for document discovery from third parties expressly incorporate two other statutory schemes: the general subpoena provisions of the Code of Civil Procedure,[7] and the business-record subpoena provisions of the Evidence Code.[8] These statutes apply to deposition subpoenas "[e]xcept as modified" in the specific Discovery Act provisions for nonparties.[9]

—Good Cause Affidavits: An important modification concerns the "good cause for production" affidavit or declaration that normally accompanies a subpoena duces tecum.[10] A general subpoena provision, adopted before the Discovery Act of 1986, still purports to require this for depositions:

> In the case of subpoena duces tecum which requires appearance and the production of matters and things *at the taking of a deposition*, the subpoena shall not be valid unless a copy of *the affidavit upon which the subpoena is based . . . is attached* to the notice of taking the deposition served upon each party or its attorney . . .[11]

However, the Civil Discovery Act has "modified" this general requirement. Its provisions for nonparty document production, whether alone[12] or at a deposition,[13] expressly eliminate the requirement that a good cause affidavit accompany the deposition subpoena.

Although a "good cause" affidavit no longer need accompany a deposition subpoena duces tecum, the party issuing such a subpoena must show good cause if the one receiving it moves to quash or seeks a protective order.[14]

—Consumer Records: Section 1985.3 sets up a complicated notice scheme to give "consumers" a chance to protect their privacy interests when a subpoena directs another person or entity to produce records concerning them. Section 2020.030 incorporates this provision for deposition subpoenas. However, it "modifies" it in two ways. First, the general statute requires that the consumer receive a copy of the good cause affidavit filed to support the subpoena.[15] Such an affidavit is unnecessary for deposition subpoenas.[16]

---

[7] Chapter 2, commencing with CCP § 1985.

[8] Evid Code §§ 1560–1566.

[9] CCP § 2020.030.

[10] CCP § 1985(b).

[11] CCP § 1987.5 (italics added).

[12] CCP § 2020.410(c).

[13] CCP § 2020.510(b).

[14] Calcor Space Facility, Inc. v Superior Court (1997) 53 Cal App 4th 216, 224, 61 Cal Rptr 2d 567, 572.

[15] CCP § 1985.3(b).

[16] See CCP §§ 2020.410(c) and 2020.510(b).

Second, the consumer records statute authorizes production 15 days after the issuance of the subpoena.[17] The deposition statutes, however, require at least 20 days between the issuance of the subpoena and the production date.[18]

§ 7.2 Production of Items During a Deposition

During discovery, a party may want a nonparty both to testify and to allow inspection of materials that the nonparty controls. The party can accomplish both goals simultaneously through a deposition.

Special Requirements: The party wishing to simultaneously obtain testimonial and documentary discovery from a nonparty must, of course, follow the procedures that govern a nonparty's deposition, mainly the service of a deposition subpoena to compel that person's attendance at the deposition.[1] However, three additional requirements apply if a party also wants to simultaneously inspect documents or other materials at that deposition.

First, the deposition *notice* sent to all the other parties in the case must specify "with reasonable particularity" the items or categories of items that the deponent must produce.[2] Second, the deposition *subpoena* must designate the items the deponent must produce.[3] It may either specify the individual items or describe categories of items with reasonable particularity. In addition, the subpoena must describe any plans for testing or sampling the items produced.[4] The party seeking production, however, no longer needs to support its deposition subpoena with an affidavit showing good cause.[5] Third, a copy of the deposition *subpoena* must accompany the deposition *notice* served on the other parties.[6]

"Consumer" Records: The procedure becomes much more complicated if the items sought by the deposition subpoena are records that the deponent maintains on someone that has done business with it. In such cases, the discovering party must refer to Section 1985.3 to learn whether the deponent is a "witness" as defined by that statute.[7] This definition includes most health care providers, professionals, financial institutions and schools.[8]

---

[17] CCP § 1985.3(b).

[18] CCP § 2020.410(c) [records only deposition subpoenas] and CCP § 2025.270(a) [testimonial and records deposition subpoenas].

[1] For a discussion of the means of compelling the nonparty's attendance at the deposition, see § 2.9.

For a discussion of the place where the deposition may occur, see §§ 2.13–2.14.

[2] CCP § 2025.220(a)(4).

[3] CCP § 2020.510(a)(2).

[4] CCP § 2020.510(a)(3).

[5] CCP § 2020.510(b).

For a further discussion of the elimination of the requirement of an affidavit of good cause, see § 7.1.

[6] CCP § 2025.240(c).

[7] CCP § 2020.510(c).

[8] CCP § 1985.3(a)(1) defines "witness" to include "physician, chiropractor, . . . pharmacist,

—Notice to Consumer: If the deponent is a "witness," the party taking the deposition must serve a copy of the deposition subpoena on the "consumer"[9] who is the specific subject of the records sought.[10] Simultaneously, that party must give the consumer a statutorily prescribed privacy rights notice.[11]

The deponent may not produce the records unless the party seeking them provides either a written authorization from the consumer or proof of service upon the consumer of a copy of the subpoena and of the privacy rights notice.[12]

The deposition date must be at least 20 days after the issuance of the subpoena.[13] Moreover, the consumer must receive notice at least 10 days before the date of production and at least five days before service on the deponent.[14] This gives the consumer time to challenge the subpoena.[15]

§ 7.3 "Records Only" Subpoena

Usually, a party seeking access to a nonparty's business records would prefer simply to inspect them without also deposing their custodian. Building on existing provisions of the Evidence Code,[1] Section 2020.410 allows a party to inspect

---

pharmacy, hospital, state or national bank, state or federal association . . ., state or federal credit union, trust company, anyone authorized by the state to make or arrange loans that are secured by real property, title insurance company, underwritten title company, escrow agent . . ., attorney, accountant, institution of the Farm Credit System . . ., or telephone corporation which is a public utility . . ., or psychotherapist . . ., or a private or public preschool, elementary school, or secondary school."

Cf. Scalise and Farmer, Disclosure of a Patient's Medical Information to Third Parties: How Much is Too Much?, 22 Law and Psychol. Rev. 199 (1998).

[9] CCP § 1985.3(a)(2) defines "consumer" as "any individual, partnership of five or fewer persons, association, or trust which has transacted business with, or has used the services of, the witness or for whom the witness has acted as agent or fiduciary."

[10] These notice provisions do not apply if the subpoena does not seek the records of any particular consumer as long as all references to individual consumers are deleted from the records produced.

[11] CCP § 1985.3(b).

[12] CCP § 1985.3(c).

[13] See CCP § 2025.270(a). This section thus supersedes the 15 day notice provisions of CCP § 1985.3(b) generally applicable to consumer records subpoenas.

Cf. Reporter's Note to CCP § 2020(d) and (e), Proposed Civil Discovery Act of 1986, Appendix D.

[14] CCP §§ 1985.3(b)(2), (b)(3). In both instances, for mailed service of notice, the consumer must receive additional time, usually five days, before production can occur. See CCP § 1013.

[15] CCP § 1985.3(g) [consumer may move to quash].

Cf. Babcock v Superior Court (1994) 29 Cal App 4th 721, 725–726, 35 Cal Rptr 2d 462, 465 [nonparty consumer can seek in camera inspection to determine circumstances, if any, of the disclosure of its records]; Lantz v Superior Court (1994) 28 Cal App 4th 1839, 1849–1852, 34 Cal Rptr 358 [a county can be a "subpoenaing party" for purposes of § 1983.5].

[1] See Evid Code § 1560(b) [in lieu of personal attendance at deposition, recipient of business records only subpoena may deliver certified copy of records to deposition officer] and Evid Code § 1560(e) [in lieu of delivery of copy of subpoenaed records at deposition, records custodian can simply make them available for inspection by the subpoenaing party].

and copy a nonparty's business records by what is tantamount to a "records only" deposition subpoena.[2] The "business records subpoena," an innovation of the Civil Discovery Act of 1986, commands the production of business records for copying without attendance at a deposition, thus allowing parties to obtain "business records" held by nonparties by simply serving them with that subpoena.[3]

However, the "records only" subpoena covers only "business records." It does not compel the production of other types of documents. For example, a transcript of a deposition is considered a product of the court reporter's business, not a "record" of that business. Therefore, a party cannot circumvent the court reporter's charge for providing a copy (no matter how unconscionable that charge may be) by subpoenaing the original for the purpose of copying it oneself.[4] Moreover, a party who wishes to inspect, sample, or test "tangible items" controlled by a nonparty still must subpoena the custodian of that property to bring the items to an oral deposition.[5]

Basic Procedure: To inspect and copy a nonparty's business records without deposing the person who has custody of them, a party simply serves a "deposition subpoena" that seeks such records only.[6] A copy of the deposition subpoena itself is sent to all other parties, and serves as a deposition notice.[7] Although this procedure foregoes the formality of testimony by the records custodian, it is still a "deposition." Therefore, the deposition "hold" still applies.[8] Thus, a plaintiff may not serve a nonparty with a "records only" deposition subpoena seeking discovery of business records until 20 days after at least one of the defendants has been served with the summons and complaint.[9]

—Contents of Subpoena: The deposition subpoena must designate the items to be produced. It may either specify the individual items or describe categories of items with reasonable particularity.[10] A party may not define the items or

---

[2] CCP § 2020.410.

[3] Urban Pacific Equities Corp. v Superior Court (1997) 59 Cal App 4th 688, 692, 69 Cal Rptr 2d 635, 638.

[4] Urban Pacific Equities Corp. v Superior Court (1997) 59 Cal App 4th 688, 693, 69 Cal Rptr 2d 635, 638.

[5] See CCP § 2020.510(a) [deposition subpoenas requiring attendance and production of "tangible things" must identify any planned "testing or sampling"]. But cf. CCP § 2020.220(c)(2) ["Personal service of a deposition subpoena is effective to require . . . any specified production, inspection, testing, and sampling"].

For a discussion of production of items during a deposition, see § 7.2.

[6] CCP § 2025.220(b).

Where the nonparty is a corporation or other type of organization, one may serve the deposition subpoena on any officer, director or custodian of its records. CCP § 2020.220(b)(2).

[7] CCP § 2025.220(b).

[8] For a discussion of the "deposition hold," see § 2.2.

[9] California Shellfish Inc. v United Shellfish Co. (1997) 56 Cal App 4th 16, 20–24, 64 Cal Rptr 2d 797, 798–801.

[10] CCP § 2020.410(a).

categories so broadly that they constitute a blanket demand for all records on a certain matter.[11] Using boldface type, the deposition subpoena must expressly caution the recipient against delivering the records to a designated "deposition officer" *earlier* than the date and time specified in the deposition subpoena.[12] However, the party seeking production need not support a "records only" deposition subpoena with a "good cause" affidavit.[13]

—Time of Production: Section 2020.410 imposes two requirements for the time of production. First, the production date must be at least 20 days after the *issuance* of the subpoena. Second, that date must also be at least 15 days after the *service* of the subpoena.[14]

"Consumer" Records: The procedure becomes much more complicated if the items sought by the deposition subpoena are records that the deponent maintains on someone that has done *business* with it. In such cases, the records-seeking party must refer to Section 1985.3 to learn whether the deponent is a "witness" as defined by that statute.[15] This definition includes most health care providers, professionals, financial institutions, and schools.[16]

—Notice to Consumer: If the deponent is a "witness," the party taking the "records only" deposition must serve a copy of the deposition subpoena on the "consumer"[17] who is the specific subject of the records sought.[18] Simultaneously, that party must give the consumer a statutorily prescribed privacy rights notice.[19]

---

[11] See, e.g., Calcor Space Facility, Inc. v Superior Court (1997) 53 Cal App 4th 216, 222, 61 Cal Rptr 2d 567, 571.

[12] CCP § 2020.430(d).

This restriction does not apply if the materials are delivered to the party's attorney for copying, since that attorney is not a "deposition officer" within the meaning of CCP § 2020.430. See CCP § 2020.420.

[13] CCP § 2020.410(c).

For a further discussion of the elimination of the requirement of an affidavit of good cause, see § 7.1.

[14] CCP § 2020.410(c).

[15] CCP § 2020.410(d).

[16] CCP § 1985.3(a)(1) defines "witness" to include "physician, chiropractor, . . . pharmacist, pharmacy, hospital, state or national bank, state or federal association . . ., state or federal credit union, trust company, anyone authorized by the state to make or arrange loans that are secured by real property, title insurance company, underwritten title company, escrow agent . . ., attorney, accountant, institution of the Farm Credit System . . ., or telephone corporation which is a public utility . . ., or psychotherapist . . ., or a private or public preschool, elementary school, or secondary school."

Cf. Scalise and Farmer, Disclosure of a Patient's Medical Information to Third Parties: How Much is Too Much?, 22 Law and Psychol. Rev. 199 (1998).

[17] CCP § 1985.3(a)(2) defines "consumer" as "any individual, partnership of five or fewer persons, association, or trust which has transacted business with, or has used the services of, the witness or for whom the witness has acted as agent or fiduciary."

[18] These notice provisions do not apply if the subpoena does not seek the records of any particular consumer as long as all references to individual consumers are deleted from the records produced.

[19] CCP § 1985.3(b).

The deponent may not produce the records unless the party seeking them provides either a written authorization from the consumer, or proof of service upon the consumer of a copy of the subpoena and of the privacy rights notice.[20]

The production date must be at least 20 days after the issuance of the subpoena.[21] Moreover, the consumer must receive notice at least 10 days before the production date and at least five days before service on the deponent.[22] This gives the consumer time to challenge the subpoena.[23]

Mechanics of Production: One seeking only an inspection of the business records of a nonparty may either direct that its attorney or attorney's representative copy them, or that a professional photocopier do so.

—Party's Attorney: Section 2020.030 incorporates[24] a provision of the Evidence Code. The latter provides that "the subpoenaing party may direct the witness to make the records available for inspection or copying by the party's attorney or the attorney's representative at the witness's business address under reasonable conditions during normal business hours."[25] Where the records are turned over to the subpoenaing party's attorney for copying, that attorney must also provide an affidavit attesting to the genuineness of the copies made from those records.[26]

—Professional Photocopier: Instead of having an attorney carry out the inspection and copying, the subpoena can direct the custodian of the records to deliver a sealed, certified copy of them directly to the "deposition officer."[27] In such cases, the deposition officer must be a professional photocopier.[28] Such a photocopier can neither have a financial interest in the action nor be related to any party's attorney.

Alternatively, the subpoenaing party can arrange to have the records turned over to a professional photocopier at the custodian's place of business. In such

---

[20] CCP § 1985.3(c).

See Inabnit v Berkson (1988) 199 Cal App 3d 1230, 245 Cal Rptr 525.

[21] See CCP § 2025.270. This section thus supersedes the 15 day notice provisions of CCP § 1985.3(b) generally applicable to consumer records subpoenas.

Cf. Reporter's Note to CCP § 2020(d), Proposed Civil Discovery Act of 1986, Appendix D.

[22] CCP §§ 1985.3(b)(2) and (b)(3). In both instances, for mailed service of the notice, the consumer must receive additional time, usually five days, before production can occur. See CCP § 1013.

[23] CCP § 1985.3(g) [consumer may move to quash].

Cf. Babcock v Superior Court (1994) 29 Cal App 4th 721, 725–726, 35 Cal Rptr 2d 462, 465 [nonparty consumer can seek in camera inspection to determine circumstances, if any, of the disclosure of its records]; Lantz v Superior Court (1994) 28 Cal App 4th 1839, 1849–1852, 34 Cal Rptr 358 [a county can be a "subpoenaing party" for purposes of § 1983.5].

[24] CCP § 2020.030.

[25] Evid Code § 1560(e).

[26] Evid Code § 1561(c).

[27] See Evid Code § 1560.

[28] CCP § 2020.420.

cases, the nonparty may choose either to copy the documents itself beforehand, or to let the professional copy them on site.[29] A nonparty who copies the documents itself need not provide a copy in a sealed envelope. However, it can insist on prepayment of its reasonable copying costs.[30]

Proof of Compliance: At the time of compliance with the deposition subpoena, the nonparty who is subject to it must also include an affidavit. This must affirm that: (1) the affiant is the authorized custodian of the documents; (2) the records described in the deposition subpoena, or true copies of them, have been provided; and (3) the documents were prepared in the ordinary course of business at or near the time of the events recorded.[31] In addition, the affidavit must identify the records and describe their mode of preparation.[32] Where the business does not have any or all of the subpoenaed records, the custodian must so state in its affidavit.

Witness Fees and Costs: A party serving a nonparty with a "records only" deposition subpoena must tender the witness fee[33] specified in the Evidence Code:

> Where the records are delivered to the attorney or the attorney's representative for inspection or photocopying at the witness' place of business, the only fee for complying with the subpoena shall not exceed fifteen dollars ($15), plus actual costs, if any, charged to the witness by a third person for retrieval and return of records held offsite by the third person. If the records are retrieved from microfilm, the reasonable cost, as defined in [Evid. Code § 1563(b)(1)], shall also apply.[34]

§ 7.4 Resisting Deposition Subpoena as Oppressive

A nonparty[1] may seek a protective order against production of items sought by a deposition subpoena where compliance with it would cause "unwarranted annoyance, embarrassment, or oppression, or undue burden and expense." Section 2025.420 details a nonexclusive list of protective orders.[2] It includes an order directing that "all or certain of the writings or tangible things designated in the deposition notice need not be produced, inspected or copied."[3]

---

29 CCP § 2020.430.

30 CCP § 2020.230(b), incorporating by reference Evid Code § 1563(b).

31 Evid Code § 1561(a).

32 Evid Code §§ 1562(a)(4) and (5).

33 CCP § 2020.230(b).

34 Evid Code § 1563(b)(6).

1 CCP § 2025.420(a).

2 CCP § 2025.420(b).

3 CCP § 2025.420(b)(11).

See, e.g., Calcor Space Facility, Inc. v Superior Court (1997) 53 Cal App 4th 216, 220, 61 Cal Rptr 2d 567, 570.

The *Monarch Healthcare* case considered whether a nonparty must move either for a protective order or to quash the subpoena in order to preserve an objection to the attempted discovery: "Nonparties *may* file a motion to quash, but is this extra step necessary or may they simply wait and object, putting the onus on the proponent to move to compel?"[4] In answering this question, the court noted that a deponent may avoid waiver of a privilege by objecting during the deposition.[5] It saw no reason to require a nonparty to do more:

> The discovery rules do not discriminate against nonparty deponents. They need not scramble to retain a lawyer to file a motion to quash in order to challenge "records only" discovery requests that seek privileged information. It is sufficient to simply object.[6]

Motion to Quash vs. Protective Order: There is no need for "protection" against a deposition subpoena that seeks irrelevant or privileged items. A nonparty may simply move to quash the subpoena because the items it covers are not discoverable. Protective orders are for situations where there is good reason to deny discovery of items although the items covered by the subpoenas are relevant and nonprivileged.

A federal case, *Hecht v Pro-Football, Inc.,*[7] well illustrates this point. Plaintiffs could not field a rival professional football team because the established league's team had an exclusive lease of the local stadium. In their antitrust action, they served a discovery subpoena upon nonparty club owners in the defendant football league. It directed them to produce financial records that would reveal the purchase price and profitability of their franchises. Additionally, the subpoena directed a former franchise owner to produce records that would reveal the sales price for his franchise. The franchise owners conceded that, if plaintiffs established the league's liability, the subpoenaed documents would help establish the plaintiffs' damages. Nevertheless, the trial judge quashed the subpoena:

> It is possible for a subpoena *duces tecum* to be unreasonable or oppressive, even though the evidence sought to be procured may prove to be thereafter relevant at the trial. . . . [¶] [E]ven if the information is not privileged, and [here] it is not, it may still be oppressive or unreasonable to require disclosure at the taking of a deposition.[8]

---

[4] Monarch Healthcare v Superior Court (2000) 78 Cal App 4th 1282, 1287, 93 Cal Rptr 2d 619, 623 (original italics).

[5] See CCP § 2025.460(a).

[6] Monarch Healthcare v Superior Court (2000) 78 Cal App 4th 1282, 1284, 93 Cal Rptr 2d 619, 621.

[7] Hecht v Pro-Football, Inc. (1969, D DC) 46 FRD 605.

[8] Hecht v Pro-Football, Inc. (1969, D DC) 46 FRD 605, 606–607 (original italics).

See also Valley Bank of Nevada v Superior Court (1975) 15 Cal 3d 652, 655–656, 125 Cal Rptr 553, 554–555, 542 P2d 977, 978–979 [applying the same principle to resist production of records by a party].

Criteria for Protective Orders: "Unwarranted annoyance, embarrassment, or oppression, or undue burden and expense" is necessarily vague. The concerns it embodies cannot be reduced to a legal yardstick. A survey of the many cases that have arisen under comparable provisions, however, reveals several common factors that judges employ when deciding if a nonparty has shown sufficient "oppression."

—Level of Relevance: First, the *level* of relevance of the items sought may influence courts in their evaluation of "oppression." For example, some deposition subpoenas may seek information only marginally relevant to the lawsuit's general *subject matter*. In such cases, judges will be slower to require nonparties to produce the information than they would be if faced with a comparable production request directed to a party:

> It is not at this point clear whether the same broad test for relevance of documents will be utilized with respect to third parties. There appear to be quite strong considerations indicating that the discovery would be more limited to protect third parties from harassment, inconvenience, or disclosure of confidential documents.[9]

At the other extreme, when the information sought is highly relevant to an issue critical to the lawsuit, courts may require a nonparty to carry a heavy burden to obtain protection against it: "Inconvenience to third parties may be outweighed by the public interest in seeking the truth in every litigated case."[10]

—Contingent Relevance: The subpoena may seek information quite relevant to an *issue* in the lawsuit. Nevertheless, if resolution of that issue may turn out to be unnecessary, the courts will hesitate before ordering the nonparty to produce it. In particular, courts hesitate to order nonparties to produce information relevant to damages where liability in the case seems shaky, or where a settlement of the suit is likely:

> This information can be obtained at the trial if the trial progresses to a point where it becomes relevant. It seems oppressive and unreasonable to require these [third] persons to disclose this information in advance when many things may happen between now and the trial that might make the disclosure unnecessary.[11]

---

[9] Collins and Aikman Corp. v J. P. Stevens and Co. (1971, D SC) 51 FRD 219, 221.

[10] Covey Oil Co. v Continental Oil Co. (1965, CA10 Utah) 340 F2d 993, 999.

See also Westinghouse Electric Corp. v City of Burlington (1965, CADC) 351 F2d 762, 767; United States v American Optical Co. (1966, ND Cal) 39 FRD 580, 586.

[11] Hecht v Pro-Football, Inc. (1969, D DC) 46 FRD 605, 607.

See also Rifkind v Superior Court (1981) 123 Cal App 3d 1045, 1051–1052, 177 Cal Rptr 82, 85 [deferring discovery of "good will" value of husband's law practice through production of his partners' compensation records until after resolution of wife's community property interest in the practice].

—**Importance of the Lawsuit:** Courts also consider the importance of the factual and legal issues presented by the particular lawsuit. In cases involving either substantial sums of money or issues of far-reaching significance, courts more willingly require nonparties to shoulder heavy burdens to provide the desired information:

> This massive discovery process is intended to provide economic data and other information essential to the proper resolution of this action, which has been characterized as one of the most important and complex antitrust cases in history. . . . This is not an action between private litigants seeking to resolve personal grievances. It is a major antitrust suit brought on behalf of all the people.[12]

—**Extent and Cost of Compliance:** Courts also consider both the extent and the costs of compliance. The volume of requests,[13] and the expense of file searches and document assembly[14] may suggest oppression. Neither factor, however, is dispositive. In appropriate cases, courts will order nonparties to produce voluminous records.[15] For sufficiently important information, courts will order them to carry out costly and time-consuming searches.[16] Often, the court's power to force the subpoenaing party to pay the search costs will mitigate against a finding of oppression.[17]

—**Alternatives Available:** Where production of the requested materials would force a nonparty to search through voluminous files, the subpoenaing party may have to content itself with the witness's generalized oral testimony about the matters contained in the records. For example, in the *Allen* case,[18] a personal

[12] United States v International Business Machines Corp. (1974, SD NY) 62 FRD 526, 528–529.

[13] See, e.g., Calcor Space Facility, Inc. v Superior Court (1997) 53 Cal App 4th 216, 220, 61 Cal Rptr 2d 567, 570 [thousands of nonparty's records fell within the broad categories in deposition subpoena duces tecum]; Premium Service Corp. v Sperry & Hutchinson Co. (1975, CA9 Cal) 511 F2d 225, 229.

[14] See, e.g., Calcor Space Facility, Inc. v Superior Court (1997) 53 Cal App 4th 216, 220, 61 Cal Rptr 2d 567, 570 [compliance with deposition subpoena duces tecum would require full-time efforts of two of the nonparty's employees for at least two and one-half weeks]; Allen v Superior Court (1984) 151 Cal App 3d 447, 198 Cal Rptr 737 [defense medical expert need not search through voluminous patient files to dig out those that involved examinations made at behest of defense bar or insurance companies].

[15] See, e.g., Democratic Nat. Committee v McCord (1973, D DC) 356 F Supp 1394, 1396.

[16] See, e.g., United States v International Business Machines Corp. (1976, CD NY) 71 FRD 88, 92 [nonparty ordered to comply with a subpoena duces tecum even though it would take from three to six months and cost tens of thousands of dollars to do so].

[17] See, e.g., Collins and Aikman Corp. v J. P. Stevens and Co. (1971, D SC) 51 FRD 219, 221.

See also FRCivP 45(c)(3)(B)(iii) [court may condition denial of a motion to quash a subpoena upon adequate assurances that the subpoenaing party will "assure that the person to whom the subpoena is addressed will be reasonably compensated"].

[18] Allen v Superior Court (1984) 151 Cal App 3d 447, 198 Cal Rptr 737.

injury plaintiff had submitted to a medical examination by a defense doctor. To help show this physician's possible bias, plaintiff's lawyers then subpoenaed the doctor's records in all other cases where he had examined people for the defense bar and insurance companies. The appellate court found that the plaintiff's ability to get this information by deposing the doctor, instead of forcing him to make the extensive search required to produce these records, justified reversal of the trial court's enforcement of the subpoena:

> The court abused its discretion when it failed to require a less intrusive method of discovery. [¶] At deposition, the medical expert may be asked questions directed toward disclosing what percentage of his practice involves examining patients for the defense and how much compensation he derives from defense work. To show bias or prejudice, [the plaintiff] need not learn the details of his billing and accounting or the specifics of his prior testimony and depositions.[19]

—Sensitive Information: "Oppression" may also result from a demand for sensitive or confidential information. For example, corporate parties frequently will subpoena a competitor to produce the sort of market and pricing data that businesses prefer to keep private. Normally, courts are "most reluctant to force a non-party competitor to divulge confidential information."[20] Nevertheless, sometimes the party's substantial and legitimate need for the data will lead the court to allow the discovery.

For example, *Covey Oil Co. v Continental Oil Co.*[21] involved an antitrust suit against a wholesale gas marketer. To justify its pricing practices, the defendant claimed that it was simply matching in good faith its competitors' prices. The defendant subpoenaed the purchasing, pricing, and sales volume records of a nonparty rival. Since establishing its competitor's marketplace conduct was essential to the defense, the appellate court upheld the trial court's refusal to quash the subpoena.

In such situations, Section 2025.420 allows a court to structure disclosure to minimize the dangers to the nonparty.[22] The court may order the information sealed. It may allow only counsel or independent accountants to access the

---

19 Allen v Superior Court (1984) 151 Cal App 3d 447, 453, 198 Cal Rptr 737, 741.

See also Calcor Space Facility, Inc. v Superior Court (1997) 53 Cal App 4th 216, 225, 61 Cal Rptr 2d 567, 573 ["As between parties to litigation and nonparties, the burden of discovery should be placed on the latter only if the former do not possess the material sought to be discovered."]

20 United States v Serta Associates, Inc. (1961, ND Ill) 29 FRD 136, 138.

21 Covey Oil Co. v Continental Oil Co. (1965, CA10 Utah) 340 F2d 993.

22 CCP § 2025.420(b)(13)–(15).

See, e.g., Covey Oil Co. v Continental Oil Co. (1965, CA10 Utah) 340 F2d 993, 999; United States v American Optical Co. (1966, ND Cal) 39 FRD 580, 587; but see People v Superior Court (1967) 248 Cal App 2d 276, 56 Cal Rptr 393.

Cf. Note: Trade Secrets in Discovery: From First Amendment Disclosure to Fifth Amendment Protection (1991) 104 Harvard LR 1330.

information. In addition, it can prohibit the information's use for purposes other than the litigation, restrict unnecessary copying, and order the records returned at the case's conclusion.

—Consumer Records: Courts are also sensitive to the normal desires of individuals not to reveal information relating to their personal or financial affairs:

> [T]hese requests seek private financial records of persons who are not parties to this litigation. . . . The right of privacy and the right to keep confidential one's financial affairs is well recognized. It seems to be part of human nature not to desire to disclose them.[23]

As discussed in the previous two sections,[24] the Discovery Act's provisions for nonparty discovery incorporate by reference Section 1985.3.[25] That statute sets up a procedure to notify designated "consumers" (e.g., patients, depositors, insureds) about a litigant's attempt to subpoena the records of the consumer's transactions with certain professionals and organizations. Section 1985.3 lets consumers who are parties to the action in which the subpoena is served seek a court order quashing or modifying the subpoena if it intrudes unnecessarily on their privacy rights.[26] Nonparty consumers need simply to serve a written objection that specifies the grounds for opposition.[27] The requesting party has 20 days from the service of the objection to move for an order enforcing the subpoena.[28]

§ 7.5 Inspection of Nonparty's Land or Premises

Most discovery from nonparties seeks only their testimony or access to their documents and tangible items of personal property. Occasionally, however, a party may wish to inspect a nonparty's land or business premises.[1]

Examples: In a product liability case, an employee injured at work by allegedly defective machinery may sue the equipment manufacturer. During the suit against

---

[23] Hecht v Pro-Football, Inc. (1969, D DC) 46 FRD 605.

See also Valley Bank of Nevada v Superior Court (1975) 15 Cal 3d 652, 125 Cal Rptr 553, 542 P2d 977 [nonparty consumers must have notice before parties to a suit can disclose documents that record the party's business transactions with the consumers].

[24] For a further discussion of CCP § 1985.3, see §§ 7.2–7.3.

[25] CCP §§ 2020.410(d) and 2020.510(c).

[26] See, e.g., Lantz v Superior Court (1994) 28 Cal App 4th 1839, 1849–1852, 34 Cal Rptr 2d 358, 364–366 [a county can be a "subpoenaing party" for purposes of § 1983.5].

[27] CCP § 1983.5(g).

[28] CCP § 1983.5(g).

[1] Annotation: Discovery and inspection of article or premises the condition of which is alleged to have caused personal injury or death. 13 ALR2d 657.

Annotation: Discovery and inspection of article and premises in civil actions other than for personal injury or death. 4 ALR3d 762.

Annotation: Independent action against nonparty for production of documents and things or permission to enter upon land [FRCivP 34(c)]. 62 ALR Fed 935.

the manufacturer, the employee may want access to the employer's premises to examine the machine itself.[2] In air crash litigation, either side may want to inspect the crash site. In environmental cases, the parties may wish to test the soil or water of adjacent land to trace the cause of the alleged pollution. In condemnation cases, an appraisal of nearby land may help value the condemned land. In a slip-and-fall case, after the accident a nonparty may have leased or bought the land or premises where the injury occurred.[3]

No Express Provision: Like the 1956 Discovery Act,[4] the current Civil Discovery Act does not expressly authorize a court to compel nonparties to open their land or buildings for pretrial inspection. Section 2020.020 only authorizes deposition subpoenas for "business records, documents, and tangible things."[5] In this regard, California differs from the current federal procedure.[6]

Independent Action: A party seeking access to a nonparty's land may consider filing an independent action in the nature of an equity bill of discovery. For example, in *Griesa v Mutual Life Ins.,*[7] a life insurance company believed that its insured had deliberately poisoned himself. The company anticipated a suit by the insured's executors to collect on a policy that excluded suicide from its coverage. The company filed a bill of discovery against the insured's widow. She owned the cemetery lot where he was buried. The company obtained a court order to exhume and examine the insured's body for traces of poison. Since the exhumation had already been carried out by the time the case reached the appellate court, it declined to rule on the propriety of this use of the bill of discovery.[8]

In *Wofford v Ethyl Corporation,*[9] the South Carolina Supreme Court allowed presuit discovery of a nonparty's business premises. There, the plaintiff's

---

[2] See, e.g., Humphries v Pennsylvania R. Co. (1953, D Ohio) 14 FRD 177, 181.

[3] These examples have been adapted from those in Note, Rule 34(c) and Discovery of Nonparty Land (1975) 85 Yale LJ 112, 113.

Cf. Bullen v Superior Court (1988) 204 Cal App 3d 22, 251 Cal Rptr 32 [where a murder defendant failed to show "good cause" and "plausible justification" for an order directing the victim's widow to grant the defendant access to the murder site, the appellate court left unresolved the trial court's power to make such an order].

[4] See former CCP § 2031, 1956 Discovery Act, Appendix E.

[5] CCP § 2020.020(c).

[6] As amended in 1991, FRCivP 34(c) incorporates the nonparty discovery provisions of FRCivP 45, which authorize "inspection of [a nonparty's] premises." See FRCivP 45(a)(1)(C).

Two states who have not otherwise adopted the Federal Rules authorize such inspections. See NY Civil Practice Law § 3120(b); Okla Court Rule 12.

[7] Griesa v Mutual Life Ins. (1909, CA8 Kan) 169 F 509.

[8] Griesa v Mutual Life Ins. (1909, CA8 Kan) 169 F 509, 512–513.

See also Lubrin v Hess Oil Virgin Islands Corp. (1986, D VI) 109 FRD 403 [employer ordered to permit injured employee's inspection of property to determine proper party for possible third party claim].

[9] Wofford v Ethyl Corporation (1994, So Car) 447 SE2d 187.

decedent had died after a fatal on-the-job injury at his employer's plant. To help decide whether the estate had a potential claim against someone other than the employer, the estate's administrator sought to inspect the employer's plant. The state version of Federal Rule 34 then in effect authorized no such inspection.[10] After the employer denied the request, the administrator filed an independent action to compel the requested inspection. In upholding an order allowing the inspection, the court concluded: "[M]odern discovery rules . . . do not totally displace the traditional equitable jurisdiction of the court to issue appropriate orders for independent discovery when effective discovery cannot otherwise be obtained and the ends of justice served."[11]

—Reform Needed: To date, no reported California decision has considered the availability of such independent equitable actions.[12] The Legislature should make this question moot. It should follow the recent federal example and fill the statutory gap by making controlled access to nonparty "premises" a feature of the California civil discovery system.

---

[10] Wofford v Ethyl Corporation (1994, So Car) 447 SE2d 187, 189 n1. South Carolina later adopted the 1991 changes to FRCivP 34(c) that expressly incorporate the nonparty land inspection provisions of FRCivP 45.

[11] Wofford v Ethyl Corporation (1994, So Car) 447 SE2d 187, 189.

Cf. Shorey v Lincoln Pulp and Paper Co. (1986, Maine) 511 A2d 1076, 1078 [courts retain traditional equitable powers to enter independent discovery orders].

[12] For a discussion of the feasibility of using a bill of discovery to achieve inspection of a nonparty's land, see Note, Rule 34(c) and Discovery of Nonparty Land (1975) 85 Yale LJ 112, 114–119.

CHAPTER 8

MEDICAL EXAMINATIONS: PHYSICAL AND MENTAL

SYNOPSIS

§ 8.1   History of Compulsory Medical Examinations

Early California Practice: In 1956, by including a provision for compulsory medical examinations in the original Discovery Act, the Legislature was simply codifying a discovery tool already well established in California case law. A half century earlier, in *Johnston v Southern Pacific Co.*,[1] the Supreme Court had approved this form of discovery for civil litigation. In that case, a passenger

---

[1] Johnston v Southern Pacific Co. (1907) 150 Cal 535, 89 P 348.

alleged that she had sustained a severe head injury when the train from which she was alighting moved suddenly. The railroad asked the trial court to order the plaintiff to submit to a physical examination by two doctors it had selected. Believing itself powerless to make such an order, the trial court denied the motion. The Supreme Court, after canvassing the authorities from other states, adopted the majority view that "courts have the power to order such examinations and should exercise it with a sound discretion."[2] Otherwise, the Court felt, the defendant would be at the mercy of the plaintiff's medical witnesses, an injustice that must be avoided even at the expense of "the refined and delicate feelings of the plaintiff."[3]

Early Federal Practice: In contrast, the adoption in 1938 of Federal Rule of Civil Procedure 35, which later became the model for Section 2032 of the original Discovery Act, departed radically from then-existing federal practice. In 1891, in *Union Pacific R. Co. v Botsford*,[4] the defendant had sought to compel the plaintiff "to submit to a surgical examination as to the extent of the injury sued for."[5] Seven members of the United States Supreme Court were horrified that "the right of every individual to the possession and control of his own person"[6] might be invaded simply because that person had sued to recover for bodily injury:

> The inviolability of the person is as much invaded by a compulsory stripping and exposure as by a blow. To compel anyone, and especially a woman, to lay bare the body, or to submit to the touch of a stranger, without lawful authority, is an indignity, an assault and a trespass . . . .[7]

The Court's other two members viewed the issue less prudishly and more practically:

> The end of litigation is justice. Knowledge of the truth is essential thereto. . . . It is said that there is a sanctity of the person which may not be outraged. We believe that truth and justice are more sacred than any personal consideration.[8]

---

[2] Johnston v Southern Pacific Co. (1907) 150 Cal 535, 541, 89 P 348, 351.

[3] Johnston v Southern Pacific Co. (1907) 150 Cal 535, 542, 89 P 348, 351.

For other pre-1956 cases, see Melone v Sierra R. Co. (1907) 151 Cal 113, 91 P 522; Anderson v United Stages, Inc. (1923) 192 Cal 250, 219 P 748; Lawrence v Pickwick Stages, Inc. (1924) 68 Cal App 494, 229 P 885; Laubscher v Blake (1935) 7 Cal App 2d 376, 46 P2d 836; Dodge v San Diego E. R. Co. (1949) 92 Cal App 2d 759, 208 P2d 37; Sharff v Superior Court (1955) 44 Cal 2d 508, 282 P2d 896.

[4] Union Pacific R. Co. v Botsford (1891) 141 US 250, 35 L Ed 734, 11 S Ct 1000.

[5] Union Pacific R. Co. v Botsford (1891) 141 US 250, 251, 35 L Ed 734, 737, 11 S Ct 1000, 1001.

[6] Union Pacific R. Co. v Botsford (1891) 141 US 250, 251, 35 L Ed 734, 737, 11 S Ct 1000, 1001.

[7] Union Pacific R. Co. v Botsford (1891) 141 US 250, 252, 35 L Ed 734, 737, 11 S Ct 1000, 1001.

[8] Union Pacific R. Co. v Botsford (1891) 141 US 250, 258–259, 35 L Ed 734, 740, 11 S Ct 1000, 1003–1004 (dissenting opinion).

A few years later, the Court retreated somewhat from *Botsford*. It ruled that in diversity cases, a federal court could compel a medical examination if the statutes of the state in which the federal court sat authorized one.[9]

Against this background, it is not surprising that a challenge to Federal Rule of Civil Procedure 35 occurred almost immediately after it took effect. In *Sibbach v Wilson & Co.*,[10] a personal injury plaintiff contended that Rule 35 broke so sharply with the former policy that it abridged a litigant's "substantive rights." Such a step, plaintiff argued, violated the statute[11] that authorized the Federal Rules: "The [plaintiff] says the phrase 'substantive rights' connotes more; that by its use Congress intended that in regulating procedure this court should not deal with important and substantial rights theretofore recognized."[12] By a 5-4 vote, the United States Supreme Court rejected this attack: "If we were to adopt the suggested criterion of the importance of the alleged right, we should invite endless litigation and confusion worse compounded."[13]

The dissenters acknowledged that "the immunity [of one's person] that was recognized in the *Botsford* case has no constitutional sanction."[14] Nevertheless, they insisted that the regard for the "inviolability of a person" that had inspired that decision has "such historic roots in Anglo-American law" that any curtailment of it as intrusive as Rule 35 required crystal-clear statutory authorization.[15]

§ 8.2   Who May Be Examined

Examination of Plaintiffs: The obvious candidates for court-ordered medical examinations are personal injury plaintiffs. Their very claims ask the court to resolve issues concerning their medical condition. Section 2032.020,[1] however, authorizes a medical examination of *any* type of plaintiff whose medical condition is in controversy. Thus, in a paternity case, the mother may be directed to undergo a blood test.[2] And in a libel case based on defamatory assertions concerning

---

[9] Camden & S. R. Co. v Stetson (1900) 177 US 172, 44 L Ed 721, 20 S Ct 617.

[10] Sibbach v Wilson & Co. (1941) 312 US 1, 85 L Ed 479, 61 S Ct 422.

[11] See The Rules Enabling Act, ch. 651, 48 Stat. 1064 (1934).

[12] Sibbach v Wilson & Co. (1941) 312 US 1, 13, 85 L Ed 479, 485, 61 S Ct 422, 426.

[13] Sibbach v Wilson & Co. (1941) 312 US 1, 13, 85 L Ed 479, 485, 61 S Ct 422, 426.

[14] Sibbach v Wilson & Co. (1941) 312 US 1, 17, 85 L Ed 479, 487, 61 S Ct 422, 428 (dissenting opinion).

[15] Sibbach v Wilson & Co. (1941) 312 US 1, 17, 85 L Ed 479, 487, 61 S Ct 422, 428 (dissenting opinion).

[1] CCP § 2032.020(a).

[2] Beach v Beach (1940, DC Cir) 114 F2d 479.

See CCP § 2032.010.

See also Monroe v Monroe (1993, Md) 621 A2d 898, 902–905 [in custody dispute, mother's right to compel ex-husband to submit to blood test to disprove paternity].

Annotation: Admissibility or compellability of blood tests to establish testee's nonpaternity for purpose of challenging testee's parental rights. 87 ALR 4th 572.

the plaintiff's medical condition, the defendant may obtain a medical examination to help establish the affirmative defense of "truth."[3]

The examinee, however, must be more than a nominal party to the action. For example, courts will not routinely order a guardian ad litem to submit to a medical examination:

> A guardian ad litem would not necessarily be a parent of the minor. The legal incapacity of a minor which requires he have an adult representative to pursue his interests offers no justification for ordering such a guardian to submit to the invasion of his body or intimate mental processes.[4]

Similarly, merely attaching the label "real party in interest" to an individual will not convert a nonparty into a party for purposes of compelling a medical examination.[5]

Examination of Defendants: Section 20632.020, like its prototype, Federal Rule of Civil Procedure 35, reaches beyond a lawsuit's original protagonists. It allows a compulsory medical examination "of a *party* to the action."[6] Thus where a defendant's physical or mental condition is "in controversy" in the case,[7] and a plaintiff has made a showing of "good cause" for a medical examination,[8] a court may compel a defendant to submit to one.[9] Most commonly, a court will order an eye test.[10] Similarly, upon a proper showing, a defendant may obtain

---

[3] Cf. Beach v Beach (1940, DC Cir) 114 F2d 479, disapproving Wadlow v Humberd (1939, D Mo) 27 F Supp 210.

[4] Reuter v Superior Court (1979) 93 Cal App 3d 332, 344, 155 Cal Rptr 525, 533.

See also Cruz v Superior Court (2004) 121 Cal App 4th 646, 651, 17 Cal Rptr 3d 368, 371; Scharf v United States Atty. Gen. (1979, CA9 Cal) 597 F2d 1240, 1243; Fong Sik Leung v Dulles (1955, CA9 Cal) 226 F2d 74, 76.

[5] T.R. v Cora Priest's Day Care Center (1993, Wash App) 847 P2d 33, 34–35 [parents of plaintiff children were not "parties" subject to compelled examination despite defendant's claim that they were the "real parties in interest"].

[6] CCP § 2032.020(a) (italics added).

[7] For a discussion of when a defendant's *physical* condition is "in controversy," see § 8.4.

For a discussion of when a party's *mental* condition is "in controversy," see § 8.5.

[8] For a discussion of what constitutes "good cause" for a compulsory medical examination, see §§ 8.6–8.8.

[9] Schlagenhauf v Holder (1964) 379 US 104, 114, 13 L Ed 2d 152, 161, 85 S Ct 234, 240.

See, e.g., Ranft v Lyons (1991, Wis App) 471 NW2d 254, 259 [driver who claims ability to resist alcohol-induced impairment despite a blood-alcohol level of .18 ordered to submit to physical examination].

Annotation: Physical examination of allegedly negligent person with respect to defect claimed to have caused or contributed to accident. 89 ALR2d 1001.

[10] Harabedian v Superior Court (1961) 195 Cal App 2d 26, 15 Cal Rptr 420.

See also Schlagenhauf v Holder (1964) 379 US 104, 121, 13 L Ed 2d 152, 165, 85 S Ct 234, 244.

the examination of a third-party defendant.[11]

Examinee Need Not Be an Adversary: As long as the examinee is a party, the one seeking the examination and the examinee need not be adversaries in the lawsuit. In *Schlagenhauf v Holder*,[12] for example, plaintiffs had been injured when the bus in which they were riding collided with the rear end of a slowly moving truck. They sued the bus company, the truck owner, and both drivers. When the bus company cross-claimed against the truck owner for the damage to its bus, the cross-defendant moved for a medical examination of the bus driver, who it maintained was the one at fault. Although the bus driver was a party to the suit brought by the passengers, he was not a party to the cross-claim. Nevertheless, the United States Supreme Court considered that, upon a proper showing of "good cause," the trial court could compel him to submit to a discovery medical examination:

> Rule 35 only requires that the person to be examined be a party to the "action," not that he be an opposing party vis-a-vis the movant. . . . Insistence that the movant have filed a pleading against the person to be examined would have the undesirable result of an unnecessary proliferation of cross-claims and counterclaims and would not be in keeping with the aims of a liberal, nontechnical application of the Federal Rules.[13]

Examination of Nonparty Minors, Spouses, and Agents: In two respects, Section 2032.020 extends beyond the actual parties to the litigation. First, it reaches one who is "in the custody or under the legal control of a party."[14] In adding like language to Federal Rule of Civil Procedure 35 in 1970, the Advisory Committee noted: "The amendment will settle beyond doubt that a parent or guardian suing to recover for injuries to a minor may be ordered to produce the minor for examination."[15] And arguably, when one spouse seeks damages for the loss of consortium of the other spouse, the other spouse is under the "control" of the one filing the action.[16]

Second, Section 2032.020, going beyond its federal model, expressly empowers the court to order a medical examination of "an agent of a party."[17] Under

---

[11] Smith v Servicemen's Group, Inc. (1989, ND Ind) 124 FRD 195 [defendant life insurance company, sued for policy proceeds by one claiming to be the child of its insured, impleaded insured's parents who had received those proceeds when they claimed that he was childless; defendant was entitled to compel the parents to submit to blood test to determine the validity of plaintiff's claim].

[12] Schlagenhauf v Holder (1964) 379 US 104, 13 L Ed 2d 152, 85 S Ct 234.

[13] Schlagenhauf v Holder (1964) 379 US 104, 115–116, 13 L Ed 2d 152, 162, 85 S Ct 234, 241.

[14] CCP § 2032.020(a).

[15] 1970 Advisory Committee Note to amended FRCivP 35(a).

[16] Annotation: Power to require physical examination of injured person in action by his parent or spouse to recover for his injury. 62 ALR2d 1291.

[17] CCP § 2032.020(a)

the California version, the trial court could order a defendant corporation, sued for its employee's alleged negligence, to produce that employee for a compulsory medical examination, even if the employee is not a party to the suit. In the *Cruz* case,[18] an action for medical malpractice brought on behalf of a child for alleged negligence during its mother's pregnancy and delivery, the court ruled that the mother is an "agent" of the child. Thus, she could be required to provide a specimen of her blood:

> We do not hold that a parent is always to be treated as the child's agent for discovery purposes. But here mother and plaintiff were contemporaneously under the care of [defendants hospital and doctor], and plaintiff's malpractice claim includes charges that his injury resulted in part from the manner in which [defendants] treated mother during her pregnancy and delivery. Furthermore, in her capacity as plaintiff's mother, she has a definable economic interest in the outcome of the suit. If plaintiff is successful in obtaining a monetary award, mother's financial burdens will be lessened.[19]

However, a court may not sanction nonparty minors, spouses or agents who refuse to undergo a court-ordered medical examination. In such event, the sanction would run against the party who has custody or control of those individuals or who is their principal. Even then that party could avoid the sanction by "demonstrat[ing] an inability to produce that person for examination."[20]

Discovery from Other Nonparties: No matter how central a person's physical or mental condition is to a particular lawsuit, a court may only order the examination of those individuals that the statute specifies. The *Reuter* case, for example, held that the trial court lacks the power to compel the mother of an injured minor plaintiff to undergo psychological testing:

> [I]t would be inappropriate for this court to expand the classes of persons who may be compelled to submit to intimate examinations. . . . [A]n examination ordered outside the scope of section 2032, and unsupported by other authority, possibly would violate a person's constitutionally protected right of privacy.[21]

The absence of a similar provision in FRCivP 35 prevents the federal courts from ordering a medical examination of a litigant's employee. Clark v Geiger (1962, ED Pa) 31 FRD 268, 270; Kropp v General Dynamics Corp. (1962, ED Mich) 202 F Supp 207.

[18] Cruz v Superior Court (2004) 121 Cal App 4th 646, 17 Cal Rptr 3d 368.

[19] Cruz v Superior Court (2004) 121 Cal App 4th 646, 652, 17 Cal Rptr 3d 368, 372.

[20] CCP § 2032.420.

See also Estate of Sanders (1992) 2 Cal App 4th 462, 468–469, 3 Cal Rptr 2d 536, 539 [in proceeding to establish heirship, the court is without power to order the two mothers of the decedent's children, neither of whom was a party to the probate proceeding, to provide blood samples for DNA testing].

[21] Reuter v Superior Court (1979) 93 Cal App 3d 332, 343, 155 Cal Rptr 525, 532.

See also William M. v Superior Court (1990) 225 Cal App 3d 447, 451, 275 Cal Rptr 103,

Examination of Corpses: Although a decedent's physical or mental condition may be in controversy in a lawsuit, his corpse is not a party to a probate action. The *Holm* case[22] held that Section 2032 of the Discovery Act of 1956 did not authorize the exhumation of the corpse for an autopsy:

> [T]he legislature, in enacting [former Section 2032], contemplated its application to requests for examinations of *living* persons. Furthermore, we see no way the express terms of the statute, even if liberally construed, could be found to encompass the body of decedent. The corpse is obviously not a "party" to the probate court action, nor can it be considered a "person."[23]

§ 8.3 Procedure for Obtaining Medical Examinations

Litigants initiate the other five discovery methods[1] extrajudicially, i.e., simply by giving notice to counsel for the other parties to the lawsuit. In contrast, discovery by compulsory medical examinations is self-executing in only two circumstances. First, the parties may always *agree* to the ground rules for a medical examination. Second, in a narrow, but common situation, a defendant may *demand* an examination of a plaintiff. In all other situations, a party must file a formal *motion*.

Examinations by Agreement: Often a litigant's medical condition will be so obviously an issue that both sides will recognize that discovery via medical examination is appropriate. In these situations, the parties may simply agree to the arrangements for the examination without troubling the trial court. These agreements most often occur when five circumstances coincide: (1) the action involves only physical injuries; (2) the examinee is the plaintiff; (3) defendant

---

105 [putative grandparents in paternity action may not be compelled to submit to a blood test, even though their son, the putative father, is dead]; Scharf v United States Atty. Gen. (1979, CA9 Cal) 597 F2d 1240, 1243 [in a proceeding seeking a declaration of citizenship, government may not compel plaintiff's putative father and mother to undergo blood testing]. Cf. Cruz v Superior Court (2004) 121 Cal App 4th 646, 652, 17 Cal Rptr 3d 368, 372 [in a child's malpractice action against the doctor and hospital that cared for his mother during pregnancy and delivery, his mother was ordered to submit to a blood test on the theory that she was the child's agent]; Smith v Servicemen's Group, Inc. (1989, ND Ind) 124 FRD 195 [defendant life insurance company, sued for policy proceeds by one claiming to be the child of its insured, impleaded insured's parents who had received those proceeds when they claimed he was childless; defendant was entitled to compel parents to submit to a blood test to determine the validity of the plaintiff's claim].

22 Holm v Superior Court (1986) 187 Cal App 3d 1241, 232 Cal Rptr 432.

23 Holm v Superior Court (1986) 187 Cal App 3d 1241, 1248, 232 Cal Rptr 432, 437 (original italics).

A federal trial court has taken the opposite view. In re Certain Asbestos Cases (1986, ND Tex) 112 FRD 427, 113 FRD 612. Cf. Walsh v Caidin (1991) 232 Cal App 3d 159, 283 Cal Rptr 326 [defendants in medical malpractice have no cause of action against plaintiff-widow because her decision to cremate their deceased patient's remains has precluded an autopsy].

For a discussion of whether a corpse may be the subject of an *inspection demand*, see § 6.9.

1 Depositions, interrogatories, inspection demands, admission requests and exchanges of expert witness information.

seeks only a physical examination; (4) the examination will be routine; and (5) the examination will occur near the examinee's residence.[2] This agreement, like any other stipulation modifying the statutory procedures, must be written.[3]

—Agreements Encouraged: In four ways, the statutes encourage parties to agree to discovery medical examinations. First, they must meet and confer before seeking a court-ordered one.[4] Second, the sanctions for an examinee's failure to submit to an examination also apply to one arranged by agreement.[5] Third, Section 2032.610 extends the right to get a report from the examiner to examinations arranged by agreement.[6] Thus, the scope of the reciprocal right to medical reports does not depend upon the method used to obtain the examination.[7] Finally, the defendant's right, discussed below, to demand the most common type of medical examination should discourage pointless refusals to consent.

Examinations by Demand: The Discovery Commission identified one situation where a party almost always should obtain discovery by medical examination. This is where: (1) the action involves personal injuries; (2) the examinee is the plaintiff; (3) defendant seeks only a physical examination; (4) no previous examination has been obtained; (5) the examination will be routine; and (6) it will occur within 75 miles of the plaintiff's residence.[8] The Commission recommended that in these circumstances the defense should not have to get judicial permission for an initial physical examination if it cannot arrange one by agreement. The Legislature adopted the essence of the Commission' recommendations: Section 2032.220 allows a defendant or cross-defendant[9] to demand[10] that a plaintiff or cross-complainant[11] submit to one physical

---

[2] See, e.g., Queen of Angels Hospital v Superior Court (1976) 57 Cal App 3d 370, 129 Cal Rptr 282; Jorgensen v Superior Court (1958) 163 Cal App 2d 513, 329 P2d 550; Grover v Superior Court (1958) 161 Cal App 2d 644, 327 P2d 212.

[3] CCP § 2016.030.

[4] CCP § 2032.310(b), referencing CCP § 2016.040.

[5] CCP § 2032.410.

For a discussion of the sanctions for failure to appear for or to submit to a compulsory medical examination, see § 8.20.

[6] CCP § 2032.610(a).

For a discussion of the examinee's right to a report of a compulsory medical examination, see § 8.18.

For a discussion of the examining party's reciprocal right to the examinee's medical reports, see § 8.19.

[7] See Queen of Angels Hospital v Superior Court (1976) 57 Cal App 3d 370, 129 Cal Rptr 282; Jorgensen v Superior Court (1958) 163 Cal App 2d 513, 329 P2d 550; Grover v Superior Court (1958) 161 Cal App 2d 644, 327 P2d 212.

[8] See Reporter's Note to Section 2032(c) of Proposed Civil Discovery Act of 1986, Appendix D.

[9] CCP § 2032.210.

[10] A copy of the demand must be served on all parties who have appeared in the action. CCP § 2032.220(e).

[11] CCP § 2032.210.

examination. Defendants may demand a physical examination as soon as they are served.[12] If they learn about the suit before they have been served, they may appear and simultaneously serve a demand.[13]

—Contents of Demand: The demand must "specify the time, place, manner, conditions, scope, and nature of the examination, and also the identity and specialty, if any, of the physician who will make the examination."[14] The demanding party may not schedule the examination sooner than 30 days from service of the demand.[15]

—Response to Demand: After service of a demand, the plaintiff must respond in writing. The response must take one of three forms: (1) a full acquiescence in the demand; (2) an assent subject to specified modifications; or (3) a refusal to comply with the demand, accompanied by a specific statement of the reasons for noncompliance.[16] The plaintiff must serve the response within 20 days after service of the demand for the examination.[17]

A plaintiff should always respond to a demand for a medical examination. By ignoring a demand, a plaintiff waives all objections to it.[18] The trial court may relieve a party from this waiver. The motion for this relief, however, must represent that the plaintiff has by then served a response.[19] In addition, the delinquent party must also persuade the trial court that the failure to respond timely was attributable to "mistake, inadvertence, or excusable neglect."[20] In any event, the delinquent party should expect to pay a monetary sanction unless it convinces the trial judge that "substantial justification" excused its tardiness.[21]

—Judicial Intervention: If the defense deems "unwarranted" any modification or refusal contained in the response, it must seek trial court intervention. Before doing so, defense counsel must try to "meet and confer" with plaintiff's attorney to try to resolve the dispute informally.[22] If no informal resolution

---

[12] CCP § 2032.220(b).

[13] CCP § 2032.220(b).

See Putnam v Clague (1992) 3 Cal App 4th 542, 565, 5 Cal Rptr 2d 25, 39–40.

[14] CCP § 2032.220(c).

[15] CCP § 2032.220(d).

Service of the demand by mail extends by five days the earliest time for the examination. CCP § 2016.050, referencing CCP § 1013(a). The trial court may shorten or enlarge this period. CCP § 2032.220(d).

[16] CCP § 2032.230(a).

[17] CCP § 2032.230(b).

Service of the demand by mail extends by five days the time for service of the response. CCP § 2016.050, referencing CCP § 1013(a). The trial court may shorten or enlarge this period. CCP § 2032.230(b).

[18] CCP § 2032.240(a).

[19] CCP § 2032.240(a)(1).

[20] CCP § 2032.240(a)(2).

[21] CCP § 2032.240(c).

[22] CCP § 2032.250(a).

occurs, and the defendant successfully moves to compel compliance with the demand, the court may impose a monetary sanction on the plaintiff.[23] If the plaintiff acquiesces initially in the demand, but later fails to submit to the examination, the court may sanction the plaintiff as if the plaintiff had disobeyed a court order to submit to an examination.[24]

Court-Ordered Examination: When a discovery medical examination involves more than a routine physical examination of a personal injury plaintiff, resistance by the projected examinee becomes more likely. Moreover, the chances diminish that counsel for the parties can arrange a discovery examination between themselves. Nevertheless, they must still try to reach agreement before seeking a court-ordered examination.[25] If no agreement results, then all mental examinations, and any physical examinations that do not fall within the ambit of the "demand" procedure just discussed, require leave of court.[26] Six types of examinations will commonly necessitate a court order: (1) a mental examination; (2) any examination of either a nonparty[27] or a defendant;[28] (3) a battery of examinations;[29] (4) a repeat examination;[30] (5) a painful or dangerous examination;[31] and (6) an examination held far from the examinee's residence.[32]

—Contents of Motion and Order: Under Section 2032.310, a motion for a medical examination must "specify the time, place, manner, conditions, scope, and nature of the examination, as well as the identity and specialty, if any, of the person or persons who will perform the examination."[33] The order granting the motion must specify the same information.[34] In addition, the order must spell out the "diagnostic tests and procedures" that the examinee must undergo.[35] A non-specific order is defective.[36] In *Schlagenhauf v Holder*,[37] for example, the

---

[23] CCP § 2032.240(d).

[24] CCP § 2032.410.

For a discussion of the sanctions for failure to appear for or submit to a compulsory medical examination, see § 8.20.

[25] CCP § 2032.310(b), referencing CCP § 2016.040.

[26] CCP § 2032.310(a).

Cf. Vinson v Superior Court (1987) 43 Cal 3d 833, 840, 239 Cal Rptr 292, 297, 740 P2d 404, 409.

[27] For a discussion of the types of nonparties who may be compelled to submit to a medical examination, see § 8.2.

[28] For a discussion of compulsory medical examinations of a defendant, see § 8.2.

[29] For a discussion of multiple court-ordered medical examinations, see § 8.8.

[30] For a discussion of successive court-ordered medical examinations, see § 8.8.

[31] For a discussion of painful, dangerous, or intrusive compulsory medical examinations, see § 8.7.

[32] For a discussion of the place for a compulsory medical examination, see § 8.11.

[33] CCP § 2032.310(b).

[34] CCP § 2032.320(d).

[35] CCP § 2032.320(d).

[36] See Harabedian v Superior Court (1961) 195 Cal App 2d 26, 29, 15 Cal Rptr 420, 422. Cf.

United States Supreme Court criticized the trial court's failure to specify the procedures permissible in the examinations it ordered:

> [T]here was no compliance with Rule 35's requirement that the trial judge delineate the "conditions, and scope" of the examinations. The internal medicine examination might, for example, at the instance of the movant or its recommended physician extend to such things as blood tests, electrocardiograms, gastro-intestinal and other X-ray examinations. It is hard to conceive how some of these could be relevant under any possible theory of the case.[38]

—Evidentiary Support: A mere recitation in the motion that some individual's medical condition is "in controversy"[39] in the case and that "good cause"[40] exists for an examination of that condition does not suffice. The movant must supply concrete data establishing both elements:

> [The "in controversy" and "good cause" requirements] are not met by mere conclusory allegations of the pleadings—nor by mere relevance to the case—but require an *affirmative showing* by the movant that each condition as to which the examination is sought is really and genuinely in controversy and that good cause exists for ordering each particular examination. . . . [¶] [An evidentiary hearing] may be necessary in some cases, but in other cases the showing could be made by affidavits or other usual methods short of a hearing.[41]

Doyle v Superior Court (1996) 50 Cal App 4th 1878, 1881–1882, 58 Cal Rptr 2d 476, 478; Bittle v Superior Court (1976) 55 Cal App 3d 489, 495, 127 Cal Rptr 574, 577 [although order itself did not specify time, place or examiner's identity, it sufficed that these particulars were contained in the notice of motion]; Amis v Ashworth (1990, Tex App) 802 SW2d 374, 379 [order failing to describe any limitations on scope of mental examination fatally defective].

37 Schlagenhauf v Holder (1964) 379 US 104, 13 L Ed 2d 152, 85 S Ct 234.

38 Schlagenhauf v Holder (1964) 379 US 104, 121 n16, 13 L Ed 2d 152, 165 n16, 85 S Ct 234, 244 n16.

See also Baqleh v Superior Court (2002) 100 Cal App 4th 478, 491–493, 122 Cal Rptr 2d 673, 683–685. Cf. Bennett v White Laboratories (1993, MD Fla) 841 F Supp 1155, 1159 ["routine pelvic examination" adequately delimited prospective examination's scope].

39 For a discussion of the requirement that the examinee's physical or mental condition be "in controversy" in the lawsuit, see §§ 8.4 and 8.5.

40 For a discussion of the requirement that there be "good cause" for a medical examination, see § 8.6.

41 Schlagenhauf v Holder (1964) 379 US 104, 118–119, 85 S Ct 234, 242–243, 13 L Ed 2d 152, 164 (italics added).

See, e.g., Russenberger v Russenberger (1994, Fla) 639 So2d 963, 965 [court need not always hold evidentiary hearing if the movant submits affidavits demonstrating that examinee's condition is "in controversy" and there is "good cause" for examination]; Hodges v Keane (1993, SD NY) 145 FRD 332, 334–335 [psychiatrist's detailed affidavit documenting plaintiff's past mental history supported order for mental examination]; Amis v Ashworth (1990, Tex App) 802 SW2d 374, 378–379 [complete absence of affidavits demonstrating how mental condition is "in controversy" and why there is "good cause" for examination warrants denial of motion].

§ 8.4 Physical Condition "In Controversy"

Narrow Scope of Discovery: Discovery via court-ordered medical examinations, and that conducted by depositions, interrogatories, inspections, and admission requests, differ markedly with respect to the scope of the discovery allowed. Litigants may use these other devices to obtain non-privileged information that is merely relevant to the general *subject matter* of the lawsuit.[1] Thus, the discovering party may avoid the more difficult question of whether the information sought relates to the precise *issues* likely to be tried.[2] In contrast, one who seeks to discover an adversary's physical condition through a medical examination must show that the condition is actually in issue in the case. Section 2032.020 does not incorporate Section 2017.010, with its broad concept of relevance to the subject matter. Instead, it restricts examinations to cases in which a party's physical condition is "in controversy".[3] Moreover, even when such a controversy exists over that condition, the examining party ordinarily must also show "good cause" for the examination:

> Determining that the mental or physical condition of a party is in controversy is but the first step in our analysis. In contrast to more pedestrian discovery procedures, a mental or physical examination requires the discovering party to obtain a court order. The court may grant the motion only for good cause shown.[4]

Personal Injury Plaintiffs: The most frequent use of the court-ordered physical examination is against plaintiffs in negligence and products liability cases. These individuals are seeking compensation for some bodily injury, and their physical condition is almost inevitably "in controversy" in the lawsuit. As the United States Supreme Court observed:

---

[1] For a discussion of "relevant to the subject matter of the action," see §§ 11.1–11.3.

[2] See Pacific Tel. & Tel. Co. v Superior Court (1970) 2 Cal 3d 161, 172–173, 84 Cal Rptr 718, 726, 465 P2d 854, 862.

[3] See CCP § 2032.020(a).

See, e.g., Estate of Sanders (1992) 2 Cal App 4th 462, 477–478, 3 Cal Rptr 2d 536, 539–545 [because the probate code does not include DNA matching as one of the ways of establishing that a decedent was the natural parent of the claimant, a court hearing a petition to establish heirship may not order the decedent's children to submit blood samples, even though they may be interested parties]; Sacramona v Bridgestone/Firestone, Inc. (1993, D Mass) 152 FRD 428, 431–432 [although lifestyle of plaintiff indicated he might have HIV, his claim for future damages did not put his life expectancy "in controversy" so as to warrant a compulsory blood test].

[4] Vinson v Superior Court (1987) 43 Cal 3d 833, 840, 239 Cal Rptr 292, 297, 740 P2d 404, 409. The post-*Vinson* addition of the "demand" procedure for certain physical examinations represents the only exception to the requirement for prior court permission for a compulsory medical examination.

For a discussion of the "good cause" requirement, see §§ 8.6–8.8.

For a discussion of the "demand" procedure for obtaining a compulsory physical examination, see § 8.3.

[T]here are situations where the pleadings alone are sufficient to meet these requirements. A plaintiff in a negligence action who asserts . . . physical injury places that . . . physical injury clearly in controversy . . . .[5]

Indeed, as long as defendants in these cases seek only one routine physical examination, they may "demand"[6] it; they need no court order. Moreover, even one who merely anticipates being a defendant in a personal injury case may obtain a physical examination of the potential plaintiff.[7]

Personal injury plaintiffs have successfully resisted a motion for a physical examination by stipulating that they have now completely recovered and will not seek damages for any present, anticipated, or permanent injury. Therefore, their physical condition is no longer "in controversy."[8]

Relevance to Liability Issues: Although disputes over a party's physical condition usually arise during the damages phase of a personal injury case, such "controversies" sometimes surface in a case's liability phase. Section 2032.020 authorizes a physical examination in such situations.[9]

For example, cases involving motor vehicle collisions often raise liability issues that concern the physical condition of one or more of the parties.[10] The condition usually implicated is a motorist's eyesight.[11] Although a court should not routinely order an opthalmological examination, it is far less intrusive than most other physical examinations. Moreover, such examinations would have

---

[5] Schlagenhauf v Holder (1964) 379 US 104, 119, 13 L Ed 2d 152, 164, 85 S Ct 234, 243 (internal citation omitted).

See also Postell v Amana Refrigeration, Inc. (1980, ND Ga) 87 FRD 706, 707.

[6] For a discussion of the "demand" procedure for obtaining a compulsory physical examination, see § 8.3.

[7] CCP § 2035.020(c).

For a discussion of the availability of discovery medical examinations before suit has been filed, see § 14.1.

[8] See Winters v Travia (1974, CA2 NY) 495 F2d 839, 840–841; Coca-Cola Bottling Co. v Negron Torres (1958, CA1 Puerto Rico) 255 F2d 149, 153.

[9] CCP § 2032.020(a).

An early case decided under FRCivP 35 took the opposite position. In Wadlow v Humberd (1939, WD Mo) 27 F Supp 210, plaintiff claimed that certain statements describing his physical condition in a medical journal were libelous. Defendant set up the affirmative defense of "truth" and sought a physical examination to confirm the accuracy of the article. The court denied the application on the ground that "the Rule looks to a situation in which the mental or physical condition of a party shall be immediately and directly in controversy and not merely in controversy incidentally and collaterally." Wadlow v Humberd (1939, WD Mo) 27 F Supp 210, 212.

[10] Annotation: Physical examination of allegedly negligent person with respect to defect claimed to have caused or contributed to accident. 89 ALR2d 1001.

[11] See also Ranft v Lyons (1991, Wis App) 471 NW2d 254, 258–259 [the defendant motorist's claimed abnormal tolerance for alcohol justified medical examination by injured pedestrian's doctors].

strong probative value in any case where a party's vision may have contributed to the accident.

Two cases provide illustrations. In the *Harabedian* case,[12] the plaintiff claimed that the father of the driver of the car in which plaintiff was riding had negligently entrusted it to a son whom he knew had a congenital eye defect that caused blurred vision. On this showing, the California court held "that the condition of defendant-driver's eyesight was and is in controversy in the principal action, and that the trial court in ordering an ophthalmological examination was not exceeding its proper authority."[13] And in *Schlagenhauf v Holder*,[14] the trial court ordered a bus driver who had run into the rear of a lighted tractor-trailer unit at night to undergo an eye examination. Plaintiffs showed that the bus driver had neither reduced his speed nor altered his course, although he had seen the truck's red lights for several seconds. Plaintiffs also showed that the driver had previously been involved in a similar rear-end collision. Although the United States Supreme Court found this showing inadequate to warrant the battery of medical examinations ordered by the trial court, the compelled eye examination gave the Court no trouble: "[W]e would be hesitant to set aside a visual examination if it had been the only one ordered."[15]

Blood-Group Examinations: As used in Section 2032.020, "physical condition" expressly includes a party's "blood group."[16] Therefore, a court may order a discovery blood examination provided there is a "controversy" concerning the examinee's blood type. Paternity proceedings present the obvious case for a court-ordered blood test.[17] Here Section 2032.020 is largely surplusage because California includes in its Family Code the Uniform Act on Blood Tests to Determine Paternity.[18] Designed for such cases, the Uniform Act details the appropriate procedure. The Legislature has expressly avoided any implied repeal of the Uniform Act by its enactment of Section 2032.020.[19]

---

[12] Harabedian v Superior Court (1961) 195 Cal App 2d 26, 15 Cal Rptr 420.

[13] Harabedian v Superior Court (1961) 195 Cal App 2d 26, 31–32, 15 Cal Rptr 420.

[14] Schlagenhauf v Holder (1964) 379 US 104, 13 L Ed 2d 152, 85 S Ct 234.

[15] Schlagenhauf v Holder (1964) 379 US 104, 121, 13 L Ed 2d 152, 165, 85 S Ct 234, 244.

[16] CCP § 2032.020(a).

[17] See CCP § 2032.010(a).

Cf. In re Letter Rogatory from Local Court (1994, ND Ill) 154 FRD 196 [under Hague Convention, federal court will honor request from German court conducting paternity proceeding that United States citizen submit to blood test]; In re Letter of Request from Boras Dist. Court (1994, ED NY) 153 FRD 31 [under Hague Convention, federal court will honor request from Swedish court conducting paternity proceeding that United States citizen submit to blood test]; Niedwiecki, Science Fact or Science Fiction? The Implications of Court-Ordered Genetic Testing Under Rule 35, 34 U.S.F. L. Rev. 295 (2000); Rothstein, Preventing the Discovery of Plaintiff Genetic Profiles by Defendants Seeking to Limit Damages in Personal Injury Litigation, 71 Ind. L.J. 877 (1996).

[18] Family Code §§ 7550–7557. Before 1994, this Act was found in Evidence Code §§ 890–897. See also Beach v Beach (1940, DC Cir) 114 F2d 479.

[19] See CCP § 2032.010(a).

The Uniform Act authorizes compelled blood-group examinations only of the "mother, child, and alleged father."[20] Section 2032.020 may reach more broadly. In a federal case, a putative child of a decedent sued an insurer to compel payment to him of a life insurance policy on his "father." The insurer had already paid the proceeds to the insured's parents, who had represented to it that their son had died childless. The insurer joined the decedent's parents as third-party defendants. Acting under Federal Rule of Civil Procedure 35, the trial court ordered the plaintiff "child" and the insured's parents to submit to a blood examination.[21]

§ 8.5 Mental Condition "In Controversy"

A court-ordered mental examination unquestionably intrudes upon a litigant's personal privacy: "The analyst in a psychiatric examination seeks by careful direction of areas of inquiry to probe, possibly very deeply, into the psyche, measuring stress, seeking origins, tracing aberrations, and attempting to form a professional judgment or interpretation of the examinee's mental condition."[1] Yet Section 2032.020 expressly empowers a trial court to enter such an order in an appropriate case.[2] Indeed, Section 2035.020 allows a court-ordered mental examination even before plaintiff has filed a law suit.[3] This power, however, covers only an *examination*; a court may not compel a litigant to undergo *therapy*.[4]

Narrow Scope of Discovery: A notable difference between discovery via court-ordered medical examinations, and that conducted by depositions, interrogatories, inspections, and admission requests, is the scope of the discovery allowed. Litigants may use these other devices to obtain non-privileged information that

---

[20] Family Code § 7551.

Cf. City & County of San Francisco v Cartagena (1995) 35 Cal App 4th 1061, 41 Cal Rptr 2d 797 [father seeking to set aside judicial determination of paternity is not entitled to compel mother and child to submit to a blood test unless and until court decides to set aside the judgment].

[21] Smith v Servicemen's Group Life Ins. (1989, ND Ind) 124 FRD 195.

Cf. Niedwiecki, Science Fact or Science Fiction? The Implications of Court-Ordered Genetic Testing Under Rule 35, 34 U.S.F. L. Rev. 295 (2000); Rothstein, Preventing the Discovery of Plaintiff Genetic Profiles by Defendants Seeking to Limit Damages in Personal Injury Litigation, 71 Ind. L.J. 877 (1996).

[1] Edwards v Superior Court (1976) 16 Cal 3d 905, 911, 130 Cal Rptr 14, 17, 549 P2d 846, 849.

[2] CCP § 2032.020(a).

See Vinson v Superior Court (1987) 43 Cal 3d 833, 838, 239 Cal Rptr 292, 296, 740 P2d 404, 408; Lester v Lennane (2000) 84 Cal App 4th 536, 547–550, 101 Cal Rptr 2d 86, 93–95; Maynard v City of San Jose (1994, CA9 Cal) 37 F3d 1396, 1402.

[3] CCP § 2035.020(c).

For a discussion of the availability of discovery medical examinations before suit has been filed, see § 14.1.

[4] In re Marriage of Matthews (1980) 101 Cal App 3d 811, 817, 161 Cal Rptr 879, 882 [parent in child custody case may not be ordered to undergo therapy or counseling].

is merely relevant to the general *subject matter* of the lawsuit.[5] Thus, the discovering party may avoid the more difficult question of whether the information sought relates to the precise *issues* likely to be tried.[6] In contrast, one who seeks to discover an adversary's mental condition through a medical examination must demonstrate that this condition is actually an issue in the case.[7] Section 2032.020 does not incorporate Section 2017.010, with its broad concept of relevance to the subject matter.[8] As with physical examinations,[9] the statute restricts mental examinations to cases in which a party's mental condition is actually "in controversy."[10] Moreover, even when such a controversy exists over that condition, the examining party must also show "good cause" for the examination:

> Determining that the mental or physical condition of a party is in controversy is but the first step in our analysis. In contrast to more pedestrian discovery procedures, a mental or physical examination requires the discovering party to obtain a court order. The court may grant the motion only for good cause shown.[11]

Personal Injury Plaintiffs: Claimants for physical injuries routinely include a prayer for the mental and emotional stress caused by those injuries. In *Stuart v Burford*,[12] a federal trial court concluded that such a prayer alone does not place the plaintiff's mental condition "in controversy." Noting both that the plaintiff had not alleged that the accident caused any mental disease and that

---

[5] For a discussion of "relevant to the subject matter of the action," see §§ 11.1–11.3.

[6] See Pacific Tel. & Tel. Co. v Superior Court (1970) 2 Cal 3d 161, 172–173, 84 Cal Rptr 718, 726, 465 P2d 854, 862.

[7] But see Cruz v Superior Court (2004) 121 Cal App 4th 646, 653, 17 Cal Rptr 3d 368, 373 [in minor plaintiff's malpractice action for claimed injury resulting from medical treatment during his mother's pregnancy and delivery, defendants were allowed to compel mother to undergo blood test on the speculation that this might show the minor's problem was traceable to the mother's genetic condition].

[8] See Doyle v Superior Court (1996) 50 Cal App 4th 1878, 1886, 58 Cal Rptr 2d 476, 482 ["Mental examinations are not authorized for the purpose of testing a person's 'credibility.'"]; Bennett v White Laboratories, Inc. (1993, MD Fla) 841 F Supp 1155, 1157.

[9] For a discussion of the "in controversy" requirement for physical examinations, see § 8.4.

[10] CCP § 2032.020(a).

See Bennett v White Laboratories, Inc. (1993, MD Fla) 841 F Supp 1155, 1159–1160 [speculation that plaintiff's claimed pain during sexual relations might have psychological overlay does not place her mental condition "in controversy" so as to warrant a court-ordered mental examination].

[11] Vinson v Superior Court (1987) 43 Cal 3d 833, 840, 239 Cal Rptr 292, 297, 740 P2d 404, 409.

For a discussion of the "good cause" requirement, see §§ 8.6–8.8.

[12] Stuart v Burford (1967, ND Okla) 42 FRD 591.

See also Smith v J.I. Case Corp. (1995, ED Pa) 163 FRD 229, 232 ["(I)n cases such as this one—your basic garden-variety tort quest for damages, to include pain and suffering—psychiatric examination should be the exception, not the rule."]

she did not plan to present psychiatric testimony at trial, the court required more information before it would order a mental examination.[13]

—Normal Distress: Section 2032.320 now embodies much the same approach. A party may stipulate that a person for whose personal injuries a recovery is being sought is making no claim for an unusual or particularly serious component of mental and emotional distress over and above that usually associated with the physical injuries claimed, and that no expert testimony regarding this usual mental and emotional distress will be presented at trial in support of the claim for damages. When a party makes this stipulation, the trial court may not order a mental examination of that party absent a showing of exceptional circumstances.[14]

—Disproportionate Distress: In contrast, where a plaintiff claims that an accident has caused mental or emotional distress disproportionate to that normally expected from the injury sustained, that plaintiff's mental condition is "in controversy" for discovery purposes:

> In addition to seeking medical treatment for his physical injuries after the accident, the plaintiff also was required to seek psychiatric treatment. Since that psychiatric treatment required the plaintiff to be confined in a psychiatric ward, it must be assumed that the plaintiff was experiencing problems which were more severe than the emotional distress which frequently accompanies personal injuries. Therefore, the nature and seriousness of the emotional distress experienced by the plaintiff after the accident is an important issue in this lawsuit.[15]

---

[13] The court directed a defense doctor who was about to conduct a physical examination to provide an opinion as to whether a mental examination was also necessary.

See also Turner v Imperial Stores (1995, SD Cal) 161 FRD 89 [no mental examination warranted where plaintiff claims only for the normal mental distress associated with a wrongful discharge]; Bennett v White Laboratories, Inc. (1993, MD Fla) 841 F Supp 1155, 1159 [plaintiff's fear that exposure to defendant's product might cause cancer did not place her mental condition "in controversy" since she did not claim any psychological or psychiatric disorder and did not plan to call any psychiatrist or psychologist as a witness].

But see Reuter v Superior Court (1979) 93 Cal App 3d 332, 340, 155 Cal Rptr 525, 530 [an allegation of "great mental pain and suffering" in the complaint of an auto tort victim "clearly placed his mental condition in controversy"]; Smedley v Capps, Staples, Ward, Hastings & Dodson (1993, ND Cal) 820 F Supp 1227, 1232 [plaintiff seeking recovery for only the normal stress connected with her wrongful discharge ordered to undergo a mental examination].

[14] CCP §§ 2032.320(b) and (c).

Sections 2032.320(b) and (c) reflect the influence of the Supreme Court's decision in a related area. See In re Lifschutz (1970) 2 Cal 3d 415, 436, 85 Cal Rptr 829, 843, 467 P2d 557, 571 [no automatic waiver of the psychotherapist-patient privilege results when a personal injury plaintiff merely claims the normal distress connected with the physical injury and not for any "unusual or particularly serious elements"].

For a discussion of the scope of the patient-litigant exception to the psychotherapist-patient privilege, see § 12.29.

[15] Anson v Fickel (1986, ND Ind) 110 FRD 184, 186.

Claims for accident-related traumatic neuroses or psychoses undoubtedly place one's mental condition in controversy.[16] However, as with court-ordered physical examinations,[17] a personal injury plaintiff who alleges only *past* mental pain and suffering and seeks no damages for severe *ongoing* mental anguish, can probably avoid a court-ordered mental examination.[18]

"Direct" Issue Required: Before an issue involving a party's mental condition is "in controversy" under Section 2032.020, it must bear directly, not merely collaterally, upon the case. In the *Reuter* case,[19] the trial court had ordered the minor plaintiff to submit to a mental examination because he claimed "great" mental pain and suffering. The child's mother happened to be his guardian ad litem. Psychiatrists customarily interview the parents of a child they examine and they often recommend psychological testing of the parents to help them to diagnose the child's condition. In addition, the defense psychiatrist who was to examine the child declared that the tests of the mother were necessary to an evaluation of the child. On this showing, the trial judge ordered the child's mother to undergo a battery of psychological tests to furnish background information for her son's examination. The appellate court, however, ruled that the Discovery Act did not, and probably could not constitutionally, empower a trial court to require someone to submit to psychiatric or psychological probing, simply because that person may have influenced the mental state of one whose condition was in controversy:

> [M]any different parties may be the main influence in any particular person's mental state—his parent, his priest, his teacher, his little league coach. Section [2032.02] does not create a power broad enough to allow the court to order all these parties to submit to a battery of tests to determine the extent of their influence on a child's mental state merely on a psychiatrist's declaration that he needs them.[20]

Sexual Harassment Claims: When a plaintiff files a claim against an employer for sexual harassment, the defendant often responds with a motion to compel the plaintiff to submit to a mental examination. In the *Vinson* case,[21] the Supreme Court recognized that such a claim does not automatically place the plaintiff's mental condition "in controversy":

---

[16] E.g., Lowe v Philadelphia Newspapers, Inc. (1983, ED Pa) 101 FRD 296, 298.

See also Benchmaster, Inc. v Kawaelde (1985, ED Mich) 107 FRD 752, 754–755 [anxiety and distress caused by defendant's tortious acts allegedly precipitated plaintiff's coronary condition]; Brandenberg v El Al Israel Airlines (1978, SD NY) 79 FRD 543, 546 [airline's neglect of plaintiff's diabetic condition allegedly caused "psychiatric" injuries in the amount of $900,000].

[17] For a discussion of the "in controversy" requirement for physical examinations, see § 8.4.

[18] Cf. Bridges v Eastman Kodak (1994, SD NY) 850 F Supp 216, 222 [plaintiff in sexual harassment case who is not claiming present mental injury or past psychiatric disorder has not put her mental state "in controversy" merely by alleging her past mental suffering].

[19] Reuter v Superior Court (1979) 93 Cal App 3d 332, 155 Cal Rptr 525.

[20] Reuter v Superior Court (1979) 93 Cal App 3d 332, 342, 155 Cal Rptr 525, 531.

[21] Vinson v Superior Court (1987) 43 Cal 3d 833, 239 Cal Rptr 292, 740 P2d 404.

A simple sexual harassment claim asking compensation for having to endure an oppressive work environment or for wages lost following an unjust dismissal would not normally create a controversy regarding the plaintiff's mental state. To hold otherwise would mean that every person who brings such a suit implicitly asserts he or she is mentally unstable, obviously an untenable position.[22]

However, the plaintiff in *Vinson* alleged that she was still experiencing various forms of mental and emotional distress because of the harassment: "Plaintiff in the case at bar asserts that she continues to suffer diminished self-esteem, reduced motivation, sleeplessness, loss of appetite, fear, lessened ability to help others, loss of social contacts, anxiety, mental anguish, loss of reputation, and severe emotional distress."[23] These allegations, the Court ruled, placed her mental condition "in controversy":

[P]laintiff haled defendants into court and accused them of causing her various mental and emotional ailments. Defendants deny her charges. As a result, the existence and extent of her mental injuries is indubitably in dispute. In addition, by asserting a causal link between her mental distress and defendants' conduct, plaintiff implicitly claims it was not caused by a preexisting mental condition, thereby raising the question of alternative sources for the distress. We thus conclude that her mental state was in controversy.[24]

---

[22] Vinson v Superior Court (1987) 43 Cal 3d 833, 840, 239 Cal Rptr 292, 297, 740 P2d 404, 409.

See also Acosta v Tenneco Oil Co. (1990, CA5 La) 913 F2d 205, 208–209 [claim for age discrimination does not place mental condition of plaintiff employee in controversy]; Ford v Contra Costa County (ND Cal 1998) 179 FRD 579 [a plaintiff in a gender discrimination case may not be compelled to submit to a psychiatric examination merely because she has included normal emotional distress as one element of damages].

[23] Vinson v Superior Court (1987) 43 Cal 3d 833, 840, 239 Cal Rptr 292, 297–298, 740 P2d 404, 409–410.

See also Ziemann v Burlington County Bridge Commission (1994, D NJ) 155 FRD 497, 501 n1 [sexual harassment plaintiff ordered to undergo mental examination where psychological injury was practically her only element of damages, and she planned to present expert testimony of a 60% permanent psychiatric disability].

[24] Vinson v Superior Court (1987) 43 Cal 3d 833, 839–840, 239 Cal Rptr 292, 297, 740 P2d 404, 409.

See also Eckman v University of Rhode Island (1995, D RI) 160 FRD 431, 433–434; Jansen v Packaging Corp. of America (1994, ND Ill) 158 FRD 409.

Compare Ali v Wang Laboratories, Inc. (1995, MD Fla) 162 FRD 165, 168 [mental examination warranted by plaintiff's claim that wrongful discharge caused change in personality], and Shepherd v American Broadcasting Companies, Inc. (1993, D DC) 151 FRD 194, 212–213 [mental examination warranted by plaintiff's claim that wrongful discharge caused post-traumatic stress syndrome], with O'Quinn v New York University Medical Center (1995, SD NY) 163 FRD 226, and Turner v Imperial Stores (1995, SD Cal) 161 FRD 89 [no mental examination warranted where plaintiff claims only for the normal mental distress associated with a wrongful discharge].

In contrast to *Vinson*, although the plaintiff in the *Doyle* case originally sought damages for mental distress attributable to alleged sexual harassment, she later amended her complaint to eliminate any claim for ongoing or current mental distress. This meant that her present mental condition was no longer "in controversy."

> [W]here a plaintiff alleges that she is not suffering any current mental injury but only that she has suffered emotional distress in the past arising from the defendant's misconduct, a mental examination is unnecessary because such an allegation alone does not place the nature and cause of the plaintiff's current mental condition "in controversy."[25]

Other Types of Litigation: A claim under a disability insurance policy that an injury has caused the insured to develop a psychosis places the plaintiff's mental condition in controversy.[26] And in marriage dissolution proceedings, in which the mental condition of one or both of the parents may bear directly on their respective fitness for child custody,[27] their mental condition is "in controversy."

Examination of a Defendant: In the vast majority of cases where a mental examination is ordered, the examinee will be the plaintiff. However, a court may also direct a defendant to submit to one. In *Schlagenhauf v Holder*,[28] the United States Supreme Court ruled that Rule 35, the federal version of discovery medical examinations, applied to defendants as well as plaintiffs.[29] The Court drew no distinction between a mental and a physical examination in this regard. A few years later, a California court ordered a teacher who was resisting a school district's efforts to remove her for alleged mental instability to submit to a psychiatric examination.[30]

In *Schlagenhauf*, however, the Court cautioned trial judges to require a strong showing of "good cause"[31] before ordering defendants to submit to a psychiatric examination. In such instances, the party seeking the examination will usually be the one who is injecting the controversy concerning their mental condition into the case: "[S]weeping examinations of a party who has not affirmatively put into issue his own mental . . . condition are not to be automatically ordered

---

25 Doyle v Superior Court (1996) 50 Cal App 4th 1878, 1887, 58 Cal Rptr 2d 476, 482.

26 See, e.g., Durst v Superior Court (1963) 222 Cal App 2d 447, 35 Cal Rptr 143.

27 Cf. In re Marriage of Matthews (1980) 101 Cal App 3d 811, 817, 161 Cal Rptr 879, 882.

28 Schlagenhauf v Holder (1964) 379 US 104, 13 L Ed 2d 152, 85 S Ct 234.

29 For a discussion of who may be ordered to undergo a compulsory medical examination, see § 8.2.

30 Board of Trustees v Superior Court (1969) 274 Cal App 2d 377, 79 Cal Rptr 58. Cf. Kees v Medical Board (1992) 7 Cal App 4th 1801, 1815, 10 Cal Rptr 2d 112, 121 [in a proceeding to revoke a medical license, reports of the bizarre conduct of the respondent doctor in dealing with his patients furnished "good cause" to require him to submit to a psychiatric examination].

31 For a discussion of the "good cause" requirement for a compulsory medical examination, see § 8.6.

merely because the person has been involved in an accident . . . and a general charge of negligence is lodged."[32] For example, a federal court has ruled that a defendant in a sexual harassment case does not place his mental condition in controversy simply by denying the plaintiff's claims.[33]

§ 8.6 "Good Cause" Requirement

Separate Requirement: The moving party must do more than merely show that the examinee's physical or mental condition is "in controversy"[1] in the law suit:

"Deciding that the mental or physical condition of a party is in controversy is but the first step in our analysis."[2] Section 2032.320 lets a court order a medical examination "only for good cause shown."[3] This requirement is "not a mere formality" that may be "met by mere conclusory allegations."[4] Rather, it is "a plainly expressed limitation on the use" of this discovery device that requires "an affirmative showing" for "each particular examination" sought.[5]

Showing "Good Cause": Sometimes the pleadings themselves will establish "good cause":

A plaintiff in a negligence action who asserts mental or physical injury . . . provides the defendant with good cause for an examination to determine the existence and extent of such asserted injury. This is not only true as to a plaintiff, but applies equally to a defendant who asserts his mental or physical condition as a defense to a claim, such as, for example, where insanity is asserted as a defense to a divorce action.[6]

In such cases, issues about "good cause" arise mostly when the moving party is seeking either a painful, dangerous, or intrusive examination,[7] or a series of examinations.[8]

---

[32] Schlagenhauf v Holder (1964) 379 US 104, 121, 13 L Ed 2d 152, 165, 85 S Ct 234, 244.

See also Vinson v Superior Court (1987) 43 Cal 3d 833, 839, 239 Cal Rptr 292, 297, 740 P2d 404, 409 ["One party's unsubstantiated allegation cannot put the mental state of another in controversy"]; Marroni v Matey (1979, ED Pa) 82 FRD 371 [claim that defendant's developmental disability rendered him incapable of understanding and complying with applicable safety rules for operating a motor boat did not automatically warrant a mental examination].

[33] Taylor v National Group of Companies, Inc. (1992, ND Ohio) 145 FRD 79, 79–80.

[1] For a discussion of when someone's *physical* condition is "in controversy," see § 8.4.

For a discussion of when someone's *mental* condition is "in controversy," see § 8.5.

[2] Vinson v Superior Court (1987) 43 Cal 3d 833, 840, 239 Cal Rptr 292, 297, 740 P2d 404, 409.

[3] CCP § 2032.320(a).

[4] Schlagenhauf v Holder (1964) 379 US 104, 118, 13 L Ed 2d 152, 163–164, 85 S Ct 234, 242–243.

[5] Schlagenhauf v Holder (1964) 379 US 104, 118, 13 L Ed 2d 152, 163–164, 85 S Ct 234, 242–243.

[6] Schlagenhauf v Holder (1964) 379 US 104, 119, 13 L Ed 2d 152, 164, 85 S Ct 234, 243.

[7] For a discussion of "good cause" for a painful or dangerous medical examination, see § 8.7.

[8] For a discussion of "good cause" for multiple or successive medical examinations, see § 8.8.

Where "good cause" does not appear on the face of the pleadings, the moving party must provide the trial court with "sufficient information" to show "good cause."[9] Normally, the moving party will make its "affirmative showing" with affidavits.[10] These affidavits should be specific; mere conclusory statements do not suffice.[11] In unusual circumstances the trial court can hold an evidentiary hearing.[12]

Statutory "Good Cause": The Legislature defined "good cause" in two common situations: initial, routine physical examinations of personal injury plaintiffs, and mental examinations of plaintiffs claiming only the distress normally expected with the physical injury alleged.

In the first situation, the "in controversy" and "good cause" requirements are virtually congruent. Recognizing this, the Legislature has made a motion in such a case unnecessary. Instead, it has permitted a "demand" for "one physical examination of the plaintiff provided the examination does not include any diagnostic test or procedure that is painful, protracted, or intrusive . . . ."[13]

The demand procedure ratifies the United States Supreme Court's view in *Schlagenhauf v Holder* that the mere filing of a personal injury complaint "provides the defendant with good cause for an examination to determine the existence and extent of such asserted injury."[14]

In the second situation, so long as the plaintiff is not supporting its claim with a mental health expert's testimony, Section 2032.320 requires "exceptional circumstances" before "good cause" will exist for subjecting that party to a psychiatric or psychological examination.[15]

Common Examples of "Good Cause": Beyond these two statutory applications of "good cause," case law provides additional examples of "good cause" for a medical examination. For example, a litigant's projected use of a medical specialist as an expert witness normally creates "good cause" for an opponent to have its own specialist examine the party:

---

[9] Schlagenhauf v Holder (1964) 379 US 104, 119, 13 L Ed 2d 152, 164, 85 S Ct 234, 243.

[10] Schlagenhauf v Holder (1964) 379 US 104, 119, 13 L Ed 2d 152, 164, 85 S Ct 234, 243.

See also Russenberger v Russenberger (1994, Fla) 639 So2d 963, 965 [party seeking mental examination may demonstrate "good cause" by affidavits and verified pleadings].

[11] See Thompson v Palos Community Hospital (1993, Ill App) 627 NE2d 239, 244 [bare assertion by defendant's counsel that the relationship between genetic disturbances and brain damage is "well documented and commonly accepted" is a "mere conclusory statement" insufficient to establish "good cause"].

[12] Schlagenhauf v Holder (1964) 379 US 104, 119, 13 L Ed 2d 152, 164, 85 S Ct 234, 243.

See also Russenberger v Russenberger (1994, Fla) 639 So2d 963, 965 [trial court need not hold evidentiary hearing if affidavits or verified pleadings demonstrate "good cause"].

[13] CCP § 2032.220(a).

For a discussion of the "demand" route for obtaining a compulsory physical examination, see § 8.3.

[14] Schlagenhauf v Holder (1964) 379 US 104, 119, 13 L Ed 2d 152, 164, 85 S Ct 234, 243.

[15] CCP §§ 2032.320(b) and (c).

Unless [its ophthalmologist] is likewise allowed to examine the plaintiff, the defendant will be at a distinct disadvantage in this "battle of experts" at trial. . . . Because the plaintiff has permitted [his own ophthalmologist] to examine him, fundamental fairness dictates that he now allow [a defense ophthalmologist] to do so also.[16]

Moreover, as the Supreme Court ruled in the *Vinson* case, the pleading of continuing and extensive injury to a plaintiff's emotional well-being alone is "good cause" to allow the defendant to obtain a mental examination:

Plaintiff in the case at bar asserts that she continues to suffer diminished self-esteem, reduced motivation, sleeplessness, loss of appetite, fear, lessened ability to help others, loss of social contacts, anxiety, mental anguish, loss of reputation, and severe mental distress. In their motion defendants pointed to these allegations. Because the truth of these claims is relevant to plaintiff's cause of action and justifying facts have been shown with specificity, good cause as to these assertions has been demonstrated. [D]efendants must be allowed to investigate the continued existence and severity of the plaintiff's alleged damages.[17]

In contrast, where an opponent *initiates* the controversy over a litigant's mental condition, "good cause" may require the moving party to first unsuccessfully explore "less intrusive methods of discovery" to obtain the desired information.[18]

Scope and Length of Mental Examinations: Even where a litigant has shown "good cause" for a mental examination, the trial court may still limit the examination to protect the examinee's privacy. For example, in the *Vinson* case,[19] the Supreme Court found that plaintiff's claim for severe mental disturbance was "good cause" for her to undergo a mental examination by a defense psychiatrist. However, the Court prohibited any probing into the plaintiff's sexual history and practices during that examination:

We cannot agree that the mere initiation of a sexual harassment suit, even with the rather extreme mental and emotional damage plaintiff

---

[16] Pastel v Amana Refrigeration, Inc. (1980, ND Ga) 87 FRD 706, 709.

See also Duncan v Upjohn Co. (1994, D Conn) 155 FRD 23, 25 [plaintiff's plan to call psychiatric witnesses constituted "good cause" for a mental examination by the defense].

[17] Vinson v Superior Court (1987) 43 Cal 3d 833, 840–841, 239 Cal Rptr 292, 297–298, 740 P2d 404, 409–410.

Duncan v Upjohn Co. (1994, D Conn) 155 FRD 23, 25 [where plaintiff pleads ongoing mental injury, the "in controversy" and the "good cause" requirements merge].

[18] See Marroni v Matey (1979, ED Pa) 82 FRD 371, 372 [psychological testing of developmentally disabled minor plaintiff injured in boating accident will not be ordered simply because defendant claims that he was unfit to operate a motor boat].

Cf. Kentucky Fried Chicken National Management Co. v Tennant (1989, Tex App) 782 SW2d 318, 321 [defendant's efforts to obtain plaintiff's prior mental history records required no "good cause" showing; they *were* a "less intrusive" means of getting sensitive medical information].

[19] Vinson v Superior Court (1987) 43 Cal 3d 833, 239 Cal Rptr 292, 740 P2d 404.

claims to have suffered, functions to waive all her privacy interests, exposing her persona to the unfettered mental probing of defendants' expert. Plaintiff is not compelled, as a condition of entering the courtroom, to discard entirely her mantle of privacy. . . . [¶] Nowhere do defendants establish specific facts justifying inquiry into plaintiff's zone of sexual privacy or show how such discovery would be relevant.[20]

The court should also consider the length of any ordered mental examination. In the *Edwards* case,[21] for example, the court limited the defense psychiatrist's to four hours. The court also let plaintiff choose between a single session or four one-hour sessions.

§ 8.7 Painful, Dangerous, or Intrusive Examinations

Explicit Statutory Restrictions: The "good cause" requirement plays a crucial role when the examination sought is very painful, unusually intrusive, or actually dangerous to the examinee. In three ways the Discovery Act manifests special concern about such examinations. First, it does not allow the "demand" procedure[1] if it will include "any diagnostic test or procedure that is painful, protracted, or intrusive."[2] However, a court should interpret this exception with common sense, not literally. In the *Abex* case,[3] for example, the plaintiff claimed that exposure to the defendant's products had caused his recurring warts. Using the "demand" procedure, the defendant sought a medical examination that would include a biopsy of the warts. Rejecting the plaintiff's objection that this was a "painful" test, the appellate court stated:

> The uncontradicted medical evidence is that the procedure will involve little pain or danger. Any procedure involving a local anesthetic arguably will produce some discomfort but given the fact that [plaintiff] scrapes the warts off himself with a pocket knife, it strains credulity past the breaking point to believe that this procedure qualifies as one that is "painful, protracted, or intrusive" within the meaning of the discovery legislation.[4]

---

[20] Vinson v Superior Court (1987) 43 Cal 3d 833, 841–844, 239 Cal Rptr 292, 298–300, 740 P2d 404, 412.

[21] Edwards v Superior Court (1976) 16 Cal 3d 905, 130 Cal Rptr 14, 549 P2d 846.

[1] For a discussion for the "demand" route for obtaining a compulsory physical examination, see § 8.3.

[2] CCP § 2032.220(a)(1).

[3] Abex Corp. v Superior Court (1989) 209 Cal App 3d 755, 257 Cal Rptr 498.

[4] Abex Corp. v Superior Court (1989) 209 Cal App 3d 755, 758, 257 Cal Rptr 498, 499–500.

See also Cruz v Superior Court (2004) 121 Cal App 4th 646, 652, 17 Cal Rptr 3d 368, 372 [no evidence that obtaining blood from mother of minor plaintiff would be other than a routine procedure]; Ghanooni v Super Shuttle (1993) 20 Cal App 4th 256, 24 Cal Rptr 2d 501 ["routine" medical examination includes right to x-ray personal injury plaintiff's back, neck, right elbow, right knee, and left ankle, since plaintiff was complaining of pain in those areas].

Second, the Legislature has noted the long-range adverse effects of cumulative exposure to radiation. Section 2032.520 provides that by making previous x-rays available, a party can usually avoid any further x-rays of the same area:

> If the examinee submits or authorizes access to X-rays of any area of his or her body for inspection by the examining physician, no additional X-rays of that area may be taken by the examining physician except with the consent of the examinee or on order of the court for good cause shown.[5]

In contrast, examinees who do not supply earlier x-rays may not refuse to undergo routine x-rays either by basing their damage claims solely upon soft tissue injuries or by expressing a generalized fear of radiation.[6]

Finally, the Legislature has required that one seeking a medical examination, whether by demand or by motion, must specify its "manner, conditions, scope, and nature."[7] Thus, the moving party must alert both the examinee and the trial court to the possible discomfort and risk attending the examination.

Judicial Balancing of Need Against Risk: Early federal and state decisions under provisions similar to California's reveal considerable judicial timidity about ordering a party to submit to any painful, dangerous, or intrusive diagnostic procedure.[8] However, as the courts have acquired more information about, and experience with, particular sophisticated medical testing methods, they have grown bolder. They now recognize that they must weigh "the probative value of the proposed examination as it relates to the litigation against the level of risk to the plaintiff."[9]

---

[5] CCP §§ 2032.520.

[6] Ghanooni v Super Shuttle (1993) 20 Cal App 4th 256, 260–261, 24 Cal Rptr 2d 501, 504 ["routine" medical examination includes right to x-ray personal injury plaintiff's back, neck, right elbow, right knee, and left ankle, since plaintiff was complaining of pain in those areas].

[7] CCP §§ 2032.220(c) and 2032.310(b). Although CCP § 2032(a) of the 1956 Discovery Act required such detail in the court's order, it left to implication whether the motion itself had to be that specific.

See Bennett v White Laboratories, Inc. (1993, MD Fla) 841 F Supp 1155, 1159 [the phrase "routine pelvic examination" is sufficiently descriptive]; Shapiro v Win-Sum Ski Corp. (1982, WD NY) 95 FRD 38, 39; Marroni v Matey (1979, ED Pa) 82 FRD 371, 372 [motion for "psychological testing" does not adequately specify the scope of the examination sought].

[8] The following cases refused to allow the diagnostic procedure sought by the defendant: Sullivan, Long, & Haggerty, Inc. v Washington (1942, CA5 La) 128 F2d 466 [X-ray examination using lipiodol]; Riss & Co. v Galloway (1941, Colo) 114 P2d 550 [spinal tap]; Burns v Aetna Life Ins. Co. (1933, Mont) 26 P2d 175 [periodic immersion of injured hand into hot water]; United States Fidelity & Guaranty Co. (1919, Neb) 173 NW 689 [x-ray procedure requiring injection of contrast substance into the kidney]; Cardinal v University of Rochester (1946, Misc) 71 NYS2d 614 [bone marrow biopsy]; Carrig v Oakes (1940, App Div) 18 NYS2d 917 [cystoscopic examination of female plaintiff]; Bartoletta v Delco Appliance Corp. (1938, App Div) 4 NYS2d 744 [stomach examination requiring consumption of barium meal].

[9] Stasiak v Illinois Valley Com. Hospital (1992, Ill App) 590 NE2d 974, 978 [magnetic resonance imaging scan].

The California courts, faced with a motion for a painful or dangerous medical test, should consider the practice adopted in New York and Illinois for balancing "the competing interest of the defendant to investigate and completely satisfy his curiosity by generally accepted medical tests and the plaintiff's interest in his own safety and comfort given the risks of a particular procedure."[10] These courts, like California,[11] initially require the motion to mention the diagnostic procedures that the examiner will use. They do not initially require the moving party to justify them. Instead, an examinee who is concerned about the pain or the risk connected with any requested examination, must file an objection. The examinee must support its objection by declarations of physicians or excerpts from recognized medical texts[12] that describe the dangers it poses. After such a response, the moving party must show that "the requested examination has a clear probative value to the litigation's ultimate issues and that there is a minimal level of risk to the plaintiff."[13] To meet this burden[14] the moving party must present competent and specific medical evidence, not conclusory statements of defense counsel[15] or physicians.[16]

When convinced both of their usefulness and their comparative safety, modern courts have ordered parties to undergo a spinal tap,[17] a coronary arteriogram,[18] a cystoscopic examination,[19] a magnetic resonance imaging (MRI) scan,[20] and

---

[10] Stasiak v Illinois Valley Com. Hospital (1992, Ill App) 590 NE2d 974, 977 [magnetic resonance imaging scan].

[11] The Discovery Commission proposed that a motion for a medical examination involving "unusual, painful, protracted, dangerous, or intrusive diagnostic procedures" must be accompanied by a physician's declaration "explaining the necessity for those procedures and the degree of pain or danger involved." Proposed Civil Discovery Act of 1986, Section 2032(d), Appendix D. However, the Legislature ultimately rejected this proposal.

[12] See, e.g., Lefkowitz v Nassau County Medical Center (1983, App Div) 462 NYS2d 903, 905–906 [excerpts from Physician's Desk Reference and gynecology textbook sufficed to show that proposed fertility test is prima facie potentially dangerous].

[13] Stasiak v Illinois Valley Com. Hospital (1992, Ill App) 590 NE2d 974, 977.
See also Lefkowitz v Nassau County Medical Center (1983, App Div) 462 NYS2d 903, 906.

[14] Cf. Stinchcomb v United States (1990, ED Pa) 132 FRD 29, 30 [court insists on clear and convincing showing of compelling need before subjecting 10-year-old developmentally disabled child with behavioral problems to lengthy, invasive, painful and stressful testing].

[15] Lefkowitz v Nassau County Medical Center (1983, App Div) 462 NYS2d 903, 906 [conclusory statements of defense counsel that test would establish fertility and was not life-threatening "are valueless because of his inability to render a medical opinion"].

[16] Stasiak v Illinois Valley Com. Hospital (1992, Ill App) 590 NE2d 974, 978 [conclusory claim that MRI scan is "necessary" and "crucial" unaccompanied by explanation of why this is so did not meet moving party's burden].

[17] Trent v American Service Co. (1947, Tenn) 206 SW2d 301, 302 [three centimeters of plaintiff's spinal fluid would be obtained by "injecting a needle into the soft tissue and between the vertebrae"].

[18] McQuillen v City of Sioux (1981, Iowa) 306 NW2d 789, 791 [procedure "involves a heart catheterization and an injection of radionuclide to permit tracing of coronary blood flow," followed by "efforts by doctor to induce the kind of angina spasm for which plaintiff was to be tested"].

[19] Klein v Yellow Cab Co. (1944, ND Ohio) 7 FRD 169 [male plaintiff claiming injury-related loss of sexual function].

a computerized axial tomographic (CAT) scan.[21] Although the level of safety of these tests for the general populace now satisfies the courts, they still insist that the individual examinee have no condition that results in an unusual susceptibility to complications.[22]

§ 8.8 Multiple, Repeat, and Successive Examinations

Issues of a court's authority to compel a litigant to submit to more than one medical examination arise in three contexts: (1) *multiple examinations*—a party may simultaneously request examinations by several different specialists; (2) *repeat examinations*—a party who has already received one examination may want to update it; and (3) *successive examinations*—a party may seek an examination of the same sort as one already conducted by another party.

Although Section 2032.020, like its federal prototype,[1] refers to "a" compulsory physical or mental examination,[2] the singular article does not limit a party to a single discovery examination:

> Nothing in the language of [then applicable] section 2032 limits the number of mental examinations. . . . Various subdivisions describe the terms on which "a" physical or mental examination "conducted under this section" is to be carried out, but no language specifically limits to one the number of examinations. Such a limit cannot be implied from the use of the nonrestrictive singular article "a."[3]

Multiple Examinations: The nature of the injuries alleged coupled with the high degree of specialization in modern medicine often supplies "good cause" to order a battery of examinations. In the *Shapira* case, for example, a defendant initially had plaintiff examined by a neurologist and a neuropsychologist. The court later found "good cause" for a psychiatric examination: "Nowhere does the Legislature specifically limit the number of available examinations, either mental or physical."[4] The federal courts have similarly concluded: "A reading of [FRCivP 35(a)] does not indicate an intent to establish a single examination limitation, and where alleged injuries fall into two entirely separate areas of medical specialization, examinations by practitioners in such fields are held to be authorized under the Rule."[5] Indeed, in a Delaware case, when a female

---

[20] Sarka v Rush Presbyterian-St. Luke's (1990, Ill App) 566 NE2d 301; Langelier v Ford (1990, App Div) 552 NYS2d 992. Cf. Rathgeber v Kiowa Dist. Hosp. (1990, D Kan) 131 FRD 195.

[21] Sarka v Rush Presbyterian-St. Luke's (1990, Ill App) 566 NE2d 301; Thomas v John T. Mather Hospital (1990, App Div) 556 NYS2d 720; Langelier v Ford (1990, App Div) 552 NYS2d 992.

[22] State ex rel. Letts v Zakib (1993, W Va) 433 SE2d 554, 557 [infant plaintiff "has a history of allergic reaction to the sedatives (chloral hydrate and phenobarbital) normally administered prior to an MRI"].

[1] FRCivP 35(a).

[2] CCP § 2032.020(a).

[3] Shapira v Superior Court (1990) 224 Cal App 3d 1249, 1254, 274 Cal Rptr 516, 519–520.

[4] Shapira v Superior Court (1990) 224 Cal App 3d 1249, 1255, 274 Cal Rptr 516, 520.

[5] Marshall v Peters (1962, SD Ohio) 31 FRD 238, 239 [orthopedist and cardiologist].

employee claimed injuries from carbon disulphide poisoning, the employer-defendant obtained an order for examinations by five different physicians: a general practitioner, a gynecologist, a neurologist, a psychiatrist, and a specialist in genito-urinary diseases.[6]

A court should order multiple examinations only where the moving party shows "good cause" for each specialty involved.[7] For example, in *Schlagenhauf v Holder*,[8] the plaintiff sought a battery of medical examinations of a defendant who had driven his bus at night into the rear of a moving, well-lit truck on a highway. The United States Supreme Court observed that the circumstances of the accident alone probably presented "good cause" for an opthalmological examination. However, absent a more specific showing, they did not warrant examinations by an internist, a neurologist, and a psychiatrist.

A party seeking examinations by separate specialists may reduce objections of expert "shopping" by making the requests simultaneously.[9]

Repeat Examinations: Obtaining one medical examination of a certain condition during discovery does not automatically rule out the possibility of getting another of the same type. Courts, however, do not routinely order repeat examinations of the same condition:

> [T]he only allegation of change [in the plaintiff's situation] is that [her treating physicians] have changed their opinions regarding plaintiff's need for surgery. There is no allegation of a change in the plaintiff's complaints or in the clinical findings since [the date of the previous examination].[10]

A significant change in the examinee's condition presents the most clear-cut example of "good cause" for a repeat examination.[11] "Good cause" also usually exists where substantial time has passed since the earlier examination, especially where the plaintiff is claiming permanent injuries and trial is approaching:

See also Peters v Nelson (1994, ND Ia) 153 FRD 635 [psychiatrist and neuropsychiatrist]; Little v Howey (1963, WD Mo) 32 FRD 322 [orthopedist and neurosurgeon].

6 Bowing v Delaware Rayon Co. (1937, Del) 190 A 567, cited in Shapira v Superior Court (1990) 224 Cal App 3d 1249, 1255, 274 Cal Rptr 516, 520.

7 Peters v Nelson (1994, ND Iowa) 153 FRD 635, 637–638.

8 Schlagenhauf v Holder (1964) 379 US 104, 120–121, 13 L Ed 2d 152, 165, 85 S Ct 234, 244.

9 Peters v Nelson (1994, ND Iowa) 153 FRD 635, 639 [defendant simultaneously requested separate examinations by a psychiatrist and a neuropsychologist].

10 Moore v Calavar Corp. (1992, WD La) 142 FRD 134, 135.

Cf. Kees v Medical Board (1992) 7 Cal App 4th 1801, 1815, 10 Cal Rptr 2d 112, 121 [in a proceeding to revoke a medical license, a repeat psychiatric examination of the doctor under investigation requires an additional finding of "good cause"].

11 See, e.g., Ziemann v Burlington County Bridge Comm'n (1994, D NJ) 155 FRD 497, 501 [serious deterioration of plaintiff's emotional state in the interim warranted a second mental examination].

Certainly, the injured party would not expect to go to trial without an up-to-date examination by his own physician. Upon what logic should the opposing party be denied the right to be equally well prepared to present the issue?[12]

"Good cause" for a second examination also exists where a plaintiff, after undergoing by agreement a pre-suit medical examination in one locale, later sues in a distant forum. Plaintiff's choice of venue has made the defense doctor's testimony obtainable only by deposition or by incurring substantial expense.[13] "Good cause" may also exist where a party shows that the first examination was inadequate or incomplete.[14] However, a party's disappointment with the conclusions of the first expert selected does not constitute "good cause" to shop for a more favorable opinion.[15]

Successive Examinations: Personal injury plaintiffs commonly sue several defendants, many of whom have interests adverse to each other. When one of these defendants conducts a discovery medical examination, an issue may arise as to whether "good cause" still exists for the remaining parties to obtain one. Little case law exists on this question. In a series of cases where one defendant was claiming indemnity from another, the New York courts have recognized that each defendant is entitled to its own discovery medical examination: "Although [orthopedic and neurological] examinations had already been conducted by third-party defendants' physicians, defendant should not be relegated to reliance upon the medical experts of his adversary."[16] Similarly, courts generally do not find that pre-suit examinations by a defendant's compensation carrier pre-empt "good cause" for a later, post-suit examination:

---

[12] Vopelak v Williams (1967, ND Ohio) 42 FRD 387, 389; see, however, Sporich v Superior Court (2000) 77 Cal App 4th 422, 428, 91 Cal Rptr 2d 752, 756 [fact that last mental exam took place over a year before hearing is not in and of itself "good cause" for another mental exam, absent any showing of a change in the examinee's condition].

See also Galieti v State Farm (1994, D Colo) 154 FRD 262, 263 [where only weeks remained before the start of trial, two years had passed since the initial mental examination, and plaintiff's present emotional condition remained at issue, court ordered a second mental examination]; Dwyer ex rel. Dwyer v Mazzola (1991, App Div) 567 NYS2d 281, 282 [nine years had elapsed since original examination of infant plaintiff].

[13] Vopelak v Williams (1967, ND Ohio) 42 FRD 387.

[14] Mayer v Illinois Northern Ry. (1963, CA7 ND Ill) 324 F2d 154.

[15] See, e.g., Loveland v Kremer (1990, Minn App) 464 NW2d 306, 309 [where party chose the first examining physician, dissatisfaction with the physician's credentials and report do not constitute good cause for a second independent medical examination by the same type of specialist]; Moore v Calavar Corp. (1992, WD La) 142 FRD 134, 135–136 [absent a change in the plaintiff's condition or original clinical findings, no good cause for a subsequent examination existed merely because defendant's physicians changed their opinions regarding the plaintiff's need for surgery].

[16] Kauderer v Mestman (1991, App Div) 569 NYS2d 256, 257.

See also Fleming v Chris Craft Industries, Inc., (1983, App Div) 469 NYS2d 3, Mignott v Sears, Roebuck & Co. (1982, App Div) 447 NYS2d 3.

> [The plaintiff] argues that he has already submitted to medical examinations by [the defendant] through its worker's compensation carrier . . . . Thus, he asserts that the present request is repetitive, cumulative, and burdensome. [Its] present position as the defendant in a Jones Act-general maritime action makes it vulnerable to general damages which are entirely different from the scheduled damages recoverable under state worker's compensation law. All of [the plaintiff's] previous medical treatment was supervised, orchestrated and paid for by [its compensation carrier] without [the defendant's] involvement.[17]

An issue concerning successive examinations by different parties may also arise where the defendants are not antagonistic to each other. Section 2032.220 gives "any" defendant the right to demand a routine physical examination of a personal injury plaintiff.[18] Had the Legislature intended that the exercise of this right by one defendant would be "good cause" to prevent a *routine* physical examination by any other defendant, it would have so provided, as it did for depositions.[19] In contrast, where one of several defendants with a common interest has already obtained, whether by motion or agreement, a mental examination or a *painful, dangerous, or intrusive* physical examination, access to the results of that examination may eliminate any "good cause" for another examination by the other defendants.

§ 8.9   Qualifications of Examiner

Mental Examinations: The 1956 Discovery Act specified that only a "physician" could conduct a discovery medical examination.[1] In the *Reuter* case,[2] a defendant sought to have a plaintiff undergo a mental examination by a psychologist. The court ruled that a psychologist did not qualify as a "physician":

> [A] psychiatrist is a physician who specializes in mental, emotional or behavioral disorders. Thus, compelling a mental examination by a psychiatrist is proper under section 2032. [¶] A psychologist, however, is not licensed as a physician and surgeon. . . . A psychologist is thus not a "physician" as defined under section 2032, and may not conduct a mental examination compelled under that section.[3]

---

17 Guerra v M.P. O'Meara Oil Co. (1992, La App) 609 So2d 1015.

18 CCP § 2032.220(a).

For a discussion of the "demand" procedure for obtaining a physical examination of a personal injury plaintiff, see § 8.3.

19 See CCP § 2025.610, which prohibits a subsequent deposition of one whose deposition has been taken by any party.

For a discussion of this one-deposition limit, see § 2.36.

1 Former CCP § 2032(b), 1956 Discovery Act, Appendix E.

2 Reuter v Superior Court (1979) 93 Cal App 3d 332, 155 Cal Rptr 525.

3 Reuter v Superior Court (1979) 93 Cal App 3d 332, 339, 155 Cal Rptr 525, 529–530 [internal citations omitted].

Other jurisdictions have stretched the word "physician" to include psychologists. Anson v Fickel (1986, ND Ind) 110 FRD 184, 186; Massey v Manitowoc Co., Inc. (1983, ED Pa) 101 FRD 304; Thynne v City of Omaha (1984, Neb) 351 NW2d 54.

The Legislature quickly annulled this decision. In 1980, it amended the statute to include psychologists with specified credentials and experience.

Thus, for mental examinations, Section 2032.020 simply restates the prior law:

> A mental examination conducted under this section shall be performed only by a licensed physician, or by a licensed psychologist who has a doctoral degree in psychology and at least five years of postgraduate experience in the diagnosis and treatment of emotional and mental disorders.[4]

Physical Examinations: Although the *Reuter* case involved a mental examination, its reasoning suggested that courts would also narrowly interpret "physician" where a physical examination was sought. The court acknowledged that in some contexts any practitioner of the healing arts could be considered a "physician," but rejected this meaning for discovery examinations: "[T]he purposes of the statute and the best interest of the plaintiff and defendant are served by limiting the term 'physician' to mean a person licensed as a physician and surgeon under the Medical Practice Act."[5]

Section 2032.020 departs markedly from this restrictive approach to the qualifications of the person who may do a physical examination. It not only authorizes examinations by a "licensed physician" but also by any "other appropriate licensed health care practitioner."[6] These include osteopaths,[7] chiropractors,[8] clinical laboratory technologists,[9] physical therapists,[10] and speech pathologists.[11]

Moreover, other types of health-care practitioners must hold a "certificate." These include podiatrists,[12] optometrists,[13] occupational therapists,[14] and acupuncturists.[15] Since 1983 the Business and Professions Code has defined

---

[4] CCP § 2032.020(c).

[5] Reuter v Superior Court (1979) 93 Cal App 3d 332, 338, 155 Cal Rptr 525, 529.

[6] CCP § 2032.020(b).

In 1991, FRCivP 35(a) was amended to permit discovery medical examinations by any "suitably licensed or certified examiner."

[7] See Bus and Prof Code § 2099.5.

[8] See Bus and Prof Code § 1000–5.

[9] See Bus and Prof Code § 1261.

[10] See Bus and Prof Code § 2630.

[11] See Bus and Prof Code § 2532.

Other licensed health care practitioners include: respiratory therapists (Bus and Prof Code § 3718) and physician's assistants (Bus and Prof Code § 3519).

[12] See Bus and Prof Code § 2472.

[13] See Bus and Prof Code § 3055.

[14] Bus and Prof Code § 2570.

[15] See Bus and Prof Code § 4935.

See also Bus and Prof Code § 2590(f) [perfusionists required to hold a certificate].

"license" as synonymous with "certificate" and "registration."[16] Thus, the Legislature most likely intended Section 2032.020 to make no distinction between "licensed," "certified," and "registered" health-care practitioners.[17]

Vocational Rehabilitation Experts: In the *Browne* case,[18] decided under the 1956 Discovery Act, the defendant learned that the injured plaintiff had consulted a "rehabilitation expert." Defendant then persuaded the trial court to order a similar examination by a defense expert. However, the appellate court insisted that only licensed physicians could conduct a court-ordered physical examination:

> [S]ince a vocational rehabilitation counselor is not a licensed physician, no affirmative authority exists under the subject statute, or otherwise, to conduct the proposed physical examination. Since the statute grants no discretion to the trial court as to the person authorized to conduct a physical examination, the order under review constituted an abuse of discretion. Whether such an examination by a qualified vocational rehabilitation counselor should be permitted in the first instance is a matter for the Legislature to determine and not the courts.[19]

The court did not rule out this type of expert's possible participation in a physical examination supervised by a physician.[20] A federal appellate court, however, held that trial courts may not condition plaintiffs' use of a vocational rehabilitation expert as a trial witness upon their consent to undergoing an examination by a similar defense expert: "Since Rule 35 does not empower the district court to compel a vocational examination by [the defendant's] expert, the district court cannot indirectly compel a vocational examination by making the testimony of [the plaintiff's] own expert conditional on [the plaintiff's] submission to the additional examination."[21]

---

[16] Bus and Prof Code § 477(b).

[17] Cf. Evid Code § 1158 [permitting pre-suit access by patient's attorney to medical records of "physician and surgeon, dentist, registered nurse, dispensing optician, registered physical therapist, podiatrist, licensed psychologist, osteopathic physician and surgeon, chiropractor, clinical laboratory bioanalyst, clinical laboratory technologist, or pharmacist or pharmacy"].

[18] Browne v Superior Court (1979) 98 Cal App 3d 610, 159 Cal Rptr 669.

[19] Browne v Superior Court (1979) 98 Cal App 3d 610, 615–616, 159 Cal Rptr 669, 672 (internal citation omitted).

Before the 1991 amendment to FRCP 35(a), the federal courts also held that examinations by vocational rehabilitation experts were not authorized. See Acosta v Tenneco Oil Co. (1990, CA5 La) 913 F2d 205, 209; Soudelier v Tug Nan Services, Inc. (1987, ED La) 116 FRD 429; Acocella v Montauk Oil Transp. Corp. (1985, SD NY) 614 F Supp 1437.

[20] Browne v Superior Court (1979) 98 Cal App 3d 610, 615 n3, 159 Cal Rptr 669, 672 n3.

See also Reuter v Superior Court (1979) 93 Cal App 3d 332, 340, 155 Cal Rptr 525, 530 [defense psychiatrist may require testing by psychologist]; Wills v Red Lake Municipal Liquor Store (1984, Minn App) 350 NW2d 452, 453–454 [defense physician required vocational rehabilitation expert's examination to complete his own evaluation of plaintiff's condition]; Moore v Missouri Pacific Railroad Co. (1992, Mo) 825 SW2d 839, 843 [physical therapist supervised by physician].

[21] Acosta v Tenneco Oil Co. (1990, CA5 La) 913 F2d 205, 210.

On the one hand, the Civil Discovery Act arguably leaves *Browne* unchanged since the State neither licenses nor certifies vocational rehabilitation experts. On the other hand, Federal Rule 35 now allows any "suitably licensed or certified examiner" to conduct a discovery medical examination.[22] One federal trial judge[23] has interpreted this new wording to include a vocational rehabilitation expert, whose only license or certificate apparently was his Masters of Science degree. A subtle difference in wording, however, exists between the current federal and California provisions. Whereas Rule 35 speaks of an examiner who is *"suitably* licensed or certified," the California statute requires an "appropriate licensed health care practitioner," not an *"appropriately* licensed health care practitioner."[24]

Blood Examinations: Tests for finding out someone's blood type are frequently done by trained laboratory technicians who are not acting under a licensed physician's supervision. These blood tests usually occur in paternity cases under the provisions of Family Code Sections 7550–7557.[25] Section 7552 of that Code, however, requires only that those performing the blood tests be "experts qualified as examiners of blood types." Lest it cause an implied repeal of these Family Code provisions, the Legislature included the following statute in the discovery provisions:

> Nothing in this section affects tests under the Uniform Act on Blood Tests to Determine Paternity (Chapter 2 (commencing with Section 7550) of Part 2 of Division 12 of the Family Code).[26]

§ 8.10   Selection of Examiner

Presumptively the Movant's Choice: When a trial court orders a discovery medical examination by a certain type of health care practitioner,[1] issues sometimes arise over the selection of the particular person who will do it.[2] Whether proceeding under the "demand" procedure,[3] or by motion,[4] the discovering party must state "the identity and the specialty, if any" of the

---

[22] FRCivP 35(a).

[23] Olcott v LaFiandra (1992, D Vt) 793 F Supp 487, 491–492.

[24] CCP § 2032.020(b).

[25] Before 1994, this Act was found in Evidence Code §§ 890–897.

[26] CCP § 2032.010(a).

[1] For a discussion of the qualifications required of the examiner conducting a discovery medical examination, see § 8.9.

[2] Annotation: Right of defendant in personal injury action to designate physician to conduct medical examination of plaintiff. 33 ALR3d 1012.

[3] CCP § 2032.220(a).

For a discussion of the "demand" procedure for obtaining a compulsory medical examination, see § 8.3.

[4] CCP § 2032.310(a).

For a discussion of motions for a compulsory medical examination, see § 8.3.

examiner.[5] This suggests that at least presumptively the choice of the examiner belongs to that party.

The compulsory medical examination's function to level the "playing field as between the parties"[6] reinforces this presumption: "If a plaintiff may select his own doctor to testify as to his physical condition, fundamental fairness dictates that a defendant shall have the same right."[7] To achieve this goal, the moving party needs wide latitude in the selection of the examiner: "Although the court may appoint any physician it chooses to conduct the examination, as a practical matter the court will usually appoint the physician requested by the moving party."[8]

The *Edwards* case[9] exemplifies this deference to the moving party's choice. There, a plaintiff ordered to undergo a mental examination objected to the designation of a certain psychiatrist because of "her expressed fear and dislike of him."[10] Although the Supreme Court recognized that the moving party's choice of an examiner is not controlling, it observed that "ordinarily" the trial court should respect that choice.[11] Examinees who want a trial court to veto that selection must do more than make "unsupported objections" to the doctor's suitability.[12]

Showing Insufficient: Only a strong showing will persuade a trial court to override the moving party's choice of an examiner. The examinee must do more than claim that the examiner is defense-minded, believes that most personal injury plaintiffs are untruthful, customarily finds plaintiffs' injuries inconsequential, or testifies professionally for insurance interests.[13] Even a charge that an expert

---

[5] CCP § 2032.220(c).

[6] Looney v National Railroad Passenger Corp. (1992, D Mass) 142 FRD 264, 265.

But see Johnson v Packing Corp. of America (1994, ND Ill) 158 FRD 409 [parties directed to agree on an independent psychiatrist to perform mental examination].

[7] Timpte v District Court (1966, Colo) 421 P2d 728, cited in Mercury Casualty Co. v Superior Court (1986) 179 Cal App 3d 1027, 225 Cal Rptr 100.

See also Powell v United States (1993, ED Va) 149 FRD 122, 124.

[8] Mercury Casualty Co. v Superior Court (1986) 179 Cal App 3d 1027, 1033, 225 Cal Rptr 100, 103.

[9] Edwards v Superior Court (1976) 16 Cal 3d 905, 912–913, 130 Cal Rptr 14, 18–19, 549 P2d 846, 850–851.

[10] Edwards v Superior Court (1976) 16 Cal 3d 905, 912, 130 Cal Rptr 14, 18, 549 P2d 846, 850.

[11] Edwards v Superior Court (1976) 16 Cal 3d 905, 912, 130 Cal Rptr 14, 18, 549 P2d 846, 850.

[12] Edwards v Superior Court (1976) 16 Cal 3d 905, 913, 130 Cal Rptr 14, 19, 549 P2d 846, 851.

[13] See, e.g., Looney v National R.R. Passenger Corp. (1992, D Mass) 142 FRD 264; Matthews v Watson (1989, ED Pa) 123 FRD 522.

But see Curry v Klein (Kan 1992) 840 P2d 443 [doctor notoriously biased in previous courtroom appearances disqualified from conducting discovery medical examinations].

has a "closed mind" about the particular medical matter at issue does not require the trial judge to veto the defense's selection.[14] This charge, even if true, merely raises issues of credibility, which cross-examination at trial may explore.[15] It does not disqualify the doctor, but merely affects the weight of his or her testimony.[16] As the court remarked in the *Mercury Casualty Co.* case: "[U]nlike expert witnesses appointed under [Evid Code § 730], the physician appointed to conduct a [discovery] medical examination . . . is not hired for the purposes of being impartial."[17] Nor need the prospective examiner be of the same gender as the prospective examinee.[18]

Showing Sufficient: In one case, affidavits stating that the selected examiner had consistently hurt prior examinees supported a plaintiff's request for a full evidentiary hearing on the doctor's suitability.[19] Although not an automatic bar, the court will usually not approve a doctor who is a client of the defense attorney.[20]

§ 8.11   Place of Examination

No matter where a plaintiff lives, the defense normally will want to conduct its discovery medical examination near the forum. This "allows the examining physician to be available conveniently for testimony."[1]

---

[14] Postell v Amana Refrigeration, Inc. (1980, ND Ga) 87 FRD 706, 708–709 [plaintiff claiming an eye injury from exposure to a microwave oven is directed to submit to an examination by an ophthalmologist who had already opined in medical journals that microwave ovens could not injure eyes].

[15] Great Western Life Assurance Co. v. Levithan (1994, ED Pa) 153 FRD 74, 77 [extent of physician's bias and interest may be fully explored at trial during cross examination].

[16] Powell v United States (1993, ED Va) 149 FRD 122, 123–124 [belief of defense doctor that two-thirds of insureds exaggerate their injury is no bar to selection of him to conduct discovery medical examination].

[17] Mercury Casualty Co. v Superior Court (1986) 179 Cal App 3d 1027, 1033, 225 Cal Rptr 100, 103.

[18] Gale v National Transportation Co. (1946, SD NY) 7 FRD 237.

[19] Miller v Holtz House of Vehicles, Inc. (1991, App Div) 578 NYS2d 102, 104.

[20] Powell v United States (1993, ED Va) 149 FRD 122, 124 ["Such a relationship would prevent the appointment of (the defendant's selection) as a medical examiner."]; Martin v Superior Court (1969, Ariz) 451 P2d 597, 600 [error for trial court to accept defense-selected physician who was also client of defense attorney, absent evidentiary showing of the extent of the relationship]; Adkins v Eitel (1965, Ohio App) 206 NE2d 573 [although prior social or legal relationship is no automatic bar, trial court abused discretion in appointing physician who was client and neighbor of defense attorney, where defense attorney refused to discuss relationship]; Main v Tony L. Scheston-Luxor Cab Co. (1958, Iowa) 89 NW2d 865, 868 [no abuse of discretion to reject defense-selected physician who was also a client of the defense attorney]; compare Louth v Wiegand (1990, App Div) 561 NYS2d 955, 956 [trial court improperly accepted defense selection of physician who was client of *plaintiff's* attorney]; Great Western Life Assurance Co. v. Levithan (1994, ED Pa) 153 FRD 74, 77 [upholding selection of examinee's former physician as examiner, despite examinee's claim that this doctor "failed" to correct his medical condition].

[1] Baird v Quality Foods, Inc. (1969, ED La) 47 FRD 212, 213.

75-Mile Radius: When the examinee's home is near the proposed examiner's office, the situs of a compulsory medical examination should be uncontroversial. Indeed, one condition for using the "demand procedure"[2] is that it be "conducted at a location within 75 miles of the residence of the examinee."[3] Within this 75-mile radius, the only issue that might arise is whether the examination should occur at the doctor's office, an attorney's office, or the examinee's home. Absent unusual circumstances, a court will follow "the common sense notion that medical examinations are more properly conducted in medical offices than in the offices of an attorney,"[4] especially if the examination requires nontransportable diagnostic equipment.[5]

Two Logistical Issues: When the examiner and the examinee are farther apart, two logistical issues may arise: (1) Should the court compel the examinee to travel to reach the doctor's office? (2) If so, who pays for this travel? The 1956 Discovery Act gave little help in resolving these issues. It merely required that the court's order specify the "place" for the examination.[6] Given this vagueness and the long distances separating prospective California examiners from many resident examinees, the dearth of California case law on either issue is surprising.

—Legislative Guidance: Section 2032.320 of the Civil Discovery Act now addresses both logistical issues. As for distance, a court may only require an examinee to journey more than 75 miles from home if "there is good cause for the travel involved."[7] As for expense, the court must condition any travel order "on the advancement by the moving party of the reasonable expenses and costs to the examinee for travel to the place of examination."

"Good Cause for Travel: No reported California case has directly considered "good cause" to compel a litigant to travel more than 75 miles for a discovery medical examination. However, in a cognate situation, an appellate court refused to require a workers' compensation claimant with a heart condition to journey 185 miles for a defense medical examination, unless no qualified cardiologist or internist was available near the worker's home.[8]

---

[2] For a discussion of the "demand" procedure for obtaining a compulsory medical examination, see § 8.3.

[3] CCP § 2032.220(a)(2).

[4] Resnick v Seher (1993, App Div) 603 NYS2d 501, 502.

See also Carmody v Kuehner (1994, App Div) 612 NYS2d 53.

[5] See Healy v Deepdale General Hospital (1988, App Div) 535 NYS2d 404; Deeley v Leo's Den, Inc. (1987, App Div) 511 NYS2d 301; Schussheim v Beam's Drug Corp. (1974, App Div) 358 NYS2d 30.

[6] Former CCP § 2032, 1956 Discovery Act, Appendix D.

[7] CCP § 2032.320(e)(1).

Cf. Hansen v Workers Comp. Appeals Board (1989) 211 Cal App 3d 717, 721, 259 Cal Rptr 506, 508 [aside from whether the 75-mile travel restriction in CCP § 2032(c)(2) applies to worker's compensation proceedings, "it is indicative of legislative intent to limit the distance for medical examination in civil actions to 75 miles."]

[8] Hansen v Workers Comp. Appeals Board (1989) 211 Cal App 3d 717, 721, 259 Cal Rptr 506, 508.

—Travel to Forum: Disputes over travel to examination sites occur most often with respect to plaintiffs who sue in a state far from their home. Absent unusual circumstances, federal courts and those in other states generally require the plaintiff to travel to the forum, despite the distance from the examinee's home.[9] In ordering such journeys courts sometimes observe that the plaintiff deliberately chose a venue far from home:

> A Georgia forum would have offered a more convenient, speedier, and possibly less expensive forum [for this Georgia auto accident case]. Plaintiff, however, chose to bring the action in this [New York] forum. Plaintiff cannot now complain that he should not be examined in this forum.[10]

However, even where jurisdictional or other restrictions precluded suit in the plaintiff's home state, courts still schedule discovery medical examinations in the forum state.[11] The examining party's need to have a local physician available for trial testimony justifies the travel order. For example, in one federal case,[12] a plaintiff from Maine who had no choice but to sue in Massachusetts resisted travelling to Boston for a physical examination. He suggested that the defense either employ a doctor in Maine, or send a Massachusetts doctor to examine him there. The trial judge found either course unfair:

> I do not think it would be satisfactory . . . for him to be examined by a physician in Maine. A Maine physician as a future witness would constitute a real handicap to the defendant. Conversely, the court will recognize that it is an imposition on a Massachusetts physician, to which most will not voluntarily submit even if adequately compensated, to go to Maine simply for an examination. This not being a hardship case, I will not require it.[13]

In any case where a court orders a nonresident party to travel to the forum for a defense medical examination, it should consider alleviating the

---

[9] E.g., Commercial National Bank v Tapp (1989, D Kan) 125 FRD 695 [Mexican plaintiffs required to travel 2,000 miles to Kansas forum]; Warren v Weber & Heidenthaler, Inc. (1955, D Mass) 134 F Supp 524 [Maine plaintiff required to travel to Massachusetts forum]; Platman v Pham Thu Duc (1993, App Div) 595 NYS2d 111 [California personal injury plaintiff required to travel to New York forum].

[10] See, e.g., Pierce v Brovig (1954, SD NY) 16 FRD 569, 570.

[11] See, e.g., Costanza v Monty (1970, ED Wis) 50 FRD 75 [plaintiff who moved to Nevada while suit was pending must return to Wisconsin forum for defense physical examination]; Platman v Pham Thu Duc (1993, App Div) 595 NYS2d 111 [California plaintiff injured in New York taxi collision required to travel to New York forum for defense physical examination].

[12] Warren v Weber & Heidenthaler, Inc. (1955, D Mass) 134 F Supp 524.

[13] Warren v Weber & Heidenthaler, Inc. (1955, D Mass) 134 F Supp 524, 525.

See also Baird v Quality Foods, Inc. (1969, ED La) 47 FRD 212.

inconvenience and expense involved by directing that the parties depose the out-of-state examinee during that same trip.[14]

—Travel Outside the Forum: Infrequently a defendant has sought to compel the examinee to travel far from the forum for a specialist's examination. With rare exceptions,[15] courts elsewhere have ordered this travel if no comparable specialist practices within the forum.[16] In contrast, they find no good cause for such travel when a qualified specialist is available in the forum.[17]

Costs of Travel: Section 2032.320's[18] requirement that the examining party advance the "costs and expenses" of travel more than 75-miles from an examinee's residence[19] leaves two matters for interpretation. First, what are "costs and expenses"? Courts will doubtlessly construe this phrase to include transportation fares and the price of necessary food and lodging during the trip.[20] Second, if the examining party prevails at trial, are these expenses an item of taxable "costs"? Travel to a medical examination site is not on the list of "allowable items" in the statute governing "costs."[21] However, the court has discretion to include in the award of costs to the prevailing party "[i]tems not mentioned in this section and items assessed upon application."[22]

---

[14] See, e.g., Warren v Weber & Heidenthaler (1955, D Mass) 134 F Supp 524; Gale v National Transportation Co. (1946, SD NY) 7 FRD 237.

[15] See Bennett v White Laboratories, Inc. (1993, MD Fla) 841 F Supp 1155, 1159 [Jacksonville plaintiff cannot be ordered to travel outside the federal district for examination by a Miami specialist].

[16] See, e.g., Fletcher v Southern Farm Bureau Life Ins. Co. (1985, CA8 Ark) 757 F2d 953 [Arkansas plaintiff may be required to travel to Colorado for special allergy testing]; Reed v Marley (1959, Ark) 321 SW2d 193, 195–196 [Arkansas plaintiff may be required to travel to Oklahoma for a physical examination].

Cf. Stinchcomb v United States (1990, ED Pa) 132 FRD 29, 30–31 [evidentiary hearing required before court would order mentally developmentally disabled 10-year-old plaintiff to travel cross-country, out of the forum, for lengthy, invasive, painful, and stressful testing].

[17] See, e.g., Blount v Wake Electric Membership Corp. (1993, ED NC) 162 FRD 102, 107 [wheel-chair-bound plaintiff need not travel four hours from his home to reach defense doctor located outside the district where case is pending]; Rainey v Wal-Mart Stores, Inc. (1991, WD La) 139 FRD 94, 94 [no good cause for ordering 270 mile trip outside the forum]; Stuart v Burford (1967, ND Okla) 42 FRD 591 [no good cause to require Oklahoma City plaintiff to travel to Tulsa for examination by an internist selected by the defense].

[18] The lack of comparable provisions makes cases from other jurisdictions unhelpful in resolving disputes that will arise under CCP § 2032.320.

[19] CCP § 2032.320(e)(2).

[20] Cf. In Re American President Lines, Ltd. (1991, CA6 Ohio) 929 F2d 226, 228 [upholding trial court's decision to make defendants pay travel costs, but not living expenses, for plaintiff's out-of-state examination]; Ewing v Ayres Corp. (1989, ND Miss) 129 FRD 137, 139 [defendant required to pay travel costs, including living expenses, for indigent plaintiff to attend out-of-forum examination by specialist].

[21] CCP § 1033.5(a).

[22] CCP § 1033.5(c)(4).

§ 8.12 Time of Examination

Issues concerning the timeliness of a compulsory medical examination usually arise when a party seeks an examination close to or even after the start of trial.[1] Although the provisions regulating discovery medical examinations do not expressly address this problem,[2] Section 2024.020 provides that all discovery as a matter of right ends 30 days before the date the action is first set for trial.[3] A party seeking a medical examination after that date must get court permission.[4] In considering a motion for a late medical examination, the trial court will need to know why it is necessary, why it was not sought earlier, and whether it will delay the trial.[5]

In the *Fairmont Ins. Co.* case,[6] the Supreme Court considered the phrase "date initially set for the trial of the action" in situations where there has been a mistrial, an order granting a new trial, or a remand for a new trial after reversal of a judgment on appeal. It held that in such cases discovery is reopened and the cutoff date is calculated based on the date initially set for the *new* trial.

Coordination with Medical Report Delivery: The trial court should not grant a motion for a late medical examination without consulting the statutory timetable governing the examinee's right to demand a report of the examiner's findings and conclusions.[7] Under normal circumstances, when the examinee demands the report, the examining party must deliver a copy within 30 days or within 15 days of trial, if that date is earlier.[8] This schedule may need adjustment when examinations occur after the statutory cutoff date for discovery.

---

[1] Annotation: Timeliness of application for compulsory physical examination of injured party in personal injury action. 9 ALR3d 1146.

See Johnston v Southern Pacific Co. (1907) 150 Cal 535, 540, 89 P 348, 351 [trial court has discretion to order plaintiff to undergo a physical examination even though the trial of the case was already in progress]; Lumerman v Dikoff (1962) 203 Cal App 2d 490, 21 Cal Rptr 402 [trial court has discretion to refuse defense request for mid-trial medical examination].

For a discussion of the right to obtain a medical examination before suit has been filed, see §§ 14.1–14.3.

[2] Section 2032.320(d) merely states that both the motion for a compulsory medical examination and the order granting the motion should specify "the time" that the examination will take place.

[3] CCP § 2024.020(a).

[4] CCP § 2024.050(a).

[5] CCP § 2024.050(b).

See Miksis v Howard (1997, CA7 Ind) 106 F3d 754, 758–759 [trial court had discretion to deny defendants' motion for a physical examination where defendants, who knew the seriousness of the plaintiff's injuries, waited until the trial date was less than three months away].

[6] Fairmont Ins. Co. v Superior Court (2000) 22 Cal 4th 245, 92 Cal Rptr 2d 70, 991 P2d 156.

[7] CCP § 2032.610(b).

See, e.g., Bennett v White Laboratories, Inc. (1993, MD Fla) 841 F Supp 1155, 1157.

For a discussion of the examinee's right to demand a report of a compulsory medical examination, see § 8.18.

[8] Cf. Shapiro v Win-Sum Ski Corp. (1982, WD NY) 95 FRD 38, 38–39 ["if defendant's physician is to examine plaintiff the examination must take place sufficiently before trial to permit a copy of the report to be prepared and delivered on time for trial"].

§ 8.13   Conducting the Examination

The actual conduct of a compulsory medical examination presents two principal questions. First, who, if anyone, may attend the procedure? For example, may the examination be witnessed by the examinee's attorney, doctor, or relative, or by the lawyer for the examining party? Second, by what means, if any, may a party record what is said and what is done during that examination? For example, may either side use a court reporter, a tape recorder, or a video camera to record what happens? As one might expect, the answers to these questions will vary depending on whether the procedure is a physical or a mental examination.[1]

Pre-1986 Case Law: The original provision for discovery medical examinations, like its federal prototype,[2] provided no explicit guidance in either of these areas. It left the answers to these questions for the appellate courts. Those courts treated the task as part of the trial court's duty to specify in its order the "conditions" for carrying out a compulsory physical examination. Both as to physical and as to mental examinations, the courts repeatedly considered whether a particular type of person might witness the event, and whether a party could employ a particular method to record what took place during the examination.[3] This sizable body of case law is the foundation for the specific provisions now in the Civil Discovery Act,[4] which answer most, but not all, of the questions relating to the witnessing[5] and recording[6] of medical examinations.[7]

§ 8.14   Witnessing a Physical Examination

Attorney for Examinee: Parties have raised two arguments for allowing the examinee's attorney to be present during a compulsory physical examination. First, this procedure is simply another stage in the lawsuit. Presumably, a litigant's right to counsel extends to every stage of a case. This general presumption has special strength when the law is compelling a party to undergo a bodily examination by the adversary's agent. Litigants should not have to fend

---

[1] Annotation: Right of party to have attorney or physician present during physical or mental examination at instance of opposing party. 84 ALR4th 558.

Annotation: Right of party to have his attorney or physician, or a court reporter, present during his physical or mental examination by a court-appointed expert. 7 ALR3d 881.

[2] FRCivP 35.

[3] See, e.g., Long v Hauser (1975) 52 Cal App 3d 490, 125 Cal Rptr 125 [finding no unqualified right for the examinee to have her own physician witness a physical examination]; Ebel v Superior Court (1974) 39 Cal App 3d 934, 114 Cal Rptr 722 [approving tape recording of a physical examination].

[4] CCP §§ 2032.510–2032.530.

[5] For a discussion of who may witness a *physical* examination, see § 8.14.

For a discussion of who may witness a *mental* examination, see § 8.16.

[6] For a discussion of recording a *physical* examination, see § 8.15.

For a discussion of recording a *mental* examination, see § 8.17.

[7] CCP § 2032.510.

for themselves in learning what their legal rights are during this drastic method of discovery.[1]

Second, the presence of the examinee's attorney forestalls improper questioning by the examiner. A physical examination normally and legitimately includes the taking of a detailed history from the examinee:

[A] physician or surgeon cannot make a complete and thorough physical examination, especially of diseases or injuries to the internal organs, without asking of the patient his various symptoms. This must be especially so in the case of a physician or surgeon who is called in a long time after the injury has occurred, and who, from the nature of the case, had no opportunity to study himself the symptoms of the patient at the time of and immediately after the injury. If a physician is not to ascertain these symptoms and weigh them in the light of his professional knowledge, his examination would not be of materially more value than that of a layman.[2]

However, this legitimate questioning will often touch upon the events that gave rise to the lawsuit and could result in statements pertinent only to the liability aspects of the case.

Codifying longstanding California case law,[3] Section 2032.510 acknowledges an examinee's unqualified right to have his or her attorney present during a physical examination:

The attorney for the examinee or for a party producing the examinee, or that attorney's representative, shall be permitted to attend and observe any physical examination conducted for discovery purposes . . . .[4]

Taking account of the potential for interference with the doctor's performance, the statute warns that the attorney "shall not participate in or disrupt" the examination. Improper conduct by the examiner or by the attending attorney is a matter for the court. The statute specifically provides that if the examinee's attorney finds the examiner to be "abusive" of the client, or to be engaging in "unauthorized diagnostic tests and procedures,"[5] the attorney may halt the examination and seek a protective order. Similarly, if the examinee's attorney begins to interfere with the examination, the doctor can suspend it to allow a similar application by the party seeking the examination. The party losing either

---

[1] Annotation: Right of party to have attorney or physician present during physical or mental examination at instance of opposing party. 84 ALR4th 558.

[2] Wunsch v Weber (1894, Misc) 29 NYS 1100, 1101–1102, quoted with approval in Sharff v Superior Court (1955) 44 Cal 2d 508, 510, 282 P2d 896, 897.

[3] Sharff v Superior Court (1955) 44 Cal 2d 508, 510, 282 P2d 896, 897; Munoz v Superior Court (1972) 26 Cal App 3d 643, 102 Cal Rptr 686.

[4] CCP § 2032.510(a).

[5] CCP § 2032.510(d).

sort of motion for a protective order should anticipate the imposition of a monetary sanction.

—Representative of Examinee's Attorney: Section 2032.510 allows the examinee's attorney to send a "representative" to the physical examination.[6] The statute does not define this word. It should include an associate who has not entered an appearance in the case, and probably would cover a paralegal or a law clerk. The attorney must identify this representative in a signed authorization.

Examinee's Physician: Either besides or instead of their attorney, examinees have frequently sought to have their own medical representative attend discovery physical examinations.[7] The attorney's presence is useful and appropriate during the history-taking portion of the procedure,[8] but during the subsequent bodily examination it could intrude embarrassingly on the client's privacy. In contrast, the presence of the examinee's physician during the actual examination has four benefits. First, it would make the examinee feel more comfortable with the medical procedures. Second, the doctor would be better able than the attorney to judge the appropriateness of the procedures. Third, the doctor's presence would inhibit the examiner from conducting an unnecessarily rough or abusive examination. Finally, the doctor could judge professionally both the adequacy of the examination and the accuracy of the subsequent report.[9] Balanced against these benefits to the examinee, however, is the possibility that this scrutiny from a fellow professional will inhibit or distract the examiner.

Only one reported California case has addressed the examinee's right to have a physician witness a discovery physical examination. In *Long v Hauser*,[10] a plaintiff arrived at the defense doctor's office with her husband, her attorney, a court reporter and her personal physician. The appellate court upheld the trial court's discretion to bar the physician. It found no "unqualified right" for the plaintiff to have her own doctor witness the examination. The court, however, had no occasion to address the trial court's discretion to *allow* the doctor's attendance.[11]

Section 2032.510 does not expressly allow an examinee's own doctor to observe a physical examination. Nevertheless, a court might permit such attendance in two ways. First, the statute expressly allows the "attorney's

---

[6] CCP § 2032.510(a).

[7] Annotation: Right of party to have attorney or physician present during physical or mental examination at instance of opposing party. 84 ALR 4th 558.

[8] Cf. Mohr v District Court (1983, Mont) 660 P2d 88 [attorney may be present during the history-taking segment of the examination, but not during the actual physical examination itself].

[9] For a discussion of the examinee's right to demand a written report concerning a compulsory medical examination, see § 8.18.

[10] Long v Hauser (1975) 52 Cal App 3d 490, 493, 125 Cal Rptr 125, 127–128.

[11] Annotation: Right of party to have attorney or physician present during physical or mental examination at instance of opposing party. 84 ALR4th 558.

Cf. Johnston v Southern Pacific Co. (1907) 150 Cal 535, 540, 89 P 348, 351.

representative"[12] to attend in the attorney's place. Arguably, this phrase includes a medical consultant.[13] Second, the court could order such attendance under its general *discretion* to decide the "conditions" for a discovery examination. The codification of previous case law establishing a *right* to the presence of one's attorney and of a court reporter may suggest that no others may attend as a matter of *right*.[14] However, nothing requires a conclusion that the statute ousts a trial court of the discretion to let others attend where the particular circumstances so warrant.

The federal courts have not recognized an absolute right to have the examinee's physician attend a discovery physical examination.[15] However, they are much more receptive to allowing a doctor to witness the examination than they are to allowing an attorney to do so.[16]

Relatives and Friends: No California case has directly addressed the propriety of an examinee's spouse, relative, or friend attending a physical examination. In *Long v Hauser,*[17] a plaintiff appeared for a physical examination accompanied by her husband and her personal physician.[18] However, since the defendant challenged only the attendance by the physician, the court did not rule upon whether the spouse could attend. As discussed above, nothing in Section 2032.510 removes a trial court's discretion to order, as a "condition" of a particular examination, that a relative or friend may witness all or part of the procedure.[19] Such a "condition" would be especially appropriate where the examinee is a child or is of a different gender from the examining physician.[20]

---

[12] CCP § 2032.510(c).

[13] Cf. Gray v Victory Memorial Hospital (1989, App Div) 536 NYS2d 679, 681 [denial of right to have psychiatrist present at mental examination infringed examinee's right to assistance by counsel].

For a discussion of the right to witness a mental examination, see § 8.16.

[14] The applicable canon of statutory construction is *expressio unius est exclusio alterius.*

[15] Sanden v Mayo Clinic (1974, CA8 Minn) 495 F2d 221, 224–225 [no abuse of discretion in refusing to allow the physician of the plaintiff-nurse to attend electromyographic study of her anal sphincter].

[16] See Dziwanoski v Ocean Carriers Corp. (1960, D Md) 26 FRD 595, 598.

[17] Long v Hauser (1975) 52 Cal App 3d 490, 125 Cal Rptr 125.

See also Golfland Entertainment Centers, Inc. v Superior Court (2003) 108 Cal App 4th 739, 748 n5, 133 Cal Rptr 2d 828, 834 n5 [defendant agreed to permit plaintiff's mother to attend defense mental exam].

[18] She was also accompanied by her attorney and a court reporter.

[19] Cf. Bennett v White Laboratories, Inc. (1993, MD Fla) 841 F Supp 1155, 1158 [as a condition for obtaining an out-of-forum examination, defendant agreed to pay for examinee's mother or husband to travel with her; court did not address whether either escort may attend the examination itself].

[20] See, e.g., Simon v Castille (1965, La App) 174 So 2d 660, 665 [the appellate court, having sustained the trial court's exclusion of the attorney's attendance, observed: "We note that the plaintiff here is a female. If she objects to being examined by a strange physician without the presence of her husband or her own personal physician or some relative or other person, this may be good cause for the imposition by the trial judge of such a condition."]

Examining Party's Attorney: No reported California case has addressed whether the *examining party* may have an attorney present during a discovery physical examination. On the one hand, one reason for letting the *examinee's* attorney attend—the right to counsel at all stages of a lawsuit—also supports the presence of the opposing attorney. On the other hand, this party already has a representative—the examining doctor.

The other reason for the *examinee's* right to counsel during the examination—the danger that the doctor's questions stray from damages to liability—does not apply. On the contrary, the presence of two opposing lawyers simply invites bickering. Courts should address disruptive conduct by the examinee's attorney through the examiner's statutory right to suspend the procedure to seek a protective order.

Moreover, the opposing attorney's attendance would intrude upon the examinee's privacy. Just because examinees might desire their own counsel's presence during a physical examination does not mean that they are willing to have a hostile lawyer there as well. Absent very compelling circumstances, the court should respect the examinee's privacy.[21]

§ 8.15   Recording a Physical Examination

Court Reporter: Codifying longstanding case law,[1] Section 2032.510 unequivocally allows a court reporter to attend and "record stenographically . . . any words spoken to or by the examinee during any phase of the examination."[2]

Audio Recording: Similarly, Section 2032.510 codifies the main holding of the *Ebel* case[3] by providing for a right "to record . . . by audio tape any words spoken to or by an examinee during any phase of the examination."[4] Unlike the *Ebel* court, however, the statute does not require advance approval from the trial court to audio record the examination.

Video Recording: Advances in video technology, coupled with the *Ebel* court's statement that a party could use "*any* mechanical device"[5] that can record an examination accurately and completely, quickly led to efforts to video tape discovery physical examinations. In the *Edmiston* case,[6] the trial court had

---

See also Section 3121 of the New York Civil Practice Act, which provides with respect to physical examinations in personal injury cases: "If the party to be examined shall be a female she shall, if she desires, be entitled to have such examination in the presence of her own personal physician and such other relative or other person as the court may direct."

[21] See High v Burrell (1987, Fla App) 509 So 2d 385, 386 [trial court has discretion to permit attorneys for each side to attend discovery physical examination].

[1] Gonzi v Superior Court (1959) 51 Cal 2d 586, 335 P2d 97.

[2] CCP § 2032.510(a).

[3] Ebel v Superior Court (1974) 39 Cal App 3d 934, 114 Cal Rptr 722.

[4] CCP § 2032.510(a).

[5] Ebel v Superior Court (1974) 39 Cal App 3d 934, 937, 114 Cal Rptr 722, 723 (italics added).

[6] Edmiston v Superior Court (1978) 22 Cal 3d 699, 150 Cal Rptr 276, 586 P2d 590.

authorized this form of recording. It required the equipment operator to be a disinterested person, the taping to be nondisruptive, and the recording to be available for the other side's viewing.

A majority of the Supreme Court, however, ruled that the trial court lacked the power to issue even such a carefully crafted order. It noted fears that "videotaping with its heavy equipment and necessary additional personnel would unnecessarily create a sideshow atmosphere at which taping was the main attraction . . . ."[7] It felt that the right to an attorney's presence and a court reporter or audiotape recorder already adequately protected the examinee's interests. Moreover, the Court read the statutory right to later demand "a detailed *written* report" from the examining doctor to imply that only "printed or typewritten" records of the examination were permissible. Finally, and most importantly, the majority saw the Court's earlier rejection of videotaped depositions[8] as signifying that video recording of any discovery procedure required explicit legislative authorization.

The two dissenters believed that a trial judge should have discretion to authorize videotaping, a procedure that, in their view, was "superior to the methods previously approved by judicial decision because it provides an impartial visual record of the physical examination."[9]

Section 2032.510 does not include video recording in its list of methods that the examinee may use to record the examination.[10] This silence, coupled with the express permission that the Discovery Act now gives to the video recording of depositions,[11] strongly suggests the Legislature's tacit approval of the *Edmiston* prohibition. *Ramirez v MacAdam*[12] upheld a trial court's refusal to allow the video recording of a discovery physical examination.

§ 8.16 Witnessing a Mental Examination

Pre-1986 Case Law: The 1956 Discovery Act[1] did not address explicitly the examinee's right to have an attorney present during a compulsory medical examination, whether physical or mental. However, even before the adoption of the 1956 Discovery Act the Supreme Court had established the examinee's right to counsel during a discovery *physical* examination.[2] When examinees began

---

[7] Edmiston v Superior Court (1978) 22 Cal 3d 699, 702, 704, 150 Cal Rptr 276, 277–278, 279, 586 P2d 590, 592–593.

[8] Bailey v Superior Court (1977) 19 Cal 3d 970, 140 Cal Rptr 669, 568 P2d 394.

[9] Edmiston v Superior Court (1978) 22 Cal 3d 699, 705, 150 Cal Rptr 276, 279, 586 P2d 590, 594 (dissenting opinion).

[10] See CCP § 2032.510(a).

[11] CCP § 2025.330(c).

For a discussion of video recorded depositions, see §§ 2.33 and 2.41.

[12] Ramirez v MacAdam (1993) 13 Cal App 4th 1638, 16 Cal Rptr 2d 911. Cf. Baqleh v Superior Court (2002) 100 Cal App 4th 478, 492 n4, 122 Cal Rptr 2d 673, 684 n4.

[1] See CCP § 2032 of the 1956 Discovery Act, Appendix E.

[2] For a discussion of who may witness a compulsory physical examination, see § 8.14.

to assert a corresponding right to have their lawyers attend mental examinations, the trial and appellate courts resisted.[3]

Finally, a score of years after the adoption of the 1956 Discovery Act, the examinee's right to the presence of counsel at a discovery mental examination reached the Supreme Court in the *Edwards* case.[4] A child, injured while using school equipment, sued for sizable damages for emotional and physical injuries. Since she had received psychiatric treatment after her mishap and remained under a psychologist's care, her attorney did not question the "good cause" for a compulsory psychiatric examination. However, he insisted on attending that examination "to protect her from improper questioning, to assure accurate reporting, and to make the examination a more comfortable experience for her."[5]

These were the very factors that had led to the examinee's right to counsel's presence during a physical examination.[6] Nevertheless, a majority of the Court concluded that they were subordinate to "the defendant's statutory right to an effective psychiatric examination conducted under circumstances best calculated to assure . . . a fair and objective evaluation of the impact, if any, of the accident in question on plaintiff's mental and emotional condition."[7] In their view, the presence of an attorney would impede the establishment of the rapport between the psychiatrist and the examinee that is so necessary for a meaningful examination:

> The analyst in a psychiatric examination seeks by careful direction of areas of inquiry to probe, possibly very deeply, into the psyche,

---

[3] Board of Trustees v Superior Court (1969) 274 Cal App 2d 377, 79 Cal Rptr 58 [upholding trial court's discretion to exclude attorney for defendant-examinee from compulsory mental examination in teacher dismissal proceeding]; Whitfield v Superior Court (1966) 246 Cal App 2d 81, 54 Cal Rptr 505 [upholding trial court's discretion to exclude attorney for personal injury plaintiff from compulsory mental examination]; see also Munoz v Superior Court (1972) 26 Cal App 643, 645, 102 Cal Rptr 686, 687.

Cf. In re Spencer (1965) 63 Cal 2d 400, 411–413, 46 Cal Rptr 753, 761–762 406 P2d 33, 41–42 [no right to counsel's presence during examination of accused by court-appointed psychiatrist]; Durst v Superior Court (1963) 222 Cal App 2d 447, 452, 35 Cal Rptr 143, 146 [no right to presence of attorney at examination by court-appointed psychiatrist under former CCP § 1871, now Evid Code § 730].

Annotation: Right of party to have attorney or physician present during physical or mental examination at instance of opposing party. 84 ALR4th 558.

Annotation: Right of party to have his attorney or physician, or a court reporter, present during his physical or mental examination by a court-appointed expert. 7 ALR3d 881.

[4] Edwards v Superior Court (1976) 16 Cal 3d 905, 130 Cal Rptr 14, 549 P2d 846.

[5] Edwards v Superior Court (1976) 16 Cal 3d 905, 910, 130 Cal Rptr 14, 17, 549 P2d 846, 849.

[6] Sharff v Superior Court (1955) 44 Cal 2d 508, 282 P2d 896.

For a discussion of the examinee's right to the presence of counsel during a discovery physical examination, see § 8.14.

[7] Edwards v Superior Court (1976) 16 Cal 3d 905, 910–911, 130 Cal Rptr 14, 17, 549 P2d 846, 849.

measuring stress, seeking origins, tracing aberrations, and attempting to form a professional judgment or interpretation of the examinee's mental condition. . . . [¶] [A]t the sensitive point of the psychiatric examination itself, given the need for a special and private rapport between examiner and examinee, we think the purposes of the examination are best served by its conduct on a one-to-one basis.[8]

The two dissenters argued that counsel's presence would give the examinee "a certain degree of comfort and support" while undergoing "the ordeal of submitting oneself to the probing inquiries of someone whom the examinee may . . . view as a hostile medical force."[9] The majority found this reason insufficient to jeopardize the examination's effectiveness:

[T]he larger the number of persons attending the examination the lesser the prospect of the necessary rapport . . . . [T]o require the addition of other persons in the examining room would be distracting, if not disrupting. . . . [O]f paramount importance is the concern that the examination be valid and have meaning, free from outside influences which might disrupt it.[10]

The strongest argument for counsel's presence at a court-ordered psychiatric examination is the intensifed need for someone to monitor the questioning. As the two dissenters stated:

This reasoning [of the *Sharff* case, allowing counsel's presence at a defense physical examination] is even more compelling in the case of a psychiatric examination, the entire substance of which is an interview between patient and doctor. Under these circumstances, the examinee is particularly vulnerable to possible efforts by his adversary's represen- tative to elicit damaging responses and information beyond the permissi- ble scope of the examination.[11]

To the majority, however, the attorney's legal training would more likely hinder than help policy the psychiatrist's questioning:

[C]ounsel does not necessarily possess the ability to define the psychiat- ric relevance of elicited answers. Many questions which would be legally objectionable, if posed in a courtroom, might be very relevant in the formulation of a sound psychiatric judgment.[12]

---

[8] Edwards v Superior Court (1976) 16 Cal 3d 905, 911–912, 130 Cal Rptr 14, 17–18, 549 P2d 846, 549 P2d at 850.

[9] Edwards v Superior Court (1976) 16 Cal 3d 905, 915, 130 Cal Rptr 14, 20, 549 P2d 846, 852 (dissenting opinion).

[10] Edwards v Superior Court (1976) 16 Cal 3d 905, 911, 130 Cal Rptr 14, 18, 549 P2d 846, 850.

[11] Edwards v Superior Court (1976) 16 Cal 3d 905, 915, 130 Cal Rptr 14, 20, 549 P2d 846, 852 (dissenting opinion).

[12] Edwards v Superior Court (1976) 16 Cal 3d 905, 911, 130 Cal Rptr 14, 17, 549 P2d 846, 849

Finally, the majority stressed that other safeguards protected an examinee from possible abuse of this discovery tool. "Conflicts regarding the questions and answers elicited at the examination can be resolved through existing procedural methods."[13] Principal among these "methods" was the examinee's right to depose the examiner. During that deposition, counsel could obtain "complete access to all the notes and records" of the doctor. In addition, counsel could ask about "the specific questions and answers exchanged between examiner and examinee." Should the deposition reveal that the examiner did elicit damaging or prejudicial admissions by improper questioning, counsel can seek at trial to "exclude or limit statements made by his client."[14]

Ten years later, in the *Vinson* case,[15] the Supreme Court reconsidered and unanimously reaffirmed its decision in *Edwards*.

Edwards Codified: The Discovery Commission concluded that the holding in *Edwards* was misguided and sought to annul it. It proposed that the Legislature expressly recognize an examinee's right to an attorney's presence during a compulsory mental examination.[16]

After much backing and filling,[17] the Legislature decided not to adopt this recommendation. Instead, it included the following statement in what is now Section 2032.530:

> [N]othing in this article shall be construed to alter, amend, or affect existing case law with respect to the presence of counsel or other persons during the examination by agreement or court order.[18]

In the *Vinson* case, the Supreme Court noted that the Civil Discovery Act has left intact the holding in *Edwards* that examinees have no categorical right to an attorney's presence during a discover mental examination: "Had the Legislature felt it desirable to have counsel present at psychiatric examinations, it would certainly have provided for this in its thorough revision of the section."[19]

---

[13] Edwards v Superior Court (1976) 16 Cal 3d 905, 912, 130 Cal Rptr 14, 18, 549 P2d 846, 850.

[14] Edwards v Superior Court (1976) 16 Cal 3d 905, 912, 130 Cal Rptr 14, 18, 549 P2d 846, 850.

[15] Vinson v Superior Court (1987) 43 Cal 3d 833, 844–847, 239 Cal Rptr 292, 300–302, 740 P2d 404, 412–414. Although the opinion was rendered after the Discovery Act of 1986 took effect, this case was decided under CCP § 2032 of the original Discovery Act of 1956.

[16] See Proposed Civil Discovery Act of 1986, Section 2032(g), Appendix D.

[17] The original version of AB 1334 embraced the Discovery Commission proposal. The Senate Judiciary Committee at first approved (June 26, 1986), then deleted the provision (July 9, 1986), and later re-inserted it in AB 169 (August 13, 1986) as Section 2032.5.

[18] CCP § 2032.530(b).

[19] Vinson v Superior Court (1987) 43 Cal 3d 833, 845 n9, 239 Cal Rptr 292, 301 n9, 740 P2d 404, 413 n9.

See also Golfland Entertainment Centers, Inc. v Superior Court (2003) 108 Cal App 4th 739, 746–748,133 Cal Rptr 2d 828, 832–834. Cf. Baqleh v Superior Court (2002) 100 Cal App 4th 478, 492 n4, 122 Cal Rptr 2d 673, 684 n4.

Discretion of Trial Court: *Edwards* had decided only that a trial court *need not* allow the examinee's counsel to attend a court–ordered mental examination. It did not hold that the trial court *could not* allow counsel's attendance after an appropriate showing. The Supreme Court carefully reiterate this in the *Vinson* case:

> We emphasize, however, that *Edwards* should be viewed as standing for the proposition that the presence of an attorney is not *required* during a mental examination. In light of their broad discretion in discovery matters, trial courts retain the power to permit the presence of counsel or to take other prophylactic measures when needed.[20]

The most likely "other prophylactic measure" would be to let a psychiatrist or psychologist accompany the examinee.[21]

§ 8.17 Recording a Mental Examination

Pre-1986 Case Law: The 1956 Discovery Act[1] did not explicitly address the examinee's right to use a court reporter or tape machine to record a compulsory medical examination, whether physical or mental. However, a few years after the statute took effect the Supreme Court ruled in the *Gonzi* case[2] that the examinee could use a court reporter during a discovery *physical* examination.[3] When examinees began to assert a corresponding right to have a court reporter attend mental examinations, the trial and appellate courts resisted.[4]

---

[20] Vinson v Superior Court (1987) 43 Cal 3d 833, 846, 239 Cal Rptr 292, 301, 740 P2d 404, 403 (internal citation omitted) (original italics).

See also Golfland Entertainment Centers, Inc. v Superior Court (2003) 108 Cal App 4th 739, 748, 133 Cal Rptr 2d 828, 834.

Compare Vreeland v Ethan Allen (1993, SD NY) 158 FRD 294 [attorney may attend], with Tirado v Erosa (1994, SD NY) 158 FRD 294, and Di Bari v Incaica Cia Armadora, S.A. (1989, ED NY) 126 FRD 12 [attorney not permitted to attend].

Annotation: Right of party to have attorney or physician present during physical or mental examination at instance of opposing party. 84 ALR 4th 558.

[21] See Lowe v Philadelphia Newspapers, Inc. (1983, ED Pa) 101 FRD 296, 299, cited in Vinson v Superior Court (1987) 43 Cal 3d 833, 845, 239 Cal Rptr 292, 301, 740 P2d 404, 413; but see Duncan v Upjohn Co. (1994, D Conn) 155 FRD 23, 26–27 [absent showing that mental examination would involve unorthodox or potentially harmful techniques, examinee not allowed to have her own psychiatrist attend the examination].

[1] See former CCP § 2032, 1956 Discovery Act, Appendix E.

[2] Gonzi v Superior Court (1959) 51 Cal 2d 586, 335 P2d 97.

[3] For a discussion of what may be used to record a compulsory physical examination, see § 8.15.

[4] Board of Trustees v Superior Court (1969) 274 Cal App 2d 377, 79 Cal Rptr 58 [upholding trial court's discretion to prohibit examinee's use of court reporter to record compulsory mental examination in teacher dismissal proceeding]; Whitfield v Superior Court (1966) 246 Cal App 2d 81, 54 Cal Rptr 505 [upholding trial court's discretion to prohibit plaintiff's use of court reporter to record compulsory mental examination]; see also Munoz v Superior Court (1972) 26 Cal App 643, 645, 102 Cal Rptr 686, 687. Cf. Durst v Superior Court (1963) 222 Cal App 2d 447, 452, 35 Cal Rptr 143, 146 [examinee has no right to use court reporter during examination by court-appointed psychiatrist under former CCP § 1871, now Evid Code § 730].

Although the Supreme Court in the *Edwards* case[5] considered only the examinee's right to have an attorney attend a mental examination, some of its reasoning rejecting such a right might also apply to a court reporter's attendance:

> [T]he larger the number of persons attending the examination the lesser the prospect of the necessary rapport . . . . [T]o require the addition of other persons in the examining room would be distracting, if not disrupting. . . . [O]f paramount importance is the concern that the examination be valid and have meaning, free from outside influences which might disrupt it.[6]

Prior to 1986, no reported case had considered whether to extend to mental examinations the examinee's right to tape-record a physical examination recognized in the *Ebel* case.[7]

Right to Make an Audio Recording: As noted in the previous section, the Discovery Commission ultimately failed to persuade the Legislature to enact an absolute right by an examinee to have an attorney present during a compulsory mental examination.[8] However, the Legislature compromised by allowing audio recording of the examination: "The examiner and examinee shall have the right to record a mental examination on audio tape."[9]

Because Section 2032.510 does not allow video recording of *physical* examinations,[10] *a fortiori* it does not allow video recording a *mental* examination.

§ 8.18   Demand for Report of Opponent's Examiner

Two Ways to Obtain Examiner's Report: After a compulsory medical examination, the examinee's counsel naturally will wish to know the doctor's conclusions. The Discovery Act contains two ways to satisfy this curiosity. If the examining party later lists the doctor as an expert trial witness, counsel may use Section 2034.210, which regulates the exchange of expert *trial* witness

---

Annotation: Right of party to have his attorney or physician, or a court reporter, present during his physical or mental examination by a court-appointed expert. 7 ALR3d 881.

[5] Edwards v Superior Court (1976) 16 Cal 3d 905, 130 Cal Rptr 14, 549 P2d 846.

[6] Edwards v Superior Court (1976) 16 Cal 3d 905, 911, 130 Cal Rptr 14, 18, 549 P2d 846, 850.

[7] Ebel v Superior Court (1974) 39 Cal App 3d 934, 114 Cal Rptr 722.

See also Golfland Entertainment Centers, Inc. v Superior Court (2003) 108 Cal App 4th 739, 750, 133 Cal Rptr 2d 828, 835–836. Cf. Villa v McFerren (1995) 35 Cal App 4th 733, 738 n3, 41 Cal Rptr 2d 719, 722 n3 [CCP § 2032(g)(2) does not apply to a mental examination required of a claimant by the terms of his disability insurance policy].

[8] For a discussion of the right to the presence of the examinee's attorney at a discovery mental examination, see § 8.16.

[9] CCP § 2032.530(a).

[10] For a discussion of recording physical examinations, see § 8.15.

information.[1] Alternatively, the examinee may always exercise the right, conferred by Section 2032.610,[2] to receive a report of the examination.

Drawbacks of Section 2034.210: Reliance on an exchange of expert witness information to learn the conclusions of an opponent's examining doctor has three drawbacks. First, those procedures operate only after the court has set a trial date.[3]

Second, they do not confer an absolute right to receive a report from a designated expert; the right is available only "if any" report was actually prepared.[4] If the party who obtained a discovery medical examination decided not to have the examiner prepare a written report, there will not exist "any" report to produce. Counsel for the examinee then could learn those conclusions only by deposing the doctor after the other side lists him or her as a trial witness.[5]

Third, provisions for expert witness exchange authorize discovery only from those experts that the other side intends to use as trial witnesses. If the conclusions of a particular medical specialist disappoint the party who procured the examination, that party is not likely to designate that individual as an expert witness for trial. Generally, until a party designates a consultant as a trial witness, the work product doctrine protects that consultant's conclusions from discovery. To overcome this protection, one must show exceptional circumstances under which it is impracticable for the party seeking discovery to obtain those facts by other means.[6] Parties who have submitted to a discovery medical examination could rarely make this showing since they have superior access to information bearing upon their own mental and physical health.

Advantages of Section 2032.610: By demanding discovery of a medical examiner's report under Section 2032.610 an examinee avoids each of these three drawbacks. The statute preserves the right of the examinee to demand a report detailing the examination results.[7] This right vests whether the examination results from a court order,[8] the "demand" procedure,[9] or an agreement between

---

[1] CCP § 2034.210(c).

For a discussion of discovery concerning designated expert trial witnesses, see §§ 10.8–10.9.

[2] CCP § 2032.610(a).

[3] CCP § 2034.210(a).

For a discussion of the time at which expert trial witnesses must be designated, see § 10.2.

[4] CCP § 2034.210(c).

For a discussion of the right to receive reports of designated expert trial witnesses, see § 10.8.

[5] See CCP § 2034.410.

For a discussion of the right to depose a designated expert trial witness, see § 10.9.

[6] See FRCivP 26(b)(4)(B).

For a discussion of discovery concerning experts consulted by an adversary, but not designated as trial witnesses, see § 13.15.

[7] CCP § 2032.610(a).

Annotation: Federal Rule of Civil Procedure 35(b)(1,) (2) and similar state statutes and rules pertaining to reports of physician's examination. 36 ALR2d 946.

[8] See CCP § 2032.310(a).

the parties.[10] Even if the examining party has not requested its examining physician to prepare or deliver a report, it must obtain one upon the examinee's demand:

> Although there is a general reluctance to order parties to produce reports not in existence, the statute clearly requires that a party who submits to a physical is entitled to a report of that examination, which must contain certain specified information. The trade-off is clear: If one party to personal injury litigation is required by his or her opponent to submit to a medical examination, at the very least he or she is entitled to a report of the information obtained by the adversary in litigation.[11]

Moreover, this right is absolute. Although both the doctor's evaluation and the report describing it are the work product of the examining party's attorney,[12] the examinee need not show "unfair prejudice," "injustice,"[13] or "exceptional circumstances" to obtain the report.[14] Nor does the right to receive the report hinge on the opponent's intention to use the examiner as a trial witness.[15] Thus, even if the examiner's conclusions are disappointing or unfavorable to the defense, the examinee is entitled to learn them:

> In addition to receiving a report detailing the examiner's findings and conclusions, the party examined may also depose the examiner free of any objections based on the work product exception. This right does not depend on whether the party demanding the examination plans to use the examiner as an expert witness at trial.[16]

Includes Earlier Examinations: Section 2032.610 entitles the demanding party to receive not only a report of the discovery examination, but also "reports

---

For a discussion of motions for a compulsory medical examination, see § 8.3.

[9] See CCP § 2032.220(a).

For a discussion of a "demand" for a compulsory medical examination, see § 8.3.

[10] See CCP § 2016.030, referencing 2019.010(d).

See, e.g., Queen of Angels Hospital v Superior Court (1976) 57 Cal App 3d 370, 129 Cal Rptr 282; Jorgensen v Superior Court (1958) 163 Cal App 2d 513, 329 P2d 550; Grover v Superior Court (1958) 161 Cal App 2d 644, 327 P2d 212.

For a discussion of agreements for compulsory medical examinations, see § 8.3.

[11] Kennedy v Superior Court (1999) 64 Cal App 4th 674, 678, 75 Cal Rptr 2d 373, 375.

[12] Cf. Williamson v Superior Court (1978) 21 Cal 3d 829, 834, 148 Cal Rptr 39, 42, 582 P2d 126, 129.

For a discussion of reports of experts as a form of work product, see §§ 13.13–13.15.

[13] See CCP § 2018.030(b).

For a discussion of the showing necessary to obtain an adversary's work product, see §§ 13.4–13.16.

[14] See Buffington v Wood (1965, CA3 Pa) 351 F2d 292, 296.

[15] Kennedy v Superior Court (1999) 64 Cal App 4th 674, 75 Cal Rptr 2d 373.

[16] Kennedy v Superior Court (1999) 64 Cal App 4th 674, 678–679, 75 Cal Rptr 2d 373, 375.

of all earlier examinations of the same condition of the examinee made by that or any other examiner."[17] For example, an injured person will sometimes voluntarily submit to a physical examination arranged by a potential defendant's insurance carrier. The examinee may not have thought to ask for a copy of that examining doctor's report. When during a later lawsuit that person undergoes a discovery medical examination, he or she can demand a report of both examinations, even though conducted by different doctors at different times.[18]

Requires a Written Demand: The examinee's absolute right to a report of a medical examination is not self-executing. The examinee must serve a written demand. Unless the examinee makes this demand, the examining party has no duty to provide a report, even if the examining doctor is later designated as a trial witness.[19]

Creates Reciprocal Right: Before exercising the right to receive a report of a compulsory medical examination, counsel for the examinee should think carefully about the consequences. By demanding a report, the examinee grants reciprocal discovery rights that its opponent might not otherwise have.[20]

—Contents of Report: Section 2032.610 "details" the report the examinee must receive. It must contain "the history, examinations, findings, including the results of *all* tests made, diagnoses, prognoses, and conclusions of the examiner."[21] This specificity addresses the concerns about the integrity and quality of discovery medical reports exemplified in the following comment by a federal trial judge:

> It is to be expected that physicians and others called upon to make written reports for use in connection with litigation, whether pending, contemplated or possible, will express their candid opinion or judgment with the idea that findings should be the same irrespective of the side to which the report is furnished. Confidential addenda or qualifications intended merely for one side seem inconsistent with the professional obligation of the doctor and the spirit of Rule 35. [¶] Counsel of course should not edit reports or suggest their being rewritten to correspond

---

[17] CCP § 2032.610(a)(2).

[18] See, e.g., Keil v Himes (1952, ED Pa) 13 FRD 451. Cf. Peritz v Kaye (1988, Civ Ct) 530 NYS2d 761, 761–763 [plaintiff, who demanded and received a report of an initial discovery examination, is also entitled to receive a report of a *subsequent* evaluation by the same physician who merely reviewed additional x-rays submitted in support of newly alleged injuries].

[19] See, e.g., Kerns v Consolidated Rail Corp. (1981, ED Pa) 90 FRD 134.

[20] For a discussion of the consequences of demanding a report of a discovery medical examination, see § 8.19.

[21] CCP § 2032.610(a)(1) (italics added).

This provision is even more explicit than current FRCivP 35(b), after which it is otherwise patterned.

See Smith v State (1993, Oregon App) 852 P2d 957, 959 [transcript of examination is not a "detailed report," because it fails to include examiner's findings, diagnoses, and conclusions as required by Oregon statute].

with partisan ideas or desires. This, too, would be inconsistent with the spirit of Rule 35 and the professionalism to be expected under the circumstances.[22]

—Timetable for Compliance: Section 2032.610 establishes a timetable for delivery of the demanded report. The statutory norm for delivery is 30 days after service of the demand.[23] However, recognizing that this is too long where the trial date is imminent, the statute also provides that delivery must occur no later than 15 days before trial.[24]

This 15-day limit indirectly restricts the timing of a discovery medical examination: it must be carried out far enough in advance to permit the preparation and delivery of the report of its results 15 days before the date initially set for trial.[25]

—Express Sanctions Provided: The original version of Section 2032 was open to the interpretation that the only sanction for failure to deliver a demanded discovery medical examination report was the examiner's exclusion a trial witness.[26] Section 2032.620 makes it clear that all the sanctions available for noncompliance with other discovery requirements[27] are also available against an examining party who fails to comply with the demand.[28] It provides that on the examinee's motion, the court may order delivery of the report and simultaneously impose a monetary sanction on the recalcitrant party for making that motion necessary. It further provides that if the examining party disobeys this order,[29] the court may then impose, as appropriate, one of the drastic sanctions: issue preclusion, evidence exclusion, dismissal, or default. Section 2032.610 leaves no room to argue that a party may suppress the unfavorable results of a discovery medical examination simply by not calling the examiner as a trial witness.

If for some reason counsel does not seek, or the court does not impose, any of these sanctions, the statute requires the exclusion from the trial of the testimony "of any examiner whose report has not been provided by a party."

---

[22] Chastain v Evennou (1964, D Utah) 35 FRD 350, 353–354.

[23] This period is increased, usually by five days, in the event service of the demand for the report is made by mail. See CCP § 2016.050, referencing CCP § 1013(a).

[24] CCP § 2032.610(b).

[25] See, e.g., Shapiro v Win-Sum Ski Corp. (1982, WD NY) 95 FRD 38 ["if defendant's physician is to examine plaintiff the examination must take place sufficiently before trial to permit a copy of the report to be prepared and delivered on time for trial."].

For a discussion of the time for a compulsory medical examination, see § 8.12.

[26] Former CCP § 2032(b), 1956 Discovery Act, Appendix E.

This reading of FRCivP 35(b) was rejected in Salvatore v American Cyanamid Co. (1982, D RI) 94 FRD 156.

[27] See CCP Title 4, Chapter 7, commencing with Section 2023.010.

[28] CCP § 2032.620(a).

[29] The Legislature did not follow the Discovery Commission's recommendation to allow the imposition of sanctions directly upon an examining doctor who refused to produce a report. See Proposed Civil Discovery Act, Section 2032(h), Appendix D.

§ 8.19 Consequences of Demand for Report of Opponent's Examiner

The previous section outlined an examinee's right to demand a report detailing the results of a compulsory medical examination. This section focuses on the consequences of making such a demand.[1] Section 2032.630 imposes two principal consequences on examinees who demand a report. First, they must surrender their own medical reports to the other side.[2] Second, they waive any evidentiary privilege and also the work product protection with respect to their own medical consultants.[3]

Reciprocal Duty to Exchange Reports: An examinee's demand for a report of a discovery medical examination triggers a corresponding right in the examining party to get medical reports from the examinee.[4] Only the examinee can initiate this exchange. The examining party cannot activate it either by announcing a willingness to exchange reports,[5] or by gratuitously delivering a report of the examination.[6]

This duty to surrender the examinee's own medical reports extends only to those examinations that relate to the "same condition" covered by the discovery medical examination. However, it includes not only reports of examinations that have occurred but also reports of any examinations of that "same condition" that will occur.[7]

The 1956 Discovery Act was open to the interpretation that by demanding the other side's report, examinees thereby had to generate a report from any of their own doctors who had not already prepared one.[8] Section 2032.640, however, specifies that the examinee's duty to reciprocate extends only to "any *existing* written report."[9]

The duty to exchange covers only "reports." Examinees need not turn over hospital records or physician's office records:

> [FRCivP 35] must be reasonably construed. It does not place upon a party the burden of procuring copies of records of hospitals or of office

---

[1] Annotation: Federal Rule of Civil Procedure 35(b)(1,2) and similar state statutes and rules pertaining to reports of physician's examination. 36 ALR2d 946.

Annotation: Pretrial testimony or disclosure on discovery by party to personal injury action as to nature of injuries or treatment as waiver of physician-patient privilege. 25 ALR3d 1401.

[2] CCP § 2032.640.

[3] CCP § 2032.630.

[4] CCP § 2032.640.

[5] See Sher v DeHaven (1952, CADC) 199 F2d 777, 781.

[6] See Hardy v Riser (1970, ND Miss) 309 F Supp 1234, 1236.

[7] See, e.g., Queen of Angels Hospital v Superior Court (1976) 57 Cal App 3d 370, 129 Cal Rptr 282.

[8] See, e.g., Weir v Simmons (1964, D Neb) 233 F Supp 657, 659–660 [a plaintiff who exercises the right to receive a report concerning a court-ordered medical examination must obtain reports from any physician who has not already prepared one].

[9] CCP § 2032.640 (italics added).

records of physicians. It is limited to medical examinations conducted at the request of the party, and the reports, copies of which are subject to production, are the reports made by the physician as the result of such an examination.[10]

Under the 1956 Discovery Act provision the delivery of the examinee's reports was to take place at some indefinite time "after" receipt of the report of the compulsory medical examination.[11] Section 2032.620, however, provides for a simultaneous exchange of reports.

Waiver of Privilege and Work Product Protection: By demanding a report of a compulsory medical examination, an examinee gives the other side easy and instant access to doctors' reports that it could already have obtained by more expensive and time-consuming discovery methods. Section 2032.630, however, also provides that the demand for that report waives "any privilege" and "any protection for work product" that the examinee may otherwise have for the reports, writings and testimony of every other health care practitioner who has examined the condition that was the subject of the court-ordered examination. Thus, by demanding the report, the examinee may also be making available medical information otherwise insulated from discovery.

As far as *treating* physicians are concerned, this waiver is not very significant under California evidence law. A plaintiff in a personal injury case will have already waived the physician-patient[12] and the psychotherapist-patient[13] privileges by suing.[14]

Physicians consulted by the examinee's attorney stand on a different footing. Under California law, the lawyer-client privilege applies to the reports of any doctors who have examined a party solely to help a lawyer learn a client's medical condition.[15] Normally, these reports are not discoverable[16] unless the consulting attorney lists[17] that doctor as a trial witness.[18]

A demand for a report of a discovery medical examination, however, waives "any" privilege, including the lawyer-client one. Moreover, the demand also

---

[10] Butts v Sears, Roebuck & Co. (1949, D Colo) 9 FRD 58, 59.

[11] Former CCP 2032(b)(1), 1956 Discovery Act, Appendix E.

[12] Evid Code § 994.

[13] Evid Code § 1014.

[14] For a discussion of the patient-litigant exception to the physician-patient privilege, see § 12.24.
For a discussion of the patient-litigant exception to the psychotherapist-patient privilege, see § 12.29.

[15] City & County of San Francisco v Superior Court (1951) 37 Cal 2d 227, 237, 231 P2d 26, 31.

[16] For a discussion of the use of the lawyer-client privilege to bar discovery of the reports of medical examinations conducted to assist the client's attorney, see § 12.11.

[17] For a discussion of the waiver of the lawyer-client privilege with respect to medical consultants designated as trial witnesses, see § 12.12.

[18] For a discussion of the right to reports of an opponent's designated expert trial witnesses, see § 10.8.

waives any applicable work product protection. For example, in the *Queen of Angels Hospital* case,[19] the plaintiff, after submitting to a discovery medical examination, demanded and received a report from the examiner. Later, the plaintiff's attorney had his client examined by a medical specialist who had not previously seen him. This new doctor's report was evidently so adverse to the plaintiff's position that his attorney decided not to use that doctor as a trial witness. When the defense demanded a copy of this report, the plaintiff claimed that the work product protection precluded its discovery. However, the appellate court held that plaintiff had waived all protection against discovery of the report by earlier demanding a report of the defense medical examination.

The waiver under Section 2032.630 reaches not only the examiner's report, it also covers the doctor's "writings" and "testimony."[20] Thus, after a waiver, an opponent may subpoena the office records and depose the doctor, though the examinee has not designated that doctor as a trial witness.[21] In addition, the opposing side can call this doctor as its own trial expert and reveal to the trier of fact that the examinee initially consulted this now-adverse witness.[22]

At first glance it may seem harsh to require the examinee to surrender even those reports of medical consultants who will not be trial witnesses.[23] However, only this course is fair and equitable. After all, the examinee can receive on demand a report of a discovery medical examination, even one whose results are so unfavorable that the party who arranged it has decided not to use that examiner as a trial witness.[24] Moreover, the examinee's counsel can avoid the problem altogether by simply not demanding a report of the other side's examination.

—**Tactical Considerations:** Before demanding a report of an opponent's medical examination, counsel should carefully review their own medical consultants's conclusions. In this way they can avoid situations like that in *Chastain v Evennou.*[25] The plaintiff's attorney, who had demanded and received a copy of the defense medical report, then discovered, to his chagrin, that one of the seven medical reports in his own files contained what the federal trial judge described as "a somewhat gratuitous comment (labeled 'confidential') concerning

---

[19] Queen of Angels Hospital v Superior Court (1976) 57 Cal App 3d 370, 129 Cal Rptr 282.

[20] CCP § 2032.630.

[21] Cf. Kennedy v Superior Court (1999) 64 Cal App 4th 674, 678–679, 75 Cal Rptr 2d 373, 375 [the plaintiff may depose the defense examiner, even if the defendant does not plan to use that examiner as a trial witness].

[22] Queen of Angels Hospital v Superior Court (1976) 57 Cal App 3d 370, 375, 129 Cal Rptr 282, 285.

[23] For a discussion of the general need to show exceptional circumstances in order to gain access to information known to those expert consultants who will not be called as trial witnesses, see § 13.15.

[24] For a discussion of the right of the party examined to demand a report of a compulsory medical examination, see § 8.18.

[25] Chastain v Evennou (1964, D Utah) 35 FRD 350.

the possible composing effect that a termination of litigation might accomplish, the precise wording of which was unfortunate."[26] Nevertheless, the court required the plaintiff to turn over the report.

Even if the examinee has not yet consulted a doctor who has formed an opinion that favors the other side, counsel should bear in mind that a demand for an opponent's report creates an obligation to turn over reports of any future examinations, no matter how unfavorable they may be.[27]

—**Deposing the Examining Physician:** The examinee cannot avoid the waiver provisions of Section 2032.630 by deposing the examiner instead of demanding a report of the examination.[28] An examinee who deposes an opponent's examining physician before his or her designation as a trial witness waives any privilege and work production protection that might otherwise apply to the examinee's own medical consultants.

Vestigial Exceptions for Malpractice Certifications: On its face, Section 2032.010 excepts two circumstances from the obligation to disclose a medical consultant's report. The first exception, however, no longer has any legal applicability, and the second has little practical applicability to medical consultants.

Under the first exception, if the plaintiff's counsel consulted a doctor solely to enable counsel to certify that a medical malpractice case has merit,[29] counsel need not disclose that doctor's identity. As of 1989, however, California no longer requires medical malpractice plaintiffs to make such certifications.[30]

The second exception applied to malpractice actions against architects, engineers and surveyors. Section 411.35 required a similar certificate of merit before a plaintiff can file such an action. Section 2032.010(b) exempted from disclosure the identity of any expert consulted to help the plaintiff's attorney make that certification. Section 411.35, however, required that attorney to consult not with health care providers, but with architects, professional engineers or land surveyors.[31] Thus, it had little practical applicability to physician's reports.

§ 8.20   Sanctions

Immediate Drastic Sanctions: Unlike the other discovery tools,[1] a party who fails to submit to a compulsory medical examination may immediately incur a drastic sanction. Section 2032.420 provides:

---

[26] Chastain v Evennou (1964, D Utah) 35 FRD 350, 353.

[27] See, e.g., Queen of Angels Hospital v Superior Court (1976) 57 Cal App 3d 370, 129 Cal Rptr 282.

[28] CCP § 2032.630.

[29] CCP § 2032.010(b) citing former CCP § 411.30.

[30] CCP § 411.30, repealed by its own terms effective January 1, 1989. Stats. 1986, c. 247, § 1.

[31] Former CCP §§ 411.35(b)(1) & (3).

[1] Under the original Discovery Act a failure to appear for a deposition or to answer interrogatories exposed a party to drastic sanctions. See former CCP § 2034(d), 1956 Discovery Act, Appendix E.

If a party required . . . to submit to a physical or mental examination fails to do so, the court, on motion of the party entitled to the examination, may make those orders that are just, including the imposition of an issue sanction, an evidence sanction, or a terminating sanction under [Section 2023.010–2023.040].[2]

This failure to "submit" to the examination can occur in two ways. First, a party may simply not appear at the appointed time and place.[3] Second, a party may refuse to undergo one or more of the procedures that are properly a part of that examination.[4] A party risks a drastic sanction whether the obligation to undergo the examination originated in a demand, a court order or an agreement.[5]

The drastic sanctions themselves vary in their severity. The least severe is the "evidence" sanction.[6] This prevents a delinquent party from introducing evidence of the medical condition that the opponent was seeking to examine.[7] More severe is the "issue" sanction.[8] This considers as proven the opposing side's claims concerning that condition. Most severe is the "terminating" sanction; this would dismiss the delinquent party's claim.[9]

—Discretion to Impose Monetary Sanction: The trial court, however, need not immediately impose one of the drastic sanctions. It may, and usually does, initially impose a monetary sanction coupled with an order that the examinee submit to the examination.[10] Section 2032.240 authorizes this milder monetary

---

[2] CCP § 2032.420.

[3] See, e.g., Fletcher v Southern Farm Bureau Life Ins. Co. (1985, CA8 Ark) 757 F2d 953.

[4] See, e.g., Ghanooni v Super Shuttle (1993) 20 Cal App 4th 256, 24 Cal Rptr 2d 501 [during discovery physical examination, personal injury plaintiff, claiming fear of radiation, refused to submit to x-rays of neck, back, and elbow]. Cf. DeCrescenzo v Maersk Container Service Co., Inc. (1984, CA2 NY) 741 F2d 17 [claiming it would cause extreme pain, examinee refused to allow doctor to touch his injured foot].

[5] See, e.g., Ghanooni v Super Shuttle (1993) 20 Cal App 4th 256, 24 Cal Rptr 2d 501 [demand for routine physical examination of personal injury plaintiff].

For a discussion of the procedures for obtaining a compulsory medical examination, see § 8.3.

[6] See CCP § 2023.010(c).

[7] See, e.g., Mraovic v Elgin, Joliet & Eastern Ry. Co. (1990, CA7 Ill) 897 F2d 268, 271 [testimony of plaintiff's expert medical witnesses excluded].

[8] See CCP § 2023.010(b).

[9] See, e.g., Schempp v Reniker (1987, CA8 SD) 809 F2d 541, 542–543 [guardian ad litem's refusal to permit minor plaintiff to undergo mental examination in private led to dismissal without prejudice]; Sloane v Thompson (1989, D Mass) 128 FRD 13, 14–16 [plaintiff's repeated failure to attend medical examination justified dismissal of her claim]; Commercial National Bank v Tapp (1989, D Kan) 125 FRD 695, 695 [defendant's unjustified failure to attend her medical examination justified striking her counterclaim]; Wolford v Cerrone (1992, App Div) 584 NYS2d 498,499 [plaintiffs' failure to submit to two medical examinations justified dismissal of their lawsuit].

[10] Garza v Delano Union Elementary School Dist. (1980) 110 Cal App 3d 303, 313–316, 167 Cal Rptr 629, 634–635 [sanction of dismissal "too harsh" when lesser sanctions had not been tried].

sanction "in lieu" of the drastic ones.[11] The courts reserve the drastic sanctions for those who persist in their disobedience.[12]

—Nonparty Examinees: Occasionally, the examinee may not be a party to the lawsuit, but a party's agent, or someone in a party's custody.[13] Nothing in the Section 2032 series provides for a sanction against such nonparty examinees. Any sanction must run against the party required to produce that examinee.[14] That party may avoid a sanction by demonstrating "an inability to produce that person for examination."[15]

Monetary Sanctions: A refusal to submit to a compulsory discovery medical examination is not the only conduct that will warrant a sanction. The following derelictions also expose one to a monetary sanction: (1) a failure to serve a response to a demand for an initial physical examination;[16] (2) an unwarranted objection to a demand for an initial physical examination;[17] (3) a monitoring attorney's disruption of a physical examination;[18] (4) the examining party's failure to furnish on demand a report of the examination;[19] and (5) the examinee's failure to exchange medical reports.[20]

—Persistent Report Exchange Failures: Where the trial court on motion has transformed a party's statutory obligation to deliver a medical report into a specific court order to do so, a disobedient party may then receive[21] a drastic "issue," "evidence," or "terminating" sanction.[22] And if the trial court has not imposed one of these drastic sanctions, it must at least exclude at trial the

---

11 CCP § 2032.240(d).

See, e.g., Ghanooni v Super Shuttle (1993) 20 Cal App 4th 256, 24 Cal Rptr 2d 501.

12 See, e.g., Fletcher v Southern Farm Bureau Life Ins. Co. (1985, CA8 Ark) 757 F2d 953 [persistent failure of plaintiff to submit to court-ordered physical examination warranted dismissal of complaint for disability benefits]; Sloane v Thompson (1989, D Mass) 128 FRD 13, 14–16 [plaintiff's repeated failure to attend medical examination justified dismissal of her claim].

13 For a discussion of the extent to which nonparties may be required to submit to a compulsory medical examination, see § 8.3.

14 Cf. Schempp v Reniker (1987, CA8 SD) 809 F2d 541 [minor's lawsuit dismissed with prejudice when guardian ad litem refused to permit her to comply with conditions for compulsory mental examination].

15 CCP § 2032.410.

16 CCP § 2032.240(d).

17 CCP § 2032.250(b).

18 CCP § 2032.510(f).

For a discussion of the right to witness a compulsory physical examination, see § 8.14.

19 CCP § 2032.620(b).

For a discussion of the examinee's right to demand a report of a compulsory medical examination, see § 8.18.

20 CCP § 2032.650(b).

For a discussion of the examining party's reciprocal right to receive medical reports, see § 8.19.

21 CCP §§ 2032.620(c) and 2032.650(c).

22 For the statutory definition of these sanctions, see CCP § 2023.030.

testimony of the health care practitioner whose report was not produced. This exclusion applies alike to examining parties who withhold demanded reports[23] and to examinees who fail to reciprocate by exchanging reports from their own physicians.[24]

—**Unsuccessful Motions to Compel:** Besides the sanctions for violation of the examination statute itself, the court may impose monetary sanctions upon any party, person, or attorney[25] who unsuccessfully makes or opposes motions to compel or prevent discovery. These would include: a motion to compel response or compliance with a demand for a physical examination;[26] a motion for a protective order based on a monitoring attorney's allegedly disruptive conduct during the examination;[27] or a motion to compel delivery of medical reports.[28] Indeed, in any of these circumstances, the court must impose a monetary sanction, "unless it finds that the one subject to the sanction acted with substantial justification or that other circumstances make the imposition of the sanction unjust."[29]

---

[23] CCP § 2032.620(c).

[24] CCP § 2032.650(c).

[25] See, e.g., Ewing v Ayres Corp. (1989, ND Miss) 129 FRD 137, 138 [where plaintiff's attorney, not plaintiff himself, bore sole responsibility for plaintiff's failure to attend medical examination, monetary sanctions imposed on attorney personally].

[26] CCP §§ 2032.240(c) and 2032.250(b).

[27] CCP § 2032.510(e).

[28] CCP §§ 2032.620(b) and 2032.650(b).

[29] CCP §§ 2032.240(c) and 2032.250(b), 2032.510(f), 2032.620(b) and 2032.650(b).

See Ziemann v Burlington County Bridge Comm'n (1994, D NJ) 155 FRD 497, 507 [although court granted defendant's motion to compel, substantial justifications for plaintiff's position warranted no sanctions].

CHAPTER 9

REQUESTS FOR ADMISSION

SYNOPSIS

---

§ 9.1   General Nature and Function

Akin to a Coerced Stipulation: The Civil Discovery Act authorizes a litigant to request another party to make an admission:

> Any party may obtain discovery . . . by a written request that any other party to the action admit the genuineness of specified documents, or the truth of specified matters of fact, opinion relating to fact, or application of law to fact.[1]

---

[1] CCP § 2033.010.

This device allows one party to ask any other party to agree, for the purpose of the pending lawsuit, that some "matter" is true or that some document is genuine. If the request yields an admission, the functional equivalent of a stipulation results. A stipulation, however, requires an adverse party's willing assent. In contrast, an admission request involves a strong element of coercion: a party who unreasonably refuses to make a requested admission may have to reimburse the requesting party for the expense of proving at trial the matter covered by the request.[2]

Admission Request as a "Discovery" Device: The admission request differs fundamentally from the other five discovery tools (depositions, interrogatories, inspection demands, medical examinations, expert witness exchanges). These devices principally seek to *obtain* proof for use at trial. In marked contrast, admission requests seek to *eliminate* the need for proof: "[T]he purpose of the admissions procedure . . . is to limit the triable issues and spare the parties the burden and expense of litigating undisputed issues."[3] Sometimes the admissions obtained will even leave the party making them vulnerable to summary judgment.[4]

This contrast between the admission request and the other five discovery methods has led some courts to question whether it is a discovery tool at all.[5] These courts have alternately described it as "more than a mere discovery device,"[6] or "not really a discovery procedure."[7] Others, however, are comfortable with describing admission requests as "a vehicle of discovery"[8] or a "form of pretrial discovery."[9] Section 2033.010 reflects this latter view: it says that a party may use an admission request to "obtain discovery." This classification accords with the federal approach.[10] This view, however, did not change the

---

[2] For a discussion of the sanction for an unwarranted refusal to make an admission, see § 9.21.

[3] Shepard and Morgan v Lee and Daniel, Inc. (1982) 31 Cal 3d 256, 261, 182 Cal Rptr 351, 353, 643 P2d 968, 970; Stull v Sparrow (2001) 92 Cal App 4th 860, 864, 112 Cal Rptr 2d 239, 242.

See also Hansen v Superior Court (1983) 149 Cal App 3d 823, 827, 197 Cal Rptr 175, 177.

[4] See, e.g., Bennett v Hibernia Bank (1960) 186 Cal App 2d 748, 9 Cal Rptr 896; Buffalo Arms, Inc. v Remler Co. (1960) 179 Cal App 2d 700, 4 Cal Rptr 103.

[5] See, e.g., Freshman, Mulvaney, Marantz, Comsky, Kahan and Deutsch v Superior Court (1985) 173 Cal App 3d 223, 232, 218 Cal Rptr 533, 538.

[6] Jahn v Brickey (1985) 168 Cal App 3d 399, 404, 214 Cal Rptr 119, 122.

[7] Lieb v Superior Court (1962) 199 Cal App 2d 364, 367, 18 Cal Rptr 705, 706.

See also Miller v Marina Mercy Hospital (1984) 157 Cal App 3d 765, 769, 204 Cal Rptr 62, 65; Hansen v Superior Court (1983) 149 Cal App 3d 823, 827, 197 Cal Rptr 175, 177; International Harvester Co. v Superior Court (1969) 273 Cal App 2d 652, 655, 78 Cal Rptr 515, 517.

[8] Cembrook v Superior Court (1961) 56 Cal 2d 423, 427, 15 Cal Rptr 127, 129, 364 P2d 303, 305.

[9] Billings v Edwards (1981) 120 Cal App 3d 238, 244, 174 Cal Rptr 722, 725.

[10] See FRCivP 26(a)(1).

See Kershner v Beloit Corp. (1985, D Maine) 106 FRD 498 [rejecting contention that admission requests are not covered by the close of "discovery"].

fundamental nature of the admission device as it was under the Discovery Act of 1956.[11]

Advantages of Admission Requests: At first glance, the admission request seems to duplicate other discovery tools. After all, a party may obtain admissions from a party opponent through both depositions[12] and interrogatories.[13] As a way to pin down an opponent on a matter, however, admission requests have four advantages over depositions and, to a lesser extent, over interrogatories.

—Tighter Control of Responses: The admission request gives the propounding party a better chance to control the wording of the response. Party-deponents may lace their answers with ambiguity, shading, hedging, qualification, and equivocation. Admissions obtained by interrogatories accentuate this shortcoming since the responding party has substantial time to consult with counsel before wording the answer. In contrast, the party requesting an admission has substantial control over its phrasing, since the request itself supplies the language describing the "matter" it covers.[14] A responding party who is willing to admit that "matter" will frequently do so "as expressed in the request itself."[15] (This control over the admission's wording, however, is not absolute. The responding party is permitted to rephrase the request "reasonably and clearly" and admit the matter only as so qualified.)[16]

—Duty to Inquire: The recipient of an admission request must make reasonable inquiries before answering.[17] During a deposition, a party's lack of personal knowledge may effectively end any further testimony on a given matter. In contrast, a party may not properly deny an admission request simply because of a "lack of personal information or knowledge." Instead, Section 2033.220 obliges that party to reasonably investigate the truth of the matters involved in the request and adopt the results of that investigation when they appear correct.[18]

—Usefulness at Trial: An admission obtained by a discovery request has significantly more utility at trial than one obtained by other discovery methods. Evidence rules may make deposition testimony and interrogatory answers inadmissible at trial. For example, answers based on hearsay or inference, though

---

[11] Former CCP § 2033, 1956 Discovery Act, Appendix E.

[12] For a discussion of the admissibility at trial of the *deposition* testimony of a party-opponent, see § 2.38.

[13] For a discussion of the admissibility at trial of answers to *interrogatories* of a party-opponent, see § 5.22.

[14] CCP § 2031.010.

[15] CCP § 2033.220(b)(1).

[16] CCP § 2033.220(b)(1).

For a discussion of express admissions as a form of response to admission requests, see § 9.10.

[17] For a discussion of the obligation of the recipient of an admission request to undertake a reasonable investigation as to the truth of the matters involved, see § 9.12.

[18] CCP § 2033.220(c).

A party receiving *interrogatories* also has must make reasonable inquiries concerning matters as to which that party may have no present knowledge. See § 5.16.

valuable for discovery, may be objectionable when offered in evidence.[19] To prove at trial the matters they cover, a party will have to resort to other, admissible evidence. In contrast, the admissions obtained via a discovery request establish the matters they deal with for purposes of the trial. Consequently, developing admissible evidence of these matters becomes unnecessary.

—Conclusive Effect: Only admission requests can produce admissions that are conclusive. Even when they are admissible at trial, admissions contained in deposition testimony and interrogatory answers are merely evidentiary. As such, a party who honestly but mistakenly gave them may contradict them by other evidence at trial.[20] An unambiguous admission in response to a discovery request, however, disposes of the matter at trial.[21]

Focus of Chapter: This chapter focuses on topics peculiar to the *mechanics* of admission requests. Matters and issues common to the entire discovery process, whatever the particular method of discovery used, are discussed elsewhere. Thus, the reader should refer to the appropriate chapters of this treatise when, during the use of this device, an issue arises concerning the *relevancy* of a particular line of inquiry,[22] the validity of a claim of *privilege*,[23] or the discoverability of an adversary's *"work product"* materials.[24]

§ 9.2 Initiation and Cutoff

Extrajudicial Operation: The admission request process mainly operates extrajudicially. A party usually need not apply for court authorization to use this tool.[1]

---

[19] CCP § 2033.220(c).

For a discussion of the use of the *deposition* answers of a party opponent at trial, see § 2.38.

For a discussion of the use of answers to *interrogatories* at trial, see § 5.20.

[20] For a discussion of the extent to which a party's evidence at trial may vary from his or her *deposition* testimony, see § 2.38.

For a discussion of the extent to which a party's evidence at trial may vary from his or answers to *interrogatories*, see § 5.20.

[21] For a discussion of the effect of admissions at trial, see § 9.20.

Cf. California Shellfish Inc. v United Shellfish Co. (1997) 56 Cal App 4th 16, 22, 64 Cal Rptr 2d 797, 799–800.

For a discussion of withdrawing or amending an admission, see § 9.18.

For an excellent elaboration of these advantages of an admission secured by the request procedure, see Finman, The Request for Admissions in Federal Civil Procedure (1962) 71 Yale L J 371, 376–382.

[22] See §§ 9.5–9.6 and Chapter 11.

[23] See § 9.7 and Chapter 12.

[24] See Chapter 13.

[1] Cembrook v Superior Court (1961) 56 Cal 2d 423, 427, 15 Cal Rptr 127, 129, 364 P2d 303, 305.

Under the 1993 amendments to the Federal Rules of Civil Procedure, admission requests also continue to operate extrajudicially. FRCivP 36(a). However, without obtaining leave of court, no party may make admission requests (or engage in any other form of discovery) until the parties have met and conferred to develop a proposed discovery plan. FRCivP 26(d) and (f).

—**Initiation by Plaintiffs:** Before plaintiffs may serve admission requests on a particular defendant, they must ordinarily[2] wait until 10 days after that defendant either has received service or has appeared.[3] Section 2033.020 implicitly prohibits the submission of admission requests to defendants who have neither received service nor appeared:

> A plaintiff may make requests for admission by a party . . . at any time that is 10 days after the service of the summons on, . . . or appearance by, *that* party, whichever occurs first.[4]

However, where a suit names several defendants, plaintiff need not wait until the court gets jurisdiction over all of them before submitting admission requests to those already served or appearing in the case.[5] A plaintiff remains a "party," entitled to make admission requests, even after the court has sustained a demurrer to the complaint, provided it has also granted leave to amend.[6]

—**Initiation by Defendants:** Unlike plaintiffs, defendants need not wait before submitting admission requests. They may serve them "at any time."[7] Therefore, a defendant who acts promptly during the 10 days immediately after service of process can get a head start in the use of this discovery device.[8] However, a defendant who intends to challenge the court's personal jurisdiction should be careful to limit any admission requests to jurisdictional matters.[9] The service of requests dealing with matters that go to the merits of the case is a general appearance.[10] Moreover, an unserved defendant who responds to admission requests addressed to it may thereby be making a general appearance in the lawsuit.[11]

---

[2] A plaintiff may apply for leave of court to serve admission requests earlier. CCP § 2033.020(c).

[3] Unlawful detainer plaintiffs may serve requests within five days from the service of summons. CCP § 2033.020(b). In addition, any plaintiff may apply for leave of court to serve admissions requests earlier. CCP § 2033.020(c).

[4] CCP § 2033.020(b) (italics added).

[5] Cf. Waters v Superior Court (1962) 58 Cal 2d 885, 891–892, 27 Cal Rptr 153, 156, 377 P2d 265, 268.

For a discussion of the right to initiate *deposition* discovery without waiting until all defendants have been served, see § 2.2.

[6] Cf. Budget Finance Plan v Superior Court (1973) 34 Cal App 3d 794, 110 Cal Rptr 302 [plaintiffs may serve *interrogatories* even though they have not yet amended their complaint after a demurrer was sustained].

[7] CCP § 2033.020(a).

See Putnam v Clague (1992) 3 Cal App 4th 542, 565, 5 Cal Rptr 2d 25, 39–40.

[8] For a discussion of "priority" in conducting discovery, see § 2.3.

[9] Cf. Islamic Republic of Iran v Pahlavi (1984) 160 Cal App 3d 620, 628, 206 Cal Rptr 752, 756–757 [discovery in the form of a deposition, interrogatories, and a document inspection did not constitute a general appearance since only information bearing on the court's jurisdiction was sought].

[10] Cf. Creed v Schultz (1983) 148 Cal App 3d 733, 739–740, 196 Cal Rptr 252, 256 [serving notice of *deposition* constitutes a general appearance].

[11] Cf. Chitwood v County of Los Angeles (1971) 14 Cal App 3d 522, 528, 92 Cal Rptr 441, 445 [unserved defendant who serves answers to *interrogatories* makes a general appearance.

Discovery Cutoff: Discovery as a matter of right must be "completed" 30 days "before the date *initially* set for trial of the action."[12]

In limiting discovery in some circumstances by reference to the date initially set for trial, the Legislature is doubtless aware of the possibilities for abuse and for interference with the orderly preparation for trial, if a party is freely permitted to recommence discovery after every delay in trial, however trivial.[13]

Discovery by admission requests arguably is "completed" not on the date the party serves the requests but on the date the answers are due. A federal court has so interpreted a court-ordered discovery cutoff date:

> Common sense dictates that any request for discovery must be made in sufficient time to allow the opposing party to respond before the termination of discovery. . . . When the court sets a date for the termination of discovery, the parties should heed the logical import of such a deadline: the parties should complete discovery on or before that date and will not receive the benefit of court supervision of discovery which is to occur after that date.[14]

Since the responding party has 30 days to respond to admission requests,[15] the requesting party should serve them by the 60th day before the initial trial date.[16] A party using the mails to serve them should post them by the 65th day before that trial date.[17]

—**New Trial:** In the *Fairmont Ins. Co.* case,[18] the Supreme Court interpreted "date initially set for the trial of the action" in cases where there has been a mistrial, an order granting a new trial, or a remand for a new trial after reversal of a judgment on appeal. It held that, in such cases, discovery is reopened and the cutoff date is calculated based on the date initially set for the *new* trial.

§ 9.3 Mechanics of Preparation, Service, and Filing

Format: Admission requests must first identify the requesting and responding parties.[1] Each set must be numbered consecutively.[2] A set of requests may not include a preface or special instructions for responding[3] unless they are in the

---

[12] CCP § 2024.020(a) (italics added).

[13] Roe v Superior Court (1990) 224 Cal App 3d 642, 646, 273 Cal Rptr 745, 747.

[14] Northern Indiana Public Service Co. v Colorado Westmoreland, Inc. (1986, ND Ind) 112 FRD 423, 424.

[15] CCP § 2033.250.

[16] Cf. Beller v Credit Alliance Corp. (1985, ND Ga) 106 FRD 557, 560 [where local rule requires discovery to be "completed" within a four-month period, *interrogatories* must be served by the end of the third month, "thereby allowing the opposing party its full thirty days to respond"].

[17] CCP § 2016.050, referencing CCP § 1013(a).

[18] Fairmont Ins. Co. v Superior Court (2000) 22 Cal 4th 245, 92 Cal Rptr 2d 70, 991 P2d 156.

[1] CCP § 2033.060(b).

[2] CCP § 2033.060(a).

[3] CCP § 2033.060(d).

Judicial Council's Official Forms.[4] A requesting party may specially define a term repeated several times in a set of admission requests. However, each time that term appears in any individual request in that set, it must be printed in capital letters to remind the other party of that special definition.[5] Each request must be full and complete in itself. The statute prohibits subparts, and compound, conjunctive, or disjunctive requests.[6] If an admission request seeks to establish the genuineness of a document, a copy of that document must be attached to the request.[7] The responding party may then demand to inspect the original.[8]

—Interspersed Interrogatories Prohibited: Under the former Discovery Act, attorneys interspersed admission requests with interrogatories.[9] The responding party answered an interrogatory only if unwilling to make the corresponding admission.[10] Section 2033.060 now prohibits the mixing of admission requests with other discovery methods: "No party shall combine in a single document requests for admission with any other method of discovery."[11] Therefore, a party requesting admissions no longer may include in the same document a direction to the responding party to answer a related interrogatory if that party does not make a particular admission.

Judicial Council Form: In response to the Legislature's direction, the Judicial Council has prepared an "official" form of admission requests suitable for use in personal injury, wrongful death, breach of contract, and any other civil action.[12] Use of this form is optional.

The practical impossibility of the task that the Legislature assigned to the Judicial Council is evidenced by the contrast between the Council's useful form interrogatories, and the token form it developed for admission requests. An interrogatory, designed to elicit information, may often be open-ended; an admission request, designed to narrow issues, must generally be tailored to specific situations. The Judicial Council's efforts demonstrate that it far easier to craft standard *questions* than it is to devise form *statements*. Understandably,

---

[4] CCP §§ 2033.060(d) and Chapter 17 (commencing with Section 2033.710).

To date, the Judicial Council has not included any preface or instruction in its form.

[5] CCP § 2033.060(e).

[6] CCP § 2033.060(f). See People ex rel. Dept. of Transportation v Ad Way Signs, Inc. (1993) 14 Cal App 4th 187, 200, 17 Cal Rptr 2d 496, 503–504.

[7] CCP § 2033.060(g).

[8] CCP § 2033.060(g).

[9] See, e.g., Enfantino v Superior Court (1984) 162 Cal App 3d 1110, 1112, 208 Cal Rptr 829, 830; Hansen v Superior Court (1983) 149 Cal App 3d 823, 829, 197 Cal Rptr 175, 178; Billings v Edwards (1981) 120 Cal App 3d 238, 247, 174 Cal Rptr 722, 727–728; Zorro Investment Co. v Great Pacific Securities Corp. (1977) 69 Cal App 3d 907, 911, 138 Cal Rptr 410, 411.

[10] Cf. Imwinkelried and Blumoff, Pretrial Discovery—Strategy and Tactics § 11.06 (2004) [discussing the practice under the 1956 Discovery Act].

[11] CCP § 2033.060(h).

[12] CCP § 2033.710.

the Council's Official Form for admission requests is simply a gesture at compliance with the Legislature's unattainable mandate.

Service: The party making admission requests must, of course, serve a copy of them on the responding party. That party must also serve an informational copy on all other parties who have appeared in the action. The court has no express power to dispense with this requirement even for cases with many parties.[13]

Custody: The party making admission requests neither serves the original on the responding party nor files it with the court. Instead, that party must keep the original, with the original proof of service attached, as well as the original of the response, until six months after the case has ended.[14]

§ 9.4 Presumptive Numerical Limit

Genuineness of Documents: No presumptive numerical limit applies to requests to admit the genuineness of documents. Section 2033.030 provides:

> The number of requests for admission of the genuineness of documents is not limited except as justice requires to protect the responding party from unwarranted annoyance, embarrassment, oppression, or undue burden and expense.[1]

Truth of Specified Matters: Besides the genuineness of documents, a party may also request admissions of "the truth of specified matters of fact, opinion relating to fact, or application of law to fact."[2] However, Section 2033.030[3] imposes a presumptive numerical limit on such requests: a party may request, as a matter of right, no more than 35 of these admissions from any other party.[4]

Purpose of Limit: This presumptive numerical limit serves two purposes. First, it addresses concerns that litigants, left entirely unchecked, could abuse discovery with a superabundance of admission requests. In a federal employment

---

[13] Compare CCP § 2030.080, which authorizes the trial court to relieve a party from the requirement of serving informational copies of *interrogatories* where the number of parties is large. See § 5.3.

[14] CCP § 2033.270(b).

[1] CCP § 2033.030(c).

[2] CCP § 2033.010.

[3] Former CCP § 2033, of the 1956 Discovery Act, contained no numerical limit on the number of admission requests that one party could propound to another. On the contrary, it stated that there was no limit on the number of items that a party could include in a set of admission requests, or on the number of sets of requests that a party could submit. See former CCP § 2033(c), 1956 Discovery Act, Appendix E.

[4] CCP § 2033.030(a).

For a discussion of the presumptive numerical limit on *interrogatories*, see § 5.6.

Although the 1993 amendments to the Federal Rules of Civil Procedure placed a presumptive numerical limit on the number of interrogatories one party may propound to another, they did not impose one on the use of admission requests. Compare FRCivP 33(a) with FRCivP 36(a).

discrimination case, for example, the defendant made over 1,600 admission requests (many with subparts), which were 370 pages thick. This drew the ire of a federal magistrate:

> [T]he defendant's requests represent an attempt not just to nail down the core facts of the case, but also to pick every nit that a squad of lawyers could possibly see in it. Answering these requests in a conscientious and timely way would have taxed the powers of Hercules, even before he cleaned the Augean Stables.[5]

Second, the presumptive numerical limit forestalls easy evasion of the comparable limit for interrogatories.[6]

—Implementing the Presumptive Limit: Three formatting restrictions prevent easy evasion of the presumptive limit.[7] First, each request in a set must bear its own identifying number or letter.[8] Second, each individual request must be "full and complete in and of itself."[9] Finally, an individual request may neither contain subparts, nor use compound, conjunctive or disjunctive wording.[10]

Overcoming the Presumptive Limit: A party who wishes to submit to any other party more than 35 admission requests must overcome the presumption that this number is adequate. Section 2033.040 authorizes a party to propound a greater number if warranted "by the complexity or the quantity of the existing and potential issues in the particular case."[11]

—Supporting Declaration: A party who wants to exceed the presumptive numerical limit need not first obtain court permission. Instead, it simply serves requests that exceed this limit. However, the party must also attach a "Declaration for Additional Discovery" stating the circumstances that warrant the additional requests.[12]

---

[5] Wigler v Electronic Data Systems Corp. (1985, D Md) 108 FRD 204, 205.

[6] See, e.g., Misco, Inc. v United States Steel Corp. (1986, CA6 Tenn) 784 F2d 198, 206 [party sought to circumvent a local rule limiting a party to 30 interrogatories by serving over 2,000 admission requests]. Cf. Prochaska and Assoc. v Merrill Lynch, Pierce, Fenner and Smith, Inc. (1993, D Neb) 155 FRD 189, 192 [overruling objection that admission requests were "in fact interrogatories and a subterfuge to get around the court's limit on the number of interrogatories"].

[7] For a discussion of the presumptive numerical limit on the number of admission requests, see § 9.4.

[8] CCP § 2033.060(c).

[9] CCP § 2033.060(d).

[10] CCP § 2033.060(f).

The Official Form Requests for Admission prepared by the Judicial Council under CCP § 2033.5 are exempted from these restrictions.

See People ex rel Dep't of Transportation v Ad Way Signs, Inc. (1993) 14 Cal App 4th 187, 200–201, 17 Cal Rptr 2d 496, 503–504 [answer to improper compound request construed against requesting party on summary judgment motion].

[11] CCP § 2033.040(a).

[12] CCP § 2033.040(a), referencing CCP § 2033.050.

As originally adopted, this declaration required only the boilerplate statements that the information sought was "necessary for the proper preparation" of the case, and that the number of requests was "reasonably required" to obtain that information.[13] However, during the extensive amendment process between the initial passage of the 1986 Discovery Act and its effective date, the Legislature put some teeth in the declaration. Counsel for the requesting party must "state the reasons why the complexity or the quantity of issues" in the particular lawsuit warrant the increased number.[14]

Motion for Protective Order: If the required declaration accompanies the additional admission requests, a responding party who considers this quantity excessive must move for a protective order.[15] The moving party must accompany this motion with a declaration showing the steps taken to resolve the dispute informally.[16] In most other discovery disputes, the moving party establishes the need for a protective order. However, where a motion for a protective order challenges the need for more than 35 admission requests, "the propounding party shall have the burden of justifying" them.[17]

Increasing the Limit by Stipulation: The Civil Discovery Act gives parties the right "by written stipulation" to "modify the procedures" for any discovery method.[18] Accordingly, any two parties could agree to raise or to waive altogether the statutory limit on the number of admission requests that each of them may propound to the other.

§ 9.5 Scope of Requests: Relevance and Disputed Facts

Relevance to Subject Matter: Admission requests may cover "matters" that extend beyond the specific issues framed by the pleadings.[1] Like the statutes regulating depositions, interrogatories, and inspections, Section 2033.010 incorporates by reference Section 2017.010. That provision, in turn, authorizes broad discovery of any matter "relevant to the [general] subject matter of the lawsuit."[2] By expressly incorporating the broad discovery criterion for relevance, Section 2033.010 at once eliminates an ambiguity in the 1956 Discovery Act,[3] and

---

[13] Stats, 1986, ch 1334, Section 2033(c)(3), Declaration ¶ 6.

[14] CCP § 2033.050, Declaration ¶ 8.

[15] CCP § 2033.080(b)(2).

[16] CCP § 2033.080(a).

[17] CCP § 2033.040(b).

[18] CCP § 2016.030.

[1] CCP § 2033.010.

Annotation: Permissible scope, respecting nature of inquiry, of demand for admissions under modern state civil rules of procedure. 42 ALR4th 489.

[2] For a discussion of "relevant to the subject matter," see § 11.1.

[3] The prior statute simply stated that any documents or matters that were the subject of an admission request had to be "relevant." Former CCP § 2033, 1956 Discovery Act, Appendix E.

codifies one part of the Supreme Court's 1961 holding in the *Cembrook* case,[4] discussed below.

Controversial or Disputed Facts: The "matters"[5] as to which a party may request an admission go beyond "essentially undisputed and peripheral issues of fact."[6] Admission requests are more than "a means of avoiding the necessity of proving issues which the requesting party will doubtless be able to prove."[7] They may extend to "central facts,"[8] "lying at the heart of a case,"[9] that involve "major areas of dispute between the parties."[10] They are proper though a litigant has no realistic hope that admissions will result, but rather is using this discovery method "to lay a foundation for transferring to the other party a large part of the costs of the lawsuit."[11] And a party's belief that its position on the ultimate issues of liability is arguably valid "does not justify deceptive responses to particular requests for admission."[12] Nor may a party object that the admission involved might dispose of the parties' entire controversy.[13]

Section 2033.010 makes explicit what the 1956 Discovery Act left to interpretation: "A request for admission may relate to a matter that is in controversy between the parties."[14] With this provision, the Legislature rejected a line of contrary federal cases[15] and codified another part of the Supreme Court's 1961 holding in the *Cembrook* case.[16]

Cembrook illustrates an admission request that goes to "the heart of the case." This failure-to-warn product liability case centered on the plaintiff's claim that his serious stomach disorder resulted from his prolonged use of aspirin manufactured by the defendant. The plaintiff requested that the drug manufacturer admit

---

[4] Cembrook v Superior Court (1961) 56 Cal 2d 423, 429, 15 Cal Rptr 127, 130, 364 P2d 303, 306.

[5] CCP § 2033.010.

[6] Syracuse Broadcasting Corp. v Newhouse (1959, CA2 NY) 271 F2d 910, 917.

[7] Pickens v Equitable Life Assur. Co. (1969, CA5 Ala) 413 F2d 1390, 1393.

[8] Pickens v Equitable Life Assur. Co. (1969, CA5 Ala) 413 F2d 1390, 1393.

[9] Kasar v Miller Printing Machinery Co. (1964, WD Pa) 36 FRD 200, 203.

[10] Peck v Clesi (1963, ND Ohio) 37 FRD 11, 12.

[11] Peck v Clesi (1963, ND Ohio) 37 FRD 11, 12.

[12] Rosales v Thermax-Thermatron, Inc. (1998) 67 Cal App 4th 187, 199, 78 Cal Rptr 2d 861, 868.

[13] See, e.g., Adelman v Adelman (1988, D SD) 90 BR 1012, 1015.

[14] CCP § 2033.010.

Annotation: Permissible scope, respecting nature of inquiry, of demand for admissions under modern state civil rules of procedure. 42 ALR4th 489.

[15] See, e.g., Pickens v Equitable Life Assur. Soc. (1969, CA5 Ala) 413 F2d 1390, 1393 [finding objectionable a request that a beneficiary claiming double indemnity admit that the insured committed suicide]; Syracuse Broadcasting Corp. v Newhouse (1959, CA2 NY) 271 F2d 910, 917 [finding objectionable requests that antitrust defendants admit the very acts that plaintiff claims to be violations of Clayton and Sherman Acts].

[16] Cembrook v Superior Court (1961) 56 Cal 2d 423, 15 Cal Rptr 127, 364 P2d 303.

a causal nexus between his illness and its aspirin. The defendant objected that the requests related to a "controversial matter." Finding the requested admission proper, the Court explained:

> Most of the other discovery procedures are aimed primarily at assisting counsel to prepare for trial. Requests for admissions, on the other hand, are primarily aimed at setting at rest a triable issue so that it will not have to be tried. Thus, such requests, in a most definite manner, are aimed at expediting the trial. For this reason, the fact that the request is for the admission of a controversial matter . . . is of no moment. If the litigant is able to make the admission, the time for making it is during discovery procedures, and not at the trial.[17]

Irrelevant Request: Despite the great sweep of the discovery relevance standard, particular admission requests sometimes exceed even its generous boundaries. At a later stage in the *Cembrook* litigation, for example, the plaintiff sought admissions to support his conjecture that the defendant aspirin manufacturer had conspired with the news media to suppress publicity concerning his lawsuit. The Court of Appeal found that the requested admission had nothing to do with the legitimate subject of the plaintiff's product liability claim:

> [A]ll of the subject requests were related to the publicity given by news media to the ill effects resulting from the ingestion of [another brand of aspirin], and the lack or suppression of such publicity in the instant case by such news media. . . . [T]he right to a public trial does not carry the mandate that the trial must be publicized by or in the news media; nor is the subject of trial publicity by means of such media a triable issue in a case such as the one at hand. The subject of the requested admissions was not, therefore, relevant to the instant action nor was it reasonably calculated to lead to admissible evidence.[18]

§ 9.6   Opinions and Legal Conclusions

Section 2033.010 specifies that a party may request an admission not only of matters of "fact," but also of matters of "opinion relating to fact" and "application of law to fact."[1] The added language eliminates an ambiguity in

---

[17] Cembrook v Superior Court (1961) 56 Cal 2d 423, 429, 15 Cal Rptr 127, 131, 364 P2d 303, 307.

[18] Cembrook v Sterling Drug, Inc. (1964) 231 Cal App 2d 52, 62, 41 Cal Rptr 492, 498.

See also Workman v Chinchinian (1992, D Kan) 807 F Supp 634, 648 [objection to admission request sustained where the defendant physician's past practices in California were found irrelevant to the standard of care in Idaho or Washington]; Wauchop v Domino's Pizza, Inc. (1991, D Kan) 138 FRD 539, 551 [relevance objection sustained to a request that the defendant restauranteur admit that he controlled 90% of a company].

[1] CCP § 2033.010.

The Discovery Commission recommended an explicit prohibition of admission requests that would call for an "application of law to fact." See Proposed Civil Discovery Act of 1986, Section 2033(a), Appendix D. The Legislature initially went along with this recommendation. See Stats.

its original version,[2] mirrors a 1970 amendment to the Federal Rules,[3] and codifies the Supreme Court's holdings in the *Cembrook*[4] and the *Burke* cases.[5]

Opinions: *Cembrook* articulates the rationale for letting admissions extend beyond purely factual matters. In that product liability case, the Court upheld the plaintiff's request that the defendant drug manufacturer admit that its aspirin "caused various side effects and physical ailments," that his present illness "was caused by a prolonged use" of the defendant's product, and that he now needed a certain operation because of this illness.[6] These requests drew the objection that they "call for the conclusions and interpretations of the litigant [and] call for answers 'to an intricate and controversial matter involving complex medical and scientific facts.' "[7]

The Court unhesitatingly adopted the liberal (though then minority) view of the allowable range of admission requests. In a companion case it had ruled that written interrogatories calling for the expression of opinions and conclusions were not objectionable.[8] It could see no reason to treat admission requests differently:

> The reasons set forth . . . for holding such objections unsound when applied to other discovery procedures, are peculiarly applicable to requests for admissions. Most of the other discovery procedures are aimed primarily at assisting counsel to prepare for trial. Requests for admissions, on the other hand, are primarily aimed at setting at rest a triable issue so that it will not have to be tried. Thus, such requests, in a most definite manner, are aimed at expediting the trial. For this reason, the fact that the request . . . calls for an opinion, is of no moment. If the litigant is able to make the admission, the time for making it is during discovery procedures, and not at trial.[9]

1986, ch 1334, Section 2033(a). However, during the extensive amendment process that preceded the effective date of the 1986 Discovery Act, it converted this prohibition into an explicit authorization of such admission requests.

Annotation: Permissible scope, respecting nature of inquiry, of demand for admissions under modern state civil rules of procedure. 42 ALR4th 489.

[2] Former CCP § 2033(a), 1956 Discovery Act, Appendix E.

[3] FRCivP 36(a).

[4] Cembrook v Superior Court (1961) 56 Cal 2d 423, 15 Cal Rptr 127, 364 P2d 303.

[5] Burke v Superior Court (1969) 71 Cal 2d 276,78 Cal Rptr 481, 455 P2d 409.

[6] Cembrook v Superior Court (1961) 56 Cal 2d 423, 427–428, 15 Cal Rptr 127, 129–130, 364 P2d 303, 305–306.

[7] Cembrook v Superior Court (1961) 56 Cal 2d 423, 428, 15 Cal Rptr 127, 130, 364 P2d 303, 306.

[8] West Pico Furniture Co. v Superior Court (1961) 56 Cal 2d 407, 417, 15 Cal Rptr 119, 123, 364 P2d 295, 299.

[9] Cembrook v Superior Court (1961) 56 Cal 2d 423, 429, 15 Cal Rptr 127, 131, 364 P2d 303, 307.

See also Chodos v Superior Court (1963) 215 Cal App 2d 318, 30 Cal Rptr 303 [in action seeking an injunction after a partial landslide, the plaintiff may request an admission that the lot the defendants had created by filling a ravine now "presents a greater probability of falling and sliding that it did" before the landslide].

Application of Law to Fact: The *Burke*[10] case considered whether an admission request could properly embrace a matter that would entail the application of some law to the underlying facts of a lawsuit. In an action for wrongful attachment, the plaintiff sought recovery for the legal fees it had incurred in successfully defending the action in which the attachment had occurred. The victim of a wrongful attachment must mitigate damages. If the attachment was invalid on its face, this duty would have required an immediate motion by the plaintiff to have the court dissolve it. If it was not, such a motion would have been futile. Accordingly, the plaintiff requested that the defendant admit that the particular attachment of its property was regular on its face. The Court upheld this admission request though it called for an application of the law of damages to the particular facts of the case:

> [W]hen a party is served with a request for admission concerning a legal question properly raised in the pleadings he cannot object simply asserting that the request calls for a conclusion of law. He should make the admission if he is able to do so and does not in good faith intend to contest the issue at trial . . . .[11]

—Pure Questions of Law: There are two restrictions on the use of admission requests that call for a legal conclusion. First, in line with the federal practice,[12] courts should not allow a party to request an admission that a particular proposition is a correct rule of law.[13] A party wishing to raise such a purely legal issue should do so by a general demurrer, a motion for judgment on the pleadings, or a motion for summary judgment. A dictum in the *Lieb* case indicates that California courts will follow this interpretation:

> It may well be doubted whether requests which seek admissions as to questions of law may be properly required. Certainly the words of the statute do not impose such a requirement. It has been held in this state that binding stipulations may not be made on questions of law. But we need not decide this question here.[14]

---

[10] Burke v Superior Court (1969) 71 Cal 2d 276,78 Cal Rptr 481, 455 P2d 409.

[11] Burke v Superior Court (1969) 71 Cal 2d 276, 282, 78 Cal Rptr 481, 488, 455 P2d 409, 416.

[12] See Advisory Committee Note to 1970 amendment to FRCivP 36 ["The amended provision (allowing admission requests to require 'the application of law to fact') does not authorize requests for admissions of law unrelated to the facts of the case."]

[13] See, e.g., Adelman v Adelman (1988, D SD) 90 BR 1012, 1015 [court should strike request for admission of a legal proposition unqualified by the facts of the case, even if the responding party has failed to object]; Morris v Marshall County Board of Education (1983, ND WVa) 560 F Supp 43, 45 [although the recipient of a request to admit that a third-party defendant had properly removed the case to federal court made no response, it was not "estopped" to challenge the court's jurisdiction].

[14] Lieb v Superior Court (1962) 199 Cal App 2d 364, 367–368, 18 Cal Rptr 705, 707 (internal citations omitted).

—*De Facto* **Interrogatories:** Second, courts should prevent admission requests from usurping a function that belongs to interrogatories. In a product liability action, the manufacturer requested that the plaintiffs admit that they "know of no facts" that would "support a cause of action against it," or would "support a claim that [the manufacturer] was negligent in the design or manufacture" of the product involved. The court concluded that these were not really admission requests, but rather an effort to discover information better sought by interrogatories: "If a person desires to sound out an adversary's knowledge relative to the existence of facts, he should resort to other discovery methods . . . ."[15]

§ 9.7   Privileged Matter

Although the "matter" covered by an admission request meets the discovery test for relevance, some privilege, such as the lawyer-client privilege,[1] the marital communications privilege,[2] the governmental secrets privilege,[3] the taxpayer's privilege,[4] or the privilege against self-incrimination,[5] may nonetheless insulate it from discovery. Privileges for confidential communications, however, protect only the communications themselves. They do not preclude requests tailored to secure an admission of the facts that were the subject of the confidential communication. Thus, a request that a party admit *telling an attorney* that he or she ran a red light is objectionable. A request that the party admit that *he or she ran a red light* is not. The responding party should admit or deny the fact without revealing any confidential communication by which the party learned that fact.

Self-Incrimination: The assertion of the privilege against self-incrimination in response to an admission request poses an issue not encountered with the other discovery devices. An admission made in response to a discovery request is "made for the purpose of the pending action only. It is not an admission by that party for any other purpose, and it shall not be used in any manner against that party in any other proceeding."[6] This limitation has led parties in several federal

---

[15] International Harvester Co. v Superior Court (1969) 273 Cal App 2d 652, 655, 78 Cal Rptr 515, 517.

[1] See, e.g., Shawmut, Inc. v American Viscose Corp. (1952, DC Mass) 12 FRD 488, 489.

For a discussion of the lawyer-client privilege as a restriction on discovery, see §§ 12.8–12.12

[2] Cf. Walsh v Connecticut Mut. Life Ins. Co. (1939, ED NY) 26 F Supp 566, 572.

For a discussion of the marital communications privilege as a restriction on discovery, see §§ 12.15–12.16.

[3] See, e.g., Kenyatta v Kelly (1974, ED Pa) 375 F Supp 1175, 1177–1179.

For a discussion of the official information privilege as a restriction on discovery, see § 12.33.

[4] For a discussion of the taxpayer's privilege as a restriction on discovery, see §§ 12.35–12.36.

[5] Cf. Metalworking Machinery, Inc. v Superior Court (1977) 69 Cal App 3d 791, 138 Cal Rptr 369.

For a discussion of the privilege against self-incrimination as a restriction on civil discovery, see §§ 12.2–12.7.

[6] CCP § 2033.410(b).

cases to argue that it is not valid to object to an admission request by asserting the privilege against self-incrimination.

For example, in one federal case, the FDIC requested that the defendant admit certain facts concerning his defaults in his dealings with an insured bank. He objected that his responses might incriminate him. The agency argued that Federal Rule 36(b)'s prohibition against the use of a discovery admission "against [defendant] in any other proceeding" negated the privilege claim. The appellate court concluded that this prohibition did not confer the type of immunity necessary to annul the privilege claim:

> But [FRCivP 36(b)] does not prevent the use of facts set forth in the admission by the criminal prosecutor as a confirmation that facilitates preparation of the criminal case, or perhaps as a lead to other evidence, which is part of the protection of the constitutional privilege.[7]

A California court took a similar approach in a paternity case.[8] The defendant asserted the privilege against self-incrimination in response to a request that he admit facts that, if true, would create a conclusive presumption that he had fathered a certain child. The appellate court believed that a mere prohibition against use of a discovery admission in another proceeding was an inadequate tradeoff for the protection conferred by the privilege. It noted that in any later criminal prosecution for wilful nonsupport based on his conduct to date, the paternity judgment would be admissible in evidence. Thus, it held that the trial court could compel a response to the admission request only if it first granted the defendant use immunity. To be effective, this immunity would have to prohibit, in any later criminal action based on his past nonsupport, the use not only of any admission itself, but also of any paternity judgment.[9]

§ 9.8   Protective Orders

Grounds: Section 2033.080 empowers the trial court to issue a protective order when compliance with admission requests would cause a party "unwarranted annoyance, embarrassment, oppression, or undue burden or expense."[1] This provision differs from the 1956 Discovery Act[2] in three minor respects. First, it adds to the original trio of annoyance, embarrassment and oppression a fourth ground for seeking the court's protection, namely, the "undue burden and

---

[7] Gordon v Federal Deposit Ins. Corp. (1970 DC Cir) 427 F2d 578, 581.

See also Le Blanc v Spector (1974, DC Conn) 378 F Supp 310; Federal Deposit Ins. Corp. v Logsdon (1955, WD Ky) 18 FRD 57; State v Ott (1990, Ariz App) 808 P2d 305, 311–312 [Arizona equivalent of FRCivP 36(b) does not provide full use immunity sufficient to overcome privilege against self-incrimination].

[8] Smith v Superior Court (1980) 110 Cal App 3d 422, 168 Cal Rptr 24.

[9] For a discussion of "use immunity" as a device for overcoming in civil litigation a claim of the privilege against self-incrimination, see § 12.7.

[1] CCP § 2033.080(b).

[2] Former CCP 2030(c), 1956 Discovery Act, Appendix E.

expense" that a response will entail. Second, it uses the adjective "unwarranted" to underscore that mere "annoyance" and "embarrassment" are not grounds for avoiding an answer. Third, it includes a nonexclusive list of the protections that a responding party may request.

—Relief from the Obligation to Respond: Section 2033.080 allows the trial court to order that an entire set of admission requests or particular requests in a set "need not be answered at all."[3] This provision would be redundant if it applied to admission requests concerning irrelevant, privileged, or work product matters.[4] In the protective order context, it signifies that even if admission requests are unobjectionable on those three grounds, the court may still relieve a party from the obligation to respond to some or all of them. For example, the responding party may want to avoid any response to requests served after the close of discovery.[5]

In other situations, the recipient of a set of admission requests may wish to postpone answering some or all of them until the court has ruled on a pending motion that could moot the need for the information sought. A motion for a protective order can accomplish this postponement. Class actions provide an example. The trial court may rule that a party need not respond to admission requests relating to the merits of the underlying cause of action until it has decided whether the case may proceed as a class action.[6] It may also postpone answers to merits-related admission requests pending its disposition of a jurisdictional challenge[7] or a motion to stay or dismiss for forum non conveniens.[8]

—Challenging the Need to Exceed the Presumptive Limit: Section 2033.040 allows a party to propound more than the presumptive limit of 35 admission requests[9] if an accompanying declaration sets forth the need to exceed the limit.[10] The recipient of such a set of requests may challenge the showing by moving for a protective order.[11] Normally, the party seeking some protection

---

[3] CCP § 2033.080(b)(1).

[4] See CCP § 2033.230(b).

[5] See, e.g., Central Maine Power Co. v Foster Wheeler Corp. (1987, D Maine) 115 FRD 294, 295 [plaintiff not required to answer complicated admission requests made more than two weeks after discovery deadline].

[6] Cf. Coriell v Superior Court (1974) 39 Cal App 3d 487, 493, 114 Cal Rptr 310, 315 [recognizing that it is appropriate to defer answers to *interrogatories* on liability issues until the trial court resolves issues relating to class worthiness].

[7] Cf. Investment Properties Intl., Ltd. v IOS, Ltd. (1972, CA2 NY) 459 F2d 705 [quashing deposition notices].

[8] Cf. Fitzgerald v Texaco, Inc. (1975, CA2 NY) 521 F2d 448 n3 [postponing document discovery].

[9] See CCP § 2033.030(a).

This limit does not apply to requests for admission of the genuineness of documents. CCP § 2033.030(a).

[10] CCP § 2033.040(a).

For a discussion of the presumptive numerical limit on admission requests, see § 9.4.

[11] CCP §§ 2033.040(a) and 2033.080(b)(2).

against answering admission requests must persuade the court that the task would cause unwarranted annoyance, embarrassment, oppression, or undue burden and expense. Where, however, a party seeks to request more than the presumptive limit of 35 admissions, Section 2033.040 squarely requires the requesting party to convince the court that the greater number is necessary:

> If the responding party seeks a protective order on the ground that the number of requests for admission is unwarranted, the propounding party shall have the burden of justifying the number of requests for admission.[12]

—**Extensions of Time:** The receiving party may need more than 30-days for responding to some or all of them.[13] If the requesting party will not agree to an extension, a motion for a protective order can get this additional time.[14]

—**Confidential Information:** Admission requests may pertain to information that, while otherwise discoverable, is nevertheless quite sensitive or confidential. Trade secrets are the classic examples. The trial court can suspend or modify the recipient's duty to respond.[15] It can also seal or restrict access to answers involving such information.[16]

—**Other Grounds:** The list of five protective orders in 2033.080 is illustrative, not exclusive. "For good cause shown" the trial court can issue a protective order to prevent any form of "unwarranted annoyance, embarrassment, oppression, or undue burden and expense."[17]

"Objection" and "Protection" Distinguished: Strictly speaking, "objections" to admission requests and protective order motions are not interchangeable. A motion for a protective order is improper when the only ground for resisting discovery is that an admission request addresses a matter that is irrelevant[18] or privileged.[19] In such cases, the responding party should serve a "response"[20] that includes an "objection" to any questions that are outside the scope of permissible discovery.[21] Moreover, where a party propounds more than 35

---

[12] CCP § 2033.040(b).

[13] CCP § 2033.250.

[14] CCP § 2033.080(b)(3).

[15] CCP § 2033.080(b)(4).

[16] CCP § 2033.080(b)(5).

[17] CCP § 2033.080(b).

Cf. Torres v Superior Court (1990) 221 Cal App 3d 181, 188, 270 Cal Rptr 401, 405 [trial court issues unlisted type of protective order in connection with demand for disclosure of *expert witness information*].

[18] For a discussion of relevance issues peculiar to admission requests, see § 9.5.

For a general discussion of the discovery criterion for relevance, see Chapter 11.

[19] For a discussion of privilege issues peculiar to admission requests, see § 9.7.

[20] CCP § 2033.210.

[21] CCP § 2033.230.

For a discussion of a response that asserts an objection to an admission request, see §§ 9.13–9.14.

admission requests[22] *without* the required justifying declaration, the responding party should state in the "response" an "objection" to all requests over the statutory limit: "Unless a [justifying] declaration . . . has been made, a party need only respond to the first 35 admission requests served . . ., if that party states an objection to the balance . . . on the ground that the limit has been exceeded."[23]

Protective orders should be reserved for admission requests that are, at least arguably, within the scope of allowable discovery, yet nonetheless warrant trial court intervention. However, as long as the motion for a protective order clearly informs the other party of the basis for objecting to a request, it would elevate form over substance to deny the motion simply because the "response" is the correct vehicle for raising it.[24]

The reverse situation raises different concerns. Courts have sometimes been reluctant to consider "objections," in a "response," that a discovery request would be annoying, embarrassing, oppressive, or burdensome. There are two reasons for this strict attitude. First, before moving for a protective order, a party must consider the prospect of a monetary sanction if the court finds no substantial justification for the motion. The deterrent effect of this threat might be lost if a party could raise by objection issues of annoyance, embarrassment, oppression, burden, or expense of responding to admission requests.[25] Second, a protective order motion is subject to a "meet and confer" requirement;[26] an objection is not.[27]

In *Brigante v Huang*,[28] however, a case involving admission requests, the court allowed a party to assert a claim that the requests were "oppressive" in an opposition to a motion to deem the requests admitted:

> While defense counsel cited oppression as a basis for objecting to plaintiff's motion, rather than by raising it by a separate motion for protective order, its opposition performed the essential function of apprising the court and opposing counsel of its position and the basis for that position. That is a legally sufficient manner in which to raise

---

[22] This limit does not apply to requests for admission of the genuineness of documents. CCP § 2033.030(a).

[23] CCP § 2033.030(b).

[24] Cf. Ryan v Superior Court (1960) 186 Cal App 2d 813, 820, 9 Cal Rptr 147, 152 [if the responding party claims that an *interrogatory* calls for confidential information in the nature of a trade secret, it should move for a protective order instead of lodging an objection.]

[25] Cf. Coy v Superior Court (1962) 58 Cal 2d 210, 218, 23 Cal Rptr 393, 396, 373 P2d 457, 460 [objection that an *interrogatory* covered same matters as did previous deposition should have been raised by a motion for a protective order]; Zellerino v Brown (1991) 235 Cal App 3d 1097, 1101–1102, 1 Cal Rptr 2d 222, 224 [remedy of party receiving a premature *demand to exchange expert witness information* is a motion for a protective order, not an objection to the demand].

[26] CCP § 2033.080(a).

[27] See Zellerino v Brown (1991) 235 Cal App 3d 1097, 1101–1102, 1 Cal Rptr 2d 222, 224.

[28] Brigante v Huang (1993) 20 Cal App 4th 1569, 25 Cal Rptr 2d 354.

the issue; it was not necessary to file a separate motion for a protective order.[29]

Burden of Persuasion: Normally, the party seeking some protection against answering admission requests must persuade the court that the task would cause unwarranted annoyance, embarrassment, or oppression, or undue burden and expense.[30] However, when the ground for the protective order is that an opponent has not adequately supported its requests for more than 35 admissions,[31] the party propounding the additional requests must justify that number.[32]

Time for Motion: Section 2033.080 requires only that the responding party move "promptly" for a protective order.[33] Certainly, a motion made within the time to serve a "response" to the admission requests would be timely.[34]

Duty to Meet and Confer: Before moving for a protective order, a receiving party must try to resolve informally the dispute with the requesting party. A declaration setting forth these efforts must accompany the motion.[35]

Monetary Sanction: A party who unsuccessfully makes or opposes a motion for a protective order runs the risk of incurring a monetary sanction. The party can avoid the sanction by convincing the trial court that "substantial justification" existed for making or opposing the motion.[36]

§ 9.9 Response to Admission Requests: Format, Signature, Timing, and Service

Format: Absent grounds for a protective order,[1] a party to whom a set of admission requests is directed must respond using the format prescribed in Section . Immediately below the case title should appear the name of the responding and requesting parties and the same identifying number used on the

---

[29] Brigante v Huang (1993) 20 Cal App 4th 1569, 1585–1586, 25 Cal Rptr 2d 354, 365.

Cf. Coy v Superior Court (1962) 58 Cal 2d 210, 218, 23 Cal Rptr 393, 396, 373 P2d 457, 460 [after pointing out that an objection that an *interrogatory* covered the same matters as did a previous deposition should have been raised by a motion for a protective order, the Court proceeded to consider the merits of the objection]; Durst v Superior Court (1963) 218 Cal App 2d 460, 466–468, 32 Cal Rptr 627, 631–632 [claim that *interrogatories* were oppressive and burdensome was raised by objection instead of by motion for protective order].

[30] Cf. Coriell v Superior Court (1974) 39 Cal App 3d 487, 492–493, 114 Cal Rptr 310, 314–315 [party seeking protective order postponing need to answer *interrogatories* has burden of showing good cause]; People v Superior Court (Witzerman) (1967) 248 Cal App 2d 276, 280, 56 Cal Rptr 393, 397 [party seeking protective order sealing its answers to *interrogatories* has burden of showing good cause].

[31] CCP § 2033.080(b)(2).

[32] CCP § 2033.040(b).

[33] CCP § 2033.080(a).

[34] See CCP § 2033.250.

[35] CCP § 2033.080(a).

[36] CCP § 2033.080(d).

[1] For a discussion of protective orders against admission requests, see § 9.8.

set of requests itself.[2] The party must respond "separately" and "under oath" to each request in the set.[3] The individual responses should be in the same sequence and identified by the same number or letter as the corresponding request.[4] The responding party may, but need not, retype the text of the request.[5]

—Permissible Responses: As used in Section 2033.220, "response" includes either an "answer" or an "objection" to a particular request. Three types of "answers" to an admission request are possible: (1) an admission,[6] (2) a denial,[7] and (3) a statement of inability to admit or deny.[8]

Sections 2033.220 and 2033.230 reflect a serious legislative effort to eliminate hypertechnical, nitpicking interpretations of the admission requests.[9] If only part of a request is objectionable, the responding party must "answer" the balance.[10] An "answer" must be "as complete and straightforward" as the information available to the responding party allows.[11] If the "matter" asked by an admission request is only partially true or incompletely known, the "answer" should admit the true or known part and specify the untrue or unknown part.[12]

Signature: The nature of the individual responses determines who must sign. If the responses consist entirely of objections, then only the attorney needs to sign the "response" document.[13] If they consist entirely of "answers" (i.e., admissions, denials, or statements of inability to do either), then the party must sign the document; the attorney need not. If the responses include both answers

---

[2] CCP § 2033.210(c)

[3] CCP § 2033.210(a).

See Tobin v Oris (1992) 3 Cal App 4th 814, 829, 4 Cal Rptr 2d 736, 745 [joint response by two defendants to separate but identical sets of admission requests did not violate "separate" response requirement, where each defendant separately verified responses].

[4] CCP § 2033.210(d).

[5] CCP § 2033.210(d).

[6] CCP § 2033.220(b)(1).

For a discussion of answers expressly admitting requests, see § 9.10.

[7] CCP § 2033.220(b)(2).

For a discussion of answers denying requested admissions, see § 9.11.

[8] CCP § (b)(3).

For a discussion of answers stating an inability to admit or deny, see § 9.12.

[9] Cf. Thalheim v Eberheim (1988, D Conn) 124 FRD 34, 35 [court should not encourage over-qualification of responses by "crediting disingenuous, hair-splitting distinctions whose unarticulated goal is unfairly to burden an opposing party"].

[10] CCP § 2033.230(a).

[11] CCP § 2033.220(a).

See, e.g., Collisson and Kaplan v Hartunian (1994) 21 Cal App 4th 1611, 1617, 26 Cal Rptr 2d 786, 790 [it is not "straightforward" to respond from the perspective of a nonparty].

[12] CCP § 2033.220(b).

See, e.g., Apex Oil Co. v Belcher Co (1988, CA2 NY) 855 F2d 1009, 1019 [improper to deny outright a request where responding party knew truth of two elements of the request].

[13] CCP §§ 2033.240(a) and (c).

and objections, then both the party and the attorney must sign the document. However, where a response document contains a mixture of answers and objections, the failure to comply fully with the signature requirement for the client's *answers* does not invalidate those responses containing the attorney's *objections*.[14]

—Entities: Where the responding party is an entity such as a corporation, partnership, or governmental agency, an officer or agent must sign the response document.[15] Where this agent is also an attorney for the entity, the statute imposes a limited waiver of the lawyer-client privilege and the work product protection. The entity may not later assert either that privilege or that protection to block efforts to learn from that attorney "the identity of the sources" used to obtain the information in the responses.[16]

—Verification: Where the response requires the party's signature, the party must sign under oath.[17] An uncorrected failure to include a verification may lead a court to deem the requested matters admitted.[18] Unlike the provision governing verification of *pleadings,*[19] counsel for a party may not verify *admission request* responses, even when the client resides outside the county where the attorney's office is located.[20]

Attorneys should resist the temptation to have the client sign undated, blank verification forms. An attorney may not prepare a response to admission requests and then, without consulting with the client about the accuracy of the answers, simply attach a presigned verification to these responses and serve them on opposing counsel: "The *use* of a presigned verification in discovery proceedings,

---

[14] See Food 4 Less Supermarkets v Superior Court (1995) 40 Cal App 4th 651, 657–658, 46 Cal Rptr 2d 925, 928–929 [unverified response to an *inspection demand*]; Blue Ridge Ins. Co. v Superior Court (1988) 202 Cal App 3d 339, 344–345, 248 Cal Rptr 346, 349–350 [client's timely but unverified response to an *inspection demand* did not invalidate objections contained in the response].

[15] CCP § 2033.240(b).

[16] CCP § 2033.240(b).

[17] CCP §§ 2033.210(a) and 2033.240(a).

Current federal practice does not require a responding party to answer admission requests under oath. See FRCivP 36.

[18] See, e.g., Appleton v Superior Court (1988) 206 Cal App 3d 632, 636, 253 Cal Rptr 762, 764 [timely but unverified responses "tantamount to no responses at all" and subject to motion to have matters deemed admitted].

Cf. Brochtrup v Intep (1987) 190 Cal App 3d 323, 330–332, 235 Cal Rptr 390, 394–395 [under the version of CCP § 2033 in the 1956 Discovery Act, honest mistake of law regarding need for verification justified relief from deemed admissions].

For a discussion of deemed admissions, see § 9.16.

[19] CCP § 446.

[20] Cf. Brigante v Huang (1993) 20 Cal App 4th 1569, 1585, 25 Cal Rptr 2d 354, 364; Steele v Totah (1986) 180 Cal App 3d 545, 550, 225 Cal Rptr 635, 637.

For a discussion of the consequences of failing to supply the required verification, see § 9.16.

without first consulting with the client to assure that any assertions of fact are true, is a clear and serious violation of the statutes and rules."[21]

The requirement that a party's answers to admission requests be under oath seems ill-advised insofar as it covers express admissions.[22] Section 2033.410 makes any admissions that it produces effective only for the purpose of the lawsuit in they are made.[23] Given this limitation, a party should not have to swear under the penalty of perjury that an admitted fact really is true. For convenience or efficiency, a party should be able to admit both a fact that the party does not know to be true, and one that the party knows or believes to be untrue.

Time for Response: The response is normally due 30 days after service of the admission requests.[24] Service of the requests by mail extends this period, usually by five days.[25] The requesting and responding parties may agree to extend this period.[26] Any informal agreement must be confirmed in a writing that specifies the agreed response date.[27] Unless the agreement states otherwise, it extends the time not only to "answer" a request, but also to "object" to it.[28] All other parties must receive notice of any agreed extension.[29]

Failure to file a timely response waives any objections the delinquent party might have made to the requests.[30] A court may grant relief from this waiver[31] to a party who then serves a response that substantially complies with the statutory

---

[21] Cf. Drociak v State Bar (1991) 52 Cal 3d 1085, 1090, 278 Cal Rptr 86, 89, 804 P2d 711, 714 [not realizing that his client's death explained his inability to contact her, plaintiff's attorney prepared answers to *interrogatories* and attached presigned verification].

[22] For a discussion of express admissions, see § 9.10.

Current federal practice does not require a responding party to answer admission requests under oath. See FRCivP 36.

[23] CCP § 2033.410(b).

For a discussion of the effect of a discovery admission, see § 9.20.

[24] CCP § 2033.250.

On motion the court may shorten or extend this time period. CCP § 2033.250.

Cf. Winslow v Romer (1990, D Colo) 123 BR 74, 75–76 [plaintiff's desire to "'get at the truth quickly'" is an insufficient reason to shorten time to respond to an admission request].

[25] CCP § 2016.050, referencing CCP § 1013(a).

Compare Equal Employment Opportunity Commission v Jordan Graphics, Inc. (1991, WD NC) 135 FRD 126, 127–128 [30 day period for response under FRCivP 36 begins to run on the date of mailing, not on the date of receipt of the admission requests].

[26] CCP § 2033.260(a).

[27] CCP § 2033.260(b).

Cf. Hoffman v Texas Commerce Bank N.A. (1992, Tex App) 846 SW2d 336, 339 [disputed oral agreement to extend time to respond insufficient grounds to allow withdrawal of deemed admissions].

[28] CCP § 2033.260(c).

[29] CCP § 2033.260(d).

[30] CCP § 2033.280(a).

[31] CCP § 2033.280(a).

requirements[32] and whose prior delinquency was due to "mistake, inadvertence, or excusable neglect."[33]

Service: The responding party must serve the original response on the requesting party and an informational copy on all other parties.[34] The requesting party must retain the originals of both the requests and the responses until six months after the case's completion.[35]

§ 9.10 Express Admissions

Tacit Admissions Abolished: Section 2033.220 requires a party receiving admission requests to expressly admit any matter that, as described in the request, is true.[1] Unlike both the practice under the 1956 Discovery Act[2] and the current federal practice,[3] the party's "silence" does not tacitly admit the requested matter. Instead, even a party who is ready to treat a matter as true in the case must affirmatively and formally signal this willingness by responding with an express admission of that matter.[4] Failure to respond to an admission request, even one that a party is willing to concede is true, is a "misuse of the discovery process."[5] A court *must* impose a monetary sanction on any party who fails to respond by answer or objection to any particular admission request.[6]

Form of Express Admission: Section 2033.220 allows two forms of express admission. Sometimes, the responding party may be ready not only to concede a matter's essential truth but also to adopt the phrasing of this matter in the request itself. In such cases, the responding party need only identify the request by number and state that it is "admitted."[7] In other cases, the responding party may

---

[32] CCP § 2033.280(a)(1).

[33] CCP § 2033.280(a)(2).

Cf. White Consolidated Industries, Inc. v Waterhouse (1994, D Minn) 158 FRD 429 [court should evaluate of allowing *tardy response* to admission requests under same criteria that govern *withdrawal* or *amendment* of admissions].

For a discussion of withdrawing and amending admissions, see § 9.18.

[34] CCP § 2033.250.

[35] CCP § 2033.270(b).

[1] CCP § 2033.220(b)(1).

[2] Former CCP § 2033(a), 1956 Discovery Act, Appendix E [matter deemed admitted unless recipient denied, claimed an inability to admit or deny, or objected to the request].

[3] FRCivP 36(a) [matter deemed admitted unless recipient denied, claimed an inability to admit or deny, or objected to request].

[4] CCP § 2033.220(b)(1).

[5] See CCP § 2023.010(d).

[6] CCP § 2033.280(c).

See, e.g., Appleton v Superior Court (1988) 206 Cal App 3d 632, 634–636, 253 Cal Rptr 762, 763–764.

For a further discussion of the consequences of a failure to respond to admission requests, see § 9.16.

[7] CCP § 2033.220(b).

wish to qualify its answer. Section 2033.220 allows an admission "either as expressed in the request itself or as reasonably and clearly qualified."[8] For example, in a federal case,[9] a defendant received a request to admit that he had told investigators that smoldering cigarettes "must" have caused a fire. He answered with an admission that he had stated cigarettes "may" have caused it.

§ 9.11 Denials

Form: The responding party's personal knowledge or its reasonable investigation may convince it that a "matter" covered by an admission request is untrue. To preserve the issue for trial, Section 2033.220 requires the responding party to specifically deny the request.[1]

The statute requires no explanation of a straightforward denial; the simple statement in the response document—"denied"—suffices.[2] The responding party, however, *must* respond; it may not simply rely on allegations it made in a prior verified pleading to substitute for a specific denial of a subsequent admission request: "The pleadings are not to be confused with the mechanisms for discovery, nor do they perform the same functions."[3]

Partially True Requests: A responding party may not deny a request entirely merely because the requested admission is not 100% accurate. Instead, that party should deny only "so much of the matter involved in the request as is untrue."[4] Suppose, for example, a request seeks an admission that the defendants owe the plaintiff $10,000. The defendants believe that they owe only $9,000. They may not simply respond "denied" to the request. Instead, they should also admit that they owe $9,000. A federal case[5] furnishes another example. There the defendants requested that the plaintiff admit their detailed version of the way that an accident had happened. The plaintiff answered simply that he "denies that the manner in which he received the injuries was as he was requested to admit . . . ." The court criticized this response:

> [The plaintiff] does not set out the manner in which he received his injuries, nor does he state wherein the description thereof as set forth

---

[8] CCP § 2033.220(b)(1).

[9] Continental Casualty Co. v Brummel (1986, Colo) 112 FRD 77, 81 n2. Cf. Valerio v Andrew Youngquist Construction (2002) 103 Cal App 4th 1273, 1272, 127 Cal Rptr 2d 436, 443.

[1] CCP § 2033.220(b).

[2] Cf. Holguin v Superior Court (1972) 22 Cal App 3d 812, 99 Cal Rptr 653.

Annotation: What constitutes a "denial" within Federal Rule of Civil Procedure 36 and similar state statutes and rules pertaining to admissions before trial. 36 ALR2d 1192.

[3] Bank of America v Baker (1965) 238 Cal App 2d 778, 779, 48 Cal Rptr 165, 166.

[4] CCP § 2033.220(b)(2).

Compare Thalheim v Eberheim (1988, D Conn) 124 FRD 34, 35 [under FRCivP 36, courts should not encourage over-qualification of admission request responses "by crediting disingenuous, hair-splitting distinctions whose unarticulated goal is unfairly to burden an opposing party"].

[5] Wilkinson v Powell (1945, CA5 Fla) 149 F2d 335 [evasive denial ineffective to create genuine issue of material fact for summary judgment].

in [the defendants'] request for admission of facts was erroneous. The language of the denial suggests that [it is based on] some slight variation or . . . some immaterial misstatement in the submitted request . . . .[6]

Qualified Admission Appropriate: A responding party may not simply deny an admission request when a more straightforward answer would be an express admission with qualifying language.[7] In a federal case,[8] for instance, the defendant railroad received a request that it admit that its employee was performing duties in interstate commerce at the time he lost his life in a derailment. To this request the railroad responded that it "denies the accuracy of the statements contained in [the admission request], and refuses to admit the truth thereof." The court deemed this response evasive:

> [A] denial of the accuracy of a statement is not a denial of its essential truth and certainly a refusal to admit does not amount to a denial. Parties may not avoid the failure to deny matters necessarily within their knowledge by giving any such evasive answer as was given here.[9]

Denials on Information and Belief: A responding party may not deny an admission request "upon information and belief."[10] Instead, the responding party should either deny the request outright or say that it "lacks sufficient information or knowledge" to admit the matter covered by the request.[11]

Challenging Denials: A requesting party who believes that the responding party inappropriately denied an admission request can do nothing about it prior to trial. Courts will not grant a motion to compel further response.[12] Rather, the

---

[6] Wilkinson v Powell (1945, CA5 Fla) 149 F2d 335, 337.

See also Holmgren v State Farm Mut. Auto. Ins. Co. (1992, CA9 Mont) 976 F2d 573, 580–581 [where the core of an admission request involves an "indisputable historical fact," a party who disagrees with its wording in other respects may not simply deny the request; it should qualify its denial by admitting the historical fact].

[7] For a discussion of an answer in the form of an express admission, see § 9.10.

[8] Southern R. Co. v Crosby (1953, CA4 SC) 201 F2d 878.

[9] Southern R. Co. v Crosby (1953, CA4 SC) 201 F2d 878, 880 (internal citations omitted).

See also Havenfield Corp. v H & R Block, Inc. (1973, WD Mo) 67 FRD 93.

[10] Cf. Cohen v Superior Court (1976) 63 Cal App 3d 184, 186, 133 Cal Rptr 575, 576 [under CCP § 2033 of the 1956 Discovery Act, the court erred in refusing to permit relief from deemed admission based on denial "on information and belief"].

[11] CCP § 2033.220(c).

Cf. Allen v Pitchess (1973) 36 Cal App 3d 321, 330–332, 111 Cal Rptr 658, 664–665 [cost-of-proof sanctions upheld because responding party had denied an admission request on the basis of a "lack of information and belief"]

For a discussion of the requirements for a response that one is unable to admit an admission request, see § 9.12.

[12] See, e.g., Holguin v Superior Court (1972) 22 Cal App 3d 812, 99 Cal Rptr 653.

See also Foretich v Chung (1993, D DC) 151 FRD 3, 4–5 [defendant not allowed to test sufficiency of unequivocal denial on motion to compel]; Wanke v Lynn's Transportation Co. (1993, ND Ind) 836 F Supp 587, 598 [same].

For a general discussion of motions to compel further responses, see § 9.17.

requesting party will simply have to assemble evidence to establish the matters covered by the admission request. If successful at trial, the requesting party may then seek sanctions to cover the cost of proving matters denied inappropriately.[13]

In the *Holguin* case,[14] for example, plaintiffs in a medical malpractice case requested admissions as to various medical matters. Defendants denied that the requested matters were true. Contending "that certain matters which defendants have denied are so unquestionably true, that they cannot deny them," plaintiffs sought an order either requiring a further answer or declaring that the facts would be deemed admitted at the trial. The court declared: "We do not see . . . how any court can force a litigant to admit any particular fact if he is willing to risk a perjury prosecution or financial sanctions."[15] The court noted that even "the rather weaseling qualification attached to most of [the denials] that they are made on advice of counsel" did not dictate a different result.[16]

Verification: A party must deny an admission request under oath.[17] One California opinion suggests that the responding party may deny a matter it knows is true simply to force an adversary to go to the trouble of establishing it: "If [defendants] want to put plaintiffs to their proof, they may deny, risking, however, the possibility of being surcharged with costs if the plaintiffs ultimately prove the fact involved."[18] Another case, however, remarks that one who denies a request to admit facts known to be true must be "willing to risk a perjury prosecution."[19] Accordingly, a party willing to risk the "cost-of-proof" sanction simply to force the adversary to prove that matter at trial must also consider possible perjury charges.

§ 9.12 Inability to Admit

Besides an express admission[1] or an outright denial,[2] a party may respond that it "lacks sufficient information or knowledge"[3] to make the admission.[4]

---

[13] For a discussion of the sanctions that a court may impose if, after the trial, it appears that the denial was not made in good faith or with substantial justification, see § 9.21.

[14] Holguin v Superior Court (1972) 22 Cal App 3d 812, 99 Cal Rptr 653.

[15] Holguin v Superior Court (1972) 22 Cal App 3d 812, 820, 99 Cal Rptr 653, 657–658.

See also Smith v Circle P Ranch Co. (1978) 87 Cal App 3d 267, 273, 150 Cal Rptr 828, 832.

For a discussion of the sanctions that a court may impose if, after the trial, it appears that the denial was not made in good faith or with substantial justification, see § 9.21.

[16] Holguin v Superior Court (1972) 22 Cal App 3d 812, 820 n9, 99 Cal Rptr 653, 657 n9.

[17] CCP § 2033.240(a).

For a general discussion of the verification requirement for admission request responses, see § 9.9.

[18] Caddies v Superior Court (1963) 215 Cal App 2d 318, 324, 30 Cal Rptr 303, 306.

[19] Holguin v Superior Court (1972) 22 Cal App 3d 812, 820, 99 Cal Rptr 653, 658.

[1] For a discussion of express admissions, see § 9.10.

[2] For a discussion of denials of admission requests, see § 9.11.

[3] CCP § 2033.220(b)(3).

[4] Annotation: Party's duty, under Federal Rule of Civil Procedure 36(a) and similar state statutes and rules, to respond to requests for admission of facts not within his personal knowledge. 20 ALR3d 756.

Duty to Investigate: Before a party may claim insufficient information or knowledge, it must investigate the matter addressed in the admission request. This duty applies even in the early stages of discovery.[5] Codifying the case law that developed under the 1956 Discovery Act,[6] Section 2033.220 requires a "reasonable inquiry" that encompasses not only information that is already "known," but also that which is "readily obtainable."[7] Thus, a responding party may have to inquire of third persons to ascertain the truth of the matter requested.[8] Federal decisions have required responding parties to try to obtain the necessary information from their employees,[9] from their attorneys,[10] from co-parties,[11] and by letter or telephone to distant sources.[12] However, the responding party need not inquire either of another adverse party or of indisputably hostile nonparties.[13]

In a school desegregation case[14] the court held that "reasonable inquiry" required the defendants to depose the plaintiffs' experts and then consult with their own experts before they decided whether they could admit the validity of plaintiffs' statistical surveys. After all, the court remarked, the defendants will ultimately need to take these same steps to prepare their defense.[15]

—Illustrative California Decisions: The *Lindgren* case[16] was a divorce action in the era before "no fault." A deponent testified that while she was traveling with the defendant wife in Spain, the wife had an affair in Madrid. This affair, the deponent claimed, became so intense that she had moved out of their hotel

---

[5] See A & V Fishing, Inc. v Home Insurance Co. (1993, D Mass) 145 FRD 285, 287.

[6] Chodos v Superior Court (1963) 215 Cal App 2d 318, 323, 30 Cal Rptr 303, 306.

Former CCP § 2033(a), 1956 Discovery Act, Appendix E, was silent on the extent, if any, of the responding party's duty to investigate before basing an answer on insufficient information.

[7] CCP § 2033.220(c).

[8] For a discussion of the responding party's duty to consult outside sources in order to answer an *interrogatory*, see § 5.16.

[9] See Criterion Music Corp. v Tucker (1968, SD Ga) 45 FRD 534 [defendant in a copyright infringement case must inquire of its performers when requested to admit that certain musical compositions were played in his place of business]; Anderson v United Air Lines, Inc. (1969, SD NY) 49 FRD 144, 148 [defendant airline must inquire of captain of another airliner concerning observations made by him in the area of the crash].

Compare Diederich v Dep't of Army (1990, SD NY) 132 FRD 614, 620 [defendant need not inquire of former employees]; Dubin v E.F. Hutton Group, Inc. (1989, SD NY) 125 FRD 372, 376 [no requirement to inquire of former employee since that employee's unsworn recollection would not bind employer].

[10] See Hise v Lockwood Grader Corp. (1957, D Neb) 153 F Supp 276, 278.

[11] See Dubin v E.F. Hutton Group (1988, SD NY) 125 FRD 372, 374–375.

[12] See Ranger Ins. Co. v Culberson (1969, ND Ga) 49 FRD 181, 183.

[13] See Dulansky v Iowa-Illinois Gas & Electric Co. (1950, SD Iowa) 92 F Supp 118, 123 [no duty on part of plaintiff to make inquiry of defendant's truck driver].

[14] Lumpkin v Meskill (1974, D Conn) 64 FRD 673, 678–680.

[15] Lumpkin v Meskill (1974, D Conn) 64 FRD 673, 679.

[16] Lindgren v Superior Court (1965) 237 Cal App 2d 743, 47 Cal Rptr 298.

and into one named "Legunitas." After this deposition, the wife requested her husband to admit that there was no hotel in Madrid with that name. The court upheld the husband's response that he was unable to admit or deny the request:

> Here the request related to the conduct of a third person, who may have been a complete stranger to [the plaintiff], outside of [the plaintiff's] presence and, in fact, outside the country. . . . [¶] . . . Clearly it would be unreasonable to require [the plaintiff] to employ investigators in Spain in order to obtain information which would enable him to admit or deny the matters involved in the request for admissions.[17]

The *Brooks* case[18] involved a plaintiff who claimed that an oncoming bus had crossed over the center line and forced him off the road. The defendant requested that the plaintiff admit that it was he who was on the wrong side of the center line. Plaintiff's injuries had left him with amnesia about the accident. The Highway Patrol report, however, concluded from the skid marks at the scene that the plaintiff had been on the wrong side of the center line. Without contacting the officers who prepared the report, the plaintiff denied the admission request. His later tacit concession at trial that he had been across the center line led the court to award a cost-of-proof sanction against him.[19] The court would likely have imposed the same sanction if, instead of an outright denial, the plaintiff had claimed that, after a reasonable investigation, he lacked sufficient information to admit or deny the request.[20]

Statement of Reasonable Inquiry: A "reasonable inquiry" may not have yielded sufficient information to enable a party to admit or deny the requested matter. In that case, the responding party must formally "state in the answer" that it has made such inquiry and that "the information known or readily obtainable is insufficient to enable that party to admit the matter."[21]

—Sufficiency of Statement: The 1956 Discovery Act required a party who asserted an inability to admit or deny a requested matter to set forth "in detail the reasons" for the response.[22] The present statute does not explicitly require "detailed reasons."[23] This deletion raises the question whether the required

---

[17] Lindgren v Superior Court (1965) 237 Cal App 2d 743, 747–748, 47 Cal Rptr 298, 301.

For a discussion of what constitutes a reasonable effort to obtain from outside sources the information needed to respond to an *interrogatory*, see § 5.15.

[18] Brooks v American Broadcasting Co. (1986) 179 Cal App 3d 500, 224 Cal Rptr 838.

[19] For a discussion of the cost-of-proof sanction for an unwarranted failure to make a requested admission, see § 9.21.

[20] Cf. Smith v Deere & Co. (1989, ED Pa) 1989 US Dist Lexis 2685 [plaintiff should have sought readily available blood alcohol test results before responding that he was unable to admit or deny an admission request regarding the authenticity of medical records regarding the test in question].

[21] CCP § 2033.220(c).

[22] Former CCP § 2033(a), 1956 Discovery Act, Appendix E.

[23] See CCP § 2033.220(c).

statement that "inquiry has been made" substitutes for the detailed statement of "reasons" contained in the earlier statute.

To date, no California court has addressed this matter. However, in the *Asea* case,[24] the Ninth Circuit considered the adequacy of the following response to an admission request:

> Answering party cannot admit or deny. Said party has made reasonable inquiry. Information known or readily obtainable to this date is not complete. Investigation continues.[25]

It held that an answer that simply "tracks" the language of Federal Rule of Civil Procedure 36's "reasonable inquiry" obligation would reduce the duty to "a mere semantic exercise."[26] Other federal cases, however, have approved such answers. They leave it to the requesting party to seek an elaboration:

> The fairest method would seem to be to allow the answering party to merely state that he has made reasonable inquiry. Then, the requesting party may challenge the answer as insufficient because the answering party's inquiry was not a reasonable one in light of the particular circumstances.[27]

Textual differences between the provisions in the California's Civil Discovery Act and those in the Federal Rules of Civil Procedure should lead California courts to reject *Asea*. Federal Rule 36 retains the language that Section 2033.220 dropped. It still requires an answering party to "set forth in detail the reasons why the answering party cannot truthfully admit or deny the matter."[28] Moreover, Rule 36 expressly empowers the federal courts to order a matter admitted if the answer does not comply with the rule.[29] California courts, on the other hand, however, can only order further compliance.[30]

---

[24] Asea, Inc. v Southern Pac. Transp. Co. (1981, CA9 Cal) 669 F2d 1242.

[25] Asea, Inc. v Southern Pac. Transp. Co. (1981, CA9 Cal) 669 F2d 1242, 1244.

[26] Asea, Inc. v Southern Pac. Transp. Co. (1981, CA9 Cal) 669 F2d 1242, 1247.

Accord: Checker Leasing, Inc. v Sorbello (1989, W Va) 382 SE2d 36, 39 [in dicta, approving *Asea, Inc.,* for state equivalent of FRCivP 36].

[27] Adley Express Co. v Highway Truck Drivers & Helpers (1972, ED Pa) 349 F Supp 436, 452.

See also City of Rome v United States (1978, D DC) 450 F Supp 378, 383–384; Alexander v Rizzo (1971, ED Pa) 52 FRD 235, 236.

[28] FRCivP 36(a).

[29] "The party who has requested the admissions may move to determine the sufficiency of the answers or objections. . . . If the court determines that an answer does not comply with the requirements of the rule, it may order either that the matter is admitted or that an amended answer be served." FRCivP 36(a).

[30] CCP § 2033.290(a).

For a discussion of motions to compel further response, see § 9.17.

Adoption of *Asea* by the California courts would create an anomaly. As discussed in a preceding section,[31] during discovery, California courts may not examine the of an outright denial of an admission request.[32] Therefore, it would be inconsistent to let them to do so when the responding party claims that, after "reasonable inquiry," the information "readily obtainable" still leaves it unable to make the requested admission. The sanction for a responding party's failure to reasonably inquire before answering an admission request lies in the award of costs after trial. Indeed, the cost-of-proof provision in Section 2033.420 reinforces this conclusion. Unlike its version in the 1956 Discovery Act,[33] it expressly allows the trial court to impose this sanction not only for an unwarranted denial, but also for an unwarranted claim of inability to admit.[34]

§ 9.13   Grounds for Objections

Two types of "response" to an admission request are permitted: an "answer"[1] and an "objection."[2] An answer may take one of three forms: an express admission,[3] an outright denial[4] or a statement of inability to do either.[5] A party with a valid objection to a particular admission request, however, need not "answer" that request.[6] Rather, that party can "set forth an objection" to the request in its "response."[7]

No matter how objectionable a particular admission request may be, Section requires the receiving party to make some timely "response,"[8] either an "answer" or an "objection." Unless the court has entered a protective order granting relief from the obligation to respond,[9] a party receiving admission requests must use the "response" to assert any objections. As discussed later in this section, a party waives objections not set forth in a timely response.[10]

---

[31] For a discussion of outright denials of an admission request, see § 9.11.

[32] Smith v Circle P Ranch Co. (1978) 87 Cal App 3d 267, 273, 150 Cal Rptr 828, 832; Holguin v Superior Court (1972) 22 Cal App 3d 812, 820, 99 Cal Rptr 653, 657–658.

[33] See Smith v Circle P Ranch Co. (1978) 87 Cal App 3d 267, 276–277, 150 Cal Rptr 828, 834–835.

[34] CCP § 2033.420(a).

[1] CCP § 2033.220.

[2] CCP § 2033.230.

[3] For a discussion of an express admission, see § 9.10.

[4] For a discussion of a denial, see § 9.11.

[5] For a discussion of a statement of inability to admit or deny, see § 9.12.

[6] If a request is only partially objectionable, the party must answer the unobjectionable part. CCP § 2033.230(a).

[7] CCP § 2033.210(b).

[8] CCP § 2033.210.

[9] See CCP § 2033.080(b)(1).

For a discussion of a protective order that an admission request need not be answered, see § 9.8.

[10] CCP § 2033.280(a).

Validity of Objections: In assessing the validity of a contemplated objection, the responding party should remember the broad range of the "matters" on which an opponent may request an admission. Moreover, even some privilege-based objections have a more limited application to admission requests than to other discovery devices.

—Allowable Scope of Requests: Two factors greatly diminish a party's opportunity to object that a particular request asks for an admission on an irrelevant matter. First, courts do not measure a requested matter's "relevance" by its narrow relationship to a *material issue* in the case. Rather, they use the much broader *general subject matter* of the case.[11]

Second, the statute specifically makes numerous subjects appropriate for admission requests. Thus, it authorizes requests seeking admissions of controversial "matters,"[12] fact-based opinions,[13] and applications of law-to-fact.[14] It even authorizes requests on subjects as to which the responding party has no personal knowledge.[15] These explicit provisions should prevent any argument that these topics are "out of bounds" for this discovery device.

—Inadmissibility: The recipient of admission requests should realize that an admission of a matter's truth does not waive objections to its use at trial. Indeed, the approved form for admission requests under Federal Rule of Civil Procedure 36 states that any admission made will remain "subject to all pertinent objections to admissibility which may be interposed at the trial."[16] Thus, one may not object to an admission request solely because the requested matter may be objectionable at trial. Even an express admission does not preclude a trial objection. It concedes only the *truth* of the "matter" it covers, not its ultimate *relevance* to any *material issue* in the case.[17] Similarly, an admission does not waive other evidentiary objections to admissibility, such as the hearsay rule or the rule against proof of subsequent remedial conduct.[18]

---

[11] For a discussion of the requirement that a request be relevant, see § 9.5.

[12] For a discussion of admission requests concerning a "matter" known to be in controversy between the parties, see § 9.5.

[13] Chodos v Superior Court (1963) 215 Cal App 2d 318, 30 Cal Rptr 303.

For a discussion of admission requests that require the responding party to express an opinion concerning relevant facts, see § 9.6.

[14] A request that calls for a conclusion of law unrelated to the facts of a case, however, would be objectionable.

For a discussion of admission requests that require the responding party to apply law-to-fact, see § 9.6.

[15] Chodos v Superior Court (1963) 215 Cal App 2d 318, 30 Cal Rptr 303.

For a discussion of the obligation to supplement personal knowledge by reasonable inquiry, see § 9.12.

[16] Form 25, Appendix of Forms to FRCivP.

[17] For a discussion of the effect of admissions at trial, see § 9.20.

[18] Goldman v Mooney (1959, WD Pa) 24 FRD 279.

—**Privilege:** Only certain types of privilege present legitimate objections to admission requests. Some privileges entitle a party to refuse to disclose *information*. The privilege against self-incrimination[19] best exemplifies this type. Objections based on this sort of privilege stand the best chance of being a valid response to an admission request.[20] Other privileges, however, protect only confidential *communications*; they do not cloak the *information* received during these communications. For example, under the spousal communication privilege,[21] a party may properly object to a request to admit that his *wife told him* that their son had been drinking alcohol before the son drove off in the car that later then collided with the plaintiff. However, he may not object to a request to admit that his *son had been drinking* simply because he received that information during a confidential conversation with his wife.[22]

—**Form of Request:** Challenges to the form of a request provide the largest group of valid objections to admission requests.[23] A request to admit the genuineness of a document is objectionable if a copy of the document is not attached.[24] A party may object to requests that are compound, disjunctive, conjunctive, or contain sub-parts.[25] A responding party should also be able to object that a request, like comparable trial or deposition testimony, is "repetitive,"[26] "cumulative,"[27] "confusing and ambiguous,"[28] "vague,"[29] "argumentative," or "unintelligible."

§ 9.14 Making Objections

The "responses" to admission requests should be in a single document, directed to the requesting party, which contains "answers" to permissible requests and "objections" to the rest.[1] Where a particular request is only partially

---

[19] For general coverage of the operation of the privilege against self-incrimination in civil cases, see §§ 12.2–12.7.

[20] For a further discussion of the privilege against self-incrimination as an objection to an admission request, see § 9.7.

[21] For a discussion of the privilege for confidential communications between husband and wife, see §§ 12.15–12.16.

[22] For a further discussion of privilege as a limit on admission requests, see § 9.7.

[23] For a discussion of the proper form for admission requests, see § 9.3.

[24] Cf. Lieb v Superior Court (1962) 199 Cal App 2d 364, 366, 18 Cal Rptr 705, 706.

[25] CCP § 2033.060(f).

[26] Cembrook v Superior Court (1961) 56 Cal 2d 423, 427, 15 Cal Rptr 127, 129, 364 P2d 303, 305.

[27] Chodos v Superior Court (1963) 215 Cal App 2d 318, 322, 30 Cal Rptr 303, 305.

[28] Cembrook v Superior Court (1961) 56 Cal 2d 423, 428, 15 Cal Rptr 127, 130, 364 P2d 303, 306.

Cf. Milton v Montgomery Ward & Co., Inc. (1973) 33 Cal App 3d 133, 137, 108 Cal Rptr 726, 728.

[29] Dubin v E.F. Hutton Group, Inc. (1989, SD NY) 125 FRD 372, 376 [upholding objection to "vague and ambiguous" admission requests].

[1] CCP § 2033.220(b).

objectionable, the responding party must answer any unobjectionable part, and object only to the improper part.[2] A responding party should not raise objections to admission requests by a motion to "strike," "vacate," "modify," or "limit" the requests. The statute does not authorize such motions.[3]

Format: The response need not repeat the text of the admission request.[4] However, it must identify each individual request in the set by its assigned number or letter[5] and respond to it "separately."[6] Given this "separate" response requirement, a party should not use a single, general objection to respond to several requests objectionable on identical grounds. However, the statute does permit a general objection to those requests in a set that exceed the presumptive limit of 35 and are unaccompanied by the required declaration.[7] Here, the responding party need only object "to the balance . . . on the ground that the limit has been exceeded."[8]

Form of Objections: Section 2033.230 requires the "specific ground for the objection [to] be set forth clearly in the response."[9] This phrasing virtually mirrors the Evidence Code's requirements for preserving an objection for appeal.[10] Thus, neither the bare response, "Objection," nor, "Objection—Privileged," suffices. The response must identify the "particular privilege invoked."[11] Similarly, it must specifically set forth any work product protection claim.[12] Counsel should remember that a claim of the attorney-client privilege does not also assert the work product protection.[13] A party may not object piecemeal and seriatim. One objecting to a particular admission request must include all grounds for objection. Any that are not asserted are waived.[14]

---

[2] CCP § 2033.230(a).

Now that CCP § 2033.060(f) requires each request to be "full and complete in and of itself," and prohibits requests that are "compound, conjunctive, or disjunctive," it should be rare that only a part of a request is objectionable.

[3] J.R. Prewitt and Sons, Inc. v Willmon (1967, WD Mo) 20 FRD 149.

[4] CCP § 2033.210(d).

[5] CCP § 2033.210(d).

[6] CCP § 2033.210(a).

[7] For a discussion of the presumptive limit of 35 admission requests, see § 9.4.

[8] CCP § 2033.030(b).

[9] CCP § 2033.230(b).

[10] Evid Code § 353.

[11] CCP § 2033.230(b).

[12] CCP § 2033.230(b).

For a discussion of the general nature of the work product protection, see § 13.1.

[13] Sheets v Superior Court (1967) 257 Cal App 2d 1, 8, 64 Cal Rptr 753, 757 [objection based on lawyer-client privilege is ineffective to assert work product protection].

[14] Cf. Scottsdale Ins. Co. v Superior Court (1997) 59 Cal App 4th 263, 273, 69 Cal Rptr 2d 112, 118 [timely response to inspection demand asserting objection based on burdensomeness waived a later objection based on attorney-client privilege].

—Objection Waived if Coupled with Admission or Denial: In *Local 1902 v MWD,* [15] plaintiff served a response to 9 of 15 admission requests that began with an objection to each request, and then proceeded to flatly deny three of them and partially admit and partially deny six of them. When the case was tried, defendant proceeded to prove all of the matters that plaintiff had wholly or partially denied. Defendant then sought almost $27,000 as the cost of the proof of these matters.

Plaintiff contended that defendant had waived its right to the cost-of-proof sanction because it did not seek a ruling on the objections by moving for a further response. It was held that defendant had acted properly in construing the responses as unequivocal denials, and proceeding to expend the time and effort to prove the truth of these matters to the trial court. [16]

Waiver by Tardy Response: Codifying case law that developed under the 1956 Discovery Act, [17] Section 2033.280 penalizes a tardy response by treating it as a waiver of "any objection to the requests, including one based on privilege or on the protection for work product." [18] To avoid this waiver, absent judicial permission or a written stipulation to extend time, a party must respond within 30 days after service of the requests. [19] Unless the parties stipulate otherwise, any agreement to enlarge the time for response "preserves" the right to "respond" in any "manner" permitted by Sections , 2033.220, and 2033.230. [20] Since these sections treat an objection as a form of "response," a party does not waive its right to include objections in any response served pursuant to an agreement to extend time. [21]

—No Waiver Results from Unverified Response: Section 2033.240 requires a client to verify its "response" to admission requests. [22] However, a response may contain "answers" [23] to some requests and "objections" [24] to others. A response that consists entirely of objections to the admission requests needs no oath at all. [25] By implication, where a response contains both answers and

[15] American Federation of State, County and Municipal Employees, Local 1902 v Metropolitan Water District (2005) 126 Cal App 4th 247, 265, 24 Cal Rptr 3d 285, 298.

[16] Local 1902 v MWD (2005) 126 Cal App 4th 247, 268, 24 Cal Rptr 3d 285, 300.

[17] See, e.g., Coy v Superior Court (1962) 58 Cal 2d 210, 216–217, 23 Cal Rptr 393, 395–396, 373 P2d 457, 459–460; Brown v Superior Court (1986) 180 Cal App 3d 701, 708–712, 226 Cal Rptr 10, 13–16.

[18] CCP § 2033.280(a).

[19] CCP § 2033.250.

For a further discussion of the time for serving a response to admission requests, see § 9.9.

[20] CCP § 2033.260(c).

[21] Cf. City of Fresno v Superior Court (1988) 205 Cal App 3d 1459, 1465–1467, 253 Cal Rptr 296, 298–300 [involving untimely response to inspection demand].

[22] CCP § 2033.240(a).

[23] CCP § 2033.220.

[24] CCP § 2033.230.

[25] CCP § 2033.240(a).

objections, the client's duty to sign under oath extends only to the "answer" portion. Therefore, a client's failure to properly verify a response containing both "answers" and "objections" does not waive those objections:

> [T]here is no need to verify that portion of the response containing the objections. Thus, if the response is served within the statutory time period, that portion of the response must be considered timely notwithstanding the lack of verification. The omission of the verification in the portion of the response containing fact specific responses merely renders *that* portion of the response untimely and therefore only creates a right to move for orders and sanctions . . . *as to those responses* but does not result in a waiver of the objections made.[26]

—Relief from Waiver: Section 2033.280 allows a delinquent responding party to move for relief from the waiver of an objection.[27] The statute imposes two requirements on a party who seeks this relief. First, that party must have by then served a response that complies substantially with Sections, 2033.220, and 2033.230.[28] Attachment of a copy of the tardily served responses to the motion should show the court that the party has met this requirement.[29] Second, the party must persuade the trial court that its tardiness was attributable to "mistake, inadvertence or excusable neglect."[30]

Challenging Objections: To challenge an objection, the requesting party must move for a court order compelling further response.[31] The failure to so move

---

[26] Food 4 Less Supermarkets v Superior Court (1995) 40 Cal App 4th 651, 657–658, 46 Cal Rptr 2d 925, 928–929 [unverified response to an *inspection demand* (original italics)].

See also Blue Ridge Ins. Co. v Superior Court (1988) 202 Cal App 3d 339, 344–345, 248 Cal Rptr 346, 349–350 [involving a response to an *inspection demand* that contained objections as to certain of the items].

[27] CCP § 2033.280(a).

For further discussion of the consequences of the failure to serve a timely response to admission requests, see § 9.16.

[28] CCP § 2033.280(a)(1).

[29] CCP § 2033.280(a)(2).

Cf. Dolin Roofing and Insulation Co. v Superior Court (1984) 151 Cal App 3d 886, 199 Cal Rptr 37 [under prior practice, copy of "proposed" responses must accompany motion for relief under CCP § 473].

[30] CCP § 2033.280(a) supplants the discretion the court would otherwise have under CCP § 473. Zellerino v Brown (1991) 235 Cal App 3d 1097, 1107, 1 Cal Rptr 2d 222, 228 ["the Legislature's use of section 473 language in parts of the discovery act evidences its intent to supplant the application of section 473 pro tanto."]

CCP § 2033.280(a)(2).

Cf. City of Fresno v Superior Court (1988) 205 Cal App 3d 1459, 1467, 253 Cal Rptr 296, 299–300 [in case involving an *inspection demand*, court relieved party from waiver of objection where counsel both failed to study then-new statutory time limits and was facing trial in another case].Cf. Borse v Superior Court (1970) 7 Cal App 3d 286, 86 Cal Rptr 559 [discussing similar requirements imposed, under prior law, by CCP § 473]; Zonver v Superior Court (1969) 270 Cal App 2d 613, 622–623, 76 Cal Rptr 10, 15–16 [same].

[31] CCP § 2033.290(a)(2).

within 45 days of the service of the response waives any right to an "answer" to the admission request.[32] It also forfeits the right to seek cost-of-proof sanctions after proving the matter at trial.[33]

§ 9.15 Deemed Admissions: Gamesmanship

Failure to Serve Timely Sworn Response: By far the most significant change that the 1986 Act made to prior California, and still current federal, admission request law was its treatment of a responding party's failure to comply with the three-sided obligation to serve a *response* to the requests that is both *timely* and *under oath*.[1] A brief examination of the pre-1987 procedure helps explain the reasons for this major difference in California and federal discovery practice.

Under the 1956 Discovery Act version of Section 2033, a party who would not admit a requested matter had to respond with a denial, a statement of inability to admit or deny, or an objection. This response also had to be timely and under oath. A failure to respond at all led to a so-called "deemed admission." The matters covered by the requests were automatically and conclusively conceded in the pending lawsuit. Moreover, since the courts considered an untimely or unsworn response a nullity, a deemed admission also resulted when a party served a late or unverified response.[2]

Relief from Inadvertent Deemed Admission: The former statute had inherited from its federal ancestor a serious deficiency. It lacked any explicit authorization for relief from an *inadvertent* deemed admission, that is, one resulting from the party's oversight, procrastination, or ignorance. However, the courts remedied this omission by treating this failure as a form of "default" from which the trial court could grant relief under Section 473 of the Code of Civil Procedure.[3]

To take advantage of Section 473, the delinquent party had to: (1) apply for relief within six months[4] after the date the response was due, (2) accompany

---

[32] CCP § 2033.290(c).

For a discussion of motions to compel a further response to admission requests, see § 9.17.

[33] CCP § 2033.420(b)(1).

For a discussion of the sanction for an unwarranted failures to make an admission, see § 9.21.

[1] For a discussion of the obligation of a party receiving admission requests to serve a timely and verified "response," see § 9.9.

[2] Zorro Investment Co. v Great Pacific Securities Corp. (1977) 69 Cal App 3d 907, 917, 138 Cal Rptr 410, 415.

See also Brochtrup v INTEP (1987) 190 Cal App 3d 323, 235 Cal Rptr 390; Thomas v All-American Electric Corp. (1986) 181 Cal App 3d 989, 226 Cal Rptr 413; Steele v Totah (1986) 180 Cal App 3d 545, 225 Cal Rptr 635.

[3] Zorro Investment Co. v Great Pacific Securities Corp. (1977) 69 Cal App 3d 907, 917, 138 Cal Rptr 410, 415; Cohen v Superior Court (1976) 63 Cal App 3d 184, 186, 133 Cal Rptr 575, 576.

[4] This is an outside time limit. CCP § 473 provides that a motion for relief "must be made within a reasonable time, in no case exceeding six months."

the motion with a proposed response to the admission requests,[5] and (3) persuade the trial court that the failure to do so earlier was due to "mistake, inadvertence, surprise or excusable neglect."

Tardy Motions for Relief: In 1976, the *Kaiser Steel* case addressed whether Section 473, with its six-month limit, was the only avenue for relief from an unintended deemed admission. There a plaintiff neglected to verify its response denying a set of admission requests. These requests, if treated as conceded, would have validated one of the defendant's affirmative defenses. Over four years later, as the case was approaching trial, the defendant moved for summary judgment. This motion was based on the admission requests, deemed admitted because the response was not verified. By then it was far too late for the plaintiff to apply for relief under Section 473. The appellate court, relying heavily on federal precedent,[6] parsed the Discovery Act itself to "empower the trial court to relieve a party served with a request for admissions from the consequences of a defective denial."[7] More importantly, it held that this power was not subject to "the six-month limitation for exercise of judicial discretion to relieve from default" under Section 473.[8]

The Legislature reacted ambivalently to the ruling. On the one hand, it liked the idea that a trial court should have some discretion to relieve a party from the consequences of a deemed admission. On the other hand, it was decidedly unhappy with the absence of any time limit on this judicial power. It perceived this as undermining the role that admission requests play in civil discovery. Moreover, it considered even Section 473's six-month limitation to be far too long.

"Warning" and "Notice" of Deemed Admission: The year after the *Kaiser Steel* decision, the Legislature concocted a five-element approach to the deemed admission problem.[9] First, it required the party seeking admissions to include in its request a "warning" that noncompliance with the response requirements of former Section 2033 would result in a deemed admission. Second, if despite this warning a timely verified response was not forthcoming, the requesting party could serve a "notice" that a deemed admission had occurred. Third, service of this notice would start the running of a 30-day period during which the delinquent recipient of the requests could apply to the court for relief from the deemed

---

[5] Dolin Roofing and Insulation Co. v Superior Court (1984) 151 Cal App 3d 886, 199 Cal Rptr 37.

[6] French v United States (1969, CA9 Cal) 416 F2d 1149, 1152; Hartley and Parker, Inc. v Florida Beverage Corp. (1965, CA5 Fla) 348 F2d 161, 163.

[7] Kaiser Steel Corp. v Westinghouse Electric Corp. (1976) 55 Cal App 3d 737, 744, 127 Cal Rptr 838, 843.

[8] Kaiser Steel Corp. v Westinghouse Electric Corp. (1976) 55 Cal App 3d 737, 744–745, 127 Cal Rptr 838, 843.

See also Zorro Investment Co. v Great Pacific Securities Corp. (1977) 69 Cal App 3d 907, 138 Cal Rptr 410.

[9] Stats. 1978, ch. 265, § 1, p 550.

admission. If a party did not move for relief within that time, the deemed admission became carved in stone. Fourth, since Section 473 was still the source for any relief, the delinquent party had to accompany the motion with a proposed verified response to the requests.[10] Fifth, the delinquent party had to persuade the trial court that its earlier noncompliance resulted from the "mistake, inadvertence, surprise or excusable neglect" required by Section 473.

Legislative concern about a party's failure to timely and properly respond to admission requests is understandable. This failure impedes the discovery process and impairs the usefulness of this device. However, it is difficult to justify treating this failure, at least in the first instance, far more severely than other discovery misconduct, such as failure to appear for a deposition,[11] or to respond promptly to interrogatories[12] and inspection demands.[13]

Resulting Gamesmanship: Admission requests have two legitimate purposes. First, they are obviously warranted when a party reasonably believes that an opponent will concede the "matters" they cover. Second, even without much prospect for a concession, they can set up cost-of-proof sanctions if the requesting party reasonably believes that court will find that the refusal to admit was unreasonable.

However, the 1978 amendments to the then-current version of Section 2033 fostered a form of gamesmanship that subverted discovery's principal goal—the resolution of lawsuits on their merits. Litigants began routinely to serve requests covering ultimate facts in the case that, if admitted, would determine the lawsuit.[14] This was done with no realistic expectation either that the responding party would admit them, or that the trial court would later impose cost-of-proof sanctions:

> Although the admissions procedure is designed to expedite matters by avoiding trial on disputed issues, the request at issue here did not include issues as to which the parties might conceivably agree. Instead, the

---

[10] Dolin Roofing and Insulation Co. v Superior Court (1984) 151 Cal App 3d 886, 199 Cal Rptr 37.

[11] For a discussion of the consequences of failure to appear for a *deposition*, see § 2.20.

[12] For a discussion of the consequences of failure to respond promptly to *interrogatories*, see § 5.19.

[13] For a discussion of the consequences of failure to respond promptly to *inspection demands*, see § 6.13.

[14] See, e.g., Elston v City of Turlock (1985) 38 Cal 3d 227, 235, 211 Cal Rptr 416, 421, 695 P2d 713, 718; Gribin Von Dyl & Assoc., Inc. v Kovalsky (1986) 185 Cal App 3d 653, 230 Cal Rptr 50; Thomas v All-American Electric Co. (1986) 181 Cal App 3d 989, 226 Cal App 413; Steele v Totah (1986) 180 Cal App 3d 545, 225 Cal Rptr 635; Lopez v Superior Court (1986) 178 Cal App 3d 925, 223 Cal Rptr 798; Janetsky v Avis (1986) 176 Cal App 3d 799, 222 Cal Rptr 342; Freshman, Mulvaney, Marantz, Comsky, Kahn & Deutsche v Superior Court (1985) 173 Cal App 3d 223, 218 Cal Rptr 533; Burned v American-Cal Medical Services (1984) 156 Cal App 3d 260, 202 Cal Rptr 735; Hernandez v Temple (1983) 142 Cal App 3d 286, 190 Cal Rptr 853; Billings v Edwards (1981) 120 Cal App 3d 238, 174 Cal Rptr 722.

request essentially asked plaintiffs to admit that they had no cause of action.[15]

Thus, for the price of a postage stamp and some legal stationery, a litigant could spin the "deemed admission" wheel. If the requesting party was lucky, there would be no response, or it would be untimely or unverified. That party would then spin the wheel again by serving a "notice of deemed admission." At the very least, the delinquent party would be at the mercy of some trial judge's notion of what constitutes "mistake, inadvertence, surprise or excusable neglect."[16]

The *Elston* case[17] vividly illustrates this "deemed admission" game. A motorcyclist, seriously injured in a collision, sued the county for improperly designing the intersection where the accident happened. The county promptly requested that the plaintiff admit "that the intersection was not in a dangerous condition, that [the plaintiff's] injuries were not proximately caused by the allegedly dangerous condition, and the injuries did not occur in a foreseeable manner." The admission requests arrived in the office of the firm representing the plaintiff during the turmoil created by the recent departure of two of its attorneys. Somehow the requests were misplaced and did not come to the attention of the plaintiff's harried attorney until the defendant served notice that it was deeming the requests admitted. That attorney then timely moved for relief under Section 473.

Although the county showed no prejudice from the late response, the trial court refused to grant any relief from these terminal admissions. The Supreme Court ultimately held that the denial of this particular motion was an abuse of discretion. It suggested, however, that its decision might have gone the other way had the plaintiff's failure to serve a timely response been dilatory rather than inadvertent.[18]

Judicial Reaction: In the *Elston* case, the delinquent party had acted within the 30-day period mandated under then-applicable law. Had he not done so, he would have left his lawsuit, however meritorious, vulnerable to summary judgment.[19] This forfeiture was so disproportionate to the discovery delict

---

[15] Elston v City of Turlock (1985) 38 Cal 3d 227, 235, 211 Cal Rptr 416, 421, 695 P2d 713, 718.

[16] See, e.g., Carli v Superior Court (1984) 152 Cal App 3d 1095, 199 Cal Rptr 583 [trial court had denied motion for relief from deemed admission in a case where, during the disruption created by the sudden departure of an attorney from a small law firm and a need to use inexperienced secretaries, a tape containing prompt responses to admission requests was misplaced].

[17] Elston v City of Turlock (1985) 38 Cal 3d 227, 211 Cal Rptr 416, 695 P2d 713.

[18] Elston v City of Turlock (1985) 38 Cal 3d 227, 238, 211 Cal Rptr 416, 423, 695 P2d 713, 720.

[19] See, e.g., Gribin Von Dyl & Assoc., Inc. v Kovalsky (1986) 185 Cal App 3d 653, 230 Cal Rptr 50; Steele v Totah (1986) 180 Cal App 3d 545, 225 Cal Rptr 635; Lopez v Superior Court (1986) 178 Cal App 3d 925, 223 Cal Rptr 798; Janetsky v Avis (1986) 176 Cal App 3d 799, 222 Cal Rptr 342; Barnett v American-Cal Medical Services (1984) 156 Cal App 3d 260, 202 Cal Rptr 735; Billings v Edwards (1981) 120 Cal App 3d 238, 174 Cal Rptr 722.

involved that some appellate courts strained to find a way to avoid it. Several hypertechnical rulings resulted; these held that the required warning was not in the proper spot in the request,[20] or found some noncompliance with the procedure for giving the notice of deemed admission.[21] Indeed, during the decade that the 1978 scheme was in operation, the procedure it prescribed spawned almost a score of reported appellate opinions.

§ 9.16 The Current Procedure

Summary of New Procedure: The treatment of deemed admissions in Section 2033.280 of the Civil Discovery Act differs in six ways from that which prevailed pre-1987.[1] First, the party requesting admissions need not include a warning[2] of the consequences of a failure to file a proper response. Second, any failure to respond does not automatically result in a deemed admission. Its only immediate consequences are exposure to a mandatory monetary sanction[3] and a curable waiver of any objections to the requests.[4] Third, instead of sending a "notice of deemed admission,"[5] the party who requested the admission must move for a deemed admission.[6] Fourth, without any showing of excusable mistake, neglect, or oversight, the delinquent party can avoid a deemed admission by serving a proposed response to the admission requests before the hearing on the motion.[7] Fifth, failure to make a *timely* service of that proposed response ties the trial court's hands: it must grant the motion to deem the requests admitted.[8] Sixth, the delinquent party may still extricate itself from this plight

---

[20] The 1978 amendment to original version of Section 2033(a) required the warning concerning the consequences of a failure to comply with the its requirements to be "at the end thereof." Where the warning was placed anywhere other than the end of the "request portion" of the document, or at the end of the enumerated requests themselves, several courts seized upon this trivial misstep to hold that it was ineffective to created a deemed admission. See, e.g., See, e.g., Thomas v All-American Electric Co. (1986) 181 Cal App 3d 989, 226 Cal App 413; Freshman, Mulvaney, Marantz, Comsky, Kahan & Deutsch v Superior Court (1985) 173 Cal App 3d 223, 218 Cal Rptr 533; Hansen v Superior Court (1983) 149 Cal App 3d 823, 197 Cal Rptr 175; Hernandez v Temple (1983) 142 Cal App 3d 286, 190 Cal Rptr 853; contra: Steele v Totah (1986) 180 Cal App 3d 545, 225 Cal Rptr 635.

[21] See, e.g., Enfantino v Superior Court (1984) 162 Cal App 3d 1110, 208 Cal Rptr 829.

[1] For a discussion of the treatment of deemed admissions that developed under former CCP § 2033, see § 9.15.

[2] For a discussion of the "warning" required by former CCP § 2033, see § 9.15.

[3] CCP § 2033.280(c).

[4] CCP § 2033.280(a).

For a discussion of waiver of objections to admission requests and motions to obtain relief from that waiver, see §§ 9.13–9.14.

[5] For a discussion of the "notice of deemed admission" under former CCP § 2033, see § 9.15.

[6] CCP § 2033.280(b).

[7] CCP § 2033.280(c).

[8] CCP § 2033.280(c).

by successfully moving to amend or withdraw the deemed admission pursuant to Section 2033.300.[9]

Motion for Deemed Admission: To convert a party's failure to respond into an admission, the requesting party must move for an order to have the matter deemed admitted.[10] The requesting party need *not* "meet and confer" with the delinquent party before making this motion.[11] In this respect, a motion for deemed admission differs from one for either a protective order[12] or to compel further response.[13] Moreover, in contrast to a motion to compel further response,[14] no timetable applies to the motion for a deemed admission.[15]

Belated Compliance: In the time between moving for deemed admissions and the hearing on that motion, the delinquent party can avoid the consequence of its earlier failure to properly respond. If during that interval[16] that party serves a proposed response that is "in substantial compliance" with Sections 2033.210, 2033.220, and 2033.230, the trial court must deny that motion.[17]

> The single opportunity afforded a litigant to correct what could be an entirely innocent or clerical mistake . . . is the space of time between the notice of the motion to deem matters admitted and the hearing on the motion. . . . [T]his space of time represents the *only* safety valve within the statutory scheme governing defaults on admission requests.[18]

For this reason, the trial court may not shorten the time for this hearing: "To interpret the 'hearing' contemplated by [Sections , 2033.220, and 2033.230] to include a hearing on shortened time would effectively nullify the evident function of the provision."[19]

The delinquent party's pre-hearing service of a proper proposed response cuts off the trial court's power to deem the matters admitted:

---

[9] Wilcox v Birtwhistle (1999) 21 Cal 4th 973, 983 n12, 90 Cal Rptr 2d 260, 267 n12, 987 P2d 727, 734 n12.

[10] CCP § 2033.280(b).

[11] CCP § 2033.280 does not contain the meet-and-confer requirement found in CCP §§ 2033.080 and 2033.290.

[12] For a discussion of motions for a protective order against admission requests, see § 9.8.

[13] For a discussion of motions to compel a further response to admission requests, see § 9.17.

[14] For a discussion of motions to compel a further response to admission requests, see § 9.17.

[15] Brigante v Huang (1993) 20 Cal App 4th 1569, 1584, 25 Cal Rptr 2d 354, 364 [although the trial court retains equitable power to reject a tardy motion for a deemed admission, CCP § 2033 itself does not specify a time within which a requesting party must make this motion].

[16] At least 15 days notice of a motion is required if moving papers are served personally, and 20 days if mailed within California to an address within the state. CCP § 1005.

[17] CCP § 2033.280(c).

[18] Demyer Costa Mesa Mobile Home Estates (1995) 36 Cal App 4th 393, 399, 42 Cal Rptr 2d 260, 263–264.

[19] Demyer Costa Mesa Mobile Home Estates (1995) 36 Cal App 4th 393, 400, 42 Cal Rptr 2d 260, 263.

Under [Section 2033.280], the court is *required* to grant a deemed admission motion unless a proposed response is served before the hearing on that motion. What the statute does not say, but obviously implies, is that where a proposed response *is* served prior to the hearing (and there is no finding that the "substantial compliance" requirement has not been met), then the motion may *not* be granted.[20]

Objections: Any objections contained in the belated response remain subject to challenge by the requesting party that the earlier failure to serve a timely response has waived them. However, the court may, on the responding party's motion, grant relief from that waiver if the moving party establishes mistake, inadvertence, or excusable neglect.[21]

Mandatory Monetary Sanction: A belated response enables a delinquent party to avoid having requests deemed admitted. However, that party will have to pay for the costs of the delay if the requesting party has had to move for a deemed admission. Section 2033.280 requires the trial court to impose a monetary sanction on "the party or attorney, or both, whose failure to serve a timely response to requests for admission necessitated this motion."[22]

Continued Noncompliance: Where the delinquent party does not serve a proposed response to the admission requests before the hearing on the motion, the trial court *must* order the matters deemed admitted.[23] It has no discretion to give such a recalcitrant party a second chance. "The law governing the consequences for failing to respond to requests for admission may be the most unforgiving in civil procedure."[24]

The *Courtesy Claims Service* case[25] illustrates this restriction. There, two defendants served similar sets of admission requests on four plaintiffs, all represented by the same attorney. Initially, none of the plaintiffs responded to either set of requests. One defendant then moved to have matters in its request deemed admitted. Before the hearing, one of the four plaintiffs served a proposed response to the moving party's requests. In addition, all plaintiffs served a proposed response to the requests of the *nonmoving* party. Under these circumstances, the trial judge decided that the "interests of justice" warranted giving those plaintiffs who had not responded to the *moving* party's requests another

---

[20] Tobin v Oris (1992) 3 Cal App 4th 814, 828, 4 Cal Rptr 2d 736, 744 (internal citation omitted).

See also Demyer v Costa Mesa Mobile Home Estates (1995) 36 Cal App 4th 393, 400, 42 Cal Rptr 2d 260, 264.

[21] CCP § 2033.280(a)(2).

For a further discussion of waiver of objections to admission requests, see § 9.13.

[22] CCP § 2033.280(c).

[23] CCP § 2033.280(c).

[24] Demyer v Costa Mesa Mobile Home Estates (1995) 36 Cal App 4th 393, 394, 42 Cal Rptr 260.

[25] Courtesy Claims Service, Inc. v Superior Court (1990) 219 Cal App 3d 52, 268 Cal Rptr 30.

chance to avoid a deemed admission of the matters covered by the requests. The appellate court, however, ruled that the trial court exceeded its powers:

> The court's ruling was contrary to the mandatory language of [former CCP § 2033(k)]. That section makes no exception for "the interests of justice"; rather, it specifically provides that if proposed responses are not served prior to the hearing on the motion, the court *shall* make an order that matters raised in the requests be deemed admitted.[26]

The court also rejected the notion of "amending" the responses to avoid the deemed admissions. It declined to treat the proposed response to the moving party's request served by one plaintiff as if also made by the other three. It also refused to consider the responses of these three plaintiffs to the *nonmoving* defendant's requests as a response to those of the *moving* party.

The court's refusal to fabricate an "interests of justice" exception and its unwillingness to manipulate the proposed responses that were served evidently led to deemed admissions on matters dispositive of the delinquent plaintiffs' causes of action. Although Section 2033.280 does, indeed, cause such harsh results, it is less severe than the procedure that had developed under the former version of Section 2033.[27] Therefore, the appellate court was not sympathetic to the plaintiffs' plight: "The risk of eventual dismissal is one which plaintiffs assumed when they ignored [the moving defendant's] motion."[28]

Escaping Consequences of a Deemed Admission: Disapproving *Courtesy Claims Service* and its progeny,[29] the Supreme Court in the *Wilcox* case[30] fashioned a possible escape route for a party who had made deemed admissions. It read what is now Section 2033.300 to empower the trial court to rescue that

---

[26] Courtesy Claims Service, Inc. v Superior Court (1990) 219 Cal App 3d 52, 55, 268 Cal Rptr 30, 32 (original italics).

[27] For a discussion of the treatment of deemed admissions that developed under former CCP § 2033, see § 9.15.

[28] Courtesy Claims Service, Inc. v Superior Court (1990) 219 Cal App 3d 52, 57, 268 Cal Rptr 30, 33.

See also Demyer v Costa Mesa Mobile Home Estates (1995) 36 Cal App 4th 393, 395, 42 Cal Rptr 2d 260, 261 ["But woe betide the party who fails to serve responses before the hearing."]

See also St. Paul Fire and Marine Ins. Co. v Superior Court (1992) 2 Cal App 4th 843, 850–852, 3 Cal Rptr 2d 412, 416–417 [agreeing with *Courtesy Claims Service* that no relief possible from complete failure to respond].

For a further discussion of withdrawal of deemed admissions, see § 9.18.

[29] Allen-Pacific, Ltd. v Superior Court (1997) 57 Cal App 4th 1546, 67 Cal Rptr 2d 804; Demyer v Costa Mesa Mobile Home Estates (1995) 36 Cal App 4th 393, 42 Cal Rptr 2d 260; Brigante v Huang (1993) 20 Cal App 4th 1569, 25 Cal Rptr 2d 354; Tobin v Oris (1992) 3 Cal App 4th 814, 4 Cal Rptr 2d 736; St. Paul Fire and Marine Ins. Co. v Superior Court (1992) 2 Cal App 4th 843, 3 Cal Rptr 2d 412; Courtesy Claims Service, Inc. v Superior Court (1990) 219 Cal App 3d 52, 268 Cal Rptr 30.

[30] Wilcox v Birtwhistle (1999) 21 Cal 4th 973, 983 n12, 90 Cal Rptr 2d 260, 267 n12, 987 P2d 727, 734 n12.

party by permitting the withdrawal or amendment of admissions to embrace not only express admissions but also deemed admissions:

> [T]his interpretation complements the enforcement scheme created by [Section 2033.280]. Under [it] the initial penalty for failure to respond is the waiver of all objections. Once the propounding party files a motion for a deemed admission order, the nonresponding party then faces an additional penalty—mandatory monetary sanctions . . . . [Section 2033.300] then describes the consequences of failing to respond before the hearing on the motion and the resulting entry of a deemed admission order. Now, the nonresponding party can only escape a binding admission by establishing "mistake, inadvertence, or excusable neglect" and no substantial prejudice to the propounding party. The nonresponding party also faces the likely imposition of more sanctions at the discretion of the trial court. This graduated system of enforcement furthers the legislative purpose behind section 2033 by fitting the punishment of the nonresponding party to the offense.[31]

Effect of a Voluntary Dismissal: The admissions that result from the successful use of Section 2033.010 are normally effective only in the lawsuit in which they are made.[32] However, where a court enters an order deeming a matter admitted by the plaintiff in one case, that plaintiff cannot avoid the admission by voluntarily dismissing the case and then refiling it as a new lawsuit. Otherwise, a plaintiff who has been deemed to have made admissions would have a tactical advantage over a defendant in the same position.[33]

§ 9.17 Compelling Further Response

Receipt of Inadequate Response: Where there has been *no* response at all to a set of admission requests, or where a response is tardy or unverified, the requesting party should move to have the matters deemed admitted.[1] However, even where it has received a timely and sworn response, a requesting party may find inadequate or improper one or more answers or objections. An answer[2] in the response may be "evasive or incomplete."[3] A claim of inability to admit or

---

[31] Wilcox v Birtwhistle (1999) 21 Cal 4th 973, 982, 90 Cal Rptr 2d 260, 266–267, 987 P2d 727, 733–734.

For a discussion of withdrawing or amending an admission, see § 9.18.

[32] CCP § 2033.410.

For a discussion of the effect of an admission, see § 9.20.

[33] Harris v Billings (1993) 16 Cal App 4th 1396, 1402–1403, 20 Cal Rptr 2d 718, 721 [plaintiff may not dismiss if all issues in the case are deemed admitted in defendant's favor]; Miller v Marina Mercy Hospital (1984) 157 Cal App 3d 765, 770, 204 Cal Rptr 62 [same].

[1] For a discussion of motions for a deemed admission, see § 9.16.

[2] CCP §§ 2033.220(b)(1) and (2).

[3] CCP § 2033.290(a)(1).

See, e.g., Collisson and Kaplan v Hartunian (1994) 21 Cal App 4th 1611, 1617–1618, 26 Cal Rptr 2d 786, 790.

For a discussion of express admissions that qualify the language of the requests, see § 9.10.

deny[4] may be "incomplete" because it does not contain the required statement that the responding party has made a "reasonable inquiry" before responding.[5] Or an objection[6] may be meritless or insufficiently specific.[7]

Motion for Further Response: Section 2033.290 contains the procedure for obtaining clear-cut answers and overcoming objections to particular admission requests.[8] The requesting party must first try to informally resolve the dispute with the responding party.[9] If unsuccessful, the requesting party may move for an order compelling a further response.[10]

—Time Limit for Motion: Unlike the motion for a deemed admission,[11] requesting parties have a fixed time within which they may move to compel further responses. They must serve notice of their motion to compel no later than 45 days after service of the unsatisfactory response, absent a written agreement extending that time.[12] Service of the response by mail extends this period, usually by five days.[13] Failure to act within this time waives the right to have the court order a further response to the admission request. It also forfeits the right to seek cost-of-proof sanction after trial.[14] This waiver occurs even though the responding party's written opposition to the motion raises no issue about its timing.[15] A party who has let this statutory period expire may not overcome the waiver by the ploy of including the same request in another set.[16]

---

[4] CCP § 2033.220(b)(3).

For a discussion of answers claiming insufficient knowledge or information, see § 9.12.

[5] CCP § 2033.290(b)(1).

[6] CCP § 2033.230(b).

[7] CCP § 2033.290(b)(2).

For a discussion of objections to particular admission requests, see §§ 9.13 and 9.14.

[8] CCP § 2033.290(b).

See, e.g., Stull v Sparrow (2001) 92 Cal App 4th 860, 862–864, 112 Cal Rptr 2d 239, 241–242.

[9] See Obregon v Superior Court (1998) 67 Cal App 4th 424, 79 Cal Rptr 2d 62 [discussing adequacy of informal resolution of discovery disputes]. For a discussion of *Obregon*, see § 15.3.

[10] CCP § 2033.290(a).

[11] For a discussion of motions for a deemed admission, see § 9.16.

[12] CCP § 2033.290(c).

This same time limit applies to motions challenging the adequacy of a supplemental response.

[13] See CCP § 2016.050, referencing CCP § 1013(a).

[14] CCP § 2033.420(b)(1).

See, e.g., Wimberly v Derby Cycle Corp. (1997) 56 Cal App 4th 618, 636, 65 Cal Rptr 2d 532, 543.

For a discussion of the sanction for unwarranted failures to make an admission, see § 9.21.

[15] Cf. Sexton v Superior Court (1997) 58 Cal App 4th 1403, 68 Cal Rptr 2d 708 [involving inspection demand].

[16] Cf. Professional Career Colleges, Magna Institute, Inc. v Superior Court (1989) 207 Cal App 3d 490, 493–494, 255 Cal Rptr 5, 7–8 [a party who has allowed the 45-day period for compelling a further response to an *interrogatory to lapse* may not "reset the clock" by including the same interrogatory in a later set].

—Motion Unnecessary Where Objection is Coupled with Admission or Denial: In *Local 1902 v MWD*, [17] plaintiff served a response to 9 of 15 admission requests that began with an objection to each request, and then proceeded to flatly deny three of them and partially admit and partially deny six of them. When the case was tried, defendant proceeded to prove all of the matters that plaintiff had wholly or partially denied. Defendant then sought almost $27,000 as the cost of the proof of these matters.

Plaintiff contended that defendant had waived its right to the cost-of-proof sanction because it did not seek a ruling on the objections by moving for a further response. It was held that defendant had acted properly in construing the responses as unequivocal denials, and proceeding to expend the time and effort to prove the truth of these matters to the trial court. [18]

A party who unsuccessfully makes or opposes a motion to compel further response should be prepared to pay a monetary sanction if unable to persuade the trial court that substantial justification existed for its position. [19]

Disobedience of Order for Further Response: If the court orders a further response to admission requests, a party's failure to comply with this order empowers the court to deem the relevant matters admitted. [20] In addition to, or instead of, a deemed admission order, the court may impose a monetary sanction. Where the court finds a pattern of discovery abuse, it may impose a terminating sanction as well. [21]

§ 9.18 Withdrawing or Amending an Admission

Improvident Express Admission: Occasionally, later reflection, additional information, or new insights will lead a party to conclude that it has improvidently admitted some matter. Codifying longstanding case law, [1] Section 2033.300 recognizes and regulates the trial court's power to allow withdrawal or amendment of an express admission. [2]

Deemed Admission: Disapproving a half-dozen intermediate appellate decisions, [3] the Supreme Court in the *Wilcox* case [4] read what is now Section 2033.300 to permit the withdrawal or amendment of both express and deemed admissions:

---

[17] American Federation of State, County and Municipal Employees, Local 1902 v Metropolitan Water District (2005) 126 Cal App 4th 247, 265, 24 Cal Rptr 3d 285, 298.

[18] Local 1902 v MWD (2005) 126 Cal App 4th 247, 268, 24 Cal Rptr 3d 285, 300.

[19] CCP § 2033.290(d).

[20] CCP § 2033.290(e).

[21] See, e.g., Collisson and Kaplan v Hartunian (1994) 21 Cal App 4th 1611, 1617–1620, 26 Cal Rptr 2d 786, 790–792 [trial court properly struck defendant's pleading for his repeated failure to respond properly to interrogatories, inspection demands, and admission requests, and its disobedience of orders to do so].

[1] See Jahn v Brickey (1985) 168 Cal App 3d 399, 214 Cal Rptr 119.

[2] CCP § 2033.300.

[3] Allen-Pacific, Ltd. v Superior Court (1997) 57 Cal App 4th 1546, 67 Cal Rptr 2d 804; Demyer

[T]his interpretation complements the enforcement scheme created by [Section 2033.280]. Under [it] the initial penalty for failure to respond is the waiver of all objections. Once the propounding party files a motion for a deemed admission order, the nonresponding party then faces an additional penalty—mandatory monetary sanctions . . . . [Section 2033.300] then describes the consequences of failing to respond before the hearing on the motion and the resulting entry of a deemed admission order. Now, the nonresponding party can only escape a binding admission by establishing "mistake, inadvertence, or excusable neglect" and no substantial prejudice to the propounding party. The nonresponding party also faces the likely imposition of more sanctions at the discretion of the trial court. This graduated system of enforcement furthers the legislative purpose . . . by fitting the punishment of the nonresponding party to the offense.[5]

Motion for Leave to Withdraw or Amend: A party who wishes to amend or withdraw an express admission must obtain court permission to change the earlier answer. Absent a motion to amend or withdraw, the admission remains in full force.[6] In reviewing the motion, the court must agree that the original admission resulted from "mistake, inadvertence, or excusable neglect."[7] It must also find that the withdrawal or amendment of the admission will not substantially prejudice the party who obtained it.[8] Moreover, even where the moving party

---

v Costa Mesa Mobile Home Estates (1995) 36 Cal App 4th 393, 42 Cal Rptr 2d 260; Brigante v Huang (1993) 20 Cal App 4th 1569, 25 Cal Rptr 2d 354; Tobin v Oris (1992) 3 Cal App 4th 814, 4 Cal Rptr 2d 736; St. Paul Fire and Marine Ins. Co. v Superior Court (1992) 2 Cal App 4th 843, 3 Cal Rptr 2d 412; Courtesy Claims Service, Inc. v Superior Court (1990) 219 Cal App 3d 52, 268 Cal Rptr 30.

[4] Wilcox v Birtwhistle (1999) 21 Cal 4th 973, 983 n12, 90 Cal Rptr 2d 260, 267 n12, 987 P2d 727, 734 n12.

[5] Wilcox v Birtwhistle (1999) 21 Cal 4th 973, 982, 90 Cal Rptr 2d 260, 266–267, 987 P2d 727, 733–734.

For further discussion of obtaining relief from a deemed admission, see §§ 9.15–9.16.

[6] Valerio v Andrew Youngquist Construction (2002) 103 Cal App 4th 1264, 1273–1274, 127 Cal Rptr 2d 436, 443.

[7] CCP § 2033.300(b).

Compare CCP § 2033.280 [same standard for relief from waiver of objections to admission requests].

Cf. FDIC v Senkovich (1992, MD Fla) 806 F Supp 245, 250 [refusing to allow withdrawal of admission where "'mistake' was not diligently or promptly detected despite opportunities and occasions to do so"]; In re Narowetz Mechanical Contractors, Inc. (1989, ND Ill) 99 BR 850, 861 [refusing to allow withdrawal of admission on the grounds of "newly discovered evidence" where party "possessed all along the very information it eventually sought to use in order to justify its request to amend"]; Howard v Sterchi (1989, ND Ga) 725 F Supp 1572, 1576–1577] 12 F3d 218 [permitting plaintiff to withdraw former counsel's admissions made hastily and under a mistaken impression of the facts].

[8] CCP § 2033.300(b).

satisfies the trial court as to both conditions, it retains discretion to deny the motion. [9]

—Timing: The statute places no time limit on a motion to amend or withdraw an admission. Federal courts have granted such permission even during the trial. [10] Nevertheless, the closer to trial that a party files its motion, the easier it will usually be for the opposing party to show prejudice from the amendment or withdrawal. [11] Indeed, the federal courts impose a higher burden on a party who seeks to amend or withdraw an admission at trial. [12]

Prejudice to Opposing Party: Where the party that obtained the original admission never treated it as a true concession of a critical matter in the case, a withdrawal of the admission causes no prejudice. Thus, if both parties continued to debate the matter covered by the admission, the party who obtained it can hardly claim to have mistakenly believed that there was no issue over the matter it covered. [13] Moreover, the closer an admission goes to the heart of a case, the more likely a court is to find unreasonable any reliance placed on it by the party who obtained it. [14] Even where a party has treated the admission as a concession, prejudice does not automatically arise simply because that party will now have to prove a matter believed conceded: "The prejudice contemplated . . . is not simply that the party who initially obtained the admission will now have to convince the fact finder of its truth." [15] Prejudice usually occurs only when the

---

[9] Cf. Ropfogel v United States (1991, D Kan) 138 FRD 579, 582 583; Narowetz Mechanical Contractors, Inc. (1989, ND Ill) 99 BR 850, 860.

[10] See, e.g., Farr Man and Co., Inc. v M/V Rozita (1990, CA1 Mass) 903 F2d 871, 876 [where facts came to light showing that the defendant had potentially far less exposure to damages, withdrawal of admission was permitted even after trial began]; Brook Village North Associates v General Electric Co. (1982, CA1 NH) 686 F2d 66, 73.

[11] See, e.g., Ropfogel v United States (1991, D Kan) 138 FRD 579, 583 [allowing withdrawal of admissions on the eve of trial could unfairly disrupt trial preparations]; Coca-Cola Bottling Co. v Coca-Cola Co. (1988, D Del) 123 FRD 97, 107 [allowing withdrawal of admissions on eve of trial would prejudice opposing party's ability to gather evidence].

[12] Farr Man and Co., Inc. v M/V Rozita (1990, CA1 Mass) 903 F2d 871, 876 [withdrawal of admission, like an amendment of a pretrial order, allowed at trial only to prevent "manifest injustice"]; Brook Village North Associates v General Electric Co. (1982, CA1 NH) 686 F2d 66, 73 [higher standard required for withdrawals at trial].

[13] Montcalm County Board of Comm'rs v McDonald and Co. Securities, Inc. (1993, WD Mich) 833 F Supp 1225, 1230 [where both parties continued to treat the subject of a prior admission "as a major issue, and competently and fully briefed it, the plaintiff was not "lulled into believing" that the matter was settled].

[14] McClanahan v Aetna Life Ins. Co. (1992, WD Va) 144 FRD 316, 320–321 [where plaintiff, having obtained an admission that virtually conceded liability, nevertheless continued to engage in discovery, could still obtain witnesses, and had himself made an admission along the lines of the proposed amendment, allowing the change would cause no prejudice].

[15] Brook Village North Associates v General Electric Co. (1982, CA1 NH) 686 F2d 66, 70.

party who obtained the admission faces significantly greater difficulties than it had in assembling the evidence to prove the matters involved.[16]

Conditions on Grant of Leave: The trial judge can condition its permission to withdraw or amend an admission.[17] For example, the party who has been relying on the admission may now need additional discovery to prove at trial a matter believed conceded.[18] The court may require the party withdrawing or amending its admission to pay all or some of the costs of this additional discovery.[19] Sometimes the withdrawal of an admission may undercut a party's pending motion for summary judgment based on that admission. Federal courts have conditioned relief from the admission upon the responding party's payment of the costs of preparing that motion.[20]

§ 9.19 Who May Use Admission

Usually the requesting party will also be the one who uses an admission to avoid the need to prove at trial the matter covered by it.[1] Occasionally, however, someone *other than* the requesting party may seek to use that admission. Courts have addressed three such situations: (1) use by the party who made the admission, (2) use by cross-defendants, and (3) use by coparties.

Use by the Admitting Party: In a federal case,[2] the *admitting* party attempted to use her admission against the *requesting* party. A plaintiff, injured when a swivel chair that she was trying out in a furniture store suddenly tipped over, sued a chair manufacturer. The defendant pleaded alternatively that the plaintiff had not fallen from one of *its* chairs, but that, if it had manufactured the chair, the retailer's alterations to it were the cause of any defect. Pursuing the second prong of its defense, the manufacturer requested that the plaintiff admit that defendant had sold the chair to the retailer at a discount because it was not first-class merchandise. The plaintiff made this admission and then argued at trial that her admission had eliminated the issue of whether it was a chair manufactured by the defendant from which she had fallen. The court held, however, that a requested admission does not bind the one obtaining it: "The submission of

---

[16] United States v One 1984 Chevrolet Trans Star (1985, D Conn) 623 F Supp 625, 627 [in forfeiture case, the Government was allowed to withdraw admission that drivers of seized van, whose whereabouts were now unknown, had entered country illegally, since their whereabouts were unknown at the time the admission was made]; Westmoreland v Triumph Motorcycle Corp. (1976, D Conn) 71 FRD 192, 193 [defendant seeking to withdraw admission had located the missing witness whom plaintiff claimed it would need to prove the matter admitted].

[17] CCP § 2033.300(b).

[18] CCP § 2033.300(b)(1).

[19] CCP § 2033.300(b)(2).

[20] Davis v Noufal (1992, D DC) 142 FRD 258, 260.

[1] For a discussion of the effect of an admission, see § 9.20.

[2] Champlin v Oklahoma Furniture Mfg. Co. (1963, CA10 Okla) 324 F2d 74.

requests for admissions by a litigant does not, in and of itself, bind the litigant to the truth or existence of the facts contained in the answers to the requests."[3]

Use by Cross-Defendants: Often a defendant in a lawsuit will cross-complain for indemnity against either a co-defendant or a third party. These parties may seek to bind the cross-complainant on matters admitted by that party in the main action in response to a plaintiff's requests. In the *Shepard and Morgan* case,[4] decided under the version of Section 2033 in the 1956 Discovery Act,[5] a carpenter who had fallen 20 feet from a joist on which he was working sued the general contractor. Alleging that the joist was defective, the defendant cross-complained for indemnity against the joist supplier. During discovery, in response to the plaintiff's request, the general contractor admitted that it was "contending" that the particular joist was *not* hazardous for the worker. The joist supplier then used this admission to obtain a dismissal of the cross-complaint against it.

The Supreme Court, however, ruled that the contractor's admission during its defense against the injured party's claim was not binding on it in its cross-complaint for indemnity. The Court regarded the cross-complaint as a separate action. Otherwise, it reasoned, the threat of this use of their admissions would discourage litigants from seeking indemnity in the same suit and induce them to file an independent action to avoid such a result.

In effect, Section 2033.410 embodies the holding in the *Shepard and Morgan* case. By retaining substantially the same language that the Court was interpreting in that case, it, too, prohibits such use against a cross-complainant:

> [A]ny admission made by a party under this section is . . . made *for the purpose of the pending action only*. It is not an admission by that party for any other purpose, and shall *not be used in any manner against that party in any other proceeding*.[6]

Use by Co-Parties: A different issue arises when a party tries to take advantage of an admission made at the request of its co-party. Section 2033.410 provides: "Any matter admitted in response to a request for admission is conclusively established against the party making the admission in the pending action . . . ."[7] Thus, the Legislature has left intact a judicial interpretation of comparable language in the 1956 Discovery Act.[8] The *Swedberg* case[9] had held that, at least

---

[3] Champlin v Oklahoma Furniture Mfg. Co. (1963, CA10 Okla) 324 F2d 74, 76.

See also General Motors Corp. v Aetna Cas. & Surety Co. (1991, Ind) 573 NE2d 885, 890 [party who requests an admission is not bound by it].

[4] Shepard and Morgan v Lee and Daniel, Inc. (1982) 31 Cal 3d 256, 182 Cal Rptr 351, 643 P2d 968.

[5] Former CCP § 2033(c), 1956 Discovery Act, Appendix E.

[6] CCP § 2033.410(b) (italics added).

[7] CCP § 2033.410(a).

[8] Former CCP § 2033(c), 1956 Discovery Act, Appendix E.

[9] Swedberg v Christiana Community Builders (1985) 175 Cal App 3d 138, 220 Cal Rptr 544.

where identical factual and legal bases underlie the claims asserted against two defendants, one defendant may use against the plaintiff the admissions resulting from the requests of the other defendant:

> We believe the Legislature intended to allow one party in a case to enjoy the benefits of discovery obtained by other parties in that same case. In limiting an admission to the "pending action only" and to no other action, the Legislature manifested its intent on the scope of an admission. Had the Legislature intended that admissions not be used by all parties to a single action, the Legislature would have included that limitation . . . . The absence of such a limitation reflects a legislative intent that admissions may be used by all parties to a single action.[10]

Like its predecessor, Section 2033.410 contains no language restricting the use of an admission to the party who requested it.[11]

§ 9.20 Effect of an Admission

An admission obtained pursuant to a discovery request establishes only that the "matter" it covers is "true" for the lawsuit in which it was made. Additional questions, however, can arise regarding the admission's admissibility, scope, and effect.

Admissibility: The acceptance of a matter as "true" does not mean that it will be admissible at trial. A wide gap exists between the discovery standard of "relevance to the subject matter"[1] and admissibility at trial. A fact relevant to the case's subject matter may be irrelevant to the actual trial issues.

Moreover, even a fact that is relevant to the trial issues may still be excluded under some rule of the law of evidence, such as the hearsay rule or the rule against proving safety measures taken after an accident. For example, in a federal case,[2] the defendant requested that a personal injury plaintiff admit that doctors *had made* a certain diagnosis of her eye condition. She objected to the request on the ground that any such diagnosis would be nothing more than the doctors' hearsay opinion. The court held that she was misapprehending the effect of making the requested admission:

---

[10] Swedberg v Christiana Community Builders (1985) 175 Cal App 3d 138, 144, 220 Cal Rptr 544, 548.

[11] See CCP § 2033.410.

Cf. Harkins v Calumet Realty Co. (1992, Penn) 614 A2d 699, 709 [admission made by the plaintiff in response to request of defendants who are later dismissed from the case could be used by the remaining codefendants].

[1] Cambric v Superior Court (1961) 56 Cal 2d 423, 429, 15 Cal Rptr 127, 130, 364 P2d 303, 306.

For a discussion of the of admission requests covering matters relevant to the subject matter of the case, see § 9.5.

[2] Goodman v Mooney (1959, WD Pa) 24 FRD 279.

Plaintiff's reluctance to answer is apparently based upon an assumption that the answers to defendants' requests if made would be admissible in evidence at the trial of the case. We make no such assumption, and . . . we entertain serious doubts as to their admissibility in evidence at the trial. Admissible or not, however, the requests being for relevant matter, we find that they should be answered and their admissibility determined by the trial judge.[3]

Courts are reluctant to make evidentiary rulings during discovery. Therefore, a party who has admitted a particular matter pursuant to a discovery request may still object to the use of that admission in support of a motion for summary judgment or at trial. Form 25 of the official Appendix of Forms[4] to the Federal Rules of Civil Procedure highlights this right to raise evidentiary objections at trial. It indicates that a request under Federal Rule of Civil Procedure 36 should say that any admission made will be "subject to all pertinent objections to admissibility which may be interposed at the trial."

Scope: Even where a resulting admission is otherwise admissible under the rules of evidence, an issue may later arise concerning the scope of an express or a deemed admission.[5] For example, in *Redwood Empire v Gombos,*[6] an important issue was whether a road that crossed the plaintiffs' property had become a public way because of its prolonged use for public recreational purposes. Soon after suit was filed, plaintiffs requested that defendants admit that "you have no evidence of recreational use of the disputed portion of [the road]" before 1972. Defendants responded with an unqualified admission. However, over a year later, as the case was nearing trial, the defendants had obtained testimony of witnesses that showed public recreational use of the road throughout the 1950's and 1960's. Plaintiffs sought to bar this evidence on the basis of the previous admission, which had never been withdrawn, amended, or supplemented. The reviewing court rejected this argument:

Nothing in the text of the statute creates any ongoing duty to update responses. Indeed, the statute authorizes amending or withdrawing a response only where a court finds the original admission "was the result of mistake, inadvertence, or excusable neglect." [Defendants] would not have met that standard here because there was nothing mistaken, inadvertent, or neglectful about the original response. The RFA [request for admission] asked [defendants] to admit that it did not "have" the evidence in issue. When [defendants] verified and served its response to that present tense question in April of 1997, it gave the answer that

---

[3] Goodman v Mooney (1959, WD Pa) 24 FRD 279, 280.

[4] FRCivP 84 provides: "The forms contained in the Appendix of Forms are sufficient under the rules . . . ."

[5] See, e.g., Milton v Montgomery Ward & Co. (1973) 33 Cal App 3d 133, 138, 108 Cal Rptr 726, 728.

For a discussion of deemed admissions, see § 9.16.

[6] Redwood Empire v Gombos (2000) 82 Cal App 4th 352, 98 Cal Rptr 2d 119.

was true at the time. It was still true at the time of the trial (and it will always be true) that in April 1997 [defendants] had no evidence of pre-1972 recreational use of the road. Thus, there was neither a need nor even an applicable mechanism for [defendants] to amend or withdraw its response to the RFA in question.[7]

When a party uses an admission to support a summary judgment motion, courts resolve any ambiguity in it against the moving party.[8] And where a party seeks to rely on an admission at trial, the court may allow evidence to explain ambiguities or fill in gaps.[9] For example, in the *Milton* case,[10] the plaintiff admitted that on the date he slipped and fell in the defendant's garage, he already had arthritic spurs in the area he claimed to have injured; that an X-ray taken shortly after the accident showed no compression injury; that none of his treating doctors could tie his present condition to the accident with reasonable certainty; and that the place where he fell was well lit. On appeal, the defendant argued that the trial court should not have let the plaintiff introduce contrary evidence on these matters.

The appellate court concluded that although the matters admitted complicated the plaintiff's case, they did not destroy it. In particular, they did not prevent him from showing that, notwithstanding the X-ray, he did in fact sustain a compression injury; that, despite the opinions of his treating doctors, there was a causal nexus between his fall and his back injury; and that, despite the adequate lighting in the area, he had slipped on some transparent grease or oil on the floor.[11]

Effect: Section 2033.410 specifies: "Any matter admitted in response to a request for admission is conclusively established against the party making the admission in the pending action . . . ."[12] By using this language, the Legislature

---

[7] Redwood Empire v Gombos (2000) 82 Cal App 4th 352, 359, 98 Cal Rptr 2d 119, 124.

[8] People ex rel Dep't of Transp. v Ad Way Signs, Inc. (1993) 14 Cal App 4th 187, 200, 17 Cal Rptr 2d 496, 503–504 [admissions made in response to a request that was compound were construed against requesting party where additional evidence existed to contradict the apparent admission].

[9] Fredericks v Kontos Industries Inc. (1987) 189 Cal App 3d 272, 277–279, 234 Cal Rptr 395, 397–399 [an admission that a construction contract called for progress payments does not prevent a party from showing that these payments were to be dependent on the amount of work performed].

See also Frymire-Brinati v KPMG Peat Marwick (1993, CA7 Ill) 2 F3d 183, 187 [admitting party entitled to have the jury see the actual words of its admission in their narrative context].

[10] Milton v Montgomery Ward & Co. (1973) 33 Cal App 3d 133, 108 Cal Rptr 726.

[11] See also Fredericks v Kontos Industries Inc. (1987) 189 Cal App 3d 272, 276–278, 234 Cal Rptr 395, 397–398 [an admission that a construction contract called for progress payments does not prevent a party from showing that these payments were to be dependent on the amount of work performed]; Maxwell v Colburn (1980) 105 Cal App 3d 180, 163 Cal Rptr 912 [deemed admission that defendant was driving within speed limit does not establish his freedom from negligence in failing to stop his vehicle in time to avoid collision].

[12] CCP § 2033.410(a).

has sided with those courts[13] that were holding that this discovery method produced a binding *judicial* admission, not a mere *evidentiary* one.[14] As a judicial admission, it conclusively establishes the matter it covers. The party making the admission may not present evidence contradicting it.[15] Moreover, a party need not have entered the admission itself into evidence for it to have this conclusive effect.[16]

This position comports with the special role of admission requests in the discovery scheme.[17] These requests narrow the case for trial.[18] Any admissions they yield represent "a studied response, made under sanctions against easy denials," that occur "under the direction and supervision of counsel, who has full professional realization of their significance."[19] There would be little point to this method of discovery if the resulting admissions are no different from the evidentiary ones that a litigant can obtain from an opponent via deposition or interrogatories.[20]

Voluntary Dismissal: Further reinforcing the conclusive effect of an admission obtained via a discovery request are those decisions that address its interaction with a plaintiff's ability to voluntarily dismiss its case. A plaintiff cannot moot the effect of its admissions by voluntarily dismissing the case, and then refiling it as a new lawsuit. Otherwise, plaintiffs who had made admissions would have a tactical advantage over a defendant who has made them.[21]

---

[13] See, e.g., Milton v Montgomery Ward & Co. (1973) 33 Cal App 3d 133, 137, 108 Cal Rptr 726, 728; McSparran v Hanigan (1963, ED Pa) 225 F Supp 628, 637.

[14] See, e.g., Guenther v Armstrong Rubber Co. (1969, CA3 Pa) 406 F2d 1315 [plaintiff not conclusively bound even by his own trial testimony]; Alamo v Del Rosario (1938 DC Cir) 98 F2d 328 [same].

[15] Valerio v Andrew Youngquist Construction (2002) 103 Cal App 4th 1264, 1272, 127 Cal Rptr 2d 436, 442; Fredericks v Kontos Industries, Inc. (1987) 189 Cal App 3d 272, 276–278, 234 Cal Rptr 395, 397–398.

Cf. Coca-Cola Bottling Co. of Shreveport, Inc. v Coca-Cola Co. (1993, CA3 Del) 988 F2d 414, 427 [admissions conclusive only on matters contained within them, not necessarily on all the ultimate issues in a case]; Matter of Corland Co. (1992, CA5 Tex) 967 F2d 1069, 1074 [only "'deliberate, clear and unequivocal'" statements can constitute conclusive judicial admissions; where two admissions conflicted, ambiguity precluded conclusive effect]; America Auto. Ass'n, Inc. v AAA Legal Clinic of Jefferson Crooke, P.C. (1991, CA5 Tex) 930 F2d 1117, 1120–1121 [trial court may not ignore admission simply because it found evidence produced at trial was more credible].

[16] Empiregas, Inc. v Suggs (1990, Ala) 567 So2d 271, 274 [directed verdict properly refused on basis of admission even though admission not offered in evidence at trial].

[17] For a general discussion of the function of admission requests, see § 9.1.

[18] Midwest Television, Inc. v Scott, Lancaster, Mills & Atha, Inc. (1988) 205 Cal App 3d 442, 451–452, 252 Cal Rptr 573, 579 [when a fact is deemed admitted, it is laid to rest so that it does not have to be tried].

[19] McSparran v Hanigan (1963, ED Pa) 225 F Supp 628, 637.

[20] Cf. Airco Industrial Gases, Inc. v Teamsters Health and Welfare Pension Fund (1988, CA3 Del) 850 F2d 1028, 1035–1036 [comparing relative effect of admissions made under FRCivP 33 with those made under FRCivP 36].

[21] Harris v Billings (1993) 16 Cal App 4th 1396, 1402–1403, 20 Cal Rptr 2d 718, 721; Miller v Marina Mercy Hospital (1984) 157 Cal App 3d 765, 770, 204 Cal Rptr 62.

§ 9.21 Sanction for Unwarranted Failure to Admit

When a party denies[1] an admission request or claims to have insufficient information about the matter,[2] the requesting party must spend the time, effort, and money to assemble evidence to prove the truth of the matters covered by the requests. Prior to trial, the court will not review the accuracy of either response.[3] However, after proving those matters at trial, the requesting party may move for a sanction unique to admission requests: an award of the costs incurred in proving the matter.[4]

Scope: Section 2033.420 authorizes the trial court to shift the requesting party's cost of proof to an opponent who without good reason "fails to admit"[5] a requested matter of substantial importance. This phrase, borrowed from Federal Rule of Civil Procedure 37(c), covers not only outright *denials* of a requested admission but also claims of *insufficient information* to admit or deny.[6]

Eligibility: To be eligible for the cost-of-proof sanction, the party who requested the admission must actually prove the matter covered by it. A party may prepare to prove a certain matter at trial, only to find that an opponent who previously denied a request to admit that matter now formally concedes its truth. *Wagy v Brown* holds that Section 2033.420 does not authorize the award of the costs incurred in that preparation:

> [P]reparation for trial or arbitration is not the equivalent of proving the truth of a matter so as to authorize an award of attorney fees under [CCP § 2033.420]. Expenses are recoverable only where the party requesting the admission "proves . . . the truth of that matter," not where that party merely prepares to do so.[7]

---

[1] For a discussion of denials of admission requests, see § 9.11.

[2] For a discussion of claims of insufficient information to admit a request, see § 9.12.

[3] See, e.g., Stull v Sparrow (2001) 92 Cal App 4th 860, 112 Cal Rptr 2d 239; Holguin v Superior Court (1972) 22 Cal App 3d 812, 820, 99 Cal Rptr 653, 658; Smith v Circle P Ranch Co. (1978) 87 Cal App 3d 267, 273, 150 Cal Rptr 828, 832.

[4] CCP § 2033.420(a).

See Mount Olympus Property Owners Assn. v Shpirt (1997) 59 Cal App 4th 885, 896, 69 Cal Rptr 2d 521, 528.

[5] CCP § 2033.420(a).

[6] See Advisory Committee Note to 1970 amendment to FRCivP 37(c).

Cf. Lakin v Watkins Associated Industries (1993) 6 Cal 4th 644, 649, 25 Cal Rptr 2d 109, 111, 863 P2d 179, 181.

[7] Wagy v Brown (1994) 24 Cal App 4th 1, 6, 29 Cal Rptr 2d 48, 50 [defendants admitted their negligence for purposes of the arbitration hearing, although they had earlier denied a request that they admit negligence].

See also Stull v Sparrow (2001) 92 Cal App 4th 860, 865, 112 Cal Rptr 2d 239, 243 [denial of request changed to an admission on the eve of the trial: "The instant case parallels *Wagy* in that defendants' admission of liability prior to trial obviated the need for (plaintiff) to produce any proof on that element of her case."]

Although the requesting party must first prove at trial the truth of the matter covered by the request, that party need not ultimately win the case: "One need not be a prevailing party to be entitled to sanctions under this statute."[8] In *Smith v Circle P Ranch Co.,*[9] even a general finding that certain defendants were not negligent did not automatically shield them from the cost-of-proof sanction:

> Such a general finding by the jury does not . . . establish that defendants were justified in their pretrial denials of specific facts later proved true. Nor does it constitute a determination that plaintiff failed to prove all facts to which defendants' denials were relevant.[10]

Garcia v Hyster Co.[11] holds that even if the trial results in a nonsuit, the trial court may review the record and determine that the party whose admissions requests were improperly denied proved the matter covered by them.

A party who prevails on a summary judgment motion may also qualify for the cost-of-proof sanction. In the *Barnett* case,[12] plaintiff was injured while using a leased milk truck. Claiming that the side lift gate on the truck was defective, he sued the lessor. At his deposition, he testified that the injury resulted when the lift gate had collapsed as he was placing milk products on it. Defendant then requested that plaintiff admit that the lift gate was not defective. When plaintiff denied this admission request, defendant: (1) secured declarations from plaintiff's fellow workers that the lift gate on the truck functioned properly after plaintiff's mishap; (2) employed an expert who opined that a leak of hydraulic fluid had caused the gate to collapse, and that the lift would not have functioned until the leak was repaired; and (3) used this information to support a successful motion for summary judgment.

Defendant then successfully moved for a cost-of-proof sanction to recover the expert witness's fees and the charge made by its attorney for preparing the summary judgment motion. Plaintiff appealed from the imposition of this sanction on the ground that it is available only to a party who establishes the truth of the requested matter *at a trial.* The appellate court disagreed:

> [Section 2033.420] does not on its face require that an issue be proved at trial, although it does require that the party requesting the admission have proved the issue. . . . [A] party who successfully moves for summary judgment proves the facts in issue by submitting papers that

---

[8] Smith v Circle P Ranch Co. (1978) 87 Cal App 3d 267, 275, 150 Cal Rptr 828, 833.

See also Brooks v American Broadcasting Co. (1986) 179 Cal App 3d 500, 509 n5, 224 Cal Rptr 838, 843 n5.

[9] Smith v Circle P Ranch Co. (1978) 87 Cal App 3d 267, 150 Cal Rptr 828.

[10] Smith v Circle P Ranch Co (1978) 87 Cal App 3d 267, 274, 150 Cal Rptr 828, 833.

[11] Garcia v Hyster Co. (1994) 28 Cal App 4th 724, 735, 34 Cal Rptr 2d 283, 289.

See also Wimberly v Derby Cycle Corp. (1997) 56 Cal App 4th 618, 638, 65 Cal Rptr 2d 532, 544.

[12] Barnett v Penske Truck Leasing Co. (2001) 90 Cal App 4th 494, 108 Cal Rptr 2d 821.

"show that there is no triable issue as to any material fact and that the moving party is entitled to a judgment as a matter of law." [CCP § 437c(c).][13]

Award Pending Appeal: The federal courts disagree over the court's power to award a cost-of-proof sanction while the main case is on appeal.[14] No California case has considered this question.[15] Most likely, the trial court retains power to award this sanction as a collateral or independent matter not affecting the judgment.[16]

Avoiding Cost-of-Proof Sanction: Even if a party successfully establishes at trial the truth of a requested matter, an opponent who failed to make the admission may still avoid the cost-of-proof sanction by justifying or excusing this failure: "The fact that matters denied were subsequently proved by uncontradicted evidence, if true, does not make the denial unreasonable per se, in retrospect."[17] Like its federal counterpart,[18] Section 2033.420 lists four reasons on which the trial court can base a decision not to impose this sanction: (1) objections to the request were sustained or unchallenged; (2) the matter covered by the request was of no substantial importance; (3) the responding party had a reasonable expectation of prevailing on that matter; and (4) any other good reason.[19]

—Objection Sustained or Unchallenged: A court may not award the cost-of-proof sanction if earlier it had sustained an objection to the admission request.[20] Nor may it impose the sanction on a party whose objection, whatever its validity, the requesting party did not challenge upon receiving that response.[21] However, a party is under no obligation to challenge an objection that is coupled with an

---

[13] Barnett v Penske Truck Leasing Co. (2001) 90 Cal App 4th 494, 497–498, 108 Cal Rptr 2d 821, 823.

[14] Compare Kaṣuri v St. Elizabeth's Hospital Medical Center (1990, CA6 Ohio) 897 F2d 845, 855–856 [sanctions awardable despite pending appeal] with Popeil Bros., Inc. v Schick Electric, Inc. (1975, CA7 Ill) 516 F2d 772, 778 [motion for expenses under FRCivP 37(c) must be brought prior to judgment and appeal].

[15] Cf. Lakin v Watkins Associated Industries (1993) 6 Cal 4th 644, 649, 25 Cal Rptr 2d 109, 111, 863 P2d 179, 181 [order denying cost-of-proof sanction is appealable].

[16] See, e.g., Bankes v Lucas (1992) 9 Cal App 4th 365, 370, 11 Cal Rptr 2d 723, 725 [as a collateral matter not affecting the appeal, the trial court had jurisdiction to award attorney's fees as costs despite the pendency of an appeal from the underlying judgment]; Silver v Gold (1989) 211 Cal App 3d 17, 26, 259 Cal Rptr 185, 190 [trial court has jurisdiction to issue sanctions for a frivolous motion to tax costs despite pendency of appeal from underlying judgment of dismissal].

[17] Haseltine v Haseltine (1962) 203 Cal App 2d 48, 61, 21 Cal Rptr 238, 247.

[18] FRCivP 37(c).

[19] CCP § 2033.420.

[20] CCP § 2033.420(b)(1).

[21] CCP § 2033.420(b)(1), referencing CCP § 2033.290.

See, e.g., Wimberly v Derby Cycle Corp. (1997) 56 Cal App 4th 618, 636, 65 Cal Rptr 2d 532, 543.

admission or denial of the matter the party was requested to admit. In *Local 1902 v MWD,* [22] plaintiff served a response to nine of 15 admission requests that began with an objection to each request, and then proceeded to flatly deny three of them and partially admit and partially deny six of them. When the case was tried, defendant proceeded to prove all of the matters that plaintiff had wholly or partially denied. Defendant then sought almost $27,000 as the cost of the proof of these matters.

Plaintiff contended that defendant had waived its right to the cost-of-proof sanction because it did not seek a ruling on the objections by moving for a further response. It was held that defendant had acted properly in construing the responses as unequivocal denials, and proceeding to expend the time and effort to prove the truth of these matters to the trial court. [23]

A party who unsuccessfully makes or opposes a motion to compel further response should be prepared to pay a monetary sanction if unable to persuade the trial court that substantial justification existed for its position. [24]

—Matter "of No Substantial Importance": A responding party can also avoid the sanction by persuading the trial judge that the matter covered by the admission request was "of no substantial importance" in the case. [25] Only matters central to the lawsuit's disposition will have the requisite "substantial importance": "[A]s a general rule a request for admission should have at least some direct relationship to one of the central issues in the case, i.e., an issue which, if not proven, would have altered the results in the case." [26] However, the fact involved in the request need only *relate to* a central issue; it need not have determined the outcome of that issue in favor of the requesting party. [27]

The *Brooks* case [28] illustrates the court's discretion in deciding the relative importance of the matters covered by earlier admission requests. There, the plaintiff truck driver claimed that the defendant's bus had forced his rig off the highway because it was on the plaintiff's side of the road. The truck driver denied a request that he admit that it was *his* vehicle that had strayed "zero to two feet" over the centerline. Arguing later against imposition of the cost-of-proof sanction, he contended that the requested matter lacked "substantial importance." He argued that his admission of it would have meant only that his rig was a fraction of an inch over the line. The court disagreed:

---

[22] American Federation of State, County and Municipal Employees, Local 1902 v Metropolitan Water District (2005) 126 Cal App 4th 247, 265, 24 Cal Rptr 3d 285, 298.

[23] American Federation of State, County and Municipal Employees, Local 1902 v Metropolitan Water District (2005) 126 Cal App 4th 247, 265, 24 Cal Rptr 3d 285, 300.

[24] CCP § 2033.290(d).

[25] CCP § 2033.420(b)(2).

[26] Brooks v American Broadcasting Co. (1986) 179 Cal App 3d 500, 509, 224 Cal Rptr 838, 843.

[27] Brooks v American Broadcasting Co. (1986) 179 Cal App 3d 500, 509 n5, 224 Cal Rptr 838, 843 n5.

[28] Brooks v American Broadcasting Co. (1986) 179 Cal App 3d 500, 224 Cal Rptr 838.

[T]he circumstance of his truck being only slightly over the centerline might have caused him to perceive that it was the bus . . . and not his truck which was in the wrong lane. In view of [the plaintiff's] fundamental assertion that the accident was caused when he was forced to swerve in order to miss the oncoming bus, [this admission request] was dispositive of a central issue in the case—whether the truck was in its own lane at the time the accident occurred. On the facts of this case, the trial court was well within its discretion in determining that the requested admission was of substantial importance.[29]

—**Reasonable Hope of Prevailing:** A party who has failed to make a requested admission may also avoid the cost-of proof sanction by showing "reasonable ground to believe that that party would prevail on the matter" at trial.[30] In assessing the reasonableness of a party's refusal to admit, the court must do so from the perspective of that party's knowledge as of the time of the request.[31]

Obviously, a responding party who personally knows the truth of the matter covered by an admission request has no reasonable belief in prevailing on that matter at trial.[32] Even where the responding party lacks such firsthand knowledge, the required "reasonable inquiry" may have yielded "readily obtainable" information[33] as to the truth of the requested matter. In the *Brooks* case,[34] for example, the plaintiff's amnesia prevented him from remembering the events just before the accident. Nevertheless, the court held that an examination of the police accident report would have shown the plaintiff's attorney that there was no reason to believe that the plaintiff's truck was *not* across the centerline:

> [The admission request] was denied long after the Highway Patrol had prepared its report which concluded that [the plaintiff's] truck had to have been over the centerline of the road based on the tire marks it had made on the pavement. [The plaintiff's] counsel did not even bother to contact the law enforcement officers who prepared the report because

---

[29] Brooks v American Broadcasting Co. (1986) 179 Cal App 3d 500, 511–512, 224 Cal Rptr 838, 845.

See also Wimberly v Derby Cycle Corp. (1997) 56 Cal App 4th 618, 638, 65 Cal Rptr 2d 532, 544.

[30] CCP § 2033.420(b)(3).

[31] See, e.g., Board of Directors, Water's Edge v Anden Group (1991, ED Va) 136 FRD 100, 105 [responding party who initially denied a request but later stipulated to the requested matters is not subject to cost-of-proof sanction where, at the time of the denial, good grounds supporting it existed].

[32] See, e.g., Allen v Pitchess (1973) 36 Cal App 3d 321, 330–332, 111 Cal Rptr 658, 664–665; Hillman v Stults (1968) 263 Cal App 2d 848, 885, 70 Cal Rptr 295, 317.

[33] See CCP § 2033.220.

For a discussion of the duty to make reasonable inquiry before claiming insufficient information to admit or deny a request, see § 9.12.

[34] Brooks v American Broadcasting Co. (1986) 179 Cal App 3d 500, 224 Cal Rptr 838.

he "assumed" the report was ambiguous. Finally, counsel admitted that he chose not to contest the issue at trial.[35]

When a party denies an admission request but later presents at trial no evidence to contest the matter covered by the request, an award of the cost of proving that matter is mandated.[36]

—**Other Good Reasons:** Section 2033.420 concludes with a catch-all provision. It authorizes the trial court to deny the cost-of-proof sanction if the responding party shows some "other good reason for the failure to admit."[37] For example, although a requested matter later turns out to be of "substantial importance" to the central issues in a case, the responding party might reasonably have considered it trivial at the time of the request.[38]

Determining Amount of Sanction: Unless the trial court decides that one of the reasons listed in Section 2033.420 excuses the failure to admit a matter later proved at trial, it *must* impose the cost-of-proof sanction.[39] The requesting party is entitled to an order directing the responding party "to pay the reasonable expenses incurred in making that proof." These expenses may include the cost of demonstrative evidence. For example, in the *Brooks* case, the requesting party recovered a substantial part of the expenses it had incurred in staging a re-creation of the accident.[40]

The statute is explicit that one of the expenses covered by its sanction is "reasonable attorney's fees."[41] Courts have made substantial awards of counsel fees as part of this sanction. For example, in the *Hillman* case,[42] a defendant's totally unjustified denials forced the plaintiff to embark upon a protracted line of proof to establish a trust and to obtain an accounting. The appellate court

---

[35] Brooks v American Broadcasting Co. (1986) 179 Cal App 3d 500, 512, 224 Cal Rptr 838, 845.

See also Rosales v Thermex-Thematron, Inc. (1998) 67 Cal App 4th 187, 198–199,78 Cal Rptr 2d 861, 868.

[36] Wimberly v Derby Cycle Corp. (1997) 56 Cal App 4th 618, 638, 65 Cal Rptr 2d 532, 543, 544.

[37] CCP § 2033.420(b)(4).

[38] Brooks v American Broadcasting Co. (1986) 179 Cal App 3d 500, 509–510, 224 Cal Rptr 838, 843.

See also Lakin v Watkins Associated Industries (1993) 6 Cal 4th 644, 650 n1, 25 Cal Rptr 2d 109, 112 n1, 863 P2d 179, 182 n1 [reserving decision on whether trial court may deny cost-of-proof sanction if it thinks that jury included attorney's fees in its award of punitive damages].

[39] Lakin v Watkins Associated Industries (1993) 6 Cal 4th 644, 650, 25 Cal Rptr 2d 109, 112, 863 P 2d 179, 182.

See also Smith v Circle P Ranch Co. (1978) 87 Cal App 3d 267, 274, 150 Cal Rptr 828, 833; Haseltine v Haseltine (1962) 203 Cal App 2d 48, 60, 21 Cal Rptr 238, 246.

[40] Brooks v American Broadcasting Co. (1986) 179 Cal App 3d 500, 507–512, 224 Cal Rptr 838, 842–845.

[41] CCP § 2033.420(a).

[42] Hillman v Stults (1968) 263 Cal App 2d 848, 890, 70 Cal Rptr 295, 320.

ultimately upheld a $30,000 award. And in *Local 1902 v MWD*,[43] an award of almost $27,000 was upheld despite the plaintiff's coupling of an objection to its denials of nine requests.

The trial court may not award costs by picking a figure out of the air. It must create a record that will enable an appellate court to review the reasonableness of the award. In *Smith v Circle P Ranch Co.*,[44] the appellate court agreed that the defendants' denial of admission requests entitled the plaintiff to his cost of proving the matters covered. It remanded the case, however, because "there is an insufficient record to show that the dollar amount awarded was reasonably related to proofs necessitated by this misconduct."[45]

In assessing the amount of a cost-of-proof award, the trial court must exclude any costs incurred before the receipt of the negative response to the admission request.[46] Moreover, it must award only expenses connected with those portions of the request that the responding party failed to admit without sufficient reason.[47] For example, in the *Hillman* case,[48] the trial court awarded the plaintiff all the expenses, including substantial counsel fees, incurred in the presentation of his entire case. The appellate court concluded that the defendant reasonably refused to admit some of the requests. Accordingly, it halved the trial court's award of $60,000.

Appealability: In *Lakin v Watkins Associated Industries*,[49] the Supreme Court concluded that a postjudgment order denying a motion for the cost-of-proof sanction is appealable:

> [T]he order here in issue, denying an award of attorney fees requested pursuant to [Section 2033.420], is a postjudgment order that affects the judgment or relates to its enforcement because it determines the rights and liabilities of the parties arising from the judgment, is not preliminary to later proceedings, and will not become subject to appeal after some future judgment. Therefore, it is appealable.[50]

---

[43] American Federation of State, County and Municipal Employees, Local 1902 v Metropolitan Water District (2005) 126 Cal App 4th 247, 265, 24 Cal Rptr 3d 285, 298.

[44] Smith v Circle P Ranch Co. (1978) 87 Cal App 3d 267, 150 Cal Rptr 828.

[45] Smith v Circle P Ranch Co. (1978) 87 Cal App 3d 267, 280, 150 Cal Rptr 828, 836. See also Garcia v Hyster Co. (1994) 28 Cal App 4th 724, 736–737, 34 Cal Rptr 2d 283, 290–291.

[46] Garcia v Hyster Co. (1994) 28 Cal App 4th 724, 736, 34 Cal Rptr 2d 283, 290 [error to award counsel fees for the period between service of admission requests and response denying them;] Brooks v American Broadcasting Co. (1986) 179 Cal App 3d 500, 512, 224 Cal Rptr 838, 845 [where accident reconstruction experiment had already been arranged at time admission request was denied, trial court did not abuse its discretion in allowing only one-quarter of the overall cost of the re-creation].

[47] Garcia v Hyster Co. (1994) 28 Cal App 4th 724, 736–737, 34 Cal Rptr 2d 283, 290.

[48] Hillman v Stults (1968) 263 Cal App 2d 848, 887–890, 70 Cal Rptr 295, 318–320.

[49] Lakin v Watkins Associated Industries (1993) 6 Cal 4th 644, 25 Cal Rptr 2d 109, 863 P2d 179.

[50] Lakin v Watkins Associated Industries (1993) 6 Cal 4th 644, 649, 25 Cal Rptr 2d 109, 111, 863 P2d 179, 181.

CHAPTER 10

EXPERT WITNESS DISCLOSURE

SYNOPSIS

---

§ 10.1   In General

Urgent Need for Such Discovery: An ever-increasing number of trials, especially those involving personal injury claims, feature expert witness testimony. If anything, the need for pretrial discovery is greater for expert witnesses than for ordinary witnesses.[1] If a party is going to call experts at trial, the other parties must prepare to cope with witnesses who possess specialized knowledge in some scientific or technical field. They must gear up to cross-examine them effectively, and they must marshal the evidence to rebut their opinions. The drafters of the 1970 amendments to the discovery provisions of the Federal Rules put it well:

---

[1] Gallo v Peninsula Hospital (1985) 164 Cal App 3d 899, 903, 211 Cal Rptr 27, 30; Kennemur v State of California (1982) 133 Cal App 3d 907, 916, 184 Cal Rptr 393, 398.

[A] prohibition against discovery of information held by expert witnesses produces in acute form the very evils that discovery has been created to prevent. Effective cross-examination of an expert witness requires advance preparation. The lawyer even with the help of his own experts frequently cannot anticipate the particular approach his adversary's expert will take or the data on which he will base his judgment on the stand. . . . Similarly, effective rebuttal requires advance knowledge of the line of testimony of the other side. If the latter is foreclosed by a rule against discovery, then the narrowing of issues and elimination of surprise which discovery normally produces are frustrated.[2]

Problems of Timing and Scope: A procedural system that allows discovery of the identity and the opinions of an opponent's experts must address two matters. First, it must choose the appropriate stage in a lawsuit for that discovery. Practical considerations usually lead litigants to postpone this discovery until near the trial. Earlier, factual investigation preoccupies the litigants. Until they find out what these facts are, they may think it premature to seek an expert's reaction to them. Also, experts are extremely expensive. Settlement prospects engender the hope of avoiding substantial out-of-pocket outlays. Moreover, an expert is understandably reluctant to agree to testify without at least a rough idea of when the trial is to take place.

Second, even if an adversary has been consulting with experts all along, formidable legal impediments block discovery of their identity and opinions. The findings and conclusions of an expert consulted by counsel enjoy, at least initially, considerable protection from pretrial discovery. In a few situations, the lawyer-client privilege insulates them from compelled disclosure.[3] In most others, the work product protection prevents discovery absent a showing of exceptional circumstances.[4]

Case Law Temporarily Fills Statutory Gap: The original version of the Federal Rules of Civil Procedure unfortunately contained no special provisions regulating pretrial discovery of an adversary's expert trial witnesses.[5] California's Discovery Act of 1956 inherited this shortcoming from its federal prototype. Accordingly, the California courts had to shape the rules governing discovery in this area. They quickly acknowledged the fundamental need for discovery of the experts an opponent planned to call at trial.[6] They then had to work out just

---

[2] 1970 Advisory Committee Note to amended FRCivP 26(b)(4).

See also Kenney v Superior Court (1967) 255 Cal App 2d 106, 112, 63 Cal Rptr 84, 89.

[3] For a discussion of the extent to which the lawyer-client privilege covers the findings and conclusions of an expert, see §§ 12.11–12.12.

[4] For a discussion of the extent to which the work product protection applies to the findings and conclusions of experts before their designation as trial witnesses, see § 13.15.

[5] Annotation: Pretrial discovery of facts known and opinions held by opponent's experts under Rule 26(b)(4) of Federal Rules of Civil Procedure. 33 ALR Fed 403.

[6] See Sheets v Superior Court (1967) 257 Cal App 2d 1, 11, 64 Cal Rptr 753, 760; Kenney v Superior Court (1967) 255 Cal App 2d 106, 112, 63 Cal Rptr 84, 89; Scotsman Mfg. Co. v

when a party should be able, before the trial itself, to force an adversary to identify its expert trial witnesses. Finally, they had to determine the scope of discovery concerning the anticipated trial testimony of those witnesses.

—Timing of Discovery: The courts were concerned that discovery of an opponent's expert trial witnesses not occur so early that it would let a party "ride free" on an opponent's trial preparation. Accordingly, the *South Tahoe Public Utility District* case[7] held that early in a lawsuit parties may decline not only to select their expert trial witnesses, but also even to reveal the identity of their consultants:

> Were the names of the experts here released *prior* to each party's preparation for trial, full investigation of the factual circumstances would be discouraged and there is a substantial likelihood that [one party] would be able to determine its strategy at trial without independent effort on its part and would be able to base its efforts solely on [another party's] selection of experts.[8]

In the *Sanders* case,[9] the court opined that discovery of an adversary's trial experts should wait until other discovery is completed and the case is otherwise ripe for trial. It indicated that the setting of a trial date is usually the "appropriate stage" to compel the parties to elect which of their consultants would testify at trial:

> [U]pon a showing of good cause made at an appropriate stage of the proceedings, e.g., the pretrial hearing at which time discovery is presumably complete, the case at issue and ready for trial setting, a party may be required to elect whether or not to call the expert as a witness and to disclose such election to his adversary. If he elects to do so, the opposing party shall be granted a reasonable time thereafter within which to conduct appropriate additional discovery directed at securing the desired information.[10]

—Scope of Discovery: As noted above, discovery concerning expert witnesses must consider both the attorney-client privilege and the work product protection. However, the courts held that these protections largely dissolve once a party announces the intention to use a particular expert as a trial witness.[11]

Superior Court (1966) 242 Cal App 2d 527, 532, 51 Cal Rptr 511, 514; Brown v Superior Court (1963) 218 Cal App 2d 430, 442, 32 Cal Rptr 527, 534; but see Dow Chemical Co. v Superior Court (1969) 2 Cal App 3d 1, 10, 82 Cal Rptr 288, 295 [an expert's status as "a potential witness" at trial, standing alone, does not suffice as good cause to depose that expert].

[7] South Tahoe Public Utility Dist. v Superior Court (1979) 90 Cal App 3d 135, 154 Cal Rptr 1.

[8] South Tahoe Public Utility Dist. v Superior Court (1979) 90 Cal App 3d 135, 138, 154 Cal Rptr 1, 2 (original italics).

[9] Sanders v Superior Court (1973) 34 Cal App 3d 270, 109 Cal Rptr 770.

[10] Sanders v Superior Court (1973) 34 Cal App 3d 270, 279, 109 Cal Rptr 770, 777.

[11] Bolles v Superior Court (1971) 15 Cal App 3d 962, 963–964, 93 Cal Rptr 719 [allowing deposition of an expert whom another party plans to use at trial].

[T]he initial status of the expert, as consultant and possible witness, changes its character at that point in the suit when it has become known he will actually testify as a witness. When it becomes reasonably certain an expert will give his professional opinion as a witness on a material matter in dispute, then his opinion has become a factor in the cause. At that point the expert has ceased to be merely a consultant and has become a counter in the litigation, one to be evaluated along with others. Such evaluation properly includes appropriate pretrial discovery.[12]

This right to preview the opinions of an adversary's expert trial witnesses requires no showing that the party seeking discovery lacks equal access to the facts on which those experts base their opinion.[13] Rather it stems from the need to prepare for the trial testimony of those experts.

Overview of the Present Statute: Over a score of years after the adoption of the original Discovery Act, in 1978, the Legislature first enacted an elaborate, although somewhat cryptic, scheme[14] regulating discovery of an opponent's expert trial witnesses. "The clear and obvious purpose of these provisions is to remove the element of surprise from the trial of lawsuits."[15] These provisions, although substantially modified and amplified, became the prototype for provisions in the Discovery Act of 1986.[16] These latter provisions remain largely unchanged.

Under the Civil Discovery Act, discovery of an opponent's expert witnesses becomes available only "[a]fter the setting of the initial trial date for the action."[17] Efforts to obtain the opinions of trial experts earlier than, and outside of, its framework are improper:

Questions to the defendant physicians about their impressions and reasons for their action or lack of action at the time the medical procedure was performed are, of course, entirely appropriate. . . . But . . . questions about after-the-fact opinions and impressions of the physicians stand in quite another light. [¶] . . . We see no reason to disrupt the carefully crafted legislative scheme for the regulation of discovery of the identity, qualifications and opinions of expert witnesses.

---

[12] Swartzman v Superior Court (1964) 231 Cal App 2d 195, 203, 41 Cal Rptr 721, 727.

For a discussion of the decision to call consultants as trial witnesses as working a waiver of any attorney-client privilege that had previously attached to their opinions and reports, see § 12.12.

[13] Bolles v Superior Court (1971) 15 Cal App 3d 962, 963, 93 Cal Rptr 719.

But see Dow Chemical Co. v Superior Court (1969) 2 Cal App 3d 1, 82 Cal Rptr 288.

[14] Former CCP §§ 2037–2037.9, Stats 1978, ch. 1069, § 1.

[15] West Covina Hospital v Superior Court (1986) 41 Cal 3d 846, 860, 226 Cal Rptr 132, 140, 718 P2d 119, 127 (dissenting opinion).

[16] Former CCP § 2034, now redesignated CCP §§ 2034.010–2034.730.

[17] CCP § 2034.210.

For a discussion of whether this statute preempts the trial court's inherent power to order disclosure concerning expert trial witnesses before the setting of the initial trial date, see § 10.2.

The trial court order that the defendant physicians testify at deposition about their present opinion of the medical propriety of their acts, even though they have not [yet] been designated as expert witnesses, would have that effect.[18]

This discovery tool contemplates a simultaneous exchange by the parties of specified "information concerning each other's expert trial witnesses."[19] First and foremost, of course, this "information" includes the identity of all persons, including any party, who will express an expert opinion at the trial. The identification must reach not only those experts who will provide live testimony, but also any doing so by deposition.

Having required the identification of all expert trial witnesses, Section 2034.210 then distinguishes two categories of experts. The first category includes any experts, usually treating physicians, who are *not* parties to the action or employees of a party, or persons brought into the case specifically to give expert testimony. For these experts, a party need only supply their names and addresses.[20]

The second category includes those experts who are parties, who are employees of a party or who have been "retained by a party for the purpose of forming and expressing an opinion in anticipation of the litigation or in preparation for the trial of the action."[21] For these experts, three additional forms of discovery are available. First, the party designating such experts must accompany the list with a declaration setting forth, among other things, the "general substance"[22] of their expected testimony.[23] Second, if the demand for the exchange so specifies, one must also furnish any reports and writings made by the experts in preparing their opinion.[24] Third, the party designating such experts must make them available for a deposition, usually at a site near the forum.[25]

A Separate Discovery Tool: Using the expert trial witness disclosure provisions, a party can compel an opponent to submit a list identifying them, to furnish copies of their reports, and to produce them for a discovery deposition.

---

[18] County of Los Angeles v Superior Court (1990) 224 Cal App 3d 1446, 1455–1457, 274 Cal Rptr 712, 718–719.

[19] CCP § 2034.210.

[20] CCP § 2034.210(a).

For a discussion of the right to depose an expert in this category, see § 10.9.

See also Hurtado v Western Medical Center (1990) 222 Cal App 3d 1198, 1203, 272 Cal Rptr 324, 327.

[21] CCP § 2034.210(b).

[22] CCP § 2034.210(b) referencing CCP § 2034.260(c)(2).

[23] For a discussion of the "expert witness declaration," see § 10.6.

[24] CCP § 2034.210(c).

For a discussion of the types of reports and writings that must be produced, see § 10.8.

[25] CCP § 2034.420.

For a discussion of discovery depositions of designated trial experts, see § 10.9.

The statute, incorporating as it does features of interrogatories, inspection demands, and depositions, is the functional equivalent of a separate tool of discovery. Accordingly, the Civil Discovery Act lists it as the sixth method of discovery.[26]

Of course, if none of the parties to a lawsuit demand the pretrial exchange of expert witness information, the disclosure procedures never come into play. In that event, no party can legitimately claim surprise at trial when another party calls expert witnesses.[27]

Applicability: Like their predecessor,[28] the Civil Discovery Act's provisions for expert trial witness disclosure do not apply to eminent domain proceedings,[29] which have their own special discovery provisions.[30] Moreover, they regulate and restrict only the use of expert witnesses *at trial*. They do not apply to motions for summary judgment, even one made after an exchange of expert witness lists.[31] Therefore, although a party would have no right to call an unlisted expert at trial, that party could still use the testimony, affidavit, or declaration of that expert to support or oppose a summary judgment motion.[32]

Moreover, when one party uses an expert's affidavit or declaration to support or oppose a summary judgment motion, an opponent may want to depose that expert. Trial courts do not routinely permit such depositions, but they have discretion to do so upon a proper showing. "There must be objective facts presented which create a significant question regarding the validity of the affidavit or declaration which, if successfully pursued, will impeach the foundational basis of the affidavit or declaration in question."[33] The authorization of such depositions is governed by the summary judgment statute,[34] and not by the provisions of the Civil Discovery Act.

§ 10.2   Initiating the Exchange Procedures

Discovery via a compelled exchange of expert witness information is self-executing: leave of court is not required to use it.[1] However, this exchange is not automatic; one of the parties must demand it.

Based on First Setting of a Trial Date: In contrast to the other five methods,[2]

---

[26] CCP § 2019.010(f).

[27] In re Marriage of Hoffmeister (1984) 161 Cal App 3d 1163, 1171 n6, 208 Cal Rptr 345, 350 n6. Cf. Foster v Gillette Co. (1979) 100 Cal App 3d 569, 578, 161 Cal Rptr 134, 139.

[28] Former CCP § 2037.9, Stats 1978, ch. 1069, § 1.

[29] CCP § 2034.010.

[30] CCP §§ 1258.210–1258.290.

[31] Kennedy v Modesto City Hospital (1990) 221 Cal App 3d 575, 581, 270 Cal Rptr 544.

[32] See CCP § 437c(h).

[33] St. Mary Medical Center v Superior Court (1996) 50 Cal App 4th 1531, 1540–1541, 58 Cal Rptr 2d 182, 188.

[34] CCP § 437c.

[1] CCP § 2034.220.

[2] Depositions, interrogatories, inspection demands, compulsory medical examinations, admission requests.

this discovery device is not available until the final stages of a lawsuit. No party may invoke its procedures before "the setting of the 'initial trial date' for the action."[3]

—**Premature Demands:** In the *Zellerino* case,[4] the defendants "jumped the gun" by serving an expert witness demand four days before the trial setting conference. They did not discover this mistake until it was too late to comply with the statutory timetable. Section 473 of the Code of Civil Procedure authorizes a trial court "in furtherance of justice" to allow a party to correct a "mistake" in any "proceeding." The court ruled that a discovery request is a "proceeding" within the meaning of this statute. Section 2034.220, which specifies the time for serving a demand for expert witness disclosure, contains no language either permitting or precluding relief from a premature demand. Therefore, the court held that trial judges retain their discretion under Section 473 to grant relief in a proper case.

Deadline for Making Demand: Section 2034.220 contains a deadline for initiating the process: a party must demand the exchange no later than 10 days *after* the setting of the initial date for trial, or 70 days *before* that trial date, whichever is *later*. This deadline is based on the *initial* trial date; a later order of a new date for the first trial of a case does not by itself reopen a previously lost opportunity to invoke this discovery device:

> By referring to the date "initially" set for trial or the "initial" trial date, the Legislature clearly inferred subsequent, continued, new, rescheduled, or other "non-initial" trial dates might be set but the controlling date for purposes of discovery cut off is the initial, i.e., first trial date set, not a date which might be set later.[5]

An untimely demand for expert witness disclosure is ineffective. The parties are as free to call undisclosed experts as they would be if no disclosure demand was served at all.[6]

Order for a New Trial: Two appellate courts have ruled that the ordering of a new *trial* (as opposed to a new *date* for the first trial) entitles a party to institute or re-institute this form of discovery. In the *Guzman* case,[7] the trial court had granted a new trial because the jury's award was excessive. Plaintiff then sought leave to augment his expert witness list. The denial of this motion was an abuse of discretion:

---

[3] CCP § 2034.210.

[4] Zellerino v Brown (1991) 235 Cal App 3d 1097, 1104–1107, 1 Cal Rptr 2d 222, 226–228.

[5] Beverly Hospital v Superior Court (1993) 19 Cal App 4th 1289, 1292–1293, 24 Cal Rptr 2d 238, 239–240.

[6] Zavala v Board of Trustees (1993) 16 Cal App 4th 1755, 1761 n3, 20 Cal Rptr 2d 768, 771 n3 [because their demand for expert witness disclosure was made less than 70 days before initial trial date, defendants in medical malpractice case could not bar the plaintiff's use of experts on the ground that he had not disclosed them until trial].

[7] Guzman v Superior Court (1993) 19 Cal App 4th 705, 23 Cal Rptr 2d 585.

The trial court [at the first trial] found insufficient evidence of damages because no expert witness linked [the plaintiff's] belated thumb injury to his initial broken arm. But to order a new trial for this deficiency and then prohibit its remedy—by preventing plaintiff from calling expert witnesses—is an unwarranted catch-22. We find nothing in [Sections §§ 2034.010–2034.730] which requires such a circular result.[8]

Similarly, in the *Beverly Hospital* case,[9] a hung jury forced a retrial of a medical malpractice case. The plaintiff promptly served a new demand for an exchange. She then submitted a list that included six experts who were not on her original list. The defendant hospital objected to this new list as untimely. In its view the Legislature had inextricably linked this discovery device to the original date set for the *first* trial in the case. The plaintiff countered that a lawsuit does not necessarily have a single, everlasting, "initial" trial date, but may have several "initial" trial dates, each one corresponding to a different trial of the action. This argument prevailed with the appellate court: "[T]he phrase "initial trial date" should be interpreted to refer to the first date set for each trial in the action, not to the first trial date set in the action."[10] The court also commented that it would reach the same result if the new trial order resulted from a reversal on appeal.[11]

In the *Fairmont Ins. Co.* case,[12] the Supreme Court considered the meaning of "date initially set for the trial of the action" after a mistrial, an order granting a new trial, or a remand for a new trial after reversal of a judgment on appeal. Agreeing with the *Guzman* and *Beverly Hospital* cases, the Court held that in such cases discovery is reopened and the cutoff date is calculated based on the date initially set for the *new* trial.

—**Timetable for Demand:** The *Guzman* and the *Beverly Hospital* cases reached the same conclusion concerning the revived availability of expert witness disclosure once a new trial is ordered. However, although decided by the same division of the Second District Court of Appeal, the two opinions differ over the applicability of the statutory timetable in Section 2033.220 in such a situation. On the one hand, *Guzman* noted that the plaintiff moved to augment the expert witness list "[w]ell before the new trial date,"[13] thus "affording [the defendants] ample time to depose those witnesses."[14] The court did not appear troubled by

---

[8] Guzman v Superior Court (1993) 19 Cal App 4th 705, 708, 23 Cal Rptr 2d 585, 586.

[9] Beverly Hospital v Superior Court (1993) 19 Cal App 4th 1289, 24 Cal Rptr 2d 238.

[10] Beverly Hospital v Superior Court (1993) 19 Cal App 4th 1289, 1292, 24 Cal Rptr 2d 238, 239.

[11] Beverly Hospital v Superior Court (1993) 19 Cal App 4th 1289, 1295, 24 Cal Rptr 2d 238, 241.

[12] Fairmont Ins. Co. v Superior Court (2000) 22 Cal 4th 245, 254–255, 92 Cal Rptr 2d 70, 991 P2d 156.

[13] Guzman v Superior Court (1993) 19 Cal App 4th 705, 707, 23 Cal Rptr 2d 585.

[14] Guzman v Superior Court (1993) 19 Cal App 4th 705, 708, 23 Cal Rptr 2d 585, 586.

the filing of this motion less than 70 days before the date set for the retrial. On the other hand, in the *Beverly Hospital* case, the court noted that the "subsequent demand for exchange of expert witness information was timely because it was made more than 70 days before the date set for retrial."[15]

No Power to Alter Statutory Deadlines: The trial court cannot tinker with the statutory deadlines for the demand. In the *St. Vincent Medical Center Case*,[16] decided under the 1978 provisions, the trial court's sua sponte order drastically shortened the time for demanding expert witness information: it required service of the demand within five days after the setting of the trial date. This reduction of the statutory deadline exceeds the trial court's power:

> We cannot presume the Legislature has indulged in meaningless acts in enacting a statute providing a comprehensive procedure for the exchange of lists of expert witnesses and including therein specific time limitations. Accordingly, we view the time limits . . . as permitting no deviation, and hence the shorter time limits in the [court order] must be held void and unenforceable.[17]

The *County of Los Angeles* case later reached the same conclusion under the 1986 Discovery Act:

> The Civil Discovery Act of 1986 continues to expressly provide that the court may reduce only the time for the date of exchange of the expert [witness] information, not the time for the service of the demand for exchange. [CCP § 2034(b)–(c), now redesignated CCP § 2034.220.] This distinction is logical because service of the demand is the triggering step for the exchange of information about expert witnesses.[18]

Exclusivity of Disclosure Provisions: Although the expert witness disclosure procedures themselves are not available before "the setting of the initial trial date,"[19] nothing within them expressly provides that they are the exclusive vehicle for obtaining discovery about expert trial witnesses. In 1973, several years before the Legislature had first expressly provided for such disclosure, the *Sanders* case had held that the trial court had inherent power to order disclosure of trial experts "at an appropriate stage of the proceedings."[20] However, in the same breath, the court suggested that this should occur around the time the trial date is fixed.

---

[15] Beverly Hospital v Superior Court (1993) 19 Cal App 4th 1289, 1291, 24 Cal Rptr 2d 238.

[16] St. Vincent Medical Center v Superior Court (1984) 160 Cal App 3d 1030, 206 Cal Rptr 840 [decided under former CCP § 2037, the predecessor of CCP § 2034.220].

[17] St. Vincent Medical Center v Superior Court (1984) 160 Cal App 3d 1030, 1033–1034, 206 Cal Rptr 840, 842.

[18] County of Los Angeles v Superior Court (1990) 224 Cal App 3d 1446, 1456, 274 Cal Rptr 712, 719.

[19] CCP § 2034.210.

[20] Sanders v Superior Court (1973) 34 Cal App 3d 270, 279, 109 Cal Rptr 770, 777.

This is essentially the approach that taken by Section 2034.220. Given this virtual codification of *Sanders* ruling, the question arose whether it has preempted a trial court's power to order disclosure of expert witness information before the case has a trial date. In the *County of Los Angeles* case,[21] before the setting of a trial date, plaintiffs in an obstetrical malpractice case sought to depose the defendant doctors concerning their "after-the-fact opinions and impressions"[22] about the procedures they had used during the delivery. Such discovery was appropriate, they argued, because the defense would likely designate the defendant doctors as expert trial witnesses. The appellate court held that this probability did not matter; discovery of their present opinions must await the procedures, including the timetable, of former Section 2034:

> We see no reason to disrupt the carefully crafted legislative scheme for the regulation of discovery of the identity, qualifications and opinions of expert witnesses. The trial court order that the physician defendants testify at depositions about their present opinion of the medical propriety of their acts, even though they have not been designated as expert witnesses, would have that effect.[23]

Adjusting for Complex Cases: In a particular lawsuit the number of parties or the nature of the issues requiring expert testimony could make expert trial witness disclosure desirable much earlier than the times spelled out in the statute. Although Section 2034.220 appears to preempt judicial discretion to compel a disclosure before the initial setting of a trial date, a trial court may still accommodate such an exceptional case. Although unable to shorten the time for making the *demand* for expert witness disclosure,[24] it may accelerate the date for the *exchange* itself.[25] Or the court, on a showing that the time left after the exchange for deposing the designated experts is too short, may entertain a motion continue the trial date and extend the time for completion of discovery.[26]

§ 10.3   Contents and Effect of Demand for Exchange

Must Reference Chapter 18: The demand for an exchange of expert witness information is a simple document. Section 2034.230[1] specifies its contents. It

---

[21] County of Los Angeles v Superior Court (1990) 224 Cal App 3d 1446, 274 Cal Rptr 712.

[22] County of Los Angeles v Superior Court (1990) 224 Cal App 3d 1446, 1456, 274 Cal Rptr 712, 718.

[23] County of Los Angeles v Superior Court (1990) 224 Cal App 3d 1446, 1457, 274 Cal Rptr 712, 719.

See also South Tahoe Public Utility Dist. v Superior Court (1979) 90 Cal App 3d 135, 139, 154 Cal Rptr 1, 3.

[24] St. Vincent Medical Center v Superior Court (1984) 160 Cal App 3d 1030, 1033–1034, 206 Cal Rptr 840, 842.

[25] CCP §§ 2034.230(b) and 2034.250(b)(2).

[26] See CCP § 2024.250(b).

[1] CCP § 2034.230.

must start with the case title, identify the party making the demand and cite Chapter 18.[2] However, unlike the 1978 statute,[3] it need not include a warning that noncompliance waives the right to call expert witnesses.

Specification of Statutory Date for Exchange: The demand must specify the date for the exchange of expert witness information. Section 2034.230 sets this date as either 50 days *before* the initial trial date, or 20 days *after* service of the demand, whichever is *closer* to the initial trial date.[4] In specifying the date of exchange, counsel should remember that mailed service of the demand extends the statutory time, usually by five days.[5]

Reports of Experts: In addition to the identity of all expert trial witnesses, a party can demand a copy of the reports and writings submitted by those who were specially retained experts.[6] A party who wishes to exercise this right should explicitly include these reports in the demand document.[7]

Demand Now Effective as to All Parties: The initial version of the statutes regulating the exchange of expert witness information provided that "any party may serve on any party" a demand for an exchange of expert witness information.[8] In the *West Hills Hospital* case,[9] two doctor defendants in a medical malpractice case directed an exchange demand only to the plaintiff. They served an informational copy of this demand on the remaining defendant, a hospital. In complying with the demand, the plaintiff sent a copy of his witness list not only to the two defendants who had made the demand, but also to the defendant hospital. When the hospital did not reciprocate with a list of its experts, the plaintiff took the position that this failure precluded it from calling any experts at the trial. The court held, however, that "only the party who makes the demand and the party on whom it is made are required to [exchange witness lists] and not other parties on whom [informational] copies of the demand may be served."[10]

Under Section 2034.240, this is no longer true. The party making the demand must serve it on "all parties who have appeared in the action."[11] Moreover, the

---

[2] Chapter 18 of the Civil Discovery Act contains the 25 statutes (CCP §§ 2034.010–2034.730) regulating Simultaneous Exchange of Expert Witness Information.

[3] See former CCP § 2037, Stats 1978, ch. 1069, § 1.

[4] On a showing of good cause to do so, the trial court can order the exchange to take place at an earlier or a later date. CCP § 2034.230(b).

See Zellerino v Brown (1991) 235 Cal App 3d 1097, 1108–1109, 1 Cal Rptr 2d 222, 228–229.

[5] CCP § 2016.050, referencing CCP § 1013(a).

[6] See CCP § 2034.210(c).

[7] For a discussion of which reports and writings of experts are discoverable under Section 2034, see § 10.8.

[8] Former CCP § 2037(a), Stats 1978, ch. 1069, § 1.

[9] West Hills Hospital v Superior Court (1979) 98 Cal App 3d 656, 159 Cal Rptr 645.

[10] West Hills Hospital v Superior Court (1979) 98 Cal App 3d 656, 660, 159 Cal Rptr 645, 647.

[11] CCP § 2034.240.

demand is effective against "all parties."[12] Each must now participate in the exchange of expert witness information.

Custody of Original: The original of the demand document is not filed with the court.[13] Instead, the party making the demand must retain both it and the original of the proof of service until six months after the final disposition of the case. At this point, unless one of the parties has obtained a court order to the contrary, the custodian party may destroy both originals.[14]

§ 10.4   Protective Orders

Grounds for Protective Orders: Under Section 2034.250 the trial court can issue a protective order when compliance with a demand would cause a party "unwarranted annoyance, embarrassment, or oppression, or undue burden or expense."[1] This provision differs from its predecessor in the 1956 Discovery Act[2] in three minor respects. First, it adds "undue burden and expense" to the original grounds of annoyance, embarrassment, and oppression. Second, it uses "unwarranted" to underscore that mere "annoyance, embarrassment, or oppression" is not a ground for escaping the duty to exchange expert witness information. Third, it contains a nonexclusive list of six protective orders that a recipient of an exchange demand may request.

—Untimely Demand: Section 2034.220 regulates the timing of the demand for expert witness information: no later than 10 days *after* the setting of the initial trial date, or 70 days *before* the initial trial date, whichever is *later.*[3] If a party serves a tardy demand, other parties can move for a protective order.[4] Similarly, in the rare case where a party serves a demand before the court has set an initial trial date, a motion for a protective order is the appropriate way to attack it.[5]

—Changing Date of Exchange: Section 2034.230 regulates the date that the demand must specify for the exchange: 50 days *before* the initial trial date, or 20 days *after* service of the demand, whichever is *closer* to that trial date.[6] However, for good cause the trial court may change the specified date of the exchange to an earlier or a later one.[7] A party seeking to accelerate or postpone the exchange should seek a protective order.[8]

---

[12] CCP §§ 2034.210, 2034.240, and 2034.260(a).

[13] CCP § 2034.290(a).

[14] CCP § 2034.290(b).

[1] CCP § 2034.250(b).

[2] Former CCP § 2037.8, Stats 1978, ch. 1069, § 1.

[3] For a discussion of the timing of a demand for the exchange of expert witness information, see § 10.2.

[4] CCP § 2034.250(b)(1).

[5] Zellerino v Brown (1991) 235 Cal App 3d 1097, 1109, 1 Cal Rptr 2d 222, 229.

[6] For a discussion of the statutory date for the exchange of expert witness information, see § 10.3.

[7] CCP § 2034.230(b).

[8] CCP § 2034.250(b)(2).

—Ground Rules for Exchange: Section 2034.260 contains only a barebones description of the mechanics for the actual exchange: it occurs either at a meeting of counsel or by a mailing on or before the specified date. In a particular case a party may want to flesh out these procedures. For good reason, the trial court may enter a protective order that specifies certain conditions for the exchange.[9]

—Changing Time and Place for Exchange of Reports: Section 2034.270 requires the parties to turn over reports and writings simultaneously with the exchange of other required information.[10] In a particular case there may be good reason for allowing the exchange of reports and writings to occur later or elsewhere. A motion for a protective order is the appropriate step for a party who has some good reason for segregating this part of the exchange.[11]

—Limiting the Number of Expert Witnesses: The Discovery Commission was concerned about cumulative expert witness testimony. It proposed that each party be limited to the designation, as a matter of right, of no more than two employed or specially retained experts "on any issue in the action."[12] Influenced in part by the Commission's inability to define "issue" in its proposal, the Legislature rejected any presumptive limit on the number of experts. Instead, it authorized the trial court to control case-by-case the number of expert witnesses. Where there are several parties to a lawsuit, it may issue a protective order that both aggregates into a "side" those with the same interest in a particular issue and requires that court-created "side" to designate trial experts.[13] In addition, the court may order a party or a side to reduce the number of the specially retained or employee experts that it has designated.[14]

—Other Grounds: The list of six protective orders in Section 2034.250 is illustrative, not exclusive. "For good cause shown" the trial court can issue a protective order to prevent any form of "unwarranted annoyance, embarrassment, or oppression, or undue burden and expense." In the *Torres* case,[15] for example, a defendant in a medical malpractice case designated as an expert trial witness a doctor who had previously treated the plaintiff. Although the appellate court saw nothing wrong with this, it recognized the need to ensure that the doctor did not disclose to the defense any privileged information. Accordingly, it

---

Cf. Zellerino v Brown (1991) 235 Cal App 3d 1097, 1108–1109, 1 Cal Rptr 2d 222, 228–229 [trial court may change erroneously specified date where error was innocent and caused no prejudice].

[9] CCP § 2034.250(b)(3).

[10] CCP § 2034.270.

For a discussion of the duty to provide reports of expert trial witnesses, see § 10.8.

[11] CCP § 2034.250(b)(4).

[12] Proposed Civil Discovery Act of 1986, Section 2034(b), Appendix D.

[13] CCP § 2034(b)(5).

Cf. CCP § 231(c) [in multi-party civil cases, the trial court must create sides for the exercise of peremptory challenges].

[14] CCP § 2034.250(b)(6).

[15] Torres v Superior Court (1990) 221 Cal App 3d 181, 188, 270 Cal Rptr 401, 405.

directed the trial court to temporarily prohibit *ex parte* interviews by the defense and to require that all communication between the doctor and defense counsel take place via formal discovery procedures.[16]

Duty to Meet and Confer: Before moving for a protective order, the party receiving an exchange demand must try to work out informally the points of dispute with the demanding party. A declaration setting forth these efforts must accompany the motion.[17]

Monetary Sanction: A party who unsuccessfully makes or opposes a motion for a protective order should expect a monetary sanction unless that party can convince the court that, despite this lack of success, "substantial justification" existed for its position.[18]

"Objection" to Demand Not Allowed: Each of the other five discovery methods—depositions,[19] interrogatories,[20] inspections,[21] medical examinations,[22] and admission requests[23] —provides for an "objection" to challenge an unauthorized use of that device. These other five methods reserve the protective order for situations where an otherwise permissible use of the method will nonetheless cause "unwarranted annoyance, embarrassment, or oppression, or undue burden or expense".

However, the sixth discovery method—exchange of expert witness information—contains no provision for an "objection." In the *Zellerino* case,[24] for example, a defendant, mistakenly believing that a local "fast track" rule applied to the case, served a demand for an exchange of expert witness information before the court had set an initial trial date. Instead of moving for a protective order,[25] plaintiff ignored the demand until four days after the date it specified for the exchange, and then served an "objection" to it.[26]

The *Zellerino* court held that a plaintiff cannot raise a defendant's procedural misstep by an objection instead of a motion for a protective order. It noted that a party must seek a protective order "promptly."[27] There would be no such

---

[16] See also Province v Center for Women's Health and Family Birth (1993) 20 Cal App 4th 1673, 1684–1685, 25 Cal Rptr 2d 667, 674.

Cf. Easton, Can We Talk? Removing Counterproductive Ethical Restraints Upon Ex Parte Communication Between Attorneys and Adverse Expert Witnesses, 76 Ind. L.J. 647 (2001).

[17] CCP § 2034.250(a).

[18] CCP § 2034.250(d).

[19] CCP §§ 2025.410 and 2025.460.

[20] CCP § 2030.210.

[21] CCP § 2031.060.

[22] CCP §§ 2032.230 and 2032.240.

[23] CCP § 2033.210.

[24] Zellerino v Brown (1991) 235 Cal App 3d 1097, 1 Cal Rptr 2d 222.

[25] See CCP § 2034.250(b)(1).

[26] Zellerino v Brown (1991) 235 Cal App 3d 1097, 1101–1102, 1 Cal Rptr 2d 222, 224.

[27] CCP § 2034.250(a).

restriction on the timing of an objection, at least one that the statute itself does not regulate. Moreover, a party contemplating a motion for a protective order must consider the prospect of a monetary sanction if the court decides there was no substantial justification for it. The deterrent effect of this sanction might be lost if one could raise a discovery issue by an objection that the statute does not mention. In addition, a protective order motion is subject to a "meet and confer" requirement; an objection would not be. Finally, if a party were free to attack the timeliness of an exchange demand by an objection, this would make redundant the explicit provision for a protective order directing that a "demand be quashed because it was not timely served."[28]

§ 10.5   The Exchange Itself

Section 2034.360 envisions a mutual and simultaneous exchange of expert trial witness information.[1] To achieve these goals, it specifies a common date for the exchange: 50 days before the initial trial date, or within 20 days after the demand is made, whichever is closer to the initial trial date.[2] Where the demand is served by mail, the party serving the demand should increase this period, usually by five days.[3] The exchange may take place at a meeting of counsel, but any party may submit the required information by mail on or before that date.[4] Unlike the original law,[5] all parties who have appeared in the action must participate in the exchange.[6]

Depending on the categories of experts designated, a party may be supplying three different types of information: (1) a list identifying its trial experts,[7] (2) an expert witness declaration concerning them,[8] and (3) their reports and writings.[9]

§ 10.6   List of Expert Witnesses

Who Must be Listed: The list of expert witnesses must contain the name and address of any individuals from whom the party submitting it contemplates eliciting an expert opinion.[1] If that party himself or herself expects to testify

---

[28] CCP § 2034.250(b)(1).

[1] The trial court cannot, even in a complex case, issue a case management order mandating *unilateral* disclosure of an expert medical witness's identity, curriculum vitae, and opinion. Hernandez v Superior Court (2003) 112 Cal App 4th 285, 296–300, 4 Cal Rptr 3d 883, 892–895.

[2] CCP § 2034.230(b).

[3] CCP § 2016.050, referencing CCP § 1013(a).

[4] CCP § 2034.260(a).

[5] See West Hills Hospital v Superior Court (1979) 98 Cal App 3d 656, 660, 159 Cal Rptr 645, 647 [requiring participation only by the party serving and the party receiving the demand].

[6] CCP § 2034.260(a).

[7] For discussion of the contents of the expert witness list, see § 10.6.

[8] For a discussion of the contents of the expert witness declaration, see § 10.7.

[9] For a discussion of the duty to exchange reports of expert witnesses, see § 10.8.

[1] CCP §§ 2034.210(a) and 2034.260(b)(1).

as an expert, his or her name must also be listed.[2] If that party intends to offer expert opinions contained in a deposition, the deponent's name should be listed.[3]

Each party should list the experts that it plans to call at trial. A party may not just state that it reserves the right to call any expert witness listed by another party:

> This would create a trap for the unwary. Cautious attorneys would demand to take the deposition of every expert listed by all parties even if a party settles or is dismissed. This would increase the already high costs of litigation, raise legal malpractice insurance rates, and would encourage waste. Full and timely disclosure of expert witnesses encourages pretrial settlements; a salutary effect which would be lost if we were to condone the practice of adopting other parties' expert witnesses in such a wholesale manner.[4]

—**Percipient Experts:** A party must list any person whose trial testimony will include an expert opinion. If that expert is (1) a party to the case, (2) employed by a party, or (3) someone retained to form and express an opinion, the designating party must also supply an expert witness declaration.[5]

If an expert does not fall into any of these three categories, the furnishing of the expert's name and address suffices; no expert witness declaration is necessary.[6] The most common example of such an expert is a plaintiff's treating physician. As the Supreme Court held in the *Schreiber* case:

> A treating physician is a percipient expert, but that does not mean that his testimony is limited only to personal observations. Rather, like any other expert, he may provide both fact and opinion testimony. [W]hat distinguishes the treating physician from a retained expert is not the content of the testimony, but the context in which he became familiar with the plaintiff's injuries that were ultimately the subject of litigation, and which form the factual basis for the medical opinion. . . .A treating physician is not consulted for litigation purposes, but rather learns of the plaintiff's injuries and medical history because of the underlying physician-patient relationship.[7]

> [T]o the extent a physician acquires personal knowledge of the relevant facts independently of the litigation, . . . no expert witness declaration

---

[2] CCP §§ 2034.210(a) and 2034.260(b)(1).

[3] CCP §§ 2034.210(a) and 2034.260(b)(1).

For a discussion of the use of video recorded depositions of experts in lieu of live testimony at trial, see § 2.41.

[4] Gallo v Peninsula Hospital (1985) 164 Cal App 3d 899, 904, 211 Cal Rptr 27, 30–31.

[5] For a discussion of the contents of an expert witness declaration, see § 10.7.

[6] See CCP § 2034.210(b).

[7] Schreiber v Estate of Kiser (1999) 22 Cal 4th 31, 35–36, 91 Cal Rptr 2d 293, 297, 989 P2d 720, 724.

is required, and he may testify as to any opinions formed on the basis of facts independently acquired and informed by his training, skill, and experience. This may well include opinions regarding causation and standard of care because such issues are inherent in a physician's work.[8]

Even if a party plans to elicit *only* an expert's perceptions, and *not* his or her *opinions based on those perceptions*, strictly speaking, that party need not include that person on the expert witness list.[9] However, since the line between fact and opinion is often thin, slippery and tricky, the safer course is to list any witness who has relevant expertise.

Although a party need not include an expert witness declaration in order to elicit opinion testimony from a treating physician, the party must separately name each treating physician who will be asked to express an opinion at trial. A blanket designation of "any and all of the plaintiff's past or present examining and/or treating physicians" does not suffice, even if the identities of those physicians had already been disclosed during other discovery in the case. A trial court may bar opinion testimony from any treating physician who has not been identified by name in the expert witness designation.[10]

"No Expert Opinions" Statement: A party who has no present intention to present expert testimony must submit a statement to that effect.[11] The submission of this statement will preserve that party's right to later retain and designate experts upon learning that an adversary is planning to call an expert in a certain area.[12]

§ 10.7 Expert Witness Declaration

Experts to Whom Applicable: Where a listed expert is a party, a party's employee, or someone specially retained "for the purpose of forming and expressing an opinion in anticipation of litigation or in preparation for the trial of the action,"[1] the exchange of expert witness information has an added dimension. A party designating such experts must submit a declaration containing specified information about them. This declaration is made not by the expert, but by the attorney for the party who plans to call that expert as a trial witness.[2]

---

[8] Schreiber v Estate of Kiser (1999) 22 Cal 4th 31, 39, 91 Cal Rptr 2d 293, 300, 989 P2d 720, 727.

See also Kalaba v Gray (2002) 95 Cal App 4th 1416, 116 Cal Rptr 2d 570; Huntley v Foster (1995) 35 Cal App 4th 753, 41 Cal Rptr 2d 358; Hurtado v Western Medical Center (1990) 222 Cal App 3d 1198, 1203, 272 Cal Rptr 324, 327.

[9] Broffman v Newman (1989) 213 Cal App 3d 252, 262–263, 261 Cal Rptr 532, 539–540.

See also Davoll v Webb (1999, CA10 Colo) 194 F3d 1116, 1138.

[10] Kalaba v Gray (2002) 95 Cal App 4th 1416, 1422–1424, 116 Cal Rptr 2d 570. Cf. Gottschall v Daly (2002) 96 Cal App 4th 479, 484, 116 Cal Rptr 2d 882, 886.

[11] CCP § 2034.260(b)(2).

[12] For a discussion of the right to supplement an expert witness designation, see § 10.11.

[1] CCP § 2034.210(b).

[2] CCP § 2034.260(c).

A party who appears *pro se* must sign the expert witness declaration.

A party cannot avoid this obligation simply by naming someone already designated by another party. "By listing the experts of her opponent [plaintiff] assumed the burden of providing declarations regarding the expected expert testimony."[3]

In contrast, no declaration is required for nonparty experts who have acquired their information as percipient witnesses, and whose training, skill, and experience enable to them to form opinions concerning what they have perceived.[4]

However, in some situations, notably medical malpractice cases, the testimony of treating physicians may have an added dimension. They may be asked not only to describe the treatment that they themselves provided, but also to opine about the caliber of the treatment rendered by the defendant. This distinction was stressed in the *Plunkett* case:

> [T]he justification for categorizing a treating physician as a "fact witness" for purposes of discovery dissolves when his or her intended testimony extends beyond what the treating physician has observed, concluded and done, and addresses what another physician should have observed, concluded and done. [¶] When a treating physician intends to testify as to what standard of practice applies generally to practitioners in the same or a related field, or whether the standard has been breached in a particular case, such opinion testimony is extraneous to that physician's treatment of the patient; is not based solely on the treating physician's personal observation of the patient; necessarily relies on information provided by the party; and is rendered for the purpose of trial rather than treatment.[5]

Presuming that a plaintiff may not compel an unwilling treating physician to form and testify to an opinion about another doctor's care, the *Plunkett* court concluded "that a party in a medical malpractice action who elicits standard of care testimony from a treating physician necessarily does so pursuant to an agreement that the physician will exceed the ordinary role of a treating physician by providing other expert testimony for purpose of the litigation."[6] The physician then becomes "retained" under Section 2034.210,[7] even if the agreement includes no special remuneration. Accordingly, to elicit such testimony, a party must provide an expert witness declaration describing the general nature of the anticipated testimony. Any other interpretation would leave an opponent open to surprise at trial.

---

[3] Zellerino v Brown (1991) 235 Cal App 3d 1097, 1116, 1 Cal Rptr 2d 222, 234.

[4] Schreiber v Estate of Kiser (1999) 22 Cal 4th 31, 35–36, 91 Cal Rptr 2d 293, 297, 989 P2d 720, 724.

See also Kalaba v Gray (2002) 95 Cal App 4th 1416, 116 Cal Rptr 2d 570.

[5] Plunkett v Spaulding (1997) 52 Cal App 4th 114, 128, 60 Cal Rptr 2d 377, 385.

[6] Plunkett v Spaulding (1997) 52 Cal App 4th 114, 129, 60 Cal Rptr 2d 377, 386.

[7] CCP § 2034.210(b).

Expert's Qualifications: The declaration must address the expert's background. It should set forth a "brief narrative statement of the qualifications of each expert."[8] The Evidence Code describes the "qualifications" of an expert; they include the "special knowledge, skill, experience, training, and education"[9] that supports an individual's standing to express an opinion on the subject matter of his or her trial testimony. No reported case has yet considered the adequacy of an opponent's description of the "qualifications" of a designated expert witness.[10]

General Substance of Expected Testimony: The declaration must also address the expert's expected testimony. In this regard, the Discovery Commission proposed a comprehensive disclosure requirement that included: (1) a description of the information that the expert relied on; (2) a statement of the subject the expert would address; (3) any facts or opinions about that subject to which the expert would testify; and (4) a summary of the basis for the expert's opinions.[11] This detailed disclosure would have reduced the need to depose the expert, and prevented the designation of experts whom a party has not already contacted about testifying in the case.

The Legislature ultimately rejected the Commission's elaborate disclosure proposal. It evidently doubted that even this level of disclosure would induce parties to forego pretrial depositions of an opponent's expert trial witnesses. Moreover, it considered that there were more effective methods to curb wholesale listing of experts who had not yet agreed to testify. Instead, the Legislature retained[12] the requirement of only a "brief narrative statement of the general substance of the testimony that the expert is expected to give."[13] Thus the Legislature has left it to the courts to decide the level of disclosure implied by the phrase "general substance."

—Examples: Two cases decided under the identical wording of the 1978 statute indicate that it is a minimal requirement. In *Sprague v Equifax, Inc.,*[14] the expert witness declaration stated only that the trial testimony of a physician[15] would cover "the medical care and treatment rendered to plaintiff as well as [his]

---

[8] CCP § 2034.260(c)(1).

This wording is substantially the same as former CCP § 2037.3, Stats 1978, ch. 1069, § 1.

[9] See Evid Code § 801(b).

[10] Cf. Williams v Volkswagenwerk Aktiengesellschaft (1986) 180 Cal App 3d 1244, 1258 n5, 226 Cal Rptr 306, 312 n5 [plaintiff described three of her experts simply as "an independent metallurgist;" "an independent metallurgy expert" and "a professor at UCLA;" and "a mechanical engineer" and "independent accident reconstruction expert."]

[11] Proposed Civil Discovery Act of 1986, Section 2034(g)(2), Appendix D.

[12] Former CCP § 2037.3, Stats 1978, ch. 1069, § 1.

[13] CCP § 2034.260(c)(2).

[14] Sprague v Equifax, Inc. (1985) 166 Cal App 3d 1012, 213 Cal Rptr 69.

[15] The original statute required disclosure of the general substance of the anticipated testimony of *all* designated expert witnesses. Former CCP § 2037.3, Stats 1978, ch. 1069, § 1.

diagnoses and prognoses of plaintiff's physical condition."[16] The court considered this meager description a sufficient disclosure to permit the following trial testimony:

> [The doctor] testified that he had examined plaintiff at the request of the workers' compensation insurer and gave his findings and interpretation of the various tests and diagnostic procedures he had used. He testified on the general diagnosis of disc disease; explained medical terminology relevant to plaintiff's treatment; testified to his interpretation of other doctor's reports which he had seen in making his diagnosis; testified to symptoms of disc disease; answered hypothetical questions about what his diagnosis would be, given certain symptoms; and gave his evaluation of [another doctor's] X-rays and X-ray report; his evaluation of X-rays and a medical test taken by other doctors after the disability period; and his disagreement with [the other doctor's] diagnosis.[17]

In a products liability case,[18] a plaintiff submitted the following skimpy descriptions[19] of the "general substance" of her experts' expected trial testimony:

> [A metallurgist] is expected to testify regarding metallurgical issues concerning the trailing arm in question and cause of accident herein.

> [Another metallurgist] is expected to testify that the trailing arm which forms the subject of this lawsuit was defective when sold and was improperly designed, manufactured, tested, inspected and serviced. He will further testify as to the cause of plaintiff's injuries and damage to the plaintiff's vehicle.

> [An accident reconstruction expert] will testify as to the nature of the accident and design, manufacture, installation, and negligent inspection and maintenance issues concerning the subject accident.

The court considered that this level of disclosure "meets the requirements of former] section 2037.3."[20] Anything more, such as a "disclosure of specific facts and opinions . . . would defy the clear language of the section and the practical dynamics of intelligent trial preparation."[21]

The first two cases decided under the 1986 Act initially reinforced the conclusion that a very general description of the intended testimony will suffice.

---

16 Sprague v Equifax, Inc. (1985) 166 Cal App 3d 1012, 1040, 213 Cal Rptr 69, 87.

17 Sprague v Equifax, Inc. (1985) 166 Cal App 3d 1012, 1040–1041, 213 Cal Rptr 69, 87.

18 Williams v Volkswagenwerk A.G. (1986) 180 Cal App 3d 1244, 226 Cal Rptr 306.

19 Williams v Volkswagenwerk A.G. (1986) 180 Cal App 3d 1244, 1258 n5, 226 Cal Rptr 306, 312 n5.

20 Williams v Volkswagenwerk A.G. (1986) 180 Cal App 3d 1244, 1258, 226 Cal Rptr 306, 312.

21 Williams v Volkswagenwerk A.G. (1986) 180 Cal App 3d 1244, 1258, 226 Cal Rptr 306, 312. See also Jones v Moore (2000) 80 Cal App 4th 557, 95 Cal Rptr 2d 216.

In the *Martinez* case,[22] the plaintiff offered at trial an opinion of an expert that was clearly outside the area described in the expert witness declaration.[23] The court found reversible error in the exclusion of this testimony:

> [B]ecause [the expert's] identity had been disclosed to other parties in a timely fashion along with a description of his testimony, *albeit an inaccurate one*, the trial court had *no power* to limit [his] testimony at trial.[24]

In *Castenada v Bornstein,*[25] a medical malpractice case, the plaintiff's expert witness declaration stated that a designated doctor "will testify as to the negligent obstetric care and treatment of [the plaintiff] *leading to* the asphyxia injury . . . ." The trial court ruled that this statement was specific enough to permit the expert to testify that defendants were negligent. However, it found the statement inadequate to put the defendant on notice that the doctor would also be opining that this negligence caused the plaintiff's injury. Accordingly, it refused to permit him to testify on the causation issue. This was error:

> [T]his statement of the "general substance" of [the expert's] testimony was broad enough to include the issue of causation as well as the issue of breach of the standard of care. Although in strict legal terms, proof an act "led to" an injury would not be the equivalent of proof an act was the "legal cause" of an injury, we do not believe the Legislature intended a "brief narrative statement" containing the "general substance" of an expert's testimony should be written in strict legal terms. This would only result in delays during trial while the parties argued over the technical legal sufficiency of the expert witness declaration prior to the admission of each expert's testimony. . . . [¶] [T]he statement [the expert] would testify as to negligence "leading to" plaintiff's injury was sufficient to put the defendant on notice [he] would testify as to both breach of duty and causation. It is undisputed [the defendant] had the opportunity to depose [him] on both issues. If he chose not to do so based on a narrow, technical interpretation of the narrative statement, we find he has no justification to complain.[26]

Four years later, however, in *Bonds v Roy*[27] the Supreme Court disapproved both *Castaneda* and *Martinez.*

---

[22] Martinez v City of Poway (1993) 12 Cal App 4th 425, 15 Cal Rptr 2d 644.

[23] The expected testimony described in the declaration related to the design of the roadway where the accident happened; that offered at trial would have reconstructed the accident itself.

[24] Martinez v City of Poway (1993) 12 Cal App 4th 425, 432, 15 Cal Rptr 2d 644, 648 (italics added).

[25] Castenada v Bornstein (1995) 36 Cal App 4th 1818, 1828, 43 Cal Rptr 2d 10, 16 (original italics).

[26] Castenada v Bornstein (1995) 36 Cal App 4th 1818, 1828, 43 Cal Rptr 10, 16–17.

[27] Bonds v Roy (1999) 20 Cal 4th 140, 149, n4, 83 Cal Rptr 2d 289, 294 n4, 973 P2d 66, 71 n4.

For additional discussion of *Bonds*, see § 10.15.

In *Bonds*, another medical malpractice case, the defendant's declaration, after designating a vascular surgeon to testify on the issue of liability and causation, listed an orthopedist to testify only on the issue of plaintiff's damages. During the deposition of the orthopedist, he insisted that he was to testify only concerning the extent of the plaintiff's present disability and the prospects for his rehabilitation, and he confirmed that he was not to opine on the malpractice issues standard of care issues in the case.

At trial, however, when the defense called this orthopedist as its last witness, it "sought to expand the scope of [his] testimony to include two new areas . . . relating to the standard of care."[28] The trial judge ruled that any such expansion of the expert's trial testimony would be an unfair and prejudicial surprise to the plaintiff.

In the Court of Appeal the defense, relying on *Martinez*, insisted that since it had filed an expert witness declaration concerning this witness's projected trial testimony, it was free to have him range outside the areas specified in that declaration.

The Supreme Court first noted that the statute requires an expert witness declaration to include "A brief narrative statement of the general substance of the testimony that the expert is expected to give." It then stressed that expert trial witness disclosure procedures contain "an exhaustive series of requirements both for making and for granting"[29] a motion to augment an expert witness declaration "with respect to the general substance of the testimony that an expert previously designated is expected to give."[30]

Section 2034.300 speaks of excluding the testimony of an expert where a party has unreasonably failed to "[s]ubmit an expert witness declaration." This language led the defense to argue that an expert's testimony could be excluded only where the party calling that expert had failed "altogether"[31] to submit a declaration concerning that expert.

The Court rejected this argument, because it would render redundant the elaborate statutory provisions[32] for amending an expert witness declaration.[33] Instead the Court concluded that, absent a court-approved amendment under these statutes, the areas of opinion testimony given by a retained expert at trial must track those earlier described in the expert witness declaration.[34]

Cf. Kahn, Declarations: Recent Decisions have Blurred the Line between Providing Too Much and Too Little Information in Expert Witness Declarations, 28-MAR L.A. Law. 28 (2005).

[28] Bonds v Roy (1999) 20 Cal 4th 140, 143, 83 Cal Rptr 2d 289, 290, 973 P2d 66, 67.

[29] Bonds v Roy (1999) 20 Cal 4th 140, 144, 83 Cal Rptr 2d 289, 291, 973 P2d 66, 68.

[30] CCP § 2034.610(a)(2).

[31] Bonds v Roy (1999) 20 Cal 4th 140, 146, 83 Cal Rptr 2d 289, 292, 973 P2d 66, 69.

[32] See CCP §§ 2034.610–2034.630.

[33] Bonds v Roy (1999) 20 Cal 4th 140, 146, 83 Cal Rptr 2d 289, 292, 973 P2d 66, 69.

[34] Bonds v Roy (1999) 20 Cal 4th 140, 148–149, 83 Cal Rptr 2d 289, 294, 973 P2d 66, 71.

Where the description in an expert witness declaration is too vague to comply with the statute, the deficiency will usually become moot if that expert is later deposed.[35]

Assurances that Expert Has Been Retained: Section 2034.260 contains a trio of requirements aimed at eradicating the practice of submitting a laundry list of experts,[36] none of whom has yet been retained, or even contacted by the party designating them.[37] First, counsel must expressly "represent" in the declaration that "the expert has agreed to testify at the trial."[38] Second, counsel must represent that any designated expert will be able to give "a meaningful oral deposition" concerning the "specific testimony, including any opinion and its basis"[39] that the expert expects to give at trial. Finally, the declaration must set forth the expert's hourly and daily fee for submitting to a deposition.[40] An honest declaration containing these representations should ensure that counsel will have actually contacted and retained the designated experts.

§ 10.8 Reports of Expert Witnesses

Scope of Demand: A demand for an exchange of expert witness information may extend to reports and writings.[1] In this regard, Section 2034.210 has inherited an undesirable feature from its predecessors:[2] the demanding party decides whether the exchange will include reports. To insure that the later exchange will cover the reports of experts, a litigant should not wait for another party to make a demand. The safer course is to serve, within the time specified in the statute,[3] one's own demand, specifying that the exchange includes reports and writings of any designated expert witnesses.

Percipient Experts Not Included: Unlike the 1978 provision,[4] Section 2034.210 does not allow a party to demand the reports of all designated expert

---

[35] See Kennemur v State of California (1982) 133 Cal App 3d 907, 918 n5, 184 Cal Rptr 393, 399 n5. Cf. Jones v Moore (2000) 80 Cal App 4th 557, 95 Cal Rptr 2d 216.

For a discussion of the right to depose a designated expert trial witness, see § 10.9.

[36] See, e.g., Williams v Volkswagenwerk A.G. (1986) 180 Cal App 3d 1244, 1252, 226 Cal Rptr 306, 308.

[37] CCP § 2034.260(c).

[38] CCP § 2034.260(c)(3).

[39] CCP § 2034.260(c)(4).

Cf. Fatica v Superior Court (2002) 99 Cal App 4th 350, 120 Cal Rptr 2d 904 [plaintiff cannot be held responsible for the lack of preparedness for a discovery deposition on the part of a designated treating physician].

[40] CCP § 2034.260(c)(5).

[1] CCP § 2034.210(c).

[2] Former CCP § 2037, Appendix C. See also former CCP § 2037, 1956 Discovery Act, as amended by Stats 1978, ch. 1069, § 1.

[3] CCP § 2034.220.

For a discussion of the procedure for initiating an exchange of expert witness information, see § 10.2.

[4] Former CCP § 2037, 1956 Discovery Act, as amended by Stats. 1978, ch. 1069, § 1.

witnesses. Rather, that right extends only to the reports of experts who are parties, employees of parties, or specially retained to provide opinion testimony.[5] Accordingly, there is no right to demand reports of nonparty experts, such as treating physicians, who have acquired their knowledge independently of the litigation.[6]

Date of Exchange: The original statute regulating disclosure of expert trial witnesses called for the exchange of reports to occur at some specified "reasonable time" after the exchange of expert witness lists.[7] The present statute provides for the exchange to occur simultaneously with the exchange of witness lists and declarations.[8]

Reports Subject to Demand: The obligation to exchange reports extends only to those that are "discoverable."[9] This adjective implies that even after an expert's designation as a trial witness, certain reports and writings of that expert may remain insulated from discovery. The *National Steel Products* case[10] illustrates the difficulty the courts have in deciding whether a report of a designated expert is discoverable. The plaintiff claimed that the defendant's design and fabrication of a metal building built in California did not meet approved construction practices. The defendant listed as a trial expert an engineer whom it had used as a consultant in an earlier lawsuit. This other case involved the same sort of claim about the same type of building. Not satisfied with an inspection of the reports and writings prepared by the expert in connection with the present litigation, the plaintiff sought discovery of a report that the engineer had prepared on the building involved in the earlier case. The defendant maintained that both the attorney-client privilege and the work product protection insulated the earlier report from discovery.

—Attorney-Client Privilege: The court quickly disposed of the attorney-client privilege claim. It ruled that defendant waived this privilege by designating the expert to testify about the same general subject matter covered by his report in the earlier case, namely, the design and fabrication of the same kind of metal building.[11]

—Absolute Work Product: The court was not prepared, however, to find that the listing of its preparer as a trial witness ipso facto removed a report from

---

[5] CCP §§ 2034.210(c) and 2034.370.

[6] Cf. Zellerino v Brown (1991) 235 Cal App 1097, 1116, 1 Cal Rptr 2d 222, 234; Kennedy v Modesto City Hospital (1990) 221 Cal App 3d 575, 580 n3, 270 Cal Rptr 544, 547 n3.

[7] Former CCP § 2037, Stats 1978, ch. 1069, § 1.

[8] CCP § 2034.230(b).

[9] CCP § 2034.210(c).

[10] National Steel Products Co. v Superior Court (1985) 164 Cal App 3d 476, 210 Cal Rptr 535.

[11] National Steel Products Co. v Superior Court (1985) 164 Cal App 3d 476, 485, 210 Cal Rptr 535, 540.

For a discussion of the waiver of the attorney-client privilege by designating an expert as a trial witness, see § 12.12.

the work product protection. Instead, it held that the trial judge must review the report in camera and try to distinguish among three categories of information that it might contain. First, the report might contain passages that reflect the "impressions, conclusions, opinions, or legal research or theories" of the attorney who commissioned it. To that extent, the report falls under the "absolute" or "hard-core" branch of the work product doctrine, which shields it from discovery "under any circumstances."[12]

—General Work Product: Second, the report may contain passages that were "rendered in an advisory capacity" to the attorney. In other words, they were "designed to assist the attorney in such matters as preparation of pleadings, the manner of presentation of proof, and cross-examination of opposing expert witnesses."[13] These portions of the report would fall under the conditional work product protection.[14] A party would have to show that denial of this discovery would produce unfair prejudice or an injustice. For purely advisory opinions, such a showing is difficult to make. In the case before it, however, the court speculated that the trial court might find that the report in question, dealing as it did with the same general subject as the expert's projected trial testimony, had unusual impeachment value.

—Discoverable Reports: Finally, and most importantly, any reports or parts of reports containing "findings and opinions of the expert that go to the establishment or denial of a principal fact in issue"[15] in the case are discoverable. However, these passages must be "easily severable"[16] from the portions of any report that also contain protected work product.

§ 10.9 Depositions of Designated Experts

Deposition as a Matter of Right: Once a party designates someone as an expert trial witness, Section 2034.410 allows the other litigants to depose that person.[1] This departs from the original Discovery Act, which contained no such provision. Instead, the early case law had recognized the trial court's discretion to bar a discovery deposition if inspection of the expert's report would adequately reveal the content of the anticipated trial testimony.[2]

---

[12] CCP § 2018.030(a).

For a discussion of "absolutely protected" work product, see § 13.16.

[13] National Steel Products Co. v Superior Court (1985) 164 Cal App 3d 476, 489, 210 Cal Rptr 535, 543.

[14] CCP § 2018.030(b).

For a discussion of conditional work product protection, see §§ 13.6–13.12.

[15] National Steel Products Co. v Superior Court (1985) 164 Cal App 3d 476, 489, 210 Cal Rptr 535, 543.

[16] National Steel Products Co. v Superior Court (1985) 164 Cal App 3d 476, 490, 210 Cal Rptr 535, 543.

[1] CCP § 2034.410.

Annotation: Pretrial deposition-discovery of opinions of opponent's expert witnesses. 86 ALR2d 138, partially superseded by 33 ALR Fed 403.

[2] Crumpton v Dickstein (1978) 82 Cal App 3d 166, 169, 146 Cal Rptr 840, 841.

Deposition Procedures Modified: The procedures governing other discovery depositions apply, for the most part, to depositions of designated expert witnesses.[3] There are, however, some important modifications in those procedures for depositions of designated expert trial witnesses.

—Deposition Site: The first modification involves the deposition site. Normally, a litigant cannot require a deponent to travel long distances to give a deposition.[4] Under Section 2034.420, these travel restrictions do not apply where the deponent-expert is a party, an employee of a party, or someone specially retained to testify in the action.[5] These three types of experts must attend at any place that is within 75 miles of the courthouse where the action is pending.[6] However, where this travel would cause an "exceptional hardship," the trial court may fix a location more distant from the place of trial.[7]

—Compelling Attendance: The second modification concerns the method of compelling the expert's attendance for the deposition. The normal deposition procedures require service of a deposition subpoena on any witness who is neither a party nor an employee of a party.[8] This remains the case for those designated experts, such as treating physicians, who have acquired their information from personal observation.[9] However, where designated experts have been specially retained to form and express an opinion, no deposition subpoena is necessary.[10] A party that designates expert witnesses must produce them for a discovery deposition at the forum, even if they reside in another jurisdiction.[11] If a specially retained expert fails to submit to or to complete a deposition, the trial court may strike that expert from the witness list.[12]

—Cut-off Date: The third modification involves the time for the completion of discovery. Generally, parties must complete discovery by the 30th day before the initial trial date, and have motions related to discovery heard by the 15th

---

[3] For a general discussion of depositions, see Chapters 3 and 4.

[4] CCP § 2025.250(a).

For a discussion of the travel restrictions generally applicable to depositions, see §§ 2.13–2.14.

[5] CCP § 2034.420.

[6] This reflects the case law under the 1978 statute. See Tahoe Forest Inn v Superior Court (1979) 99 Cal App 3d 509, 512–513, 160 Cal Rptr 314, 316.

[7] CCP § 2034.420.

[8] CCP § 2025.280(b).

For a discussion of when a subpoena is necessary to compel a deponent's attendance, see §§ 2.9–2.12.

[9] Hurtado v Western Medical Center (1990) 222 Cal App 3d 1198, 1203, 272 Cal Rptr 324, 327.

[10] CCP § 2034.460.

Former CCP § 2037.4, of the 1978 statute, required a party to make *all* designated expert witnesses available for a deposition. See Tahoe Forest Inn v Superior Court (1979) 99 Cal App 3d 509, 512–513, 160 Cal Rptr 314, 316.

[11] Tahoe Forest Inn v Superior Court (1979) 99 Cal App 3d 509, 512, 160 Cal Rptr 314, 316.

[12] Waicis v Superior Court (1990) 226 Cal App 3d 283, 287–288, 276 Cal Rptr 45.

day before that trial date.[13] However, under Section 2024.030 a party has until 15 days before the initial trial date to complete the depositions of an adversary's designated expert witnesses, and until 10 days before that trial date to have related motions heard.

—One-Deposition Limit: A fourth modification in the normal deposition rules is unfortunately left to implication. Section 2025.610 provides generally that once a party takes any person's deposition, neither that party nor any other party who received notice of it may depose that witness again.[14] This limitation properly functions to protect an expert, once designated, from being subjected to a series of depositions. However, this one-deposition limit should not bar another deposition of an individual now designated as an expert witness simply because some party has already deposed him or her at an earlier stage in the case.

Variance Between Declaration and Deposition: Usually an expert witness may testify at trial to an opinion that falls within the general substance of the expected testimony described in the expert witness declaration. However, once an opponent has deposed the designated expert, this will not always be true. In *Jones v Moore,*[15] a wife sued the attorney who had represented her in a dissolution proceeding from 1987 until the middle of 1996. Her complaint contained general charges of legal malpractice spanning this entire period. As the trial date neared, the plaintiff identified an expert witness and broadly described his expected testimony about departures from the standard of care in terms that would also cover the entire period that the defendant-attorney had represented her.

However, when the defendant deposed the plaintiff's designated expert, that expert criticized only the defendant's actions in negotiating the terms of a property settlement agreement that had been incorporated in the final judgment at the end of 1990:

> [The expert's deposition] opinions related only to defendant's conduct with regard to the settlement agreement and further judgment entered in 1990. None of [his] opinions related to defendant's later conduct in failing to obtain substitute security [once a 1992 bankruptcy of a partnership wiped out the interest that the husband was using to secure the settlement agreement]. [The expert] specifically disavowed holding any other opinions than those he had expressed, and said if he formed any other opinions than those he had expressed he would notify defendant.[16]

When this malpractice case came to trial, the plaintiff asked her expert to opine as to whether defendant had acted negligently in 1994 when he failed to obtain

---

[13] CCP § 2034.210.

[14] CCP § 2025.610(a).

For a discussion of this one-deposition limit, see § 2.36.

[15] Jones v Moore (2000) 80 Cal App 4th 557, 95 Cal Rptr 2d 216.

[16] Jones v Moore (2000) 80 Cal App 4th 557, 564, 95 Cal Rptr 2d 216, 220.

additional security after the partnership's bankruptcy. The trial court's decision to bar any opinion as to the post-settlement actions of the plaintiff's former attorney was upheld by the appellate court:

> When an expert deponent testifies as to specific opinions and affirmatively states those are the only opinions he intends to offer at trial, it would be grossly unfair and prejudicial to permit the expert to offer additional opinions at trial.[17]

Showing Bias of Expert: During the deposition of a listed expert trial witness, an opponent may develop information that bears on the deponent's possible bias. For example, the *Stony Brook* case[18] acknowledged an opponent's right to obtain an estimate of the extent to which the doctor's practice, in the proceeding three years, has included testimony in personal injury cases for defendants as opposed to plaintiffs. However, the doctor was not required to detail the precise number of cases and the income derived from them.

§ 10.10 Deposition Fee

Costly Undertakings: Depositions of expert witnesses are expensive.[1] There are, of course, the reporter's charges for taking and transcribing the testimony. As with any other deposition, these are the responsibility of the party taking it.[2] In addition, an expert's deposition usually requires special fees and expenses. The expert will usually charge a substantial sum for the time spent testifying. Moreover, preparation for that testimony often takes a considerable amount of time, for which the expert may also expect compensation. Finally, where the expert resides some distance from the deposition site, the bill may include charges for travel time, transportation, meals, and lodging.

Former Statute: The original expert witness disclosure statute[3] required the party noticing a deposition to compensate an opponent's expert only if the deposition was taken "primarily" to obtain that expert's opinion.[4] This obligation covered not only the time spent giving the testimony, but also that spent traveling to and from the deposition site. Expressly excluded was the expert's preparation

---

[17] Jones v Moore (2000) 80 Cal App 4th 557, 565, 95 Cal Rptr 2d 216, 221.

[18] Stoney Brook I Homeowners Ass'n v Superior Court (2000) 84 Cal App 4th 691, 699–700, 101 Cal Rptr 2d 67 [trial court abused its discretion when it ordered the doctor to supply information that it would require about 90 hours to compile].

[1] See, e.g., Rancho Bernardo Development Co. v Superior Court (1992) 2 Cal App 4th 358, 360, 2 Cal Rptr 878, 879 [one party's costs for taking expert witness depositions already exceeded $20,000].

[2] CCP § 2025.510(b).

[3] Former CCP § 2037.7(a), Stats 1978, ch. 1069, § 1.

[4] In a worker's compensation case, this obligation to pay the deponent applied to any opponent's expert who was deposed. Former CCP § 2037.7(b), Stats 1978, ch. 1069, § 1.

The word "primarily" replaced "solely" as the result of a short-lived amendment that took effect in January 1987.

time. The statute did not mention the out-of-pocket costs connected with the expert's travel to the deposition site.

Types of Experts Entitled to a Deposition Fee: Section 2034.410 differs markedly from the pre-1987 law. It expressly requires the party noticing a deposition to pay a deposition fee to three types of experts: (1) one specially retained to form and express an opinion in the lawsuit; (2) a treating health care practitioner if asked to express an opinion;[5] and (3) an architect, engineer, or surveyor involved in the original project design if asked to express an opinion concerning it.

By implication the statute exempts from entitlement to such a fee three types of experts who might appear on an opponent's expert witness list: (1) a party to the action; (2) an employee of a party; and (3) an expert who is a percipient or fact witness and who will *not* be asked to express an opinion during the deposition.[6] As to the third group, *Brun v Bailey*[7] had distinguished between factual and opinion questions addressed to a treating physician:

> Questions regarding the physician's knowledge of specific facts as to the patient's condition, including past treatments provided and past diagnoses and prognoses rendered, are factual questions. Questions regarding the expert's opinion as to the patient's prognosis at the time of the deposition, or regarding the reasons for the treatments, diagnoses, or prognoses provided in the past, call for opinion.[8]

The Legislature, however, has annulled the holding in *Brun v Bailey* that treating physicians are not being asked "to express an opinion" when they are questioned during a deposition about their past diagnoses and prognoses of their patients. Section 2034.430 now explicitly entitles treating doctors to a deposition fee when they are asked "to express opinion testimony, including opinion or factual testimony regarding [their] past or present diagnosis or the reasons for a particular treatment decision," unless their testimony is limited to the translation of words and symbols in medical records.[9]

Amount of Deposition Fee: When an expert is entitled to a deposition fee, the party taking the deposition must pay it. However, this obligation extends only to "the time spent at the deposition."[10] The party who designated the expert is

---

[5] A treating physician may retain counsel to help determine whether opinions are being elicited. See, e.g., Brun v Bailey (1994) 27 Cal App 4th 641, 646, 32 Cal Rptr 624, 626.

[6] This would include not only treating doctors, and architects, engineers, and surveyors involved in the original design of the relevant project, but also any other expert with relevant factual information.

Cf. Hurtado v Western Medical Center (1990) 222 Cal App 3d 1198, 272 Cal Rptr 324.

[7] Brun v Bailey (1994) 27 Cal App 4th 641, 32 Cal Rptr 624.

[8] Brun v Bailey (1994) 27 Cal App 4th 641, 653, 32 Cal Rptr 624, 631.

[9] CCP § 2034.430(a)(2).

[10] CCP § 2034.430(b).

responsible for any charge made by the expert for preparation and for travel time, as well as for any travel expenses.[11]

The deposition fee "meter" runs from the time the expert arrives until he or she is dismissed. If an attorney's late arrival delays the start of the deposition, the tardy attorney is responsible for any part of the fee attributable to the delay.[12]

An hourly rate is the norm. A daily rate is appropriate only if the expert actually testifies for a full day, or has foregone a full day's regular business at the request of counsel who noticed the deposition.[13]

—Tender of Fee: The original expert witness disclosure statute required a tender of the deposition fee of the expert. However, it did not specify either when this tender was to occur or the consequences of a failure to make it. The *Tahoe Forest Inn* case[14] held that the party taking the deposition was to tender this fee in advance. This made sense, because otherwise a party might produce its expert at the time and place specified in the notice, only to find that the other party had canceled the deposition.

The Civil Discovery Act contains conflicting provisions with respect to when the expert witness fee is to be tendered. On the one hand, Section 2034.450 allows the party taking the deposition either to accompany the deposition notice with a fee tender or to postpone that tender until the deposition itself.[15] On the other hand, Section 2034.460 indicates that unless the fee tender accompanies the notice, that notice will not compel the party who designated the expert to produce the expert for the deposition.[16] This conflict was noted and resolved in *True v Shank,* which held "that the Legislature, by explicitly providing two different ways expert fees may be tendered, intended that expert fees could be given either way."[17] Unless the party who noticed the deposition has tendered the expert's fee by the deposition's start, "the expert shall not be deposed at that time unless the parties stipulate otherwise."[18]

If the deposition consumes more time than that reflected in the fee tendered, the party noticing the deposition must remit the additional fee within five days after receiving an itemized bill from the expert.[19]

—Limits on Amount: The expert's rate is subject to three restrictions: it must be "reasonable;" it must be "customary;" and it must not exceed the amount charged the party retaining the expert.[20] The declaration accompanying the

---

[11] CCP § 2034.440.

[12] CCP § 2034.430(c).

[13] CCP § 2034.430(e).

[14] Tahoe Forest Inn v Superior Court (1979) 99 Cal App 3d 509, 513, 160 Cal Rptr 314, 316–317.

[15] CCP § 2034.450(a).

[16] CCP § 2034.460(a).

[17] True v Shank (2000) 81 Cal App 4th 1250, 1256, 97 Cal Rptr 2d 462, 466.

[18] CCP § 2034.460(b).

[19] CCP § 2034.450(c).

[20] Unless the expert's services are being donated to a party that is a charitable or nonprofit organization.

designation of a specially retained expert must include the hourly and the daily rate of that expert for providing deposition testimony. It must also reveal the rate that the expert is charging for "consulting"[21] with the designating party. Section 2034.430 then prohibits the expert from charging the deposing party more than the retaining party.[22] The *Rancho Bernardo Development Co.* case[23] construed this limitation to refer to the fee the expert will charge the retaining party for trial testimony, not to the usually lower fee charged for pretrial investigation and advice:

> Knowing . . . experts customarily charge more for depositions than for other work, it would be nonsensical to limit the testimonial charge to the amount charged for nontestimonial work. The first measure of compensation (the reasonable fee) would always be then reduced by the second measure (the lower rate charged for ordinary services), thus making the first and presumably principal fee definition inoperative.[24]

If the "customary" deposition fee of a designated expert exceeds a "reasonable" fee, the lower amount governs.[25]

—Supporting Data: A party desiring to depose another party's designated expert witness may dispute the reasonableness of the fee stated in the expert witness declaration.[26] Before troubling the trial court, the parties must meet and confer to try to resolve this issue informally.[27] During this process the party designating the expert must supply data supporting the amount of the deposition fee. This should include: (1) the fee that the expert has previously charged others for similar services;[28] (2) the number of times that expert has received the demanded fee;[29] and (3) how often within the past two years that expert has actually received the fee he or she is demanding.[30]

—Order Setting Deposition Fee: If the parties cannot informally resolve the fee issue, the party desiring to take the expert's deposition should move for an order setting the rate.[31] This motion must be accompanied by a meet-and-confer

---

[21] CCP § 2034.260(c)(5).

[22] CCP § 2034.430(d).

[23] Rancho Bernardo Development Co. v Superior Court (1992) 2 Cal App 4th 358, 2 Cal Rptr 2d 878.

[24] Rancho Bernardo Development Co. v Superior Court (1992) 2 Cal App 4th 358, 363, 2 Cal Rptr 2d 878, 881.

[25] Marsh v Mountain Zephyr, Inc. (1996) 43 Cal App 4th 289, 296, 50 Cal Rptr 2d 493 [designated expert engineer who customarily charged $360 per hour is entitled only to receive $250 per hour from party taking his deposition].

[26] See CCP § 2034.260(c)(5).

[27] CCP § 2034.470(b).

[28] CCP § 2034.470(b)(1).

[29] CCP § 2034.470(b)(2).

[30] CCP § 2034.470(b)(3).

[31] CCP § 2034.470(a).

declaration that includes the data supplied relating to the expert's ordinary and customary fees.[32] The court may consider any other factors it considers appropriate, including what similar experts in the relevant community ordinarily and customarily charge for similar services.[33] If the court determines that the demanded fee is unreasonable, it will then set the appropriate fee for the deposition testimony.[34] Absent substantial justification the court will impose a monetary sanction on a party who unsuccessfully makes or opposes a motion to set the amount of an expert's deposition fee.[35]

Under the collateral order rule, an expert who believes that the court has abused its discretion in awarding a fee that is lower than the expert's "customary" charge may immediately appeal from the order.[36]

—**Not a Recoverable "Cost":** The prevailing parties' right to recover as costs the deposition fees they paid to experts designated by an opponent was considered in the *McGarity* case.[37] The court noted that the applicable statute[38] provides: "The following items are not allowable as costs, except when expressly authorized by law: Fees of experts not ordered by the court." It concluded that "the plain language"[39] of this statute precludes recovery of deposition fees paid to experts designated by an opponent. The *Baker-Hoey* case reached the same conclusion: "In the absence of statutory authority which makes the costs incurred in deposing treating physicians recoverable by the prevailing party, . . . such costs are not recoverable."[40]

§ 10.11 Supplementing Expert Witness Information

Second Thoughts: As the trial date draws near, the litigants sometimes will change their minds about the need for expert testimony. One party may initially decide that a particular aspect of the case does not require expert testimony. Then, the initial exchange of expert witness information reveals that another party has designated one or more experts to testify in this area. This may cause the party who has not listed an expert to decide that the safer course is to retain one. Section 2034.280 offers a way to effectuate this change of mind.[1] It provides a window of opportunity after the initial exchange during which a party may have a *right*[2]

---

[32] CCP § 2034.470(b).

[33] CCP § 2034.470(e).

[34] CCP § 2034.470(f).

[35] CCP § 2034.470(g).

[36] Marsh v Mountain Zephyr, Inc. (1996) 43 Cal App 4th 289, 299, 50 Cal Rptr 2d 493.

[37] McGarity v Department of Transportation (1992) 8 Cal App 4th 677, 10 Cal Rptr 2d 344.

[38] CCP § 1033.5(b)(1).

[39] McGarity v Department of Transportation (1992) 8 Cal App 4th 677, 686, 10 Cal Rptr 2d 344, 349–350.

[40] Baker-Hoey v Lockheed Martin Corp. (2003) 111 Cal App 4th 592, 602, 3 Cal Rptr 3d 593, 601.

[1] CCP § 2034.280.

[2] Cf. Kennedy v Modesto City Hospital (1990) 221 Cal App 3d 575, 580 n3, 270 Cal Rptr 544, 547 n3.

to make a supplemental expert witness designation. In this respect *supplementation* of an expert witness under Section 2034.280 is different both from *augmenting* an expert witness list[3] and from making a *tardy* submission of one.[4] These latter steps are not a matter of right; they require leave of court.

Eligibility to Supplement Designation: The right to supplement expert witness information is available for only 20 days after the original exchange.[5] There are four requirements. First, the subject of the expert's projected trial testimony must be one for which another party has already designated an expert.[6] One may not use this right to *supplement* as a way to inject into the lawsuit a new area for expert testimony. To do the latter, a party must seek leave of court to *augment* the exchange of information.[7]

Second, the supplementing party must not have previously designated anyone to testify in the area covered by the newly designated expert. In *Basham v Babcock,*[8] for example, there was a sharp dispute concerning the extent to which a low-speed auto collision had aggravated the plaintiff's preexisting bulging lumbar disc. Initially, the defense designated as an expert witness only the orthopedist who had examined the plaintiff during discovery. A few days later, it served a "supplemental" designation of a radiologist. It proposed to have both experts testify that the plaintiff's preexisting condition, not the collision, caused his present back pain. This was held to be an improper use of Section 2034.280: "a party who has designated an expert on a particular subject may not use a supplemental list to substitute experts."[9] Nor would it cure this error if the party calls at trial only the "supplemental" expert, and not the one originally designated: "[Defendant] simply substituted [the radiologist] as her expert to testify on matters for [the orthopedist] who had been previously retained. In doing so she violated the letter and spirit of [former] section 2034."[10]

Third, the supplementing party must not have previously retained anyone to testify on the subject covered by the new expert.[11] This restriction prevents the concealment of one's own experts until the other parties have disclosed theirs.

---

[3] See CCP § 2034.610.

For a discussion of motions for leave to augment expert witness information, see § 10.12.

[4] See CCP § 2034.710.

For a discussion of motions for leave to submit tardy expert witness information, see § 10.13.

[5] CCP § 2034.280(a).

[6] CCP § 2034.280(a).

[7] For a discussion of motions for leave to augment expert witness information, see § 10.12.

[8] Basham v Babcock (1996) 44 Cal App 4th 1717, 52 Cal Rptr 2d 456.

[9] Basham v Babcock (1996) 44 Cal App 4th 1717, 1723, 52 Cal Rptr 2d 456, 460.

[10] Basham v Babcock (1996) 44 Cal App 4th 1717, 1723, 52 Cal Rptr 2d 456, 460.

[11] CCP § 2034.280(a).

Cf. Kennedy v Modesto City Hospital (1990) 221 Cal App 3d 575, 580 n3, 270 Cal Rptr 544, 547 n3.

Fourth, the supplementing party must have participated in the original exchange of expert witness information.[12] At a minimum, this party must have submitted a statement that it does not presently plan to call any expert witnesses.[13]

Submission of Declaration and Reports: If the newly designated expert is a party, an employee of a party, or a consultant specially retained to form and express opinions in the lawsuit, the supplemental information must include an expert witness declaration,[14] as well as the discoverable reports and writings of that expert.[15]

Availability for Deposition: Usually the original exchange of expert witness information will take place 50 days before the initial trial date (45 days if the demand for the exchange was served by mail).[16] An eligible party has 20 days after the exchange to submit supplemental expert witness information. Accordingly, the trial date may be only 25 days away when a supplemental expert witness designation is served. Recognizing this, Section 2034.280 requires the supplementing party to make any newly listed experts available for a deposition "immediately."[17] This connotes that the normal 10-day notice required for a deposition[18] is not applicable to experts designated supplementally. Moreover, the statute expressly exempts depositions of such experts from the normal requirement[19] that expert witness depositions be completed 15 days before the initial trial date.[20]

§ 10.12 Augmenting or Amending Expert Witness Information

After the exchange of expert witness information, a party may want to add to, or substitute for, the experts initially designated.[1] Section 2034.610 permits, and Section 2034.620 regulates, a party's ability to *augment* an expert witness list. Less frequently, a litigant may wish to have one or more of the already designated experts testify in additional or different areas from those originally indicated.[2] The two statutes also govern such *amendments* of an expert witness declaration.

---

[12] CCP § 2034.280(a).

[13] CCP § 2034.260(b)(2).

[14] CCP § 2034.280(b).

For a discussion of the contents of an expert witness declaration, see § 10.7.

[15] CCP § 2034.280(b).

For a discussion of what reports of designated trial experts are discoverable, see § 10.8.

[16] For a discussion of the time for the exchange of expert witness information, see § 10.3.

[17] CCP § 2034.280(c).

For a discussion of the right to depose a designated expert witness, see § 10.9.

[18] For a discussion of the usual amount of notice for a deposition, see § 2.7.

[19] See CCP § 2024.030.

[20] CCP § 2034.280(c).

[1] For a discussion of the duty to identify expert trial witnesses, see § 10.6.

[2] For a discussion of the duty to disclose the general substance of the anticipated testimony of expert trial witnesses, see § 10.7.

Preconditions: Unlike the *supplementation* of expert witness information, which is a matter of right,[3] both the augmentation[4] and the amendment[5] of expert witness information require leave of court.[6] To receive this relief, a party must meet four conditions. First, it must have "engaged in a timely exchange of expert witness information"[7] in the first instance.[8] Second, the proposed expert must have been "subsequently retained."[9] This requirement reduces the temptation to deliberately hold back disclosure of an expert until a party has seen an opponent's list. Third, the party must "promptly" notify all other parties of the identity of any new expert and the general substance of any new testimony.[10] Fourth, the party must have attempted to "meet and confer" to see whether the parties can agree to the augmentation. A declaration setting forth these efforts must accompany the motion.[11]

Timing of Motion: A motion to augment or amend must be made "promptly"[12] after a party decides to use a new expert or to present different testimony.[13] Moreover, a party must usually make the motion soon enough so that, if it is granted, the other parties will still have time, before the cut-off date for expert witness discovery,[14] to depose any expert who is added or whose topic areas are changed.[15] However, under "exceptional circumstances,"[16] the trial court may entertain the motion later, probably even during the trial itself.[17]

The contents of the original exchange of information may become relevant to the court's consideration of the motion. In this event the parties should lodge with the court the demand for the exchange and the expert witness lists and declarations generated by it.

Ruling on the Motion: Even if all these conditions have been fulfilled, the trial court should not automatically grant the motion. Section 2034.620 instructs the court to consider other parties' reliance on the information previously

---

[3] For a discussion of the limited right to *supplement* an expert witness list, see § 10.11.

[4] CCP § 2034.610(a)(1).

[5] CCP § 2034.610(a)(2).

[6] CCP § 2034.610(a)

Richaud v Jennings (1993) 16 Cal App 4th 81, 90, 19 Cal Rptr 2d 790, 795.

[7] CCP § 2034.610(a).

[8] For a discussion of the circumstances under which a party may make a *tardy* designation of expert witnesses, see § 10.13.

[9] CCP § 2034.610(a)(1).

[10] CCP § 2034.620(c)(2)(B).

[11] CCP § 2034.610(c).

[12] CCP § 2034.620(c)(2)(B).

[13] See Martinez v City of Poway (1993) 12 Cal App 4th 425, 432, 15 Cal Rptr 2d 644, 647.

[14] This cut-off date is 15 days before the initial trial date. CCP § 2024(d).

[15] CCP § 2034.610(b).

[16] CCP § 2034.60(b).

[17] Cf. Sprague v Equifax, Inc. (1985) 166 Cal App 3d 1012, 1038, 213 Cal Rptr 69, 85–86.

submitted.[18] The court must deny the motion unless it determines that no party opposing it will suffer prejudice in presenting its claim or defense.[19] *Dickison v Howen*[20] interprets this requirement. "Prejudice" does not result simply because the new expert's testimony could affect the outcome of the case. Rather it connotes a concern that the opposing party, "due to its reliance on the previous list of experts, is not prepared and cannot be prepared in time."[21]

Even if the trial court is satisfied in this regard, it must still assess the moving party's failure to include the information during the initial expert witness exchange. It must consider two overlapping criteria. First, the court must consider whether the moving party acted without "reasonable diligence"[22] by omitting the expert or subject area in the initial exchange.[23] Second, the court must consider whether this omission resulted from that party's "mistake, inadvertence, surprise, or excusable neglect." The *Dickison* case[24] upheld a trial court's ruling that "surprise" occurred when one of the designated experts proceeded to give deposition testimony diametrically opposed to that anticipated. In contrast, a case decided under the 1978 statute concluded that neither "reasonable diligence" nor "surprise" was shown by a party who left an expert off its list because it expected that individual to be called by a codefendant, who then settled with the plaintiff.[25] The most clear-cut situation warranting leave to augment or amend is when a designated expert, through no fault of the designating party, becomes unavailable to testify at the trial.[26]

Conditions for Granting Motion: The trial court must require the moving party to make any affected expert "immediately" available for a deposition.[27] "Immediately" connotes that the normal 10-day minimum notice[28] does not apply.[29]

The trial court may impose additional conditions in the interest of justice.[30] These may include: (1) leave to other parties to designate new experts[31] or to

---

[18] CCP § 2034.620(a).

[19] CCP § 2034.620(b).

[20] Dickison v Howen (1990) 220 Cal App 3d 1471, 270 Cal Rptr 188.

[21] Dickison v Howen (1990) 220 Cal App 3d 1471, 1479, 270 Cal Rptr 188, 193.

[22] CCP § 2034.620(c)(1).

[23] CCP § 2034.620(c)(1).

[24] Dickison v Howen (1990) 220 Cal App 3d 1471, 1477–1478, 270 Cal Rptr 188.

[25] Gallo v Peninsula Hospital (1985) 164 Cal App 3d 899, 904, 211 Cal Rptr 27.

[26] Cf. Richaud v Jennings (1993) 16 Cal App 4th 81, 89–90, 19 Cal Rptr 2d 790, 795.

[27] CCP § 2034.620(d).

For a discussion of the right to depose an opponent's designated expert witnesses, see § 10.9.

[28] For a discussion of the usual amount of notice for a deposition, see § 2.7.

[29] For a discussion of the similar requirement of "immediate" availability for a supplemental expert, see § 10.11.

[30] CCP § 2034.620(d).

See, e.g., Dickison v Howen (1990) 220 Cal App 3d 1471, 1480, 270 Cal Rptr 188, 193.

[31] CCP § 2034.620(d).

expand the coverage of the testimony of experts already listed by them;[32] (2) a continuance of the trial;[33] and (3) an award of costs and litigation expenses to those opposing the motion.[34] These "litigation expenses" may include the attorney's fees incurred both in resisting the motion and in the duplication of trial preparation efforts caused by any continuance of the trial date.[35]

A party who unsuccessfully makes or opposes a motion to change its expert witness information should be prepared to incur a monetary sanction. To avoid such a sanction that party must show substantial justification, or that circumstances make imposition of that sanction unjust.[36]

§ 10.13 Tardy Submission of Expert Witness Information

Parties who have failed to submit expert trial witness information either at all or on time may still be able to cure this delinquency by seeking leave of court to make a tardy compliance with the exchange demand.[1]

Preconditions: To be eligible to seek this relief, the delinquent party must act "promptly" in three respects. First, that party, after becoming aware of the delinquency, must "promptly" serve all parties who have appeared in the case with a copy of the tardy expert trial witness information.[2] Second, the party must "promptly"[3] meet and confer with opposing counsel in an effort to obtain their consent to the belated submission.[4] Third, if this meeting is unsuccessful, the party must "promptly" move for leave to make a late submission of expert witness information.[5] This motion must usually be made soon enough so that, if granted, the other parties will still have time, before the cut-off date[6] for expert witness discovery to depose the tardily designated experts.[7] Under "exceptional circumstances,"[8] the trial court may entertain the motion later, probably even during the trial itself.[9]

Ruling on the Motion: Although a party has fulfilled these three conditions, the trial court should not routinely grant the motion. Section 2034.720 enjoins it to consider other parties' reliance, if any, on the moving party's apparent

---

[32] CCP § 2034.620(d).

[33] CCP § 2034.620(d).

[34] CCP § 2034.620(d).

[35] See Estate of Maron (1986) 183 Cal App 3d 707, 711, 228 Cal Rptr 402, 404.

[36] CCP § 2034.630.

[1] CCP §§ 2034.710–2034.730.

[2] See CCP § 2034.720(3).

[3] See CCP § 2034.720(c)(2).

[4] See CCP § 2034.710(c), referencing CCP § 2016.040.

[5] See CCP § 2034.720(c)(2).

[6] CCP § 2024(d) [This cut-off date is 15 days before the initial trial date.]

[7] CCP § 2034.710(b).

[8] CCP § 2034.710(b).

[9] Cf. Sprague v Equifax, Inc. (1985) 166 Cal App 3d 1012, 1038, 213 Cal Rptr 69, 85–86.

forfeiture of the right to present expert testimony at trial.[10] The court must deny the motion unless it determines that the late submission will not "prejudice" any party opposing it in presenting a claim or defense.[11] Prejudice in this context does not result simply because the testimony of the tardily designated experts could affect the case outcome.[12] Rather it connotes a concern that an opposing party, due to the tardy submission of the information, would be unable to adequately prepare to meet it in the time remaining before trial.

Once the moving party shows that the tardy submission will not prejudice the other litigants, the trial court must still consider whether failure to comply with the statutory deadline was attributable to "mistake, inadvertence, surprise, or excusable neglect."[13] If the noncompliance was deliberate or inexcusably careless, the court should deny the motion.

Conditions for Granting Motion: The trial court must require the moving party to make any affected expert "immediately" available for a deposition.[14] "Immediately" connotes that the normal 10-day minimum notice[15] does not apply.[16]

The trial court may impose additional conditions in the interest of justice. These may include: (1) leave to other parties to designate new experts or to expand the scope of listed experts' testimony; (2) a continuance of the trial; and (3) an award of costs and litigation expenses to those opposing the motion.[17] These "litigation expenses" may include the attorney's fees incurred both in resisting the motion, and in the duplication of trial preparation efforts caused by any continuance of the trial date.[18]

A party who unsuccessfully makes or opposes a motion to submit tardy expert witness information should be prepared to incur a monetary sanction. To avoid this sanction, the party must show substantial justification for its position, or that circumstances make that sanction unjust.[19]

---

[10] CCP § 2034.720(a).

[11] CCP § 2034.720(b).

[12] Cf. Zellerino v Brown (1991) 235 Cal App 3d 1097, 1107, 1 Cal Rptr 2d 222, 228 ["the Legislature's use of section 473 language in parts of the discovery act evidences its intent to supplant the application of section 473 pro tanto"]; see also Dickison v Howen (1990) 220 Cal App 3d 1471, 270 Cal Rptr 188.

[13] CCP § 2034.720(c)(1).

[14] CCP § 2034.720(d).

For a discussion of the right to depose an opponent's designated expert witnesses, see § 10.9.

[15] For a discussion of the usual amount of notice for a deposition, see § 2.7.

[16] For a discussion of the similar requirement of "immediate" availability for a supplemental expert, see § 10.11.

[17] CCP § 2034.720(d).

[18] See Estate of Maron (1986) 183 Cal App 3d 707, 711, 228 Cal Rptr 402, 404.

[19] CCP § 2034.730, referencing CCP § 2023.010.

§ 10.14 Permissible Use of Undesignated Experts

A party usually acquires the right to call an expert witness at trial by listing that individual during the initial exchange of expert witness information.[1] In a few instances, that right results from the naming of the expert on a supplemental list.[2] Under certain conditions the trial court will allow a party to augment an expert witness list,[3] or even to submit a tardy list.[4] However, in two situations, a party may present the testimony of an *undesignated* expert.

Expert Later Deposed: Section 2034 confers a limited right to use an expert whom some other party has designated as a trial witness. This right accrues once *any* party has taken the deposition of any one who was listed as an expert trial witness by any other party.

> A party may call as a witness at trial an expert not previously designated by that party if . . . that expert has been designated by another party and has thereafter been deposed . . . .[5]

This right is probably most valuable where the party designating that expert later settles before trial[6] or decides not to call that expert as a witness. However, it is not limited to these circumstances. In the *Powell* case,[7] for example, the plaintiff deposed one of the doctors on the defendant's expert witness list. This allowed the plaintiff to call that doctor as part of its case in chief,[8] even though the defense was still planning to call him during its case.

—Expert Already Deposed: The right to use an opponent's expert does not accrue immediately upon the designation of that expert. Rather, some other party must have "thereafter"[9] deposed the expert. In the *County of Los Angeles* case,[10] the defendant in a medical malpractice case received a deposition notice for one of its designated experts. It promptly withdrew that individual from its list but continued his services as a consultant. The court held that the plaintiff acted

---

[1] For a discussion of the exchange of expert witness information, see §§ 10.5–10.8.

[2] For a discussion of supplemental expert witness information, see § 10.11.

[3] For a discussion of motions to augment or amend expert witness information, see § 10.12.

[4] For a discussion of motions to make a tardy submission of expert witness information, see § 10.13.

[5] CCP § 2034.310(a), referencing CCP § 2034.410.

For a discussion of the right to depose an opponent's designated expert witnesses, see § 10.9 at the trial.

[6] Gallo v Peninsula Hospital (1985) 164 Cal App 3d 899, 904, 211 Cal Rptr 27.

[7] Powell v Superior Court (1989) 211 Cal App 3d 441, 444–445, 259 Cal Rptr 390.

[8] See also Alef v Alta Bates Hospital (1992) 5 Cal App 4th 208, 217–220, 6 Cal Rptr 2d 900, 906–907; Salasguevara v Wyeth Laboratories, Inc. (1990) 222 Cal App 3d 379, 386–387, 271 Cal Rptr 780, 784; Dickison v Howen (1990) 220 Cal App 3d 1471, 1474–1475, 270 Cal Rptr 188, 190.

[9] CCP § 2034.310(a).

[10] County of Los Angeles v Superior Court (1990) 222 Cal App 3d 647, 271 Cal Rptr 698.

improperly in contacting this expert[11] and in seeking to augment the plaintiff's list by adding his name:

> [A] party may, for tactical reasons, withdraw a previously designated expert witness, not yet deposed. If that expert continues his or her relationship with the party as a consultant, the opposing party is barred from communicating with the expert and from retaining him or her as the opposing party's expert.[12]

Any other rule, the court felt, would make too great an inroad on the work product protection by licensing experts, once withdrawn by the party initially designating them, to "shop" their opinion to another party.

Use in Rebuttal: In addition, a party may call an undesignated expert for rebuttal. The 1978 statute allowed a party to call an undesignated expert for "impeachment."[13] This choice of words was unfortunate, because the Evidence Code defines "impeachment" so broadly that it includes showing "the existence or the nonexistence of any fact"[14] testified to by another witness. This led to the contention that once another party called a designated witness to express an opinion, any other party could call in rebuttal an unlisted expert to contradict that opinion. The appellate courts uniformly rejected this interpretation: "Calling an expert witness to testify to an opinion *contrary* to the opinion of another expert witness is not 'impeachment' within the meaning of [the expert witness disclosure statutes"].[15] As the court pointed out in the *Kennemur* case:

> If a liberal rule of interpretation were adopted to permit impeachment by contradiction of an expert's opinion, the legislative intent manifested in the expert witness disclosure statutes (i.e., reasonable notice to the opposing party of the expert's expected testimony) would be thwarted . . . .[16]

---

[11] Cf. Easton, Can We Talk? Removing Counterproductive Ethical Restraints Upon Ex Parte Communication Between Attorneys and Adverse Expert Witnesses, 76 Ind. L.J. 647 (2001).

[12] County of Los Angeles v Superior Court (1990) 222 Cal App 3d 647, 657–658, 271 Cal Rptr 698, 705.

See also Shooker v Superior Court (2003) 111 Cal App 4th 923, 928, 4 Cal Rptr 3d 334, 339–340 [plaintiff designated himself as an expert trial witness, responded to defendant's deposition notice, and gave preliminary testimony, but then revoked the designation before making any disclosure of the content of his communications with his attorneys. Held: a party's designation of himself as an expert trial witness "is not itself an implied waiver of the party's attorney-client privilege . . . . If the designation is withdrawn before the party discloses a significant part of a privileged communication . . ., the privilege is secure; if the party provides privileged documents or testifies as an expert (such as by stating his opinion in a declaration or at a deposition) the privilege is waived."]

[13] Former CCP § 2037.5, Stats 1978, ch. 1069, § 1.

[14] Evid Code § 780(i).

[15] Sprague v Equifax, Inc. (1985) 166 Cal App 3d 1012, 1040, 213 Cal Rptr 2d 69, 87.

[16] Kennemur v State of California (1982) 133 Cal App 3d 907, 924, 184 Cal Rptr 393, 403.

Kennemur held that an undesignated expert, called as a rebuttal witness, may only contradict foundational facts relied on by another party's expert to support an opinion. The rebuttal expert may not contradict the opinion itself.

Section 2034.310 codifies the *Kennemur* holding: a previously undesignated expert may be called in rebuttal "to impeach the testimony of an expert witness offered by any other party at the trial.[17] This impeachment may include testimony to the falsity or nonexistence of any fact used as the foundation for any opinion by any other party's expert witness, but may not include testimony that contradicts the opinion."[18]

—**Illustrations:** *Stark v City of Los Angeles*[19] arose out of a right-angle collision between the plaintiff's auto and one driven by a traffic violator pursued by a police car. The police had not turned on their siren. An expert called by the City opined that the failure to use the siren had not caused the collision. He based this conclusion on his belief that the police car was too far away for its siren to be heard by a motorist traveling at right angles to it. The court held that the trial judge properly permitted the plaintiff to call in rebuttal a previously undisclosed expert who testified to certain tests conducted by him that showed the siren would have been audible at that distance.

In contrast, in *Fish v Guevara*[20] the plaintiffs claimed that the septic system on defendant's property directly across the street was discharging waste onto their property. Defense experts opined that the permeability rate of the type of soil surrounding the septic system was an inch per *year*. Plaintiffs then offered in rebuttal the testimony of an undesignated expert that the permeability rate of such soil was no more than an inch per *hour*. The appellate court upheld the trial judge's exclusion of this testimony:

> Plaintiffs did not assert that [their undesignated expert] had performed a permeability test on the soil that would permit him to testify on permeability as a matter of *fact*. Consequently, the proposed testimony of [the undesignated expert] was merely another contradictory *opinion* on the permeability rate of the soil.[21]

In *Mizel v City of Santa Monica,*[22] the plaintiff's treating physician and designated expert testified that from his training and experience, he had developed such a keen sense of smell for alcohol that he could detect its odor even in a patient whose blood/alcohol level was significantly lower than .08. Defendant was not allowed to present in rebuttal the opinion of an undesignated expert that alcohol's odor can only be detected when a person's consumption is at least .08.

---

[17] CCP § 2034.310(b).

[18] CCP § 2034.310(b).

[19] Stark v City of Los Angeles (1985) 168 Cal App 3d 276, 214 Cal Rptr 216.

[20] Fish v Guevara (1993) 12 Cal App 4th 142, 15 Cal Rptr 329.

[21] Fish v Guevara (1993) 12 Cal App 4th 142, 146, 15 Cal Rptr 329, 331–332 (original italics).

[22] Mizel v City of Santa Monica (2001) 93 Cal App 4th 1059, 1066–1068, 113 Cal Rptr 2d 649, 654–655.

And the *Howard Contracting* case[23] held that the trial court acted properly in excluding an undesignated expert's testimony where it was offered not to contradict a foundational fact used by opposing party's expert in his estimation of damages, but rather the very results reached by that opposing expert's use of a standard damages estimation formula.

§ 10.15 Exclusion of Testimony of Undesignated Experts

Sanction for Noncompliance: A party who fails to properly disclose its expert trial witnesses faces exclusion of any affected expert's opinion testimony.[1] Noncompliance usually takes the form of a failure to timely disclose the expert's identity.[2] However, where a party has specially retained an expert to testify at trial, noncompliance may also result from a failure to submit an expert witness declaration,[3] to produce the discoverable reports of the expert,[4] or to make the expert available for a deposition.[5]

In the *Zellerino* case,[6] for example, plaintiff completely failed to comply with the expert witness disclosure requirements or to seek forgiveness under any of the applicable provisions. The court upheld the exclusion of the plaintiff's expert witnesses even though this ruling resulted in a nonsuit:

> [The plaintiff's] real complaint appears to be that the discovery act does not permit a party to conceal a vacuum in its case. What she seeks is a return to cat-and-mouse discovery, where each side tries, as do Tom and Jerry, to sandbag the other.[7]

> [The plaintiff] failed to comply with any of the requirements of the expert disclosure statute thereby frustrating the purposes of the discovery act. Her actions were not mere infractions. The record discloses a comprehensive attempt to thwart the opposition from legitimate and

---

[23] Howard Contracting, Inc. v G.A. MacDonald Construction Co, Inc. (1999) 71 Cal App 4th 38, 52–53, 83 Cal Rptr 2d 590, 597–598.

[1] CCP § 2034.300.

[2] CCP § 2034.300(a).

See, e.g., Province v Women's Center for Health and Family Birth (1993) 20 Cal App 4th 1673, 1681–1684, 25 Cal Rptr 2d 667, 671–674; Richaud v Jennings (1993) 16 Cal App 4th 81, 19 Cal Rptr 2d 790; Fish v Guevara (1993) 12 Cal App 4th 142, 15 Cal Rptr 2d 329; Zellerino v Brown (1991) 235 Cal App 3d 1097, 1115, 1 Cal Rptr 2d 222, 233; Gallo v Peninsula Hospital (1985) 164 Cal App 3d 899, 901, 211 Cal Rptr 27, 29. Cf. Crumpton v Dickstein (1978) 82 Cal App 3d 166, 146 Cal Rptr 840.

[3] CCP § 2034.300(b).

[4] CCP § 2034.300(c).

[5] CCP § 2034.300(a).

Zellerino v Brown (1991) 235 Cal App 3d 1097, 1116–1117, 1 Cal Rptr 2d 222, 233–234. Cf. Stanchfield v Hamer Toyota, Inc. (1995) 37 Cal App 4th 1495, 1503–1505, 44 Cal Rptr 2d 565, 570–571.

[6] Zellerino v Brown (1991) 235 Cal App 3d 1097, 1115–1118, 1 Cal Rptr 2d 222, 233–235.

[7] Zellerino v Brown (1991) 235 Cal App 3d 1097, 1115, 1 Cal Rptr 2d 222, 233.

necessary discovery. [The plaintiff's] conduct prejudiced the defense, which did not have the ability to counter the testimony of the belatedly disclosed experts. The trial court properly granted the in limine motion [to exclude her experts].[8]

The *Province* case[9] reversed a trial judge who allowed the testimony of a treating doctor, not designated as an expert, to range beyond his perceptions and into the area of opinion.

Not Applicable to Summary Judgment Motions: A reading of the various statutes regulating the exchange of expert witness information[10] discovery via expert trial witness disclosure makes it abundantly clear that these procedures are applicable only to expert *trial* witnesses. They do not apply to the use of expert witnesses in support of or in opposition to a summary judgment motion, even one filed after an exchange of expert trial witness information. Therefore, even though a party might have no right to call a certain undesignated expert at trial, these statutes would not preclude the use of the testimony or affidavit of that expert in connection with a summary judgment motion.[11]

Eligibility to Invoke Sanction: The sanction (more properly perhaps called a "consequence") provided by Section 2034.300 is invoked by objecting at trial to the opinion testimony of the affected expert. However, eligibility to seek that sanction requires that the objecting party have made a complete and timely exchange of expert witness information.[12] Of course, if none of the parties has served a demand for exchange of expert witness information, its sanction will never come into play. In that event, no party can claim surprise when at trial another party calls expert witnesses.[13]

Deficient Description of Expert's Anticipated Testimony: The Discovery Commission's proposal,[14] which was initially adopted by the Legislature,[15] called for the imposition of the sanction if a party had failed to state in an expert witness declaration "the general substance of the testimony of that expert." However, before the new statute took effect, the Legislature watered down this segment so that now the sanction becomes available only if a party fails *altogether* to "submit an expert witness declaration."[16] This change serves to prevent the

---

[8] Zellerino v Brown (1991) 235 Cal App 3d 1097, 1117–1118, 1 Cal Rptr 2d 222, 235.

[9] Province v Women's Center for Health and Family Birth (1993) 20 Cal App 4th 1673, 1682–1683, 25 Cal Rptr 2d 667.

[10] CCP §§ 2034.010–2034.730.

[11] Kennedy v Modesto City Hospital (1990) 221 Cal App 3d 575, 582–583, 270 Cal Rptr 544.

[12] CCP § 2034.300.

Zellerino v Brown (1991) 235 Cal App 3d 1097, 1113, 1 Cal Rptr 2d 222, 232.

[13] See In re Marriage of Hoffmeister (1984) 161 Cal App 3d 1163, 1171 n6, 208 Cal Rptr 345, 350 n6. Cf. Foster v Gillette Co. (1979) 100 Cal App 3d 569, 577–578, 161 Cal Rptr 134, 139.

[14] Proposed Civil Discovery Act of 1986, Section 2034(k), Appendix D.

[15] Stats 1986, c 1336, § 2 [former CCP § 2034(j)].

[16] CCP § 2034.300(b).

exclusion of an expert's opinion because of minor shortcomings in the declaration's description of it. [17]

Unfortunately, the effort to achieve this merciful goal threatened to pull the teeth from the requirement that a party describe the "general substance" of the expected testimony. In the *Martinez* case, [18] the plaintiff offered at trial an opinion of an expert that was clearly outside the area described in the expert witness declaration. [19] The court found reversible error in the exclusion of this testimony:

> [B]ecause [the expert's] identity had been disclosed to other parties in a timely fashion along with a description of his testimony, *albeit an inaccurate one*, the trial court had *no power* to limit [his] testimony at trial. [20]

Six years later, the Supreme Court, in *Bonds v Roy*, [21] disapproved the holding in the *Martinez* case. In that medical malpractice case, the defendant's declaration, after designating a vascular surgeon to testify on the issue of liability and causation, listed an orthopedist to testify only on the issue of plaintiff's damages. During the deposition of the orthopedist, he insisted that he was to testify only concerning the extent of the plaintiff's present disability and the prospects for his rehabilitation, and he confirmed that he was not to opine on the standard of care issues in the case.

At trial, however, when the defense called this orthopedist as its last witness, it "sought to expand the scope of [his] testimony to include two new areas . . . relating to the standard of care." [22] The trial judge ruled that any such expansion of the expert's trial testimony would be an unfair and prejudicial surprise to the plaintiff.

In the Court of Appeal, the defense, relying on the ruling in the *Martinez* case, insisted that since it had filed an expert witness declaration concerning this witness's projected trial testimony, it was free to have him range outside the areas specified in that declaration.

The Supreme Court first noted that the statute requires an expert witness declaration to include "a brief narrative statement of the general substance of

---

[17] See Sprague v Equifax, Inc. (1985) 166 Cal App 3d 1012, 1040, 213 Cal Rptr 69, 87 [decided under former CCP §§ 2037.3 and 2037.5].

For a discussion of the requirements for an expert witness declaration, see § 10.7.

[18] Martinez v City of Poway (1993) 12 Cal App 4th 425, 15 Cal Rptr 2d 644.

[19] The expected testimony described in the declaration related to the design of the roadway where the accident happened; that offered at trial would have reconstructed the accident itself.

[20] Martinez v City of Poway (1993) 12 Cal App 4th 425, 432, 15 Cal Rptr 2d 644, 648 (italics added).

[21] Bonds v Roy (1999) 20 Cal 4th 140, 149 n4, 83 Cal Rptr 2d 289, 294 n4, 973 P2d 66, 71 n4.

Cf. Kahn, Declarations: Recent Decisions have Blurred the Line between Providing Too Much and Too Little Information in Expert Witness Declarations, 28-MAR L.A. Law. 28 (2005).

[22] Bonds v Roy (1999) 20 Cal 4th 140, 143, 83 Cal Rptr 2d 289, 290, 973 P2d 66, 67.

the testimony that the expert is expected to give." It then stressed that expert trial witness disclosure procedures contain "an exhaustive series of requirements both for making and for granting"[23] a motion to augment an expert witness declaration "with respect to the general substance of the testimony that an expert previously designated is expected to give."[24]

Section 2034.300 speaks of excluding the testimony of an expert where a party has unreasonably failed to "[s]ubmit an expert witness declaration." This language led the defense to argue that an expert's testimony could be excluded only where the party calling that expert had failed "altogether"[25] to submit a declaration concerning that expert.

The Court rejected this argument, because it would render redundant the elaborate statutory provisions[26] for amending an expert witness declaration.[27] Instead the Court made it abundantly clear that, absent a court-approved amendment under these statutes, the areas of opinion testimony given by a retained expert at trial must track those earlier described in the expert witness declaration:

> In short, the statutory scheme as a whole envisions timely disclosure of the general substance of an expert's expected testimony so that the parties may properly prepare for trial. Allowing new and unexpected testimony for the first time at trial so long as a party has submitted any expert witness declaration whatsoever is inconsistent with this purpose. We therefore conclude that the exclusion sanction . . . applies when a party unreasonably fails to submit an expert witness declaration that fully complies with the content requirements of [present Section 2034.260] including the requirement that the declaration contain "[a] brief narrative statement of the general substance of the testimony that the expert is expected to give." This encompasses situations like the present one, in which a party has submitted an expert witness declaration, but the narrative statement fails to disclose the general substance of the testimony the party later wishes to elicit from the expert at trial. To expand the scope of an expert's testimony beyond what is stated in the declaration, a party must successfully move to amend the declaration . . . .[28]

Variance Between Expert Witness Declaration and Expert's Deposition: Usually an expert witness may testify at trial to an opinion that falls within the general substance of the expected testimony described in the expert witness declaration. However, where an opponent has deposed the designated expert, this

---

[23] Bonds v Roy (1999) 20 Cal 4th 140, 144, 83 Cal Rptr 2d 289, 291, 973 P2d 66, 68.

[24] CCP § 2034.610(a)(2).

[25] Bonds v Roy (1999) 20 Cal 4th 140, 146, 83 Cal Rptr 2d 289, 292, 973 P2d 66, 69.

[26] See CCP §§ 2034.610–2034.630.

[27] Bonds v Roy (1999) 20 Cal 4th 140, 143, 83 Cal Rptr 2d 289, 292, 973 P2d 66, 69.

[28] Bonds v Roy (1999) 20 Cal 4th 140, 148–149, 83 Cal Rptr 2d 289, 294, 973 P2d 66, 71.

will not always be true. In *Jones v Moore,* [29] a wife sued the attorney who had represented her in a dissolution proceeding from 1987 until the middle of 1996. Her complaint contained general charges of legal malpractice spanning this entire period. As the trial date neared, the plaintiff identified an expert witness and broadly described his expected testimony about departures from the standard of care in terms that would also cover the entire period that the defendant-attorney had represented her.

However, when the defendant deposed the plaintiff's designated expert, that expert criticized only the defendant's actions in negotiating the terms of a property settlement agreement which had been incorporated in the final judgment at the end of 1990:

> [The expert's deposition] opinions related only to defendant's conduct with regard to the settlement agreement and further judgment entered in 1990. None of [his] opinions related to defendant's later conduct in failing to obtain substitute security [once a 1992 bankruptcy of a partnership wiped out the interest that the husband was using to secure the agreement]. [The expert] specifically disavowed holding any other opinions than those he had expressed, and said if he formed any other opinions than those he had expressed he would notify defendant. [30]

When the malpractice case came to trial, the plaintiff asked her expert to opine as to whether defendant had acted negligently in 1994 when he failed to obtain additional security after the partnership's bankruptcy. The action of the trial court in barring any opinion as to the post-settlement actions of the plaintiff's former attorney was upheld by the appellate court:

> When an expert deponent testifies as to specific opinions and affirmatively states those are the only opinions he intends to offer at trial, it would be grossly unfair and prejudicial to permit the expert to offer additional opinions at trial. [31]

Motion Required to Avoid Sanction: The Discovery Commission proposed that any of the forms of noncompliance with expert witness disclosure obligations that are now listed in Section 2034.300 would require the trial court to impose the sanction of excluding the expert's testimony at trial. [32] However, an eleventh-hour amendment provided for exclusion of the expert's testimony only if the delinquent party acted "unreasonably" in its failure to comply with the statute. Read literally, this amendment would undercut the elaborate provisions for obtaining leave of court to augment one's original list of trial experts. [33] To obtain

---

[29] Jones v Moore (2000) 80 Cal App 4th 557, 95 Cal Rptr 2d 216.

[30] Jones v Moore (2000) 80 Cal App 4th 557, 564, 95 Cal Rptr 2d 216, 220.

[31] Jones v Moore (2000) 80 Cal App 4th 557, 565, 95 Cal Rptr 2d 216, 221.

[32] See Section 2034(j) of the Proposed Civil Discovery Act of 1986, Appendix D.

[33] CCP §§ 2034.610–2034.630.

this augmentation a party must act "promptly" and with good cause.[34] The *Richaud* case[35] describes the dilemma created by the amendment:

[I]t would be anomalous to conclude that . . . [a] party could then simply show up at trial with expert No. 2, announce that expert No. 1 is dead, and insist on calling expert No. 2 as a replacement witness without having first sought to augment that party's expert witness list to include expert No. 2. . . . Since the adverse party ordinarily has a right to depose the opponent's expert and that right is contingent upon listing the expert under the code, failure to properly list the expert would affect deposition rights.[36]

The court refused to undermine the expert witness disclosure provisions by such a construction:

The spirit of [the expert witness disclosure statutes], though apparently not the letter of [Section 2034.300] itself, implies that a party who wishes to call at trial an expert who was not designated when expert witness information was exchanged and who is intended to take the place of a previously designated expert but now unavailable expert, must *make* a motion under [Section 2034.610] to augment that party's expert witness list to include the new expert. The party cannot do nothing and then insist that the replacement expert can be called at trial on the ground that the party's failure to list the replacement expert when expert witness information was exchanged was not "unreasonable."[37]

In effect, the court is holding that a party who realizes the need to substitute an expert, yet does not promptly seek leave of court to do so, is estopped to claim at trial that the failure to list that expert in the first place was "reasonable."

§ 10.16 Recovery of Expert Witness Fees as Costs

The presentation of expert testimony in support of one's lawsuit can be an expensive proposition.[1] It is only natural that the prevailing party will seek to include the fees charged by expert witnesses testifying at the trial as an item of costs. The principal statute governing the right of the prevailing party to recover litigation costs is CCP § 1032. The term "costs," as used in that section, is defined in CCP § 1033.5. Expert witness fees are expressly "allowed" as a "cost" if the expert testimony was "ordered by the court."[2] On the other hand,

---

[34] For a discussion of motions to augment an expert witness list, see § 10.12.

[35] Richaud v Jennings (1993) 16 Cal App 4th 81, 19 Cal Rptr 2d 790.

[36] Richaud v Jennings (1993) 16 Cal App 4th 81, 90, 19 Cal Rptr 2d 790, 795.

[37] Richaud v Jennings (1993) 16 Cal App 4th 81, 90–91, 19 Cal Rptr 2d 790, 795–796 (original italics).

[1] See, e.g., First Nationwide Bank v Mountain Cascade, Inc. (2000) 77 Cal App 4th 871, 879, 92 Cal Rptr 2d 145, 151 [expert witness fees of prevailing party in construction defect case exceeded $59,000].

[2] CCP § 1033.5(a).

experts whose testimony was not so ordered are expressly made nonallowable costs absent specific statutory authorization.[3]

In the *Sanchez* case,[4] a medical malpractice action in which the plaintiffs prevailed, they persuaded the trial court that where expert testimony is required by law in order to make out a prima facie case, the experts retained are in effect "ordered by the court." The Court of Appeals rejected this contention: "The fact that an expert is necessary to present a party's case does not mean that expert has been ordered by the court for purposes of recovery of expert witness fees as costs."[5]

It is common to include in written contracts a provision for recovery of attorney's fees and *costs*. One appellate case read such a provision to include any disbursement by the prevailing party's attorney that is ordinarily billed separately to the client, and it held that expert fees fell within this category.[6] However, several other decisions have rejected this argument.[7] In the *Davis* case, the Supreme Court noted this conflict among the Courts of Appeal, but found it unnecessary to resolve it in the case before it.[8]

---

[3] CCP § 1033.5(b).

[4] Sanchez v Bay Shores Medical Group (1999) 75 Cal App 4th 946, 89 Cal Rptr 2d 634.

[5] Sanchez v Bay Shores Medical Group (1999) 75 Cal App 4th 946, 950, 89 Cal Rptr 2d 634, 637.

[6] Bussey v Affleck (1990) 225 Cal App 3d 1162, 1164–1167, 275 Cal Rptr 646.

[7] Carwash of America-PO v Windswept Ventures No. I (2002) 97 Cal App 4th 540, 118 Cal Rptr 2d 536; Fairchild v Park (2001) 90 Cal App 4th 919, 931, 109 Cal Rptr 2d 442, 450; Steiney & Co. v California Electric Supply Co. (2000) 79 Cal App 4th 285, 293–294, 93 Cal Rptr 2d 920, 926; First Nationwide Bank v Mountain Cascade, Inc. (2000) 77 Cal App 4th 871, 92 Cal Rptr 2d 145; Robert L. Cloud & Associates, Inc. v Mikesell (1999) 69 Cal App 4th 1141, 82 Cal Rptr 2d 1431; Ripley v Pappadopoulos (1994) 23 Cal App 4th 1616, 28 Cal Rptr 2d 878.

[8] Davis v KGO-T.V., Inc. (1998) 17 Cal 4th 436, 446 n5, 71 Cal Rptr 2d 452, 458 n5, 950 P2d 567, 573 n5.